CW01184259

ns on the 20th Century*
Ponder Anew
Reflections on the 20th Century

PONDER ANEW

Reflections on the 20th Century

by

John Graham

SPELLMOUNT
Staplehurst

British Library Cataloguing in Publication Data:
A catalogue record for this book is available
from the British Library

Copyright © John Graham 1999

ISBN 1-86227-068-6

Published privately in 1999 by Spellmount Ltd on behalf of the author
in a limited edition of 300 copies, designed for presentation
to family members and friends
of proven discretion and sound judgement

The right of John Graham to be identified
as the author of this work has been asserted by him
in accordance with the Copyright, Designs
and Patents Act 1988

All rights reserved. No part of this publication may be
reproduced, stored in a retrieval system or transmitted in
any form or by any means, electronic, mechanical,
photocopying, recording or otherwise,
without prior permission in writing from
Spellmount Limited, Publishers,
The Old Rectory, Staplehurst, Kent TN12 0AZ.

Typeset by Palimpsest Book Production Limited,
Polmont, Stirlingshire
Printed in Great Britain by
T.J. International Ltd Padstow, Cornwall

Contents

		List of Maps	vii
		List of Plates	viii
		Introduction and Acknowledgements	xii
I	1923–40	Antecedents, Adolescence and the Outbreak of War	1
II	1940–44	From Dad's Army into the Argylls 'The Pride of Them All'	24
III	1944–45	With the New 93rd in the British Liberation Army	55
IV	1945–48	Palestine and Parachuting	103
V	1948–52	Four Czech Years	124
VI	1952–60	With the Argylls in Scotland, British Guiana, Cyprus and West Germany and Marriage	141
VII	1960–61	With NATO in Fontainebleau (HQ AFCENT) A Coup that Failed	174
VIII	1961–62	HQ AFCENT (cont'd) A Medley of Memories	203
IX	1963–64	With 2 PARA I am introduced to the Persian Gulf; and Episodes in Normandy and the Congo	231
X	1964–67	Commanding 1 PARA Group in Aldershot, Bahrain, Aden and Aldershot again	263
XI	1967–70	Staff College, RHQ The Parachute Regiment and Beaconsfield	293
XII	1970	Muscat and Oman: A Dismal Situation	308
XIII	1970–72	The Sultanate of Oman: From Darkness into Light	340
XIV	1973	With the Indian National Defence College, and in Parts of South-East Asia	380
XV	1974–78	Back to HQ AFCENT, Wales as GOC, and Retirement	404
XVI	1978–88	Foreign Affairs in Kent and Home Affairs in Barnes	420
XVII	1988–99	Visits to Oman, PARA 90 and our Move to Barbados	439

Epilogue		455
Appendix I:	Military Government in the British Zone of Germany, 1945–6 by Noel Annan	457
Appendix II:	A Ballad of Two Tropic Nights	460
Appendix III:	A Mulatto's Prayer	466
Appendix IV:	Lieutenant-Colonel Said Salem Al Wahaibi: An Outline Biography	467
Appendix V:	My personal diary entries (unedited) made each evening during the official visits of Rosemary and myself to Iran and Jordan in late September – early October 1972	481
Appendix VI:	Address given by JDCG at the Funeral of my Mother	489
Appendix VII:	Address given by JDCG at the Memorial Service for Brigadier Colin Maxwell	491
Appendix VIII:	Sermon given by the Bishop of Peterborough, 22 June 1990	495
Appendix IX:	British Guiana Revisited, 1991	497
Family Tree		501
Index		503

List of Maps

1 The Moves & Operations of the 2nd Bn Argyll & Sutherland
   Highlanders (The New 93rd) 1940–1945   43
2 Normandy: *Operation EPSOM*   58
3 2 A&SH Operations: September 1944 – March 1945   78
4 British Guiana (Guyana) and the Caribbean   150
5 Cyprus post 1975   161
6 The Arabian Peninsula and the Persian Gulf   233
7 The Sultanate of Oman   311
8 Dhofar   318
9 The Indian Sub-Continent   382

List of Plates

1. Tommy Carew-Hunt, my Maternal Grandfather
2. Max Graham, my Paternal Grandfather
3. Thomas Graham of Balgowan, Lord Lynedoch *(Sir Thomas Lawrence)*
4. The Honourable Mrs Graham, née Mary Cathcart *(Thomas Gainsborough)*
5. My Father, John Alexander (Jack) Graham
6. My Mother, Constance Mary (Jane) Graham, 1921
7. Jane Graham in India, 1934
8. Cosmo Graham
9. JDCG, Colchester, 1933
10. Elspeth Graham with JDCG, 1949
11. Tommy Carew-Hunt with his second wife, Mida
12. My Mother with my Brothers, Moray and Alastair, 1942
13. Lieut-Colonel J W Tweedie, DSO, CO 2nd Bn The Argyll & Sutherland Highlanders (2A&SH), 1943–44
14. Lieut-Colonel D R Morgan, DSO MC, CO 2nd Bn Argyll & Sutherland Highlanders, 1944–45
15. The Officers of 2nd Bn Argyll & Sutherland Highlanders shortly before embarking for Normandy, 1944
16. JDCG with No 8 Platoon, 'The Plums', May 1944. Pte McLeod (back row far right)
17. My 2A&SH Intelligence Section at our 1993 reunion in York. From left: Maurice Tucker, John Park, Harry Oakley, Alf Horsley, Maurice Lester-Mallinson
18. CSM Leslie, 5 PARA in Husum, 1948
19. Moray and Alastair, Versailles, 1949
20. Sir Pierson Dixon with Colonel Francis Blake and Major Guy Wheeler, Prague, 1950
21. Holyrood House, Edinburgh, 26 June 1953. Queen Elizabeth after presenting new Colours to 1st Battalion The Argyll & Sutherland Highlanders, with General Sir Gordon MacMillan far left
22. HMS *Implacable*
23. Sir Alfred Savage, Governor of British Guiana, The Queen's Birthday Parade, 1954
24. The Pipes and Drums of 1st Bn The Argyll & Sutherland Highlanders, Georgetown, 1954
25. Our wedding, St James's Church, Piccadilly, 17 November 1956

List of Plates

26. Lieut-Colonel Hugh Spens MBE, CO 1st Bn The Argyll & Sutherland Highlanders with citizens of Lemgo, 1960
27. Tim and Mouse Macpherson with Rosemary, 1960
28. Fontainebleau 1961. Generals Lauris Norstad (SACEUR), Jacquot (CINCENT), Brigadier-General Costa de Beauregard and Captain Loic Eon-Duval (ADC)
29. General Jacquot with his subordinate commanders. Air Chief Marshal The Earl of Bandon (Comd Air Forces Central Europe), Air Marshal Sir John Grandy (Comd 2 ATAF), Major-General Marias (FAF), General Sir James Cassels (Comd Northern Army Group), General Speidel, Lieut-General André Dulac (COS HQ AFCENT), General Bruce Clark (Comd Central Army Group), and Vice-Admiral van Erkel
30. General Dr Hans Speidel (Comd Land Forces Central Europe)
31. Le Cabinet: Hubert Jeschke, JDCG, Bill Wildman, Captain Dicharry and Robert Allard de Grandmaison
32. General Maurice Challe
33. Lord Bandon, Sir James Cassels, General Speidel (back to camera) and Sir John Grandy
34. Mr Julian Amery (S-of-S for Air) and General Jacquot, Fontainebleau, 24 November 1961
35. Brigadier-General Costa de Beauregard greets Admiral of the Fleet The Earl Mountbatten of Burma (Chief of the UK Defence Staff), 13 July 1961
36. Captain Dicharry (Comd HQ AFCENT Provost & Security Detachment)
37. Rosemary and JDCG at the Versailles Ball, 1961
38. With the Pipes & Drums and Military Band of 1st Bn The Argyll & Sutherland Highlanders, Fontainebleau, November 1961. (Pipe-Major Pitkeathley and, back to camera, Drum-Major Malloch)
39. JDCG, April 1962
40. JDCG, Rosemary, Pinky and Christopher, Oxford, 1962
41. Our Latimer Common Market party, 1962. JDCG, Rosemary, Valerie and Adrian Rouse
42. On exercise near Sharjah, 1965, showing our 'Hats Afrika Korps'
43. Hamala Camp, Bahrain, 1965. JDCG (CO 1 PARA), and RSM Cole with our contractor, Ghulam Hassan and his team
44. Sheikh Isa bin Sulman Al Khalifa, Ruler of Bahrain, at the 1 PARA Tattoo in Hamala Camp, October 1965. Behind HH are General Sir Kenneth Darling (Colonel Commandant of The Parachute Regiment) and my Mother, Jane Graham
45. With Colour-Sergeant Gordon Burt and the 1 PARA Cross Country Team, 1966
46. Rosemary on our first visit to Kirchberg, 1967
47. Colin Mitchell and Field Marshal The Viscount Montgomery of Alamein ('Monty') at Isington Mill, near Farnham, 1969

48. His Highness Said bin Taimur, Sultan of Muscat & Oman
49. Colonel Hugh Oldman, Sultanate Defence Secretary, with reporter from Radio Dubai, July 1970
50. Lieut-Colonel Teddy Turnill, CO Desert Regiment, and 2nd Lieut Miran Sabil, Salalah, 1970
51. Sultan Qaboos bin Said being greeted by JDCG on arrival at Bait al Falaj on 30 July 1970.
52. Sultan Qaboos inspects Guard of Honour, commanded by Major John Cooper, prior to the Accession Ceremony at Bait al Falaj, 30 July 1970
53. His Majesty Qaboos bin Said, Sultan of Oman and Commander-in-Chief of the Armed Forces, 1972
54. HE Lieut-Colonel Said Salem Al Wahaibi, Minister of Royal Court Affairs, 1985
55. Said bin Geyr, an early defector from the communist enemy ranks, with local colleagues, Salalah, early 1970
56. Major Spike Powell with Major Vyvyan Robinson in rear
57. Colonel Mike Harvey (Comd Dhofar Brigade) with Lieut-Colonel David Glazebrook (Senior Adminstrative Staff Officer, HQ SAF)
58. Major Vyvyan Robinson (OC Baluch recruit training centre at Rayzut) and David Glazebrook
59. Mr Donald Hawley, the first British Ambassador to the Sultanate, with Major-General Roland Gibbs (Comd British Forces Gulf) 1971
60. Muscat harbour; Fort Mirani, and in foreground, the sole quay
61. Major Paul Wright (Jebel Regt) and Colonel Courtney Welch (British Defence Attaché) 1972
62. Former SAF colleagues at a lunch hosted by JDCG in Browning Barracks, Aldershot on 23 July 1990 to celebrate the 20th anniversary of the Accession of HM Sultan Qaboos
63. At the Taj Mahal in Agra, India, 1973
64. General Ernst Ferber (CINCENT), Brunssum, The Netherlands
65. Air Chief Marshal Sir Lewis Hodges (Comd Air Forces Central Europe), General Alexander Haig (SACEUR), General Dr Karl Schnell (CINCENT on retirement of General Ferber) and Major-General Zwyner (NL Military Representative at Supreme Headquarters) 1975
66. The Silver Jubilee of The Queen, Cardiff, 1977. Her Majesty inspecting the Guard of Honour found by The Royal Regiment of Wales outside the City Hall
67. The Queen with JDCG (GOC Wales)
68. Chevening, view from the south-west
69. Jacqueline (Pinky) with Roland Dane on their wedding day, Chevening, 5 June 1982
70. Sir Geoffrey Howe (S-of-S for Foreign & Commonwealth Affairs), Lady Howe and 'Budget', Chevening, 1986

List of Plates

71. Rosemary and JDCG in Kirchberg, summer 1985
72. The 50th anniversary of the Raising of British Airborne Forces, London, 22 June 1990. The March from St Paul's Cathedral to Guildhall after the Service of Thanksgiving
73. Contingents of serving and retired members of The Parachute Regiment march past The Prince of Wales, our Colonel-in-Chief, the Lord Mayor, Sir Hugh Bidwell, the Aldermen, Commoners and Sheriffs, St Paul's Churchyard
74. The wedding of Christopher (Didi) and Cynthia (Tia) Brus, 26 October 1996, St James's Parish Church, Barbados
75. JDCG, 1948 (5th [Scottish] Bn, The Parachute Regiment)
76. JDCG, 1963 (2nd Bn The Parachute Regiment) outside the lines of F (Sphinx) Battery, 7th Royal Horse Artillery, Hamala Camp, Bahrain
77. JDCG, 1972 (Comd The Sultan's Armed Forces), Bait al Falaj, Oman
78. Rosemary Graham, neé Adamson, 1970
79. HM Sultan Qaboos bin Said, 1998

Introduction and Acknowledgements

During many periods of my life I kept diaries, a medley of notebooks in which I scribbled my recollections of each day and pasted extracts from journals which I had read with especial interest or delight.

After retiring to the Caribbean I took it into my head to transcribe these daily jottings, making copies only for my closest family members. But friends took an interest and, having read bits, urged me to write for a wider readership, to omit little but rather to expand my story using regimental and other histories already in print. The result is this dauntingly large tome. Few will read it all, but I hope that colleagues will dip into it and find episodes which evoke pleasing memories of shared experiences.

My paramount purpose, however, is to give to my Grandchildren and to their descendants an understanding of the 20th century; of the events which shaped my life, of my joys and sorrows and, particularly, of my good fortune to have been born British, serving for most of my life in the Armed Forces of our country, with by my side a gem of a wife.

I make no apology for describing aspects of our routine Service business such as Recruits' training in wartime, or of peacetime unit administration, for our military procedures will seem to future historians as quaint as do those of Wellington's army to us. About financial worries I have written frankly for they overshadowed the lives of many of my generation; and I have done so in the hope that those who come after us in the Services will have fewer concerns on that account.

I have included many photographs: all from my own collection. Some I took myself; others were generously given to me by, for example, the Public Relations personnel of the organisations, such as the NATO Headquarters in which I was employed. For the fine portrait (Plate 53) of His Majesty Sultan Qaboos I am indebted to Major Charles Butt, a colleague in the Sultan's Armed Forces. Others to whom I express my thanks are the Right Reverend William Westwood, Bishop of Peterborough, for allowing me to include the text of his sermon in St Paul's Cathedral and to HarperCollins Ltd for permission to reproduce the extract (at Appendix I) from Noel Annan's book *Changing Enemies*; also to Mr James Wilson of Spellmount Publishers for his counsel and encouragement. I am grateful too to Brigadier Robert Gordon CBE and his Staff in the Ministry of Defence for vetting, as is required, what I had

Introduction

written, and for their advice on the presentation of certain sensitive events narrated therein.

Those who are interested in the history of the Sultan's Armed Forces may like to note that a comprehensive collection of reports, operation orders, maps, photographs, ciné film and other documents relating to my period in command is held in Oxford, in the Oman Archive of St Antony's College.

These Reflections will, I trust, give pleasure to many but offence to none. To this end I have deliberately altered the names of individuals whose inclusion might distress them.

JDCG
Christ Church
Barbados
April 1999

For

Elaine Maud Adamson

To my Compatriots:

Praise to the Lord, who doth prosper thy work and defend thee;
Surely His goodness and mercy shall daily attend thee;
Ponder anew what the Almighty can do,
If to the end He befriend thee.

Hymns Ancient & Modern

The History of England is one of Mankind's outstanding successes.
It is instructive to probe the secret of a destiny as impressive as that of
ancient Rome.

André Maurois

CHAPTER I
1923–1940

Antecedents, Adolescence and the Outbreak of War

I first put on khaki in September 1937. At Cheltenham College it was obligatory for boys to join the Officer Training Corps on entering their second year. As far as I can recall only one boy managed to avoid enrolment in the OTC. He was Welsh, a budding poet, and came from a family of conscientious objectors. He was nevertheless to perish as did many of our contemporaries in the Second World War which broke out two years later.

I had been born into a military family on 18 January 1923. That date was the 52nd anniversary of the founding of the German Empire by Count Otto von Bismarck in the Hall of Mirrors at Versailles in 1871. It was perhaps that fact which implanted in me at an early age an enduring interest in, and a certain respect for, Germany and things Teutonic. But there were other affinities.

My Maternal Great-Grandfather, Henry Carew-Hunt, himself an amalgam of Irish Carews and Devonian Hunts, spent most of his life in the Consular Service. His postings included Haiti, Bordeaux and New Orleans, where he died in 1923. His penultimate tour of duty was in East Prussia, where he lived for seventeen years and where his first wife is buried. He later married a German lady. His sons by his first wife, Thomas Edward and George Ward, absorbed from their upbringing in Königsberg and Danzig three things: proficiency in the German language, thrift, and a reverence for good order and social discipline.

Thomas became my Grandfather. He, Tommy, was an Army Officer commissioned into the Royal Berkshire Regiment in 1897. The next year he married Ethel Emily Nicholson, a descendent of the General Sir John Nicholson of Indian Mutiny fame. She had a rather long nose and a censorious nature, and it was gossiped that Tommy, gentle, modest and totally orthodox in all things, was not all that happy wedded to her. I am told, however, that she was extremely fond of me, her first grandchild. I wish I had clearer memories of her, but she died of peritonitis in 1931 having produced only one child, my Mother, Constance Mary, born on 10 March 1900.

It is strange that in an age of large families my Mother, Jane as she was universally called, came to marry a man who was also an only child.

PONDER ANEW

John Alexander Graham, my Father, was the son of Malcolm David (Max) Graham. Max was the youngest son and seventh child of the sixteen born to the Honourable Robert Graham, who after some years in Scotland and Australia returned in 1850 to South Africa where he rose to high office in that colony's administration.

The links of the Graham clan with that beautiful country date from 1805 when Colonel John Graham, Max's Grandfather, was posted to the Cape of Good Hope as a Major in the 93rd Highlanders. The next year he raised a Corps of Hottentots, later named the Cape Regiment, and was appointed Commissioner responsible for the defence of the eastern frontier of Cape Province against 'the Kafir Hordes'. The city of Grahamstown was named in testimony of his success in carrying out that assignment.

This John Graham was a kinsman of General Thomas Graham whose beautiful but consumptive wife, Mary, had been painted by Gainsborough and who, as a divisional commander under the Duke of Wellington, was created Lord Lynedoch after his victory over the French under Marshal Victor at Barrosa, near Cadiz, on 5 March 1811.

I never saw my Grandfather, Max Graham, but I am told that he saw me when I was three days old. The next day he embarked on a liner for a cruise round the world, but left the ship at Cape Town and settled in Durban where he died penniless in 1941.

Born in Cape Province in 1865, Max had been educated in England at Haileybury and the Royal Military College, before being commissioned into the Northamptonshire Regiment. In 1890 he found himself back in South Africa, seconded for service with the Mashonaland Expedition, and while in Cape Town, he met Helen Magdalen Abercrombie, the daughter of a prominent surgeon. They had a protracted engagement, but Helen followed Max to England and they were married at Frimley in 1896.

From this union, allegedly lukewarm on Max's part, was born on 21 January 1898 my Father, John Alexander Graham (Jack for short). The three of them soon went off with the Northamptons to India, but Helen Graham died there of cholera in 1903. The few pictures and accounts we have of her tell us that she was blond, petite and shy. She could not have had an easy life with Max, whose stronger personality and egotism contrasted with her self-effacing temperament. Helen must have been a very nice young woman who deserved affection. She lies buried at Kasauli near the hill-station Simla.

Her death left Max, who never remarried, with the problem of bringing up a boy of five when he, a professional soldier, would be abroad for much of the time. The problem was solved for him by his unmarried sister, Albinia Ellen, who set up house in Camberley, and she, Ellie Graham, took over the care of young Jack from his return from India on his Mother's death until he went off to fight in France in 1917.

Holidays from school in the house of a spinster Aunt cannot have been other than dull. Very small, shy but alert, Jack seems to have resembled his Mother remarkably closely both in character and physique. But the absence of brothers, sisters or companions of his own age turned him into a lonely boy. This loneliness he sublimated in classroom achievement, first at Stubbington House and later at Cheltenham. He won numerous prizes for a variety of subjects, shone at gymnastics and cricket, and had no difficulty in meeting the standards demanded for a regular commission in the Corps of Royal Engineers. He had impeccable manners, but all his life remained timid, incapable of vulgar argument and reluctant to stick up for his rights or his beliefs. Of the world beyond the schoolroom or the Sappers he seemed extraordinarily apprehensive, and to face it ill-equipped. His leisure time he devoted to collecting stamps and butterflies – he built up fine collections of both – and to woodwork. He was, I suppose, the natural creation of an absent Father, a maiden Aunt and an era when little boys were to be seen but rarely heard.

Alas, his marriage to my Mother ultimately brought him little of the comfort or companionship he needed and for which he doubtless craved. The marriage had come about thus.

In 1912 his Father was promoted Lieutenant-Colonel and transferred into the command of the First Battalion of the Royal Berkshire Regiment. In that battalion, then in Aldershot, Tommy Carew-Hunt was commanding a company. I got to know quite a lot about the Berkshires of 1912–14 when I myself was in Aldershot in 1969, and succeeded in tracking down three men who had been in that battalion while Max was CO. It seems that initially Max was not all that popular. He was strict, and being brought in from another regiment to take command is usually resented. But he was energetic, experienced and a good trainer of men, and he brought the Berkshires up to a high pitch of efficiency and self-confidence. His foresight and leadership were especially appreciated when the battalion was sent to France in August 1914 as part of the immortal BEF – British Expeditionary Force, rated by the German Kaiser as 'a contemptible little army' – and took part in the Retreat from Mons (where Tommy commanded the Rear Guard Company) and the battles of late 1914 which were the twilight of Britain's incomparable pre-war Regular Army. Although said to be short-tempered and highly-strung, Max Graham was clearly a competent commander in the field, but his active service was cut short in November 1914 when he was grievously wounded by a shell, losing a leg and an eye. He spent the rest of his life on crutches as he found an artificial leg too painful to wear. After convalescence he went to the War Office as Deputy Military Secretary, and later became ADC to King George V. He finally retired in 1922 and, invested with many honours and awards, British and foreign,[1] sailed away to live out his life in South Africa, the land of his birth.

Although Max and the Carew-Hunts had served together in Aldershot, it was not until he came back wounded from the Front that they became closely acquainted. Emily, Tommy whenever he was home on leave from France, and Max lived in the same part of London and the Carew-Hunts used to keep an eye on his well-being. They were however surprised and sometimes exasperated by the extent to which young women were attracted to their crippled friend. 'Sorry, can't ask you in tonight, Hunt,' a preoccupied Max would whisper through the door when they called round at his flat. But their daughter, Jane, had never come across anyone with the charm and glamour of Max. She was young, impressionable and she idolized him. And of course she got to know his son, Jack.

For her Jack was certainly a good catch. Attractive, polite, bright, with an allowance from his Father to boost his service pay, he was regarded as having a golden future in the Army and on the cricket field. He played for the Band of Brothers, the Free Foresters and the I Zingari as well as for his Corps. Furthermore, marriage to Jack would keep her in touch with her hero, Max. It was probably inevitable that they would wed, for like him she was shy and inexperienced; also her health was a bit fragile. Neither of them seemed to have had close friends of the opposite sex; but they had Max in common. They were married on 7 September 1921 in St Mark's Church, in North Audley Street near Hyde Park, and they had twelve years of comfort and reasonable contentment together in the garrisons of Chatham, Dover and Colchester during which they produced me (1923), and my Brothers, Moray (1929) and Alastair (1932). Rather foolishly Jack allowed his hobbies to divert him from the task of studying for the important entrance examination to the Army Staff College. He sat the exam once but without success. This failure was undoubtedly a handicap in his future career.

When in 1933 they went to India, to the Command Headquarters at Naini Tal in the foothills of the Himalayas, his professional star began to fade; by contrast Jane's health, self-confidence and personality grew markedly stronger. She was always to claim that those Indian years were the best of her life. It is easy to see why. She had Nanny Kirby from Kent to look after the kids, a pleasant bungalow overlooking a lake, many servants and plenty of time for painting, amateur dramatics and parties; and the incessant attentions of unattached young Officers gave her ego a boost she could not have enjoyed in a more inhibited garrison town in England.

But education problems loomed, and Jane brought Moray and Alastair back home in 1936 to rejoin me, leaving Jack on his own in India. His separation from us was prolonged by the outbreak of war in 1939 as he was kept in India until being sent to Egypt. Money was chronically short for our divided family; and his career of which Jane, and many others, had originally had such high expectations, petered out despite the opportunities for promotion and recognition which wartime should have opened to him. Jack finally returned to England in 1947 to a disappointed and unsympathetic wife, to sons who barely knew him, and he himself disillusioned in mind and wasted in body. Employed at the War Office in a Retired Officer's appointment, he lived in a London boarding house while Jane continued to live on the Isle of Wight.

He died in a London hospital of an aneurism which surgery had failed to put right. He was 59.

I was fond of my Father, and when I survey the path down which his life had taken him I feel very sad.

For many of my generation the shadows of the Great War of 1914–18 dimmed the joys of childhood, for we were born into the period when Britain was reflecting with horror[2] on that ruinous conflict and grieving deeply for her Empire's million dead.

It was a time when in every village, town and city in the land memorials to the Fallen were being unveiled; and when taken in a pram into Chatham or Rochester I saw widows who would live out their lives in mourning black and, sitting resignedly on the pavements, stricken men, blind, amputees or with shell-shocked minds, wearing their medals and bearing placards on which were written appeals such as 'Wounded Ex-Serviceman: Please Help', and who sought, by selling from little trays suspended from their necks, matches, shoelaces or buttons, to secure some pennies for daily bread. Others, less crippled, drew on the walls with coloured chalks portraits, landscapes and often replicas of their regimental badges. The depth of the nation's grief was demonstrated each year on Armistice Day. At the eleventh hour of the eleventh day of the eleventh month, the precise end of that terrible war was commemorated throughout the land by two minutes of silence. And it was a perfect silence. From the groups of villagers gathered round rural memorials to the Londoners who in their thousands joined with their Sovereign to pay homage at Lutyen's Cenotaph in Whitehall, the whole nation paused bare-headed. All movement ceased. Those on foot stood still; motor cars and horse-drawn vehicles pulled into the kerbside. No flying machines disturbed those sacred seconds; in the air only birds flew. Even on the railways some drivers are said to have slowed down their trains so that their passengers might share in that ritual observance which united the nation each November.[3]

We were living then in Chatham, in a house halfway between the garrison Church, where I was baptised on Palm Sunday 1923, and the gates of Brompton Barracks, the home of the Royal Engineers, the Sappers, whose Colonel Commandant had the stirring name of General Sir Bindon Blood. My Father was on the staff of the School of Military Engineering (the SME), and I have many memories of the parades and ceremonies held on that large rectangular parade ground where, near the statue of General Gordon of Khartoum mounted on his camel, stood the grey stone monuments erected in honour of Sappers who had given their lives in the campaigns and wars in which Britain had engaged since Queen Victoria ascended the throne. One very clear memory I have is of the day in March 1926 when, aged 3, I sat with my Mother watching from a window in the Officers' Mess as King George V, bearded, booted and wearing a heavy overcoat, for he was 61 years old, inspected the SME and the RE Depot. These units had then a total establishment of 208 Officers and 1,803 Other Ranks. On fine days we at home in Mansion Row could plainly hear the music of the Corps Band, and there also often came to us from the adjacent naval dockyard the sounds of a Royal Marine band and the smell of rope and tar. I have ever since adored military bands and their marches which raise the spirits and quicken the pace.

In 1928 my Father was posted to Dover. Our home there, an army quarter, was one of half-a-dozen small bungalows each named after a Flanders battlefield. Ours was called Messines. It was at the end of the row, nearest to the great Norman castle which loomed over our valley and the harbour beyond. A few yards from our bungalow is the field on which the shape of a monoplane has been set in concrete, marking the very spot where Louis Blériot had landed on 25 July 1909 after the first ever successful aerial crossing of the English Channel.[4] From our garden in front of Messines one day in 1929 I saw flying towards London on her round-the-world journey the long silver German airship, the 'Graf Zeppelin'. (Her sister-ship, the 'Hindenburg', was totally destroyed by fire in 1937 when mooring in New Jersey.) And over us one night in 1930 there also passed that ill-fated British airship, the R101, which, too hastily despatched on a voyage to India with among her passengers a Secretary-of-State, crashed into a hill near Beauvais with great loss of life.

By this time I was beginning to fathom the pattern and logic of our garrison existence and something too about the wider world into which it fitted. I was daily discovering new facts, new names and new sensations. It was exciting and I especially enjoyed my first lessons in English and French at my Dover day-school, St George's; and watching my Father's prowess on various Kentish cricket fields. The hours between tea and bedtime were filled by stories of Winnie-the-Pooh and Christopher Robin, and by the voices of the soprano Amelita Galli-Curci and the beloved Maurice Chevalier flowing from our wind-up gramophone. And Father's car, a Lancia (Number NE 2803), a gift from Max Graham in South Africa, sometimes carried us as far afield as London, and one summer came with us on holiday to Jersey.

Some experiences however were disagreeable. Witnessing for the first time the accusations and tears of parental discord, then as so often in the future about that perpetual preoccupation money. And one day in a shop I overheard a man, a well-dressed man who I thought should have known better, maligning in public our King. To my young ears that was a sort of treason, and very shocking. The innocence of the nursery was being rapidly eroded as my knowledge of the world was enlarged by the reports in the newspapers and by the conversation of the adults around me.

After two years in Dover, my Father was posted to the 7th Field Company of the Royal Engineers in Colchester, then as in Roman times an important garrison town. We rented a comfortable house with a large garden and my Father, now a Captain could, thanks to his allowance from Max, afford a Nanny, a living-in cook, and a parlour maid.

I was sent as a weekly boarder to a nearby private school, Holmwood House, run by a Mr and Mrs Duggan. I performed adequately on the sports ground and at all lessons except algebra. I can recall with great clarity how Mrs Duggan with blackboard and chalk introduced us to the symbols x and y and explained how they can be combined to create z. But by the end of that lesson I was still totally mystified by the subject.

And so I remained for seven long years until at Cheltenham College there loomed a Great Test, the London Matriculation Exam. My Housemaster, aware of my deficiencies, made me attend extra lessons in arithmetic as well as algebra. This involved getting up at daybreak several mornings a week, walking to College on an empty stomach and reporting to a little Welshman named Ritchie-Williams. He was fierce, intolerant of sloth or stupidity and free with verbal and corporal abuse. He was, as the Americans say, awesome. I was terrified of the man and, like my fellow duffers, sat on the edge of my chair hanging on to every syllable he uttered. He taught us brilliantly, and when the examination results were published that autumn, I found that I had been awarded a credit – a pass with distinction – in every subject.

I am eternally grateful to Ritchie-Bill for the clarity of his teaching, the harshness of his classroom regime and the confidence he instilled in us. I commend his methods to other teachers; as I do his timing, for perhaps the brain absorbs instruction best soon after dawn and unencumbered by breakfast.

We had a grand piano, a Bechstein, later destroyed by an air raid while in store in London, on which my Mother, Jane, and Grandfather, Tommy, used to play. Tommy came to stay with us for a bit after his wife, Emily, died in 1931. Jane knew I was fond of music, and one evening asked me if I would like to take music lessons at school. I reflected for a few moments before replying 'No'. In those days boys could only engage in music by reducing the hours devoted to the standard subjects such as Latin, Greek, History, Maths, etc. I knew that I would have to win a scholarship if my parents were to send me, and in due course my Brothers, to public schools; and music lessons would distract me from that goal. Nevertheless, I have always envied people who can entertain roomfulls of guests with a piano or rouse the very angels with chords from a great cathedral's organ.

I was quickly learning about the structure and customs of the British Army, or at least that part of it that embraced our family. The social stratification would amaze the onlooker of today just as it surprised me, then a small boy of 9. Near us in Colchester there lived another Army family with a son of about my own age with whom I used to play. His Father was in the Royal Army Ordnance Corps; for the purposes of this story I shall call him Captain Brown. I liked the Browns very much. My parents did quite a lot of entertaining, and one evening my Mother came to tuck me up in bed. She was all dressed up and wearing jewellery, so I said to her: 'Who are you having to dine tonight?' She told me. I then said: 'When are you going to invite the Browns who are so kind to me?' She seemed rather shocked by my question for she replied: 'The Browns; we really can't have them, they're Ordnance!' It was then pointed out to me that members of certain Corps – the Medical, Dental, RASC and RAOC – were considered the social inferiors of Gunners and Sappers; and by the same order of social precedence the Sappers (Mad, Married or Methodist was their reputation in the Service) were looked down on by the Cavalry, Guards and wealthier Line Regiments.

Lying at home in bed I could hear the trumpet and bugle calls that regulated the routine of the regiments in the Colchester barracks, and I became aware too of the poor state our Army had been brought down to through Government parsimony. Thanks to unemployment during those years of the Depression, there was no shortage of recruits; but the pay was poor and training, based on the equipment, the drills and the tactical doctrines of 1914–18, was cramped by lack of funds. Furthermore, a cardinal tenet of our national defence policy since 1919 had been the Ten Year Rule: the assumption that 'the British Empire will not be engaged in any great war during the next ten years, and that no Expeditionary Force will be required'. This assumption was not abandoned until 1932, by which time much harm had been done to the efficiency and morale of our Servicemen.

My peripheral childhood observation of the nation's neglect of its Armed Forces caused me during the Second World War to marvel at Britain's extraordinary good fortune in being served at that time of great peril by such men as Slim, Montgomery, Dowding, Cunningham, Ramsay, Alanbrooke and their companions on the long, hard road to victory. These wartime leaders were endowed with professional skills and a dedication exceeding anything the country had a right to expect. Despite the way the electorate had during the inter-war years deprived the Armed Forces of funds, encouragement and status, these men had remained faithful to the Profession of Arms and were on hand when the storm broke. Why was this?

There were, I believe, two fundamental reasons. Firstly, in spite of the poor pay and public indifference, Officers and Men enjoyed in their barracks, ships or air stations a degree of material security, well-being and comfort greater than most civilians could count on. For very many, life in a regiment or ship under caring Officers and alongside proven friends was congenial and protective; just like being a member of a proud and united family. Secondly there was India: service overseas in Imperial garrisons where sunshine, servants, sport and sometimes bullets made life stimulating and professionally interesting.

The retrenchment imposed on the Armed Forces was a symptom of the attempts made by successive governments to cope with Britain's economic difficulties. Because during almost the whole of my life to date British Governments have been facing a seemingly unbroken series of economic crises, I have included at this point a summary, extracted from official documents, of the economic problems which beset Britain in the years between the two World Wars and the policies adopted in the attempt to solve them.

The boom which followed the Armistice of November 1918 had suggested that the return to a peacetime economy would be quick and prosperous. The output of British industry in 1920 was as high as in 1913. But it was a false dawn: as *The Economist* commented: 'In April 1920 all was right with the world. In April 1921 it was all wrong.' Britain had a National Debt of £7,000 million; many other countries were also deep in debt. Thus British goods no longer sold as readily as in the nineteenth century, and our trading position had been further weakened by the sale during the war of about a quarter of Britain's overseas investments. Our invisible earnings were now less than before 1914. Moreover the pound sterling had in the period 1914–20, lost more than half its buying power. In consequence inflation pushed up the cost of British goods, many of which were produced with outdated machinery by industries designed to meet the needs of the previous century. Britain was losing her competitive edge.

In 1920 Lloyd George's government raised the interest rate from six to seven per cent in an attempt to check inflation, but this made it more expensive to borrow money for investment and modernisation. The boom ended quickly. Unsold goods led to reductions in output and to unemployment. From that time until the Second World War there were in Britain never fewer than one million unemployed (out of a population of about forty-five million); the basic industries which had thrived during the nineteenth century being the hardest hit. By 1921 it was clear that 'the land fit for heroes to live in', which Lloyd George had hoped to create, was one of unemployment and inequality. Hope gave way to disillusionment and anger.

Lloyd George eagerly consulted experts and businessmen whose advice, often confused and confusing, was essentially conservative. Early in 1922 a committee of businessmen under Eric Geddes advocated widespread cuts in government spending, and under the 'Geddes Axe' education, housing and the Armed Forces suffered. These cuts did nothing to tackle the fundamental problems of the British economy; they gave root, however, to the view that any expenditure on social welfare or any kind of government planning was certain to plunge the country into bankruptcy. This hidebound view was bitterly resisted by the Labour Party, the TUC and by JM Keynes. The latter argued that government spending, far from being undesirable, would aid a depressed economy by providing work, reducing unemployment and increasing purchasing power. Britain's ills were compounded by events outside the country: the horrendous inflation which devastated millions of Germans in 1923, the Wall Street Crash of October 1929, the Great Depression, the failure of the Austrian Credit Anstalt bank and widespread financial panic. Governments were shaken almost everywhere. In Germany the Depression played a considerable part in bringing the National Socialists to power in 1933, and in the USA persuaded the American voters to reject Hoover and the Republicans and to turn in 1932 to the Democrats, Franklin Roosevelt and his New Deal. By contrast with the USA, in Britain the emphasis remained on engendering new confidence in sterling through balanced budgets; no more money being spent by government than it received in revenue.

The May Committee, set up in March 1931 to examine government spending, like Geddes ten years earlier recommended substantial cuts in the wages of teachers, civil servants, policemen and members of the Armed Forces. One consequence of these cuts was that the men in Royal Navy ships based at Invergordon mutinied – though more in anger over the inept manner in which the cuts were announced to them than over the Government's policy itself.

These cuts were again fiercely opposed by the Labour Party and the TUC. Ramsay MacDonald resigned as Prime Minister and from the Labour Party, but was immediately appointed by King George V to head a 'National Government of Personalities' backed by the Conservatives, some Liberals and by a handful of those Labour MPs who supported the policy of retrenchment. This new government abandoned the Gold Standard, and reduced the level of cuts. The run on the pound, which had fallen to $3.30, was checked and the pound swung back to $5. MacDonald called a general election in October 1931 asking the voters to give him a 'Doctor's Mandate' to cure the country's ills. The Conservatives supported him, and the outcome of the election was a massive vote of confidence in the National Government, only fifty-two Labour Members being returned to the House of Commons.

During 1932 the Bank Rate fell to two per cent (it was to remain at about that level until 1951), but having arrived at a policy of cheap money, the

National Government did almost nothing to make use of it. By building public amenities and modernising the nation's infrastructure the central government could have given a lead in reviving the British economy and reducing unemployment, as did governments in the USA and many parts of Europe. The policy of MacDonald, and after 1935 of Baldwin and Chamberlain, lacked initiative and creative enterprise.

Chamberlain carefully balanced his budgets and went on looking for ways to cut official spending further. The Means Test provided one such way. It was detested by the working class and was to prove a factor in the Labour Party's landslide victory in the election of 1945. But Chamberlain's careful calculations were derailed by the need to rearm, belatedly, to meet the military threats of the Axis Powers, Germany, Italy and Japan.

But Government alone could not be blamed for the state of our military affairs. Within the Services themselves there was too much argument and lack of precision about the fundamental roles of the Royal Navy, the Army and the Royal Air Force, and what they should be equipped and trained to do. In the Cavalry regiments there was fierce controversy about mechanisation. The advocates of retaining the horse, sword and lance hotly disputed the views of those military thinkers who predicted that the future of cavalry lay in armoured protection, powerful guns and good cross-country performance. All that had been briefly proved by the tank in the last year of fighting on the Western Front, but too many of our Defence Planners ignored the evidence. Over in Germany the leaders of the Reichswehr and the men who were to become commanders in Hitler's Wehrmacht were drawing the opposite lessons.

It must have been with some relief that my parents received orders to go to India. Because there were in India no schools suitable for European children of my age, I was taken to Haslemere and put into a large boarding school named Fernden set in spacious and well-kept grounds. My poor Mother was very distressed at having to leave her first-born child behind in England, but such separation had always been one of the penalties of Empire, and it was eased only when the aeroplane replaced the steamship as the principal means of travel between the Motherland and her overseas possessions.

Fernden was run by the Brownrigg family, had an excellent reputation and about a hundred boys. There I stayed for three years from early 1933 when my parents, two Brothers and Nanny Kirby sailed off in a troopship to Bombay and thence by train and motorcar to their lakeside bungalow in Naini Tal.

Having no uncles or aunts meant that for the bulk of the school holidays I remained in Fernden. I was not alone: there were two German boys, an Argentino and an Indian princeling. His name was Surendra Singh and he came from the State of Alirajpur. I got to know him pretty well as we were in the same dormitory and usually opened the batting for the school's First XI. He was a slim, lithe, active and engaging young man, popular at Fernden. In the autumn of 1936 we parted company as I went on to Cheltenham while he entered some other English public school. We did not keep in touch but I never forgot him.

Many, many years later, in December 1973 I was coming to the end of my year's attachment to the Indian Services, and was in the Gymkhana Club in New Delhi talking to a Colonel of their Special Forces.

I suddenly remembered Surendra Singh and I asked the Colonel: 'Have you heard of a state called Alirajpur? I cannot find it on any map.' He replied: 'No wonder, it is indeed a very small state; but I do know it. Why do you ask?' I explained about Fernden and our time together there some forty years earlier, and said to the Colonel: 'I am shortly to leave India but it would be so nice, for old times' sake, to send Surendra Singh a telegram, letter or some message to show him he's not forgotten. Can you help me to get a message to him please?' The Colonel replied: 'I can do better than that. If you turn round,' he said, 'you will find Surendra Singh ten feet in front of you at the bar.'

The Brownrigg family, Norman the Headmaster and Esther his wife, did all they could to give us interesting and varied holidays. In summer we went down to a farmhouse in Devon, not far from the grim Dartmoor Prison; and in the Aprils of 1934 and 1935 to France where we lodged for a fortnight in an hotel in Dinard. In those days one English pound bought eighty-two French francs, and much of my pocket money I spent on the most delicious chocolate cakes filled with real cream. They were the best thing about France: everything else I found rather dreary. Much of the time it rained, and Dinard out of season, like most seaside resorts, had an empty, decayed look, and the unsmiling faces of its citizens seemed to me to reflect France's anguish in the Great War and their anxieties over the unending political turmoil in Paris. Most days in Dinard I felt profoundly depressed. I had a bad conscience about this for I felt that I really should be more exhilarated and interested in that foreign land to which the Brownriggs – and my Father's payment of the school fees – had brought me. The cause of my depression became clear half a century later. In 1984, together with my wife and two friends, I went back to Dinard.

I had no difficulty in finding the hotel in which I had stayed all those years before, and was pleased to see that it, like much of the town, had been given an extensive facelift. Much money had been spent on tarting up the hotel's exterior. I went inside, and as I ventured up the stairs to seek out my former bedrooms, that old melancholy struck me like a blow to the head. Inside, the hotel had changed not one jot. The dark paint on the walls, worn carpets, sunless corridors and feeble electric lights all combined to recreate the identical atmosphere which had made my boyhood sojourn in that building so unjoyous.

Other things too began to cloud our young lives. Norman Brownrigg took to creeping around the dormitories in his stockinged feet after dark and with a hairbrush laying into any boy he caught whispering or reading or in any way displeasing him. As his temper grew worse he had to be kept increasingly away from us, and during my last term at Fernden he was permanently bed-ridden. He died of cancer shortly after I left the school, and his son Charles took over its running.

The school staff were pretty good, caring and talented. They introduced us to the works of Gilbert and Sullivan, and also to the Boy Scout Movement in which I rose to become Patrol Leader of the Woodpeckers. It is claimed that a former Fernden boy, when asked to agree with the statement that 'Time at school spent on scouting was time wasted' replied thus: 'I used to think that but something happened last year which caused me to change my mind.' He went on: 'I was motoring with my family through the Alps. Early one morning we were the first people to come across the scene of an accident; an omnibus had collided with boulders which had fallen onto the narrow road. There was broken glass, injured passengers and a lot of blood around.' He continued: 'At that moment I realised how lucky I was to have learned First Aid with the Fernden Scouts, for I remembered to put my head between my legs and I didn't feel faint.'

My favourite Master was Sergeant King, the PT Instructor at whose hands I developed a love for gymnastics. The Matron, Miss Fishwick, and her pretty Assistant, Miss Vickers, looked after our physical well-being as wisely as the science of medicine in those days permitted. To ward off illness and to make us grow up straight and tall, Matron used to give each of us daily a small glass of milk with in it a drop of iodine. The taste was quite pleasant but what good it did us I do not know.

Comparing my school days with those of my own children some thirty years later, I am struck by the frequency with which severe illness and even death came upon us. I was lucky to have been spared – thanks to Miss Fishwick's iodine cocktail? – for scarlet fever, diphtheria and tuberculosis were common killers. The boy in the bed next to mine, Derek Dore, died in my second term undergoing lung surgery; young Lee never recovered from having his appendix taken out; Bruce-Poole was crippled by polio, and the elder of the two Langrishe boys died in the sick-bay: of what we were never told.

My time at Fernden coincided with the years in which the world started to slide inexorably towards another Great War. I personally have always regarded 1931 rather than 1939 as the start of the Second World War. One day that summer as my parents, Moray and I were getting into the car at Frinton-on-Sea to return home to Colchester after a picnic on the beach, a boy walked past selling evening newspapers headed in great black letters 'JAPAN INVADES MANCHURIA'. And so it went on.

While we were at school the news which reached us from outside was largely of Test and County cricket matches and personalities which we followed avidly, or of events in Germany and Italy. Adolf Hitler and Benito Mussolini featured more and more in the papers and in the conversations of the adults around us. Most of these seemed to have a high regard for Hitler, the new Chancellor of Germany, and sympathy for what he was seeking to achieve within that country. This sympathy changed to alarm in 1936 when he sent in the German Army to re-occupy the Rhineland in breach of the Versailles Treaty.

About Benito Mussolini, the Italian Duce, we knew less. By draining some marshland around Rome and by making the Italian trains run on time, he seemed to have earned in English eyes quite a few 'Brownie Points', but this rather benign image was shattered in 1935 when Italian Forces invaded Abyssinia, defeated the local armies, and drove Emperor Haile Selassie, the 'Lion of Judah', into exile. The wickedness of the Italians was pointed out to us by the Headmaster who ordered the whole school into the chapel to pray for the salvation of the Abyssinians; and also for the League of Nations whose reputation and effectiveness were to be increasingly tested in the years leading up to 1939.

In 1933 the students of the Oxford Union had passed a resolution that 'This House will in no circumstances fight for its King and Country'; Oswald Mosley's British Fascist Movement was growing in numbers; and pacifist organisations were publishing a variety of books and pamphlets depicting the horrors of war. One book of gruesome photographs of dead and mutilated soldiers on the Western Front, published under the title, *A Covenant with Death*, shocked our young minds despite the efforts of our elders to conceal the book from us. All this gave me little confidence that our country would take early and effective steps to deter Germany, Italy and Japan from further acts of international banditry.

My Mother, Moray, Alastair and Nanny had come back from India in early 1936 and took rooms in an hotel in Haslemere so as to be near me at Fernden. There then began for Jane a harrowing period.

Both my Brothers went down with measles, caught on the boat that brought them home. Complications set in, and Moray would have died if a specialist from London had not operated on him in the hotel bedroom. I too was living in the hotel as the Brownriggs had banned me from Fernden while in quarantine on account of my Brothers' measles. To add to my poor Mother's worries she found herself with no money to pay either the doctors' fees or the mounting hotel bill. This happened because my Father in India received his pay monthly in arrears and then had to have it transferred, in those days by a laborious and unreliable procedure, to a London bank account where Jane could, if in credit, draw on it. At one stage, desperate for help, she appealed to her Father. He lent her five pounds!

I shall not forget those Haslemere weeks and the strain they imposed on my Mother. They were for her and my Brothers a dismal homecoming from India and one I felt powerless to alleviate. Grandfather Tommy really should have done more to help Jane; she had no other relative to whom to turn. Fortunately the Manager of the hotel and his wife were sympathetic and tolerant of our family misfortunes.

I joined Cheltenham College in September 1936 and was enrolled in Newick, a House with a good reputation run by Mr Hereward Wake and his plump little wife, Sheila. Having been taught Greek for only two terms – the Brownriggs had difficulty in finding someone to teach that subject – I failed to win a scholarship, but the College was good enough to award me an exhibition, a minor scholarship, the following year.

I have to confess that my first years at Cheltenham were the most unhappy of my life. I was an undersized, pallid and solitary boy with a dread of being stared at by crowds. This phobia had started when as a page-boy aged 3, and all dressed up in velvet for a big London wedding, I entered the church to find row upon row of grown ups staring round at me. I turned in terror and fled down the street. Thus for me, put into the choir whose stalls were in the centre of the College chapel under the direct gaze of all, every Divine Service was an ordeal from which I used to emerge shaking.

I kept these anxieties to myself; indeed even if there had been someone in whom I could have confided, to have done so would have been thoroughly 'wet'.

During my second year a merciful Providence stepped in to give me a respite from these tribulations. Something went wrong with Grandfather Max's financial affairs in South Africa and he suddenly cut off my Father's allowance. This was a severe blow to my parents who, amongst other problems, found themselves unable to pay my College fees. In consequence I had to miss a term and had four far more agreeable months at home.

Jane had rented an attractive house on the Suffolk bank of the River Stour in the village of Bures. There I enjoyed my extended holiday by gardening, fishing and operating the splendid model railway set of Bassett-Lowke trains which my Father had passed on to me. Of school work I did the absolute minimum; throughout my life I have inclined to the maxim 'Do not strive to do today what can safely be put off to the morrow'. When my parents got their finances sorted out I returned to College, uttering to those who enquired, some rather unconvincing explanation for my long absence.

That was a period when Cheltenham College was going downhill in morale, achievement and, I believe, in reputation. When I joined, the Headmaster was Roseveare; colourless and little known. He was not a success. In 1937 he was replaced by Victor Pite, a splendid man whose background and charisma led us to expect that he would do great things for Cheltenham. Alas he died of a heart attack after only two terms with us. The next Head was John Bell, a fat little man who came to us from St Paul's School in London. I have to say that Bell, like Roseveare, made no positive impression on the lives of my contemporaries and me. More effective, and remembered by me with especial warmth, were two of my Form-masters, W. L. King and C.T. (Jaw) Priestley. Hereward and Sheila Wake ran Newick at least satisfactorily, but we did not see much of them as the House routine and discipline were administered by the Prefects. It was they who flogged those of us who broke the House rules, and sitting at our desks doing our evening 'prep' we could hear the running feet of the Prefects and the swish of the cane; and as the chastened victim crept back to his place among us, we glanced up to see if he had taken his punishment with tears or fortitude. In Newick tears were rare, as, I am glad to say, was flogging.

It was in Newick that we sat round a wireless set in December 1936 listening to the Abdication speech of King Edward VIII. When we grasped the fact that this man, so popular as Prince of Wales, was actually going to renounce the throne we realized that something had gone very wrong at the highest levels of our nation's leadership. As he spoke of the impossibility of ruling 'without the help and support of the woman I love' our reaction was one of contempt. 'How gutless to run away from his duty on account of some woman: a foreign divorcee to boot!'

However, it soon became clear that Edward's replacement on the throne by his Brother, the Duke of York, had been a blessing. At no time was this to be more apparent than in the Second World War. The behaviour of Edward, then Duke of Windsor, was often self-centred, and unhelpful to our overburdened wartime Government; whereas the conduct of King George VI and his Queen, Elizabeth, and the example they set to the nation, were admirable.

As so often happens, Providence had known how best to arrange the course of events for Britain's good.

A subject about which we adolescents in the thirties were extraordinarily ill-informed was sex. In our household the subject had never been discussed. I had no sisters, and the little I knew at the age of 13 about how babies were conceived and born I had gleaned from one of the foreign boys at Fernden. He was well acquainted with the female anatomy, but as he described in words and drawings the process of human procreation we were filled with astonishment. We simply could not believe that the Almighty had designed Mankind to reproduce itself through such crude and uncomfortable exertions.

The day before I set off for Cheltenham, Jane said to me quietly: 'After you have settled down at College someone will explain to you about sex and where babies come from. In the meantime I want you to be very careful and avoid being attacked by bigger boys.' That was the sole occasion in the whole of her long life – she died in her 88th year – that the subject was ever mentioned between us. In due course I began to fathom what she had meant by her reference to 'attacks by bigger boys', for distasteful gossip about the periodic pairing of senior students with the youths of their fancy – their 'bijoux' – was constantly whispered around College. These relationships, it seemed to me, brought considerable kudos to the older partner, but to his bijou an enduring notoriety. My Mother was quite right; that was truly a situation to steer clear of.

One evening during my second term at Newick a group of us was summoned into the Housemaster's study. This, we guessed, was for our long-awaited Official Lesson on Sex. We sat down. An embarrassed Mr Wake started by announcing that we had reached an age when certain marked changes would take place in our bodies; also in our thoughts and attitudes, particularly about girls.

All this was entirely natural and we were, he adjured us, in no way to get alarmed about these developments. He went on: 'If however any of you begin to feel urges which are too strong for you to resist, you must come and talk to me and I'll tell you what to do about the problem. Do any of you wish to ask me a question?' No one did, so we quietly and unenlightened returned to our evening studies. The Great Lesson was Over!

For me enlightenment came the following year. Cosmo Graham, a cousin of my Father, was a Captain in the Royal Navy. He was in every sense a big man and I remember him with admiration and affection. He died soon after the war in the rank of Rear Admiral. He and his wife, Elspeth, owned a large house called Monk's Park in Wadhurst where they invited me to spend three weeks in the long summer holidays of 1938. Their elder and favourite son, Keillour, a Subaltern in the Argyll and Sutherland Highlanders, had been killed with two companions in March 1936 in Kashmir by an avalanche. Elspeth never wholly got over Keillour's death, but she became uncommonly kind and affectionate towards me, and I like to think that our close association during the next forty years brought her some recompense.

Elspeth had an older brother, Patrick. He was an expert on China, the Chinese, their art and languages. Although he spent most of his life abroad, a room was kept for him in Monk's Park and it was into his room that I was put for my stay. Sent to bed earlier than anyone else – for I was the youngest person in the house – I looked around for something to read during the evenings that lay ahead. On two walls of the room were shelves lined with books, dozens of them, but alas every one seemed to be in Chinese. I looked more closely and found on a lower shelf two volumes in English. The title of one was *A History of European Morals*; of the other *An Encyclopaedia of Sexual Knowledge*. By the time I left Monk's Park my knowledge of sex, or at least the theory of the thing, had been considerably widened.

Today it is, I think, generally admitted that our national attitude to sex and all its ramifications had from Queen Victoria's reign until well after the Second World War been repressive, inhibited and unnatural; certainly quite at variance with the frank, open and red-blooded way the English had traditionally viewed such matters. Many of my generation were brought up to look upon sexual topics as obscene and the sex act as sinful. This was so deeply engrained that some young men convinced themselves that if ever they indulged in illicit sex they would not survive the war.

While at Fernden I got the idea that the most worthwhile way in which to pass one's adult life is to make people happy. I proposed therefore to be a writer of plays. I actually wrote two pieces which we put on at Christmas for the Brownriggs. But that charitable ambition was soon replaced by a tremendous urge to be a surgeon and I devoured any medical book that was within reach and comprehensible. My tutors at Cheltenham, however, knew what was best for me and quickly steered me away from Science into classes which concentrated on History, French and German.

Once the London Matriculation Exam was behind me, I started to prepare for the next examination hurdle, the Higher Certificate of Education, scheduled for 1940. I had by now set my sights on a career in the Diplomatic Service as I relished languages and history, and I took up Spanish in order to qualify for the scholarship to Oxford University reserved for Cheltonians who had studied that language. I had grown a lot in size and self-confidence, and was now happy at College and eager to set off down the path I had mapped out for myself.

All these plans were brought to nought in September 1939 by Adolf Hitler. The German attack on Poland did not surprise us, for the worsening situation in Europe had become obvious to all: the Saar plebiscite, German rearmament, the Austrian Anschluss, the Civil War in Spain, the Sudeten crisis and our humiliation at Munich in 1938, the German invasion, unopposed, of Czechoslovakia six months later, the Italian occupation of Albania – and now Poland. The one event which came upon us like a bolt from the blue was the Pact signed in the very last days of peace between those two bitter enemies, Nazi Germany and the Communist Soviet Union. The evidence of the slide to war had indeed been clear to see, but as late as the spring of 1939 we in Britain deluded ourselves that the League of Nations, with France and Britain in the van, would muster its collective strength and halt the aggressive actions of the Axis Powers. Moreover few believed that any nation in civilised Western Europe would allow itself to be led again into a cataclysm such as the continent had endured from 1914 to 1918. We were wrong. But Marshal Ferdinand Foch, the victorious Generalissimo of the Allied Armies, had been right when, on reading in 1919 the clauses of the Treaty of Versailles imposed on the vanquished Germans, he cried: 'This is not Peace; it is merely an Armistice for twenty years.'

I was with my family in Seaview in the Isle of Wight – we had moved there from Suffolk the previous year – listening to the wireless as Neville Chamberlain, the Prime Minister, saddened by the failure of his work for peace, announced that war with Germany had begun. Many men and women had already volunteered for various wartime duties, principally in the field of ARP (Air Raid Precautions): Auxiliary Firemen, Special Constables, Air Raid Wardens, Rescue Teams, nursing and so on. I had offered my services as an Evacuation Officer, and with a companion had gone round the village compiling a list of householders willing to take in some of the children being moved to safety out of the likely target areas for bombing in London, the Midlands and the big ports. Jane had made for me an armband embroidered with the letters E.O. but I never wore it as for some reason none of the expected evacuees arrived in Seaview. So the afternoon of the first day of the war I spent on the beach helping to fill sandbags.

The summer ended without any enemy activity coming to our part of the world. All remained peaceful. But I did not return to Cheltenham as the College buildings had been requisitioned by the Army and all Cheltonians were instructed to report instead to Shrewsbury. There the Salopians were to share with us the good facilities of their famous school, while we invaders from Cheltenham were dispersed in twos and threes among hospitable households in the town. Another boy from Newick House, Christopher Little, and I were taken into the home of a Mr and Mrs French. He was the Manager of a local branch of the National Provincial Bank; she, Sylvia French, ran a beauty parlour. We did not at first see much of the Frenches save at weekends, because we were either at the school doing sports or lessons, or upstairs doing our homework. Christopher and I shared a comfortable room, with a stove to keep out the worst of the winter cold, and were given plenty to eat. We were in good hands. I was soon to find however that they were uncommon ones.

The household on which we were billeted consisted of Mr French, 'EJ' we called him for he was everywhere known more by his initials than by a Christian name. Middle-aged, stoutish and rather taciturn he was kind and helpful to us two newcomers from Cheltenham. He was, I guess, ten years older than his wife who was tall, pale of complexion, with dark hair and a figure that was thin rather than slim. In contrast to her rather stolid husband she was vivacious and well groomed. They had two sons but we never met them as they were away at boarding school.

One Sunday evening in early November Mrs French and I were alone in the dining room and were chatting about nothing in particular. It was actually the first time we had ever been left alone for an uninterrupted conversation à deux, and Sylvia French knew little of me or my background and nothing whatsoever of my plans for the future.

All of a sudden she announced: 'You are a very lucky young man! Do you know that your life is being watched over by someone who is very fond of you?' She said this in a particularly calm and deliberate voice. I must have appeared a bit startled but she went on: 'There is a woman protecting you and she is standing right behind your chair now, in this room.' I turned round but saw no one: Mrs French and I were still quite alone. As she continued to talk in the same measured tones she began to describe the general pattern which my life was to take, its trends and main events. And as she spoke she from time to time glanced over my shoulder as if to seek from my invisible protectress confirmation of her predictions. After perhaps two minutes her voice petered out having, it seemed to me, either become drained of images of my future or she had detected some happening she felt compelled to conceal. 'Anyway,' she said finally: 'Do not worry about it.' She got up and left the room.

Sylvia French never spoke of the matter again, nor did she do or say anything to indicate that this extraordinary episode had even occurred.

Although I recorded it in my diary, I gave little thought to her conversation with me at the time. But as I grew older and more concerned with the future and the hazards and opportunities it might bring, I began to reflect increasingly on what she had told me; and I became aware that her predictions were proving uncannily accurate. I long ago ceased to ask myself unanswerable questions about the motives behind her interest in me. Was it caused by maternal or even amatory feelings? If so, why me? Was she a charlatan? Was I merely a gullible schoolboy easily duped by an older female? Now, all these years later I am convinced that she had a genuine ability to foresee the future accurately. The principal events of my life have certainly come to pass in the way and in the sequence she predicted. Moreover I was to discover from random conversations with neighbours and others who were acquainted with the French family, that Sylvia was known to be what the Scots call fey – clairvoyant and somehow in contact with the world we term the supernatural. All this has been a comfort to me, for in my moments of greatest depression and anxiety I was to remind myself of her optimistic predictions and of her reference to the Protectress she had seen standing behind my chair in that dining room. She is, I believe, my Grandmother, Emily Carew-Hunt, who had died in 1931. I revere and thank her profoundly for all she has done for me.

There remains however one thing which has puzzled me about Sylvia French's powers of prophesy: in all the weeks that we were under her roof she never revealed that my room-mate, Christopher Little, would win a scholarship to Oxford but die of pneumonia before he took it up. Perhaps she knew, but out of kindness decided to keep silent.

* * *

The first seven months of the war took a course totally different to what had been expected. On land the German Army overcame in four weeks all resistance in Poland, and the Red Army, advancing in collusion from the east, completed the subjugation of that gallant but ill-fated nation.

On the western front the French Army in its Maginot Line defences and the British Expeditionary Force, deployed along the frontier of neutral Belgium under the command of General Lord Gort, lay opposite the Germans through the long, cold winter. The French Government was adamant that no action should be taken by the Allies which might provoke the enemy into retaliation against ill-defended French cities and an inadequately prepared population. Thus the deliberate inactivity at the front was broken only by intermittent and small-scale patrolling.

In the air the Luftwaffe carried out some bombing raids against naval installations in Scotland, but the onslaught by massed bombers against our cities which many experts had predicted had not occurred, although Londoners had been driven into their shelters within a few minutes of the Prime Minister's broadcast on 3 September by a false air raid alarm.

Though the Royal Air Force had carried out some small raids on coastal areas of Germany, their principal mission was to drop on the inhabitants of western Germany millions of leaflets urging them to turn against Hitler and to end the war. This was widely regarded in England as a waste of effort and an insult to the aircrews.

Many delusions were in fact being spread around our country at this time. 'The Germans had only enough oil for a war of three months' duration; the General Staff were plotting to do away with Hitler, and a high percentage of the tanks in the panzer divisions were made of cardboard, dummies paraded to hearten the dim-witted German citizenry and to intimidate the neutrals, but exposed by the eagle-eyes of the British Secret Service.'

Concurrently, however, perturbing stories were reaching England of weaknesses in the French Army, standing so idle, poorly trained, ill-led and infected with communist anti-war propaganda. That the tribulations of the French since 1870 and the political turmoil in Paris in the 1930s had quenched the military ardour of that nation was soon to be revealed to an astonished world.

Those seven months of bizarre inactivity in the air and on land were labelled by the English-speaking world the 'phoney war'. And so they were – except at sea. The Royal Navy was already being harshly tested, though not yet seriously by the German surface fleet. An important action had been won when a cruiser squadron under Commodore Harwood caused the destruction of the pocket battleship *Graf Spee* off Montevideo in December and the suicide of her captain, Langsdorff. The navy had almost completed too the task of ridding the oceans of enemy shipping and of establishing the economic blockade of German territory; and it was preparing to meet again the formidable challenge of the submarine.

Admiral Doenitz's U-boat fleet scored significant successes when they sank the aircraft carrier *Courageous* in the third week of the war, and when on 14 October Lieutenant Günther Prien, in a fine feat of navigation and daring, steered his U47 through the block ships, booms and hazardous currents into the great naval anchorage of Scapa Flow. There he sank HMS *Royal Oak* with the loss of over 800 lives including that of Able Seaman Brading, the son of our village butcher in Seaview. The honour of the German navy had however been sullied when, on the very first day of the war, a U-boat sank without warning an unarmed liner, the *Athenia*, carrying across the Atlantic to the safety of the New World many women and children.

The chief anxiety of the Royal Navy during the last three months of 1939 was the magnetic mine, a device dropped from the air or laid by submarine in shallow water, which detonated electronically when a ship passed over it. This novel weapon was designed to cripple our ports and coastal shipping, and it caused much alarm and damaged many vessels before it was neutralised by the valour and skill of a team of sailors and scientists.

Although the battlefields of western Europe lay silent, a bloody conflict broke out in Finland which the Soviet Union attacked on the first day of December. High in morale, tough and well equipped for fighting in snow, the Finns inflicted severe losses on the Red Army, but after four months the superior numbers and the revamped strategy of the Russians prevailed and the Finns sued for peace.

This brief and distant campaign had two important consequences. It caused many onlookers to underrate the competence and resilience of the Red Army, alleged to have been sapped by Stalin's purges of its senior ranks three years before. That Army was to prove victorious over Finland but even more gloriously over Germany in 1945 at the end of the most barbarous war fought in modern times between European nations. The 'Winter War' in Finland also led the politicians and military leaders in Paris and London to divert their attention from the main, western, battleground. They deluded themselves that Hitler was reluctant to attack there. They saw little immediate threat from over the Rhine, through the Ardennes or across the Meuse, but they perceived in Finland an opportunity to strike at German interests in the Baltic and in northern Scandinavia.

Much energy and thought was devoted to assembling and fitting out an Anglo-French expedition to go to the aid of the Finns, a charitable but wholly futile project, and when the Finns capitulated it was decided instead to put an end by force of arms to German naval and commercial activities in Norway and in Norwegian waters. Alas, the German Army got there first. The people of England could not foresee the melancholy outcome of this Norwegian venture – a 'ramshackle campaign' Churchill was to call it – as they passed the winter months of 1939-40 perplexed by the 'phoney war', resentful of the restrictions placed on them by the blackout and other regulations, and generally lulling themselves into a state of monumental complacency. The Government's failure to dispel this foolishness was epitomised in Chamberlain's unfortunate pronouncement on 4 April that 'Hitler has missed the bus'.

Complacency and wishful thinking were widespread. On 1 January 1940 Jane and I had gone by taxi into Ryde to see a film. With us was a couple from Seaview, an elderly lady and her grown-up son.

During the journey the conversation turned to the war and the course it would take during the New Year, born that day. The old lady said to me, aged 16: 'What do you think will happen this year?' I replied, instinctively and without any prior reflection: 'Oh, the Germans will attack in the west as soon as spring comes and they will be in Paris in six weeks.'

This statement horrified my listeners: 'How dare you say such a thing!'; 'That is almost treason,' said the other; 'Do you really believe what you've just said?' asked my Mother. 'Yes, I do,' I replied, and gave them some reasons which seemed to me valid. And so they proved. When winter was over the Wehrmacht launched its ambitious and successful attacks; in April on Denmark and Norway, and in May against the Low Countries and France. I was not, however, wholly correct in my prediction, for when the Germans attacked France they were to take only five weeks to reach and occupy Paris.

At that dismal moment in the fortunes of the British and French nations, Benito Mussolini brought Italy into the war on the side of Hitler's seemingly invincible Germany.

Notes

1. The Orders and Medals awarded to Colonel M.D. Graham were:– The Order of the Bath (Military), Order of St Michael and St George, Royal Victorian Order, Order of the White Eagle of Serbia, Order of Wen Hu (Striped Tiger) of China, Order of the Rising Sun of Japan, Order of St Anne of Russia, Belgian Order of Leopold, The French Legion of Honour, Union of South Africa Commemorative 1910 Medal, 1914 Star with August-November Bar, 1914–18 War Medal, 1914–18 Victory Medal, Belgian Croix de Guerre.
2. And with pride also; for Haig's sixty divisions which Britain had by 1918 built up were the undisputed masters of the European battlefield.
3. The losses suffered by the other major combatants were greater, but for Britain which had no previous experience of a mass conscript army the Great War was a unique social and psychological trauma.
4. M. Blériot took off from Baraques, near Calais, at sunrise in his monoplane and crossed the Channel at a speed of about 45 miles per hour at a height of 250 feet. After passing over Dover Harbour he spotted his friend, Monsieur Fontaine, who was waving a large French tricolour to denote the point where he was to land. The flight had taken twenty-three minutes.

CHAPTER II
1940–1944

From Dad's Army into the Argylls
'The Pride of Them All'

Early in the spring of 1940 the War Office wrote to my Mother stating that arrangements were being made for the four of us to be shipped out to India to be reunited with Father. It was Government policy to evacuate from the British Isles to various parts of the Empire as many women and children in our situation as practicable, and she was instructed to await embarkation orders which would be 'issued shortly'.

My Brothers, Moray and Alastair, continued with their education at a local prep school, Little Appley, but Jane cancelled my return to Cheltenham for the summer term and I happily remained in Seaview to help her prepare for the voyage to India, where, it was planned, I would try for a commission in the British-Indian Army, while my Brothers went to one of the boarding schools being established by the Raj.

Because my appendix had started to 'grumble', our doctor, Dockray, advised that it be removed without delay rather than risk it blowing up under less convenient circumstances. Thus, in early May, I was taken into a Ryde nursing home to have the operation. Recovery was swift, but that bit of surgery was to give rise to complications which eleven years later nearly proved fatal, and which for the rest of my life have caused me, periodically, spells of real distress.

In May 1940 our thoughts were dominated by the march of events across the Channel. The great German offensive in the west had been launched on 10 May and their *Blitzkrieg* tactics had in less than six weeks brought about the subjugation of Holland, Luxembourg and Belgium, the eviction from the continent of the British Expeditionary Force, the defeat of the French Army, the capitulation of the Vichy Government of Marshal Pétain, and the occupation of the entire coastline of Europe from the North Cape of Norway to the Pyrenees. It was a staggering achievement by the Wehrmacht, and in those lovely days of sunshine and calm seas we listened with consternation to the wireless bulletins reporting the chain of calamities befalling the Allied armies on the other side of the Channel.

We listened too with muted admiration, for the Germans had in forty days achieved by force of arms far more than in the four years of the Great War of 1914–18; and with dismay that the French Army, so valiant and tenacious in that earlier conflict and so highly rated in the peace that followed, should have collapsed so ignominiously in the face of the German onslaught. But we listened too with a deep sense of thankfulness.

Firstly, because the Government of our country was now in the hands of Winston Churchill; secondly, because the majority of the BEF – and many French soldiers – had been rescued from off the Dunkirk beaches, albeit having jettisoned everything but their lightest weapons and equipment; and thirdly, because the British people now stood alone in our 'island fortress'. We no longer had continental commitments to distract us, no more Allies to let us down. Henceforth we were to stand or fall by our own efforts. The next and decisive match in the dread contest was to be a Home Fixture. It was all a great relief; and the sense of excitement and national unity at that time of unprecedented crisis was universal and unforgettable. It was a splendid time to be alive, young and in the south of England.

As July followed June, the true significance of those military disasters and the precariousness of our situation began to sink in. The German land and air forces, on their performance since September 1939, seemed to be invincible, and we had no doubt that before winter set in an attempt would be made to invade England; the seaborne assault being preceded by heavy and widespread bombing, and by the dropping of parachute troops, some disguised, as the Dutch had alleged, as nuns.

As far as we in Seaview were concerned, the period between the Dunkirk evacuation, completed by the beginning of June, and the outbreak of the Battle of Britain in August, was one of anxious assessment, much rumour and calm preparation. Government issued sensible leaflets to every household telling us what to do in the event of an invasion, how to grow more food and how best to cook it; appeals for scrap metal for armaments, exhortations about Air Raid Precaution (ARP) drills and warnings about the dangers of careless talk: ('Be like Dad, keep Mum!', 'Walls have ears', 'Careless talk cost lives', etc.). We became inveterate listeners to the bulletins of news, information and advice put out by the BBC and, largely for amusement, to the seductive English-language broadcasts from the German propaganda stations by 'Lord Haw-Haw', William Joyce, a traitor whose life was to end after the war on the gallows of Pentonville Prison.

The seaward defences of the Solent were strengthened, minefields laid and metal booms constructed from shore to shore. Naval gunnery practice at Gosport increased, all yachting and offshore leisure activities were forbidden, and movement between the mainland and the Isle of Wight, now designated a Special Defence Area, was henceforth strictly controlled.

Activity in the air above us increased too as our fighter patrols over the Channel became more frequent, and German intruders on reconnaissance or dropping mines into shallow waters by night set off the air raid warning sirens. We soon learned to identify enemy aircraft by the sound of their engines which produced, we avowed, a sound different to those of the RAF. The Air Ministry contradicted this claim, but many of us continued to place as much reliance on our own ears as on the air raid sirens.

As the weeks passed it became pretty clear that the project to export families like us would be delayed. Therefore Jane prepared to see the war out in the Isle of Wight, and we lived in a succession of rented houses in Seaview until my Grandfather and his second wife, Mida, suggested in 1942 that we move into her family home, the White House, about half a mile inland at Nettlestone. This would prevent, they said, 'that nice empty house being requisitioned for the brutal and licentious' – a reference to the battalion of the Black Watch then stationed in our bit of the island.

Late one night in early June gunfire could be heard from the Southampton end of the Solent and we could see, held in the crossed beams of many searchlights, the shine of an aeroplane and around it the twinkling bursts of anti-aircraft shells. This spectacle continued for a good quarter of an hour until the plane flew lower and was lost to view. The next morning we learned that it had been brought down and was lying in the grounds of my Brothers' school two miles away. Jane and I therefore caught an early bus and were soon standing on the Little Appley School playing field. The plane, badly damaged, was lying on the edge of the cricket pitch. The engine had broken off and in falling had missed the boys' dormitory by a few feet, ending up in a flower bed. Our confidence in the air defences of the United Kingdom was dented, however, when we saw that it was no German machine: a squad of airmen was busy painting out the RAF roundels. They told us it had got lost on a night navigation exercise, was picked up by the searchlights and, having failed to identify itself as friendly, was shot at and eventually downed. The pilot was picked up out of the sea having come down by parachute.

The highlight of our lives, and I think of the lives of everyone in the British Isles at that time, were the speeches to Parliament, or broadcasts to the nation by the Prime Minister, Winston Churchill. With an eloquence seldom surpassed, and in phrases remembered to this day, he told the country how our fortunes stood, warned us of what lay ahead, and inspired both the nation and our friends worldwide to a degree I have witnessed since in no other politician. We had total confidence in his wisdom, leadership and his stamina, and I believe it is correct to state that every one of his colleagues in the Coalition Government held until the war's end the respect and trust of the British people. No less admired than Churchill were the King and Queen who set a fine example of devotion to duty and genuine concern for the injured and bereaved. Queen Elizabeth was especially beloved for the marvellous way she supported and gave strength to her husband, King George, a quiet, exceptionally good man who had never wished or expected to wear the crown, and who was striving with success to overcome the speech impediment which had handicapped him since youth. Britain in those dramatic and testing years was very greatly blessed in the calibre of her leaders.

The leaders of our enemies were in a different category of humanity. Benito Mussolini, the Italian Duce, we regarded as an inept buffoon, completely dominated by his ally, Hitler. He, the German Führer, during his rise to power we had regarded as a comic but earnest low-class Austrian. By 1940 however he was seen as an unstable megalomaniac; 'a bloodthirsty guttersnipe' Churchill was to call him, but who nevertheless from his unbroken chain of political and military victories seemed to have procured the Devil himself as an ally. As the war went on and evidence emerged of German barbarities in the occupied territories and of the Holocaust, our perception of Adolf Hitler changed to one of the personification of Evil. From about 1941 onwards we all realized that the war had, beyond question, become a deadly conflict between Good and Evil; but that no matter how disastrous the situation or how costly the struggle, Britain would emerge from the war on the winning side. We had absolutely no idea of how that victory would be won, but in our hearts we knew that it was inconceivable that Almighty God could permit the victory of a criminal gang as ignoble and savage as Germany's Nazi rulers.[1]

We used to boast that more German aircraft passed over the Isle of Wight than over any other part of the UK; allegedly because the flight paths of two Air Fleets on their way to targets in the Midlands and north-west England merged at a point just south of Ventnor. True or not, we certainly believed it at the time, and the amount of aerial activity over our heads from the autumn of 1940 onwards seemed to justify the claim. Up to the day when I left Seaview in September 1941 to join the Army, I kept a diary. Although my comments on the events and people of that time now seem childishly naive, those daily entries are interesting in that they record, to a much greater extent than memory can recall, the effect of the war on our village. At the height of the 'Blitz', the air raid sirens sounded as much as six times in one day, enemy bombs fell almost as often on peaceful rural areas as on military or industrial targets, and occasionally German planes flew above the rooftops or the surface of the Solent so low that we could watch the figures of the crews, the bombs falling and the machine guns firing. On 10 January 1941, during a heavy night raid on Portsmouth, about 200 incendiary bombs fell on Seaview, some right outside our house, but all were quickly extinguished by householders equipped with sandbags and stirrup pumps, and by the village Fire Brigade.

A continuous hazard were the splinters from our anti-aircraft shells which rained down when the guns put up a barrage. Quite a number of people lost their lives from this cause; it was this danger rather than fear of German bombs which made us shelter indoors during air raids.

Surprisingly perhaps, we on the ground at the east end of the Island did not see much of the daylight engagements between the RAF and the Luftwaffe during the Battle of Britain. Most took place out of our sight, either above the clouds or over the mainland. The course of the battle we could follow from the vapour trails, but to identify individual aircraft at that height with the naked eye was seldom possible.

There were, however, some memorable exceptions. The Battle of Britain opened on 8 August with enemy attacks on shipping in the Channel and against radar and other key installations along the south coast. The weather was superb; hot windless days of blue skies and warm sea. Jane, my Brothers and I spent as much time as we could on the beach, usually taking a picnic and our bathing togs. On the 12th, the fourth day of the German offensive, we left our house in Seafield Terrace at about eleven o'clock, looking forward to a happy day down in Seagrove Bay. As we left home Jane said: 'I don't think we should go very far today.' So we settled down instead in an inlet near the Yacht Club and began to eat our sandwiches. While we were still eating Jane exclaimed: 'We must pack up and go straight home.' She said this in such decisive tones that we did not protest but hurried home beside her. Once indoors I switched on the wireless to listen to the mid-day news, but all I could hear was a steady roar punctuated by drum beats. As I adjusted the set Moray, who was by the window, cried out: 'Good God, look up there!' A wide and seemingly endless column of German aircraft – there were actually about fifty of them in that wave – was moving at about eight thousand feet quite slowly across the sky over our village towards Portsmouth. From the mass of shell bursts around the Germans we knew that the AA gunners of the Nettlestone battery were hard, but fruitlessly, at work. Nothing deflected the German stream; every plane flew unfalteringly on over the Solent. When we looked towards Portsmouth we could see a pair of Messerschmidts methodically shooting down in flames the protective cordon of barrage balloons to allow the leading flights of dive-bombers and then the Heinkels and Dorniers to release their bomb loads. Soon the harbour and city of Portsmouth, Gosport and much of Southsea were hidden by a wall of flame and smoke. We were about three miles away and, our guns having ceased firing, an extraordinary silence descended, broken only when the All Clear sounded about forty minutes later, long after the Germans had turned away back towards their bases in France. It looked to us as if they had got away unscathed, but we heard that our fighters had destroyed several out over the Channel. Air power, as I was to realise four years later in Normandy, is normally applied over the horizon, unseen and unheard by those it is most designed to protect. That night the BBC news announced that Portsmouth's harbour railway station, a jetty and a brewery had been damaged and two small boats sunk, but our local ARP Wardens told us that the damage was actually far greater and more widely spread, and that many people had been killed. Mercifully the naval dockyard and HMS *Victory* escaped.

The Home Guard had been formed in May 1940. This nation-wide force of uniformed volunteers was initially called the LDVs – Local Defence Volunteers – but at Churchill's insistence this was changed to the more stimulating and enduring title. Our bit of the Isle of Wight Home Guard, the Seaview Platoon in which I enrolled, was part of the Nunwell Battalion commanded by a retired General, Sir Charles Oglander-Aspinall, said to have been Hamilton's Chief of Staff in the Dardanelles campaign of 1915–16. Our Company Commander, Sir Ralph Gore – nicknamed 'Ruddigore' by some – was a big wheel in local yachting circles. Both he and the General were encouraging and helpful to me when the time for me to enlist in the Regular Army approached. The Seaview platoon consisted of some two dozen men whose ages ranged from over 60 down to adolescence. I was the youngest member, but despite this was soon elevated to the rank of Lance Corporal on the strength of having passed Certificate 'A', a test of basic military skills, while in the Cheltenham College OTC. Our physical abilities were equally varied. While age and corpulence slowed down many, several of our members were more severely handicapped. My own section Corporal, Marcus Smith, a gentleman of leisure, had one hand crippled in the Great War; Henley, the baker's boy, was a consumptive; Reynolds, a former signaller, had a pronounced limp, while the chap whom I got to know best, since we were habitually paired together for guard duty, a retired naval stoker and a survivor of the Battle of Jutland, Mick Curran by name, suffered chronically from faulty plumbing. The rumblings and wind which his insides produced were a continuous accompaniment to our activities. Our Sergeant, Neville Chichester, who had fought in the Boer War, was the oldest in the platoon and by far the best rifle shot of us all. They were all interesting characters with, just as in the TV series 'Dad's Army', an engaging variety of eccentricities. One, Jack Majorcas, who was an immigrant from north Africa, had opened a shop in the village selling sweets and tobacco. He was a great walker, also a strict vegetarian, and we often met him striding homewards in his large sandals, clutching enormous bundles of nettles and other greenery he had plucked from the hedgerows. Once, when he fell ill, my Brothers and I scoured the fields for him so he wouldn't go hungry. We were a happy bunch of chaps and got on well together. Extraordinarily keen too were some of us, considering the demands of daily work and family commitments, and several devoted their leisure hours to extra training whenever an instructor from a nearby Regular unit could be obtained. All service in the Home Guard was voluntary and unpaid, but as Allen, the village electrician, declared: 'A man's honour becomes involved once he signs the Enrolment Form.' Being in the Home Guard, however, absolved a man from the obligations of joining the Auxiliary Fire Service and of nightly Fire Watching duties. For routine training we used to parade for Lieutenant Love, our Platoon Commander and the manager of the principal village pub, one evening a week and most weekends. Sometimes we were taken off to other parts of the Island for rifle shooting, live grenade throwing, or to a gas chamber to test our respirators. Occasionally we took part in a large-scale exercise organised by the Army's District Headquarters.

Even though the Luftwaffe, defeated in the Battle of Britain, had been forced to switch their major bombing attacks, the 'Blitz', to the hours of darkness, the threat of a German invasion remained, and in consequence each of our Home Guard sections went on operational duty every fifth night. We assembled after tea at Platoon HQ in the village dressed in khaki battledress, leather boots, gaiters and belt, forage cap with the badge of the Hampshire Regiment (on which, I must add, we proudly displayed on the first day of August a red rose in commemoration of the regiment's performance at the Battle of Minden in 1759). For sustenance we provided ourselves with sandwich boxes and thermos flasks which we got our womenfolk to fill. Our armament consisted of a .300 calibre P14 rifle made in the USA and a long bayonet. Tom Love I think had a pistol, and various types of grenades were kept in boxes for distribution as the need arose. Thus equipped we drove or marched a couple of miles up towards St Helens to a building known as the Priory, surrounded by large fields in which cows and sheep grazed. The Priory was our base for the night, and from it we emerged in pairs to patrol the fields for two hours on the lookout for enemy parachutists or other intruders, and from this hilltop we had a grandstand view of the air raids on Cowes, Portsmouth or Southampton, and on cloudless nights of London burning some seventy miles away. At first light we left the building and, with bayonets fixed and magazines charged, moved down to the beach to confront any of the long-awaited German Army who might have arrived during the night. We searched the shore, the caves and the deserted houses in Priory and Seagrove Bays all the way along to Seaview. Our sections did this every night from early in the winter of 1940 through to the autumn of 1941, but, alas, without ever finding any Germans alive or dead; and as we, feeling rather let down by the Hun, walked back at dawn to our homes, we consoled ourselves with the knowledge that we would in due course each receive the sum of one shilling and three pence to reimburse us for the cost of our tea and sandwiches, and with the hope expressed as we dispersed: 'Never mind, perhaps they'll come next time we're on.'

We were, we believed, adequately trained and equipped to give a good account of ourselves. Our morale was high, and though this self-confidence was in retrospect grossly ill-founded, we would have spontaneously engaged any Germans who appeared in our sector of the island until the ammunition ran out. Then, I suppose, we would have taken to our heels or been scuppered. But we would have done what was required of Home Guard units; to find, report and engage the invaders and thereby gain time for the Regulars with their heavier firepower and greater numbers to appear on the scene and take them on.

After the Wehrmacht turned east and attacked the Soviet Union in June 1941, German aerial activity in our part of the world dropped off significantly, and the likelihood of an invasion of the British Isles became more remote. The family had by then given up all hope of joining Father in India, so we settled eventually into the White House where Jane was to stay until Father's death in 1957, and I decided to join the Army voluntarily rather than wait to be conscripted.

The nearest Army recruiting office was in Southsea, so there I went on 25 August, a volunteer for 'the duration of hostilities'. After the medical and taking the oath of allegiance, I signed the Document of Attestation which the clerk had filled in with my particulars. I had already reckoned that I was not bright enough to join a technical corps and, rather to my Sapper Father's disappointment, had decided to go for the Infantry.

The Grahams of Fintry had substantial links with two Scottish regiments, the Cameronians (Scottish Rifles) which Thomas Graham had raised in 1794 as the Perthshire Volunteers, and the Argyll and Sutherland Highlanders, formerly the 91st and 93rd Highlanders. The Cameronians wore trews, the Argylls were kilted. I chose the latter.

When asked by the clerk which regiment I wanted to join, I had replied; 'The family regiment, the Argyll and Sutherland Highlanders'. On reading the Attestation form, however, I saw that he, presumably because I lived on the other side of the Solent, had enlisted me into 'the Argyll and Sutherland Islanders'. These formalities completed, I was given five shillings – one day's pay plus a week's ration allowance – and a railway warrant to Perth where I was to report on 5 September.

In the grey Scottish city of Perth, the Queen's Barracks was the Headquarters and Depot of the Black Watch, responsible at that time for training recruits both of the Black Watch and the Argylls. Our intake, about forty strong, assembled in the City Hall where we were issued with uniforms, eating utensils, a straw-filled mattress and three blankets. Our first afternoon was taken up with 'bulling' our new army boots, an operation whose object was to give the toe-caps a mirror-like shine. This was achieved by massaging the leather with a toothbrush handle, black polish and spit. My fellow-recruits knew more about this technique than I did, and quite a fierce rivalry developed between them as to who could get the best shine quickest. My own efforts were noticed by a blond lad named Caddow who took my boots away and returned them that evening gleaming like glass. Caddow and I were to meet again seven years later in the Scottish Parachute battalion.

A group of our colleagues, mainly Glaswegians, were in the meantime furtively sewing razor blades onto their bonnets behind the large Argyll badge whose tip protruded just above the bonnet's rim. The aim of this exercise, one confided to me, was as follows. In the Perth area at that time were stationed cavalry units of the Free Polish Army. Their uniforms were more colourful than the plain battledress normally seen around Britain, and these Poles had a particular appeal for the local Scottish girls. The plan therefore was that when a party of these toughs encountered a Pole out walking with a girl, the bonnets were removed and the tip of the badge with the hidden razor blade was brought smartly down across the Pole's face. He, in consequence, took himself off to a doctor while my Glaswegian colleagues walked off with the girl. That at least was the theory behind the razor blades.

It took me several weeks before I could understand everything my fellow recruits said. Their Scottish accents and vocabulary were as strange to me as my own southern English public school speech must have seemed to them. Off parade, their conversation was dominated by two topics: football and sex; and their free time in the evenings and on Saturday afternoons was wholly devoted to copulation; the search for sexual partners, all of whom seemed to be called Sadie, being conducted in the cinemas and dance halls. Today much space in the newspapers and on TV is devoted to 'child abuse', and healing the trauma inflicted on the young gives employment to legions of social workers and psychiatrists. My own experience of working and sleeping cheek-by-jowl in 1941 with those young men from deprived homes, as most of them were, in Scotland's meanest streets, taught me that what we now call 'child abuse' was then a widely accepted fact of life in large families sharing perhaps a single bedroom and in which the husband seldom went to bed sober.

It didn't seem to me that any of the chaps I was living beside in Perth had been unduly scarred by that aspect of their upbringing.

Coming from a sheltered home in England, I found their raw, uninhibited behaviour, with its profanities and boasts of sexual prowess, alarming at first, but I have to say that those fellows, varied rough diamonds all, soon developed, thanks to Army discipline and a healthy routine, into good soldiers and comrades. I became fond of them and especially admired their lack of resentment against a social order in which they had been placed pretty near the bottom of the pecking order.

Our instructors were mostly regular NCOs in Highland regiments. Their conversations were virtually incomprehensible to the likes of me as their speech was interlarded with words and phrases from Urdu, Chinese and Arabic they had picked up during their service in Imperial garrisons. Our platoon Sergeant was a short, dark-haired man named Dow, a firm, fair and a gifted teacher. We made good progress under his tutelage, and soon developed a remarkable team spirit and collective loyalty to him and to each other. I was sad to learn later that Sergeant Dow was killed when his troopship was torpedoed.

The Officers we seldom saw. There were two Argyll subalterns who came occasionally to watch us at training. Wearing service dress complete with Sam Browne belt and badgerhead sporran, they had little to do but with their canes cut the heads off the daisies around us.

With our Company Commander, a Major in the Black Watch, I had one unexpected confrontation. This was after our platoon moved out of Queen's Barracks into Kinfauns Castle, a mansion on the Dundee road. It so happened that a neighbour of my family in the Isle of Wight, Angel Whitcombe whose Gunner husband had been taken prisoner with the Highland Division in 1940, was temporarily living in Perth. She kindly had invited me to her house on Saturday afternoons for tea and, more important, a bath. One day I turned up at her house covered with insect bites picked up from the field where we had been doing weapon training, so I asked Angel to let me have some disinfectant to put in the bath water. That did the trick and I forgot all about the bites. But in the middle of the following week when we were all standing by our beds for some inspection, the door burst open and in strode the Sergeant-Major with the Company Commander at his heels. 'Which one is Private Graham?' cried the CSM, whereupon the Major barked at me, 'Show me your blankets.' I gave them to him. 'How dare you go around saying that your bed is flea-ridden!' My appeal to Angel Whitcombe for disinfectant had somehow reached the ears of the Colonel commanding the Depot who ordered the affronted Major to investigate this slur on the hygiene of his men.

The CO of the Depot, Lieutenant-Colonel Holt, we saw once. Just before we left Perth at the end of our training, he addressed us all. I particularly remember him telling us to abstain from bad language. 'Call it a toothbrush,' he exclaimed, 'not a f***ing toothbrush.' He was of course quite right, but I fear his counsel has been all too little heeded.

The man whom we all respected and feared mightily was Regimental Sergeant-Major Drummond. As far as we were concerned he was the King of the Depot. A rebuke from him was crushing, but a word of praise gave us a major uplift. He was exceedingly smart and in his bearing faultless. It was said throughout the Black Watch that, one day when he was out shopping in Perth with his family, the Colonel drove past in his staff car, whereupon RSM Drummond was heard to give the order 'Wife and Child, Eyes Left!' It was also said of him that, to keep his subordinates up to the mark in foot drill, he used to have two barrack tables placed end to end, thus forming a platform measuring twelve feet by three feet, which he then mounted and made his NCOs drill him along and across the tables without causing him to fall off.

I have mentioned some of the impressions I gained of my fellow recruits. I am sure they thought me equally odd: different, rather naive and a bit wet. One day Sergeant Dow called for volunteers for the platoon team to take part in an important relay race around the North Inch, a large park in Perth. Four runners were needed and three of our platoon put their hands up at once, but only three. I had never run a distance with either pleasure or success, so I remained mute in the rear rank. 'What about you, Graham?' said Dow. 'Have a go!' I could not refuse.

At this, some of the platoon started to mutter and predict certain defeat at the inclusion in our team of such a weed as I.

On the day of the race I was placed to run last in our team, and when the baton was eventually handed over to me we were trailing badly. But somehow I managed to overtake all the others during that long, awful, flog around the park, and by coming in first I secured victory for our platoon. As I lay gasping on the ground I saw bending over me Andy Drummond exclaiming, 'Well done, laddie. Bloody well run.' I could have asked for no greater prize. But above all it made me realize how much I owed to my Mother for the sensible way she had fed me – good food and few cigarettes, a diet markedly different from that which my fellow recruits had been brought up on.

This episode sufficed too to alter somewhat my colleagues' view of me. But I must say, they had never shown towards me any hostility or resentment. And at no time during our weeks together in the ranks did I have anything stolen. Alas, I cannot say the same thing about my time as an Officer Cadet or after being commissioned.

On completion of the recruit phase of our training we moved by train to Fort George to join A Company of the 70th (Young Soldiers) Battalion of the Argylls.

Built between 1748 and 1769 on a promontory jutting out into the Moray Firth as part of General Wade's plan for the suppression of the Scots after the crushing Hanoverian victory in April 1746 at Culloden Moor, Fort George was the Depot and regimental home of the Seaforth Highlanders. I developed a deep respect and affection for the Seaforth. The light in Morayshire has a magical quality and the air a crispness which seemed to give us a greater zest for life, and certainly the people who live out their lives in Seaforth country have a rare charm, good manners and a quiet self-esteem beside which most other people seem brash and unrefined: lesser breeds.

We young soldiers lived on the Carse, the common outside the Fort, in Nissen huts with some twenty men to each hut and two bunks at the end for Corporals. It was winter and we occasionally awoke to find our beds covered by snow forced by the gales through crevices in the walls, but the two great, iron, coal-burning stoves ensured that anything cold was soon warmed and anything wet dried. The most disagreeable things were being marched to breakfast in the pitch dark bitter cold, and the primitive lavatorial arrangements. As their title implies, Young Soldiers battalions were composed mainly of lads too young to be sent overseas. Nevertheless they had operational roles in the event of a German invasion. Ours was to defend a stretch of coastline and certain airfields.

Our training was more ambitious than had been possible in Perth, and around the Fort we had plenty of scope for tactical exercises, ranges for shooting, a gymnasium and so on. We seldom moved anywhere by lorry, for petrol was rationed. Long distances we covered by train, those of ten miles or less we marched. We did a lot of marching, and as we marched we sang or whistled airs such as 'Ten Green Bottles', 'Waltzing Matilda', 'Green Grow the Rushes Oh', or 'The Quartermaster's Stores' ('My eyes grow dim, I cannot see . . .').

Our company favourite was a music-hall song which embraced all the regiments of the Highland Brigade except, oddly, the Highland Light Infantry. It went like this:

> 'You can talk about your Gordons and your Camerons so braw, Your silver-streaked Seaforths and your gallant Forty-Twa, But give to me the regiment of the lads that look so fine, The Argyll and Sutherland Highlanders, The Thin Red Line.'

This epithet, The Thin Red Line, was accorded to the 93rd Highlanders (who under the Cardwell reforms of 1881 became the 2nd Battalion The Argyll and Sutherland Highlanders) for their feat at Balaclava in the Crimean War when they repulsed a charge by Russian heavy cavalry while still drawn up in three ranks. For Infantry to repel such an attack without forming square had been considered impossible. There was another popular ditty:

> 'It's an Argyll for me, it's an Argyll for me;
> If you're nae an Argyll you're nae use to me.
> Keep your Camerons so braw, your Seaforths and a'
> But give me an Argyll, the Pride of them All.'

Because of the importance and frequency of marches we Infantrymen had to pay especial attention to our feet, socks, boots and equipment-fitting, and the subaltern Officers and NCOs who would be disgraced if any of us in their charge fell out of the line of march kept a strict eye on each of us. The manner too in which the march was conducted was precisely regulated with look-outs in front and rear to warn road traffic, and sentries posted at halts to give warning of air or gas attack. And after each fifty minutes of marching a halt was called and everyone save the sentries lay down, with feet higher than head and took out their water bottles. Drinking was water only and only at halts.

On reaching our destination two things were done before anything else. All weapons were thoroughly cleaned and the feet of each man were examined by his Officer. This was not a particularly congenial duty but was laid down as an essential part of a young Officer's responsibility for the well-being and efficiency of his Men.

In the years that followed the war this custom faded; but then, as the Infantry has become mechanised so has the art of marching – except, thank Heavens, in the Royal Marines and The Parachute Regiment whose roles still demand of All Ranks a very high degree of all-round physical prowess.

Another custom has long since passed. With the growth of terrorism and the complexity and cost of small arms, rifles, pistols and so on, all now have to be kept locked up in secure armouries. But up at Fort George in 1941 we each kept our personal weapon, a .303 Lee Enfield rifle, clipped to the wall at the head of our bed. Every evening, before the lights were put out at ten-fifteen sharp, we would clean our equipment for the next day's parades and pull-through and oil our rifles. Then we would grip the rifle with the left hand, take aim and, with a penny coin balanced on top of the foresight protectors, with the right hand we would open and close the bolt as many times as possible before the coin fell off the rifle. This was a good way to improve one's steadiness of aim and rapidity of fire. By such practice had the British Army of 1914 achieved the steady marksmanship which so devastated the oncoming Germans.

We were very fit and, although there was not much to do in our spare time apart from going down to the Alma pub in Ardersier, we were pretty content with our lot. We had three substantial if rather monotonous meals each day: breakfast, lunch and tea, the latter around 5pm. If we wanted more we had to buy it at the NAAFI.[2] Every unit in the Army had a NAAFI, and from NAAFI we could get almost everything we needed, including beer, but no spirits.

Pay parade was held weekly on Friday afternoons, the cash having been collected from the bank by an Officer and the pay forms, called Acquittance Rolls, written out by hand in triplicate by the Colour Sergeant. The company fell in, and starting with those whose names began with 'A', we were called in turn to the pay table, saluted, received the money from the Officer with the left hand, signed the Roll, saluted again and returned to the ranks. At that time, in November 1941, as a Trained Soldier in the rank of Private, I was entitled to the weekly sum of seventeen shillings and sixpence. But I did not get that, as one shilling was deducted for the barber's fees, and one shilling and sixpence for the Barrack Damage Repair Fund. Thus we had to exist for seven days on fifteen shillings. With that, seventy-five pence in 'modern' money, we had to buy supper, Blanco, Brasso, Silvo, boot polish, soap, toothpaste, stamps, papers, cinema tickets, pay bus fares, and so on. And we could! Indeed, during the whole of my service in the ranks from September 1941 until I was commissioned in August 1942, my Mother only once had to send me money 'to keep me going'. She sent me a single ten-shilling note (fifty pence).

The culmination of each week's activities was the Saturday Morning Inspection. Preparations for this ordeal began on Friday afternoon immediately after pay parade. Outside our huts the weeds had to be removed, stones whitened and firebuckets refilled. Inside, the windows were polished, walls wiped, stoves blackened and the floor scrubbed with soap and water. On our beds we had to display every item of our military kit precisely in accordance with the Company Kit Layout Plan. To ensure that the position of each article on every bed was identical, we stretched lengths of string from each end of the hut to serve as guidelines. By these means did we achieve by Saturday morning a satisfying degree of cleanliness and symmetry. But despite our pains the inspecting Officer usually managed to find some fault with our presentation.

All this meant that we seldom slept in our beds on Friday night; we slept on the still damp floor using newspaper for insulation.

People reading today of this weekly ritual will doubtless decry it as an example of absurd, pettifogging, time-wasting military 'bull'. I ask them, however, to note that no one in authority demanded such efforts from us. We decided to take such pains each Friday entirely off our own bats. We did it simply because we wanted our hut on the Saturday morning to outshine the huts of the other platoons. And the lads in those other platoons thought and acted exactly as we did.

By and large we were well commanded, administered and trained. Among our superiors in 70 A&SH were men destined for greater fame in the post-war world. Our CO, Lord Rowallan, became the Chief Scout, and our Company Commander, Major Chew, the Headmaster of the prep school to which the future Prince of Wales was sent. Of the NCOs my own favourite was Corporal Jock Leslie, a Gordon Highlander. He married the prettiest of the Fort George NAAFI girls, and years later was to find himself my Company Sergeant-Major in the Scottish Parachute Battalion, 5 PARA.

On Christmas Eve 1941 I received out of the blue one of the nicest presents of my life. I was made a Lance Corporal. Because I have spent most of my life in the Service, I have been favoured with many promotions, but none has given me such pleasure as that first one at Fort George – out of the ranks of the Led into the body of the Leaders, a first but most significant step. Three months later I was given a second stripe.

The rank of Corporal I found particularly agreeable. All difficult tasks were undertaken by Sergeants while the easy ones could be delegated to Lance Corporals. And the pay was substantially better than anything I had received so far. I was lucky, and my good fortune endured during the war in that I seldom went home on leave in the same rank twice. By early 1945 I was a Major although aged only 22.

Though in Morayshire we were far from any fighting, we knew from the BBC and the newspapers roughly how the war was going. Pearl Harbor and the entry into the war of the United States on our side was a relief, but we did not expect much help from that quarter for many months. But to our German enemy was now added a formidable and savage Asiatic foe; all the more alarming, we discovered, since the Japanese had been consistently under-rated by our military commentators. For me, the blackest of the many black days in the early part of the war came in the winter of 1941–2 when Hong Kong fell to the Japanese, when those two mighty warships, *Prince of Wales* and *Repulse*, were sunk off Malaya, and when two months later General Percival surrendered the great island base of Singapore to an inferior Japanese force. The one thing which sustained our self-respect in that dismal period was the knowledge that the 2nd Battalion of our regiment, the Argylls, had fought under Colonel Ian Stewart with a success and distinction unmatched by any other British unit in that theatre.

Nevertheless, the fall of Singapore was, we realized, the greatest military disaster in our nation's history and a mortal blow to the status in Asia of the European.

Our youthful lives soon, however, regained their normal unworried stride and optimism. We were confident that, however long the war lasted, Britain would come out on the winning side. We could not explain how this would come about: it was merely an article of our faith.

Nor could we foresee the disasters into which Hitler's 'intuition' would lead the German nation; and while the Wehrmacht fought its way eastwards across those broad and bloody Russian battlefields, we trained and marched, marched and trained in preparation for the day when we could take our place in one of Scotland's famous fighting formations.

At that stage in the war no permanent commissions in the Army were being granted, only 'emergency' ones. Everyone aspiring to be an Officer had to start off in the ranks and, if approved by Selection Boards at unit and Command level, complete a course at an Officer Cadet Training Unit (OCTU).

Before going to an OCTU most Potential Officers – that is how we were labelled – were sent on a short preliminary course to ensure that everyone had attained roughly the same standard of military competence.

Each arm of the Service ran one or more OCTUs: the one to which I was sent was No 163 at Heysham Towers, near Morecombe in Lancashire. The institutions at which our pre-war equivalents, 'Gentlemen Cadets', had been educated, the Royal Military Academy at Woolwich and the Royal Military College at Sandhurst, now served as OCTUs for the Royal Artillery and the Royal Armoured Corps respectively.

For my pre-OCTU course I went to Brentwood where the Essex Regiment had their Depot in Warley Barracks. Warley had once housed troops of the Honourable East India Company, and even to me, coming from a hut on a highland heath, it seemed an appallingly primitive place. Sunk into the walls on each floor of the ill-lit staircases were open urinals, and on the barrack-room walls one could still see some of the hooks from which rows of blankets used to hang, screening the sleeping area of the unmarried soldiers from that of the married men and their women. One day, as part of our 'grooming', we were taken to see the Officers' Mess, and I recall a comfortable and homely group of rooms of which the centrepiece was a large and impressive oil painting of 'The Last Stand at Gandamak', an episode in the Afghan War of 1842 in which the forebears of the Essex Regiment, the 44th Foot, had died to a man during the disastrous retreat from Kabul to the Khyber Pass. Other things I remember from my brief stay at Brentwood were pleasure at being back in a town with buses, shops and cinemas; and our Instructor. He was a Sergeant-Major (I've forgotten his name) and he had a limp caused, we were told by one who knew him well, by leaping one night into the deep end of a waterless swimming pool. He was an exceptionally bad tempered fellow. Perhaps it was his injuries that made him so, or maybe he resented having to instruct youngsters like us destined for a status beyond his reach.

I greatly enjoyed my four months at Heysham Towers where I reported in May 1942. We lived in what before the war had been a Butlin's holiday camp, and we slept two by two in comfortable chalets. The Officers' Mess, the administrative offices, lecture hall and cinema were in the Mansion: our normal classes were held in Nissen huts. The weather during those summer months was good, the air bracing and our training areas in the Lancashire countryside were varied, pretty and close at hand. An additional attraction was nearby Morecombe, a major seaside resort, and in 1942 the place where thousands of young women, recruited into the Womens' Royal Air Force, were being introduced to life in the Armed Forces.

The training we were put through was designed solely to fit us for our first appointments in an Infantry battalion: to command, train and look after a platoon of some three dozen soldiers – and to lead them in battle. I consider that the syllabus and the way it was put over to us met that requirement very well. Indeed for many years I queried the need for the much longer and more expensive procedures deemed essential to prepare young men for their commissions in peacetime, but I came to realize that the difference between the two systems was fully justified. Sandhurst aims to lay in Cadets just out of school the foundations of a long career, at least to the rank of Major, in many cases to Colonel and in a few to General Officer. By contrast, the ceiling for an OCTU Cadet was, if he was lucky, Captain; for the reality of our situation was that a high proportion of us would inevitably be killed or wounded within a short time of going into battle with our platoons.

But we did not worry our heads about such matters. At Heysham Towers we were well taught, well fed, fit, and pretty confident about our grasp of Infantry skills and the right way to do things. I passed out of 163 in August 1942. They were good enough to give me the highest grading and an encouraging report, and I went home on a week's leave before joining the unit in which I was to start my life as an Officer, the 2nd Battalion of The Argyll and Sutherland Highlanders, then stationed in Orkney.

The business of kitting oneself out involved, even in wartime, spending much money and quite a lot of time. To begin with, one had to find a tailor to provide the uniforms and accoutrements peculiar to one's regiment. Not surprisingly, no such tailor existed near my home in the Isle of Wight, so I had to look to London. My initial order included a khaki service dress tunic and kilt, greatcoat, Sam Browne belt, Officer-type bonnet, silver regimental badge, glengarry cap, two sporrans, hose, skean-dhu, black brogue shoes, raincoat and regimental cane.

Each Scottish regiment had its own tartan. The Black Watch and the Argylls both wear the dark 'Government' tartan, their kilts differing in the pleats and in the panel with its silk rosettes worn by Officers and Warrant Officers.

Getting a kilt was about the simplest part of the business, for on the establishment of 2A&SH were a Master Tailor and his two Assistant Kiltmakers. Within a day of getting to Orkney I located this tailoring trio tucked away behind the Quartermaster's Department and in no time these helpful Scottish craftsmen, Sergeant Todd, Private Greenbaum and Private Zimmerman, made my kilt; longlasting, heavy and so warm that nothing was ever worn beneath it. One had to learn, though, how to sit down without pubic exposure.

Towards the cost of all these acquisitions I duly received from the Paymaster the Uniform Allowance of £25. Of course, this nothing like covered the expense then; moreover, after the war, when I was in the Regular Army, all sorts of additional uniforms came into regimental vogue: scarlet mess dress, green and gold No 1 dress, an ornate full-dress sporran, diced hose, dirk, claymore and so on. These had to be paid for out of one's own pocket or scrounged from generous retired Argylls. During the post-war decades, we Argyll Officers seemed to be endlessly altering our uniform. Whenever the CO of the battalion changed or someone new took over the colonelcy of the regiment, we were required to get a new pattern of headdress, a different type of strap or chain for our sporrans, or new shirts. All to suit the whim of our new Chief. Shirts we changed frequently, going through a whole range of materials and styles: flannel, poplin, cotton; collars attached or removable and with the colour varying from dark khaki to light green to blue-gray. The latter is attractive and distinctive; I wish the regiment had adopted it from the beginning.

Our wartime battledress uniform was issued to us free. Every CO with a spark of imagination regarded the blouse as a splendid means of displaying regimental individuality without breaking the rules of military uniformity. Earnest discussions were held – even, I remember, in the front line in Holland in 1944 – about the merits of having the collars faced and the cuffs turned back and lined. (I should add that the Colonel who led that battlefield discussion had been a model for the publication *Tailor and Cutter*; matters sartorial interested him greatly.)

The War Office had quite early on sensibly decreed that a variety of identification insignia were to be sewn onto the sleeves of the BD blouse: the divisional sign, the arm-of-service bar (red for Infantry), the brigade number – all these in addition to wound, length of service stripes and specialist badges awarded to the individual soldier.

These embellishments were good for morale and fostered unit esprit. Most of the formation signs were objects of venerated significance and were worn with pride; for example the Pegasus of Airborne Forces, and the Desert Rat of the 7th Armoured Division. Above these, at the top of the sleeve, was worn the name of the regiment. Most Infantry regiments had their names, in full or abbreviated, embroidered or printed on cloth. Some, however, shunned such lettering; Scottish regiments mostly wore a patch of their particular tartan. The Argylls, however, adopted in 1944 a strip of red and white dicing, a tribute to the 93rd Highlanders, our pre-Cardwell forebears, who at Balaclava had won the immortal title 'The Thin Red Line'. (If one peers along the strip where the red and white chequered squares meet, a thin red line is plainly visible.) In this distinction we were unique and very proud of it.

From what I have written above it will be clear to the reader that dress, embellishments and emblems played a big part in the life and traditions of the British Army. They did, and without doubt they did more good than harm, for they emphasized the individuality of each unit and of its every member. This tradition also gave substance to the perception many of us had that there really existed no such entity as the British Army; rather that our Service consisted of a variety of highly individualistic corps and regiments. And it was to these that the Soldier, like the Officer – and the Officer's wife – committed his allegiance, his energy, and in retirement, his charity. Should this thread of devotion to the regimental family ever be broken or even weakened, the Service and the nation will be harmed. Nevertheless these complex matters of dress did cause much work; particularly to Adjutants who took pains to set out in Regimental Dress Regulations the minutiae of when and how each bit of our assorted uniforms should be worn. Despite their labours, it was rare to find even on the most formal occasion two Argyll Officers dressed exactly and correctly alike.

Quite rightly, the allowance now paid to young Officers to fit themselves out with uniforms and the associated articles has been vastly increased beyond the £25 I received in 1942. Also, the Army has simplified the whole question of dress for training, for combat, for formal and social occasions. That is good. But it has to be said that we who served during and after the Second World War find the Army of today, with its daily dress of unrelieved dark green, drab to look at; and, I suspect, a bit depressing to wear.

The battalion which I joined as a subaltern in September 1942 was stationed on Pomona, the largest of the ninety islands which constitute the county of Orkney. Sunnybank Camp was a collection of Nissen huts, which housed Battalion Headquarters, Support Company and the administrative platoons, about a mile to the west of the principal town, Kirkwall, on the Stromness road. The four rifle companies were in similar, smaller camps scattered around Kirkwall.

Three miles to the south of our camp under the waters of Scapa Flow lay HMS *Royal Oak*; even three years after she was sunk many people were telling new arrivals like me that 'the U-boat could never have got in and out of the great anchorage but for the precise information about the defences which that watchmaker in Kirkwall had passed to the Germans.' After the *Royal Oak* disaster the Fleet was moved to anchorages on the west coast of Scotland, but had returned to Scapa Flow in the spring of 1940, by which time the defences on land and to seaward had been substantially improved. As the main threat was reckoned to be from the air, a great number of anti-aircraft guns were brought in, and once a year, in mid-summer, all these guns fired a practice barrage in unison and the dense aerial umbrella of black shell-bursts over the Flow was extremely reassuring.

To protect Orkney from any German invasion there was in addition an infantry brigade which in 1942 consisted of battalions from the South Lancashire Regiment, the Gordon Highlanders and the Argylls. The Argyll battalion had been raised as the 15th Battalion The Argyll and Sutherland Highlanders, but after the fall of Singapore and the loss of our renowned 2nd Battalion, the King decreed that 15 A&SH should have the honour of assuming the seniority, privileges and responsibilities of the lost battalion, and in May 1942 it was formally renamed 2nd

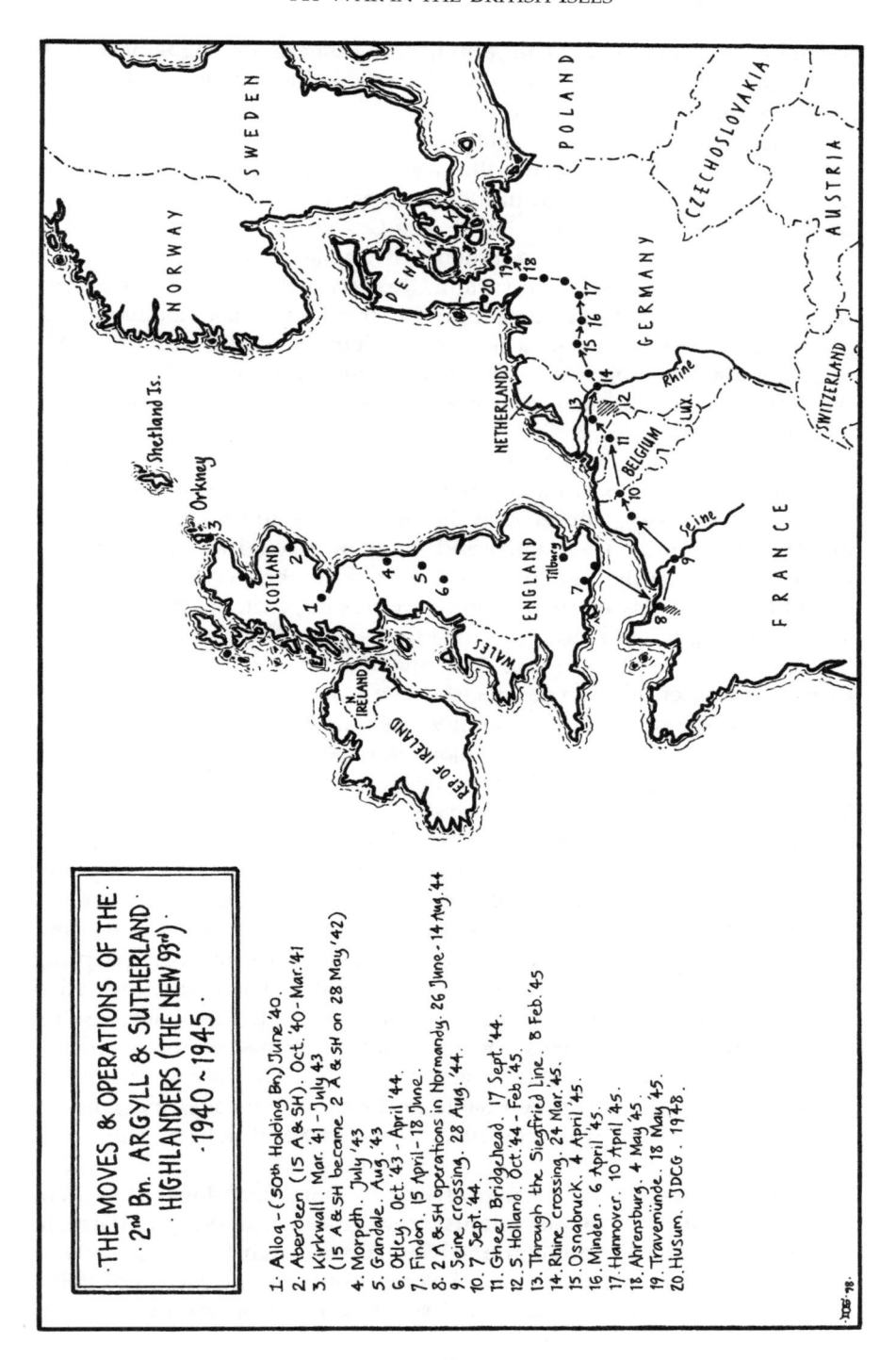

THE MOVES & OPERATIONS OF THE
2nd Bn. ARGYLL & SUTHERLAND
HIGHLANDERS (THE NEW 93rd)
· 1940 ~ 1945 ·

1. Alloa - (50th Holding Bn) June '40.
2. Aberdeen (1S A & SH). Oct. 40 - Mar. 41
3. Kirkwall. Mar. 41 - July 43
   (1S A & SH became 2 A & SH on 28 May '42)
4. Morpeth. July '43
5. Gandale. Aug. '43
6. Otley. Oct. 43 - April '44.
7. Findon. 15 April - 18 June.
8. 2 A & SH operations in Normandy. 26 June - 14 Aug. '44
9. Seine crossing. 28 Aug. '44.
10. 7 Sept. '44.
11. Gheel Bridgehead. 17 Sept. '44.
12. S. Holland. Oct. '44 - Feb. '45.
13. Through the Siegfried Line. 8 Feb. '45
14. Rhine crossing. 24 Mar. 45.
15. Osnabruck. 4 April '45
16. Minden. 6 April '45.
17. Hannover. 10 April '45
18. Ahrensburg. 4 May '45
19. Travemünde. 18 May '45
20. Husum. JDCG. 1948.

Battalion (Reconstituted) The Argyll and Sutherland Highlanders; in regimental parlance the 'New 93rd'. This was the battalion I joined on commissioning.

Orkney was not a popular station with its bleak, treeless hills, gales and long, long hours of winter darkness. 'Orkney, bloody Orkney' was the title of a poem engraved in the memories of many Servicemen who wore the wartime badge of OSDEF, the Orkney and Shetland Defence Force. Our 11th Battalion was stationed in Shetland at the time.

Sailors probably had a worse time than us, for their periods ashore were limited, and their facilities for amusement and relaxation were still primitive; but for none of us was there much in the way of comfort, sport or entertainment. I suppose though that the men who suffered most were the many Italian prisoners of war employed on constructing buildings and shore defences.

We could do little infantry training, as much of the ground was bog and guard duties took up many hours by day and night. In any event, none of us seriously believed that the Germans would try to invade our inhospitable islands. I was surprised therefore when I met in Germany in 1960 a Major in the Bundeswehr who told me that while I was doing my bit to protect Orkney, he was in Norway being trained for an airborne assault against Scapa Flow.

Everyone was entitled to ten days' leave every four months, and the chance to get away from the island was eagerly looked forward to. But there was one impediment to this enjoyable experience: the Pentland Firth. This strip of narrow water flowing between the southern island of the Orkney group and the coast of Caithness in northern Scotland was where the Atlantic Ocean and the North Sea clashed. The three-hour passage in the small ship, the *Zetland*, between Stromness and the mainland harbour of Scrabster could be smooth and enjoyable, but normally once the boat had passed that rocky column, the Old Man of Hoy, the sea became extremely rough and we used to disembark in Scotland pale, weak and empty, hoping only for an undisturbed journey down the single railway track through the Highlands to Perth, the 'Gateway to Civilisation'. But sometimes the gales and currents of the Pentland Firth inflicted on us a double ordeal, for the *Zetland*, having struggled across to Caithness, would be unable to steer safely through the narrow harbour entrance and was ordered to turn about and fight its way back to Stromness.

Life on Orkney was certainly different to that which most of us had experienced hitherto: the inhabitants too were different, being Norsemen rather than Scots. One day I was told to go and fetch the Mess's ration of eggs from a nearby farm, so I left the camp and walked along the narrow road that led to Blackhill Farm. I knocked on the door which was soon opened to me by a pleasant dark-haired woman in her late twenties.

– 'Good afternoon. May I please have the eggs for the Argyll Officers' Mess?'
– 'Of course. Wait a minute while I fetch them.'
When she came back I asked:
– 'I'm new here; that is Kirkwall, isn't it?' (pointing towards the town)
– 'Yes, that is Kirkwall.'
– 'Can you please tell me when is Early-Closing Day in the shops, Tuesday or Wednesday?'
– 'I'm sorry, I do not know. You see,' she said, 'I haven't been into the town for some twenty years. My Father took me in there in the cart when I was a child but the journey made me sick and I've never been since.'

Kirkwall with its impressive cathedral named for St Magnus, houses and shops, lay at the most two miles from where we were standing.

But there were some marvellous compensations. The air was wonderfully pure and stimulating, as was the light in that northern latitude whenever the sky was free of cloud; and we were young, fit and pretty well looked after.

Almost all the Rank and File were men conscripted into the Army for the duration of hostilities, and on account of the limited size of Scotland's population, a great number came from England, Yorkshiremen predominating. However, they took quite naturally to the kilt and Tam O'Shanter bonnet and they made splendid Highland soldiers. The key members of the Warrant Officers' and Sergeants' Mess – the backbone of all regiments – were long service Regulars, as were the Commanding Officer, the 2IC, the Adjutant and the Quartermaster. The other thirty-odd Officers were either like me, on 'wartime commissions' or former Territorial Army Officers: the latter commanded the six companies which made up the battalion. Up to the time when I got to the battalion few young, fit Officers had stayed long, most being soon posted overseas to units in the British-Indian Army for active service in North Africa or Burma. Luckily the batch who joined with me were retained in 2A&SH and we had, I imagine, a more congenial war than they did.

There are two things about military life in Orkney in 1942–3 which I remember with some distaste: punishment drill and censorship. Soldiers who transgressed were often sentenced to extra drill, confinement to barracks and detention, the normal punishments under the Army Act, being hardly appropriate in view of the restricted life we all led on those islands. These men had to spend hours with rifle and full equipment marching at speed up and down the parade ground in view of us all. It was a hard punishment, but not intolerable or unjust. The thing which caused the distaste was the glee with which the Provost Sergeant inflicted this exhausting exercise on the malefactors.

We junior Officers had an unusual task which occupied many hours each evening. Because Orkney was such an important area for the Royal Navy and to a lesser extent for the RAF, the reporting of information about military activities, ship movements, the weather and other facts which could help the enemy was strictly controlled. All letters written by Servicemen from Orkney had to be censored, and each evening a pile of our soldiers' mail was brought to us for examination. There was a list of prohibited subjects, and if we came across a mention of any we cut the offending sentences out before sealing the envelope and signing it. Any soldier who wished to write about a sensitive personal matter could apply for a specially printed envelope and we did not examine those letters. They were, however, liable to be opened by the Base Censor.

Our soldiers accepted without resentment this essential but disagreeable breach of their privacy and I believe they knew that, although we censored their mail conscientiously, what they had written 'went in one eye and out of the other'. Very little of what we read registered in our minds. But some things did, and the procedure did give us a glimpse of what was passing through their minds and hearts, and revealed to us individuals who were particularly anxious about some matter; and thus they could be helped.

But we who were obliged to read our soldiers' letters were horrified by the illiteracy of so many and their inability to express themselves in other than the most basic terms; and by the narrow range of topics they wrote, and presumably thought, about. It was a shaming commentary on the state of the nation's pre-war education system.

The CO of the New 93rd was Lieutenant-Colonel John Bedford-Roberts. He was tall, erect, with iron-grey hair and moustache. We youngsters named him 'Ramrod' and we trembled in his presence, for he was stern and unbendingly strict; above all, he knew from long experience what made the Jocks tick. In my view JB-R was the ideal man to mould that inexperienced collection of Officers and Men, and by imprinting on each of us the need for excellence in all things, he laid the foundations of a unit which was in time to be acclaimed as a first-class battalion on and off the battlefield.

I was, to begin with, sent to C Company as a platoon commander. The company was at the time commanded by a captain who not long before had been a corporal in another Highland regiment; but he, alas, soon came unstuck and was court-martialled for selling rum on the black market and other indiscretions; and I had the experience of acting as his escort while he was in close arrest.

Shortly after this novel introduction to military law, the CO brought me into his Headquarters in the appointment of Battalion Intelligence Officer;

and I remained in that post until the 93rd had landed in Normandy in June 1944.

As IO, I was in charge of the Intelligence Section. There were eight of us: Sergeant Tucker from Yorkshire, six NCOs or Privates and, youngest of the lot, me. We stuck together through all the months of movement, training and increasing pressure which were our preparation for the battles in north-west Europe and, I like to think, never let the battalion down. Inevitably, some of the Section became casualties in that campaign and had to be replaced, but the original spirit which bound us together as friends as well as comrades-in-arms lasted until the end of the war. And long after; for we have kept in touch, meeting when possible, by telephone more frequently; and in June 1993 six of us sat down in Maurice Tucker's house for a reunion lunch. Not a bad record on the part of that small Intelligence Section who had first come together in Orkney fifty-one years earlier.

The huts in which we slept were primitive, with roofs of curved corrugated-iron sheets, rough concrete floors, an electric light or two and the minimum of furniture. The CO nevertheless insisted that all Officers using his Headquarters Mess should conform to the regimental conventions of peacetime. Thus I had to acquire promptly a blue patrol tunic and tartan trews, and each evening, dressed in these, I would pick my way over the mud to the Mess hut to await my colleagues, the Colonel, and, in due course, the evening meal.

Regimental custom required me, the newest joined subaltern, to be the first to arrive in the Mess and, unless called away to some duty, the last to leave after dining. Good manners also dictated that we junior Officers did not take up a newspaper or occupy one of the more comfortable chairs if someone senior was present who might wish to use either.

This discipline was good for our souls and the Colonel was right to demand high standards in the Mess no less than in our duties towards our soldiers. The two are in truth complementary.

I shared a hut with two other subalterns: Harry Dunning and David Scott-Lyon. Harry, a sugar-beet farmer from Fife, was the Pioneer Platoon commander and a very good one he was too. Popular with girls, calm, humorous, and laid back, he was fond of his bed; and even when Orderly Officer, he used to put off until the last moment the ordeal of getting up in the cold, unheated hut, and to save time, often did not dress himself fully, but merely threw on stockings, shoes, greatcoat and hat before rushing down to the parade ground at dawn to dismount the Night Guard.

This was one of the key events in the camp's daily routine and it was a formal affair as it involved ensuring that the mens' rifles were emptied of live ammunition and made safe. Sometimes the Adjutant or the RSM would come to watch the parade and satisfy himself that we young Officers were performing correctly.

That Harry had been slower than usual to get out of bed became evident one morning, for, as he stood barking orders at the Guard, two blue striped pyjama trouser legs rolled slowly down below his greatcoat.

David Scott-Lyon, the Signals Officer, was quite different. Punctilious, conscientious, with very high principles and rosy cheeks, David was a bonny lad. I liked him very much and was delighted when he asked me to be his Best Man at his marriage to Alison in Oxted in 1947. He was ordained into the Church of Scotland and spent much of his life in India. I mention Harry and David not only because we were good friends but because they, like our abusive but efficient Quartermaster, John Kenny, were the only Officers who served with the 93rd throughout the campaign in north-west Europe and who returned home afterwards alive and unwounded.

On one wall of the mess anteroom we hung large maps, and with the aid of coloured pins traced the course of the war on the Russian front and in North Africa. For some reason we ignored the war with Japan: perhaps it was too far away and the Pacific theatre too vast – or maybe I was unable to get hold of the right map.

The tide of war was now turning dramatically with the Eighth Army's success at Alamein, the Allied invasion of North Africa and, three months later, the destruction of the German Sixth Army at Stalingrad. We realized that our tedious vigil over Scapa Flow would soon end, and that the 93rd would be summoned to take part in adventures altogether more challenging and fateful.

We bade farewell to Orkney in the early summer of 1943 and, after a brief interlude in Northumberland, moved into a camp of comfortable wooden huts in Farnley Park just outside the Yorkshire town of Otley. The park was part of the estate owned by the Houghton-Fawkes family in whose home, the 15th-century Farnley Hall, the painter Joseph Turner had spent some twenty years of his life.

By now the 93rd, like our sister battalion from Orkney, the 2nd Battalion of the Gordon Highlanders, had been incorporated into the Order of Battle for the invasion of Europe. The whole tempo of our lives, collective and individual, changed into a higher and more exciting gear. With the 10th Battalion The Highland Light Infantry, the Gordons and ourselves formed an infantry brigade commanded by Brigadier Ronnie Mackintosh-Walker, a Seaforth, an experienced soldier and a charmer. When the Highland Division was trapped in France in 1940 he had evaded capture and made his way back to Britain. Our brigade, 227 (Highland), was part of the famous 15th (Scottish) Infantry Division and we were proud to display on our sleeves and vehicles the formation sign, the red Lion of Scotland, encircled by a white letter 'O' ('O' being the fifteenth letter of the alphabet), the whole bordered by black in mourning for the division's Fallen in the Great War.

The divisional commander was an Argyll, Major-General Gordon MacMillan, 'the Babe', and under him the 15th Scottish was to make a signal contribution to the victory in Europe, and many historians were to rate it the most reliable and successful infantry division in Sir Miles Dempsey's Second Army.

Preparations for the assault on Europe hugely enlarged our personal military skills and confidence and the efficiency of the battalion. Many Commanding Officers were being replaced by younger men since General Sir Bernard Montgomery, now the designated Commander-in-Chief of the 21st Army Group which was to carry out the assault on Europe, regarded anyone over 35 as too old to command an infantry unit in battle. John Bedford-Roberts had therefore left us while we were still in Orkney and another Argyll, Lieutenant-Colonel John Tweedie, took over. At the same time our 2IC, Major Eddie Colville, left to take over 2 Gordons.

Physically large and robust, John Tweedie had a complexion which, normally pink, was transformed when he was angry through crimson to purple. Angered he often was, for he had a quick temper, but his explosions of wrath, like squalls of rain, soon blew over. A devout Catholic, he was in fact a sensitive and very kind-hearted man. He had a sound but orthodox background of regimental soldiering which had included a spell on the north-west frontier of India; but he was a worrier, prone to periods of self-doubt. As his Intelligence Officer and subsequently Adjutant, I got to know him well and I understood him better, I believe, than the Majors and Captains who, coming from civilian professions, had a more relaxed attitude to matters military than he; initially they tended to view him as a bit of a joke. It was, however, Colonel Tweedie who transformed us, a totally inexperienced unit, within eighteen months into a first-class infantry battalion. After we had been in Normandy for two months, he took over another Argyll unit and in due course reached the rank of Brigadier. In the post-war decades I used to visit him as often as I could. His last years saddened me: a lonely widower in poor health, he constantly reproached himself over every Officer and Soldier who had been killed while under his command.

John Tweedie had as his 2IC an outstanding Officer and a man who is still remembered as a paragon of military leadership. Major Russell Morgan was tall, athletic, extremely good-looking and immaculate in dress. Known throughout the regiment as Hank, he captured and retained the admiration and affection of every Jock. He had a quick wit, a generous and engaging personality and a stimulating tongue. His calmness and tact smoothed many feathers ruffled by the temperamental outbursts of his cousin, the CO. Nevertheless when vexed or caught by surprise Hank's automatic exclamation invariably was: 'F**k me with a Green Banana!' I know that his pretty actress wife, Eve, and the Colonel disapproved, but we youngsters all tittered mightily. To live and work alongside Russell Morgan was fun, and instructive too. He was to be our CO during the drab months of fighting in Belgium, Holland and Germany. The 93rd could not have been in better hands.

The battalion's tactical knowledge and fitness for battle were, when we settled down in Yorkshire, zero. Colonel Tweedie had put us through two simple test exercises, but the result was a disquieting shambles. The battalion had had no experience at all of operating as a cohesive unit or of cooperating with anyone else. Thus we arrived in Otley with an enormous amount to learn. We learned fast.

General Sir Bernard Paget was in charge of the whole organization for training the Army for the battles to come, and an exhilarating variety of courses of instruction were run and drills invented to cover every aspect of modern combat, supplemented by demonstrations, lectures, pamphlets and films.

I was sent to the School of Military Intelligence at Matlock where I found myself studying alongside Officers from almost every regiment of the British Army and from the Allied armies also, including several from the United States Army which had already arrived in Britain in strength. The experience brought home to every one of us the breadth and latent vigour of the Grand Alliance, its unity of purpose and the marvellous world-wide communion created by the English language. None of us had any illusions though about the grim task that lay ahead, nor of the urgency of the need to liberate the peoples of Occupied Europe; for evidence of Nazi atrocities was being laid daily before us. The half, however, was not being told us then: the full facts about the death camps, the Holocaust, slave labour, the savage reprisals and other German barbarities were not revealed to the horrified world until Hitler was dead and Germany in ruins and overrun.

From the summer of 1943 onwards the War Office organised a series of large-scale exercises which ranged over great areas of the British Isles and which alone could rehearse senior commanders and their staffs in the control of very large numbers of men, vehicles, guns and tanks. We took part in many, 'Blackcock' and 'Eagle' being the most memorable because they were the longest and the most demanding. To and fro over the Ridings and rivers of Yorkshire we practised all the operations of war, with Infantry working with tanks and the ground forces being supported by the Air Force. All this movement, digging, cutting vegetation for camouflage, using barns and so on for Headquarters did a lot of damage to the roads, walls, hedges and farmland; the Army did have, however, an effective repair organisation and paid compensation promptly. The pressures on each of us living out in the field through many days and nights of rain, sun, snow and frost ensured that we crawled back to

Farnley Park exhausted, wet, dirty and hungry. But the experience had been invaluable. All we lacked now was exposure to real combat: to a live enemy firing live bullets, bombs and shells.

But even our mock battles on those exercises claimed the lives and limbs of many men: through vehicle accidents, crews crushed as they slept on soft ground beneath their tanks, exhausted infantrymen run over by tanks as they lay invisible in the dark, drownings during river-crossing practice, accidental explosions, ill-aimed bullets, carelessness, recklessness and plain bad luck. The Battle Schools with their liberal use of live ammunition had a high casualty rate. It was rumoured that for each course to lose up to five percent of its students through death or injury in the interests of realism was acceptable.

'Spartan' was a very big exercise. It was laid on for another Corps so 15th Scottish Division was not involved. Of Spartan it was said that the Germans were able to publish in the Wehrmacht's magazine, *Signal*, a full and accurate account of the exercise; of who fought whom, where, when, how and who won, merely by listening on the continent to the wireless nets of the British units exercising in England. Happily, our wireless procedures and discipline improved markedly in time for D-Day in June 1944.

My stalwart colleagues in the Intelligence Section and I became particularly skilled at controlling the battalion's moves by day and night, from harbour area to harbour area, to assembly area and so on right up to the forward positions on the battlefield; and in such a way that every element got to its appointed place precisely as required, in good order and unseen by the enemy. Through being the Commanding Officer's Battle Staff, we normally knew what was going on before anyone else in the battalion. This was useful, as all sorts of people from the Majors downward strove to keep in our good books in order to glean from us morsels of news about what was being planned.

As D-Day for the invasion drew nearer, a succession of famous and important people came to visit us. Our Corps Commander, that little terrier of a Cameronian, General Sir Richard O'Connor; Monty with his beret and two badges, his piercing blue eyes, and his air of total self-confidence; Eisenhower, the Supreme Allied Commander; Winston Churchill, the Prime Minister; and His Majesty the King.

We knew now that we were on the verge of great events. Our hectic training programme was relaxed somewhat, and sporting and social events took temporary precedence. And as we circulated among the other units, our feelings of confidence and divisional pride grew; and we made many fleeting friendships outside the ranks of our own battalion.

As part of the final inspections by the Brigadier of his three battalions, Ronnie Mackintosh-Walker descended early one day on the Gordons' Transport Platoon. The Gordons knew he was coming and had devoted much time and effort to making their jeeps, trucks, lorries and Bren carriers immaculate inside and out. Our Argyll drivers, however, had resolved secretly to take the Gordons down a peg or two, and during the night they crept undetected into the Gordons' camp. Morning brought consternation, for as the brigade team pressed on with the inspection, they found hidden in the engine compartments and other crevices of the Gordons' vehicles birds' nests, dead mice, and such-like garbage.

'An enemy has done this!' cried Colonel Colville. 'And I know exactly who that enemy is!' He was referring to our Argyll Transport Officer, Tom Spencerley, a large, kindly man well-known for his practical jokes. This little coup meant that the 93rd had to be especially vigilant during the final days at Otley lest the Gordons took revenge on us, but I do not recollect them succeeding. Tom Spencerley was to take his own life the following year: he is rightly remembered as much for his care for his subordinates as for his eccentricities.

I remember the spring of 1944 particularly for its wonderful weather and my own feeling of physical well-being. In company with the rest of the Division the 93rd moved from Yorkshire down the south coast of England, into a tented camp in the village of Findon under the Sussex Downs. To broaden our experience and to give us a break from Intelligence duties, the CO sent members of the Section out to the rifle companies. I temporarily took over command of No. 8 Platoon; 'The Plums' of Major Kenneth's A Company, we called ourselves. During my month's attachment, which I enjoyed very much indeed, a Private McLeod volunteered to be my Batman and to look after me. A Glaswegian with dark wavy hair and a pencil-thin moustache, McLeod was dapper, talkative and amusing. We got on well together and I was sorry that I had to leave him in A Company when I went back to my job at Battalion HQ. Forty-four years later I was in France lecturing to a party of English tourists about the Battle for Normandy. They decided to stop the coach for a leg-stretch and to 'spend pennies', so we drew up in a little village to the west of Caen named Brouay. Behind the church and its clusters of graves, monuments, crosses and urns was a small military cemetery in which some two hundred British soldiers lie buried. The cemetery was beautifully laid out and cared for as they invariably are the world over. I went in and looked along the neat rows of headstones. Noticing that three bore the badge of the Argyll and Sutherland Highlanders, I looked more closely and saw that one marked the grave of my Batman and colleague of May 1944, No 899 Private J. McLeod. He had been severely wounded at the end of our first big battle and had died the next day in a Field Hospital in the vicinity of Brouay. He was, incidentally, the only man I have ever met who wished the Communist Party of Great Britain to take power. He was convinced that they alone could cure the ills which beset our country – unemployment, inequality and class-divisions.

By 1944 the manpower of Britain could no longer provide for the Armed Forces Officer material in the numbers and of the calibre needed, and to alleviate this shortage, young trained Officers of the Canadian Army were seconded to British units. This CANLOAN scheme was a great success. Our battalion received in all about a dozen of these stalwarts. They were popular and efficient, and, I am glad to say, several have to this day kept in close touch with the Regiment.

Our pre-battle programme of sporting and social events culminated just before D-Day in an Assault-at-Arms, a demonstration of the military and athletic skills of every unit in 15th Scottish Division. Held in the Brighton stadium under blue skies and in bright sunshine, this colourful and uplifting day ended with the Beating of Retreat by the massed Pipes and Drums of the Division. It reminded some of us of the ball given by the Duchess of Richmond in Brussels in June 1815 on the eve of Waterloo.

For the launching of Operation OVERLORD, the invasion of Europe, the British Isles from South Wales to Norfolk had been transformed into a vast concentration area, and into it flowed, by train, in lorries or on foot, the armies who would fight in France. In the West Country the Americans; along the south coast and in East Anglia the British and Canadian formations and the units of Poles, Free French, Belgians, Dutch, Luxembourgers and Czechs who, far from their German-occupied homes, had trained alongside us.

In the south-eastern counties too a phantom army had been created with dummy tanks, guns and wireless nets, all designed to deceive German eyes and ears into believing that the invasion fleets would fall not on the coast of Normandy, but on the nearer shore of the Pas de Calais.

Beside the railway lines, roads and airfields of southern England, in meadows and woods, were built up great dumps of ammunition, shells for the artillery and bombs for the Air Forces; of fuel; motor parks with row upon row of jeeps, trucks and armoured vehicles; tons of engineer and ordnance stores, rations, medical equipment, stationery: the complete arsenal essential for the defeat of the Wehrmacht and which would all soon be consumed in the fire and destruction of modern war.

This intricate, complex and crucial timetable of movement, concealment and deception, coupled at all stages with thoughtful care for the well-being of the soldiers involved, seemed to go like clockwork. So that the Germans, their agents and sympathizers should discern no details of the OVERLORD plan, the British Government imposed on everyone who lived in the south of England a blanket of security measures of unprecedented rigour. Travel, mail, the press, broadcasting, telephone communications, all were controlled and censored. Even foreign diplomats in the United Kingdom had their privileges in respect of travel and communication by wireless and courier suspended.

Before departing for Europe, the invasion units were moved into special 'sealed' camps out of which it was forbidden to post letters, make telephone calls or walk. Only when we had been thus isolated from the rest of the Army and from all civilian contacts were we told about our destination, our journey there and our probable tasks on reaching France. Money, maps, information sheets, phrase books, escape kits, extra medical equipment – everything which the soldier might need on arriving over there was issued in these camps.

To be even a small cog in the huge, unstoppable and perfectly operating invasion machine was a wonderful and rather awesome experience. It had on most of us, I believe, three effects. Firstly, it gave us tremendous confidence in our political and military leaders. After such flawless preparations in England, failure in France was unthinkable. Secondly, our faith in ultimate victory was confirmed, even though some, perhaps many of us, would not live to see it. For Good would in the end conquer Evil. Thirdly, it struck us that if our nation could, after four years of war, plan and carry through with such marvellous precision this vast, complex business of mounting OVERLORD, surely we should be capable of surmounting every sort of problem or peril which the post-war years might bring us. A nation with such proven discipline, resolution and expertise was equipped to tackle anything.

The enemy Intelligence Services failed, lamentably from the German viewpoint, to detect the magnitude of the armadas being assembled along our Channel coast or to predict the sectors of their Atlantic Wall on which the Allied blow was to fall. However, a week after D-Day, the Germans launched against London and the Home Counties the first of their 'Retaliation' (*Vergeltung*) weapons, the V1, which the British called the Flying Bomb or 'Doodlebug'. These small, pilotless flying machines, fitted with a powerful explosive warhead, were propelled from ramps set up in northern France. Just under nine thousand in all were launched against England. They killed many people and did a lot of damage to built-up areas and undoubtedly rattled very many of those who lived in or near the target areas. But this novel weapon had, as far as I could tell, absolutely no effect on the flow of men and material across the Channel.

The invasion was launched on 6 June, D-Day, and by 10 June the American, Canadian and British assault formations had linked up to form a single firm bridgehead up to twelve miles deep in Normandy. 15 Scottish Division played no part in the initial operations, for we were a 'Break-Out' Division. Our task would be to attack through the forward troops and punch a hole in the German defences through which our armoured units would penetrate deep into the rear of the enemy. For this reason we remained encamped in England until the third week of June. Eventually the order came to embark, and the Brigade drove in a long convoy past groups of well-wishers in the hamlets and villages of Sussex and onto the quays at Newhaven.

Looking from my vehicle at the lorries on the road ahead I could see the happy, waving Jocks, and floating above them, bunches of long white balloons. 'Heavens' I exclaimed, 'where did the Men get so many balloons from?'. 'Sir,' replied my driver, 'them's not balloons, them's French Letters!'.[3]

Thus did we innocents set sail to confront in France the veteran German Army.

Notes

1. When in January 1933 Field Marshal Paul von Hindenburg, the aged German President, appointed Hitler Chancellor, his former Chief of Staff, General Erich Ludendorff, rebuked him with the warning 'that accursed man will assuredly lead Germany to destruction'.
2. NAAFI; Navy, Army and Air Force Institute.
3. Now called condoms.

CHAPTER III
1944–1945

With the New 93rd in the British Liberation Army

For the move to France the battalion passed into the hands of an efficient Movement Control Organization which split us into three parties. The Vehicle Party under the command of the 2IC, Russell Morgan, embarked at Tilbury. So that a single torpedo should not destroy an entire unit, half the Argylls travelled from Newhaven in one ship under Lieutenant-Colonel Colville with half of his 2 Gordons, while Colonel Tweedie embarked in another with the other two half battalions. I sailed with Eddie Colville's party in *The Maid of Guernsey*. The ships moved out of the port under clear skies in the evening sunlight, anchored in the Channel and when the rest of the convoy had assembled we headed for France. It was Sunday 18 June.

At dawn we found ourselves rolling about in an exceptionally severe gale within sight of the coast of Normandy, and it was not until late on 21 June that the first heavily laden and sea-sick Highlanders could be landed onto the long heaving pontoons of the Mulberry harbour, one of two artificial ports constructed in secrecy in Britain, towed in segments across the Channel and assembled on the shores of Calvados.

The gale of 19 and 20 June had destroyed the Mulberry harbour in the

US sector off Omaha Beach and severely damaged the one at Arromanches where we landed, and through which the British and Canadian divisions were supplied. One consequence was that the ammunition for some artillery batteries had been rationed to five shells per gun per day. Also the concentration of our VIII Corps was delayed causing the start of our first major operation to be postponed until 26 June.

From Arromanches we set out on the twelve-mile march to our concentration area at Vaux-sur-Seulles. Our Vehicle Party had had a particularly tedious journey from Tilbury. They were at sea for a week, and it was not until the afternoon of 23 June that the whole of 2 A&SH was reunited in a large field bordered by thick hedges, deep ditches and well-kept woods, disturbed only by the sound of artillery fire a mile or so to the south and by the passage overhead of aircraft.

There we set about planning for Operation EPSOM, to be launched two days later. In this battle I had to act as Adjutant to Colonel John Tweedie since Alan Fyfe had been kept in England with a bout of pneumonia. I had no difficulty in that appointment as I had, as Intelligence Officer, been Tweedie's Battle Adjutant on all those gruelling exercises in Yorkshire, except that I failed to master the essential art of compiling from busy and dispersed parts of the battalion the data demanded each day by Brigade and higher Headquarters concerning ration strengths, petrol and ammunition consumption, and such like. Hitherto these things had been attended to by the Quartermaster and the Orderly Room Sergeant, but these experts were now way back in B Echelon and I was on my own, up front with the CO and F Echelon, the fighting elements of the battalion. The routine staff work of the 93rd was poorly rated by Brigade HQ while I was groping with it.

Many of us were surprised by the attitude of the French civilians we encountered in Normandy. Uncommunicative and unwelcoming they did not seem to be all that pleased to have been liberated. We were disappointed and a bit shocked. Being newly arrived we forgot that liberation for them had occurred two weeks earlier; since then the bridgehead had been deepened and the battlefield had moved farther inland. Their relief at the ejection of the Germans had worn off and had been replaced by a reluctant acceptance of our presence on their land and consternation at the cumulative destruction of their property and livelihood which our weapons and vehicles, and our pilfering, were causing. Whenever I returned to Normandy in the post-war years I took up with them the matter of our grudging reception in 1944, and I came to appreciate why this had been.

Calvados was a rich agricultural province of France, little touched until the invasion by Allied bombing or coastal raids. Although German soldiers and German fortifications, defence works, regulations, restrictions and requisitions were disagreeable, life under the Boche was, if one 'kept one's nose clean', by no means intolerable. The German units were disciplined, industrious and, being to a great extent composed of men from rural backgrounds, they were sympathetic to the French farmers; helping them when off-duty with sowing, harvesting and caring for the livestock, and paying well and promptly for the things they purchased. Thus relations between the Germans and the local French were polite, often warm and sometimes even intimate. Furthermore we British, admirers of General de Gaulle and the Free French whom he led, overlooked the fact that the lawful government of France was the one set up in Vichy whose figure-head was the aged hero of Verdun, Marshal Pétain, but whose real head was the odious Pierre Laval. Laval had long declared that the interests of France were best served by cooperating with Hitler's regime, even to the extent of recruiting forced labour for German factories, deporting Communists and Jews into the hands of the German exterminators, and hunting down those French men and women who were working for an Allied victory and the agents trained in England and inserted into France to encourage and equip them.

We worked away on the plans for the forthcoming operation for which we had so frequently practised our role: to break out from the Allied bridgehead and, in conjunction with armoured forces, to punch a hole deep into the German defences. The River Odon, which lay obliquely across our front until it flowed into the River Orne near Caen, was not wide but its steep wooded banks made it an effective tank obstacle. The task of 15 Scottish Division in Operation EPSOM was to attack through the FDLs[1] of the 3 Canadian Division, to clear the area up to the line of the Odon, to seize crossings over that river, and to enable a strong British armoured force to pass through and establish itself on the large feature, Hill 112, which dominated the whole area between the valleys of the Odon and Orne to the south-west of Caen. For 2 A&SH was reserved the honourable but formidable task of seizing the two principal crossing places over the Odon, the bridges at Tourmauville and Gavrus. These lay some five miles behind the German front line and to reach them the Division had to fight its way through very close country, all woods and orchards and fields of uncut corn standing chest-high, bordered by thick double hedges with deep ditches and buttressed by clusters of buildings in farms, hamlets and villages grown prosperous on the produce of the rich countryside and each with its thick stone walls forming for the enemy a sturdy fortress. This Norman bocage country was ideal for the German defenders, entrenched, camouflaged, invisible and tenacious. For our advancing Scottish Infantry and our accompanying tanks it posed many hazards. But our Higher Command had promised while in England that when 15 Scottish went into action for the first time it would be 'committed on the right foot'.

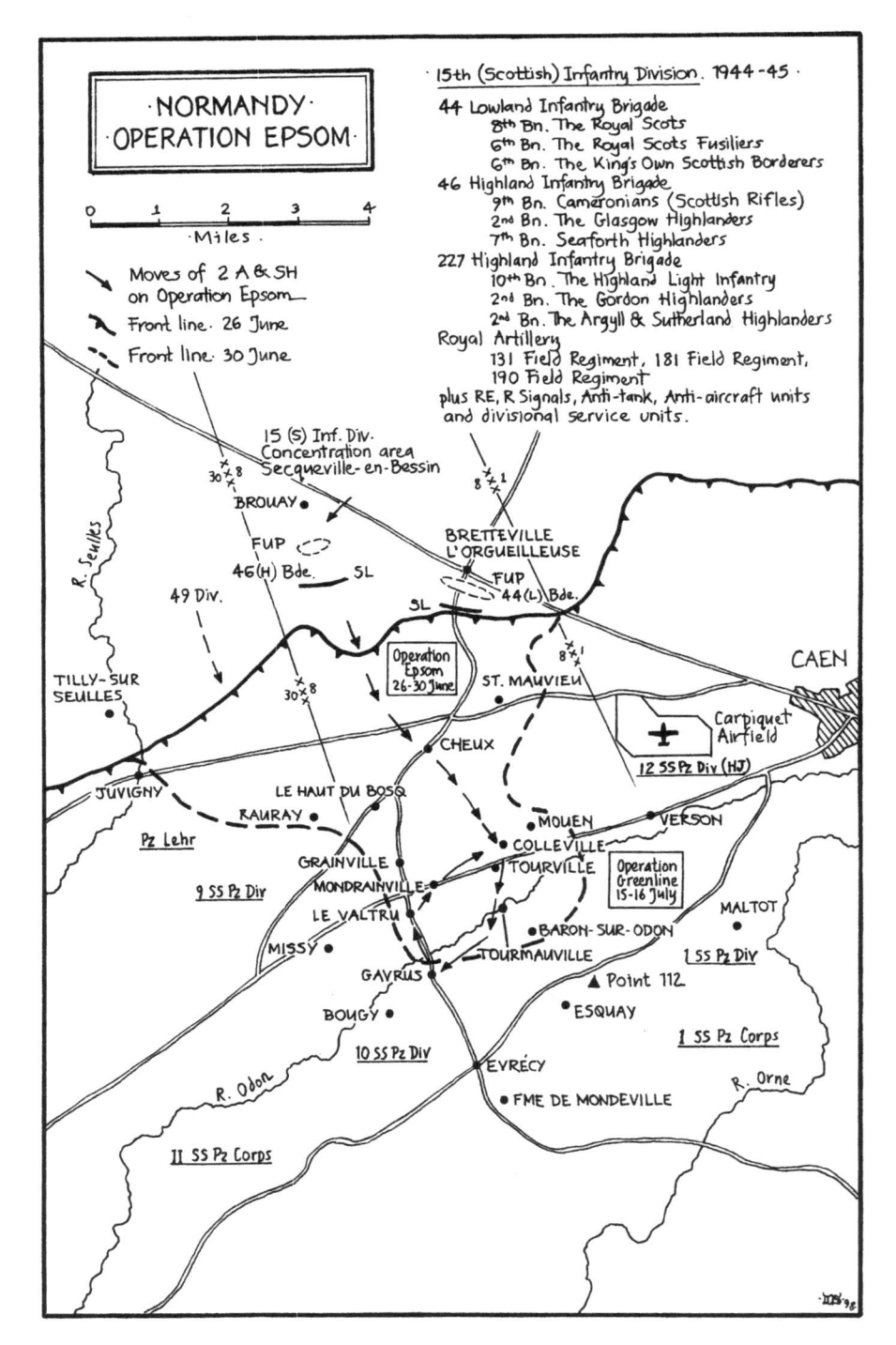

NORMANDY OPERATION EPSOM

15th (Scottish) Infantry Division. 1944-45

44 Lowland Infantry Brigade
    8th Bn. The Royal Scots
    6th Bn. The Royal Scots Fusiliers
    6th Bn. The King's Own Scottish Borderers

46 Highland Infantry Brigade
    9th Bn. Cameronians (Scottish Rifles)
    2nd Bn. The Glasgow Highlanders
    7th Bn. Seaforth Highlanders

227 Highland Infantry Brigade
    10th Bn. The Highland Light Infantry
    2nd Bn. The Gordon Highlanders
    2nd Bn. The Argyll & Sutherland Highlanders

Royal Artillery
    131 Field Regiment, 181 Field Regiment, 190 Field Regiment
plus RE, R Signals, Anti-tank, Anti-aircraft units and divisional service units.

Legend:
- Moves of 2 A & SH on Operation Epsom
- Front line 26 June
- Front line 30 June

Map locations: 15 (S) Inf. Div. Concentration area Secqueville-en-Bessin; BROUAY; FUP 46(H) Bde.; 49 Div.; BRETTEVILLE L'ORGUEILLEUSE; FUP 44(L) Bde.; TILLY-SUR-SEULLES; Operation Epsom 26-30 June; ST. MAUVIEU; CAEN; Carpiquet Airfield; CHEUX; 12 SS Pz Div (HJ); JUVIGNY; LE HAUT DU BOSQ; RAURAY; Pz Lehr; MOUEN; VERSON; GRAINVILLE; COLLEVILLE; 9 SS Pz Div; MONDRAINVILLE; TOURVILLE; Operation Greenline 15-16 July; MALTOT; LE VALTRU; MISSY; GAVRUS; BARON-SUR-ODON; 1 SS Pz Div; TOURMAUVILLE; Point 112; BOUGY; ESQUAY; 1 SS Pz Corps; 10 SS Pz Div; EVRÉCY; R. Odon; FME DE MONDEVILLE; R. Orne; II SS Pz Corps; R. Seulles

Thus our pre-battle briefings were helped by a generous issue of maps and air photographs overlaid with intelligence about the enemy defences, gun positions, headquarters, and so on.

The initial attack into the crust of the German defences by the other two brigades in our Division was to be supported by a barrage from some nine hundred field and medium guns of the British and Canadian artillery, by naval gunfire, by close air support and by armoured units. The latter sadly were not to be the 6th Guards Tank Brigade whom we had got to know so well in Yorkshire, for that splendid formation of Grenadiers, Coldstream and Scots Guards with their Churchill tanks was not yet ashore.

The Battalion left Vaux on the afternoon of Sunday 25 June and, after a march of only about five miles, settled down for the night in a field right in among the batteries which were to support the attack the next morning. The weather which had been lovely for the past three days had turned wet, but the going was still good for tanks and the drizzle at least kept the dust down. At first light the barrage opened up and those who had been prudent enough to bring cotton wool for the purpose stopped their ears against the racket. Breakfast was served and the 93rd prepared to move off into its first battle.

Unless he was moving on foot the CO of an Infantry battalion exercised command from a Bren carrier, a lightly armoured tracked vehicle in which he was accompanied by the I.O. (his Battle Adjutant), and the signallers and the No 18 wireless set into which all the sub-units of the battalion were 'netted'. The Rear Link No 11 set was manned by a detachment of Royal Signals operators mounted with the Adjutant in a separate vehicle farther to the rear, and through this set passed all the radio messages to and from Brigade Headquarters and flanking units. When we were about to leave Vaux for the Assembly Area there had arrived a vehicle with which we were wholly unfamiliar. It was a semi-tracked lorry, lightly armoured, with a canvas roof, larger than our own Bren carrier and driven by a young soldier from the Royal Corps of Signals. The General Staff had decided to issue these vehicles at short notice to enable battalion commanders to have, unusually, both their Forward and Rear Link wireless sets beside them in a single vehicle.

I suppose it was my fault: on the eve of battle and with my preoccupations as Adjutant I paid little heed to the young signaller who had arrived out of the blue with his half-track. When in the morning of the next day it was time for the Battalion to move off, this man was nowhere to be found. Lonely, unused to sleeping in the rain surrounded by strange Scottish Infantrymen and frightened out of his wits by the incessant firing of the guns in the fields all around us, he had taken himself off: disappeared. Colonel John Tweedie was not pleased and I endured one of his choleric outbursts at finding himself immobile beside a driverless vehicle with whose gears and steering mechanisms we were unacquainted. Then our sterling Intelligence Sergeant, Maurice Tucker, came to my rescue. He remembered that a fellow Yorkshireman, an Anti-tank Gunner, had once been on a course and had come across vehicles of this type. The man was located, asked if he was capable of driving us into battle and, much to the vexation of his Anti-tank Platoon Commander, was bundled into the driving seat beside an apoplectic Colonel and me, a hugely relieved Adjutant.

The divisional plan visualized an attack in three phases. For the first, Brigadier Colin Barber's 46 Highland Brigade on the right were to go for Cheux and 44 Lowland Brigade under Brigadier Douglas Money for St Mauvieu. For the second phase our 227 Highland Brigade was to move forward from the firm base thus established on a two-battalion front, the 10 HLI passing through 46 Brigade to capture Grainville-sur-Odon and the 2nd Gordons on the left directed through Colleville[2] on to Tourville. We in the 93rd were then to pass through in two half-battalions, the group on the right under the CO to seize and hold the two bridges at Gavrus, the group on the left under the 2IC to go for the bridge at Tourmauville. It was hoped that the whole attack would be completed in one day and that by nightfall the Argylls would be consolidating their two bridgeheads for the armoured divisions to cross the next day.

Quite early as we moved down the axis of the 46 Brigade's attack, I saw lying on the edge of a cornfield a dead British soldier. He was the first corpse I had ever seen in my life. He was a Corporal in the Cameronians, the regiment raised in 1794 by Thomas Graham of Balgowan.

Phase I was successful in that 44 and 46 Brigades both captured their objectives, but they did not do so until late in the afternoon, and by the time the HLI and the Gordons went through it was pretty clear that the 93rd was unlikely to be committed that day. In fact the HLI were unable to get beyond their start-line on which they encountered German tanks, suffering heavily and being thrown into some confusion before digging in on the southern outskirts of Cheux. The Gordons managed to get two companies into Colleville but these were pulled back as night fell having suffered fairly heavy casualties.

We in the Argylls passed a rather maddening day moving forward by fits and starts, halting frequently when the cry went up 'Sniper fire'[3] or to roll and unroll our waterproof gas capes as the weather alternated between hot sun and drenching showers. When we finally dug in for the night in open fields around the cross-roads just north of Cheux, we were pretty tired and wet. It rained heavily throughout the night. Even though I was manning the Rear Link set, the information I got from Brigade HQ about the course of the battle up front was very sparse, but when we reached our destination it became clear that our two sister battalions in the brigade had had a sticky time and we were told to send our Medical

Officer, Captain Jones, and the Padre to the HLI Aid Post to help deal with their dead and wounded. We also learned that 49 Division, whose task was to advance on our right flank, had made little progress and had failed to clear the Rauray feature from which the Germans continued to fire into the corridor which 15 Scottish was opening up in its advance to the Odon.

The battalion spent a miserable night in those muddy fields. At 0545 hours Colonel Tweedie was called to Brigade Headquarters for orders.

There followed by contrast to the day before a mad scramble of activity. As Major McElwee wrote in the Battalion's History: 'Companies had to be on the move by six-thirty and were mostly just starting breakfast when the "O" Group was called for. There was only just time to get orders to the platoon commanders, and they had to brief their men as best they could as they moved off. It was something of a tribute to the battalion's training in Battle Procedure that it was managed at all; and although everybody felt at the time that it was all far too hectic and confused, the proof of the pudding is in the eating, and the fact remains that the start-line was found, that all the companies knew their objectives and tasks, that the CO was in control throughout, and that the final objective was captured exactly as planned'. The final objective was the bridge at Tourmauville – the one originally planned for the left half-battalion. The start of our advance was exasperating. Cheux was a heap of ruins with streets flooded and partially blocked by fallen masonry among which parties of enemy were still staunchly resisting. There were few usable routes forward, and these were full of HLI and Argyll carriers trying to get round British tanks stationary among the rubble and water, closed down and with their commanders ignoring all attempts to communicate with them. Trying to get through Cheux was an infuriating business. However the CO and I found a track which led out of the village in the direction we wanted to go and across which lay the mangled bodies of a cow and of an HLI officer over whom a tank had been driven. The rifle companies soon got out into the more open country and advanced steadily, clearing their axes of small parties of enemy machine gunners and riflemen despite the intervention of armoured cars and, near Mondrainville, of two Tiger tanks. These were seen off by a couple of our 6-pounder anti-tank guns which Captain Willie Muirhead had rushed up to Bill McElwee's B Company position. After establishing with A Company and Battalion HQ a firmish base round the cross-roads at Tourville, the Colonel sent the other three rifle companies forward to clear the mile of fairly open country which separated us from the Tourmauville bridge. During all this activity I was rather astonished to see circling at about five thousand feet above us a trio of German aircraft. Round and round they flew in a tight circle observing and reporting, I assumed, our progress down the slope towards the Odon Valley.

C Company's dash to the bridge was probably the most classic manoeuvre carried out by the Battalion at any time in the campaign. The three companies moved forward in turn, from firm base to firm base. The final assault by C Company, down across the open cornfields against three spandau positions was brilliant. As the Battalion History records, Major Hugh Fyfe's plan and orders would have got ten out of ten in any School of Infantry test, and he led the attack himself with a dash and gallantry which earned him a Military Cross and which carried his company and Sergeant King's section of the Carrier Platoon across the river with miraculously few casualties.[4] Thus was the first Odon crossing established. We were relieved to find the bridge intact and unmined, but were rather disappointed to see how small it was. Short but solidly built it was an unremarkable structure. Nevertheless it was indispensable for the move of our tanks across the Odon. The Battalion consolidated a small bridgehead not more than two hundred yards in diameter half expecting a violent German counter-attack to regain the bridge. But none came. (Years later, while at the Camberley Staff College, I learned that on our advance southward from Cheux on that day, 27 June 1944, we had by good luck found a gap in the German defences which their two divisions, 12 SS Panzer (Hitler Jugend) to the east and Panzer Lehr on our western flank, were too hard pressed to fill. Consequently the ground over which 15 Scottish Division had fought was fairly lightly defended, the principal resistance being put up – very creditably – by the SS Divisional Engineer Regiment and by a battalion of artillery led by an energetic and brave Colonel who was killed during the first night of our offensive.)

But our whole situation felt very unsafe. The 93rd had advanced from Cheux four miles deep into enemy territory; the HLI and the Gordons were a mile or more behind us, while both flanks of our division were open with the enemy still holding Rauray and Verson. But apart from the arrival at Battalion HQ of a wounded SS-man and a salvo of *nebelwerfer* ('Moaning Minnie') bombs near the bridge causing a fearful noise but no damage, the afternoon passed peacefully. The rain had stopped in mid-morning and a warm sun shone down from blue skies. About seven o'clock in the evening the first tanks of 11 Armoured Division swung down the twisting narrow road into the river valley, over the bridge and up the slope through our small bridgehead. Cheering them wildly some of us shouted 'On now to Hill 112'. Others, more optimistic, cried 'Next stop Paris!'. The Gordons moved forward and dug in around Tourville and in the fields over which Major Fyfe's force had manoeuvred in their assault on the bridge. Being on a forward slope and under enemy observation from the higher ground around the village of Baron, the Gordons were to suffer many casualties. There the impressive memorial to our 15 Scottish Division was erected after the war, beside the road which runs down to the Tourmauville bridge.

That night the Quartermaster and Transport Officer came up to our position with a hot meal and to replenish our vehicles with petrol and ammunition. They told us that the name of the Argylls was on everyone's lips on the strength of our having captured the bridge, and we settled down for a night of full alertness in our small perimeter feeling that we had written a proud page in the history of the 93rd Highlanders. But, of greater significance to those of us to whom they reported, John Kenny and Tom Spencerley stated that the whole of our line of communication through the 'Scottish Corridor' back to beyond Cheux was under enemy small-arms fire from either side of the road. That evening our Brigade Major, John Lochore, was killed by mortar fire as he sorted out the traffic congestion at the Tourville cross-roads.

About noon on 28 June we sent two patrols, each commanded by one of our Canadian Officers, up the river to report on the situation at the Gavrus crossing place. By four o'clock they radioed to say that these two bridges over the Odon were intact and undefended. The whole battalion was at once ordered to move to Gavrus. This was not easy, for the road linking Tourmauville with Gavrus ran through enemy-held territory on the ridge to the south of the river. Our only route therefore lay through the thick woods which lined the river banks. It was a nightmare trek; the going was vile, we expected at every minute to fall into a fatal ambush, and the Battalion's progress was greatly slowed by the need to manhandle the anti-tank guns over a succession of obstacles.

But the 93rd arrived intact and complete at the Gavrus crossing place just before dark. The Commanding Officer made a quick tour of the area, issued his orders for the defence of the two bridges and the Battalion started to dig in.[5] Just as night fell the enemy fired a long burst of *spandau* fire from a position about three hundred yards up river, wounding Sergeant King whose Carrier Platoon section had accompanied Hugh Fyfe in the capture of the Tourmauville bridge.

29 June dawned grey and drizzly but the sun came out early. The 93rd passed a fairly quiet forenoon disturbed only by fruitless attempts to engage an enemy armoured car moving around the lanes to the west of Gavrus. But behind us things were hotting up. The road from Cheux was still under small arms fire for most of its length, and a series of German attacks was developing against Grainville and against Le Valtru where 7 Seaforths were being hard pressed. We, right up at the sharpest end of the Scottish Corridor, were hardly aware of these developments and were in fact preparing to move to Missy about two miles to the west. Those preparations were abruptly halted just after three o'clock in the afternoon when B Company's forward platoon in Gavrus saw tanks and half-tracks filled with infantry driving towards them from the direction of Bougy. For more than five hours the attacks were incessant, with accurate mortar and shell fire being directed onto the

three companies on the south bank. In Gavrus itself one Tiger tank was destroyed by a PIAT[6], another was immobilized and three others driven off, but the positions of those companies became more precarious as enemy infantry worked their way round to the river bank. Though the Germans showed at times great toughness and excellent field craft, they never pushed their attacks home with an infantry assault: the battle remained a fire-fight. This activity at Gavrus was part of the long-expected attempt by the Germans to drive the British and Canadians back to the beaches of Normandy. The principal punch in this counter-attack was delivered by General Paul Hausser's II SS Panzer Corps. This formidable and experienced force had been transported from Poland, but bombed railway lines and damaged bridges delayed their arrival in Normandy where attacks by Allied aircraft on their Headquarters and assembly areas caused further confusion and casualties. Nevertheless the threat this force presented to the exposed flank of the 15 Scottish, and of the 53 Welsh Division behind us, and to the communications running forward along the Scottish Corridor through Cheux to the Odon and beyond, caused the High Command to pull all British armoured units back behind the river. One consequence of this withdrawal was that the Germans strengthened their grip on the dominating feature Hill 112 which was only captured by the 43 Wessex Division after a month of most bitter fighting. By soldiers of both sides Hill 112 is remembered as a place of particular horror. While the attacks against our companies around Gavrus and the Seaforths at Le Valtru persisted throughout the afternoon of 29 June, the positions of D Company and Battalion HQ were subjected only to spasmodic mortar and machine-gun fire. A German soldier was brought to me. Very blond and well nourished he was certainly an amenable prisoner; perhaps even a deserter though that was improbable since he was an SS man. As we sheltered under a vehicle he gave me his pay book and told me about his family and military experience. He was convinced that Germany had lost the war. He had recently been moved from Tarnopol on the Eastern Front with his comrades in SS Panzer Divisions 9 (Hohenstaufen) and 10 (Frundsberg) with the task of destroying the Allied bridgehead in Normandy. I have forgotten his name but he told me his Father was a chef on the Berlin-Istanbul express. He was killed the next day when the Germans shelled our positions whence it had not been possible to evacuate either him or our own wounded.

The next morning the Germans switched their attention to the north bank, where Battalion HQ with its radios were dug in overlooking the river valley, and with D Company entrenched along the hedges around us. In order to ensure our timely resupply our soft-skinned A Echelon vehicles had been sent forward by Brigade HQ, and these were dispersed off the road between us and Le Valtru. At about noon another attack was put in against our positions around Gavrus, but this did not amount to much. It was, however, preceded by heavy and very accurate mortar and small arms fire onto Battalion HQ and D Company and the Mill began to burn fiercely.

At one point it was believed that enemy snipers had got into our cornfield, and at Colonel Tweedie's urging Major Vyvyan Cornwell, the commander of our affiliated 495 Field Battery, brought fire down into that field. His gunners performed with quite remarkable skill, the shells falling accurately less than a hundred yards from where we were crouching in our slit trenches. Above the sound of the explosions I heard a sudden whizz and a thump as a red-hot fragment of 25-pounder shell six inches long thudded into the earth grazing my helmet. The enemy fire intensified and our casualties mounted, and by one o'clock every radio was off the air and much damage had been inflicted on our vehicles. We no longer had any radio communication with the companies on the far side of the river, or with Brigade HQ; nor with our supporting artillery for Cornwell's set had been damaged and he himself wounded. Moreover it was clear that the Germans had such good observation over us that their accurate fire pinned us down in our holes. The CO shouted out the order to move, and during a lull in the enemy's fire he, Russell Morgan and I together with a group of Jocks ran across the road for about two hundred yards into a clover field where two large pits had once contained German anti-aircraft guns. But the enemy spotted our move, and it was not long before mortar bombs and tracer bullets started to fall around us. Our new shelter was even more exposed than the ones we had so hastily vacated, so somewhat unnerved we dispersed again into whatever fresh cover we could find. I flung myself into a disused trench; it had alas been used as a latrine. In due course the enemy fire died down and I discussed with the few Jocks near me what we should do. We crept back to the shambles of our former position in the cornfield, extremely thirsty, knackered and mentally confused. Of John Tweedie and Russell Morgan there was now no sign. Someone stated that 'the CO and 2IC have gone off along the river to get help', and as the afternoon wore on the rumour circulated that both had been killed. If true this meant that command had devolved on Bill McElwee on the other side of the river where our companies had had a fairly peaceful day. At that moment I saw a tank emerge from the distant woods behind us in the direction of Le Valtru. It was a Churchill tank. With my helmet in my hand I ran towards it. It halted and the commander, a Sergeant, put his head out of the turret and asked me 'Are you the Herefords?'[7] I put him briefly in the picture about the 93rd and told him to send back on his radio the gist of what I had told him. This he did. He then reversed his tank and disappeared into the trees whence he had come. As I made my way back to our cornfield I saw a silver object glinting in the sunlight on the side of the road. It was an article I had often seen before and knew to be Russell Morgan's pocket knife. I picked it up relieved to know that our 2IC had not after all gone down to the river and that he was probably therefore not dead.

Soon a troop of tanks appeared, led by a subaltern who told Willie Muirhead and me: 'You Argylls are to withdraw from the Gavrus bridges and my tanks are here to cover your withdrawal'. Willie and I got a carrier to take us across the river and we found Bill McElwee to whom we passed on the tank Officer's instruction. But Bill rightly refused to move without a direct order properly conveyed. About an hour later a Liaison Officer whom we knew well arrived in a scout car with a written order signed by the Brigade Commander. By half-past nine the remnants of the three companies were safely across the river, and together with the surviving Battalion HQ personnel we all moved back on foot led by D Company. Our withdrawal was watched by a Gunner Captain named Gordon Campbell[8] who, knowing that Vyvyan Cornwell was out of action, had come forward from the position of 2 Gordons around Tourville with a radio set that worked. As we passed through Le Valtru a row of Germans was being laid out beside the road. Fair-haired and already rigid in death in their distinctive camouflaged SS overalls, they looked mere school-boys but they had given the Seaforths a stiff fight.

Eventually we got back to Colleville where John Kenny, our Quartermaster, was waiting with a hot meal and blankets, and where after a night's sleep we stood by to reinforce a Welsh unit which was under heavy pressure in Grainville. Our CO and 2IC were still missing. They turned up the next day safe and sound but with the following tale to tell. After we were driven in confusion out of the gun pits in the clover field John Tweedie and Russell Morgan had taken themselves off independently in search of a unit with a wireless. Their search took a long time and it was dark when they met up again in our former Battalion HQ position. By that time the 93rd, unknown to them, had been pulled out and was back in Colleville. Huddled together in a slit trench they listened with growing trepidation to the voices of Germans who had come up during the night to search the area. Just before dawn the alarm clock, which Russell always carried in his haversack, for some reason went off. John Tweedie's vexation waxed mightily as he sought to stifle the infernal clanging, but even he realised that he could not on this occasion give vent to his anger with his usual apoplectic explosion. He managed to restrain himself. The Germans seem to have heard nothing, and the Argylls got away without being challenged. But John Tweedie had to pay a price for that extreme and uncharacteristic self-control: a month later he went into hospital with a severe attack of piles. The next night the battalion was moved back to Bretteville l'Orgueilleuse for a much needed rest and refit. For our part in EPSOM the 93rd was awarded one DSO, four MCs and five MMs[9] But we had lost in killed, wounded and missing seven officers and

182 Other Ranks. The newspapers christened us 'the Crossing Sweepers' on the strength of the three bridges we'd captured in two days.

Replacing the men we had lost was for the Staff easier than replacing the equipment and the many vehicles written off or left behind when we were pulled out of the Gavrus area.

Personnel reinforcements joined us almost immediately. Many were old friends, LOBs[10] who had deliberately been excluded from EPSOM, but most were total strangers, men from English country regiments who found themselves arbitrarily transformed into Highlanders. As the campaign went on the heavy losses incurred by Infantry battalions in the bocage country gave rise in Whitehall to much anxiety, and from the autumn of 1944 onwards those who came to top up our ranks were either wounded Argylls rejoining from hospital or former Gunners from the UK's Anti-Aircraft Command which, having driven off the Luftwaffe and overcome the V1 Flying Bomb, was being run down with many of its soldiers hastily converted into Infantrymen. Looking back I find it remarkable how well those chaps settled without audible complaint into the habits and uniforms of our Scottish tribal regiments. But this transmutation of the nation's dwindling manpower exposed the great defect in the Regimental System: the inability of weakly populated areas to sustain through a long and costly war their traditional county regiments.

The gales of late June had slowed down the flow of supplies into the Allied bridgehead, but the Ordnance Corps and Quartermasters worked hard and by 7 July all the essentials had been delivered and the 93rd was again fit for action.

While out of the line we had a grandstand view one evening of the destruction of Caen by Bomber Command of the RAF. That ancient Norman city should, according to Montgomery's initial plan for OVERLORD, have been captured by the British 3rd Division on D-Day, but in early July it was still in enemy hands. For the Germans Caen was the hub of important road communications and the hinge of their defences in Normandy; for the British and Canadians it was a barrier to our advance over open country towards the River Seine. The sight of the Lancasters and Halifaxes over that city, and the smoke, dust and flames which erupted as their bombs burst gave us no joy. Our thoughts were wholly with the French civilians caught in the inferno. The Germans had, we suspected, moved out of the target area or into deep shelters. The result of the bombing of Caen, and in the months to come of so many built-up areas in the path of the Allied advance, was to create even more formidable obstacles to our own forward movement, while for the German defenders the rubble and ruins provided enhanced protection.

Battlefields are no place for the superstitious. To begin with, some of us were dismayed that our activities at the front were accompanied by processions of single magpies[11], seldom by the more encouraging pairs or trios; and our battles too often seemed to start on Sundays. (Desecration of the Sabbath – or doing God's work, which?) One feature of the campaign remained until the end of the war a source of either encouragement or apprehension. This was the identity of the Corps Headquarters responsible for planning the successive operations to which our division was committed. In VIII Corps and its commander Dick O'Connor we had from our Yorkshire days great faith, and we never lost it. But under Neil Ritchie's XII Corps we found ourselves in ill-starred battles, victims of over-optimistic planners. We experienced the first of these 'cock-ups' in our second operation, GREENLINE.

The primary object of this operation was to gain possession of the high ground round the Ferme de Mondeville which lay to the south-west of Hill 112 and about four thousand yards south of Tourmauville. The plan was exceedingly complicated, consisting of four phases and involving most of 15 Scottish Division and two regiments of tanks. Problems arose right at the start. It was impossible to carry out an adequate reconnaissance owing to the fact that the enemy held the reverse slopes of Hill 112, whence they had a clear view of the ground over which we had to advance, and their SS Panzer Grenadier Regiments reacted very strongly to any movement by the 43rd Wessex Division on the southern edge of Baron village. I went with Colonel Tweedie and the COs of 10 HLI and 2 Gordons to examine the ground forward of Baron. It was a pretty fruitless activity as it was not possible to approach the crest of Hill 112 and so we could identify only our allotted Start Line but nothing beyond that.

We had to creep through the FDLs of an English county regiment where the unburied corpses of their own soldiers suggested that the fighting spirit of that West Country division had reached a low ebb, and that they could not be relied on in the essential task of neutralizing the Panzer Grenadiers dug in on Hill 112 before our division's operation began. Unfortunately 43 Division considered it unnecessary to clear the reverse slopes with Infantry, believing that the SS defenders could be rendered harmless by artillery, mortar and machine gun fire alone. This judgement was to be proved incorrect with evil consequences for the whole operation.

Late on 14 July, Bastille Day, the 93rd moved out of Bretteville to a concentration area near Mouen where, like 10 HLI just to the east of us, we were continuously shelled. In the early evening of the next day, 15 July – too early, for the enemy observed what we were up to – we marched forward accompanied by the vehicles of our F Echelon into a rather cramped assembly area in some orchards at the north end of Baron. It transpired that Baron had been the site of a German Corps HQ, and that night 2 A&SH experienced the heaviest and most prolonged shelling of the whole campaign. Before darkness fell the 2 Glasgow Highlanders of 46

Brigade moved down to clear and hold Esquay, and 44 Brigade advancing along the south bank of the Odon occupied Gavrus and Bougy. It was then the turn of our 227 Brigade to commence our attack towards the Ferme de Mondeville and Evrecy. 2 Gordons went first and got within two hundred yards of their first objective, but as they started down the forward slope, they paid the penalty for the SS positions on the reverse slopes of Hill 112 having been left uncleared. Well sited and firing on fixed lines the machine guns of the Panzer Grenadiers brought the advance of the Gordons to a halt.

As Alan Fyfe had returned to the Battalion I reverted to my job as I.O. and with my Intelligence Section had the tasks of marking the 93rd's Start Line, just beyond Baron church, and of guiding the Battalion, company by company, from the assembly area, through the village and up to the Start Line. It was an exceedingly unpleasant duty with shells falling continuously among the houses, and collapsing walls and bits of roof onto us as we made our way forward through the village in the semi-darkness. 2 A&SH left the Start Line punctually, negotiated the gap through a minefield and slowly advanced down the sloping cornfield followed by 10 HLI believing that the Gordons' hold-up was only temporary. As the brigade piled up in the dark in rear of the halted Gordons, all we could do was lie down in the bare, open field and wait. We were still there when dawn broke; three battalions of 227 Brigade, three squadrons of tanks and other sub-units, all jammed together in an area of about 800 yards by 300 yards, on a forward slope under the direct observation of the Germans on Hill 112 and beyond the River Orne. To compound the situation our Brigade HQ was off the air. In the shelling of Baron, Brigadier Ronnie Mackintosh-Walker had been killed and the HQ had pulled back to Mouen. While the CO of the Gordons, Eddie Colville, went back to take over command of the brigade, Colonel Young of the HLI and John Tweedie came to the decision that the most prudent way out of our predicament was for our two battalions to get back to Baron before the sun got up and we presented the Germans with an even more unique target. This sensible arrangement was messed up, however, for some of our accompanying tanks got into difficulties while withdrawing through the badly marked minefield and blocked the gap. The whole brigade was therefore obliged to remain for several hours exposed on that forward slope while our Gunners fired a great quantity of smoke-shells to blind the enemy's vision. That worked. By noon we were all back behind Baron whence we were soon directed to our old position in Tourmauville. On 17 July we were relieved by units of the 53rd Welsh Division. In Operation GREENLINE the 93rd without ever being in contact with the enemy lost seventy-one Officers and Men including young Neil Dunning, the young brother of our excellent Pioneer Officer, killed by a direct hit on his slit trench soon after we reached Tourmauville.

A principal component of Montgomery's master-plan for the Battle of Normandy was that the bulk of the German armour should be drawn onto the Caen sector. This meant that during June and July the heaviest fighting would have to be endured by the British and Canadian forces. His plan succeeded. At the end of June the US forces in the west were opposed by only 140 tanks, whereas 725 were in action against the British and Canadians; on 25 July the numbers were 190 and 645 respectively. This had enabled the Americans to complete the clearance of the Cotentin Peninusula, to capture the port of Cherbourg and to prepare their break-out, Operation COBRA, launched on 25 July after a massive aerial bombardment of the German front-line formations. COBRA was to bring about the encirclement of the German Seventh Army and the liberation of Brittany and the U-boat bases and airfields there which were so important to the enemy in the Battle of the Atlantic. By then the 15 Scottish Division had been moved west into the Caumont sector[12] where our brigade took over the positions of the 11th Infantry Regiment of the 25th US Division. It was a quiet sector: nothing much had happened there since the middle of June and, after the ruins and torn-up fields of our Odon battles, the sight of undamaged houses and tranquil green fields was refreshing.

As in EPSOM our task was to break through the German defences and to penetrate southwards deep into enemy territory while the Americans developed their right hook along the general line St Lo – Flers – Argentan – Evreux – the Seine.

For this operation, BLUECOAT, the 93rd was commanded by Major John Kenneth, a Territorial Officer and a member of a lowland family well known in the coal industry. This was because Colonel Tweedie was in hospital and Russell Morgan had been taken away to command 10 HLI whose CO had been wounded. This time we had the support of 3 Scots Guards and their Churchill tanks with whom we had trained so effectively and happily in England. The attack which started on 30 July was part of an offensive by VIII and XXX Corps to gain the line running west to east through the town of St Martin des Besaces. The objective of 15 Scottish was the town itself and the high ground to the east on which stood the hamlet of Les Loges. Les Loges was the objective allotted to our battalion. On our left 43 Wessex Division was required to conform with the advance of 15 Scottish. The operation, preceded by bombing by Halifaxes of the RAF, had been planned in great and complicated detail. The country was very close and the Germans put up some tough resistance which slowed up the Gordons through whom we had to pass in order to reach the Start Line for our phase of the attack. John Kenneth therefore led the battalion round their left flank, but our leading platoons were soon engaged by other enemy infantry and we Argylls found ourselves prematurely in the battle. Nevertheless our companies advanced methodically despite German resistance, a minefield and the thick woods and high hedges which made it difficult for junior leaders to find their way and keep direction.

By mid-morning however it was clear that the 93rd was confronted by more enemy sited in depth behind those who had held up the Gordons, so Kenneth halted the advance and, with his gunner and tank representatives, made a new plan. The attack was resumed soon after mid-day with the guns firing a series of timed concentrations (each given the name of a disease – 'Measles', 'Mumps', 'Pleurisy', and so on). From this point all went well and the three squadrons of Scots Guards, whose tank Besa fire had been particularly effective in demoralising the enemy, were on their objectives two hours later. By three o'clock our C Company was established in Les Loges with the other companies on the high ground to the south-east, Hill 226.

The 93rd had reached its objectives, having advanced some six thousand yards through, we were later told, three enemy battalion positions with the loss of only twenty-four men. Many prisoners had been taken, among whom were a number of Poles, Russians and Yugoslavs who had joined the Wehrmacht either voluntarily or under duress.

In many ways BLUECOAT was the smoothest operation that the battalion ever carried out, a model of its kind for which a large share of the credit is due to John Kenneth personally. His leadership of a large group of all arms in complicated circumstances and in difficult terrain was clear-headed and resolute throughout. For 227 Brigade also the operation had been an unqualified success. 10 HLI had reached Hervieux on our right, but our two battalions were a mile deeper into the enemy positions than anyone else had yet penetrated; moreover, our left flank was completely exposed as the Wessex Division had hardly been able to make any progress. Fortunately no counter-attack was mounted against us, but two powerful self-propelled guns emerged from hiding on our left and with their 88 millimetre guns knocked out ten of the Scots Guards' Churchills in the space of a few minutes before disappearing eastwards unscathed.

After three days the brigade moved some ten miles farther south without meeting any significant opposition. On one of those days two unarmed deserters approached me. They were Yugoslavs and very hungry. When they had finished eating what I was able to give them I sent for an escort and, in jest, announced that, as we had taken so many prisoners, we were running out of food and I was therefore going to have those two taken back to the German lines. On hearing this one threw himself at my feet crying: 'Please, not that. They will kill us'. The other man, older than his companion, merely looked at me and said: 'The English are gentlemen. You will not do that to us'. I replied: 'But we here are Scots, not English'. He said: 'That is the same. We are safe with you'.

We had already read in the Intelligence Summaries reports of the bid made by a group of senior Officers to kill Hitler at his Headquarters in East Prussia. None of us foresaw the appalling consequences this failed coup would have on German families of the highest rank and greatest prestige, nor the savage retribution that was to befall the conspirators. We at the front line assumed that even though Hitler was not dead the cohesion of the German nation and the loyalty of the Armed Forces would disintegrate, that the dominance of the National Socialist Party had been mortally impaired and, above all, that the end of the war had by that one event been brought much nearer. My own initial reaction was rather one of surprise that the assassination attempt, plotted and carried into execution by eminent members of a General Staff, long regarded in Germany with reverence and elsewhere with awe, should have been so bungled. Although enemy soldiers who fell into our hands thereafter wearily exclaimed in increasing numbers 'Deutschland kaputt!', we discerned neither at that time nor in the next eight months of the campaign a marked lessening in the devotion to duty of the German Officer or Soldier in the field. Indeed the survival as if by a miracle of Adolf Hitler, their Supreme Commander, appeared rather to stiffen the staunchness of some of our opponents.

The enemy High Command now starkly realised the dangers which Dollmann's Seventh Army faced from the British armoured thrust southeastward from Caen,[13] from our Corps' BLUECOAT offensive and from the sweep by General Omar Bradley's powerful mechanized right-hook round their western flank and rear. To escape from encirclement in the pocket now visibly taking shape, the wise course for the Germans was to commence without delay an orderly fighting withdrawal eastward to the line of the River Orne or even farther behind the Seine. Hitler, however, forbade his soldiers to yield any ground; retreat, he decreed, was not to be considered. He went further. He ordered the hard pressed Seventh Army to assemble a powerful armoured force and to launch it westwards towards the coastal town of Avranches so as to halt Bradley's advance by severing the van of the American columns from those behind. Such a thrust in the face of the overwhelming Allied air superiority was doomed: it was a costly failure. Against our pressure in the Caumont sector the Germans now organized a desperate defence, creating in every village nests of machine guns and mortars supported by dug-in tanks. It was a network of these manned by the SS round Estry and Vassy that 227 Brigade was ordered to attack. There the country was hilly and open giving the Germans good fields of fire. Against such a dogged and well-sited resistance no rapid advance was possible and the brigade paid a high price for the ground won. There, in the death of Major Alan Fyfe, the 93rd sustained on 7 August the worst single loss of the entire campaign. Alan, brother of Hugh Fyfe who had captured the Tourmauville bridge, had been our Adjutant since 1942. Efficient, charming and beloved he had done more than anyone else to make the 93rd a happy and united battalion. In the reorganization before our BLUECOAT operation Alan was promoted to major and given command of B Company; I became Adjutant in his place.

By the evening of 6 August the Gordons and HLI were pinned down on the north side of Estry. Our own attack in the direction of Vassy had been halted about a thousand yards south of the La Caverie cross-roads and the battalion had dug itself in in darkness some three hundred yards short of a feature held by men of the 9th SS Division. An inspection at first light of the Argyll dispositions made Colonel Tweedie, out of hospital and back in command, uneasy about the security of our left flank and he decided to improve it by pushing forward a couple of hundred yards across two fields to occupy a small hill. Two companies, B and D, advanced supported by artillery and mortars, but they were driven back by the great volume of German fire, leaving more than a score of men lying dead or wounded in the open. Mortally wounded Alan Fyfe died in the RAP.[14] But some of our wounded lay too far out, so Major Law Moreton, commanding C Company, got hold of a Red Cross flag and walked out across the fields. A German Officer came out to meet him, the two shook hands and agreed a thirty-minute truce so that the wounded could be moved to safety by the stretcher-bearers of both sides. For this act Moreton was awarded the Military Cross.[15]

By 12 August it was evident that the enemy were pulling out. Thirty miles away to the east the jaws of the pincers were about to close as the British, Canadian and Polish divisions pressing down from beyond Caen met near Falaise the leading elements of the American right-hook.

The Battle of Normandy ended on 19 August. It had lasted seventy-five days and claimed the lives of ninety members of the 93rd. Allied casualties totalled 170,000 killed and wounded. Although a large number of Seventh Army managed by moving in darkness to make their way out of the Falaise pocket, enemy losses in equipment, fighting vehicles and transport were very great. They have been summarized thus[16]

Army, Corps and Divisional Commanders killed or captured	20
Army Commanders wounded (Rommel and Hausser)[17]	2
Supreme Commanders dismissed (von Rundstedt and von Kluge)	2
Divisions eliminated or savagely mauled	about 40
Guns captured or destroyed	over 3,000
Tanks destroyed	over 1,000
Total enemy personnel losses	250,000 (+/-)

This victory, master-minded by Montgomery, was definite and complete.

We believed that it was also decisive. No nation, we said to each other, could suffer such a military disaster and maintain an army to fight on effectively in the field.

Before we left the Caumont sector to join the rest of Dempsey's Second Army in the pursuit of the vanquished Germans, Colonel Tweedie was transferred to command an anti-tank regiment; so John Kenneth again took over the battalion. The casualties incurred by the British Infantry had been heavy and units like us seemed to go through an almost continuous process of reorganization and change, particularly in the Officers.

I think my most indelible memories of the campaign in north-west Europe are two-fold. Firstly, the thirst and tiredness which battle brings; secondly, the persistent draining away from the Battalion of one's comrades and friends, mostly through death or wounds but also from accidents, illness or routine postings. These frequent changes of their Officers must have been unsettling for the younger Soldiers and placed an important responsibility on the Warrant Officers and Sergeants who tended to remain for longer periods in the same sub-unit. The transient passage of Officers through the Battalion seemed such a relentless process that we all knew that it was almost inevitable that our own individual fates could be no different.

Nor did seniority confer protection. We had lost our brigade commander, killed at Baron in July. In mid-August our GOC, Major-General Gordon MacMillan, was wounded and Colin Barber, nick-named 'Tiny' because of his great height, took over 15 Scottish. Gaps in our ranks were being filled in part by Officers from Staff appointments. Some like Barclay Pearson were Regular Argylls, but others came to us from other regiments, English, Welsh and Canadian; some even from colonial forces. One of the latter, Major Fergusson, had absconded from the Reinforcement Organization and made his way to the 93rd instead of reporting as ordered to the Black Watch. An amusing and likeable character, he played the mouth organ with gusto, but as his most recent service had been with the Camel Corps in the Sudan his appointment to lead a company of Highlanders in battle caused some quiet tooth-sucking.

As it happened our division was not employed in the sealing-off of the Falaise pocket, so we spent a week or so moving via the Orne valley towards the Seine which we were warned off to cross by assault. The weather was glorious, the enemy far ahead of us and, unlike the rather sullen Normans, the French people all along our route feted the battalion with wine, fruit, flags, cheers and kisses. It was a memorable welcome which brought home to our Jocks for the first time the real significance of our invasion of Europe and of the cause for which we were fighting. But while in bivouacs at a place named Barbéry, the 93rd was attacked in moonlight just before midnight on 20 August by six enemy aircraft, and the shower of fragmentation bombs which fell around Battalion HQ killed

Captain Bill Sloan and seven members of his Mortar Platoon and seriously wounded seventeen others. It was a grievous blow and one which came from an unexpected quarter, as hitherto the Luftwaffe had never once troubled us. David Lyon, the Signals Officer, and I were sleeping in a farmhouse and took cover under the kitchen table when woken by the noise, but John Kenneth and Padre Jamieson in the adjoining room were badly hurt. Command of the Battalion thus devolved through seniority and the hazards of war on our newly arrived colleague from the Sudan, Simon Fergusson[19]; and with him playing his harmonica and me reading the map, we led 2 A&SH on towards the Seine Valley.

Part of our route followed one of the roads along which the German Army had tried to escape from the Falaise pocket and where they had been caught in dense confusion by our artillery and the rockets and cannon fire of the RAF's Typhoons. For seven miles we drove, slowly on account of the destruction, past burnt-out tanks, wrecked vehicles and abandoned guns. Equipment of every kind was to be seen spread wide on both sides of the road. But pervading everything was the indescribable stench from the hundreds of corpses, human and animal, that lay among the wreckage, still unburied under the blazing sun. The sight of so many dead horses harnessed to the carts and limbers which formed much of the Wehrmacht's transport affected us the most deeply; and to see French men and women hacking portions of flesh from the carcasses of those poor animals was sickening. Our experience that day changed, in most of us I believe, our attitude towards the war. Up to that point we had glibly proclaimed: 'The only good German is a dead one'. Henceforth we vowed: 'This must never be allowed to happen again'.

227 Highland Brigade crossed the Seine in daylight on 27 August in the big loop of the river to the east of Louviers. The assault was opposed by a small number of Germans, the Gordons losing many men when three of their boats were sunk by machine gun fire, but by dawn the next day the three battalions were across and a bridge was being built by the Sappers. The 93rd, in reserve for the assault, spent three days enlarging the bridgehead and mopping up enemy lurking in the woods and buildings.

Great events had occurred elsewhere. In mid-August a large Allied force (Operation DRAGOON) landed on the Mediterranean coast of France and were advancing up the Rhone valley, and on 25 August Paris was liberated by an American column spearheaded by General Leclerc's 2nd Armoured Division of the Free French Army. Brussels was freed in the first days of September by our Guards Armoured Division. On 1 September two important changes were made in the Allied command structure. General Eisenhower himself took over from Montgomery personal command of the ground forces, Bradley's 12th Army Group and Montgomery's 21st army Group; and Russell Morgan left 10 HLI and returned to us, his old battalion, in permanent command.[20]

The next day we were sent on ahead to secure a bridge over the River Somme, and from there moved on to St Pol where we paused while the brigade caught up with us. This was a wonderful period of elation and journeys in lorries covering many map sheets, under blue skies through villages and towns decorated with flags and flowers by the inhabitants for whom, when we halted overnight, we put on our kilts and had our Pipes and Drums beat 'Retreat' in the Town Squares. We in the BLA, the British Liberation Army, felt very proud of our country and of ourselves: the local populations made us feel so.

As we approached St Pol a German soldier, a middle-aged man with greying hair who had been found hiding near the road-side, was put into my vehicle. He was the Sergeant-Major of some infantry company and from amongst his possessions he produced for me a book. It was an ordinary school exercise book, printed with faint lines, and on its separate pages he had recorded in neat bold manuscript the Nominal Roll of the men for whom he was responsible in his unit.

There were almost two pages of names of those killed in action; the list of wounded filled more than three; the names of those missing covered about two-thirds of a page. The page, however, which shocked me contained, I remember, at least six names – for the list filled half the page. It was headed in capital letters with one word: *SELBSTMORD* (suicide) That perhaps more than any other incident in the whole campaign brought home to me the reality of front-line service in the German Army at that time; and how blessed by Providence my fellow-Argylls and I were to be in our efficient yet fundamentally humane and caring Army – and on the winning side. Surely one of the most poignant features of the fighting from July 1944 onwards was the steadfastness of the mass of the German soldiers; ordinary, plain men, like us of European stock, enduring terrors unknown to most on our side in the defence of a doomed state governed by a gang of criminals. I gave the book back to him.

Our euphoria and hopes of an early end to the German war evaporated during the third week of September. Along the line of the Albert canal German resistance was stiffening. Disregarding conventional service structures, the enemy High Command with skill and energy was creating out of the survivors of the Normandy disaster, and men bought forward from the Fatherland, ad hoc battle groups which, deployed under implacable commanders behind the successive water obstacles which abound in Belgium and Holland, could only be dislodged by set-piece attacks supported by artillery and air power. The Germans were demonstrating remarkable powers of recuperation. For convinced Nazis the Führer's escape from assassination was an omen of the invincibility of the Third Reich; others took heart when the bombardment of England by Hitler's second secret weapon, the V2 rocket, commenced; moreover the declared Allied insistence on Unconditional Surrender left that nation with no course of action other than to fight on.

The onrush of the Canadian, British and American armies was slowed too by escalating logistical problems. Everything needed to keep them fed, mobile and fighting had still to be brought forward from the Normandy coast. The great port of Antwerp was not to be opened until early November; and enemy garrisons and demolitions still denied us the use of the Channel harbours such as Calais, Boulogne and Le Havre. Although we at my level did not learn this until after the war, there was already arising between Eisenhower and Montgomery a fateful conflict of opinion concerning the strategy to be adopted to bring about the final defeat of Germany. Eisenhower, mindful of public opinion in the USA and not willing to deny to his subordinate American commanders the chance to be 'in at the kill', determined on a general advance to the frontiers of Germany and beyond on a broad front. Montgomery, conscious of the still weak but stiffening opposition and the war-weariness of the people of Britain, advocated a single powerful thrust by British and American mobile units, under American command if politically desirable, on a narrow front through Holland, over the Rhine and onto the North German Plain whence the Allies could encircle the Ruhr, the heartland of German industry, and sweep east to occupy Berlin before the Russians, still at the gates of Warsaw, could seize that crowning prize. Eisenhower's strategy would require time for the essential supplies to be delivered to all the armies; it would also mean the abandonment of hopes of victory in 1944. For Montgomery's strategy to succeed four things were required:—

1. Self-denial by many American formations in that they would have to renounce offensive action in the interests of the forces actually engaged on the single northern thrust.
2. Whole-hearted logistical support to be given by everyone to those engaged on that thrust.
3. The quick agreement of Eisenhower and the Allied political leaders to the single thrust concept.
4. Luck.
All these Montgomery was to be denied.

The wrangling over the strategic course of action to be adopted had not been resolved in mid-September. Montgomery had, however, tasked the Canadians to capture Boulogne and Calais and, of especial importance, to enable full use to be made of Antwerp. The port had been taken by the British but the approaches up the estuary of the River Scheldt were still in German hands. In the same directive he ordered Second British Army as its first task 'to operate northward and secure the crossings over the Rhine and Meuse[21] in the general area Arnhem – Nijmegen – Grave. The

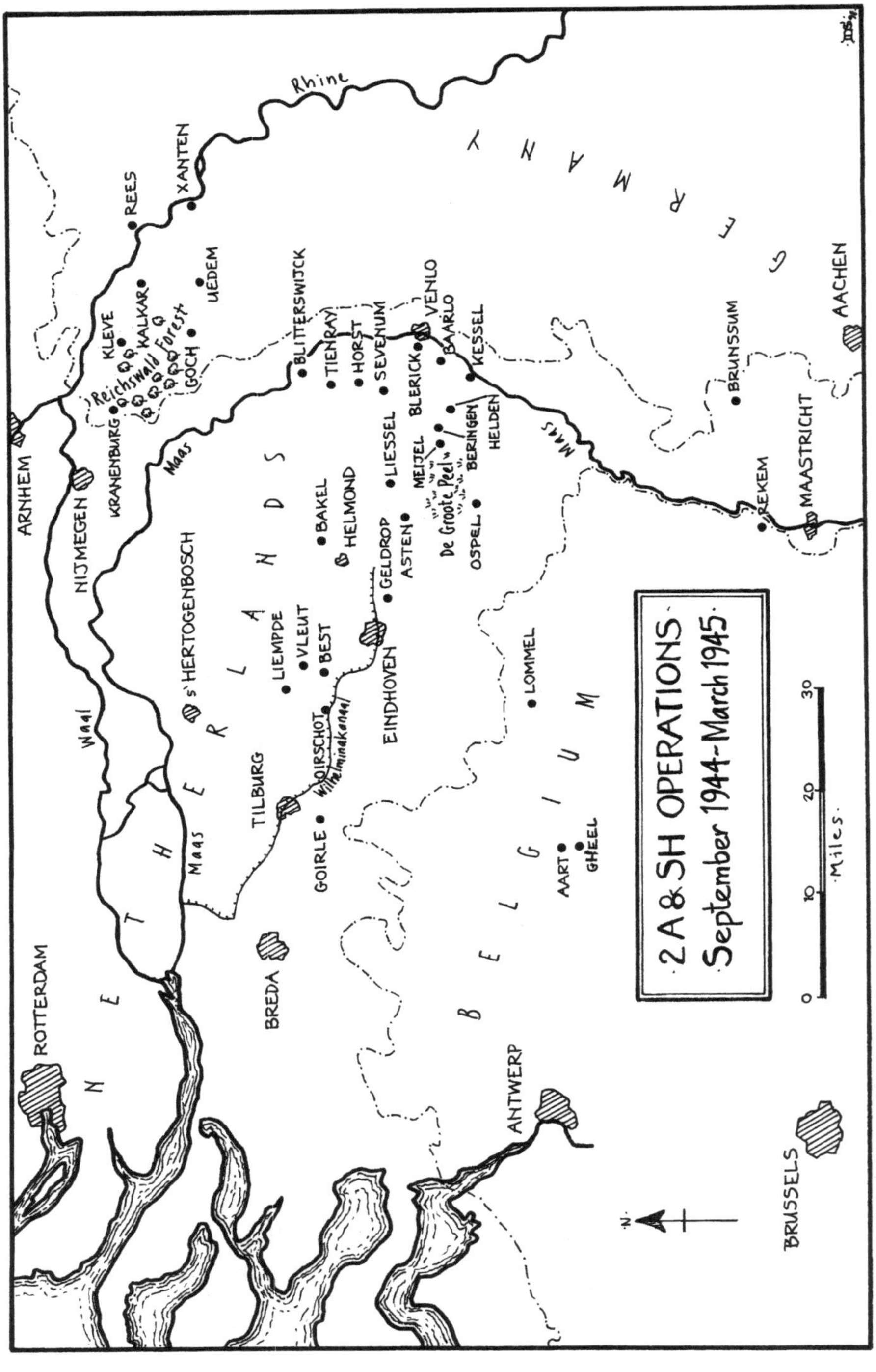
2 A & SH OPERATIONS
September 1944-March 1945
GERMANY
NETHERLANDS
BELGIUM
Rhine
Maas
Waal
ROTTERDAM
BREDA
TILBURG
GOIRLE
OIRSCHOT
Wilhelminakanaal
s' HERTOGENBOSCH
LIEMPDE
VLEUT
BEST
EINDHOVEN
GELDROP
HELMOND
BAKEL
ASTEN
LIESSEL
MEIJEL
De Groote Peel
OSPEL
BERINGEN
HELDEN
BLERICK
BAARLO
KESSEL
VENLO
SEVENUM
HORST
TIENRAY
BLITTERSWIJCK
ARNHEM
NIJMEGEN
KRANENBURG
Reichswald Forest
KLEVE
KALKAR
GOCH
UEDEM
REES
XANTEN
ANTWERP
BRUSSELS
AART
GHEEL
LOMMEL
REKEM
MAASTRICHT
BRUNSSUM
AACHEN
Miles
0
10
20
30
N

thrust northward to secure the river crossings will be rapid and violent, and without regard to what is happening on the flanks'.

The Army was then to establish itself in strength (south of the Zuider Zee) on the general line Zwolle – Deventer – Arnhem, facing east, with deep bridgeheads on the east side of the Ijssel river. From this position, he ordered, it was to be prepared to advance eastward to the general area Rheine – Osnabruck – Hamm – Munster. Concurrently the First US Army was to capture Bonn and Cologne and to establish a deep bridgehead on the east side of the Rhine 'prior to advancing eastward round the south face of the Ruhr in a movement carefully coordinated with the move of Second British Army round the north face of the Ruhr'.

The first phase of this ambitious but potentially decisive offensive was the launching on 17 September of Operation MARKET GARDEN in order to secure crossings over Dutch waterways as follows:–

Over the Wilhelmina canal at Son	by the 101st US Airborne Division
Over the Zuid Willemvard canal at Veghel	
Over the River Meuse/Maas at Grave	by the 82nd US Airborne Division
Over the River Rhine/Waal at Nijmegen	
Over the Neder Rijn (Lower Rhine) at Arnhem	by the 1st British Airborne Division and the Polish Parachute Brigade.

The 'rapid and violent' thrust to link up with the airborne troops at these five locations was entrusted to XXX Corps (General Horrocks). As this Corps with the Guards Armoured Division in the van moved north along the corridor formed by the airborne 'carpet', two other corps were to widen the corridor – Ritchie's XII Corps on the west side and O'Connor's VIII Corps on the east.

MARKET GARDEN was successful in that four of the five crossings were captured and held, and a belt of Dutch territory, forty-five miles long between the Meuse-Escaut canal and the Waal at Nijmegen, was cleared of the enemy. This was to prove of immense value as a stepping stone for the battles of the Rhineland that were to follow. But with the defeat of 1st British Airborne Division at Arnhem the concept of establishing a strong force between Arnhem and the shore of the Zuider Zee and thereafter encircling the Ruhr was vitiated.

The Battle of Arnhem is remembered today as a great feat of arms, albeit a glorious failure. Naturally during my years of service with The Parachute Regiment I have closely studied that battle, visited the scenes of the fighting and met personally many of the Officers and Soldiers who took part. The failure can not be laid at their door. The causes however are well known. I summarize them as follows:–

1. The Airborne Division was put down too far from the Arnhem bridge. Dropping and landing zones could have been found nearer to that vital objective and the risk of losses from enemy anti-aircraft fire accepted.
2. Shortage of aircraft and deteriorating weather meant that the arrival of the parachute and glider troops was spread over several days; the division was concentrated neither in time nor space.
3. German resistance was greater and more rapidly mounted than had been anticipated. II SS Panzer Corps[22] was known to be stationed in the Arnhem area refitting after the fighting in and retreat from Normandy. They and other units available were effectively gripped and quickly committed to the tasks of containing, isolating and destroying our airborne units piecemeal. In this the Germans were helped by the fortuitous presence of General Kurt Student[23] and the retrieval from the body of a British Officer of a copy of the Airborne Division's operation order. The enemy thus learnt early in the battle the composition of the British airborne force and the operational plan.
4. XXX Corps' route to Arnhem was along a single highway. It was in places embanked and devoid of cover. Vehicles moving along it presented easy targets to enemy artillery and anti-tank weapons. Because of the nature of the ground it was at many points not possible for tanks and other vehicles to deploy off the road. The clearance of the enemy from the axis of the advance had therefore to be carried out by infantry on foot: a slow process. Furthermore the road was frequently cut after the fighting echelons had passed, stranding the convoy of 'soft skinned' lorries for long periods. The Germans and our airborne soldiers fought with desperation; the former to stave off their country's defeat, the latter to reach and hold the vital bridge and thereafter for survival.
5. Montgomery did not receive from Supreme Headquarters or the American 12th Army Group the priority in logistical and air support he needed for his thrust onto the North German Plain; a priority to which he believed Eisenhower personally had agreed.

My own personal belief remains this: the plan was too ambitious. Without the whole-hearted backing of the Americans the thrust towards the Ruhr, even if the Arnhem bridge had been secured, could not have been sustained. In the event the German reaction proved at Arnhem to be too resolute and their remaining field armies too strong for 1st Airborne Division and XXX Corps alone to have overcome; and the widening of the corridor along the flanks of the advance by VIII and XII Corps was to prove more laborious and costly than anticipated. I know, because the 93rd was engaged in that task as part of O'Connor's VIII Corps.

Defeat at Arnhem was a deep disappointment. It was indeed 'a Bridge Too Far'. But the events that occurred there in those nine days in September 1944 added a golden page to the annals of the British Army. They did something more. They created between 1st Airborne Division and its heirs and the citizens of that city a remarkable bond of friendship, gratitude and respect. The succour given by the Dutch to the British in their shared ordeal, comforting the wounded, sheltering the survivors and honouring the dead, is remembered to this day. Those spontaneous and selfless acts of heroism and Christian charity, and the prolonged suffering which German retribution was to inflict on the population, have given Arnhem an enduring and very special place in British emotions.

French rejoicings were almost nothing compared with the delirious joy of the Belgians when we crossed the frontier on 7 September at Mouscron and drove through an orgy of embraces, fruit, eggs and wine via Bossuit to Machelan, and to Deynze where Major Moreton and his company were given a civic reception, a champagne dinner and a dance. This interlude in Belgium was wonderfully uplifting and culminated in a brief stay in the Brussels area which allowed every man to spend three hours in that attractive and undamaged city.

The next day, 12 September, we were warned to move into battle in the area of Antwerp. The Albert canal had already been crossed but the enemy held the line of the Meuse-Escaut canal and our leading companies and the tanks of the Sharpshooters came under quite heavy fire as they raced for the bridge at Donck which they found to be already blown.

We spent four days there in expectations of having to make an assault crossing but none materialized. In the meantime a small bridgehead over that canal had been won at a place named Aart, just north of Gheel, by 8 Royal Scots of 44 Lowland Brigade after some bitter and costly fighting. Their bridgehead had been enlarged by their two sister battalions, 6 Royal Scots Fusiliers and 6 King's Own Scottish Borderers, and we were told to take over the positions of the Fusiliers in what will always be grimly remembered as the Gheel Bridgehead.

We moved in on 17 September, the opening day of MARKET GARDEN, and the airborne divisions passed over us that afternoon on their way to Nijmegen and Arnhem. The state of affairs in our bridgehead was very confused; the place was congested, the Lowland units rather mixed up and many dead bodies were lying amid the ruins of the village. We stayed there for four days being continuously shelled and mortared and twice heavily attacked by infantry and SP-guns, the Germans on the last occasion being halted with many casualties only about two hundred yards from our positions. D Company had earlier had the unfortunate experience of being attacked by RAF Typhoons whose pilots had wrongly identified features on the ground.

In war such incidents occur quite frequently and casualties inflicted by 'friendly fire' invariably provoke anger and inter-service or international recriminations. The American troops were to suffer more from errors made by the US Army Air Force than we did from the RAF. The Germans were equally aware of the dangers of misdirected air support and used to exclaim to us: 'When the British bomb the Germans take cover; when the Germans bomb the British take cover; when the Americans bomb everybody takes cover'.

Conditions at Aart were most unpleasant, and the congestion increased when the HLI and Gordons joined us. Movement in and out of the place was hazardous as, in addition to the accurate shelling of the crossing site and the road from Gheel, the Germans had *spandau* machine guns firing along the canal from both flanks of the bridgehead. This fire had forced the Sappers to abandon the construction of a bridge and in consequence everything had to be ferried across by assault boat and ropes. Nevertheless the Quartermaster and his team ensured that every meal and other daily requirements reached the men punctually and intact.

On 20 September the decision was taken to give up the bridgehead and the tricky business of pulling out commenced almost at once. The rifle companies and battalion HQ moved after darkness fell; heavy equipment such as the anti-tank guns had to be left behind to be retrieved later, after the enemy had also withdrawn. Just before midnight our last man was safely back over the canal and the episode of the Gheel Bridgehead was ended. The graves of a hundred and fifty Scottish soldiers and over two hundred Germans remained as testimony to the bitterness of the fighting.

It had been a most trying experience which cost the 93rd sixty-seven killed or wounded; the six Officer casualties included Major Moreton, killed while making a routine visit to his platoon positions. By now few of the 93rd's Officers who had landed in France fifteen weeks before were still with the battalion.

We had been too preoccupied with our own activities and problems to follow the course of the operations in the Arnhem corridor. After our withdrawal, however, we were told by the Corps Commander that the purpose of our division's operations at Gheel had been to create a diversion; to draw off enemy forces so as to allow another bridgehead to be established out of which XXX Corps was pressing forward to link up with the American, British and Polish airborne units.

With the fight for the Nijmegen bridge not yet won and the long struggle around Arnhem of 1st Airborne Division still going on, the situation of XXX Corps was far from secure. The long precarious salient running up through Eindhoven was far too narrow for comfort and the Germans had several times cut the over-crowded main axis. It was vital that this corridor should be widened with all possible speed. XII Corps was advancing slowly on the western side in the direction of Turnhout, Tilburg and Boxtel. Our Corps, VIII, was on the east side. The 93rd crossed the Escaut canal into the Lommel bridgehead on 22 September and, having crossed the Dutch frontier, concentrated near Eindhoven for operations in the direction of Best. We did not find it easy to know for sure whether we were in Belgium or Holland. The writing on the signposts and shops seemed the same in both countries, the terrain not much different and the weather identical.

We did notice, however, that the architecture was different; the Dutch gardens neat as in England, and the people whom we saw were rather more stolid and less excitable than the Belgians. Actually we saw few people; the land was more deserted than the places we had passed through recently. We knew that the Dutch, having been neutral during the Great War of 1914–18 had been greatly angered by the German onslaught in 1940 and by their behaviour as the Occupying Power since, and that the Germans who still held most of Holland were giving the population a hard time. We knew too that the Queen of the Netherlands, unlike the King of the Belgians, had escaped to England in a ship of the Royal Navy to carry on the fight against Hitler. We soon learned, however, to identify countries we found ourselves in by the uniforms of the postmen and police officers; and by the flags. On 25 September we assembled in the heather and scrub country just north of the Wilhelmina canal, while the Gordons attacked westward along the canal in the direction of Oirshot without making much headway against strong opposition. The next day we were ordered to form up along the road from Best to Tilburg and clear the country up as far as the thick woods south of Liempde. At first all went well and we took some prisoners and made good progress despite the close country. Things became more difficult during the afternoon in the approaches to Liempde. The enemy lay concealed in the undergrowth and shadows of the woods, opening fire at short range and we quickly lost three officers killed, two of whom were company commanders.

It was slow and depressing work, but we cleared the Liempde woods before the day ended. We were then pulled back and dug in near Vleut with the task of preventing any enemy penetration onto the Eindhoven-Nijmegen road. There we remained for a week, busy with patrol activity, skirmishes with the enemy and taking prisoners. Some reinforcements joined us but the number in no way made up for our losses. Of the local civilians we hardly saw any apart from the occasional farmer tending his fences. On 3 October we moved in lorries to Bakel, about twenty miles to the east, beyond Helmond, for a greatly needed period of reorganization and to brush up on weapon handling and minor tactics, the essential skills of the Infantryman. I do not remember whether we knew about the events at Arnhem or not; I suppose we did. Nor do I know what happened in the business of widening the corridor after we moved from Vleut. I do recollect, however, that the impetus of the Allied advances slowed down dramatically, that we realised that the war would go on, a long slog, until sometime in 1945, and that the weather turned wet.

It was no longer possible to maintain four rifle companies in our Battalion, so B Company was temporarily disbanded. Some forty of the more experienced soldiers were kept together in a special 'Battle Group' and command of this novel outfit was given to me, my job as Adjutant being taken over by David Lyon. Though small in numbers the Battle Group was heavily armed with Bren guns, light mortars and anti-tank weapons. We were not really capable of holding ground at night with such small strength, but with our fire-power we could act as a firm base for an attack, do patrolling and be available for Commando-type tasks. There were two disadvantages to being in the Battle Group. Because of our weaponry we each had abnormally heavy loads to carry, and every time the 93rd moved forward towards the enemy we were put in the front. But we were a happy team, rather proud of our unorthodox status and organization, and we stayed together for some three months. The period at Bakel was both constructive from the training aspect and enjoyable for the social activities we managed to arrange, such as hot baths and concerts, film shows and football matches against our sister units and the Bakel Town XI whom we defeated. The massed Pipes and Drums of the Division gave an impressive public display in the grounds of Helmond Castle on 7 October, and on the 17th there occurred at Geldrop an event rare in our Regimental history; the Beating of Retreat by the Pipes and Drums of three Argyll battalions – our 93rd, the 91 Anti-tank Regiment and the 7th Argylls, the latter belonging to 51 Highland Division. During this period of retraining and relaxation there were continual threats of impending action, Warning Orders to move, planning conferences and so on, but nothing came of them until 20 October when we were sent back to the Vleut area.

Because patrolling is an important and risky activity, the British Army teaches that if a party of men has to go out on patrol at, say, last light, they ought, ideally, to be warned at the beginning of that day so as to ensure that they are properly briefed, rehearsed, fed, rested and inspected before setting out. In the middle of one morning Battalion HQ sent me a message stating that 'the Brigade Commander wants a Patrol tasked to find out how close the enemy are, the Battle Group is to provide the patrol and the information is to reach Brigade HQ by 1500 hours'. This was a fairly fast ball and a bit unfair on my Soldiers, so I decided to lead the patrol myself accompanied by an experienced NCO named Corporal Fee. After rushed but adequate briefing and preparation, we moved out through the HLI position. The weather was fine after several days of heavy rain, and we made our way forward through the belts of trees which grew in ordered lines out of otherwise empty fields and along hedges until we came to a wide muddy track bordered by high banks and crossed at intervals by water-filled ditches. The track gave a good field of view towards the HLI, so I guessed that if there were any Germans around they were probably quite close to us. But we needed to get off that bare track, so when Cpl Fee pointed to a ditch leading to a thick hedge-row about fifty yards away to our right I whispered to him: 'We'll move up the ditch to the corner of the hedge and see what lies on the other side'.

Leaving two men with a Bren gun to cover us, we got gingerly into the ditch and edged our way forward through waist-deep water followed by three of my soldiers. We were half-way along the ditch when a figure suddenly stood up on the other side of the hedge. It was a German soldier; tall, with a countryman's weather-beaten face and grey hair, he was wearing an overcoat with his rifle slung from one shoulder and on his head not a steel helmet but a peaked cloth cap. He turned and began to walk slowly away from us up the hedge. It was pretty certain that he had not seen us crouching about twenty yards from him; most likely he was going off to relieve himself or fetch the rations or something similar. The Jock behind me took aim at the man. At that instant I had a vision of an elderly Hausfrau weeping as she learnt that her husband had been killed, and the question flashed into my mind 'By taking the life of that unsuspecting old man would we bring the end of the war nearer by even one minute? Of course not!'. And I pushed the end of the man's rifle down leaving the German to amble off up the hedge. But he had not been alone. As Fee[24] and I began to ease our way forward, grenades thrown by other Germans hidden behind the hedge fell around us. We were in a dicey situation. We had located the enemy as ordered, and the correct thing now was to get back with the information, so, expecting to be gunned down at any moment, we managed to escape to some trees while our covering party kept the enemy's heads down. The Germans added to the noise by firing some mortar bombs in our direction, but we all got back to the HLI lines safely but very wet. I have never reproached myself for leaving that German alive. Perhaps I should. But I have thought about that incident often since because of something that happened to me some four weeks later. We were moving up to the Maas through desolate country and awful weather, and I fell asleep alone in a small deserted farm shed. I awoke as it was getting light and found sitting beside me a German soldier armed and equipped for battle. In the darkness of the wet and windy night he had made his way between our sentries and into the hut where I was sleeping. 'I have come to surrender,' he said as I woke up, 'but did not want to disturb you while you slept'. A case of Quid pro Quo?

The operation planned for 27 October was the liberation of Tilburg. Farther north the 53rd Welsh Division were fighting their way through to s'Hertogenbosch and 51 Highland Division were going for Boxtel. The general object was the clearance of all south-west Holland up to the Maas. For this attack 227 Brigade rode for the first time in Kangaroos; armoured troop-carriers converted from a Canadian type of tank. We followed 44 Lowland Brigade across the Wilhelmina canal and into Tilburg from the south. The advance was desperately slow; the great number of mines laid along the road, blown bridges and mud all made movement difficult, but by the evening we were well into the town and had cleared all the western edge. The remainder was cleared the next morning. Few Germans were encountered but many Dutch citizens came out of the buildings and gave us a great welcome; slightly more restrained than what we had experienced in Belgium, but no less sincere. Tilburg was little damaged, seemed prosperous and we were looking forward to getting to know the town and to making friends with the dignified and hospitable people whom we had just freed from the German scourge. This was not to be.

On the day before, the enemy XLVII Panzer Corps had launched a spoiling attack against a thinly held sector where a United States armoured division was in the line. This attack met with some initial success, capturing Meijel and pushing on down the road towards Helmond. Our division, and later the Highland Division, was sent down to seal off the penetration. The 93rd left Tilburg late on 28 October and arrived in the Asten area, about five miles north-west of Meijel, before dawn. My Battle Group was given a road-junction to defend and we dug in quickly in the dark on some flat ground behind some walls. When it got lighter we could see that we had established our defences in the church-yard; in the burial ground in fact, and I regret that our digging had disturbed some of the graves. But we put that right when daylight came. We could then see the effect of the German thrust. The open fields had been where one of our artillery batteries, which curiously had made contact with the enemy ahead of us in the Infantry, had engaged some Germans at short range – over open sights; and as we looked around we saw a disturbing number of Sherman tanks and self-propelled guns which appeared to have been abandoned undamaged by their American crews. No Germans came near Asten while we were there, and we began to develop a close and memorable association with the inhabitants. That move to Asten ushered in one of the most uncomfortable periods of our campaign. The country was flat, boggy and intersected by numerous waterways. The villages and farms had been badly knocked about in the fighting and the weather degenerated into almost continuous rain. All the tracks had been thickly sown with *schumines*[25] and movement off the tracks in the waterlogged fields was almost impossible. In this area 15 Scottish was to remain for the next three months; first stabilizing the situation; then in clearing the enemy-held area up to the line of the Maas, and finally holding the west bank while the Allied armies farther south dealt with the powerful German offensive in the Ardennes, called 'the Battle of the Bulge'. Our, the Argylls', initial role was to strengthen the defences behind the Americans along the Asten-Liesel road. We had some sharp little actions and carried out some successful patrols but German machine guns, mortar, artillery and mines took a continuous toll of our chaps. In that boggy country there was not much we could, at that stage, do in retaliation.

However, the people of Asten, safe now from the threat of reoccupation by 'the Moffe',[26] began to take our Jocks to their hearts and some lasting friendships were formed during that otherwise particularly dreary phase of the war. And not only by Asten; Tilburg had adopted our Scottish Division as her favourite bit of the British Army and a Rest Centre, the Red Lion Club,[27] was set up in the town with, as its first Commander, my name-sake in the 93rd, Major FGS Graham. He was the only one of our company commanders to have come through the campaign unharmed.

The 93rd was left in Asten for only two days before being sent down the road to Ospel to relieve an American infantry regiment. My Battle Group's task was to take over a feature standing about a hundred feet above the flat, wet, scrub-covered countryside and overlooking a wide depression formed perhaps by a meteorite in prehistoric times. Our ridge was crowned by a clump of straggly trees and was, like the whole of the battalion's location, under enemy observation from the far side of the Deurne canal.

The American sub-unit holding the place which I had to take over numbered almost two hundred, so my group of fifty-odd Jocks was going to be a bit thin on the ground. But this was acceptable as the whole area had been strewn with *schumines* by the Germans and it was improbable that they would try to attack us on foot. I went up in daylight to reconnoitre the position and, with the American company commander, made a plan for our change-over that night. It was very dark when I led the Battle Group up the taped path cleared through a minefield and onto our hill. The path was wide enough for men to walk safely in single file but when our Gunner FOO[28] came up in his carrier its tracks set off several of the mines. When I reached the trees I neither saw nor heard anyone. The place seemed deserted and we began to suspect that the Americans had left without waiting for us. Then I heard a whisper, 'Who's that?' coming from a slit trench about five feet from me. I whispered back: 'The British: we're here to relieve you as agreed this morning'. 'Thank God you've come,' the figure said as it climbed out of the trench. He was the only American who addressed me that night, and within ten minutes the whole lot of them had lined up and disappeared down the hill, leaving us to settle in unguided as best we could. The real surprise came the next morning when we had a chance to inspect our new area. Our Allies had gone off leaving behind many items of kit, radio batteries, boxes of ammunition, stationery, blankets, and a machine gun complete with its tripod and many belts of ammunition. I suppose that these were too heavy to carry with comfort and that Uncle Sam would in any case replace them without demur. That is how my Battle Group became the elated possessors of a Browning 50-calibre water-cooled medium machine gun[29], and Privates Brown, McCoole and Doyle nursed that bulky weapon until a vital part broke in early 1945. The Germans sent over a lot of shells and mortar bombs during the battalion's week near Ospel and life was thoroughly unpleasant and dangerous. Sergeant Skinn and a patrol from my Group successfully tracked an enemy patrol back to its base one night and thereby got some useful information, but the next night he lost three men in a minefield and in the confusion one of the patrol's Bren guns got left behind. The Commanding Officer was not pleased and made Skinn go out again the next night to retrieve the weapon.

On relief by the Gordons we moved into Meijel in preparation for the advance to the Maas which we began on 20 November, the 51st Highland Division having commenced its attack two days earlier. Our experiences during the following ten days must have resembled those of our Fathers serving in the trenches of Flanders during the First World War. I quote from the Regimental History: 'Every farm, and Meijel itself, seemed to have suffered even more severely than any village in Normandy. Almost every house that was not totally ruined was booby-trapped; and there was more than a fair share of shelling. The tracks which 227 Brigade used as axes for the advance had never been intended for more than occasional farm traffic, and they were soon cut to pieces and feet deep in mud; and though the Sappers performed many wonders, the supply route running back from the leading battalions rapidly became a trail of churned up mud dotted all the way with groups of weary soldiers struggling to get a carrier or jeep moving again. Sometimes a friendly tank would lend a hand with a tow. Even men on their feet got stuck fast sometimes and it took four men hauling on a rope to drag a chap clear.' All the Bren carriers were taken off their proper tasks and used solely to keep the flow of supplies going forward. It was as well that few Germans were around for bringing up large amounts of ammunition would have been almost impossible. No boots or waterproof clothing could keep out such mud and such rain. Slit trenches filled with water the moment they were dug; and there were no means of getting the men warm and dry.

We have ever since termed that area of Peel country in the Holland of 1944 'an abomination of desolation'. But our discomforts paled into insignificance when compared with the miseries of the long columns of refugees which passed down the line the other way during the first two days. The enemy was setting the farms on fire as he withdrew so as to leave no cover for us, and the inhabitants came stumbling back, struggling through the mire with prams and wheelbarrows. For most of the Jocks it was the first scene of its kind they had witnessed and it produced in them an anger greater than any they had shown in Normandy; and a grim determination that, if there were to be any more columns of fleeing refugees, they should at least be Germans who in great measure had brought that fate on themselves.

The advance went slowly but steadily on, through Beringen and Sevenum up to the little town of Horst which the 93rd entered on 23 November. The Germans had withdrawn twenty-four hours before, but from time to time shelled us quite heavily, so we were glad to move forward again on the 25th by which time the weather had cleared up a bit.

We occupied Tienraij while the HLI and Gordons cleared Blitterswijk and Megelsum. Tienraij presented the now familiar picture of ruined houses, mined roads and felled and booby-trapped trees, but most of the soldiers had become pretty skilful at negotiating such hazards without casualties. The shelling was at times intense and my Battle Group and the Carrier Platoon, established in a prominent convent at the top end of the village, had a particularly trying time. On 28 November troops of the British 3rd Division began to take over from 15 Scottish and we Argylls found ourselves once more back in Asten with its friendly and hospitable people.

It was now obvious that the Army would be stuck in Holland for the winter. The pace of operations slackened and more emphasis could be put on training, maintenance and recreation. After beating 'Retreat' in the Town Square on St Andrew's Night, 30 November, the Officers entertained the Burgomaster and the leading citizens and their wives to a cocktail party at which the Burgomaster delivered a nicely turned speech of welcome and thanks which our Liaison Officer, Henry Chabot, translated for us.

Henry, attached from the Royal Netherlands Army, had joined us in mid-October and was to stay with the 93rd until we were well established in Germany after the war. He was an indispensable colleague; energetic, helpful, always cheerful and a real friend. The Officers and Sergeants were not the only members of the battalion to celebrate. Again to quote from the Regimental History: 'On 1 December the Battle Group gave a really excellent dance in the Town Hall with plenty of tea, biscuits and beer provided by the YMCA. Sergeant Andres danced a Sword Dance and a Highland Fling for the entertainment of our Dutch guests after a short explanatory speech by Henry; and successful stage-management scored a final triumph when all the lights went out for about half an hour half-way through the evening!'

This pleasant interlude ended on 8 December when the Brigade took over a very large sector of the line on the River Maas beginning a quite distinct phase in our war experience and one which was reminiscent of accounts of the 1914–18 war. From the Reichswald down to the Roer the opponents were dug in on opposite banks of the river, sniping at each other, patrolling by night, but principally engaged in combatting first the damp, and then the cold. From the second week in December the ground froze iron-hard and was covered with snow. This was unpleasant for the troops who had to spend every night in a slit trench but was more healthy than the mud and rain of the preceding weeks. 15 Scottish was kept in the line for about six weeks while the situation in the Ardennes, where von Rundstedt launched on 16 December his large-scale offensive against a weakly held part of the American First Army's front, was stabilised. As far as our 227 Brigade was concerned, this meant a routine inter-change of areas amongst ourselves, keeping two battalions forward on the river bank at Baarlo and Kessel, and one a few miles back at Helden in reserve. There was little danger, but it was monotonous and an anti-climax to the hard fighting and rapid advances we had lived through since June. Because the brigade area was so large, and because the Germans quite frequently sent strong patrols over to our bank, everyone, even when in reserve, was kept at a high state of readiness to react. And because so many of our outposts had to be placed right forward on or very near the bank itself, there was permanent anxiety about keeping in touch with them, which gave the line-laying signallers a lot of work under trying conditions, and about rescuing them should the enemy attempt to cut them out. We were forbidden to cross over to the far bank. It would have been too dangerous as the German occupants enjoyed good cover and observation over us; also it was heavily mined. We would have lost men to no good purpose.

The Germans, however, were bolder. We suspected that some of their men who intruded by night onto our territory had been sent over as punishment, but there were several instances of them mounting sharp, skilful little attacks which lifted isolated parties of Jocks silently out of their lonely and exposed posts.

A lot of our time was taken up with road maintenance since all the local roads and tracks had broken up completely; also with training. The newly joined Officers and Men had much to learn from the 'Old Hands', and the junior leaders promoted in the field to fill gaps caused by deaths and wounds knew little about the teaching and management skills essential for all NCOs.

The cold really did become very severe at one stage, to the extent that oil in vehicles and in the recoil systems of artillery equipments froze. But quite soon we were given a generous issue of leather jerkins and white snow clothing, and the occasional rum issue. It was interesting to learn that in the First World War our soldiers used to be given rum <u>before</u>

setting out on a dangerous mission since it was believed that alcohol put fire in their bellies and made them braver. In 1944 the medical experts declared that to be all wrong: the purpose of rum is to help a man to sleep well <u>after</u> he has come in from some cold and exhausting activity; so our Jocks got their rum issue only after they'd earned it! One of the best gadgets issued to us during this static and semi-Arctic period was self-heating soup. These were tins of soup wrapped around with some sort of wick which when touched with the glowing tip of a cigarette burned slowly and with perfect safety and produced after a few minutes really excellent hot nourishment.

Christmas came and went with various alarms about enemy incursions onto our side of the Maas, one of which was true, as in a nice little operation they removed four men of the HLI from their post on the river bank. Being Scots we played down Christmas but kept Hogmanay (New Year's Eve) zealously, and despite the circumstances we ushered in 1945 with proper style.

Most of the Dutch civilians had fled before we arrived and few had returned to their properties in the battle zone, but there were some around with whom we shared our festivities. New Year's Day 1945 was also memorable for producing the Luftwaffe's final fling against the Allies. They struck a wide-ranging and unexpected blow against our aircraft on the ground and various ground installations and did a lot of damage. We engaged some of them as they raced overhead, but even our Browning machine gunners could claim no hits; however anti-aircraft units farther back and the RAF inflicted heavy losses on the Germans who, as far as I can recall, never again troubled us from the air. Actually, the exchanges of sniping and artillery fire across the Maas during the first week of January gave us plenty of excitement and we made life for the 'Moffe' opposite us at Kessel abnormally disagreeable since, for once, we could observe them better than they could see us.

A leave scheme to the United Kingdom started at about this time and the lucky names of the chaps who had had no time off since landing in France were pulled out of a hat by the Padre. Reinforcements had lately been arriving in encouraging numbers. They came from an extraordinary variety of military backgrounds, some hastily converted from other Arms into Infantrymen. I was astonished to find among a party sent to join my company a tall, pale young man whom I had known in earlier years to be the Laundry-Boy in my home village in the Isle of Wight and reputed to be medically unfit for military service.

This influx of new, albeit immature and ill-trained, soldiers allowed B Company to be reformed out of the Battle Group with me becoming 2IC to Bill McElwee. But shortly after my 22nd birthday I was promoted to command D Company in the rank of major. Many changes had occurred in the ranks of the 93rd's Officers, and it was a different battalion to the one which had entered Holland in September that moved up to Blerick, a suburb of Venlo, on 20 January. There we were in due course relieved by troops from 6 Airborne Division and sent back to Goirle, not far from Tilburg. 15 Scottish Division was preparing to breach the Siegfried Line.

Ever since the failure at Arnhem it had been clear that the northern extension of Hitler's Siegfried Line[30] would have to be breached and the German territory lying between the Maas and the Rhine cleared before a major assault across the Rhine and into the heart of Germany could be launched. While the Generals were completing their plans, the 93rd enjoyed in Goirle and Tilburg despite the rain a really pleasant week, with concerts, film shows and a variety of dances. Our Officers gave a most successful Ball, held in a large house kindly lent for the evening by some good friends of the Battalion, and at which the young ladies of Tilburg wore the gowns that they had carefully packed away during the German occupation.

On 4 February the general plan for the operation was disclosed to all Officers at a divisional briefing in a Tilburg cinema by the Corps Commander, General Horrocks. He made it clear that a very big battle indeed was to be expected. The main object was not only to penetrate the Siegfried Line defences but also to jockey the enemy into committing his main forces to battle on the near side of the Rhine. The operation had the code-name VERITABLE and was to be launched on 8 February. First Canadian Army were responsible for making the attack, using British forces, both infantry and armour, grouped in XXX Corps for the actual assault. 15 Scottish Division was to assault on the extreme left of the line, with initially a completely exposed flank on our left or north side. VERITABLE had originally been planned for early January when the ground was frozen hard and perfect for tanks, but the German Ardennes offensive had upset that timetable and now, in February, the incessant rain, the mud and the floods made it doubtful if any tracked vehicles at all would be able to get through with the foot-soldiers onto their objectives. Nevertheless the plan went ahead, and for the assault we were supported by a really formidable artillery barrage. More than a thousand guns and rocket tubes were allotted and a huge quantity of shell was dumped at each gun position. It was all to be very much like the beginning of an attack during the Great War of 1914–18, with the soldiers advancing through thick mud behind a barrage of artillery shells which moved forward slowly, at a rate of three hundred yards in twelve minutes, with yellow smoke being fired to mark the end of every pause and the next lift of the barrage. It was stressed time and again that the Infantry must keep up with the barrage, keeping station about two hundred yards behind the line of the shell bursts, and thus arriving on top of the Germans before they could recover from the deluge of fire. 227 Brigade, on the left of the division, was to operate in the flat ground between the wooded foothills of the Reichswald Forest and the main road to Kleve, with our final objectives at Klinkenberg and in the triangle formed by the road and railway north-east of Kranenburg. On our right 46 Highland Brigade was to clear the northern spur of the forest and establish themselves in Frasselt. The division would then be poised about a thousand yards short of the main anti-tank ditch of the Siegfried Line ready for a dash through by 44 Lowland Brigade mounted in kangaroos and supported by tanks as they had done so successfully when they captured Blerick. The move to Nijmegen was slow and difficult on account of the thaw and of the need to move in the dark without lights so as to conceal from the enemy the enormous concentration of troops which was taking place. Nijmegen was crammed to overflowing and we spent two days hidden in two large schools completing our preparations for the battle. With the other Company Commanders I went up to the Canadian observation posts and saw the terrain that we had to cross. Flat, wet, featureless and lying between the steep hills of the Reichswald and the totally flooded plain on our left, we knew that keeping direction would be difficult; also that until 46 Brigade cleared the Frasselt area we would be under enemy observation throughout. We had excellent air photographs and the briefings we got, and which we were able to give to our men, were extremely detailed and accurate. This was just as well for many of our soldiers were newly joined reinforcements who had never before been in action.

We left our Nijmegen billets at three o'clock in the morning and rode slowly on the Churchill tanks of 3 Scots Guards up to the gun area and then on through to the forward Assembly Area by the woods just west of Hooge Hof, about a mile from the German frontier. The eastern sky was lit up by fires and explosions and tracer shells as the RAF bombed Kleve, Goch and Udem, and soon the artillery started to shoot the preliminary counter-battery serials of their massive programme of fire tasks.

The noise was deafening but reassuring, and we had a quick breakfast before the barrage proper began at nine o'clock. Already it was clear that the going would be terrible; and the chances of vehicles being able to keep up with the Infantry were slim. This was serious for casualty evacuation and for the maintenance of wireless communications with Brigade, but it had happened before and we coped. A greater difficulty was presented by an American-laid minefield which had not been fully marked or cleared, and the mud churned up by the tanks was so thick that the carriers with the Sappers' and Pioneers' mine-clearance equipment never got up to the Start Line. Our two leading companies lost some men in that minefield and also from German shelling. Around midday 10 HLI came up to advance on Kranenburg and the 93rd crossed the frontier into Germany to attack the enemy strong-point at Elsenhof. This enemy post had been very severely hammered by our Gunners and our B Company took over eighty prisoners as they emerged from their deep shelters, and also an unused 88-mm gun. I brought my D Company up beside B Company to clear the hamlet of Hettsteeg, losing my CSM to a *schumine* on the approach and coming under sporadic but increasing enemy machine gun and mortar fire. Luckily the mud deadened the explosions of shells and mortar bombs. While we managed to keep up with the barrage as exhorted, advancing about two hundred yards behind the line of bursting shells, one troop of our artillery persisted in firing two hundred yards short, and in consequence its shells were falling amid my right forward platoon; but harmlessly thank God, as the mud absorbed the blast and shrapnel. I actually saw one man thrown right up into the air as a shell burst beside him. He spun round, landed on his feet and continued to walk forward unscathed. We plodded on against pretty light opposition and consolidated our position at the end of the day beside the village of Frasselt whence, before darkness fell, we watched 9 Cameronians putting in a most spirited attack against the northern spur of the Reichswald Forest. Although 44 Brigade had passed through us and breached the main defences of the Siegfried Line, the hoped for break-through to the Rhine Valley did not occur. On our left the flood waters were still rising and parties of Canadians could be seen rowing from farm to farm in assault boats, and the single axis forward from Kranenburg became clogged with the vehicles of our Division and those of 43 Division tasked to push on to Kleve. The whole affair became messy and disjointed; logistical preoccupations taking priority over battle plans. We had a short spell up on the Materborn feature with its splendid views over the low ground to the east and John Codner, my FOO, and his Gunner colleagues had some good shooting at distant Germans. My D Company was able to make a singular contribution to the business of extricating vehicles from the floods as we had discovered in a barn near Frasselt an abandoned enemy tracked vehicle of a type we'd not seen before and it was put to good use rescuing our A Echelon back in Kranenburg.

At this time we welcomed back into the 93rd a number of our friends who had been wounded early on in Normandy, but their arrival could not disguise the fact that, like I believe all Infantry battalions, many of our new Officers were a mixed bunch of inexperienced chaps from a variety of regiments and young raw Private Soldiers. The second half of February I remember as a period of order, counter-order and subsequent frustration. The Germans put up a strong resistance west of the Rhine and there was some stiff fighting for places such as Kalcar, Goch and Udem, and during this period the Highland and Welsh Divisions were having a very trying time clearing the deep, gloomy, rain-soaked forest. We in the 93rd had one difficult day when we were given the task of capturing a group of villages between Goch and Udem, for Buchholt proved to be quite a costly objective as the enemy artillery fire was unusually heavy and the smoke and mist caused two of our companies to lose their bearings and they got caught in machine gun cross-fire.

Since the beginning of the month we had lost nineteen killed or died of wounds, but at Buchholt alone we took almost two hundred prisoners. Other divisions were by now making good progress against weakening resistance, and on 25 February 2A&SH was pulled back to our Dutch 'Home Town', Tilburg, to prepare for a major role in the crossing of the Rhine, that last formidable obstacle protecting the western side of Hitler's Reich. Now with the whole of 15 Scottish Division concentrated in and around the town the Dutch population surpassed themselves. Nothing could have equalled the hospitality which they extended to all our Jocks and to us Officers, or the patience with which they tolerated the inevitable but numerous discomforts which the billeting of so many troops inflicted on them at a time when they themselves were recovering from years of occupation, oppression and privation. They gave us an unforgettable welcome. The phrase which I remember so well hearing from countless Dutch householders as we made our way across their country, tired, wet and generally anxious about what lay ahead, was 'Slapen is goed voor soldaten', as they insisted that we take over their best beds.

The 93rd had long boasted privately that we were the best turned-out unit in the BLA and Colonel Morgan opened our stay in Tilburg with a full-scale drive on smartness. In a Highland Regiment this meant clean battle-dress with new badges sewn on, knife-edge creases in our trousers and properly pressed kilts when off-duty, and our bonnets had to be stiffened with hoops of wire. All this was achieved to a satisfying degree and I personally was extremely gratified by the efforts made by my D Company Jocks who were judged to have attained the highest standard in the Battalion.

Newcomers to the 93rd were heard to wonder. 'What the . . . must life be like in the Guards if this is what it is in a Highland regiment?'

The Divisional Commander, 'Tiny' Barber, was clearly pleased when he came to inspect us and I am pretty sure that our Dutch friends felt heartened by the peace-time atmosphere of the parade ground which our activities created in their midst. Sadly this was the Battalion's final spell in Holland, for early in March we were lifted out of Tilburg and taken to Rekem, a small Belgian village where the River Maas provided the essential conditions for practising how to cross the wider River Rhine. But before we left Tilburg we gave another even more colourful and ambitious Ball in honour of our Dutch friends; and we took it as a compliment that so many pretty girls turned up to dance with us.

After nearly three weeks of planning and rehearsals the 93rd crossed the Rhine near Xanten at 2 a.m. on 24 March. The leading companies of the assault divisions, our 15 Scottish and 51 Highland, were mounted in Buffaloes, amphibian armoured vehicles crewed by men of a Yeomanry regiment. Our artillery fire concealed the noise as we edged towards the crossing points and into the current of Europe's widest waterway, and the darkness of the still spring night was transformed by the 'moonlight' artificially created by the beams of searchlights reflected off the clouds.

I never set foot on the enemy-held bank and have retained only a hazy memory of the events of that night and of the day which followed. I remember that the Leader of our flight of Buffaloes had had difficulty in finding a stretch of firm ground on which to exit from the water, and that I was standing up peering over the side as we climbed up the bank. There was a bright flash, an explosion and something struck me hard on the side of my head below the protective rim of my helmet and I found myself lying on the floor of the empty vehicle with a field dressing round my benumbed head.

Some hours later, in the bright light of morning, I was on a stretcher in an ambulance which after travelling for about twenty minutes halted and one of the sitting patients, a Welsh Guards subaltern, and the ambulance driver got out and excitedly described the scene as the streams of aircraft flew overhead carrying the parachute and glider-borne troops into the battle. This assault from the sky, by a whole corps of British, Canadian and American units, was the largest airborne operation of World War Two and the most successful. That evening I found myself in a hospital near Brussels in a bed next to that of a lively young Officer of the 52nd Light Infantry. Before the week was out he fell madly in love with the pretty blond nurse who twice a day gave us injections of a newly invented antibiotic named penicillin. After two weeks my head had healed and, as no fracture had occurred, I was discharged and moved to a Military Convalescent Depot in the Belgian sea-side resort of Knocke-Le Zoute. That bit of Belgium had been liberated by the Canadians without much fighting, and apart from empty gun emplacements and the remnants of beach obstacles in shallow water, there were no visible reminders of Nazi occupation or hostilities. We were accommodated in hotels and life became extremely agreeable. The weather was good, the beaches close by and cleared of mines and other perils, and there was great rejoicing that the war was ending.

The news of President Roosevelt's death shocked us, for FDR had been a great and noble American leader and a true friend to Churchill and Britain. His judgement, alas, faltered in the final months of his life and the consequences for the people of Central and Eastern Europe were to endure for almost half a century. We heard with satisfaction of Adolf Hitler's suicide but felt a tiny twinge of pity for Eva Braun who had joined that most evil man in a macabre marriage ceremony and immolation in a Berlin bunker. Churchill's victory speech broadcast over loud-speakers set up in the main square outside our billets ended with the exhortation, so characteristic of that great patriot, 'Advance Britannia, God save The King', and was for me the climax of that euphoric period; and my thoughts turned to my comrades in the 93rd, now deep inside conquered Germany, who could enjoy their first summer of peace for six years; and to my Mother and Father whose lives had been warped by two World Wars.

The prediction that within three months Mr Churchill was to be rejected as Prime Minister by the electorate of Britain would in our circles have been received with total disbelief. Certain matters were already jolting our euphoria as the first days of peace in Europe passed. Stories were circulating about the unfriendly attitude towards the Americans and the British by the Red Army Generals, and of Marshal Stalin's malevolence towards the Western Allies. But as horrified Mankind learned of the barbarities carried out in the Concentration and Extermination Camps on millions of human beings whom the Nazis stigmatised as racially inferior, the retribution being systematically wreaked through rape and pillage by vengeful Slavs on the vanquished German population was viewed by us with understanding though not with approval.

For those of us in the British forces with no prospect of early demobilisation – this category included me as I had been granted a Regular Commission – a constant consideration was Japan. She had not been defeated, and to achieve that the Allies would have to invade the Japanese homeland and there overcome a resistance more fanatical and deadly than that which Slim's 14th Army had encountered in Burma or the US Marine Corps had encountered on those blood-stained Pacific islands. It was not an agreeable prospect, but we tucked it away in the back of our minds as we enjoyed life on the beaches of Belgium.

The small circle of convalescent Officers of which I was one was befriended by a group of attractive, well-heeled and generous French-speaking Belgians. I did not discover what the men of the group did during the war but had the feeling that their occupations were both lucrative and undangerous. They certainly had more to say about the gaffes and eccentricities of individual Germans with whom they had rubbed shoulders than about the exactions inflicted on their fellow-countrymen by the German Occupiers. Actually, it appeared to me that their principal anxiety at that time stemmed from the political ambitions of the Flemish-speaking half of Belgium and the effects of these on the fortunes of our charming hosts. One member of our group, however, was singular; very special, an extremely pretty girl in her mid-twenties with a small, blond son, 2½ years old.

Netchou Richard was beloved by us all, Belgian and British, and especially deeply by the Welsh Guards subaltern whom I had met in the ambulance during the Rhine Crossing battle and who had joined us in our Convalescent Depot. In 1943 Netchou's husband had been deported for forced labour in Germany. She had received no news of him until, the war ended, deportees, prisoners of war and others released from captivity started to arrive back in their homeland. Like her friends, Netchou was buoyed up (for she loved her husband very much) by the reports she received from early returnees that 'Your husband is alive and is on his way home', 'Do not worry, you'll see him again in a few days' and such like. But Richard did not come back to his wife and baby son; the reports, albeit well-meaning, related to another Belgian with identical names and a similar description. Netchou's husband had been put to death soon after reaching Germany two years earlier.

Like my colleagues in the British Army of 1945 I was appalled by the scale of the cruelty and misery inflicted in Belsen and Auschwitz, but the emaciated bodies there recorded in film and photographs seemed alien, remote; as if on another planet. Netchou Richard was a lovely person and one of our group, and for her and for her infant son, Jean-François, we grieved.

In June I rejoined the Argylls, by now well established in Travemunde on the Baltic coast near Lübeck. It was an excellent place for the victorious Jocks to end up; the area had suffered little damage but was crowded by refugees from the bombed towns and from the advancing Russians whose Occupation Zone bordered on our Battalion's area. Travemunde was an important hospital and convalescent centre for the Wehrmacht, and we used to watch the patients being taken for exercise in the streets and park. They were grouped according to infirmity. Thus, one party would consist of amputees whose left legs were missing; the next those with no right legs; another of blinded men. Frostbite on the Eastern Front had caused a fearful toll of limb amputations. The destruction I had seen on my journey from the Belgian coast through western Germany up to the Baltic was fearful too. The railway system with tracks and bridges severed, rolling stock up-ended and installations burnt out resembled a child's Hornby train-set on which a man in boots had stamped and kicked and ground his heels into the rails, locomotives, carriages and wagons. I was driven for five miles through the great city of Hamburg without seeing a building intact. Most had no roofs and only three walls, and the stench of death which rose into the sunshine from beneath the rubble was nauseating. It was hard not to be overcome by compassion for the citizens who had endured so much and who were having to live with the consequences of Total War, albeit a war that they had started. As we looked on the scenes of devastation which constituted north-west Germany in the summer of 1945, we openly declared: 'It will be at least fifty years before Germany has recovered from all this'. As so often, we vastly under-estimated the energy and powers of recuperation of the German people – and the generosity of the United States whose Marshall

Plan was to make such a marvellous contribution to the rebuilding of war-torn Europe.

When I reached Travemunde much of Central Europe was in chaos with thousands of prisoners trying to reach their homelands, tens of thousands of Displaced Persons and refugees wandering westward away from the Russian zone, and former Slave Labourers, now no longer confined in German mines and factories, roaming the countryside in search of food, women or loot, aflame with hatred for members of Hitler's Master Race. The part which the British Army played, together with the Control Commission Germany (the CCG), in restoring order, a functioning administration and the supply of food and fuel to prevent the population in the first post-war winter from dying of starvation and cold has in general been ill recognised. Because the British Zone in Occupied Germany was the most densely populated of the four, and contained the greatest proportion of industrial plants, the British task was the most formidable and the most urgent.[31]

But I was not in Germany to see this achievement with my own eyes, for in July I was posted away to join the First Battalion of the Argylls in Lincolnshire. Many others were by now leaving the 93rd; the Regulars like me to other units and other campaigns, or the majority, the conscripts, in their due turn for demobilisation and 'civvy street'.

When I enlisted in 1941 I had no intention of becoming a career soldier, but by late 1944 my views had changed. I was holding the rank of major (albeit temporary), was for my age well informed and experienced in matters military, and I was enjoying the comradeship, sense of purpose and the respect which membership of a good regiment confers. So why throw all that up and embark on the uncharted waters of civilian life? Moreover, my attitude was already being influenced by a conviction that the defeat of the Axis Powers would be followed by no long period of peace such as Europe had enjoyed after 1815, but rather by a variety of upheavals as colonies broke away from the grip of declining empires, and as the malignant Soviet Union strove to erode the economic and strategic strength of the Christian democracies. Indeed, there were dark moments when some of my colleagues and I came to accept as inevitable the outbreak of World War Three, and we deliberated over the question: 'Should one not, out of self-interest and patriotic duty, remain in khaki and prepare to fight or, more optimistically, work to master the Profession of Arms and thereby in a small personal way contribute to the policy of Armed Deterrence which the Western Powers, now acutely aware of their failures in the 1930s, would have to adopt?'

Mercifully, the policy of constant vigilance and sustained strength, which the North Atlantic Treaty Organisation (NATO) embodied, was successful; confrontation with the Communist bloc never escalated into the dreaded Hot War. But the Cold War and the turbulent phase of Retreat from Empire have kept the British Armed Services fully employed until the end of the century. I have never regretted my decision to spend my working life in their midst.

A few days before I left Travemunde that wonderful man, Russell Morgan, who had played such a memorable part in our lives since the Battalion left Orkney, was promoted to the command of 15 Brigade in the 5th Division. We gave him the traditional Argyll send-off; he stood in his car which was drawn by the Warrant Officers and Sergeants, with the Pipes and Drums at their head, through the ranks of cheering, grateful, admiring Jocks. By God, we were indeed lucky and privileged to have had Russell as our Commander, guide and friend. Command of 2A&SH then passed temporarily into the hands of the new 2IC, Major Kenny Muir. He was to win the Victoria Cross serving with the First Battalion in the Korean War which broke out five years later.

I returned home to the Isle of Wight for three weeks leave.

The First Battalion which I was to join was under orders for India and we assumed that we would be part of the Allied force committed to the invasion of Japan and the final defeat of that enemy.

My leave was almost finished when the BBC announced that the Americans had dropped atom bombs on Hiroshima and Nagasaki. By 15 August the Emperor of Japan had ordered his forces to lay down their arms. World War Two was over. It had lasted for seventy-one months and is said to have killed over fifty million human beings; a war which surely could have been averted if the nations, victorious in 1918, had stood up to Adolf Hitler and Benito Mussolini with greater unity and resolution.

The use against those two heavily populated Asiatic cities of the atomic bomb, a novel weapon of mass destruction, has been widely criticised. My own views on the matter have never altered since the day when I heard with such enormous relief that those two bombs had brought about the surrender of Japan.

Firstly, the Japanese forces, even though defeated in Burma and in the Pacific, would have fought desperately to defend their remaining possessions and their homeland. Secondly, if the United States had renounced the use of that weapon, a weapon they alone possessed, the war would have been prolonged and the death toll and suffering would have far exceeded the death toll in those two Japanese cities. Thirdly, as the effects of those atomic explosions were comprehended throughout the world, the concepts of nuclear deterrence and a nuclear balance of power came to create a priceless stability and averted a major conflict between the Western Democracies and the Communist nations of the Soviet Empire.

Would mankind have enjoyed those years of immunity from World War Three if in 1945 President Truman had announced to Marshal Stalin: 'The United States has produced the atomic bomb but it is a weapon of such devastating power that for humanitarian reasons we shall not use it'? Surely to become a convincing deterrent, a weapon of dread, the effects of nuclear explosions on man-made installations and on human beings HAD to be demonstrated in an irrefutable manner.

To President Truman and to the victims of Hiroshima and Nagasaki we owe a great debt. Those who like me were spared from going to the Far East to invade the Japanese homeland owe perhaps the greatest debt of all.

During this blood-stained century now ending there have been two World Wars. Only two countries fought every day in both – Germany and Britain. The other belligerents either joined late or left early; from both wars Germany emerged defeated and Britain victorious. Although it is inconceivable that Almighty God would have permitted the eventual triumph of Hitler's Germany, four other factors, it seems to me, ensured Britain's survival during the second war and her victory in 1945, (bought at less cost in blood than in 1918).

a. The English Channel, the barrier which the German Forces proved incapable of surmounting.
b. The might of American industry and the dynamism and generosity of the people of the United States, the arsenal of democracy.
c. The valour of the people of the Soviet Union and their armies, who on the Eastern Front at terrible cost bled the Wehrmacht white, and who thereby made possible the successful Anglo-American campaigns on the mainland of Europe.
d. The criminal lunacy of Adolf Hitler.

When I reflect on the good fortune of my country, and when with colleagues I celebrate the anniversaries of D-Day in 1944 and of VE-Day in 1945, I remind myself of the debt we British owe to our former Russian Allies, a debt forgotten in the antagonisms of the Cold War.

Notes

1. FDLs = Forward Defended Localities
2. It is an odd fact that the name of the Gordons' first objective in the campaign sounded the same as that of their Commanding Officer.
3. In fact few Germans were encountered by the 93rd during our move forward that day. The bullets and bombs which caused these sniper alarms were 'overs' from the fighting ahead of us. We were too inexperienced to realise this.
4. 2A&SH lost that day three killed and eleven wounded
5. Three rifle companies, A, B and C, were on the south side of the Odon, dug-in in woods and in some of the buildings of Gavrus village astride the road which ran down over the two branches of the river, here about two

hundred yards wide. On the north bank the Carrier Platoon was dug-in near the bridges with Battalion HQ on the elevated edge of a cornfield overlooking a large mill building and the two bridges. D Company was dug-in around Battalion HQ.

6. PIAT = Projector, Infantry, Anti-Tank.
7. A battalion of 53rd Welsh Division in rear of 15th Scottish.
8. Later the Rt Hon Lord Campbell of Croy and a friend of my wife and myself.
9. DSO: Distinguished Service Order; MC: Military Cross; MM: Military Medal
10. LOBs: Officers and Soldiers selected to be Left Out of Battle to provide in the event of a disaster the nucleus of a new unit.
11. The well-known jingle about these birds went: 'One for sorrow, two for joy, three for a girl and four for a boy'.
12. Caumont lies 15 miles SSW of Bayeux and 13 miles east of St Lo.
13. Operation GOODWOOD launched on 18 July.
14. Regimental Aid Post.
15. Moreton was killed in action in Belgium six weeks later.
16. See The Memoirs of Field-Marshal The Viscount Montgomery of Alamein.
17. Field Marshal Rommel was seriously wounded by RAF ground attack aircraft on 17 July. Implicated in the bomb-plot of 20 July against Hitler he was compelled to commit suicide by poison on 24 October 1944.
18. Field Marshal von Kluge was brought from the Russian Front to replace von Rundstedt as C-in-C West in early July. He committed suicide after the attempted assassination of Hitler.
19. He later took Holy Orders. His Brother Bernard, a General, became Governor-General of New Zealand.
20. The King promoted Montgomery to the rank of Field-Marshal on the same day.
21. In Holland named the Waal and the Maas respectively.
22. The opponents of 15th Scottish Division on EPSOM in June.
23. The 'Father' of German airborne forces. He had planned the capture in May 1941 of Crete by troops brought in by parachute, glider and transport aircraft.
24. Cpl Fee was killed in action ten days before the war ended in the rank of Sergeant.
25. An explosive device constructed of wood and plastic and therefore difficult to detect, which when trodden on removed a man's foot above the ankle. The Germans scattered these in great quantities during the fighting of the autumn of 1944 onwards.
26. A Dutch term of hatred for the Germans equivalent to the English 'Hun'.
27. So named because the divisional emblem of 15th Scottish is the Red Lion of Scotland.
28. Artillery Forward Observation Officer.
29. The British equivalent was the excellent Vickers .303-inch calibre medium machine gun.
30. The Germans called it the West Wall.
31. For a description of conditions in the British Zone 1945–6, see Appendix I.

CHAPTER IV
1945–1948
Palestine and Parachuting

The First Battalion had a disappointing war. In mid-1940 they moved from Palestine to Egypt and took part in General Wavell's highly successful – and for the British nation hugely cheering – attack on the large Italian Army positioned along the Libyan frontier. The battle honour Sidi Barani testifies to the 91st's contribution to that feat of arms.

In the spring of 1941 they were belatedly moved to Crete to reinforce General Freyberg's units deployed against the imminent German sea- and airborne invasion, but by the end of the ten days' fighting the enemy airborne forces had conquered the whole island, and of the Argylls fewer than half got back to Egypt. The 91st thereafter played no significant part in the fighting until March 1944 when they entered the Italian battlefield as part of 8th Indian Division. They returned to the UK at the end of the war in Europe, and I joined them in the Lincolnshire village of Market Rasen and took over A Company. The spirit and general tone was a bit depressing to newcomers like me who had trained and fought in other battalions. The CO, Richard Lumley Webb, known throughout the Army as 'Squire', was a gallant old-fashioned Edwardian gentleman, expert with rod and shotgun, but he was no Russell Morgan. However, my own spirits were lifted when the battalion was brought into the Air-landing Brigade of the renowned 6th Airborne Division to replace the 12th Devonshires. We were a pretty bogus glider unit as only a few of us got as far as learning how to get in and out of those flimsy machines, but we at once enjoyed the benefits of belonging to an airborne formation with its distinctive steel helmets, superior web equipment, higher establishment of Officers and Soldiers, and a general scale of weapons, radios and those operational gadgets which make field-soldiering more agreeable. Instead of going to India, we were to go to Palestine to maintain law and order in that small country where the rights of the Arab inhabitants and the obligations to them of the British Mandatory Power were being assailed by Zionist pressures, increasingly strident and vilifying, egged on by influential Jewish elements in the United States.

Along with several thousand assorted members of 6th Airborne, we embarked in October in the troopship *Ascania*. The soldiers had to do all the loading of the boat unaided as the Liverpool dockers were on strike, a condition which was to exemplify post-war Britain and fill us in the Armed Forces with anger – and with anxiety too about the path down which our country already seemed to be heading. We docked in Haifa some ten days later, and were driven down the coast road in a long convoy of Jewish-owned buses, and we settled into our camp near the seaside resort of Nathanya alongside the 2nd Battalion The Royal Ulster Rifles. During the voyage All Ranks had been made to attend a series of lectures by experts on Palestine, its problems and the pitfalls which lay ahead of us in our new role of Imperial Policing, officially termed 'Aid to the Civil Power', so different from the total war against the Axis armies in which we had been engaged for six years.

Every one of us got off that boat exceedingly well informed about the Palestine situation, aware of the irreconcilable demands of the Arabs, the British and of the Jews who had experienced the ghastliness of Hitler's 'New Order'; and between Arab and Jew we were, when we set foot in that country, wholly without bias or prejudice. This did not last.

It soon became apparent that the Jocks, and to a lesser extent we Officers, were developing a dislike of the Jew, but for the Arab a tolerant affection such as a parent has for an incorrigibly naughty child. The young Arabs who crossed our paths were rogues. They flattered, they cheated and they stole; but they did it all with a smile, and with a skill and daring which we much admired. On their first night in Camp 21 a section of the Field Ambulance went to sleep in a tent pitched near the thick belt of barbed wire which marked the camp's perimeter. When dawn broke they found that the tent and all their belongings had vanished over the wire. None of the sleeping medics had been disturbed.

The Jews, however, seemed to be totally without humour or consideration for the rights of other people. And the ultra-devout, with their black raiments, long beards and skins pallid from lack of healthy exercise and fresh air, appeared to many of us like creatures from an underworld: repellent. Their treatment under German rule had placed them in a unique category of persecuted humanity, but their arrogance and self-pity dampened the sympathy we felt towards those survivors of the Holocaust. This initial sympathy was transformed into contempt when terrorists acting in the Zionist cause started to murder our people, men and women, civilians and military; the same British who had expended much blood and treasure to bring about the destruction of Nazi Germany which alone saved European Jewry from extinction. We began to notice too that the Jews already in Palestine were not united in zeal for the Zionist cause. The older ones who had come to Palestine in the 1930s, mainly from Germany and Austria, and who had built up fertile, well-ordered and law-abiding settlements, whispered to us of their dismay that the swarms of Jews now demanding unrestricted entry into Palestine included 'such rabble from the Balkans, Poland and

Russia'. And rumours that the Soviet government, our wartime ally, was providing money and shipping for this exodus from Eastern Europe seemed a thoroughly unfriendly act designed specifically to embarrass us British. We heard too of the soul-searching which went on amongst the boatloads of immigrants as they headed for Palestine. Individuals were being asked by their companions: 'What did you do to save your skin?' 'How come the Holocaust left you alive and healthy?' All were perplexed and ashamed that few Jews had taken up arms against their persecutors. Most had simply acquiesced in their denunciation, herding together for deportation and eventual extermination in the process known as The Final Solution.

But that extensive, Europe-wide process was not kept operating solely by Germans. The lesser functionaries who did the vilest work at German behest in national Police forces, in the Councils in the ghettoes, in Death Camp administration and in the physical handling of each batch of victims, were non-Germans. It began to dawn on us also that the venom which was being poured out against Britain by the Zionist press was to an extent generated by bad conscience and shame at what Jew had done to Jew during those terrible years.

Acts of terrorism against our bit of the Army began in quite a mild way. The Brigade Major, Paddy Brett, was taken out of his hotel on the coast, tied up and flogged: a reprisal for some alleged harsh treatment of Jews by members of the Division.

The Jews hated and feared the 'Red Berets', the soldiers of the Airborne Division, and called them *Kalionets*, their word for poppy – a red flower with a black heart.

Our own activities during those weeks in Nathanya were largely confined to cordon-and-search operations; cordoning areas to stop people moving around while the Police and Army searched for arms and wanted criminals. I do not remember any of these lengthy actions yielding up much of interest. Either the information on which they were based was faulty, or the stuff was too expertly hidden or, most usually, the Jews got wind of our intentions and the wanted men fled before the cordon was in place.

It was all a bit frustrating, but the Jocks carried out their tasks with patience and good humour. Discipline was strict and certainly in our battalion discourtesy or loutish behaviour towards any civilian was forbidden. This was not a matter of enforced discipline; the British soldier is by nature and upbringing kindly and good humoured, and it was not until Jews' acts of terrorism and murder became really vicious in 1946 that the Jock began to apply the boot and rifle butt in place of the smile and friendly gesture natural to him.

One day my Company had to search a factory in which explosives were known to be hidden. The factory made kitchen utensils of every description, and the main store room consisted of long, high racks on which were stacked hundreds of kettles, pots, pans, mugs, containers of every type and size, all made of aluminium and each capable of concealing dynamite, bullets, grenades or pistols. Every article had to be taken down, inspected and carefully replaced exactly where found. Colonel Webb, who was present, was adamant on this latter point.

Although we were engaged increasingly on active operations, the CO and 2IC strove to get the Battalion, or at least us Officers, into the routine and frame of mind appropriate for peacetime soldiering; early morning lessons in Highland Dancing were attended with ill grace. The episode that is best remembered though was when, having forced our way into a Jewish settlement through very hostile inhabitants and carried out an extensive search, the Mess Sergeant was ordered to lay out lunch for the Officers in full view of the same settlers, on tables covered with white cloths and the regimental silver.

While we were in Camp 21 the government at home brought out a Defence White Paper outlining the principles by which the Armed Forces were to be recruited, manned, deployed and administered during the years of peace which lay ahead. Conscription, or National Service as it was called, would continue indefinitely alongside a substantial Regular element; the Services would be deployed widely across the globe to safeguard the interests of Great Britain and her Empire, to protect the King's subjects and Imperial trade, and Regular Servicemen would as far as possible be accompanied by their families when despatched to garrison our overseas military bases and outposts. This was of particular interest to those who, like me, had chosen a career in the Regular Army; but we were not all convinced that those principles were sound or, from the viewpoint of the British taxpayer, prudent. Colin Mitchell, the only Regular Officer in my Company, and I spent much time discussing the implications of that White Paper. He became famous in 1967 when in command of the First Argylls he reoccupied the Crater District of Aden and put an end to terrorist activity there.

The British Army of the post-war era was to be spread from Jamaica in the New World to Hong Kong in farthest Asia, with large bases in the United Kingdom, West Germany, the Suez Canal area, the Persian Gulf, East Africa, Malaya, Singapore and Hong Kong with smaller garrisons, airfields and naval facilities on islands such as Malta and Cyprus and in certain colonies.

Garrison service accompanied by families committed HMG to the building and maintenance to European standards of offices, quarters, schools, military hospitals, leave centres, clubs and the other facilities that wives and children overseas would require. If the political situation in any of these places turned sour, and British lives and property became endangered, they would have to be guarded, probably by additional units brought in, while the front-line units stationed there carried out the operational tasks for which they had been deployed originally. India had already been promised her independence: if other places won their independence or demanded the removal of the British military presence, what would happen to the expensive and complex installations that HMG was now proposing to build for the benefit of her Servicemen and their dependents? To us in early 1946 it seemed that these plans, designed largely to sustain the Regular element in the Forces, were founded on excessive optimism about the durability of a worldwide British military presence, about the passivity of the native populations alongside whom the Army would be living, and that they misjudged the long-term financial interests of our country. Would it not be more prudent and cheaper, we pondered, to scrap the plans for schools, quarters, family passages by air and sea, and other facilities and instead to pay the Regulars in the Forces more generous salaries? That would enable them to buy their own houses in the United Kingdom in which their families could put down roots, enjoy an unbroken education, and rely on the local National Health Service? To these privately owned homes the Serviceman could return for his leaves and retire on leaving the Colours. And moreover, if he wished, he could on his improved salary afford to bring his relatives out for holidays to the part of the world where he happened to be stationed. After all, many civilian expatriates acted thus.

Years later, when I observed the immense difficulties that our Soldiers were encountering in their search for accommodation to buy or rent on their discharge from the Army, and when I watched the vast and expensive military complexes being handed over to Third World governments as Britain withdrew from the global stage, the memory of those discussions in our Palestine tents came back to me.

Under the emergency laws then operating, the illegal possession of arms and explosives was punishable by death. We therefore had to take extreme care that no Service weapon or ammunition fell into the hands of Arab or Jew. Arms and ammunition were kept under guard in special armouries and subject to constant checking. My Company Arms Kote was a large tent, isolated by belts of wire and never left unattended, in which the rifles and Bren guns were chained to racks and the smaller items locked in strong-boxes. Every weapon had to be counted once a day by an Officer, the numbers checked against the register, and the details of the inspection recorded. It was a tedious but extremely important task for the Company Orderly Officer. One of my subalterns was a Glaswegian; pale, wiry and immature. I am still at a loss to know how he obtained a King's Commission, but he was already in the 91st when I joined them in Lincolnshire.

When we had been in Camp 21 for some weeks he committed some minor military folly for which I awarded him as punishment three days' extra duty as Orderly Officer. Four days later I said to Sandy Simpson, my Company Sergeant-Major: 'I am going to check the weapons myself. Come and give me a hand.' We counted, checked, recounted and rechecked, three times in all; each time with the same result. One Browning 9-millimetre pistol was missing. This was a most grave matter. 'When were the weapons last checked and by whom?'

'Mr McCarthy [authors' note: this is not his real name] checked them during each of the past three days and here in the Inspection Record are his signatures and the dates and the times,' said Simpson. McCarthy was summoned. Yes, he had been Orderly Officer for the past three days. Yes, those were his signatures in the book certifying that he had completed the daily checks and found all correct. But no, he admitted, he had not actually counted every weapon each day. He'd signed the book without doing a proper, full check.

The Colonel, when McCarthy was brought before him, took a very dim view of that admission and exclaimed: 'By this act of gross neglect and deceit you have very badly let down your Company Commander, me and the Regiment. It is a disgraceful thing that you have done. But you have not been with us long and you are very young. I'll therefore give you a choice of punishment. You can either stand trial by General Court Martial or volunteer to transfer immediately to The Parachute Regiment!' He chose the latter course and soon left the 91st. His confession and banishment did not, however, explain how the pistol had gone missing. That came later.

When I took over A company in Market Rasen there was already in its ranks one Private Morris. This man had been taken prisoner in France in early 1940 and had remained in German captivity until repatriated in May 1945, by which time his account with the Regimental Paymaster had accumulated a credit balance of several hundred pounds. By the time I joined the Company, Morris had acquired a wife, had blown all his credits and, being in debt, was undergoing Restrictions of Pay.

A couple of weeks after the drama of the missing pistol CSM Simpson said to me: 'You know that Private Morris is in debt, is on short pay and has a wife in Scotland. How then is he managing to go up to Jerusalem once a week by taxi to visit a girlfriend?' This called for further investigation but Morris flatly denied any connection with the missing pistol.

'An Arab friend owns the taxi and my girlfriend pays the bill.'

I decided to call in expert help and a very cocky Morris was ushered into the Company Office for questioning by two NCOs of the Special Investigation Branch (SIB) of the Military Police. Simpson and I waited in another room. After about forty minutes a grey-faced Morris tottered out and was taken straight to the Guard Room in close arrest. He had broken down under questioning and had confessed all. He had taken the pistol and had sold it to an Arab. He also disclosed something else. Another Private Soldier, a friend of Morris, had sold to the same Arab a Belgian-made pistol, a war souvenir which he had illegally retained. Morris was duly sentenced to five years' imprisonment and the second soldier to two years.

Major Sandy Bardwell had been taken prisoner in Crete and had rejoined the 91st as our Second-in-Command shortly before we left England. In early 1948 he married and with his bride flew out to honeymoon in the West Indies; but the aircraft, the Star Tiger, crashed and all on board were killed. David Wilson, a cousin of mine and a member of a distinguished family of Argylls, had become 2IC in his place. This brought a new zest to the Battalion for David was a most energetic and enthusiastic Officer and the whole tone of the 91st improved.

Not all battalion 2ICs were as productive. Some were elderly Majors with no chance of promotion, and each seemed to have a different idea of what the duties of a 2IC consisted. This was, after all, very much a matter to be decided between the CO and the 2IC, taking into account their respective interests and abilities; like so much in the Army, it was largely – and quite sensibly – a 'matter of personalities'.

One famous regiment had a balding bachelor of great charm, much loved by his soldiers. He considered that his prime responsibility was to keep his finger firmly on the pulse of the Other Ranks – to know exactly what they were thinking, their grievances and hopes, and to keep his CO constantly informed on such matters. In our desert camps the latrine arrangements consisted of deep pits over which circular concrete structures were erected, each partitioned into cubicles with wooden seats, doors and walls rather like segments of cheese as sold in round boxes. In those cubicles the troops attended to their natural functions and, because these Deep Trench Latrines (DTLs) were down-wind of the camp and fairly soundproof they were also convenient places for the buglers and pipers to sit and practise their musical skills. Thus, they were much frequented during daylight hours. One day this Major concealed himself in one of the ORs' latrines. After a few minutes two men came and occupied the adjacent cubicles and began a conversation over the head of the unseen 2IC. Putting on his best Jocks' accent the Major started to join in the conversation with questions such as: 'What do you think of the new RSM?' 'The food's getting worse, isn't it?' and 'Isn't so-and-so a bit of a bastard?' To his questions he got no reply, but after a hasty rustling of paper and a slamming of the latrine doors, two little soldiers were seen running across the sand towards their Company Office crying: 'Sergeant-Major, come quickly! The Second-in-Command's in our shit-house and he's gone clean off his rocker.'

At the end of 1945 I made a couple of brief excursions; one to Beirut and the other to Bethlehem. The Lebanese countryside was refreshingly green in comparison with the coastal plain of Palestine, and Beirut, deeply French in administration, architecture, ambiance and gastronomy, seemed an oasis of tranquillity and good living. My trip to Bethlehem on Christmas Eve I still regret. My companions and I queued in the bitter cold for a long time to see the spot where our Saviour was born, surrounded by hundreds of sightseers and pushed into line by bad-tempered members of the Palestine Police. Eventually we descended a stone stairway, briefly examined a plaque set into the floor to mark the place where the newborn Jesus had lain, and, pressed forward by the impatient throng behind us, we stumbled up the opposite steps to emerge into the town square with its neon lights and garish commercial advertisements. For me the solemnity of this once-in-a-lifetime pilgrimage was spoiled above all by the stench of garlic and curry powder which followed us into the Manger.

In the spring of 1946 the 91st moved up to Jerusalem, left the Airborne Division and came under command of 31st Infantry Brigade. Battalion Headquarters was established in the heart of the city in the Hospice de Notre Dame, but I was sent to the suburbs to occupy with my own A Company and Support Company a large complex known as the Syrian Orphanage; in military parlance Camp 417 or 'Fortress B'. The significance of this orphange was that it housed the 90th Battalion of the Royal Army Pay Corps and the pay accounts of all the troops in the Middle East and the financial records of the British Army in that command. It was therefore thought to be a tempting target for sabotage, and because the bulk of the clerical staff were local civilians, an unusually soft target. The task of my Argyll force was to guard 'Fortress B' and to act as a Quick Reaction Force for operations in north-west Jerusalem.

We Argylls and the Pay Corps chaps got on well, shared messes and the limited sports facilities. The 90th Battalion was commanded by a tall likeable Colonel named Charlie Holmes. I remember him with affection for he was exceedingly kind to us; also because he wore a most colourful uniform. In those days senior Officers wore hat bands and collar patches in the colour of their Corps or Department. Holmes was the only Officer I ever saw with his service dress embellished in bright yellow.

My Jocks lived in huts aligned along one side of the orphanage grounds. They were comfortable and surrounded by neat flower beds, but as they were overlooked from the other side of the low perimeter wall by Jewish-occupied houses I was constantly anxious about the vulnerability of my sleeping soldiers. But the expected fusillade never came. Our work consisted of frequent night patrols inside the Jewish quarter, normally a monotonous, uneventful, activity etched in my memory by the balmy night air, the smell of garbage rotting on the pavements and the squeals of mangy cats, the only living things to be seen during the hours of darkness. Dusk-to-dawn curfews were being increasingly imposed as communal punishment and to curb the movement of arms and gangsters by the chief terrorist organisations, the Irgun Zvi Leumi (IZL) and the Stern Gang. A very big operation, AGATHA, was mounted at the end of June in which, inter alia, the Jewish Agency was occupied by the Royal Ulster Rifles and thoroughly searched.

When off duty our soldiers were normally allowed out of camp but only in uniform, armed and in parties of three or more. Thus, they could go to cinemas, shop and visit the Holy Places. To enter the homes of either Arabs or Jews was very unusual. One subaltern who had become over-friendly with a Jewish family was quietly sent back to England to protect him from an unwise marriage or from the danger of being taken hostage.

I took the company one day down to the Dead Sea where we lay on the water reading books, prevented by the salinity from sinking, but in agony if the water got into one's eyes or mouth. At the end of the day, sunburnt and sore, we drove back up the long winding road from the Dead Sea and its potash factories and awesome aridity, crossed the unexpectedly modest River Jordan by the Allenby Bridge and back to the Orphanage. Thus for the first months we were in Jerusalem life was fairly normal. We were constantly vigilant, always armed, but could carry out training exercises, routine patrols and essential off-duty activities without much fear of being gunned down. Terrorist attacks were things which seemed to happen to softer targets such as administrative units from whom the Jews could seize weapons and ammunition without the certainty of getting a bloody nose in the attempt. The bombing of the King David Hotel changed the whole tenor of life in Palestine and altered irrevocably relations between the inhabitants and the British Administration and Armed Forces.

The hotel was a large white building in the centre of Jerusalem. Being large it provided not only high-class restaurant and sleeping accommodation but one wing was occupied by the Headquarters of the British Forces in Palestine whose personnel shared with the hotel staff and its clientele many of the hotel's facilities.

The Manager was, I believe, Swiss. Soon after we arrived in Jerusalem we had invited him to some regimental function and in return he had invited me to a lunch party he was hosting on 22 July.

I left off work early that morning, changed into clean uniform and, to kill time before setting out for my lunch appointment, played a game of table-tennis in the Mess with a Pay Corps colleague.

'I must go now as I've a lunch appointment in town.'
'What time do you have to be there?'
'One o'clock.'
'No hurry then; we've time for another game.'

So we played a second game of 'ping-pong' and I joined Privates Greenwood my driver and Whitehead my escort and the jeep headed off towards the centre of the city. When we were still about four hundred yards from the King David there was a massive explosion, the sound dulled by the buildings around us, and a column of smoke and dust rose up ahead of us above the rooftops. The alarm sirens sounded almost immediately, and Greenwood turned the jeep round and we sped straight back to the Orphanage where the Jocks were already standing-to under arms.

The manner in which this atrocity was carried out by the Jews is well known. Indeed men who were to become leaders in the State of Israel have boasted about the part they played in the planning and execution of this, their most blood-stained blow in Palestine against the British.

A party of Jews, members of the IZL led by Menachem Begin disguised as Arabs, drove up to the hotel ostensibly to deliver a routine consignment of milk in large churns. The churns, however, contained explosives which some moments after the 'Arab' deliverymen had departed, were detonated by a timing device. The damage to the hotel was substantial; the part which housed the military HQ collapsed, burying the occupants, many of whom were young women, telephone operators and orderlies, whose duty shifts were changing over at the moment of the explosion. In all ninety-one people were killed and a further twenty remained unaccounted for. It was a most shocking and atrocious act.

Jerusalem and the Jewish quarters of the chief towns were again placed under curfew, and as more and more evidence about the murder gang was gathered by the CID, the search for individual terrorists was intensified. The sense of outrage created by the bombing of the King David was heightened by another atrocity. The Stern Gang, named after its leader Abram Stern, kidnapped two military Policemen, Sergeants Pearce and Robinson. These two NCOs, the gang announced, would be put to death if the British authorities proceeded with the execution of a convicted terrorist, Dov Gruner. The law took its course and Gruner was hanged. The Stern Gang carried out their threatened reprisal and passed a message stating that the corpses of Pearce and Robinson were hanging in an orange grove near Tel Aviv. Moreover, the bodies had been booby-trapped deliberately to kill or injure the medical team sent to recover them.

Among the Jocks any lingering sympathy for the Jewish cause was now extinguished. All Ranks were determined to insist that the punitive measures imposed on the population were complied with to the letter. There was little brutality on the part of the Argyll soldiers but there was in their manner a new firmness, a disregard for entreaties or excuses and a deep contempt for Jews of all sects, ages and backgrounds.

This unbending conduct, so uncharacteristic of the British soldier in his normal dealings with civilians, and the inconvenience inflicted on the citizenry by these prolonged curfews, searches and random questioning naturally antagonised many people who had been lukewarm in their support for the Zionist cause. We were still a bit naive and had yet to experience to the full the complexities and hazards of Imperial Policing. As the time to impose the evening curfew approached, our platoons would move out of camp accompanied by vehicles loaded with coils of barbed wire, and with these road blocks were set up, invariably at the same hour and at the identical places. On the third day of one curfew operation a series of small bombs concealed in the walls on either side of several of our road blocks exploded. With hindsight we really should have foreseen this possibility and varied our routine. Our failure to do so cost the lives of two Argylls and the wounding of eight others.

This incident also proved to be the undoing of our Colonel. Squire Webb liked his gin, and when he called a Press conference had already had his fill. He was angry about his dead and wounded soldiers, irked by the media's pro-Jew attitude and he deliberately had the journalists held in his Hospice for a couple of hours. They took exception to this treatment and complained; the military authorities caved in and relieved Webb of his command. We in the 91st thought he had done rather well: in slanging the Jews and the Press he had merely expressed the sentiments of everyone in the battalion. Happily Squire Webb thereafter had a congenial appointment as OC Troops on a troopship, a job in which he made many more friends, lived comfortably and not too strenuously with adequate spells ashore at his home in Kent.

The rising level of terrorism, the inflow of immigrants, the anti-British bias of much of the world's Press, especially in the United States, and the burden of administering the mandate was to persuade Ernest Bevin, our Foreign Secretary, that Britain must pull out of Palestine. This was done in May 1948, and resulted for the Jews in the creation of the State of Israel. For the Palestine Arabs however, the long-established inhabitants, it was a catastrophe, and for them many of us who have served there have lasting feelings of both guilt and compassion. I had by that time accumulated an entitlement to a long spell of post-war leave in the UK, and after a sea voyage from Port Said, travelled across a frozen France from Toulon to Calais in an unheated troop-train, arriving home in the Isle of Wight a few days before Christmas.

The winter of 1946-7 was exceptionally cold. Living with my Mother in the White House, we had enough coal to keep the fire in the small study burning and thus one room warm, and for cooking we relied on the excellent Aga which she had bought in 1937. But very many people in the Kingdom suffered, the snow and ice having caused widespread disruption to the transport network and to the delivery of coal to the power stations. Moreover, the average dwelling in Britain at that time had no insulation, the water pipes were fixed to the exterior walls and therefore froze in only a few degrees of frost, and central heating was a luxury found only in the homes of the wealthy. The chaos and misery caused by the long spell of Arctic weather gave rise to much criticism of the Labour government and of Mr Shinwell, the Minister of Fuel and Power, in particular. My own memories of those weeks in the Isle of Wight are of watching the snow fall out of a lilac-coloured sky, the flakes blown almost horizontally by the blizzard, and of making my unsteady way down to the edge of the Solent at the Duver to walk out on the frozen sea for more than a hundred yards from the shore.

Though only 23 years old I was still holding Major's rank; my true, substantive rank in the peacetime Army was Lieutenant. After the war it was normal for Officers to drop back in rank; to revert from commanding a brigade to command a rifle company was not uncommon. While I was on leave however David Wilson, in command of the Argylls since the departure of Squire Webb, wrote me a most helpful letter, the gist of which was: 'The older and more senior Officers who were on the Staff or prisoners during the war are now beginning to come back to regimental duty with the 91st. Rather than have to drop down to your substantive rank, why don't you volunteer for a tour with Airborne Forces? I know how keen you have long been to join the "Maroon Machine": now is your chance and I wish you the best of luck.'

It was a glorious day in the spring of 1947 when I reported to Perham Down Camp near Ludgershall in Hampshire to join the 5th (Scottish) Battalion of The Parachute Regiment, thus beginning a happy relationship which would continue to the end of my life.

'I'm sorry, Sir,' said the Mess Sergeant as he showed me to my quarters. 'The whole Battalion is out on a brigade exercise. Actually,' he added, 'there is one Officer left in the camp: he's in the room at the end of your hut.'

When I had unpacked I wandered down to introduce myself. Lying on the bed was Lieutenant McCarthy! Hanging down the wall behind him was a parachute strop. 'My Batman's' he said, 'he was killed recently when his 'chute malfunctioned, and as lightning never strikes the same spot twice, I've kept it to ward off such a calamity from myself'. McCarthy was in trouble again; in arrest and awaiting a Court Martial.

5 PARA was raised in 1943 and manned principally by volunteers from Scottish regiments. We wore a patch of Hunting Stuart tartan on our red berets behind The Parachute Regiment badge and the battalion had Pipes and Drums, but otherwise we wore the service dress of our parent regiments, with Highlanders in the kilt and the chaps from Lowland regiments in tartan trews. Although soldiers could transfer permanently out of the regiments in which they had enlisted and been trained into the Army Air Corps, of which The Parachute Regiment was part, Officers were only loaned – seconded was the term used – for tours with parachute units of two or three years. This scheme had undoubted advantages for the young Parachute Regiment in that it could absorb a lot of what much

older regiments had learned in the field of man-management, etiquette, traditions and peace-time standards from their long histories, but it had the inherent defect of subordinating the excellent Parachute Soldier and NCO to a stream of Officers who remained with him for perhaps only one year of duty in a battalion and whose long-term loyalty was to their own parent regiments. Thus the system was changed in 1961, and with the creation of a Permanent Cadre of Officers, The Parachute Regiment adopted the career-long, family-like, regimental system that has been an enduring source of strength to the British Infantry.

5 PARA was part of 2nd Parachute Brigade which had fought in Italy and the South of France, and from October 1944 to February 1945 had played a notable role in cleansing Athens of communist forces in that bitter Greek civil war. In Palestine the Battalion had been victims of one of the first acts of Zionist terrorism when seven Jocks were murdered by the Stern Gang in Tel Aviv.

The battalion I joined in Perham Down had a real mixed bag of Officers. Some had come out of the war highly decorated; some were eccentric, some like me were new to Airborne Forces; all had character and most an unforgettable charisma. The CO was a fine looking Cameron Highlander, Sandy Munro, but he alas broke his thigh jumping. He was replaced by Colonel Pat Sandilands, a Scots Fusilier, quite different to Sandy in looks and manner but clever, very kind and with an enviable record of gallantry on the battlefield. The 2IC, Jack Churchill, was a Seaforth who had made his mark in the Commandos by silencing German sentries with his longbow and arrows. George Cassidy, who had won the MC, used to eat glass. When bored with waiting for the next course to be brought to him at the table, he would pick up a wine-glass, bite off the thick base and stem and chew the rest up and swallow it.

My Company Commander was Jock Hawley, a Highland Light Infantryman with a great drooping moustache, and his Sergeant-Major was Jock Leslie, my friend from Fort George days. My fellow Officers in Hawley's company were all good men: Alan Munro, Jamie O'Connor, son of Dick O'Connor, our Corps Commander in Normandy, and Ronnie Adam, a tall Seaforth. In the Battalion I had friends from the Argylls, Gerald Hadow and Neil Campbell-Baldwin; and in Bill Corbould, from the Coldstream Guards, a life-long friend. The Regimental Sergeant-Major, Jim Aitken from the HLI, remained in The Parachute Regiment for many years and ended as the senior Quartermaster in the Army holding the rank of Lieutenant-Colonel. And there was Angus Grant, son of Colonel Aeneas Grant who had commanded the 7th Seaforth in June 1944 at the sharp end of the 'Scottish Corridor'. Young Angus was to go to war a few years later, in Korea as ADC to the GOC of the Commonwealth Division, General Jim Cassels, himself a distinguished Seaforth and a future CIGS. While there Angus was shot dead by mischance by a British sentry. Truly the good do die young.

Our neighbours in Perham Down were the 6th (Welsh) Parachute Battalion whose mascot was a goat. On the last day of 1947 two Jocks of 5 PARA went into their Company Store: 'Have you got any paint, Colour?'

'Yes, what do you want it for?'

'We want to give the Welsh goat a proper Scottish coat of paint for Hogmanay. Can you let us have two brushes and a tin of Stuart tartan paint?'

When I had been in 5 PARA for a couple of months I got a vacancy on the parachute training course. But before starting that, we had to go to Aldershot for a fortnight of intensive testing of our physical and mental stamina at the hands of a special unit of Airborne Forces known, as it still is, as P Company. About a hundred of us, of all ranks and from a great variety of regiments and corps, formed up in Maida Barracks, the Depot of The Parachute Regiment, to start the dreaded selection process.

The first morning was devoted to all manner of activities in the gymnasium; running, jumping, climbing and groundwork, and by mid-morning we were already pretty knackered. But there was to be no relief, for Field Marshal Montgomery, CIGS and Colonel Commandant of the Regiment, was visiting Aldershot and a meticulous programme had been worked out for his itinerary. The Great Man was due to arrive at our gymnasium at 1145, so our PT Instructors had built our activities up to a peak of fury for that moment. Alas the Field Marshal was delayed; he reached us twenty minutes later than scheduled, by which time few of us were capable of remaining upright.

The first week of P Company passed in pain. By the Thursday I was discovering muscles I never knew existed: from fingers to toes I ached terribly. To hold a knife and fork, to climb stairs and, most agonising of all, to sit on a lavatory seat, were excruciating. But by the Saturday the body had recovered and with it a gigantic appetite. The initial strain and pain were immensely worthwhile, for at the weekend I found I had reached a degree of physical fitness never attained before and all too rarely since. Walking through the town was like walking on air, and the marvellous feeling of bodily well-being was accompanied by a mental serenity, a euphoria, wonderful to experience. I have ever since pitied those whose working conditions and lifestyle condemn them to living out their lives in ignorance of true health and vigour.

At the end of that first week we had been put through a psychiatric test, the chief part of which consisted of the Invigilating NCO holding up in rapid succession a series of cards printed with short simple words such as 'house', 'water', 'mother', and so on. We were required to write down the first thought which entered our heads on reading each word. Not a difficult exercise, but a deceptive one I discovered when we assembled on the second Monday. Many of our colleagues were absent. I asked the reason.

'A few have asked to go back to their units, some have been rtu'd[1] for not being fit enough but many have been rejected as a result of the "trick-cyclist's" test; they were found to have sexual aberrations and other weaknesses and are therefore unsuitable for Airborne Forces.' I am glad to say that soon afterwards that test was discontinued.

About half of us got through the P Company Selection process successfully, and we moved to the Parachute School at RAF Upper Heyford in Oxfordshire. In the British Armed Forces the greatest number of parachutists are in the Army. Their training, supervision and despatching from aircraft or balloons are nevertheless an RAF responsibility. This works well. The RAF's Parachute Jumping Instructors (PJIs), a skilled and much admired band of specialists, took us through every stage of the training course. We were organised in groups (sticks) of ten men; each stick was in the sole charge of a PJI. Our routine military administration was exercised by The Parachute Regiment through a small unit at the PTS called the Parachute Course Administrative Unit (PCAU). When our batch reported to the PCAU at Upper Heyford in 1947 it was commanded by a distinguished and popular Officer of the Regiment; but someone must have had a grudge against him, for on our arrival we were confronted on the mat outside his office by a giant human turd.

To begin with, we spent many hours on ground training, learning how to land, fall and roll; and on the synthetic apparata mastering the essential drills inside the aircraft, how to exit and the techniques for controlling the 'chute while descending. In 1947 we were still using the X-type parachute with its 28-foot diameter canopy proven by much use in the war. We carried no reserve 'chutes. Personal weapons such as rifles were placed in padded sleeves and strapped on to us: heavy kit such as radios and mortar barrels were packed into large strong kitbags which we attached to one leg and, after the parachute had developed fully, we lowered on a nylon cord to hang beneath us like a pendulum. To qualify as a trained parachutist we had to complete eight jumps; two from a balloon and six from aircraft, including at least one in darkness. The aircraft we used was the DC 3 Dakota, with a single door on the port side. Every jump is approached by everyone with some degree of trepidation; the first one, from the side of the balloon cage, with particular nervousness as it is the first time we were required to do something so foolish and unnatural as stepping out into a void while 800 feet up in the air. But the second jump, through a hole in the bottom of the cage, was the least agreeable on account of the fear of disfigurement should one misjudge the centre of the hole and bang one's face against its solid wooden rim. This type of exit had to be practised, since in certain aircraft then in service it was the only way of getting out. Although anyone was free to withdraw from the course at any time up to the award of the parachutist's badge, I cannot recall anyone on my course opting out, and very, very few during the rest of my time in the Army.

Our morale at Upper Heyford was high and we had great confidence in our equipment and our instructors. Indeed the chief factor in getting through the eight jumps was our individual determination not to let the rest of the stick down and above all not to disappoint our PJI. Being an Officer and the senior chap on the course helped to turn my innate funk into fortitude. I was in stick K3 of Course No 228. Our stick Instructor was a short blond Welsh Sergeant named Dai Rees. He had a great sense of humour and we enjoyed being in his charge. The least enjoyable episode of the course was the last jump, a night descent. A succession of foggy nights had grounded all aircraft and the postponements of our last jump was causing administrative problems. The decision was therefore taken for us to do it from a balloon out on the DZ at Weston-on-the-Green. It was a dark, bitterly cold night with quite a stiff breeze as six of us entered the cage with Sergeant Rees and started to climb to jumping height. But the winch which controlled the cable jammed, and we were kept hanging at about 400 feet, too low for safe parachuting, while the cage swayed to and fro in the freezing air and the wind whistled through the rigging of the balloon from which we were suspended. After about thirty minutes someone got the winch going again, we went up to 800 feet and we all got down to earth very cold and much relieved. The ground was frozen hard and one chap broke his collar-bone on landing. The next day, pleased with ourselves but rather sorry to be leaving the team in which we'd worked our way through the course smoothly and happily, we received from the Station Commander the coveted blue and white badge of the qualified parachutist – and the entitlement thereafter to additional parachute pay at the rate of two shillings per diem (taxable).

Parachute pay has continued to be given to those whose military role requires them to jump from aircraft, and now, of course, it is at a much higher rate than in 1947. I have always privately queried the need for this financial perk to be paid in peacetime. The casualty rate, fatalities and serious injuries, was never large. There are surely professions or activities more dangerous and yet with no extra financial inducement attached. How many volunteer as parachutists primarily on account of the extra money? And how many would quit the comradeship and pride of an airborne unit if this small extra payment were discontinued? But I would not dream of advocating this economy. The Airborne Soldiers of the British Army deserve every penny that can be prised out of the Treasury. They are a credit to our nation. As Montgomery wrote of them: 'Every Man an Emperor'.

In early 1948 we went across to Germany to become part of the British

Army of the Rhine (BAOR) and we were stationed in the province of Schleswig-Holstein, on the map just below Denmark. 5 PARA went to Husum, on the west coast, where we occupied barracks built for the German Air Force. They were excellently designed and the whole place was built to a standard and equipped with facilities unknown in military establishments in Britain. We lived in style. The camp chores were all done by Germans and some of us kept horses. My Batman was a curious little gnome-like chap with big ears. He was a good servant and we got on well. He had come through the war unscathed, and he told me that of all the countries to which his Army service had taken him, the one he liked best was Bulgaria. 'The people there were very good to us Germans, and the fields and valleys of roses filled the air with perfume. A wonderful place.'

My job was to run a long course for training NCOs drawn from the whole brigade. This work was thoroughly rewarding, for the keenness of my Instructors and of our NCO pupils was excellent; the weather was good and we were very fit. The weeks flew by and our expeditions took us over to the Baltic coast and to the Plön area with its lakes and superb beech woods. It was one of the happiest periods of my life.

While with 5 PARA I had an extraordinary bit of luck. I record it in some detail as it is testimony to the helpfulness of two Military Policemen, the alertness of an RAF Sergeant, and to the honesty of a German civilian. I had been ordered to command a Guard of Honour for the C-in-C, General Sir Brian Robertson, in Hamburg, so Lieutenant Derek Willows and I travelled there by train with the soldiers who were to form the Guard. Coming back we had to get off the train at Schleswig station and complete the journey to Husum by lorry. It was a Sunday evening, and to kill time until the lorries arrived, we all went into the nearby Church of Scotland canteen where the doorman indicated that we should put our luggage in the cloakroom before entering the restaurant.

The building was crowded with Servicemen, mostly RAF types from the many airfields in that flat bit of Germany. When the time came for us to embus for Husum, Derek and I found that our luggage was missing. There was no trace of it in the building, nor could the doorman, a Pole whose knowledge of English was slight, give us a clue as to who might have removed our things. This was particularly vexing as our luggage contained our best and most expensive uniforms and certain prized possessions. In mine, a canvas bag with a zip-fastener opening, were my best kilt, tunic, Sam Brown belt, dress sporran, shirts, etc., and a Kodak camera. I told Derek to take the soldiers back to Husum while I stayed in Schleswig to search for the missing kit with the help of two Military Police NCOs who had by that time been summoned to the canteen. There was a chance that whoever had pinched our stuff might be spotted returning to their camp or barracks, so at the suggestion of the Police Sergeant, I was driven to several of the nearest airfields to alert the Guard Rooms where everyone who had been out of camp had to report back in before midnight. Before going on to the last of the airfields on the other side of the town, the MPs drove me to the barracks in Schleswig. They stood on the edge of a large lake, an inland sea really, formerly a sea-plane base, and in addition to housing our Brigade Headquarters and a variety of administrative units they contained a large building in which parachute troops slept before jumping early the next morning onto the Rendsburg DZ. This block, a sort of transit hotel, was constantly in use. I got out of the Police jeep and went over to the Guard Room where a long line of soldiers was filing through to report in. Standing alone near the Guard Room was an RAF NCO; in the half-light he looked familiar. It was Sergeant Rees who had got me through the parachute course the year before at Upper Heyford. I had no idea that he was in Germany. He greeted me warmly and I explained my preoccupation with the missing luggage.

Rees said: 'I'll stay here and keep my eyes on the blokes coming through this Guard Room while you go off with the Red Caps.' Half an hour later we got back to Schleswig after a fruitless journey. Sergeant Rees was waiting for us. 'It's not much to go on,' he said, 'But as I stood watching the dozens of men passing through here I noticed that two of them didn't keep hold of the cases they were carrying but left them outside the Guard Room until they had reported in. One of the cases looked a bit like the missing bag you had described to me.'

'Have you any idea of the unit those two men belong to?'

'Yes; they are both Parachute Gunners, probably from the Anti-Tank Battery since that lot's in here for the night as they are jumping tomorrow.'

'Right,' said the Military Police Sergeant, 'I know which rooms they are in. Leave this to us, Sir. I'll get a vehicle to run you back to Husum while the Corporal and I get on with our investigations here. I'm not optimistic, but I'll give you a ring tomorrow if we find anything which could belong to Mister Willows or you.'

Monday passed but no telephone call came. On Tuesday however: 'Sir, we went through the kits of all the men in that battery before they left Schleswig and one of them had in his possession a bit of red garter ribbon like what Scotsmen wear round their legs. Can you come over and identify it?'

It was indeed a garter flash from the uniform of a Highland soldier: it could be nothing else. I said: 'It is exactly the same as the two I wear and which were in the case with all my service dress. Where is the man whom you found with it?' 'We're holding him on suspicion as we believe he knows where the rest of your kit is.' I went to bed in Husum grateful to the MPs but not hopeful that I'd get my stuff back intact. Two days passed with no further news from the Police, but on the Friday I got a call from the Camp Commandant at Brigade HQ. 'Captain Graham? We think your kit has turned up. When can you come over to see the case and its contents?'

In his office was a very wet, stained, air-travel bag, and in it damp but unharmed were my missing things – kilt, sporran, tunic, shaving things, underwear – everything except the one garter flash and my Kodak camera.

'Yes, this is my case and these are my things. Where did you find them? How did the case get so wet?'

'Tomorrow, Saturday, is the Brigade Sports Competition and we've been getting the ground marked out and ready all week; and because we've had so little rain we've had to keep watering the running tracks. Yesterday one of our German labourers was pumping water out of the lake. His hose suddenly went dry so he went and found the end of his hose was blocked by your case. It must have been floating out there and been gradually sucked onto the end of the hose. The German saw that the case contained things belonging to a British soldier so he brought it straight into this office.'

I can no longer recall the name of that most honest German workman, but I rewarded him, adequately I hope. The temptation to keep for himself, in those days of post-war deprivation, articles such as my shaving kit, shirt, shoes and so on must have been great. The Gunner whom the MPs were holding eventually confessed. He had stolen the case, removed the camera and, for some strange reason, one of the red garters, and had flung the case far out into the lake. Luckily he had done up the zip-fastener opening, so it remained afloat. The camera he had concealed in his water-bottle and I got that back undamaged a few days later. He was tried by Court Martial and sent to prison. I am sorry to say that Derek Willow's luggage was never found, nor did the Police discover who had stolen it. The Gunner clearly knew but he would not tell.

There lodged in our barracks for several days a Captain and two soldiers of a Graves Registration Unit who had the task of identifying before burial the corpses which were still occasionally being washed up on the coast of Schleswig-Holstein. They were paid a special allowance for every day that they were actually in contact with dead bodies. When one of our chaps commiserated with the Captain on the pay cut he and his assistants had inevitably suffered because of the scarcity of corpses so long after the war, the latter waved a hand stained orange by nicotine saying, 'We've solved that problem. In a box in our 15-cwt truck we keep a dead seaman whom we have not yet managed to identify, and until we've worked out who he is and had him buried we can go on claiming the allowance with a clear conscience.'

While we were enjoying life in north Germany the wider European scene was darkening as tensions rose between the USSR and the three other Occupying Powers, Britain, France and the United States. Stalin's hostility towards the western democracies was becoming increasingly evident, and his determination to create a communist satellite empire in eastern Europe could no longer be disregarded. The milestones in the steady westward path of Soviet expansion into the heart of Europe were the Prague coup of February 1948, the Russian withdrawal from the Four-Power Government of Berlin, with the establishment by them of a separate administration in East Berlin, and the Soviet blockade of West Berlin which was frustrated at great expense and considerable fortitude by the Anglo-US Airlift. Two years later Communist North Korea was to attack South Korea. Winston Churchill had been right when, in his speech at Fulton, Missouri in 1946 he had drawn attention to the Iron Curtain which had descended across Europe from Stettin on the Baltic to Trieste on the Adriatic, dividing the democratic nations of western Europe from communist east Europe.

We soldiers in Husum were too preoccupied with our own regimental duties and private aspirations to pay much heed to all this evidence of Soviet antagonism which was now worrying politicians and diplomats. The Germans had been warning us, or such of us who sought opportunities to converse with them, of the Bolshevik menace and of the certainty of a Third World War, a fight to the death, between the Christian nations of the west and the Barbarians from the east, but we had tended to treat such talk as wishful thinking or sour grapes on the part of people smarting from their defeat by the Russians.

The blockade of Berlin opened our eyes and those of us who, like me, had a chance to fly along the Air-bridge, the *Luftbrücke*, realised the grim situation into which the Russians had deliberately placed the Berliners and the Allied contingents in the city, and the scale of the air operation which had to be mounted and sustained for eleven months to keep Berlin free and her 2½ million inhabitants alive. I flew with a Dakota-load of coal from RAF Wunsdorf to Berlin-Gatow; but I was to become more deeply affected by the events in Central Europe when the War Office issued a letter requiring Officers who had a knowledge of east European languages or who were willing to learn them, to offer themselves for special employment. From Cheltenham I had planned to go to Oxford with a view to entering the Diplomatic Service and had therefore in my studies concentrated on French, German and Spanish to the exclusion of maths and science; and during the months between leaving College in May 1940 and joining the Army in September 1941, I had begun to learn Russian with the aid of a 'Teach Yourself' primer. In Husum I had been introduced to the elderly wife of a local Pastor and had persuaded her to give me lessons in Russian, her native tongue.

Palestine and Parachuting

Thus when I read the War Office letter I could truthfully claim to have some acquaintance with that language. To learn Russian was not the main reason for my volunteering for a change of job. The RAF transport aircraft were now fully committed to the Air-lift and none could be spared for parachute training or airborne exercises. In addition to being grounded, we learned that our beloved 6th Airborne Division was soon to be reduced to a single Parachute Brigade. This reduction was to involve the amalgamation of the existing parachute battalions, the 5th Scottish forming the 2nd Battalion of the new 16th Independent Parachute Brigade Group. Parsimony and retrenchment were to be the immediate lot of the serving soldier.

The Colonel took the view, given the circumstances of the day, that I might be of greater use to the nation working in an Embassy, where the custom of relying on local-born men and women for daily contact with the citizenry could no longer be permitted. Communist blackmail and pressures, and threats against their relatives, had placed such employees in jeopardy and rendered them no longer reliable in British eyes. They were now unacceptable security risks; hence the appeal for commissioned Officers with a bent for languages to replace them. So with the CO's blessing I filled in the form stating my qualifications and agreeing to be taught Russian with, as my second choice, Czech. I knew little about Czechoslovakia apart from what I had read in the newspapers during the Munich crisis of 1938, and of their language I knew nothing except that it is akin to Bulgarian, Russian, Polish and Serbo-Croat. However, at Fernden with me had been two boys from that country and I quite liked them. They were in fact Sudeten Germans, but no matter; they were a link with Czechoslovakia, so I had put down Czech.

The application was speedily accepted, and by early October I was back in London, enrolled at the School of Slavonic Studies in Russell Square and living in a tiny room at the top of a cheap hotel in the Cromwell Road, then known throughout south-west London as 'The Polish Corridor' on account of the many East Europeans who had settled there at the end of the war rather than return to their own countries, now Soviet satellites.

My Father, recently returned from Egypt, had a job at the War Office and lived in a boarding house in nearby Courtfield Gardens, so I was able to get to know him after a pretty unbroken fifteen years of separation.

Note

1. Returned to (parent) unit.

CHAPTER V
1948–1952
Four Czech Years

The School of Slavonic Studies is an impressive building in London's Russell Square. There were only two of us in the Czech class, Dudley Thornton, a Captain in the Welch Regiment, and me. Our studies at the school finished at one o'clock, but we still had hours of homework ahead of us for Czech like all Slavonic languages has a complex grammar and some sounds unused by English tongues. It is often said, and I am sure there is truth in the maxim, that foreign languages are easiest and most agreeably learned on the pillow. Alas neither married Dudley in Bromley nor I in my garret in No 127 Cromwell Road could enjoy that facility, so we found the Czech language hard going.

That was not the fault of our teacher who knew intimately the structure of her native tongue and the complexities of its syntax, and whose grasp of English enabled her to explain everything with lucidity and wit.

Marketa Slonkova was a delicate, brisk, bird-like woman in her late thirties with large horn-rimmed glasses and a lump of a teenage son named Bob. Mr Slonek, from whom she was long divorced, was seldom mentioned, but from the remarks she occasionally let drop it was clear that she had had a pretty unenviable life in Central Europe from the day the Germans marched into the Republic in March 1939 until the summer of 1946 when she and Bob came to Britain. She was Jewish in appearance but no longer, she said, by faith; sanctuary in Clapham where she rented a small flat had however made her fervently pro-British. Dudley and I got to like her very much, and to admire her, and we applied ourselves assiduously to our studies not least to make her happy and to demonstrate that her efforts and kindnesses were appreciated.

Other students we met only on the stairs or in the lavatories, for Dudley and I had no occasion to use any of the canteens or public rooms. Mme Slonkova did however introduce us to another Instructor with whom she was on close terms. He was an interesting man – Mann was his name – for he was one of the few Englishmen well acquainted with Albania, that once-Moslem republic of mountains, forests and Balkan brigands which in 1946 had embraced atheism and its own rabid form of Communism. Of Professor Mann two things were claimed.

Before the Italians occupied the country in April 1939 he was the representative in Tirana, the capital, of the British Council. He decided to illuminate his house with electricity and to that end procured a generator. The nearby Palace had only candles and oil lamps until Mann by a kindly act ran an extra cable from his machine across the gardens and roads so as to brighten the lives of King Zog and his pretty Queen Geraldine. It was also said that Professor Mann possessed the largest intact collection of books written in Albanian, so many having been destroyed by the Turkish rulers who had proscribed the use of the Albanian language and customs.

Our stay in London and our studies with Mme Slonkova ended in July 1949. The next stage of our tuition began, learning to speak and understand Czech as spoken by the man in the street. Dudley Thornton went to Paris to live with an émigré Czech family. I was, the War Office stated, more fortunate as I was to be attached for a year to the British Embassy in Prague where I arrived in August 1949 by the Orient Express from Paris.

Czechoslovakia came into existence as an independent state only in 1918 after the break-up of the Austro-Hungarian empire. It consisted originally of the Bohemian crownlands, Moravia and Slovakia; to the latter the victorious Allies added in 1919 a slice of Ruthenia. Besides the related Czech and Slovak peoples, the new country included substantial minorities, chiefly Germans and Hungarians. But despite the problems of welding into one nation such a mixed group of peoples, the Czechoslovak Republic made great political and economic progress under the leadership of Thomas Masaryk, a Moravian of humble birth. He was President from 1918 until 1935 when he handed over to his disciple and friend Eduard Beneš. The rise of Hitler to power in Germany and the economic conditions plaguing Europe in the thirties spurred the minority groups in Czechoslovakia into making increasing demands for autonomy or for reincorporation into their former motherlands. These demands were amplified and distorted by anti-Czech propaganda agencies and their foreign controllers.

The role of Konrad Henlein and the Sudeten German element in undermining the authority of the Prague government and in promoting Hitler's aggressive plans is well documented, but other minorities such as the Poles and Hungarians had their own 'little Henleins' active during that period.

Eduard Beneš was unable to withstand these pressures. Moreover he was not supported by those very Allies who had brought his country into existence twenty years earlier; France, Britain, Italy and the United States.

The abandonment of Czechoslovakia by the French and British was born out of their dread of another Great War in Europe; of their military weakness viewed against the forces of the Axis Powers, Germany, Italy and ultimately of Japan also; and of misplaced faith in the effectiveness of the League of Nations and the doctrine of Collective Security. All these factors were humiliatingly demonstrated in September 1938 when Britain and France, without consulting Beneš and his people, signed away to Hitler substantial areas of Czech territory, areas important to the Czech economy and vital to her defence. By capitulating to Hitler at Munich the Prime Ministers of France and Great Britain, Daladier and Chamberlain, deferred for twelve months the outbreak of war with Germany, and during that period of respite those two countries were able to repair some of the grave deficiencies in their Armed Forces. This proved to be of cardinal importance to the effectiveness of the Royal Air Force in the Battle of Britain in 1940. Winston Churchill and others, however, have stated their belief that the Wehrmacht used that year to greater advantage; furthermore, that by encompassing at Munich the emasculation of the Czechoslovak nation, Britain and France cast aside the potential of the Czech Army. Well trained and positioned along strong natural and artificial defences, it would have been a most substantial asset in a conflict with Germany; undoubtedly a greater asset than the Polish Army was to prove in September 1939.

Six months after Munich German Forces occupied the whole country thereby gaining for Hitler's Reich all the industrial and agricultural resources of the Republic, together with its war-making potential. Bohemia and Moravia were converted into a German Protectorate; Slovakia became autonomous, allied to and dominated by Nazi Germany.

The principal benefit gained from the Munich agreement was that Hitler by invading Czechoslovakia in March 1939 was seen by the world to have broken a pledge there given by him to France and Britain. By that outrage the fundamental justness of the Allied cause in the Second World War against Germany was shown to be incontestable and was so acknowledged by the bulk of the human race.

The Czechs and Slovaks endured six years of German occupation until May 1945 when they were liberated by the Red Army advancing from the East.

A strong contingent of the US Army had already entered Bohemia but was prevented by the Roosevelt-Stalin agreement at Yalta from driving on to Prague. That ancient and beautiful city was in consequence destined to languish within the Communist Empire for more than forty years.

Old Prague is one of the architectural gems of Europe, lying with her eleven bridges astride the River Vltava and dominated by the hill on which stand the Cathedral of Saint Vitus and the Hradčany Palace.

The newer suburbs of factories and workers' tenements are by contrast purely functional and very ugly. I am told that those drab, charmless, concrete constructions were characteristic of all industrial areas in Communist states. In 1949 however the two Pragues, the ancient Christian and the modern Socialist, had one thing in common: decay. No building, however precious or interesting, was cared for. This neglect might have been excusable during the years of German occupation and war, but its continuance under a peacetime Czech government was less pardonable. The people too had the same greyish, decaying appearance. Food, petrol and clothing were strictly rationed and the war-time privations and the disciplines imposed on the population by the Germans were now replaced by those imposed on the Czechs and Slovaks by their own government, and also by the class warfare being waged on behalf of the Workers against the Bourgeoisie, the Liberals and the Imperialists; a war in which the Secret Police (the StB) and the armed Peoples' Militia were the ubiquitous evidence.

The Czechoslovak Communist Party had seized power in February 1948. This coup d'état had been planned some months before by Klement Gottwald, the Party's General Secretary, during clandestine meetings in the Kremlin and was invested with a degree of legality by an election process in which the voters were over-awed by the combined forces of the Socialists and Communists, backed by Soviet money and tactical direction, whereas the Conservatives and Liberals in government, parliament and among the masses of the electorate were subjected to harassment, intimidation and restrictions on their use of the media. Furthermore the Police and the Army, by tradition looked to for ensuring fair play and the curbing of the more blatant electoral excesses, were confined to barracks, isolated from the squares and streets where the campaign for the votes of the people was being conducted. The Minister of Defence, General Ludvik Svoboda, who had thereby made a significant contribution to the Communists' victory, had not long before been made a KBE by the King of England.

Few Czechs or Slovaks fully understood the significance of that February coup or foresaw that they would for forty-two years be ruled by an immovable left-wing government and bound militarily, economically and culturally to the Soviet Union. Jan Masaryk, Foreign Minister in the defeated Cabinet and son of the country's great first President, understood; but he was soon to die beneath a high window from which he had jumped in a deliberate act of suicide, or, as many Czechs whispered, from which he had been pushed by agents of the new regime.

The western democracies, resigned to the incorporation into the empire of Joseph Stalin of east European capitals such as Sofia, Bucharest and even Warsaw, were dismayed that Czechoslovakia with her liberal westernised culture and traditions should have been duped into following the same path. With hindsight we can now state that the two events which most clearly demonstrated the malevolence of the USSR were the Prague coup of 1948 and the Russian blockade of West Berlin. This awareness and the anxiety it engendered in the west brought about the Western European

Union and soon after the great defensive alliance of the North Atlantic Powers, designed to contain the huge armed forces of the Soviet bloc. NATO's steadfastness was rewarded in the final decade of the century by the collapse of the Communist system in Eastern Europe.

The British Embassy occupied a fine building in old Prague; in Thunovska, a narrow street at the foot of the Hradčany Hill and not far from the famous Charles Bridge. The Ambassador, Sir Pierson Dixon, was to end his career as British Representative at the Headquarters of the United Nations. He and his handsome Greek wife headed the small British community and defended British interests in Czechoslovakia with skill and charm. They were highly respected and popular. He had the unenviable task of trying to interpret to Whitehall the actions of the new Czech government and to forecast what its members and their overlords in Moscow might do next. I was slotted into the office of the Military Attaché, Francis Blake, a large, jovial bachelor Gunner Colonel. The Assistant Attaché was a Cavalry Officer, Guy Wheeler. Also in that office was a young Warrant Officer in the Royal Army Service Corps, Alex Blair. I was to work closely with him during my ten months in Prague; we became friends and have remained in touch to this day.

I had not before worked in a diplomatic environment and was soon struck by one feature of Embassy life very different to that which I had experienced in the Army. It is a British military tradition that the Officers should care for their Soldiers' families; help them with their problems of housing, health, finance and so on. Man-management and paternalism are given a high priority and the British Army is proud of the relationships between ranks and the family spirit ingrained in our Regiments and Corps. I was therefore surprised to find in our Prague Embassy, even though it was headed by eminent Officers of the Foreign Service, a marked gulf between the upper and the lower echelons of the staff. Although everyone worked closely and harmoniously in working hours, the senior diplomats seemed to take little interest in their subordinates' lives off-duty or to be aware of their living conditions, pastimes or problems. Maybe in the Foreign Service, with its high intellectual standards and emphasis on foreign personalities and affairs, everyone was expected to be self-sufficient and capable of looking after themselves. Of some, posted to a country behind the Iron Curtain, this was asking too much.

On the small staff of the British Council in Prague was an English girl. She held a junior position, was physically unattractive and she was lonely. She felt, she was to exclaim, neglected by her superiors at work and ignored by her compatriots during her leisure hours. By 1949 however it was no longer possible to ignore her, for her picture was seen in every Czech newspaper together with a list of allegations she had made to the authorities about espionage, subversion and other activities hostile to the Czechoslovak peoples being carried out by British officials in the Embassy and Council. Lonely and neglected by her compatriots, she had been targetted by the Czech Secret Service, deliberately befriended and in due course seduced by one of its agents. In consequence she was willing to confirm all the anti-British stories concocted by her lover and his controllers.

The first sign of Czech hostility towards Britain and the western democracies had been the persecution of those many Czechs who had returned home having fought the war in or alongside our Armed Forces. The witch-hunt conducted by the Communists against these patriots was nation-wide and remorseless. All who were suspected of 'imperialist attitudes' or who had past associations with the West were deprived of their jobs and liberty. Most monstrous of all, the doyen of the returned Servicemen, General Pika, was put to death[1]. In this virulent anti-western programme the Czech government was, of course, complying with instructions issued in Moscow. Nevertheless it did not seem to me that the ordinary Czech man or woman objected to this xenophobic campaign. Betrayed by the French and British in 1938 at Munich, and liberated in 1945 at great cost in Russian lives by the Red Army, the Czech people in general appeared to despise, or at least to distrust, the West European nations and their American allies. By contrast they felt towards Marshal Stalin and the USSR genuine admiration and gratitude; also a Slavonic kinship. Furthermore the Czechs reckoned that, being more intelligent and civilised than Russians, they could at any time bamboozle the latter and escape at will from the clutches of the Russian bear.

The attitude of the Czech population to the Germans I never understood. That the Germans had committed some atrocious acts during the six years of the Protectorate was undeniable, and the execution or imprisonment of war criminals in the immediate post-war years, and the expulsion from Czech soil of thousands of men and women of German blood were inevitable and justified.

But the Czechs had not as a whole suffered deeply from German oppression and bestiality. By comparison with those who lived in German-occupied Poland and Russia, the Czechs had had an enviable wartime experience. 'Provided,' some told me, 'you were not a Jew and obeyed all the regulations, life was quite good. There was plenty of work in the factories and farms, the Germans paid good money, the streets were kept clean and the trains ran on time; there was little crime and, very important, there was no fighting on Czech soil until 1945.'

Even of Obergruppenführer Reinhard Heydrich, that Nazi tyrant appointed by Hitler Protector of Bohemia and Moravia, Czech memories were, to me, sometimes surprisingly forgiving. One woman recounted to me at length how Heydrich met his death at the hands of a group of Czech parachutists despatched from England expressly to kill him.

Ambushed in late May 1942 while routinely driving without an escort on his daily journey from his residence to his Headquarters in Prague, he 'handsome, blond and immaculate in his uniform, for twenty minutes put up a magnificent fight before expiring'. The extraordinarily ambivalent attitude of some Czechs towards that most evil German and others of his race can perhaps be better understood when one remembers two things. The eight Czech soldiers who carried out this assassination of Heydrich were themselves soon betrayed and perished; and when in 1950 I visited with Alex Blair the ruins of Lidice, the Bohemian village reduced to rubble in June 1942 and whose entire male population was massacred by the SS as a reprisal[2] for Heydrich's death, the sole monument to tell of that atrocity carried out by Germans against Czechs had been erected by Russian soldiers. The Czech contribution to the memory of Lidice was the provision of a car-park and a coffee bar for visiting sightseers.

As seems to happen in the development of all revolutionary movements, the Communist Party began to devour its own members, and a number of veterans, heroes of the class-struggle, were put on trial charged with various aspects of what the Marxist-Leninists classed as heresy: deviation from the Party line, religious worship, consorting with agents of the western nations, anti-Soviet statements, and such like. The most prominent of these Czech victims was Rudolf Slansky. A Jew and convinced Communist of long standing and of proven devotion to the Party creed, he nevertheless signed the confession which inevitably led him to the gallows. Slansky's show trial was watched with close attention by the western Powers and our own Embassy was keen to assess the mood of the ordinary Czech towards Slansky and his co-defendants as opposed to the vitriolic and biased articles in *Rude Pravo* and the rest of the media. Because I was then about the only chap in the Embassy who spoke the language, I was briefed by the Head of Chancery one Saturday to make myself inconspicuous and to attend the next day a rally organised in one of the city's parks by the Party to 'express the peoples' hatred for the traitor Slansky and his accomplices'. Having done what I could to dress like an impecunious foreign student, I made my way to the park and inserted myself in the flank of a large crowd, composed mostly of middle-aged men and women, who were being addressed by a series of youths and girls, several wearing the uniform of the Communist Youth Organisation. After about half an hour the speakers ceased their ranting and their leader shouted out the question: 'What do you want done with Slansky and his like?' The reply was immediate and seemed to me to come from the mouth of every person in that crowd of ordinary, commonplace, conventional citizens. 'Hang them, hang them!' was the response. At that moment I realised that to conform, to go along with the prevailing current, is the instinctive act of a human being. Courageous and rare are those who remain firm in their beliefs and do not waver in their loyalties. Peter, in denying Christ, could not, being human and until that moment untested in his faith, have acted otherwise. Peter was to redeem himself a few years later; the men and women of Czechoslovakia did not do so fully until 1989 when they threw off the yoke which the Party had imposed on them four decades earlier. While in that park, I did not hear anyone specifically link Slansky with British institutions or personalities. When I reported to the Ambassador he seemed to draw some comfort from this.

Each year since 1945 the liberation of the country from German rule had been celebrated in early May throughout the land by large military parades and other festivities. The main celebrations were of course held in the capital and to these were invited the chief personalities of friendly nations including, in 1949, representatives of the western democracies. Invitations to view the parades were much sought after for they gave service attachés a rare opportunity to observe the Czech Forces and their equipment at close quarters.

In 1950, however, the Czech government decreed that all officials of western countries would be excluded from the events: no invitations and no reserved seats. This was a sign of the times and not wholly unexpected. A plan was therefore concocted within the Embassy to ensure that the military parade would nevertheless be covered from a variety of vantage points. At the time I was living in the flat of an elderly widow on the Belcredi Avenue, far from the areas where the parade was to assemble and march. I was therefore told to go to a part of Prague called Letna and from the apartment of one of the Embassy secretaries watch the contingents as they formed up in the broad street below. Thus on the eve of the parade I walked from the Embassy to the Consulate building on Waldstejnska Street, had supper and generally killed time before setting out for my one-night-stand in Letna.

Catching a tram in Prague was simple. All one had to do was stand on one of the many raised concrete islands positioned in the middle of the road and step into the first tram going in the desired direction.

Klarov Square was in reality a large open triangle with on one side the River Vltava, on the second side a large area of grass with clumps of bushes and shrubs beyond which stood a large block of flats, and on the side nearest to the Consulate a continuous line of houses, shops, garages and such like flanked the carriageway winding up to the summit of Hradčany Hill.

It was already dark when I left the Consulate and crossed the road onto the Klarov tramstop and stood, wearing a duffle-coat – for the nights were still chilly – and clutching a canvas bag containing my pyjamas, toothbrush and camera. But no tram came. Not a single car moved along that normally busy road. All was silent and still. Standing in the middle of the road under the bright electric lamp I felt alone in the world. But as my eyes became adapted to the darkness I discerned to my left movement on the pavements leading up the hill, among the bushes to my right and under the bridge and along the river-bank behind me. The movement was of men, standing about in groups as if waiting for a signal. A figure strode towards me across the grass: it was a Lieutenant in the Police, the SNB. He was coming to remove me from my conspicuous isolation in the middle of the road, but before he could do so a motorcycle roared up from behind, stopped briefly between us and the uniformed rider shouted to the Police Officer: 'Look out, they're coming!' or some such warning. The Lieutenant, his attention diverted from me, blew a whistle, whereupon the dim figures I had noticed on all sides moved rapidly into the open and lined both sides of the highway from the bridge behind me all the way up the hill, as far as my eyes could see. Most were in uniform and armed; some were in plain clothes. I remained, a solitary young foreigner holding a canvas bag on a brightly lit platform in the middle of the road. Almost immediately the procession began to pass me.

There were two columns of black civilian limousines with armoured cars at the head and tail of each column. The columns passed, one behind and one in front of me as I stood under my lamp. I could see quite clearly into each vehicle; indeed I could have touched them with my hand.

In the first was the President, Gottwald, with Madame Bulganina, wife of the senior Soviet delegate; next rode Martha Gottwaldova, the President's wife (known to her compatriots as 'the Gasometer' on account of her size), with beside her Marshal Bulganin easily recognised by his trim white beard. Then members of the Czech government, their wives, the Soviet Ambassador, followed by Hungarians, Poles, Indo-Chinese, Generals, assorted moguls from the fraternal socialist countries and more Czechs. They had, for it was part of the annual Liberation Day ritual, been to the National Theatre on the far side of the river to see Smetana's opera 'The Bartered Bride' and the performance over, they were being conveyed to a reception in the Hradčany Palace. The police had cleared every person and every vehicle off the processional route but I, quite fortuitously, had slipped into the middle of the road and remained there, a most interested observer. Standing in the turret of the last vehicle, an armoured car, was an SNB Colonel. I have never forgotten the look of anger on his face as he hatless, balding and perspiring, caught sight of me. As Francis Blake remarked the next day when I told him of my unexpected encounter: 'What a pity your case contained only pyjamas and a toothbrush. A few grenades might have done the world a useful service.'

The Czech government's attitude greatly reduced our working relationships with their officials and, combined with the language barrier, limited our scope for establishing the sort of friendships which normally spring up in a country between natives and visitors; between hosts and guests.

This had the happy effect of drawing the westerners together into a circle of warm intimacy and social solidarity. As might have been expected the British, Canadians and the Americans supported each other generously and by entertaining, arranging picnics, film shows and the occasional full-dress Ball, made a significant contribution to the well-being and morale of our nationals. The Belgians and Italians also became enthusiastic members of that cheerful community of 'reactionary Imperialists' in Prague.

The Communist hierarchy nevertheless seemed happy enough to be entertained in our Embassies. We were no longer permitted to invite, say, an individual Minister by name: indeed to have done so would have placed him under suspicion. The procedure required us to inform the Ministry of Foreign Affairs of the details of the function and of the number and status of the Czechs we wished to entertain. The Ministry and the Party Secretariat selected the appropriate individuals and usually, but not always, let us know who was coming. To maintain Party vigilance they normally sent a trio.

At our 1950 reception to mark the birthday of King George VI two such worthies spent most of the time at the buffet unashamedly filling both their mouths and their pockets, and on their departure, while thanking the Ambassador for 'the very enjoyable afternoon' the senior Czech added the whispered plea: 'And could you let me have five hundred cigarettes?'

I do not recall any of us having overt contacts with the Armed Forces, so the facts we needed to keep up to date our assessment of their readiness for war, possible roles and the extent to which the Russians could in time of war depend on them, had to be gleaned from other sources. One of the difficulties we faced in identifying units was that they were not, as in Britain, designated as, say, the 5th Tank Regiment or Fighter Squadron 201. Czech units were allotted cover numbers, a seemingly random jumble of four digits, and solely by these were units mentioned in the Press, be it to be praised for good work on manoeuvres or in a provincial football match.

The newspaper which habitually contained the most references to the Armed Forces and their chief personalities was *Obrana Lidu* (The People's Defence). One of my tasks was to mark the articles of interest and produce translations. We suspected that the cover numbers were based on a simple transposition code: crack the code and the identification of each unit by Arm and formation would be revealed. Thus the first thing I did on studying each new issue of *Obrana Lidu* was to ring with a blue crayon every cover number that caught my eye. In this way we built up a large collection of cover numbers. The papers were kept locked away, for we worked on the assumption that the woman who cleaned our offices, Mme Zemanova, was also employed by the StB. In early 1950 Alex Blair and I spent a couple of days at Harrochov watching the ski-jumping contest. On our return I found that pages of *Obrana Lidu*, with my markings, were being used as toilet paper in the office loo. The supply of proper paper had run out and a newcomer to the staff had in desperation taken pages of *Obrana Lidu* out of the cupboard. Our assumption about the role of Mme Zemanova seemed to be confirmed for, from the following week onward, far fewer cover numbers appeared in that newspaper.

Six months earlier, in October 1949, Alex and I had spent four days travelling round the country by train. We went first to the easternmost part of the country, where Slovakia adjoins the Ukraine in the foothills of the Carpathian Mountains. From Prague we took the southern route which followed the frontiers with Austria and Hungary, via Brno, the chief town of Moravia, and stopping overnight at Bratislava, the capital of Slovakia, lying on the wide River Danube with its disappointing brown and unromantic water. Our return trip followed the frontiers with Poland and the Democratic Republic of (East) Germany. The principal object of our expedition was to see what work was being done to increase the capacity of the railways running from the Soviet Union westward through Czechoslovakia, and to discover if any new military installations were being constructed in those mountain valleys. From Bratislava eastwards the train was pretty empty, and to the few travellers who came into our compartment we indicated that we were students from Scotland engaged on a geography project. As the train passed each new railway construction or new-looking barracks we took notes and photographs. This involved us making in turn unnaturally frequent visits to the lavatory. The transparency of our actions caused an old farmer as he left the train at some small rural station to mutter to the other man in our compartment: 'Some students!' Finding himself alone with Alex and me, the latter, a middle-aged and well educated fellow, became quite animated, declaring himself to be a Slovak patriot who detested equally Czech Communists and Soviet Bolsheviks. For the next hour or so, as the train trundled eastwards, he told us about the places we passed and the work being done to improve the railway and to modernise the military installations in his homeland. In fact this activity did not amount to very much, but nevertheless it all went into our notebook. Our informative fellow-traveller parted from us in high spirits at Košice, a railway junction about forty miles from the frontier with the USSR. But when we got to our hotel the notebook was missing. This was an alarming discovery and we jumped to the conclusion that our helpful companion, having gulled us with his anti-Communist talk, had in the darkness stolen the book while the unlit train was moving through a very long tunnel on the approach to Košice.

We anticipated early arrest and accusations of espionage. But, we reflected, it was just possible that the notebook had not been stolen; I might have mislaid it on the train. There was only one way to find out. It was nearly midnight when I walked back to the station and I located without difficulty the sidings on which several trains stood, empty and silent. After about ten minutes examining the carriages I found the very compartment in which we had travelled. Under my seat, in the litter of the past day, the notebook lay intact. Breathing prayers of thankfulness I made my way back to the hotel to a rejoicing Alex and to a few hours of relieved sleep. I still marvel that I was never challenged during my groping round the sidings. Young foreigners are not, in Communist countries, normally allowed to prowl by night round such places as key railway junctions.

The next morning we moved on to Poprad, a small town in the Tatra Mountains, close to the frontier and some seventy miles south of the Polish city of Krakow. It was a Sunday, the day was fine with clear blue skies and a gentle autumn breeze, so we decided to get as high up into the mountains as we could to enjoy the views which the hotel owner told us were marvellous. The dominating peak in that area of the High Tatras is Gerlach. Some nine thousand feet above sea-level it had recently been renamed Stalin's Emblem (*Stalinuv Stit*) in honour of the great Soviet Liberator. This expression of adulation was fully justified for the Dukla Pass, the battlefield where the Red Army had fought its way into Slovakia, suffering enormous losses at the hands of the Germans, was not far from Poprad in the north-east corner of the country. The summit of Gerlach still had patches of last winter's snow and in any case was accessible only to climbers who were properly equipped and clothed. We were not, so we went by bus to the foot of a sister-peak, Lomnicky Stit, only slightly lower than Gerlach, where a narrow-gauge railway took us about halfway up, the rest of the ascent being by *lanovka*, a cable-car. This *lanovka* carried us high over the dense pine forests which covered much of the lower slopes of the Tatras, and through which few footpaths ran. The whole of this bit of Slovakia looked wild, rarely visited by humans and, except in the valleys, uninhabited. We left the *lanovka* and walked the last few hundred metres to the top. Alex and I had taken careful note of the time at which the last car would leave the summit: the timetable was clearly printed and the Sunday schedule shown separately. A few sightseers had come up with us on the railway to the halfway point but in our ascent by cable-car we were alone. I was surprised to find, sitting on a rock on the highest pinnacle of our peak, a solitary Norwegian girl; and I was even more surprised to see that her trousers were made of the distinctive tartan of my Highland regiment. After a brief conversation with us she wandered off leaving Alex and me to gaze at the views on that clear autumn afternoon: Poland a few miles to the north; behind us, in Slovakia, the mountains of the Lower Tatra range; far to the east of us the Carpathians with the Ukraine to their rear; and to the west, invisible to our eyes, the lower lands of Moravia and Bohemia. We remained up there, moving from view-point to view-point and taking photographs, for over an hour before walking down in good time to catch the last cable-car. But not a soul was there and the machinery was silent and motionless. The operators had assumed that everyone had left the summit and had, it being Sunday, switched off the engine and gone home early. The sun was already going down behind the surrounding peaks and a cold wind blew up. There was no moon and we had no torch; nor were we dressed for a long descent on foot through pine woods and over rocks in pitch darkness. But there was no alternative. We set off down the mountain-side following as best we could the line of the cable system above us. As the night grew colder and darker we heard growls and barks of wild animals and we discussed what we should do if confronted by a bear or wolves. But we encountered nothing and no one. The last but longest part of our walk was easier for we moved down the track of the mountain railway, stepping clumsily from sleeper to sleeper. We reached the valley after, I suppose, some three hours, found a taxi and got back to Poprad footsore and exhilarated but too late for supper in the hotel restaurant.

The next day we spent travelling back to Prague along the railway which ran through the northern regions of the country stopping at nineteen stations before coming to rest in the capital. We neither saw nor experienced anything of note during this final leg of our expedition and we were quite glad to get back into the familiar atmosphere and routine of Embassy life.

During the summer of 1950 relations between East and West deteriorated further and we believed that in the Soviet satellite states a fresh campaign of intrigue, intimidation and harassment against western institutions and individuals behind the Iron Curtain was being prepared. During my secondment to the Prague Embassy I held only a supernumerary appointment, had no diplomatic passport nor the protection that fully accredited members of the Embassy enjoyed. Furthermore, if HMG should expel from Britain a Czech or other East European official, it was to be expected that the Eastern bloc would retaliate by making life difficult for British citizens in positions like mine. After consultations between the Ambassador and Whitehall it was decided that I should return to England two months earlier than originally planned. I learned of this decision with some relief for I had, amongst other reasons, come to the conclusion that scope for bettering my fluency in spoken Czech was less than if I had gone to live with an émigré family in Paris, as my colleague Dudley Thornton had done, or in London where there was a sizeable Czech community. Also I was yearning to get away from the overheated and melancholy Belcredi apartment and the widow's unattractive meals.

There were other reasons for my relief at going home. To help me learn the language I had been put in touch soon after my arrival with an elderly Franco-Jewish couple. They left Prague before the end of 1949 but before they moved they introduced me to a Czech girl, twenty years old, very blond and strikingly pretty. Eva Robachova was the daughter of a former industrialist and the family was now classed as 'bourgeois enemies of the people'. I do not know what they had done to be so censured and I was surprised by the vehemence with which my landlady condemned them, for I found Eva's parents to be gentle and considerate to all. They kept a low profile and seldom left their attractive small house halfway up the Hradčin Hill.

Our Air Attaché had a Swedish wife. She was fond of Eva who from time to time looked after her children and she did much to encourage Eva and me in a relationship from which I should emerge as a proficient linguist coached by my attractive and well educated blond. I came to realise that the Swede's intentions extended beyond that. She saw in me a means of getting Eva away from her rather hopeless life behind the Iron Curtain, with a British passport and the protection she would enjoy if wed to a Briton. The Swede had planted in Eva's mind hopes along those lines as she knew that some Czech women had got out of that country by contracting marriages with kindhearted men in the British and other West European communities in Prague. But I had been left in no doubt concerning British official views about East European liaisons, so one evening I had to tell Eva as gently as I could that marriage was for the two of us an impossibility. This was one of the most disagreeable things I have had to do, for she was a lovely person and I was apprehensive about her future under Communist rule.

The acting Head of the British Council in Prague, Rene Burrow, and his vivacious French wife Andrée, had taken me under their wing and showered me with hospitality in their spacious apartment conveniently close to the Embassy and, a particular treat, took me with them at weekends when they and their friends went up to Pec, a hamlet in the Krkonoše Mountains where the borders of the German Democratic Republic, Poland and Czechoslovakia joined. There we learned to ski the hard way – for there were no instructors – to drink beer, and to chat with Czechs from Prague whom we knew by sight but who during the week did not wish or even dare to smile at us. In the snow and mountain air everyone shed the political inhibitions and conventions of the capital, relaxed, became more human and laughed together. Those days in Pec were God-sent: good for the soul and essential for the body. My skiing has never amounted to much but my French came on marvellously. The Burrows and I remained in close touch for several more years until they were posted to the Far East and I returned to Scotland for a spell of regimental duty.

A further reason why I was glad to get back to Britain was a medical one. I had been feeling increasingly run-down, depressed and thoroughly below par. It was the autumn of 1951 before I discovered the cause.

The process of getting away from Czechoslovakia was not entirely straightforward as a number of forms had to be completed certifying all manner of things; and to ensure that I took out of the country no more currency or articles than I had brought in the previous year, I had to spend a whole morning helping two uniformed members of the Customs Service to write down meticulously the description of every bit of clothing, books, toilet gear and so on as I placed it in my suitcases. I left Prague by train on 20 June after an all-night session of drinking and talking with Francis Blake.

I had an uneventful journey back home and joined my family in the Isle of Wight, stopping only for a few interesting hours amid the tragic ruins of bombed Nurnberg and a couple of days in Versailles. I got back in time to visit at Winchester my brother, Alastair, then Head of his House but about to become the senior Prefect of the College, and to watch, with many of my regimental friends and Old Comrades, King George presenting the first Colours to the three Regular battalions of The Parachute Regiment on the Queen's Parade in Aldershot. It was a memorable ceremony, impeccably carried through and brilliantly recorded by Terence Cuneo in the large oil painting which hangs to this day in the Regimental Headquarters Officers' Mess.

In July 1950 I was taken on by the Intelligence community and on posting to MI8, the branch which handled Signals Intelligence (SIGINT), was sent to work in GCHQ (Government Communications Headquarters). This large and important organisation had its genesis during the Great War of 1914-18 in Admiralty Room OB40, and its contribution to the Allied victory in the Second World War, through its skill in intercepting, decrypting and analysing Axis radio transmissions in its huts at Bletchley Park, was outstanding.

GCHQ has long been established in Cheltenham, but in my time it was located in West London, at Eastcote. I joined a very small team of men and women, all civilians, whose job it was to translate and assess the material which came to GCHQ from the Royal Signals Intercept Unit in Cyprus and from United States sources.

The material on which we worked throughout my twenty-two months with MI8 were radio messages between the Headquarters and the dispersed units of a single large section of the Czechoslovak Armed Forces. These messages had been transmitted in a low-grade cipher but were decrypted before reaching our room in the form of Czech language plain texts. The quantity of the messages we received was great; the quality, however, varied greatly and many contained corrupt or unintelligible portions. Nevertheless, within a few months of working on this stuff, we had acquired an extensive knowledge of that bit of the Czech Armed Forces; the location of every sub-unit and the names of most of the Officers and of many senior NCOs. Moreover, two of us, working on my Prague theory about unit cover numbers, succeeded in figuring out the elementary substitution system on which they were based. This was especially gratifying since we achieved it ahead of our more numerous American colleagues who were working on the same material on the other side of the Atlantic.

Secrecy and silence were fundamentals of life in GCHQ. Our little group worked in isolation from all others. We had no knowledge of what went on in other rooms in that labyrinth of corridors at Eastcote, nor did we ever seek to know. Before any recruit to GCHQ was initiated into the work and methods of the SIGINT world, a vow of secrecy was taken and solemn declarations signed. Furthermore, no visits during a period of five years after joining GCHQ were permitted to any place where there was a risk of falling into Communist hands. It was this prohibition which barred me from taking part in the Korean War which began in August 1950, a few weeks after I had been initiated into MI8 and for which my Regiment, the Argylls, and the Middlesex Regiment were to leave Hong Kong to help our South Korean and American allies to repel the invasion by the Communist North Korean forces.

As I had joined the Army to be an active soldier rather than a sedentary egg-head, this enforced absence from my proper place in the 91st Highlanders was something I much regretted. But as so often in my life, Providence knew what was best for me. While working at Eastcote I lived in a large country mansion named Swakeleys Manor in Ickenham, then used as the Foreign Office Sports Club. There I shared a room with a Major in the 4th/7th Dragoon Guards, Leslie Curtis, who worked in one of the GCHQ Hungarian sections. During 1951 I felt increasingly unwell without knowing why. I managed to do my work OK, played the odd game of tennis and cricket and enjoyed many weekends with Aunt Elspeth in her cottage near Canterbury, Pheasants Hall, which she and Cosmo had bought shortly before his sudden death in 1947. I had managed to pass the Civil Service Interpretership Exams in Czech and French, though with lower marks than I had hoped, for much of the zest had gone out of my life. In September 1951 my internal plumbing packed up completely. Paralysis set in and I became seriously ill.

Leslie Curtis, disbelieving the breezy diagnosis of the visiting Medical Officer, summoned an ambulance and had me whisked into Hillingdon Hospital. I can remember quite a lot of what happened during my stay in that large, friendly public ward. Although I was unaware of it, my parents had been told that I was unlikely to live, but thanks to the skill of Mr Gordon Scorer, a surgeon from Ivor in Buckinghamshire, and of a splendid team of nurses, I did recover sufficiently to be moved six weeks later to the King Edward VII Convalescent Home for Officers near Cowes where I spent a further six weeks. This establishment in Queen Victoria's home, Osborne House, in the Isle of Wight, was extremely well run; it was also near my family home at Nettlestone, and I was able to return to my work in Eastcote early in 1952 albeit medically down-graded for three months. The cause of the abdominal obstruction and the paralysis which followed was adhesions which had formed inside my guts in consequence of my appendix operation in May 1940. To the National Health Service, its members who worked so hard and successfully on me at Hillingdon Hospital, and to Leslie Curtis who had just in time delivered me into their care, I have ever since felt a debt of sincere gratitude.

In early 1952 King George VI, our Sovereign during the perilous years of the Second World War and the straitened period which followed, died. His daughter, Elizabeth, and her husband Philip, Duke of Edinburgh were in Kenya at the time and the last photograph we, his subjects, were to see of him was taken as he waved farewell as their aircraft left London. That picture of the King, pale and haggard for he was already much more ill than we supposed, was to remain in the memory of millions of us for the rest of our lives. George VI was a truly good Monarch and Man. He endeared himself to his peoples by an exemplary family life, a strong sense of duty and the courage to overcome a speech impediment.

The grief of the nation and of countless visitors from other lands was movingly demonstrated in London by the thousands including myself who stood for several hours in a dense column over a mile long in the freezing fog of a February evening waiting to file through Westminster Hall where his body lay in state before burial at Windsor.

England now had a young and radiant Queen whose Coronation in the June of the following year was to be the most spectacular royal event ever broadcast by television.

In the spring of 1952 I left the confinement and inhibited atmosphere of GCHQ and returned to regimental duty at the Headquarters of the Highland Brigade in Fort George, deep in Seaforth country, where I had first gone as a Private Soldier in 1941. I much enjoyed that Scottish summer and the first of the several military Tattoos I was to be associated with and which, performed on the sloping esplanade in front of Edinburgh Castle were and still are a most popular and colourful ingredient of the annual Festival in Scotland's capital. By the autumn I was fully fit again and I remained in Edinburgh to await the Argylls' return from the Far East.

Notes

1. Alex Blair wrote to me: 'The scoundrel behind the trials of these Servicemen was one Bedrich Reicin. A Jew, he had been a sergeant in the Czech Army in the USSR and it was believed that he had been born Reizinger. He eventually rose to the rank of Brigadier-General in charge of the 5th Department of the Ministry of Defence before being himself hanged as a traitor.'
2. On the orders of Governor Frank. After the war he was hanged in Prague in the courtyard of Pankrac Prison. Tickets for admission to witness the execution were sent to the British Embassy.

CHAPTER VI
1952–1960

With the Argylls in Scotland, British Guiana, Cyprus and West Germany – and Marriage

The Argylls had won further renown while in the Far East. In company with the Middlesex Regiment – the Diehards of Albuera in 1811 – our First Battalion, the 91st Highlanders, had been the first British troops to go to the defence of South Korea when that country was invaded in August 1950; and during that savage early demonstration of East-West hostility which was to be sustained for forty years thereafter, they had won another Victoria Cross, awarded posthumously to Major Kenny Muir.

In late 1952 they came home to a great welcome from the citizens of Edinburgh and settled down in nearby Colinton, occupying one of the two Redford barrack complexes, whose buildings with their large windows, broad verandas and wide corridors were highly unsuited to the cold winds of the Lothians. It was alleged that in the previous century a War Office clerk had muddled the architects' drawings and the barracks designed for Malta had been put up in Colinton in error.

When the 91st arrived in Edinburgh from Hong Kong they had fifty-six men in arrest, nearly all VD cases. In those days venereal disease was regarded by Parliament and the Service as a self-inflicted injury, punishable under the Army Act by detention and loss of pay. AIDS had not yet been identified, but syphilis and gonorrhoea had become a serious problem for the whole Army with its units dispersed around the world and composed mainly of young National Servicemen far from home and parental supervision. The problem, if not properly tackled, could have had sombre consequences for the Army's efficiency and the nation's health. Fear of punishment was driving some men to conceal their infection or to seek treatment privately, sometimes in squalid premises from native doctors. On the other hand a permissive official attitude would, the moralists claimed, be tantamount to condoning promiscuity; quite apart from enraging parents whose boys had been conscripted by an uncaring government and exposed by the Army overseas to dreadful foreign temptations and perils. Many intellects were brought to bear on the problem; the solution adopted was the PAC, the Prophylactic Aid Centre. This was a room or hut set aside near the entrance to every barracks and military camp in which a man would find the medications and other devices necessary for cleansing himself together with simple instructions on how to apply the stuff to his anatomy. That done, he was required to write his name on a slip of paper and drop it into a sealed box. The next morning the box was opened by the Medical Officer and the names recorded in a confidential book, proof that the soldier had used the facilities in the PAC. He thereby acquired a two-fold immunity; hopefully from VD, more certainly from punishment.

Having been away from the Argylls for six years I rejoined them in Redford Barracks. I had now been in the Army for eleven years, had fought Germans, held the rank of Major, and since the end of the war had served in Germany, Palestine and Czechoslovakia. My eyes had been opened and my horizons widened; and I was still young and unmarried. I began seriously to question the wisdom of spending my life in the peacetime Army.

I assumed that having missed the Korean War, my chances of commanding the Argyll and Sutherland Highlanders were reduced: others would deserve that honour more than I. My experiences in the War, in the Prague Embassy and in GCHQ had whetted my appetite for Intelligence work and in that field I would, I reckoned, be given a more positive and interesting part to play in the East-West confrontation than if I stayed in khaki awaiting opportunities for military action in a Cold War which might never turn Hot.

So I was heartened when, out of the blue, I was discreetly approached with the suggestion that I should transfer into the Secret Intelligence Service on a permanent basis, and shortly afterwards I was summoned to London for an Interview Board.

A few days later I was informed that, should I decide to leave the Army, I would be accepted into the SIS.

To complete the Staff Training Course at Camberley and to get the letters '*psc*'[1] after one's name in the Army List was the ambition of most Officers. Very few reached high rank without that qualification, but for those with it the future held encouraging possibilities. Success in the Entrance Examination was therefore of crucial importance to one's career and future lifestyle. Officers were obliged in those days to study for the exam in their spare time, by private reading and, most rewarding, by taking a correspondence course. The Army gave little formal instruction to candidates. The exam was a stiff hurdle and each year some 800 Officers competed for approximately 100 places.

I sat the exam in Edinburgh in February 1953 and came away not confident of success. But I kept my fingers crossed and asked my contacts in the SIS to be patient and to wait for the eventual publication of the exam results. I had by now also been earmarked in the Battalion for the appointment of Adjutant. This was quite a compliment and one not to be turned down lightly.

One day in March the CO, Lieutenant-Colonel Church, said to me: 'I know you have just sat the Staff College Exam; how do you think you got on?' I replied: 'I shall be surprised if I pass but I have not lost hope'.

'I see. I have a special request to put to you.' The CO went on: 'You are due to take over as Adjutant this summer; should you find that you have passed the exam, would you consider postponing your entrance to Camberley for a year, to go in January 1955 instead of in ten months' time? It would do your career good to have an extra year at regimental duty and it would help the Battalion enormously to have you as Adjutant for eighteen months rather than six.' He added: 'It would also be a considerable kindness and help to me personally. You probably do not know it, but my wife Elizabeth is having an affair with the Duke of Roxburghe and she is going to leave me for him when the Coronation and the royal visit to Scotland are over. I shall have to divorce her and this divorce business will take up a lot of my energy and time. So I would like you to stay on and help me to run the Battalion during this difficult period. I do so hope that you will agree.'

Elizabeth Church was a pretty, brittle blond who seemed to be playing her part as CO's wife adequately, so I was shocked by what Jim Church had just told me. And saddened too that he should be dealt such a blow at the peak of his career, in command of his regiment in an exceptional year distinguished by the Coronation Parade in London, the Queen's visit to Scotland and the Presentation of new Colours to the 91st by Her Majesty, our Colonel-in-Chief. My generation had been brought up to obey the dictum of Service before Self, and that one's prime loyalty was to the Regiment. I therefore gave little further thought to the possible consequences for my career or my life, and I gave Jim Church straightaway my word that I would delay my entrance to Camberley should I be so lucky as to win a place; and also any early move out of the Army into the SIS.

To see the Coronation I joined my parents in London. Like everyone else we rose early. The weather was dull but dry and as we made our way to Green Park in a packed underground train the word on every lip was 'Everest'. The expedition led by Colonel John Hunt had conquered Mount Everest: the New Zealander, Edmund Hillary, and the Sherpa Tensing had reached the summit – the first men to do so – several days earlier, but the news had sensibly been held back until the dawn of our young Queen's Coronation Day.

Seated on the first floor of a building in St James's Street we had an excellent view of the whole long procession; bands, horsemen, marching columns made up of detachments from every uniformed part of British and Commonwealth life; coaches with foreign dignitaries and royalty – a colourful stream of movement and music. My brother Alastair carried the Regimental Colour of the First Argylls. By mid-morning the rain was falling heavily, soaking his blue bonnet; and as it shrank, being new, the brim cut into his head like a vice. Needing both hands to hold the Colour he could only grit his teeth and long for the end of the fourteen-mile processional route from and back to their billets at Olympia.

The dignitary who most caught the affection of the dense crowds along the route was Queen Salote of Tonga. A large, beaming Lady, she waved enthusiastically to everybody and, despite the rain, she was clearly enjoying herself immensely. Less happy was her companion in the open carriage. Sitting facing Queen Salote was a small fellow, a Malaysian prince I believe; wet through and dwarfed by the majestic Tongan, he looked miserable.

'Who is that unhappy little fellow riding with Queen Salote?'

'Her lunch,' came the answer, attributed to Noel Coward. It was an apt reply because the Crown Prince of some other South Pacific people had travelled to Britain by sea. As his liner was nearing the end of its long voyage the Prince, it was related, went into the Dining Room for luncheon. A waiter handed him the menu but he waved it aside with the words:

'I've sampled all that already; please now bring me the Passenger List.'

When the last files of marching men and horses had passed us we were able to watch the Queen's arrival at Westminster Abbey and the Coronation Service on television. For most of us this was the first time we had watched a great national event through that new medium, and the black and white images on the TV screen were superbly complemented by the words of that Master of Commentators, Mr Richard Dimbleby.

Not only was Coronation Day a great spectacle, it gave the peoples of Britain and the Commonwealth a wonderful uplift. The whole ceremonial had been planned to perfection by the Earl Marshal, the Duke of Norfolk, and every participant performed impeccably, above all the young Queen herself. The drabness, anxieties, restrictions and shortages of wartime and the post-war years evaporated on that wet summer's day, and people now spoke and wrote excitedly of the 'second of June 1953 marking the birth of a great new Elizabethan era' in which a proud Britain would again enjoy prosperity, self-confidence and pre-eminence in military skill, commercial success and diplomatic influence. The whole nation was buoyed up with patriotism and united in hope. These were sentiments wonderful to experience.

The reality of our nation's status was made clear only three years later by the fiasco of Suez.

The summer months of 1953 were all busy and colourful; it was a memorable period for the Argyll and Sutherland Highlanders especially. I was happy to have by my side my brother, Alastair, who was coming to the end of his two years of National Service in the Regiment. The Queen came to Scotland in mid-June and was crowned again in St Giles' Cathedral in Edinburgh, and on 26 June presented new Colours to the Battalion in the grounds of Holyrood House in a flawless ceremony and perfect weather. The next day Elizabeth Church left her husband, the Regiment, and Redford; in due course she married the Duke and produced the heir he had so long desired.

Sitting in the Mess I picked up *The Times* and quite by chance found listed the names of the Officers who had passed the Staff College exam and had been selected for Camberley. *Mirabile dictu*! I had not only passed, I had come in the top five and been awarded a 'competitive vacancy' guaranteeing me a priority place on the course starting in January, only six months away. But the CO had pressed me to stay for the extra year and I had consented, so the War Office had to be persuaded to delete my name from the 1954 course and to reserve for me a place in 1955. To turn down a competitive vacancy was, they said, unprecedented, but after some pleading by Jim Church at Scottish Command and some tooth-sucking in London the request was granted. I took over the Adjutancy of the 91st expecting to work beside Colonel Church for a clear eighteen months while he sorted out his domestic difficulties and we together kept the battalion in good order.

During the summer of 1953 the 91st was occupied almost continuously with ceremonial duties. This was inevitable for an Infantry battalion stationed in Scotland's capital city in Coronation year. I have been told that the regular soldiers of pre-1939 vintage were perfectly content to perform endless rounds of sentry-duties and ceremonial parades in preference to field training, but the Jock of the 1950s viewed such parades with a more jaundiced eye, although he would be the first to admit to a feeling of uncommon pride and well-being at the conclusion of a well-run drill parade or a ceremony impeccably carried out under the public's gaze.

In March some 400 Officers and men had spent a week in the hills near Aberfoyle enacting the battle scenes for the technicolor film 'Rob Roy' which Walt Disney's company was making. The leading actor, Richard Todd, had served in The Parachute Regiment so was better qualified than most to play the title role, except that he was skinny and short of stature. These deficiencies were overcome by padding on his limbs and torso and by the camera crew adjusting the angle of shooting to make him appear taller.

For the period of the Queen's stay in Edinburgh our bit of Redford Barracks resembled a large hotel, housing various units taking part in one ceremony or another; and we got on particularly well with the Household Cavalry and the Royal Scots Greys, the Queen's Mounted Escort, who lived under our roof. Our regimental mascot, a Shetland pony named Cruachan, was in his element too in the stables surrounded by so many beautiful mares, and like all of us was saddened by the news that his friend Pompey, the magnificent Drum Horse of the Life Guards, had died during the journey back to England.

The Battalion's unexpected and sudden move from Scotland to South America was one of its most memorable experiences and a novel end to an exceptionally busy year. As soon as the Queen left Edinburgh we were split up so as to provide some two hundred men for the Tattoo, five Officers and over one hundred men for the Royal Guard at Balmoral Castle, and the remainder were scattered round different camps to instruct or minister to units of the Territorial Army and Cadet Forces. At the end of September the 91st, less the Balmoral Guard, assembled in Yorkshire for a much-needed spell of field training. On 2 October, as Jim Church was giving out his orders for the first exercise 'battle', a dispatch rider appeared with a message: the Argylls were to return at once to Edinburgh and prepare to move overseas at forty-eight hours' notice. East Africa or Indo-China were assumed to be our most probable destinations. The CO and I took the night train to London to be briefed at the War Office.

Trouble was brewing in Guiana, Britain's only colony on the South American continent. The Governor had suspended the constitution and had called in the Royal Welch Fusiliers from Jamaica to maintain law and order. 1A&SH was required to embark in southern England, cross the Atlantic and, having relieved the RWF, to remain in British Guiana for a year. Because there had been no British garrison in that colony for over fifty years, few facilities existed to support one. Thus we had to take with us the full range of vehicles, stores and impedimenta needed to keep us going for a long period in an equatorial country about which no one at that meeting seemed to have convincing knowledge. When at the end of the briefing I asked which phrase books we should take to talk to the natives – Spanish or Portuguese? – the fact that the population spoke only English did not seem to have been hoisted in.

None of those present could describe the conditions we would meet on arrival in that remote land of rivers and jungle, but those of us who collected postage stamps, with a page or two at the back of our albums reserved for the Guianas, at least knew where the place was and were aware that it was rich in butterflies, birdlife, trees and aboriginal tribes; and the keenest philatelists knew that British Guiana had issued one of the world's most valuable stamps, the penny black of Queen Victoria's reign. This ignorance about the colony was understandable. The place had remained for most of the time since the British acquired it from the Dutch a relatively peaceful backwater. In consequence Guiana had attracted little attention in Whitehall. Our faith in Imperial management was not improved when, while at sea, we listened to a BBC talk given by a Member of Parliament in which he referred to British Guiana as 'that troublesome West Indian island'.

To embark with us were teams of specialists from the logistic corps; supply and ordnance experts, medics, mechanical engineers and a detachment of Royal Signals personnel together with their various equipments.

Everyone worked extremely hard, and exactly seven days after receiving that warning order in Yorkshire, the 91st, without a single absentee, was on its way by train to Devonport. Our Royal Guard had been peremptorily withdrawn from Balmoral, the responsibility for the Queen's protection being handed over to the local Police.

To be a member of that Guard was for Officers and Men alike an agreeable experience. The duties were not heavy, were entirely routine and everyone got a kick out of serving at close quarters our young Sovereign, our Colonel-in-Chief. The Officers were invited to join the Royal Family for shooting parties and the Jocks enjoyed acting as beaters. Walking back to the Castle after one of those shoots Princess Margaret suddenly exclaimed, 'What was that extraordinary noise?'. John Somerville, an Argyll subaltern, replied: 'That, Your Royal Highness, was one of the whistles used by the ghillies to control the dogs'. He added: 'Its pitch is such that it's audible to dogs but rarely to human ears'. 'How interesting; thank you,' replied the Princess, to which the Duke of Edinburgh, walking beside her said, 'Maggie, that's the first time in your life a young Officer has implied that you're a bitch and got away with it'.

A further anecdotal incident concerns another of our young Officers who, when in Crathie Church in company with the Queen and the Royal Family, opened the singing of the National Anthem with the words: 'God save our gracious King'.

The Royal Navy vessel in which we were to embark was an aircraft carrier, HMS *Implacable*. She was a training ship, so in addition to her crew of 1,400, she had on board over six hundred trainees and a full complement of instructors. Her big lower hangar had been converted into classrooms and the upper hangar into mess decks and recreational space. *Implacable* now had to take on board some nine hundred additional bodies of the A&SH Group together with our transport and stores. The forty-odd lorries, bren carriers and jeeps were secured on the after end of the flight deck, and in the upper hangar rows of steel hawsers were laid down to which could be lashed in bad weather the hundreds of camp beds on which our soldiers were to sleep in that vast dormitory. 'It was obvious that there was nothing that the Navy wouldn't do for us; that Service is famous for its hospitality and versatility but on this day it excelled itself.' So reads the account in the regimental journal, 'The Thin Red Line', and by the morning of Saturday 10 October *Implacable* was ready to receive us on our arrival alongside after a train journey which had begun seventeen hours earlier in Edinburgh's Gorgie Sidings.

PONDER ANEW

By a happy historical coincidence, the Captain of *Implacable* was Captain Alan Campbell RN, whose brother, Lorne, had won the Victoria Cross in the North African campaign while commanding our 7th Battalion. This personal relationship between *Implacable* and the Regiment made our expedition all the more enjoyable, and the Captain's obvious pride at being chosen to carry his 'family regiment' was reflected throughout the ship's company. The embarkation routine ran like clockwork, and by the time the great ship got under way at 5.30 in the evening, the Jocks already felt quite at home in their new surroundings. Leaving Devonport was an emotive experience. The troops lined the forward end of the flight deck and the Pipes and Drums alternated with the ship's Royal Marine band in playing *Implacable* on her way; and as she moved slowly out of the harbour in the reddening dusk, the strains of a lone piper on the breakwater came to us across the waves. We sailed past the watching crowds on Plymouth Hoe, and with the flag of our 91st Highlanders flying from the yardarm HMS *Implacable* headed west.

The voyage was generally calm and pleasant. A ship travelling at twenty-three knots is bound to heave a little but the soldiers by and large weathered the first two days rather better than the trainee matelots; many of our longer-serving soldiers had acquired more sea-time than the conscripted sailors. I was very well looked after by Captain Lionel Edwards whose cabin and Batman, Marine Hunt, I shared.

Apart from the cramped accommodation an aircraft carrier makes an excellent troopship. The big flight deck gives plenty of room for PT and games; and for training. Nobody knew what lay ahead, so while hoping for the best we prepared for the worst; and every day was taken up with weapon handling practice, shooting at balloons and anti-riot drill. A mis-thrown tear-gas grenade caused some consternation in the bowels of the ship when the vapour got sucked into an engine room air intake.

After four days at sea it was announced that our initial destination was to be Trinidad, where we would all tranship into smaller vessels which, unlike *Implacable*, could negotiate the shallow silted waters off the north-east coast of South America. So on the morning of a sweltering Sunday 18 October, a week after leaving Devonport, *Implacable* dropped anchor off Port of Spain, and along one side of the carrier the Royal Navy frigate *Bigbury Bay* tied up and on the other the dust-covered bauxite ship, the *Sunjarv*, borrowed from Saguenay Terminals. The navy began the evolution to transfer the kit and vehicles into the two smaller vessels, and in the process a number of items, mishandled by Jocks who were trying to be helpful, fell into the sea and were lost. Locating the great quantity of crates containing our stores had caused the biggest headache, for the naval personnel had worked round the clock in Devonport to get everything loaded before the battalion arrived and these had been randomly stowed in any empty space that could be found. But everything was retrieved from the ship in the end – except B Company's document box which was never found. This was exasperating for the Company Sergeant-Major but a bonus for the Jocks whose conduct sheets were in the box.

The following evening we parted company with *Implacable* and headed south-east down the coast of Venezuela and across the mouths of the Orinoco and Essequibo rivers towards Georgetown, the capital of British Guiana.

HMS *Bigbury Bay* docked in Georgetown on the morning of 21 October, Trafalgar Day, and John Parnell's company moved immediately to New Amsterdam, a coastal town some sixty-five miles farther east. The rest of the battalion group in *Sunjarv* steamed slowly up the River Demerara to the jetty at the former US airbase at Atkinson Field where we disembarked thirty-six hours after leaving Trinidad. The Second-in-Command, Alastair Troup, had flown out ahead of us and brought news of the situation and what our tasks were likely to be.

The colony of Guiana, formally ceded to Britain by the Dutch in 1814, was about three times the size of Scotland, and had a population of more than 600,000, mostly East Indians brought as labourers from the sub-continent and the descendants of slaves transported from Africa. The Indians narrowly outnumbered the Negroes; the majority of both lived and worked in the narrow belt between the mud of the shoreline and the forest-covered interior. The population had become restive during 1953 and a coup by the Peoples' Progressive Party led by Cheddi Jagan was only averted by the action of the Governor, Sir Alfred Savage, in suspending the constitution and bringing in the RWF from Jamaica.

Jagan, a 35-year old dentist of Indian blood, had been educated in the USA and became an influential politician in his native Guiana. He held strongly nationalistic and Marxist views; furthermore his wife, Janet, an American with the family name of Rosenberg, was alleged, wrongly in fact, to be closely related to the two Rosenbergs, Julius and Ethel, whom the Americans had recently executed for treason. Instability in Guiana came at a time when the British were beginning to divest themselves of their Imperial commitments, yielding to nationalist and financial pressures and the anti-colonialist propaganda vented by the USA and the USSR since the end of the Second World War. Jagan's behaviour in 'BG' was a vexation to Her Majesty's government, but by the United States government was viewed as an incipient threat to the security of the whole region and a fresh symptom of Communist Cold War activity. It was therefore primarily in response to United States demands that London took what seemed to us to be excessive measures to control Jagan and the PPP.

Our task was to give confidence in law and order, bolster the prestige of the Governor and the colony's Administration, to deter the lawless, and generally win the respect and friendship of the locals, be they Indian,

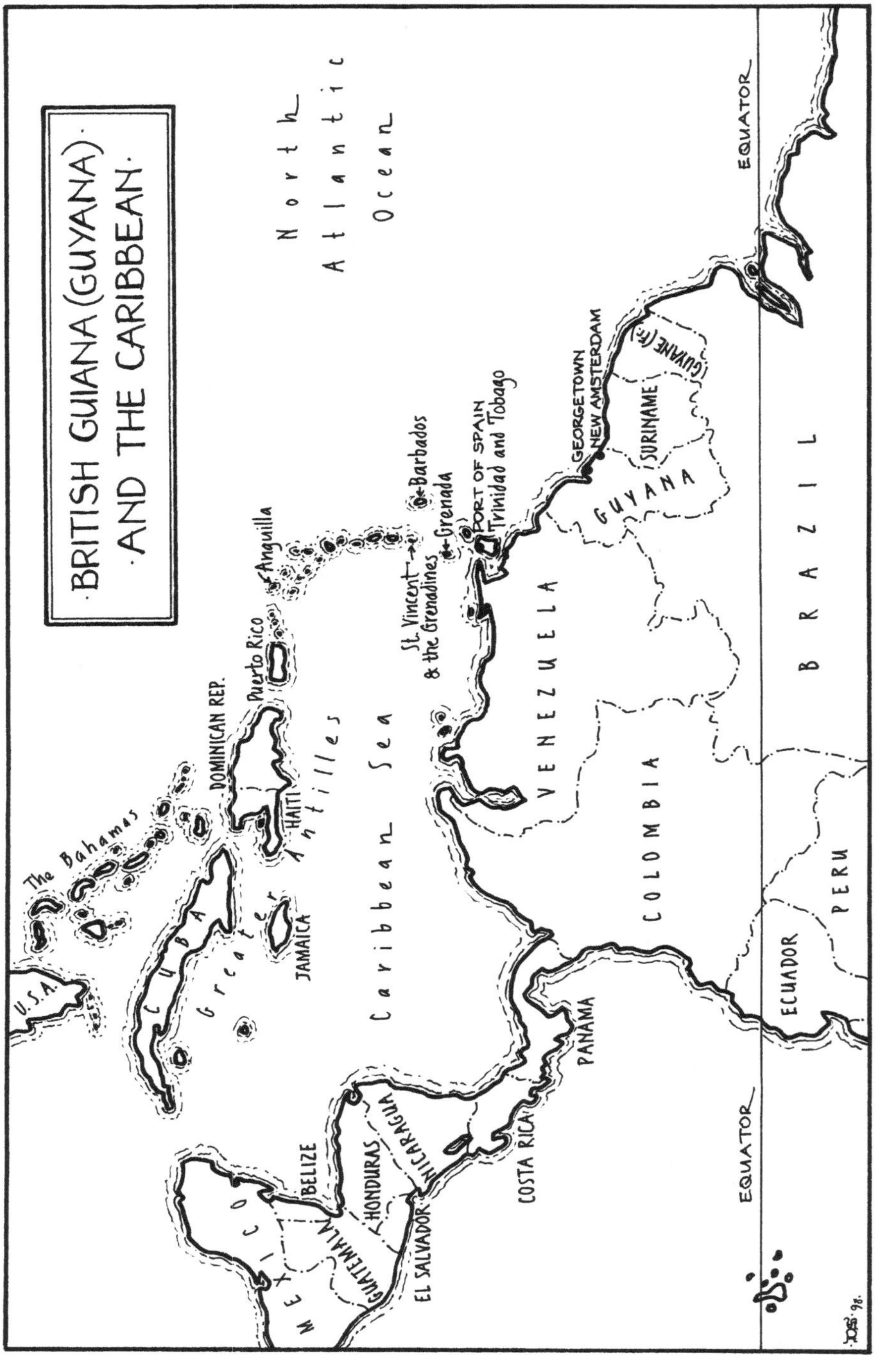
BRITISH GUIANA (GUYANA) AND THE CARIBBEAN
North Atlantic Ocean
The Bahamas
U.S.A.
CUBA
Greater Antilles
JAMAICA
HAITI
DOMINICAN REP.
Puerto Rico
Anguilla
St. Vincent & the Grenadines
Barbados
Grenada
PORT OF SPAIN
Trinidad and Tobago
GEORGETOWN
NEW AMSTERDAM
SURINAME
GUYANE (Fr.)
GUYANA
Caribbean Sea
VENEZUELA
COLOMBIA
BRAZIL
PERU
ECUADOR
PANAMA
COSTA RICA
NICARAGUA
HONDURAS
EL SALVADOR
GUATEMALA
BELIZE
MEXICO
EQUATOR
EQUATOR

African, Chinese, Portuguese, English, of mixed blood, or members of the indigenous Amerindian tribes dwelling on their jungle reservations.

First impressions of the place were not inviting; indeed the more ingenuous among us were dismayed to find that this bit of our world, proudly coloured red in atlases, should be so seedy and rundown. The 'Thin Red Line' recorded what we felt about our new surroundings.

> 'The coastal plain of British Guiana was retrieved from swamp and sea by a system of dykes and drainage, so that much of it is up to 6 feet below sea level at high tide. Through this flat, featureless landscape flows the Demerara river, wide, sluggish, and the colour of milk chocolate. On both sides of the river are sugar estates with the occasional tall chimneys of their factories. Apart from these factories, the only visible habitations appear to be the wooden shanty-houses of the estate workers. Over the whole land there is the sickly-sweet cloying smell of sugar, molasses, and rum, which soon becomes part of the normal background.
>
> Atkinson Field could be any disused air base anywhere in the Tropics, although, in spite of its general air of desertion, it is used as a staging point by the regular airlines serving South America and the Caribbean.
>
> The first depressing impression is not helped by the 26 mile drive into Georgetown over a disgracefully dilapidated road. The road runs through sugar estates with such high-flown names as Diamond, Providence, Houston, and La Penitance. It also runs past the estate workers' houses – a series of ramshackle wooden huts built on stilts. Many of these houses, in fact, are comfortable and often well-furnished, belying their shabby-looking exteriors. But many also are relics of the infamous 'ranges' – long huts like rows of racing stables, with each dark, squalid earth-floored horsebox housing a family. In spite of a growing drive to re-house the sugar workers, these ranges still exist in a large number of places, a fertile breeding ground of vice, disease, and intrigue.
>
> From the ramshackle Atkinson Road into the ramshackle streets of Georgetown itself . . . Georgetown, like almost everything else in B.G., is built of wood, and the fact that the town is well planned, with a clean modern town centre and beautiful tree-lined avenues, still cannot dispel the general impression that much of it could do with a good overhaul and a coat of paint.
>
> This ramshackle appearance is largely explained by the population, whose easy-going, lackadaisical attitude and friendly leave-it-till-tomorrow approach is at once captivating and infuriating.
>
> Since our first arrival, parties of men have been able to go up country through the grandeur of the forest to the magnificent hill

scenery towards the Parakaima mountains; but first impressions are hard to dispel, and it is in the muddy coastal belt that the population is concentrated, and where our work lies.

It is, of course, inevitable that at some time they would station Highlanders six feet below sea level, but the real compensation has been in the friendliness and generosity of the local population. The welcome received by the Battalion has been most heart warming. It is true that occasionally, there are shouts of 'Limey, go home!' in the streets, but we have heard ruder things shouted in other parts of the world.

Our only casualty so far has been Pte. Mannion, unfortunately killed in a car accident – the first British soldier to die in British Guiana on service for 100 years.

It is strange to serve in a place where they are so unused to soldiers that they cannot tell the difference between a Major and a Lance Corporal – anyway, not by the badges he wears.

In spite of anything you may read to the contrary, our stay here has been peaceful and looks like remaining so. (If you still aren't quite sure exactly where we are, find a map of South America, look at the coastline at the top, and you will find us about half-way along, next to Venezuela.)

And when, eventually, we come calypsoing down the gangway on our return home, it is pretty certain that a lot of us will look back on this sport-crazy, party-mad corner of South America with gratitude, if not with affection.'

The rifle companies rotated every three months or so between New Amsterdam, Atkinson Field and Georgetown. The troops in the latter moved out of their requisitioned hotels into comfortable and spacious barracks which the Public Works Department built for us at Eve Leary. Battalion Headquarters, which included me, remained throughout our year near the sea-wall in Georgetown working in the former Immigration Department's offices and with the Officers eating and sleeping in the Mariners' Club opposite.

Colonel Church, at whose urging I had agreed to remain in the Battalion for an extra year as his Adjutant, left us after a few weeks and remained in Scotland in order to handle his divorce proceedings. Alastair Troup acted as CO until March 1954 when Barclay Pearson came out to take over. Thus I was Adjutant to three COs in the space of a year. Barclay and I had served together briefly in the 93rd in France and Belgium before he was promoted to take command of the 8th Royal Scots in the Lowland Brigade of our Division. He had won the DSO for, inter alia, the capture by his battalion from the Germans of the Dutch town of Blerick in one of the first attacks carried out by British Infantry mounted in armoured vehicles.

Regimental Soldiering and Marriage

Support Company, split up in Scotland so as to reinforce the rifle companies, was partly reformed early in 1954 with a mortar and machine-gun platoon. One of our Majors, Ian Scheurmier, when he heard that this was proposed, kept appealing to me to put in a word for him, for he was very keen to be given the command of that recreated company. I was successful on his behalf and Colonel Pearson granted his wish. That was a fateful appointment for the next year, while in Germany, Ian Scheurmier attended with many hundreds of spectators a demonstration of Support Weapons organised by HQ BAOR. In the course of a live shoot by Vickers machine-guns Ian dropped dead, killed by a stray bullet through his head. No one around him was touched. A sad thing about that tragedy was that his wife had been married earlier to a Royal Navy aviator who had been killed in a flying accident; on duty too, as Ian was on the day of his death.

By now several plane-loads of wives and children had come out to join the Battalion Group and everyone had settled into a calm, relaxed, peacetime routine disturbed only by spells of torrential rain and swarms of mosquitoes, which though not malarial in the Georgetown area at that time, raised large lumps on our bodies. The Band and Pipes and Drums were especially popular in that land of the calypso and steel band. All Ranks became very fit, starting the day with compulsory road-runs followed by jungle patrols and sporting fixtures. Our sports teams had a full programme of matches against local players. We usually carried off the soccer prizes, held our own on the rugger field, got beaten at cricket and thrashed in the boxing ring. As well as playing in the cricket and rugger teams I, the 31-year-old Adjutant, for a brief spell held the record for running up the rough jungle tracks from the base to the summit of the magnificent Kaieteur Falls, at 822 feet five times higher than Niagara, on the Potaro River.

The PT Staff really earned their pay. This emphasis on physical fitness was not only a military obligation and an agreeable way for the troops to pass their days and weeks; it was an essential antidote to the hazards of service in that lush and most hospitable country, rum and women.

These temptations were in large measure averted by the wise combination of education and punishment, together with the good sense of the bulk of the soldiers; and by placing Out of Bounds on the advice of the local constabulary the reddest of the red-light districts. Nevertheless, a small core of hardened Jocks continued to give the Regimental Police a lot of work and to spend much of their lives in the cells.

Regimental Sergeant-Major Boyde, Rex to his family but Paddy to the Regiment, was a large, bull-necked, very upright man with a florid face. He was a fine soldier, highly decorated, not too bright and devoted to the Regiment. He had a faultless sense of what makes Jocks tick and a battalion's reputation envied by the rest of the Service. RSM Boyde's virtues had been noted too by the representatives of many nations, for he had served behind the Iron Curtain with the British Mission (Brixmis) to the Soviet Forces in East Germany and later at SHAPE in France. The soldiers both feared and loved him. Boyde was just the right man to have as our RSM in the conditions of Guiana. We worked very closely together through all the vicissitudes of that year and remained good friends until his death.

One night he and I decided to go out with one of our Police patrols. We had learned that a Private Soldier, one of our really hard cases, had failed to return to barracks before midnight and was to be found in a forbidden brothel in one of Georgetown's more squalid streets. We left the jeep quietly and with two RPs, entered the building and tiptoed along its single corridor. A woman ran out of a door through which, plainly visible in the dim light of an oil lamp, was our quarry, lying stark naked on a bed smoking a cigarette. He too must have heard our approach but without looking up, whispered: 'Is that you, darling?' 'No, Private Kyle, it is me,' replied Paddy Boyde. The consternation on the man's face as he leapt to his feet was a fine reward for our nocturnal diligence.

The Guianese were famed throughout the western hemisphere for their hospitality, and the Argylls were to experience this from our first days in their country. The Jocks were invited, individually or in groups, to parties organised for them by the plantation owners and in Georgetown by the sporting clubs and more prosperous businessmen and their wives; and the ladies of the numerous branches of the Christian faith vied with each other in kindness and culinary prowess on the Regiment's behalf.

We had been warned by the Governor's staff that we Officers would find it harder to 'get our feet under a Guianese table', and although this advice proved in the long term to be incorrect, it was evident that the locals were initially more reserved in their approaches to the members of the Officers' Mess than to our NCOs and Private Soldiers. I had learned from Mess gossip that a group of young Georgetown ladies had organised a Hallowe'en dance in aid of some charity and had sent an open invitation to our subalterns. Having a free evening – for the CO and I had by then overcome the teething problems we faced on arrival in South America – I took into my head the idea that as the Adjutant I ought to go along to see what our young Officers were being led into. Everyone was to meet up at the home of the girl organising the party. I arrived at her substantial and well furnished house just as all the others were coming down the wide staircase to move off by taxi to the principal hotel as a prelude to going on to the dance. Descending the stairs was an attractive, dark-haired girl in a pale pink crinoline skirt with a matching bolero, worn with a pretty Victorian amethyst set of jewellery. Escorting her was our Medical Officer whom I knew to be married. Some silent compulsion told me that I, a bachelor, had a greater claim than he in the quest for a Hallowe'en dancing partner, so I arrogantly eased the Doctor into the front of the taxi and sat myself down beside the girl for the short ride to the hotel. I learned that her name was Rosemary Adamson, that she lived with her widowed Mother and a young Brother almost next door to the Governor's residence, and that she, only a few days before we disembarked, had arrived back in Guiana after four years in a Berkshire boarding school. I found that we had much to talk about and the more we talked the more I became attracted by her voice, her looks and her nature.

I monopolised 19-year-old Miss Adamson for the whole of that evening, and our meetings were to become increasingly frequent as the months of our stay in Guiana passed. While I joined her family for many suppers or picnics in the country, she came to most of our Mess functions as my partner and was invariably rated the prettiest girl present. We became inseparable and I was to learn that her beauty was matched by a sterling character and a wisdom unusually rare in one so young. As I got to know her my admiration for her grew in step with our affection for each other, and I came to realise that in her I had found a jewel of a person – a real pearl – and to hate the prospect of returning to Britain leaving her behind in that colony with its political instability, racial antagonisms and uncertain prospects; and from which, although it was the land of her birth, her years in a school overlooking Watership Down and at work in London had estranged her. I decided to make her my wife and quietly told Rosemary's Mother and her of my intention.

Rosemary Adamson had been sent to school in England at the age of fourteen in order to distance her from an unhappy family situation. Her Father, James Basil Adamson, an Officer in the colony's Customs & Excise Service, was an exceptionally popular man; he was also a noted philanderer. This addiction led to his murder. No one was convicted of this crime but the circumstances were widely known, and his Daughter, Rosemary, who was deeply affected by the death of her Father, has described the episode in a partially fictionalised version, included here as Appendix II, 'A Ballad of Two Tropic Nights'.

Our growing friendship was watched by most of my fellow Argylls in silence. Some of the senior Officers and the leading personalities in Georgetown's white element said openly or behind my back: 'Of course he'll not be such a fool as to marry the girl'. And Rosemary for her part was constantly urged by her Guianese relatives and friends not to become too attached to me or to any British Officer for, they warned, 'He'll never marry you. They'll all go back to Scotland, forget about Guiana and settle down wedded to their own kind'. But not all were so bigoted. There were individuals among the Argylls and in Rosemary's circle of friends who, looking beneath skin colour, came to discern in Rosemary the same qualities as I had found; and for their quiet words of encouragement I have remained to this day grateful.

The attitude, vocal or silent, of the majority was not however based solely on colour prejudice nor on any dogma of racial superiority. There was a dread of miscegenation, the mixing of blood and genes of different races and of the consequent emergence of 'khaki-coloured babies'. These progeny of mixed marriages would, it was believed, be condemned to blighted lives, bring shame on their parents, and end up in the ranks of the criminal classes. Only three years earlier public sentiment in Britain had been aroused by the case of Seretse Khama, a black African tribal monarch who had married a white English girl named Ruth. The UK government, under pressure from the white South African architects of the apartheid system, and from much of the British electorate, had deprived Khama of his throne and banished him from his home, his tribe and his wife. In the end popular feelings changed and with change came a degree of restitution. Khama was to the great joy of his subjects restored to his throne and, knighted by the Queen, became Sir Seretse. Ruth, Lady Khama, continued to live long after her husband's death, in his kingdom beloved and respected by all who knew her.

To the successive Commanding Officers of the 1A&SH Group during our year in Guiana the Whitehall attitude to the matter of Anglo-Guianese marriages was made consistently clear. They were instructed to take all practicable measures to prevent such marriages. To permit units of the British Army to return home with coloured wives would lower the Army's prestige and infuriate the parents of those soldiers, mostly immature conscripts abroad for the first time in their lives, who had married them. The Army's reputation and the feelings of the families of those in its charge had to be safeguarded. Furthermore, and this was a weighty factor in determining official policy, the Guianese girls, pretty, educated, from relatively prosperous backgrounds and brought up in the climate and culture of that equatorial colony, had to be deterred from rashly entering into marriages which could condemn them to living in the Scottish climate in a Glasgow slum. As Adjutant I had to support this policy; certainly not to be seen overtly undermining its application. Despite our efforts the 91st returned to Britain in October 1954 with, on board the troopship *Dilwara*, eleven Guianese wives varying in colour from café-au-lait to tar black. Our arrival at Southampton caused much excitement, boldly expressed in newspaper headlines. Two of the brides vanished almost immediately: they had married Jocks solely as a means to getting a UK passport and a free passage to their Mecca, Britain; but the others, I am told, settled down well and were a boon to their husbands and to the Regiment.

The Battalion and its families flew out from Atkinson Field to Trinidad in the civilian aircraft which brought in the Black Watch; a novel air relief operation which I organised in collaboration with BWIA officials. It was considered to have been a smooth prelude to our journey to the hutted camp in Morayshire where I left the 91st.

The news, brought in the summer of 1954, that we were to be relieved by a battalion of the Black Watch was to cause a frisson of eager anticipation among the local population, and they were visibly disappointed to find that the members of the 'Forty Twa' looked very much like us in the 91st but, alas, quite different to the coloured colonial regiment their name had led the Guianese to expect.

Rosemary and I had some daunting obstacles to overcome. I had anticipated some opposition to my engagement but was unprepared for its weight and persistence. My marriage plans, discreetly announced, came to my Mother as a great shock and brought to her a degree of distress which she never wholly managed to conceal. I had long suspected from the odd remark she had made about her years in India that she disliked coloured people, but not until she and Rosemary met did I comprehend how deep-seated was her prejudice. By the end of her life she had inflicted on my wife, her daughter-in-law, through cutting remarks and disparaging actions, much accumulated hurt. My Father, already an ill man with only four years of life ahead of him, was much less hostile and went out of his way to be kind to Rosemary, but he had neither the strength nor the will to stand up to his wife's lamentations about the choice of bride of their eldest son. My Brother, Moray tended to reflect his Mother's attitude; Alastair, however, has grown to be a staunch friend to us both and, like his wife Penelope, an appreciative admirer of Rosemary and our children.

I had sent Rosemary an engagement ring through the post. I bought it in Southsea. It was made of gold with an emerald and two diamonds and it cost £25. I was able to afford it because Aunt Ellie had just died and left me that sum in her will. The family maxim, 'Graham and green should never be seen', has always struck me as a flawed superstition seeing that our clan tartan is largely green in colour. Nevertheless, until Rosemary replaced the emerald with a ruby, our marriage plans continued to be messed about in deference to the wishes of other people.

Rosemary had left her family and home in May 1955 to join me in England. By that time I had entered the Army Staff College in Camberley, one year behind my peers on account of my delayed entry at Colonel Church's entreaty. The Staff College year is pretty demanding on students and instructors alike, and every student is motivated by the belief that his future career is largely determined by his performance on that course – incidentally the only year of an Army Officer's service in which his Confidential Report is not shown to him.

Aunt Elspeth[2] took a great liking to Rosemary, whom she called Juanita, and we spent many weekends down in her country house near Canterbury, though we mostly stayed in London where Rosemary had taken a room in Regents Park and a job as Secretary with the White Fish Authority in Petty France. We had a great time exploring London and its suburbs cheaply from the upper deck of those famous red omnibuses.

We had planned to be married early in 1956, on my Father's birthday, 21 January, but a few weeks before the end of the Staff course I was summoned to the office of a senior chap in the Regiment, Brigadier Freddie Graham, who was at the time Assistant Commandant of the Royal Military Academy in nearby Sandhurst. He had sent for me on the instructions of the Colonel of the Regiment, General Sir Gordon MacMillan, to whom I had written as duty required to tell him of my plans. Freddie Graham, well known by his black-and-white moustache, was not related to me and he left me in no doubt about the view the regimental hierarchy, and indeed the whole Highland Brigade, would take if Rosemary and I went ahead with our plans, and about the calamitous effect such a marriage would have on my military career.

He quoted at length from MacMillan's letter and finally asked me at least to comply with the General's request that we 'put any marriage plans off for a period'. We were to have a period for reflection imposed on us. General MacMillan was a most distinguished soldier and an exceedingly nice man.

Moreover, he had commanded our 15th (Scottish) Division until he was wounded in the third month of the Normandy campaign. I was reluctant to spurn the advice and wishes of the honoured 'Father' of the Regiment; Elspeth backed me in my decision, and Rosemary concealed her disappointment and anxiety with remarkable understanding and self-control. The whole period from the day she landed in England to join me until we eventually married nineteen months later was overclouded by a succession of pressures, strained loyalties, family recriminations and heart-searchings. For Rosemary, far from family and homeland, and feeling herself to be the cause of the military and domestic pressures, those months were an acid test of her perception, fortitude and faith. She came out of that test admirably. But her experiences during those months in England left deep scars, invisible to all save those who know her intimately, and thereafter the prospect of having to socialize with a certain type of English man or woman has filled her with apprehension, and moved her many years later to compose in verse 'The Mulatto's Prayer' (which I have included here at Appendix III).

After leaving Camberley I had gone to Fremington in Devon to study Amphibious Warfare, followed by three months on the newly established course at the Royal Military College of Science at Shrivenham, where Rosemary and I shared several happy weekends in the glorious Wiltshire countryside.

Despite the pressures from family and superiors, I was determined to make Rosemary my wife. It had become a point of honour; but even more compelling, I knew that in her character, her looks and her devotion I had found a unique companion. We were married in St James's Church, Piccadilly in the middle of the Suez crisis and while the 91st was engaged on that short campaign, conceived by foolish politicians and conducted by a General Staff which seemed to have forgotten many of the lessons and military skills learned during World War Two. As Rosemary and I drove away from the Church to our reception in the United Services Club (founded by my ancestor Lord Lynedoch) in Pall Mall, I asked her: 'What is to-day?'. She replied: 'Our wedding day, Saturday 17 November 1956!'. But do you know that it is also the birthday of Field Marshal Montgomery and of Colin Mitchell?' The former, the victor of El Alamein and our Commander-in-Chief in Normandy, was a hero to most of my age group; the latter a regimental colleague, a close friend and a soldier of promise.

After our reception at the Club we had dinner in Soho, at a restaurant that we have never succeeded in finding again, and then went back to the Green Park Hotel. So ended the day on which I did the most sensible and rewarding thing in my life.

Early the next day, being Sunday, we returned to St James's Church for Holy Communion before catching the train to Edinburgh to settle into the small quarter the Army had provided for us behind Redford Barracks, at 18 Redford Bank. My Father had come to King's Cross to see us off. It was almost the last time I saw him alive.

Although my new job at the Headquarters of the Scottish Command was neither demanding nor particularly interesting, the War Office had done us a kindness in posting me to Edinburgh. Rosemary made our quarter in Redford Bank into a warm and admirable nest and I did my best to convert the wilderness in the rear into a colourful garden.

Almost before we had settled in we were roped into the local Army Drama group who were rehearsing Kenneth Horne's comedy about marriage, 'Fools Rush In'. The intention was to produce the play before Easter, but with people being posted and other interruptions it was early September before we were ready to face the public. We gave three performances; at Command Headquarters, in the Glasgow military hospital, and to the Staff and inmates of Edinburgh's Saughton jail. They were enthusiastic audiences; and no wonder, for there were some odd happenings in our production. I played the part of the bridegroom; my bride, a rather pretty little blond ATS girl, had a mental blackout in the last act which put me on my mettle; while my real wife, by then very visibly pregnant, had to be chased round the stage by an oversexed best man. As Rosemary's Mother was to write: 'Pregnant brides are these days two-a-penny alas, but who has heard of a pregnant bridesmaid?'

The medical care provided by the National Health Service coupled with the staff of the Simpson Memorial Hospital made Edinburgh a good place for Rosemary to have her first baby; our daughter was born on the last day of September 1957 and, just like her Mother, under the sign Libra. The previous evening I had taken Rosemary into the hospital and before going to bed took Fudge, our cat, into the garden. Looking up to the north I saw glorious multi-coloured columns of light, like the beams of many searchlights, brightening the sky over the city. Until then I had never seen the aurora borealis, and such a fine display so far to the south was, the papers announced, an exceptional event. Two other events which coincided with our daughter's arrival was the glow of the Soviet earth satellite Sputnik, launched on 4 October, orbiting our planet, in about one hundred minutes, a few hundred miles up; the precursor of the many more complex objects, some carrying Man, which the human race was to launch into space during her lifetime. The other event was the cost in Britain of posting a letter. It went up from 2½d to 3d.

But the most wonderful experience for me was my first glimpse of my wife, radiant and so pretty, holding our pink, blond, infant. We called her Jacqueline, a whimsical combination of Jack, my Father's nickname, and the Lynn of Rosemary's Mother. But from the first moment I saw her, Pinky she became and the name has stuck. She was christened on my 35th birthday in the tiny Chapel of St Margaret in Edinburgh Castle, a privilege reserved for the Governor and his personal staff of which I was a junior and quite undistinguished member.

Those were good days and from then on I started to record on 8-millimetre ciné film our more interesting domestic and professional experiences and the great number of places we were to visit. I did so initially with the small ciné camera which my Father left to me on his death in Millbank Military Hospital that August, and I continued to build up that film collection until the invention of the video camera rendered my film equipment obsolete. Thanks to Rosemary's Mother in Guiana we were able to buy our first car, a Morris Traveller, and in it the three of us toured the western part of Scotland.

By the autumn of 1958 I had done my stint on the Staff and was due to return to regimental duty with the 91st. They were in Cyprus, where a sizeable portion of the Army was engaged in hunting down the Greek-Cypriot terrorist organisation EOKA, which under the leadership of Colonel George Grivas, and the political direction of the Orthodox Archbishop Makarios, was by a campaign of sabotage and murder seeking to win for the island independence from Britain and bring about a union of Cyprus and Greece. This aim was flawed for three reasons. Cyprus had a large Turkish population, and no government in Ankara, it seemed to me, could accept the incorporation of Cyprus into the kingdom of Greece, which although a fellow-member of the North Atlantic Treaty Organisation (NATO) was Turkey's traditional enemy. Also, despite the support which many Greek Cypriots gave to Grivas and his guerillas in

CYPRUS.
Post 1975.

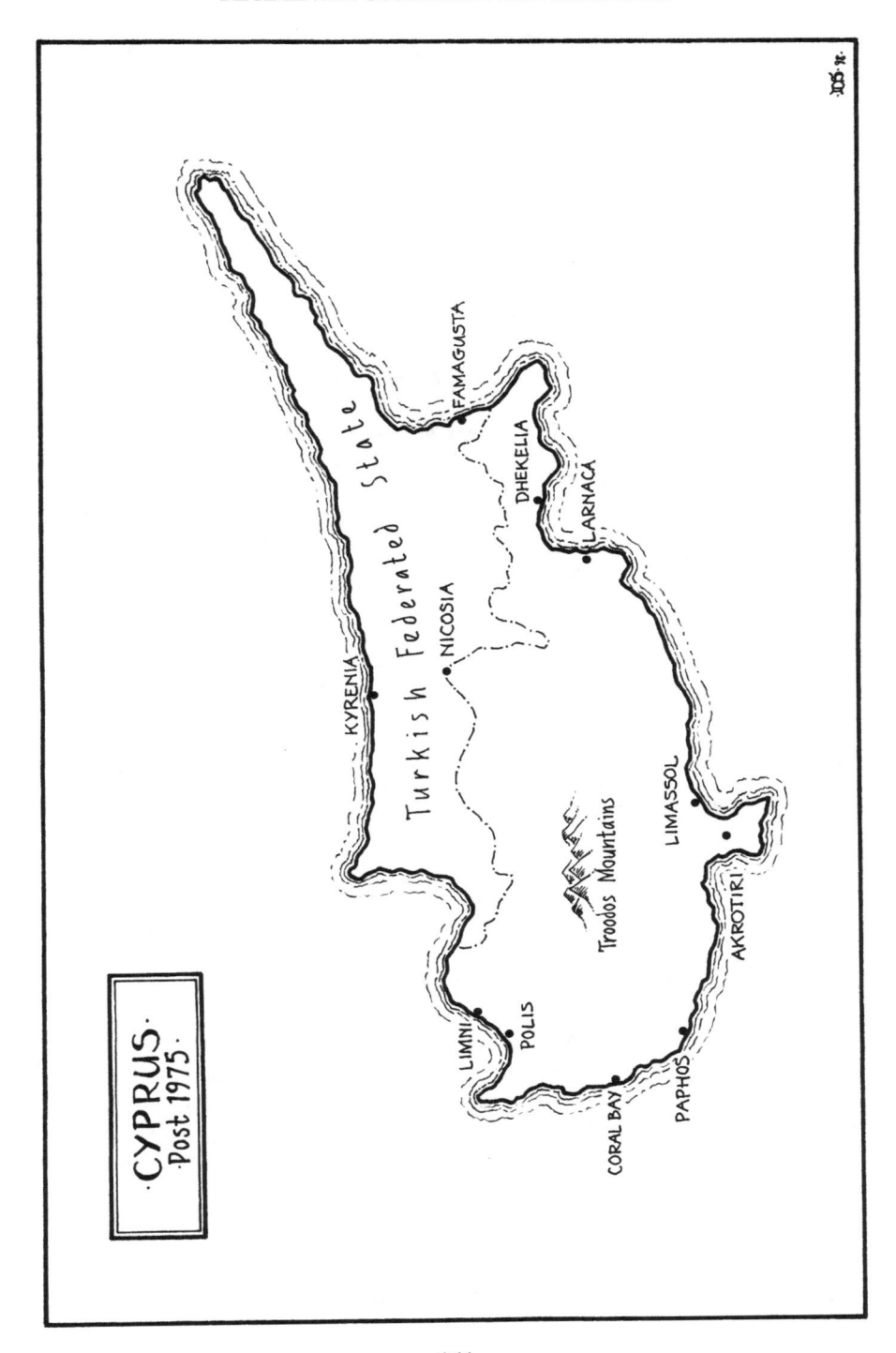

their anti-British activities, it seemed improbable that the wealthier and more influential of them would, when push came to shove, accept the lowering of their standard of living, measured in terms of prosperity and governmental competence, down to the level tolerated by the inhabitants of mainland Greece. Furthermore, it was unthinkable that Britain could be driven by force of insurgent arms to abrogate her interests in Cyprus and the responsibilities which she had shouldered there since 1878.

Nevertheless the defeat of the EOKA terrorists required the stationing on the island of a large number of units, the expenditure of a great deal of British taxpayers' money, and a distressing amount of British blood. Grivas and his followers achieved very little against organised groups of British Servicemen; the greatest number of casualties in our experience was caused by forest fires – the Gordon Highlanders had suffered particularly badly – and from burning tents. Smoking in bed had to be prohibited. EOKA turned instead to the killing by bomb and pistol of individual Servicemen and their wives, and Nicosia's Ledra Street became infamous as a place in which Britons alone out shopping or pushing prams were gunned down. The reports of these murders in the British newspapers, and on the black-and-white television screens which since the Coronation had been acquired by many households in the UK, angered the British public. They also alarmed it and spurred our government into reaching with the Greek Cypriots a political settlement before the total defeat of EOKA had been completed by our Armed Forces. The flaws in that settlement were visible from the day it was signed; most clearly to the local Turkish community and to the government of mainland Turkey, only forty miles away to the east; and a consequence was that about ten years later the Turkish Army invaded Cyprus and established in the north of the island a Turkish protectorate. The Greeks, we concluded, had not played their hand well in the matter of Cyprus.

In September I went out by troopship leaving Rosemary and the baby in London where she rented a flat in the hopes that the situation in Cyprus would soon calm down sufficiently to allow Service families to join their menfolk out there. I rejoined the 91st at Limni, in the north-west corner of the island, took command of a rifle company, and engaged in the busy series of patrols, guards, area searches, vehicle checks and other tactics used to catch EOKA members or at least to curb their activities. We were not very successful: large groups of conscripts are seldom effective against small, highly motivated bands of guerillas operating in their native environment. But on the reverse side of that coin, the only person, as far as I remember, who caused our battalion any trouble was a well-known, red-haired, female British Member of Parliament, Barbara Castle.

Before I arrived at Limni Camp one of the 91st's road convoys was ambushed and a soldier wounded. When the nearby village was cordoned off and searched some of our infuriated Jocks roughed up the inhabitants.

Barbara Castle heard of this and publicly voiced her disapproval of the Argylls' conduct. Although the Jocks' reaction had been reprehensible, her criticism did not go down at all well in our ranks and was generally viewed as further proof that the Labour Party was soft on terrorism and disloyal to the nation's Servicemen.

However, concealed beneath the mutual recriminations and unknown to most people, was the fact that later that year and for several years to come Mrs Castle and our Sergeants' Mess happily exchanged Christmas cards. The only other thing of any significance I remember about Limni Camp was its proximity to Aphrodite's Pool, the inlet where Venus had risen naked out of the sea in ancient times. One of our young colleagues had been permitted to have his bride out to Cyprus for a holiday, and being an attractive and enterprising girl she disrobed and copied what the legendary goddess had done many centuries earlier. Moreover she persuaded her husband, since they were quite alone at the Pool, to photograph her. No one else would have known of this performance if her husband had kept the photographs and negatives securely hidden, but he failed to do so and soon a greatly enlarged print of the regimental Venus of 1958 was circulating among the tents of the poor fellow's comrades.

Just before Christmas we left Limni and moved into a fine barracks in Dhekelia, one of the sovereign base areas in the now independent Cyprus retained by Britain under the settlement and important for her military role as a member of the alliances created to contain Soviet aggression in that region, NATO and the Baghdad Pact. Two months later Rosemary and Pinky were flown out by the War Office along with other families and we lived in a small house on the outskirts of Larnaca, a seaside town a mere ten minutes' drive from Dhekelia. Although we continued to carry out anti-terrorist operations, the heat had gone out of the situation and the battalion was freer to concentrate on training and reorganisation. As part of the former, John Slim and I set up a remote camp in the Troodos Mountains, and there ran a satisfying series of courses for our Regulars to bring their tactical skills and knowledge of counter-revolutionary warfare, as the subject came to be called, to a much higher standard than had been possible hitherto. Reorganisation was inevitable as the 91st, like the whole of the Army, was having to prepare for the end of National Service. About sixty per cent of our Officers and Men were conscripts, and apart from the few who opted to remain in the Service, all would be gone by 1962.

The peacetime Army composed solely of volunteers was going to require skills and a degree of motivation difficult to attain in a largely conscript Army with its continual flow of men passing through, some resenting the obligation to serve for two years imposed on them by Parliament in 1947.

Much has been written about the disadvantages of a system of recruitment to the Armed Forces based on conscription. It did disrupt the career-plans of those called up, and regiments continuously losing men just as they had been brought to a good state of military effectiveness could not attain the degree of cohesion and skill that combat and the increasing use of technology were demanding. Further, a tiny element of disaffected conscripts could hamper the smooth running of a unit. For although the Service with its centuries of experience, its traditions, code of discipline and the obligation to enforce it was more than a match for individual malcontents, the latter were never deprived of their right to complain to their Members of Parliament; and any subsequent Ministerial Inquiry demanded prompt and time-consuming investigation and a comprehensive personal report from the man's Commanding Officer. Soldiers most frequently complained of boredom, that the service forced them to spend much time on meaningless chores or on tasks beneath their dignity and qualifications. This charge was heard most from those in large static units such as administrative establishments and RAF Stations; much less in an infantry battalion with an operational role. The 91st was kept consistently busy; and as a happy youth is one who goes to bed tired, tedium and insomnia were rarely found in our barrack rooms.

A good regiment is a remarkably united family; and a compassionate one too. No matter what problem afflicts either Officer or Soldier, he is surrounded by comrades-in-arms to whom he can turn for advice and practical help; and if he is an Other Rank it is his Officers' duty to listen and help. If the problem is beyond their competence to solve, there exist the extensive resources of the Army on whom they can call. Some soldiers alas got themselves, or their wives got them, into such deep water before seeking help that the process of unravelling the resultant can of worms was a protracted and vexing business. Good Officers found the command of conscripts to be a rewarding experience, and I have encountered very few of my former soldiers, now civilians, who did not concede that they emerged from their period of National Service the better for having done it, and with memories in which the enjoyable far eclipsed the regrettable. The overwhelming majority made the best of their two years, resolved to enjoy the many activities which Service life offered, and to make a positive contribution to the platoon or whatever sub-unit they found themselves in.

For the Army, conscription based on a period of two years or less with the Colours was a burden and a disadvantage which could only be mitigated if the period was extended to three years or more. That, however, was politically unacceptable to the British. It was better therefore to end the obligation and to create, as we have done, a volunteer, all-regular Army. What that professional Army has achieved during the past thirty-seven years proves the correctness of that decision. But for many of the nation's young men and women from disadvantaged backgrounds the cessation of compulsory service has been a grievous loss, for they have been deprived of the experience of physical and mental well-being which comes, to an extent rarely found in civilian organisations and in too few families, from comradeship, enhanced self-esteem and pride in belonging to a well-led team usefully employed. And the moral fibre, the attitudes and in consequence the reputation of our country has slumped since the end of National Service; replaced by the soccer hooligan, the drug addict and the long-term unemployed.

As a *Daily Telegraph* leader declared in 1992 when lamenting the departure from the streets of London of the last shoe-shine man, the British tradition of cleaning one's shoes died with the end of National Service; and at this late stage in my life it seems to me that other fundamental virtues and national standards died too.

I had gone back to England in the autumn for a short intensive course on clandestine warfare during which we learned about some of the techniques used by our agents while operating with local resistance forces and about the counter measures used by our enemies. I was rather vexed that the Cyprus campaign fizzled out before I could put my new knowledge into practice, but a happy sequel to my brief passage through London was the birth in July of our son, Christopher. He arrived two weeks late, jaundiced and weighing ten pounds, which in mid-summer was all a bit of a trial for his Mother, but the RAMC team at the Dhekelia Military Hospital helped her through the event and all in all we have very happy memories of Cyprus. So much so that if Christopher had been a girl I should have been tempted to call her Larnaca or Dhekelia; after all, they are quite attractive feminine names. He was baptised in the Regimental Kirk on 27 September, his Mother's birthday.

A particular pleasure for us was having in nearby Nicosia 'Dusty' Miller, a stalwart Royal Engineer Captain with whom I had worked closely in Edinburgh, and his attractive wife, Maisie. In our branch of Headquarters Scottish Command, 'Dusty' and I had had as a colleague another Sapper Officer. This chap went off his head and had to be sent away for treatment in Netley, the Services' Psychiatric Hospital. While there he passed his time doing crossword puzzles; from one of them he won the huge sum of £500. Another of our fellow Officers was also a qualified Driving Examiner.

Rosemary and I had just acquired our first car, but I had no civilian licence. To get one I had, like every other citizen in the land, to pass a Driving Test. This was quite a stiff examination laid down by government, and one's future on the road was therefore determined by the Examiner. I was determined to pass the test first time so I approached the fellow with the following proposition: 'Andrew, the time for writing Annual Confidential Reports has arrived: it is my job to write yours. You, I know, are hoping to get a good one: for my part I urgently need to pass the Driving Test to get a licence. Can we work out an arrangement to our mutual advantage?' I got my licence.

Towards the end of the 91st's stay in Cyprus my Mother came out for Christopher's baptism and we had a happy week in the NAAFI Leave Camp up in the cool air of the Troodos Mountains; Colonel Hugh Spens came out to take over command from 'Chippie' Anderson and in October we embarked, in *Dilwara* again, for the journey back to Europe where the battalion was to become part of the British Army of the Rhine.

After a short stay near London, we four set out for the Republic of West Germany in our grey Morris Traveller which had been to Cyprus and back with us. The journey took two days' driving via Dover-Ostend-Liège and Aachen. We got to know the road from Ostend to Aachen well during the next two decades, and never failed to note a feeling of relief on entering West Germany with her splendid autobahns and civic orderliness; a contrast to the monotonous red brick buildings along the cobbled roads of Belgium whose drivers were alleged to be the worst in Europe and where the signs in Flemish offend both eye and ear.

Many Belgians I like very much; but I had long regarded the Kingdom of Belgium as an unnecessary country, and often conjectured with colleagues how different the course of recent European history might have been if that portion of the continent had remained divided between France and the Netherlands as it had been before the creation in 1839 of an independent Belgium. Would the Schlieffen Plan have directed von Kluck's thirty-four divisions, the right wing of the German Army, through those Belgian provinces if they had in 1914 been Dutch?

And would Britain have gone to war in August 1914 if that solemn guarantee of Belgium's neutrality, Bethmann-Hollweg's 'scrap of paper', had not existed? And would our Expeditionary Force have fared better there in May 1940 if the defence of that region had been the duty of authorities, other than a King and government in Brussels, with a less parochial vision of what had to be done to counter the German menace?

I thus gave Belgium a lower rating than Germany or France. This personal opinion, superficial, foolishly prejudiced and, many will say, wholly wrong I was able to justify to myself by recalling to mind the public lavatory at the Aachen frontier crossing point. That long building stood half in Belgium, half in Germany, invisibly bisected by the line of the frontier. Many times have I been obliged to use the conveniences maintained therein by the two nations. The German half was invariably immaculate – hygienic, odourless, with paper, soap and other requirements restored daily. The Belgian half was in these respects habitually horrendous, and the sight and smell of that midden lingers still.

But that was long ago and the two lavatories have no doubt been 'harmonised' under the influence of the European Union; and the memory of the welcome we had received from the people of Belgium in 1944 on entering their country as liberators, in contrast to that of the grudging French, has now caused me to revise my anti-Belgian prejudice.

Our new home, already our fourth in three years of marriage, was in Lemgo, a small attractive town near Bielefeld. Our well-built quarters on the outskirts of the town stood below the wooded slopes of a high hill in an attractive tree-lined street named after a former Mayor. In April 1945 he had decided to surrender the town to the advancing Canadians rather than inflict on Lemgo pointless damage and bloodshed, but a group of local Nazis, murderously inflamed by the imminent collapse of Hitler's Reich, deemed his compassion to be treason and killed him.

Lemgo lies a short distance to the west of the River Weser, that major barrier astride the North German Plain which would be the pathway for any onrush of Soviet armoured forces heading out of East Germany and Poland for the Rhine crossings, the Channel coast and even, the most gloomy scenarios pictured, the Pyrenees. The possibility of a Soviet attack on west Europe was always in our minds; fear of Communist aggression and the measures necessary to contain it had, since the late 1940s, been a constant factor in determining the policies world-wide of Britain, our west European friends and of our Allies in the new world, Canada and the United States. Faced by the secretive, monolithic empire of the USSR and her satellite states, and chastened by post-war confrontations in Greece, Berlin, Korea and SE Asia, the western democracies had created a system of alliances for their collective defence against the Communist threat. But in 1959, on the continent of Europe, they were outnumbered on land, at sea and in the air; and also in the vital field of nuclear armaments; and when the Argylls arrived in Lemgo to join BAOR we were living through anxious times. As political and economic strains began to surface in parts of the Red Empire, as they already had in East Berlin and in Hungary (both bloodily repressed), grounds for taking seriously the prospect of a war between the Warsaw Pact and NATO had become more rather than less valid.

The 91st's barracks which we took over from the Royal Hampshire Regiment were, like all German military establishments of the Nazi era, solidly constructed and provided space, facilities and central heating of a standard rarely enjoyed by Servicemen in Britain; and Lemgo had a further attraction in that it was a single-unit station. We Argylls had the place to ourselves. So we settled down quickly, resolved to enjoy life on the continent and to master our new role as part of NATO's 'trip-wire' defence strategy. And for Rosemary and me the prospect of living with our two infants in an excellently appointed German house for at least a year was both exciting and comforting. This agreeable spell of domestic bliss was enhanced by Lisa Schrader, a local girl who fell in love with Christopher's huge brown eyes and serene disposition and enlisted herself as his Nanny. Lisa was to stay with us for nearly three years.

The 91st was now part of 20th Armoured Brigade and each of our three rifle companies was affiliated to one of that formation's tank regiments. In order to keep up with their tracked Centurions and Conquerors we, Infantry, became mechanised, mounted in Saracens, wheeled armoured vehicles, in those days driven and maintained by a squadron of the 14th/20th Hussars.

This mechanised role was great fun for all of us in the companies; much less fun for our Colonel, Hugh Spens. He had been our Brigade Major in the war, having replaced a Seaforth, John Lochore, killed during our division's first operation, EPSOM. Hugh had intended to be a lawyer but he did well in the war so stayed on in the Army of so-called peacetime. It was his misfortune to command the Regiment at a time when the responsibility for its administration and discipline fell squarely on his shoulders but without the stimulus of having the complete battalion operating as one unit under his leadership. Thus he bore the burdens of command but enjoyed few of the perks. This was bad luck as he was an exceedingly fair, intelligent and sensitive man, and an experienced soldier. I like to think that our regard and affection for Hugh and his charming wife, Mary, made up in part for that deprivation.

For me, that year in Lemgo was a period of great happiness and professional fulfilment. My D Company of Argylls was affiliated to the 3rd Royal Tank Regiment, and with Colonel Peter Vaux, his ebullient 2IC, Bryan Watkins, and their squadrons my little band of Jocks soon established an excellent relationship. We did our stuff on the many exercises in which we combined with, I believe, versatility and zest. Those were good days. But it was just as well that those were only exercises, not real war; for I was always conscious of how greatly the tank crews relied on us Infantrymen for their protection at night and in close country, and yet we had to do all that with only about one hundred men; and once dismounted from our Saracens we would be vastly more vulnerable to the perils of the battlefield than our friends in their heavily armoured tanks. In a real war we would, I calculated, soon be reduced by casualties and exhaustion to ineffectiveness. A ratio of one mechanised battalion to each armoured regiment would have been more realistic. Fortunately, like so many of the BAOR units of that era whose operational commitments exceeded their human and material capabilities, we were never put to the test.

We also took the opportunity to develop a close association with a local unit of the German Bundeswehr, a Panzer-grenadier brigade in Augustdorf commanded by an amiable Colonel whose name, if anglicised, was Pancake. We rather envied the equipment and clothing of those conscripted young Krauts, now our NATO colleagues.

I was fortunate in my Company's Officers. The three platoon commanders, Andrew Dewar-Durie and Andrew Younger, both sons of the Regiment, and Calum Murray were engaging young men and sensible managers and leaders of their soldiers. My 2IC, Tim Macpherson, was a very special person. Sturdy in physique and sterling in character, he had a broad, slightly freckled complexion, nearly always brightened by a teasing smile and crowned by straight chestnut coloured hair. At Sedbergh School and at Sandhurst he had been an incorrigible prankster, but with his commission into the Argylls came maturity and deliberation in his actions and in his speech. Tim had a host of interests; whether on duty with his Jocks, on the sports field, shooting, hunting or exploring the hills and inlets of the Western Highlands he engaged himself totally; and in almost everything he undertook he outshone his peers.

His bride, christened Deirdre Higham but always 'Mouse' thereafter, whom he married shortly before joining us at Lemgo, was his exact opposite in appearance; but in character and interests they were very much alike. Tim and Mouse made an admirable couple. They both came from happy, secure homes. Tim was born in Calcutta in March 1936 as his South African-born Father had come to Oxford on a Rhodes Scholarship, married Joan from the well-known Suffolk family of Olivers, and they spent much of his working life in India, while the Olivers looked after Tim in loco parentis. Both the Highams and the Macphersons had a great love for Scotland, for the Army and for country life. But Mouse's chiefest love was for Tim whom she adored from the first time they met.

Blond, sylph-like, vivacious and tireless she enlivened the waking hours of everyone around her; from her lips ideas, observations, anecdotes and encouragements flowed like a glistening stream. She had a child-like innocence. Animals recognised this too. Throughout her life Mouse enjoyed a remarkable relationship with living things, and it was quite normal to find her car or house a crowded sanctuary for tamed hawks, wounded birds, orphaned kittens, nests of field mice and colonies of caterpillars. Her chief talent, however, was as an artist; at the age of 16 she had been the youngest painter to exhibit in the Royal Academy, and her sketches, water colours and oil paintings are treasured possessions of a legion of her friends; and in the Argylls' home in Stirling Castle her pictures constitute a fine record of regimental feats of arms. To further enrich their lives (and ours), Mouse and Tim produced three gifted and attractive daughters, Louise, Kate and Iona, to the eldest of whom my Rosemary became a devoted Godmother.

It was wholly in Tim's character that, after a year with the 91st in Lemgo and a change of company commander, he should seek a fresh military challenge, and he put in for the stiffest challenge going – selection for the Special Air Service Regiment, that remarkable band of versatile British soldiers known the world over as the SAS. An injury to a knee, alas, put paid to his hopes of being selected; it also resulted in him being classed as permanently unfit for service in a combat-ready Infantry unit. Tim could have stayed in the Army but only by transferring to an administrative corps. This he was unwilling to do, so in 1961 he left the Service and Associated British Maltsters took him on as a trainee barley buyer. He and Mouse entered a testing phase of life in a civilian career, starting near the bottom of the ladder, working alongside people whose attitudes and standards contrasted ill with those of his former colleagues, and being paid little for long hours of work and travel.

Tim and Mouse bought a house in the Thames Valley, near Wallingford, and when in 1963 I was sent, unaccompanied by my family, to the Persian Gulf, they in the kindest of many kind acts took Rosemary and our two kids into the top half of their Elm House. Tim, marvellously supported by Mouse, impressed everybody with the tenacity with which he grappled with his new career in the world of malt and barley, and his reliability and worth were soon recognised. He climbed his way steadily up the ABM ladder, reaching the appointment of Managing Director in 1980 and soon after being made a Director of Dalgety UK. He became a highly respected senior figure and to the diversity of farmers, brewers, distillers, retailers and workmen engaged in that industry he became a true and long-remembered friend.

Rosemary, Pinky, Christopher and I kept in close touch with Tim and his Four Mice – the affectionate epithet by which they were universally known – and because we had not seen each other for some time, Tim and I arranged to meet at the Regimental Dinner in London in the spring of 1986. Tim never arrived. Pressure of work had delayed him; and as he, Mouse and Iona, now almost 21 years old, were about to fly off for a long-awaited holiday in the Indian Ocean, Tim stayed at home to finish packing and all the other last-minute essentials. On 3 May their aircraft, the flagship of the Air Lanka fleet, was preparing to take off from Colombo airport for the Maldive Islands when a bomb concealed, it is thought, in a crate of vegetables in the baggage hold, blew off the entire rear section of the aircraft, incinerating ten rows of seats and scattering debris over a fifty-yard radius. Tim, Mouse and Iona were killed instantly; with them died twenty-eight other passengers, forty-one more being badly injured. Responsibility for the explosion was claimed by one of the several Tamil groups who had for fifteen years been waging a guerilla war with the Sri Lankan Government for an independent Tamil state. When the newspapers named the Macphersons as the three Britons killed by that atrocious act, the effect on their friends was devastating; it was incomprehensible that such a family should be murdered while fleetingly passing through a civil war of which they probably knew nothing.

A Memorial Service was held the next month in the Church of St Mary Magdalene in Newark-on-Trent, not far from their home in the Lincolnshire village of Walcot. It was attended by some six hundred mourners including many of their Argyll friends and a host of Tim's associates from the malting industry. It was a wonderful assembly of people united in shock at the manner of their deaths, but also in pride at having been privileged to know those three fellow human beings during their short time on this earth.

Rosemary commissioned Marion Smith, the well-known sculptor, to design for us a lasting tribute to the Macphersons who had brought into the lives of the Graham family much joy and friendship. The finished work is of a sheaf of corn with, playing on it, five harvest mice. It is now in the possession of their eldest daughter, Rosemary's Godchild, Louise.

One of the pleasures of living on the continent is the opportunity it gives for visiting the centres of Christian civilisation and European pleasure grounds readily and without the hassle and expense of the Channel crossing. From the time of our arrival in Lemgo we got to know Europe well, though not of course those forbidden countries behind the Iron Curtain; and until Rosemary and I started our life in the Caribbean thirty years later, we cheerfully devoted time and money to continental excursions.

We were fortunate in being physically fit, owning a car and during the children's infancy in having Lisa Schrader to take charge of them.

The British soldier has many admirable qualities but in the 1960s enterprise was not one of them. Throughout my years with the Jocks and the Toms I was often dismayed by their lack of initiative. Few of them at weekends ventured beyond the limits of the married quarters and the NAAFI Club; and their long leaves were more often than not dutifully spent with Mum and Dad back in Scotland or England. Even the excellent and varied expeditions which the Army of the Rhine organised for All Ranks, and in large part paid for, were undersubscribed. Few of my compatriots attempted to learn the local language, a fact which many Germans regarded both as a discourtesy and proof of British insularity and sloth; and at the British taxpayers' expense, arrangements had to be made to bring into the barracks and quarters of the British Servicemen in West Germany English television programmes. For the lethargy demonstrated by our soldiers when off-duty some blame could be laid on their wives. Semi-educated, callow, for the first time in their lives separated from Mum, many were ill-fitted to cope in a foreign land with the business of running a house, raising children, controlling the household budget and contributing positively to their husbands' careers. Mercifully the British Army's duty of care for all its members, and traditional regimental dedication, kept many a military marriage off the rocks and transformed numerous immature brides into confident and productive women. Our nation has never properly recognised the amount of energy, time and money the wives of our senior servicemen expended in mothering the young marrieds in their ranks, and in many cases having to unravel, with no specialised training for the task, domestic dramas of extraordinary complexity. Nor could the nation know of this devotion: to the commissioned and Warrant Officers of my generation and our wives, it was an accepted part of regimental life. The Service came first, and its Officers were the reticent guardians of every subordinate however exasperating or demanding.

I noticed too that relationships between our units and the German population were pretty slender. Intercourse, collective and individual, between Briton and Boche was restrained. Relations became closer during the later years of the British military presence on German soil, due chiefly to the influence of some far-sighted senior commanders in BAOR; and simultaneously the British soldier of the professional Regular Army, more imaginative, ambitious and better paid than the conscripts of earlier decades, ventured farther afield and used his off-duty time to greater advantage.

Those who married German girls and stayed to live out their lives in that country seem to have made a wise decision; most have found there contentment and substantial material rewards, for the skills, discipline and attitudes they absorbed while in khaki have stood them in good stead in German society.

But in Britain in the 1960s the memory of the two World Wars and the misery inflicted by the Empires of Kaiser Wilhelm and Adolf Hitler were fresh in our minds. For our younger colleagues the barbarities of the Third Reich were visible close at hand within our sector of Germany, while recorded in print and on film were the centres, in the Slav lands farther east, of even greater brutality and mass extermination. I had been taken to see the Concentration Camp at Bergen-Belsen in 1948. I returned there in 1960. By then the rows of huts, rusting wire, discarded helmets of guards and the other detritus of war had been removed. The area was orderly, clean and the mass graves of the thirty thousand victims were decently grassed over. But Belsen even fifteen years after liberation by Field Marshal Montgomery's victorious army was a place of total silence and stillness. Most visitors, appalled by the monuments they examined, attributed the absence of birds and insects to Nature's revulsion. The true reason, however, was chemical: the quantities of quick-lime that had of necessity been thrown down into that place of death had destroyed all insect life and made of Belsen Camp a desert incapable of sustaining bird life.

German rule had created places of equal but less known infamy. One day while out on a training area near Paderborn, a group of us paused to eat lunch on the edge of a grassy field, in the centre of which stood a small granite pillar, half hidden by brambles and thistles. We examined it more closely and on a small metal plaque found an inscription in German and Russian recording the burial during the years 1941–5 of more than eighty thousand Russian prisoners-of-war. Later that day, back in the Training Area Mess, we enquired of the barman, a German too young to have served in the war, about the camps in which those unfortunate Russians had been confined and the reasons why so many had died in German hands. 'Was it not,' we asked, 'shameful that Germans had permitted such a fearful mortality among humans, albeit captive enemy, in their charge?' The young man was totally unmoved by our question. 'What do you expect?' he retorted, for he spoke excellent English, 'when so many men, already under-nourished and illiterate, are brought out of their warm, dry, savage homelands in Central Asia and confined for many months in the damp and cold of Westphalia?' Truly, Germans differ from other nations of the European community, in part on account of history, of religion, conquest and culture. But it seems to me that the greatest differences are to be seen within Germany itself, between German and German; between the inhabitants of those provinces once conquered by Roman arms and those which were not. In the former the seeds of west European law, order, religion and morality were planted; in the latter, in which the Romans did not settle, Teutonic vision and energy over the following centuries were in the main engaged in savage wars against the tribes pressing in from the East – Poles, Balts, Swedes, Muscovites and Mongols.

Have not the recent woeful experiences of the peoples of Europe been caused primarily by the character, ambitions and fury of Prussia, supported by the stern and disciplined societies of Pomerania, Thuringia and Brandenburg, German lands which Rome failed to embrace within her Empire?

Not far from Lemgo is a range of tree-covered hills, the Teutoberger Wald; and, standing high above the trees, is a memorial to the German warrior chieftain, Arminius. Each day parties of Germans and interested tourists climb up the slope to the foot of the immense bronze statue. I once asked an elderly man why he and his wife made a habit of walking up to Hermannsdenkmal (as the statue to Arminius is termed). 'Because he was the great leader of the German tribes who near this place in AD 9 crushingly defeated the invading Roman legions of Varus, and I salute him.' I asked him: 'But might it not be said that by his victory over Varus your Hermann, in the long term, did to the German nation lasting harm? For his victory halted the armies of Rome; and thus the spread eastwards of Roman rule and all its benefits did not extend much beyond the valleys of the Rhine and of the Danube?'

We were sorry to leave Lemgo in November 1960, and it seemed that my D Company also regretted our departure. The Jocks presented Rosemary and me with an engraved silver salver and a set of wine glasses, and the Military Band, whose President I was, well and truly fixed me with round upon round of doctored drinks at our farewell party. Although no one knew it at the time, incurable diseases were soon to claim the lives of Hugh Spens, our clever, gentle and kind CO, of Glen Kelway-Bamber, our elegant and charming 2IC, and of my Company Sergeant-Major, Jim Harrison.

But new and exciting pastures lay before us, for my new job was to be in France at the centre of the organisation responsible for deterring an attack on western Europe and North America by the Soviet Union and her Warsaw Pact partners; and should that deterrent fail, for striking back, using as appropriate, the forces of the Alliance, conventional and nuclear.

Notes

1. Passed Staff College
2. Elspeth Graham came from central European stock; her maiden name was Sauer. She used to emphasize her englishness by exclaiming: 'Abroad is bloody and all foreigners are fiends'. In that era our continental neighbours were commonly referred to by the Englishman-in-the-Street as 'Frogs, Huns, Wops and Dagoes'.

CHAPTER VII
1960–1961
With NATO in Fontainebleau (HQ AFCENT)
A Coup that Failed

The fifteen nations of the North Atlantic Treaty Organisation (NATO), including since 1955 the Federal Republic of Germany, contributed land, sea and air forces to the defence of west Europe. Responsible for planning and coordinating their operational roles, harmonising training standards and effectiveness was the Supreme Allied Commander Europe (SACEUR). This appointment was always held by a distinguished United States Officer of five-star rank. In 1960 he was General Lauris Norstad, a handsome, blond airman of Scandinavian parentage. His Headquarters, SHAPE, were at Rocquencourt, near Paris. Subordinate to SACEUR were four geographical commands, Allied Forces Northern Europe (AFNORTH), Allied Forces Southern Europe (AFSOUTH), Allied Forces Mediterranean (AFMED) and Allied Forces Central Europe (AFCENT). The Headquarters of each was manned by an international staff of armed forces personnel and civilians, and were located respectively near Oslo, in Naples, on Malta, and at Fontainebleau. Throughout NATO business was conducted in the two official languages, English and French. I spoke French and was being sent to Fontainebleau to join the personal staff of the Commander-in-Chief (CINCENT) as his Military Assistant in the rank of Major.

France: A Coup That Failed

Our house at No 12 rue François Millet in Avon, was in a pretty depressing condition with an antique central heating system, crude sanitation, dim lighting and sombre paintwork. It was also costly to rent but there was no alternative. Lisa Schrader, who had never before set foot beyond the limits of her German home-town, was shocked by the housing conditions that the French, and we their guests, had to put up with; but we soon got cracking with paint brushes and disinfectant. Behind the house was a long, high-walled garden, excellent for the children to play in and for growing dahlias. Our communist neighbour, a garrulous pensioner, had two passions: gardening – most of my superb dahlias were gifts from him – and denigrating the President of the Republic. 'De Gaulle,' he used to call out to me, 'what claim to fame has he? In the first war a prisoner of the Germans, in the second a prisoner of the English: pouf!'

Another man we got to know and to respect was M. Grandpré. He had served for many years in the French Army, fighting in that long unsuccessful war in Indo-China against the brutal Viet-Minh and afterwards in Algeria against the FNL. Eight times wounded, he was discharged from the Military a deeply bitter man. He took a part-time job with the local Fire Brigade, but to make ends meet went round the houses of NATO officers stoking our boilers at dawn and sunset. The thing which most embittered him after his life in the service of his country was the complete indifference of the politicians in Paris to the ordeals which he and his colleagues had been put through in furtherance of the doomed policies of successive governments in metropolitan France. Thirteen years later soldiers of the United States were to drink from the same poisoned chalice on their defeat by the Viet Cong in the same Indo-China.

Our house was very ill-designed for entertaining, but in Rosemary's hands nevertheless became a happy home for us, and for our friends a place of laughter and good food. We look back on our time there with real warmth. It was near the shops in Avon and Fontainebleau, a thirty-minute drive from Paris up a first class road and only a ten-minute walk through the Park to my office. This daily journey caused a few titters at first as I was the only kilted chap in that bit of France. The variety of badges, hats, tartans, mess kits and sartorial idiosyncracies which distinguish the individual regiments and corps of the British Army was a source of perplexity and amusement to our Allies with their more uniform uniforms; but of esteem too, for it was recognized that our Army's long record of success can be largely attributed to Regimental Pride and Tradition. In my days at Fontainebleau NATO was commonly described as 'an organisation the Americans pay for, the British run and the rest attend.'

This contained an element of truth. Of the NATO Allies the British and French alone since 1945 had unbroken experience of active military operations, but the latter tended not to place their best Officers in international staff appointments. They treated the highest appointments allocated to France as posts for recuperation between stressful tours overseas.

The Federal Republic of Germany was represented by some very able and experienced men, many of whom had been through the crucibles of the Eastern Front and Normandy; but that country had only joined the alliance in 1955 and members of the newly created Bundeswehr, mindful of the catastrophe of 1945 and the appalling record of Hitler's Third Reich, kept a low profile and chose to walk delicately in the corridors of NATO. The American contribution in World War Two had been extensive and superlative in both the European and Pacific theatres, but apart from an unhappy experience in Korea in 1950-3, they were to engage in no significant military operations until they got into the quagmire of Viet Nam in the 1960s. In matters concerning Europe and Europeans they were still on a learning curve.

The British contingents at SHAPE and AFCENT were, by and large, recognized as containing high quality Officers; even junior chaps such as I had not only served in the War but had since 1945 been engaged on operations in Palestine, Malaya, Korea, East Africa, Cyprus and Suez. They were also rated to be the best trained for staff work and to demonstrate initiative with less prompting than their equivalent ranks in other armies. Of course our contingents included some weak links – chaps posted to NATO jobs for compassionate or medical reasons – and some of the wives were pretty unattractive representatives of our country. Nevertheless, the proven quality of the British Serviceman of that era had secured for the United Kingdom in the Treaty Organisation positions of influence and responsibility in excess of what our nation's size and wealth entitled her. British Officers, for example, held the appointments of Deputy SACEUR, the commands of AFNORTH, of the air forces of AFCENT, of the Northern Army Group, of the Second Tactical Air Force and the naval command of the Channel. Air Chief Marshal Sir Harry Broadhurst's Air HQ and the Naval HQ of the Dutch Admiral van Erkel were located on the outskirts of Fontainebleau in Camp Guynemer, named after a French air ace of the Great War. CINCENT and his Personal Staff and the HQ of General Dr Hans Speidel[1], formerly Chief of Staff to Field Marshal Erwin Rommel in the Normandy campaign of 1944 and now Commander of the Land Forces, were housed more prestigiously in the Château de Fontainebleau and in the adjoining Aile des Princes built on the four sides of a splendid courtyard, la Cour Henri IV, access to which was through a fine archway leading off the main town square, la Place d'Armes.

Next to the Château and virtually unoccupied was the Palais, best known outside France perhaps as the place where the Emperor Napoleon bade farewell to his Army on his abdication and exile to Elba in April 1814. The Palais and the Château both backed onto extensive and well kept lawns with gravelled paths and trees, and an artificial lake, l'Etang des Carpes, filled since before the time of Napoleon with fish of extraordinary size and appetites. Taking the kids to feed the voracious carp became an exciting part of our Sunday routine.

The French tell a nice story about this lake. In the autumn of 1940 when the RAF had won the air battle over Britain and the Germans had failed to invade England, Hitler, it is said, arranged a meeting at Fontainebleau at which he, Mussolini, his Italian ally, and Churchill discussed the military stalemate and would come to some arrangement for ending the war on terms favourable to the undoubted victor, Germany. The three men spent the whole morning and much of the afternoon in fruitless argument: Churchill despite all the evidence of German superiority and strategic advantage would not concede victory to Adolf Hitler. Tea time arrived but still no concession from Churchill. Hitler, enraged by the Englishman's refusal to acknowledge the obvious facts of the military situation, looked at his watch and exclaimed: 'Enough of this time-wasting talk. I am a very busy man and I have to get back to Berlin tonight'. To Churchill he said: 'I understand that you English like sporting competitions and often solve your disputes by gambling and wagers, so I'll make a special proposition to you.' Pointing at the Carp Pond he said: 'See those fish? Do you agree that the first one of us three who catches a fish without using any normal fishing equipment shall be declared the winner of the war?'. To his surprise Churchill replied, 'Yes, I agree'. Whereupon Hitler pulled out his revolver and fired off a stream of bullets into the lake. That killed no fish. The Führer then seized his Italian friend and pushed him into the water with the order: 'Duce, stay in the water until you've caught a fish!'. About half an hour later an exhausted, sodden Mussolini crawled back onto the path; no fish caught. Hitler turned to Churchill with the words: 'Your turn now', but he was not wholly despondent for, he reasoned, how could an elderly Englishman achieve what the younger and more vigorous Axis partners had failed to do? Winston Churchill placed his cup and saucer on the table but keeping the teaspoon in his hand moved across to the Pond, then kneeling down he began to throw the water, spoonful by spoonful, over his shoulder onto the grass behind him. They stared at him with amazement. 'What in God's name are you doing?' Churchill looked up at his two opponents and grunted: 'It will take a long time, but I shall win the war'.

The Personal Staff of CINCENT, le Cabinet, which I now joined, was headed by Colonel Sengès of the Foreign Legion, supported by Lieutenant-Colonel Bûchet and four Service Assistants. The French Assistant, Commandant Robert Allard de Grandmaison, was an excellent fellow and his advice and help were invaluable to us three foreigners: Major Bill Wildman, a likeable teddy-bear of an Air Assistant from the US

Air Force, married to a petite, dynamic wife who bullied him, and Korvetten-Kapitän Hubert Jeschke, a wartime U-boat Officer and an amusing bachelor with a love of French wines and gastronomy. He was to marry the following year a French girl whom we all liked; but until then spent much of his time, for as Naval Assistant he had too little to do, asleep at his desk next to mine. And there was I, the Military Assistant. We were a happy trio and soon were given the individual nicknames of the missile weaponry then in service with NATO. I was 'Honest John', Bill Wildman 'Blue Streak' and Hubert 'Sea Slug'.

General of the Air Force Maurice Challe welcomed me into his cabinet with a nice little speech – he spoke no English – and throughout our short collaboration I found him to be considerate, appreciative and on occasions amusing. But from our first meeting I got the impression that he was tired and preoccupied. Aged 55, short and thick-set, he was widely regarded in French military circles as a quiet man of great intelligence and professional ability. Born in the Vaucluse he had entered the Air Force in 1927, and from 1942 organised with considerable skill and of value to the Allied cause an intelligence network within the French Resistance. After the Second World War he had served in Germany, Morocco and Paris, but in 1958 Maurice Challe's thoughts and actions, and like that of so many of his compatriots, his fate became consumed by events in Algeria. That broad and productive area of North Africa, French since 1830 with a population of over ten million, predominantly Muslims of Arab or Berber blood, had been created and enriched by the toil and enterprise of those many French settlers who had made that country their home, and whose common destiny with France had since 1881 been recognised by the status of Algérie Française as a part of metropolitan France. That this status should remain immutable and permanent was fundamental to the thinking of the French settlers, the *colons*; and in this they were long supported by the thinking of the population of France, by successive governments in Paris and by a significant number of native Muslims who accepted French rule, enjoyed its benefits and who in the end were to suffer grievously for their loyalty to France.

By the 1950s Arab nationalism was becoming a dominant factor in the Middle East and North Africa. The overthrow of the pro-western monarchies in Iraq, Egypt and in Libya, the rise of Colonel Nasser in Egypt and his enhanced reputation after the fiasco of the Anglo-French intervention at Suez in 1956, and western support of Israel despite the injustices inflicted on the Palestinian Arabs, all these events caused an upsurge in the Arab world of militancy and Islamic brotherhood. In Algeria an armed struggle for independence broke out in 1954 headed by the FNL (National Liberation Front), and as the conflict

1 *Above left:* Tommy Carew-Hunt, my Maternal Grandfather

2 *Above right:* Max Graham, my Paternal Grandfather

3 Thomas Graham of Balgowan, Lord Lynedoch *(Sir Thomas Lawrence)*

4 The Honourable Mrs Graham, née Mary Cathcart *(Thomas Gainsborough)*

5 *Below right:* My Father, John Alexander (Jack) Graham

6 *Below left:* My Mother, Constance Mary (Jane) Graham, 1921

7 *Above left:* Jane Graham in India, 1934

8 *Above right:* Cosmo Graham

9 JDCG, Colchester, 1933

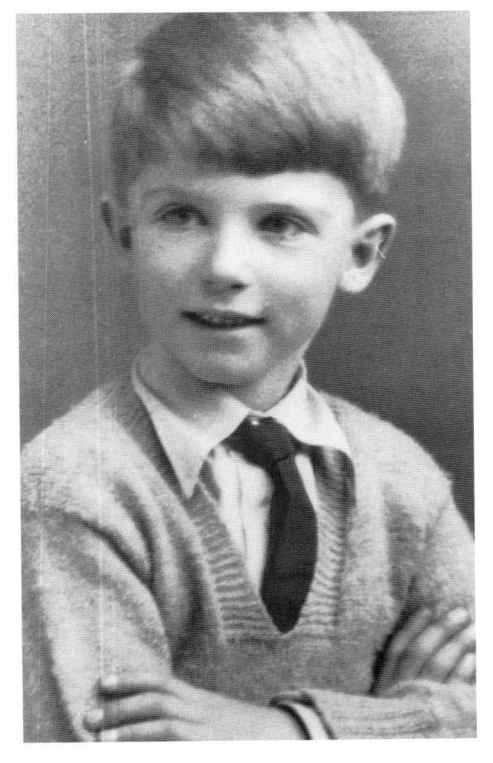

this page

10 *Above left:* Elspeth Graham with JDCG, 1949

11 *Above right:* Tommy Carew-Hunt with his second wife, Mida

12 *Left:* My Mother with my Brothers, Moray and Alastair, 1942

opposite page

13 *Top left:* Lieut-Colonel J W Tweedie, DSO, CO 2nd Bn The Argyll & Sutherland Highlanders (2A&SH), 1943-44

14 *Top right:* Lieut-Colonel D R Morgan, DSO, MC, CO 2nd Bn The Argyll & Sutherland Highlanders, 1944-45

15 The Officers of 2nd Bn The Argyll & Sutherland Highlanders shortly before embarking for Normandy, 1944

Officers of the 93rd, Findon, June 1944. *Left to right, back row:* Lieuts. Williamson, Robertson, Mackenzie, Morris, Murdoch, Cornish. *Third row:* Lieuts. Brady, H. Dunning, Capts. Sloan, Lyon, Lieuts. Graham, Macfarlane, Beck, McCall, J. Dunning, Dobson, Sword. *Second row:* Capt. Jones, R.A.M.C., Lieuts. Graham, Gillies, Capts. Phillips, Bruce, Spenceley, McElwee, Muirhead, Kenny, Caskie, R.A.Ch.D. *Front row:* Capt. Moreton, Majors Fyfe, Graham, Morgan, Lt.-Col. Tweedie, Capt. Fyfe, Majors Kenneth, MacKinnon, M.C., Capt. Robertson

16 JDCG with No 8 Platoon, 'The Plums', May 1944. Pte McLeod (back row far right)

17 My 2A&SH Intelligence Section at our 1993 reunion in York. *From left:* Maurice Tucker, John Park, Harry Oakley, Alf Horsley, Maurice Lester-Mallinson

18 CSM Leslie, 5 PARA in Husum, 1948

19 Moray and Alastair, Versailles, 1949

20 Sir Pierson Dixon with Colonel Francis Blake and Major Guy Wheeler, Prague, 1950

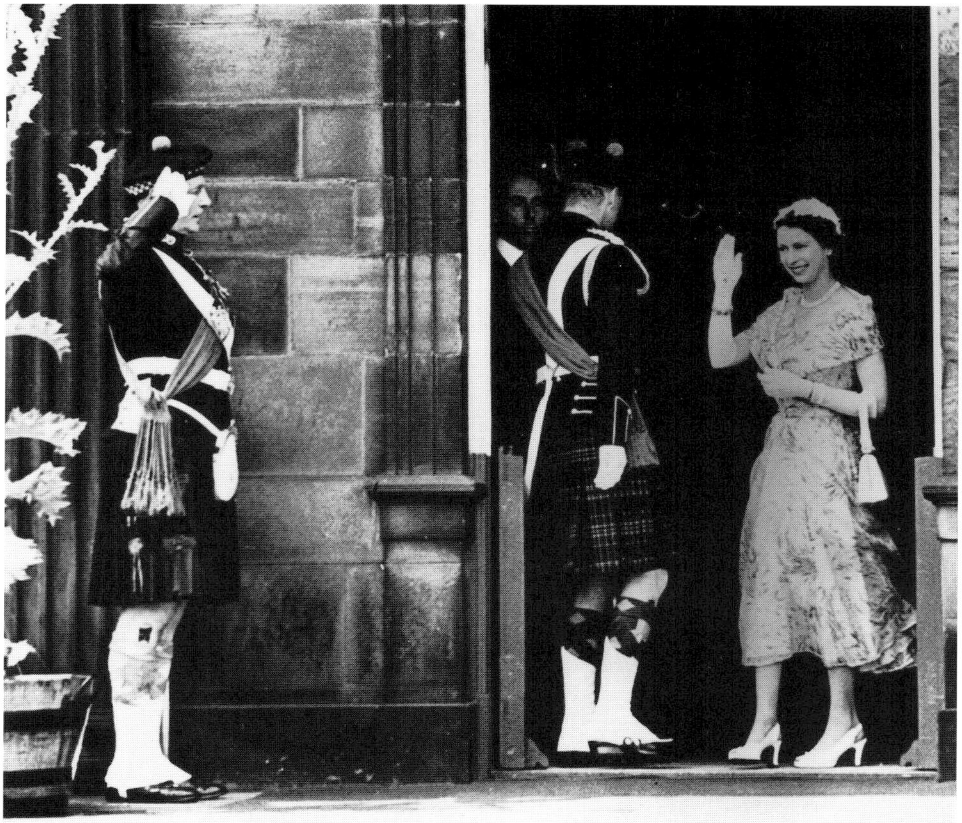

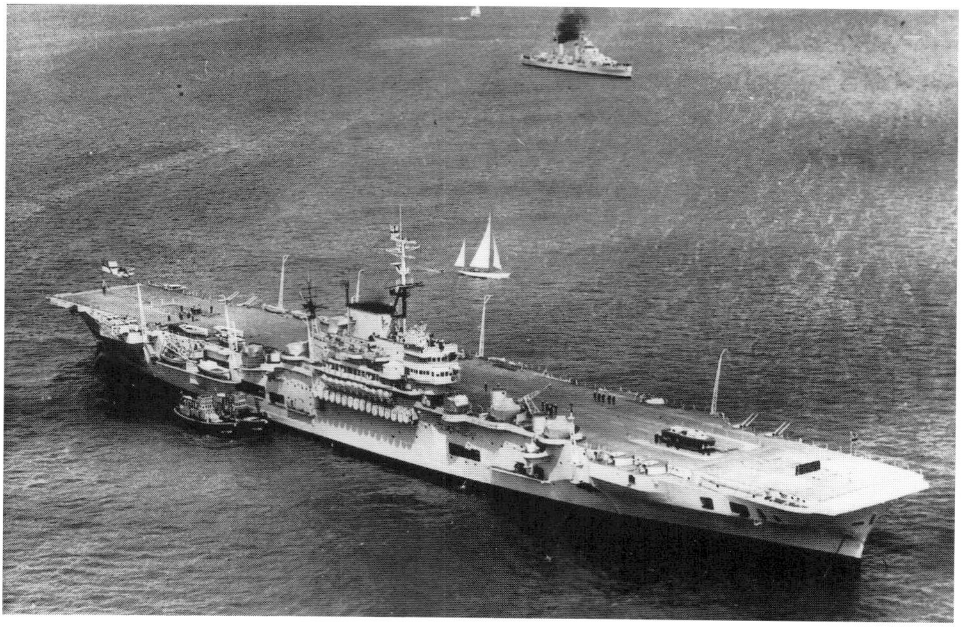

opposite page:

21 Holyrood House, Edinburgh, 26 June 1953. Queen Elizabeth after presenting new colours to 1st Battalion The Argyll and Sutherland Highlanders, with General Sir Gordon MacMillan *far left*

22 HMS *Implacable*

this page:

23 Sir Alfred Savage, Governor of British Guiana, The Queen's Birthday Parade, 1954

24 The Pipes and Drums of 1st Bn The Argyll and Sutherland Highlanders, Georgetown, 1954

25 Our wedding, St James's Church, Piccadilly, 17 November 1956

26 Lieut-Colonel Hugh Spens MBE, CO 1st Bn The Argyll and Sutherland Highlanders with citizens of Lemgo, 1960

27 Tim and Mouse Macpherson with Rosemary, 1960

28 Fontainebleau 1961. Generals Lauris Norstad (SACEUR), Jacquot (CINCENT), Brigadier-General Costa de Beauregard and Captain Loic Eon-Duval (ADC)

29 General Jacquot with his subordinate commanders. Air Chief Marshal The Earl of Bandon (Comd Air Forces Central Europe), Air Marshal Sir John Grandy (Comd 2 ATAF), Major-General Marias (FAF), General Sir James Cassels (Comd Northern Army Group), General Speidel, Lieut-General André Dulac (COS HQ AFCENT), General Bruce Clark (Comd Central Army Group) and Vice-Admiral van Erkel.

30 General Dr Hans Speidel (Comd Land Forces Central Europe)

31 Le Cabinet: Hubert Jeschke, JDCG, Bill Wildman, Captain Dicharry and Robert Allard de Grandmaison.

32 General Maurice Challe

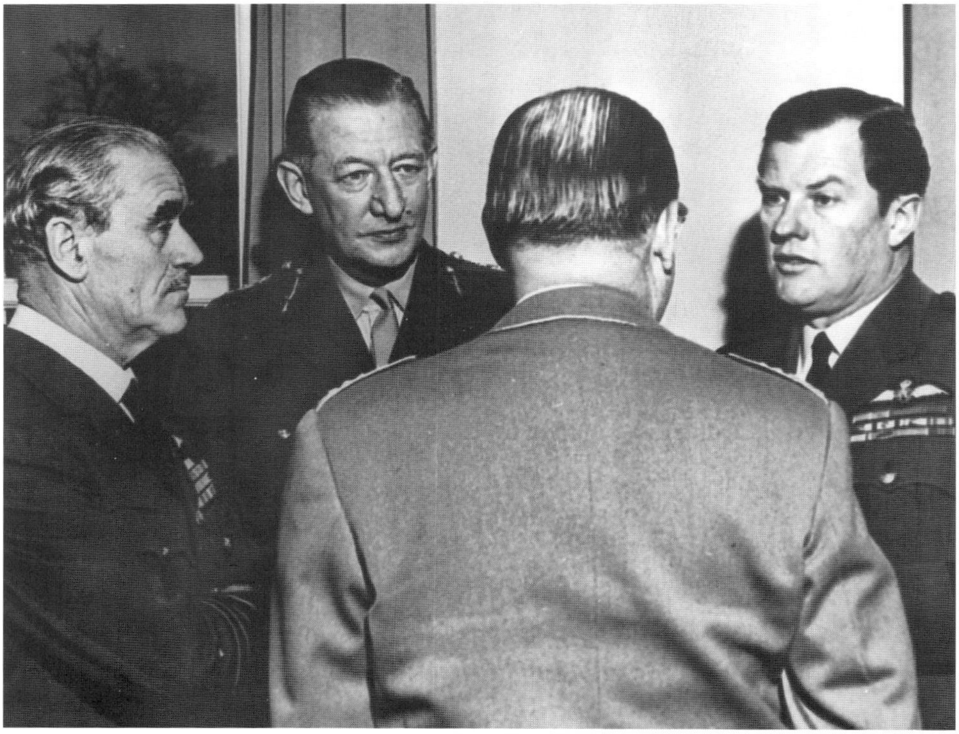

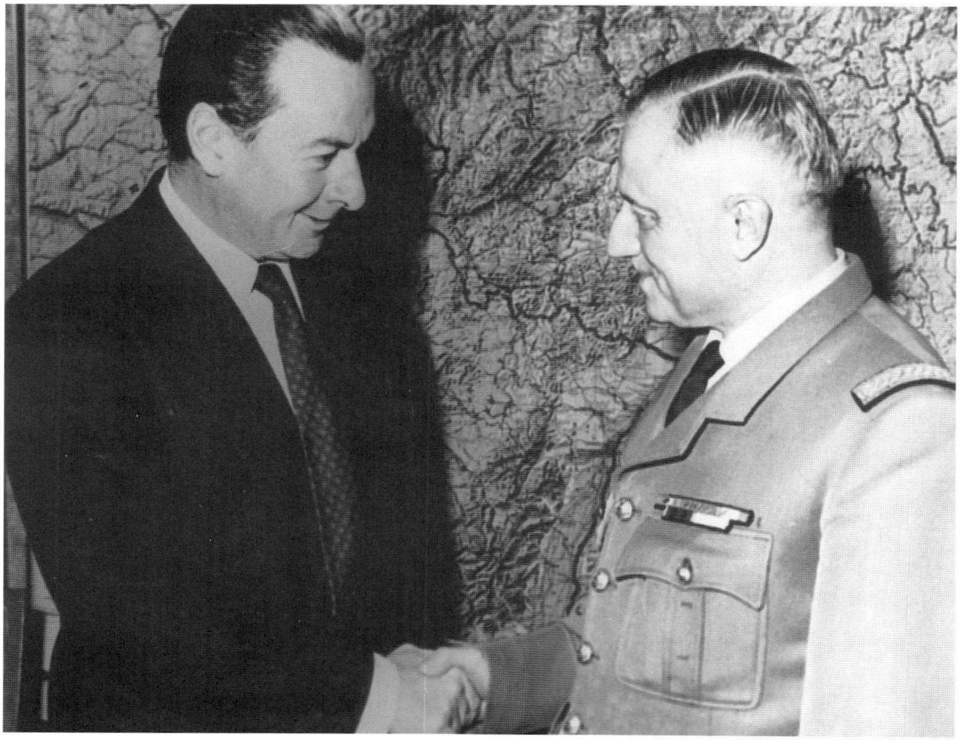

opposite page:

33 *Above:* Lord Bandon, Sir James Cassels, General Speidel (back to camera) and Sir John Grandy
34 *Below:* Mr Julian Amery (S-of-S for Air) and General Jacquot, Fontainebleau, 24 November 1961

this page:

35 *Top left:* Brigadier-General Costa de Beauregard greets Admiral of the Fleet The Earl Mountbatten of Burma (Chief of the UK Defence Staff), 13 July 1961
36 *Top right:* Captain Dicharry (Comd HQ AFCENT Provost & Security Detachment)
37 Rosemary and JDCG at the Versailles Ball, 1961

38 With the Pipes & Drums and Military Band of 1st Bn The Argyll & Sutherland Highlanders, Fontainebleau. November 1961. (Pipe-Major Pitkeathley and, back to camera, Drum-Major Malloch)

39 JDCG, April 1962

intensified, with growing brutality on both sides, nearly half a million young Frenchmen, mostly conscripts, were dispatched to quell the revolt. These servicemen from metropolitan France were initially sympathetic to the demands of the *colons* who were fanatic in their determination to keep Algeria French, and who had an abundance of weapons in Algeria and political leverage in Paris to sustain them. Among the Officer Corps the obligation to keep Algeria French was intensified by experience of FNL terrorism and cruelty, and by the spectre of Arab nationalism combining with Soviet Communism to erode the sources of Western, Christian power and wealth. The French Army had also become infected with distrust and contempt for the politicians of the Fourth Republic.

General Challe was a close friend of Prime Minister Mollet and had been closely associated with him in planning the Suez expedition. When General de Gaulle returned to power in 1958, Challe was sent to Algiers as Operational Assistant to General Salan whom he succeeded two months later as Commander-in-Chief. Challe had already recognised the alarming discontent seeping through the Army in Algeria, and in that post which he held until March 1960 he won great prestige and popularity with the Armed Forces. He introduced a new strategy and tactics that were largely responsible for achieving military supremacy over the FNL guerilla bands; and the construction of the immense barrage of wire and mines along the Tunisian frontier, with the aim of cutting the FNL bands off from their sources of supply and reinforcement, was effected by him.

But as de Gaulle's conviction of the inevitability of Algerian independence grew, and his policies edged towards an Algerian Algeria, Challe's known preference for Algérie Française was bound to involve him in a hidden confrontation with the Head of State. General Challe, torn between his allegiance to the Paris government and his personal predilections, had already been placed in an invidious position when suppressing the Algiers insurrection of January 1960, and more became known about his ambivalent attitude during the course of the so-called 'barricades trial' held in Paris in the aftermath of that disgraceful episode in which a group of Gendarmes were murdered by rioting French settlers while Army units stood by watching but unwilling to intervene.

In one of his rare interviews Challe had stated his views on the future of Algeria to a Spanish reporter with force and clarity. It was reproduced in *Le Monde* on 27 January 1961. General Challe declared: 'La sécurité du monde occidental impose à la France la permanence en Algérie. Ce que représente l'Algérie n'est qu'une bataille dans l'immense conflit où se débat aujourd'hui le monde libre. Abandonner l'Algérie serait perdre une bataille; c'est-à-dire reculer et perdre du terrain à l'Est. L'avenir de toute l'Europe occidentale et de sa civilisation s'y joue.'

His recall from Algeria and his appointment in May 1960 to the command of AFCENT was generally regarded as entirely consistent with de Gaulle's policy of relieving disgruntled commanders and placing them in positions of reduced authority.

When I joined his Headquarters it was already being whispered that Maurice Challe was not the man NATO needed to bear the chief responsibility for defending the vital Central European Front which stretched from the border of Schleswig-Holstein to the frontier of Italy. Intimate only with his immediate personal staff and keeping himself aloof from the Officers of the eight nations in Fontainebleau whose Chief he was, Challe's relations with his most senior and experienced colleagues, General Speidel and Air Chief Marshal Broadhurst, were known to be strained. I had been warned by the War Office about this lack of harmony at the highest level in AFCENT, and General Sir Hugh Stockwell, Deputy SACEUR, had told me: 'General Challe is a difficult man and always relates everything to how it affects himself personally. No good at all!'.

Nevertheless, in the eyes of the broad mass of those who made up the AFCENT community, the civilities were properly observed. General Speidel and Sir Harry Broadhurst remained dignified models of military etiquette, and an atmosphere of NATO amity and togetherness was engendered by the approach of Christmas festivities and the three-day Exercise Hostage Gris. This annual AFCENT conference was run by General Challe in the NATO building at the Porte Dauphine in Paris and attended by about fifty of the top brass from our land, air and naval commands. It was preceded by a cocktail party for eight hundred persons hosted by General Challe and his wife, Madeleine. It was the first time that many Officers had seen their Commander-in-Chief at close quarters. Bill Wildman and I made the introductions – a good way to learn faces and names.

During Hostage Gris the presentations by the senior commanders and the discussions which followed were extremely interesting to me, a newcomer to the NATO stratosphere after months of low-level regimental duty. Because progress in operational planning and in improving NATO's military capabilities was almost totally dependent on the political will of each of the fifteen Allied nations, the problems highlighted during Hostage Gris 1960 had been raised on previous occasions. They no doubt would remain unresolved for many years to come, for over NATO matters the national political mills ground very slowly indeed. But because of their significance and their interest to me personally I made a lengthy entry in my diary and I reproduce here the list of those matters which at the end of 1960 were causing greatest anxiety to the senior commanders on our Central Front.

1. Inadequate logistic backing for the ground and air forces, and inadequate protection of Army Rear Areas.
2. Shortages of engineers and engineer equipment.
3. Shortages of reliable communications and communication equipment.
4. Tactical atomic weapons are essential to NATO as our conventional forces are not strong enough to contain and repulse a full-scale Soviet attack.
5. Problems of air reconnaissance after Phase 1 of the conflict.
6. How to deploy nuclear weapons and their warheads in time to prevent them being destroyed by an initial Soviet attack.
7. Training of radar operators of Early Warning equipment in 'reading through' Soviet ECM (electronic counter-measures) jamming.
8. Political decisions about the evacuation of civilians, their control and the vast refugee problem that will arise.
9. Standardisation within the Alliance of weapons, ammunition, vehicles and spare parts.
10. Naval protection of North-West German and Danish ports.

Until I came to AFCENT the magnitude of the Soviet nuclear threat was unknown to me and I was appalled by what I learned during my first two months there. Our own nuclear stocks were said to have reached a high level, in quantity and quality, by late 1960; but since NATO could not strike first, we ran the risk of losing much under the initial Soviet nuclear attack unless we got warning of that attack and moved our forces into safety beforehand.

I was impressed by the setting, organisation and comfort of the Hostage Gris building and its management; especially by the simultaneous translation setup. It was all a pleasant change after life with an Infantry Company with its basic Quartermaster's furniture.

General Speidel's concluding remarks were a plea for more commanders on our side with 'le feu sacré' (the light of battle) in their eyes.

A few days after Christmas I went up to the NATO Defence College, located in a wing of the Ecole Militaire on the Place Joffre, to hear a lecture by Field Marshal Montgomery on 'NATO in the context of the World Struggle between West and East'. Aged 72, he didn't look more than 55 and spoke with great clarity, good humour and with his tongue firmly in his cheek. He made some sharp digs at the Germans (which they found amusing), at the Americans (which they did not like), and at politicians in general. He gave de Gaulle a big pat on the back: 'the only real Leader the West has got'. His main points were:

1. War is a consequence of national policies and the errors thereof; it is not inevitable.
2. Our attitude must be founded on two fundamentals:—

– The Atlantic Alliance must remain firm and solid
– Strength means Peace

3. NATO has prevented war in Europe. Such a war is now unlikely. NATO must therefore be reorganised.

4. Russia and China are not ready yet for a full-scale war. Nevertheless Communist aggression will go on, by economic and political means, and chiefly in Asia and Africa.

5. In ten years' time half the world will be Communist. China with a thousand million souls will be a nuclear power by 1965.

6. War is 'not on' for humanity; the deadlock has got to be broken. This means personal contact between the leaders of East and West.

7. Germany, the greatest immediate source of fear to the USSR, must remain divided. China must be brought into the United Nations in place of 'that awful setup in Formosa'.

8. Reduce the fear, then get disarmament. Keep nuclear weapons until the last stage; the first stage is to get all forces back into their own countries. Take NATO nuclear weapons off the land and put them at sea. Nations need strong armies backed up by good air transport resources.

9. The European fear, that if US forces pull back to America, that nation will not honour her obligations, is 'a monstrous suggestion'.

10. Tackle the Communist threat to Asia by massive aid.

11. Help Africans to redraw a new and more natural map of Africa.

12. Keep the Arab bloc, Yugoslavia and Scandinavia neutral.

13. Train the Youth in our countries in moral and spiritual values. Teach them about the millions who died in the two World Wars and then ask three questions:—

– Are we worth their sacrifice?
– What are we doing about it?
– Are we, the present, contributing as much to the future as the past has bequeathed to us?

A couple of weeks later I accompanied General Challe to Camp Guynemer for a discussion by the top brass of a directive sent to CINCENT by SACEUR, stating that, in exercises and planning, less stress should thenceforth be placed on the use of nuclear weapons. This of course brought up at once our capacity to wage a conventional war in Europe. General Sir James Cassels, the Commander of the Northern Army Group, stated that the ground forces could do so quite effectively but only for a short time. This was accepted. But from what Sir Harry Broadhurst said it became clear that the air forces were becoming ill-equipped for such a war; if the trend to replace aircraft with missiles continued they would be virtually incapable of playing a significant part in a conventional conflict.

Everyone agreed that there were grave dangers in NATO ground forces adopting a conventional defensive posture from which it might be difficult, even hazardous, to move rapidly to a 'nuclear' posture. The greatest threat to Western Europe lay in the Soviet ability to launch a sudden and overwhelming nuclear attack. The paramount task therefore facing the governments and military leaders of NATO nations at that time, 1961, was to prepare their populations and armed forces to survive that attack; and then to retaliate against the enemy homelands with our own surviving nuclear strike forces. The safety of those strike forces could only be assured if they were moved from their peacetime locations immediately any warning of an enemy attack was acquired. Because of a number of factors, vertical or horizontal dispersion were not yet feasible solutions; so the approved immediate action was, the speaker explained, for all the committed strike aircraft to fly off on their pre-planned operational tasks. This struck many of us in that assembly as being a most inflexible method of waging war; and the consequences for the human race would be catastrophic. The targets to be struck had been selected in the following order of priority:

– Centres of government control
– Enemy nuclear delivery capacity
– Centres of enemy military control
– Major industrial targets.

A sombre and detailed summary of the facts of life and death in the planning for the East-West conflict, which was regarded by a substantial number of politicians and Servicemen as inevitable, was delivered to us on that bright winter's morning in Fontainebleau by a tough-looking but soft-spoken Colonel in the US Air Force. No wonder Monty had declared that war is 'not on' and urged the political leaders on both sides to get together to break the deadlock.

Two weeks after Montgomery's lecture, John Fitzgerald Kennedy was installed as President of the United States at the age of 43. He looked even younger. As *The Observer* had written on New Year's Day: 'Every living person must share the hope that he will reveal himself to be as wise as he has already shown himself to be dynamically active . . .' He did, but after thirty-five months as Leader of the West and the idol of millions he was cut down by an assassin's bullet. I believe that if Kennedy had listened to Monty's lectures he too would have applauded loud and long. They had much in common in their care for the human condition and their conviction that peace can only come through strength.

On the last day of January a party of us assembled in Paris at the Gare de l'Est to catch the Orient Express to Nurnberg to observe the winter manoeuvres of the US Seventh Army, Winter Shield, held on the vast Grafenwöhr-Hohenfels Training Area in Bavaria. We were a very jolly party. Our leader, the British Brigadier Waldron, was a delightful man and an excellent representative at AFCENT of our country. Formerly a Gloster, he had commanded a battalion of the Green Howards in the war and a battalion of Gurkhas in the Malayan emergency. He, his wife and daughter had been exceptionally kind to Rosemary and me since our arrival in France; and he and I had a sort of family link in that his first names were John Graham Claverhouse. I remember him with much affection and was sad to read of his death in 1994. The other members of our little party were the Belgian General Ducq, the American General Alger, much liked by everyone, and the German Colonel Lambrecht. General Ducq was accompanied by an engaging Belgian Major from SHAPE, Pierre Roman, who had spent the early months of the war in Britain, had an English wife and a splendid sense of humour. He was to go far in the service of his country. On the train I shared a berth with an American Colonel of Engineers, but we did not see much of him when we got to our destination as he forgot to off-load his luggage and thus spent much of the exercise period in tracking down his missing kit.

At Nurnberg we were met by a group of American Escort Officers and driven to Vilseck, the US Army Training Centre. Most unusually for early February the snow was melting and the day temperature was well above freezing point. This raised considerable problems of manoeuvre damage, for deployment off the roads and for river-crossing operations by the US Vth and VIIth Corps. This unexpected thaw was estimated to increase the Manoeuvre Damage Bill by more than one million dollars.

The Escort Officer allotted to Brigadier Waldron, Colonel Lambrecht and me was Lieutenant John C. Farley, of the 2nd Missile Battalion of the 84th Artillery Regiment. He was a mass of energy and goodwill: we could not have been better looked after. The arrangements made for the reception, housing, feeding, briefing and transportation of the 800-odd Guest Observers from eighteen nationalities were staggering: faultless in execution and in cost seemingly unlimited. Only the Americans could do it.

It soon became apparent that Winter Shield 1961 would develop into an armaments trade fair and demonstration of weapons and equipment rather than a tactical manoeuvre. For the participants in the field, forbidden to get off the roads, held up by exercise 'demolitions' and pestered at every level by inquisitive Observers such as us, the affair turned into a battle against slush, mud and rain. Movement and traffic discipline by the US forces were poor: saluting by all ranks was impeccable.

Those elements of the French 11th Mechanised Brigade whom we visited displayed a disturbingly low standard of training and discipline and, on the part of their junior Officers, a lack of zeal and gumption. Their equipment looked pretty good, but their handling of it, with the exception of the new Gillois bridging equipment, was unimpressive. And we found no senior French Officer present to note and correct their many faults. The contrast with the German infantry was striking. Whereas the

France: A Coup That Failed

French, ordered to construct and defend a roadblock, were content to bar the carriage-way with a couple of vehicles while the soldiers, many unshaven, swanned around the farms or sat about munching sandwiches, the German infantry were made by their NCOs at every halt to get out of their vehicles and shovel mud and ice off the road until forward movement started again. We heard later that the French on Winter Shield had suffered eighteen cases of frostbite due to ignorance on the part of Junior Leaders more accustomed to the conditions of Indo-China and North Africa.

The tactical doctrine of the German mechanised infantry differed from that in the British and US armies. I had noticed this the year before in our collaboration with 21 Panzer Brigade at Augustdorf; they used their armoured personnel carriers (APCs) more as mobile pill-boxes, firing at the enemy through port-holes. They seldom dismounted. These tactics, they told us, served them well on the Russian front. We British took the line that unless Infantry dismount and fight on foot, it is not possible to ensure that ground such as woods, buildings, defiles and so on are properly cleared of enemy; especially of a resolute and crafty enemy such as dug-in Russians or Chinamen. It was interesting too to note that during the operation to bridge the very swollen and fast-flowing Danube, remarkably well executed by the US and German Engineers, the German infantry in the main stayed with their APCs waiting for the bridge to be opened. To seize and hold the bridge-head on the far bank, essential for the protection of the bridge-builders, the only troops employed on that task were two weak, dismounted companies of a Reconnaissance Battalion.

Colonel Wolf Lambrecht and I had a most interesting conversation about the cold experienced by the Wehrmacht units in Russia in the winter of 1941-2. Lambrecht was an Officer in an infantry company which marched on foot and whose transport was almost wholly horse-drawn. When Operation BARBAROSSA was launched on 22 June 1941, he and his men advanced in the Russian summer heat in their shirt-sleeves. As autumn approached the cries went up: 'Where are our greatcoats? What about winter clothing? Remember what happened to Napoleon Bonaparte!'. The reply from the General Staff was: 'Don't worry. Everything you will need is held in depots near Warsaw and will be delivered to you long before the first snow falls'. It did not reach Lambrecht's unit until the New Year. Winter in Russia comes twice. Initially there are sharp frosts which harden the ground, make trench digging difficult but speed the movement of tracked and wheeled vehicles. This then thaws and the land becomes covered with glutinous mud, so thick as to bring the movement of armies to a halt. Then, some nights later, the real Russian winter arrives, in the quiet darkness of the small hours. As the French experienced in 1812, men died by the hundred while sleeping or sitting round camp fires. Death came silently and unrecognised in their final moments of life by those it claimed.

In Lambrecht's company the first days of winter reduced the company's strength from two hundred to seventy. Many just died at their posts, some wandered off to find shelter and expired, some shot themselves. It was a ghastly ordeal, and one which hundreds of thousands of German soldiers sent into that savage climate endured. But, Lambrecht went on to explain, once the men had learned certain techniques, conditions became reasonably tolerable. The many Russian prisoners kept in each unit as labourers taught their German captors tricks such as stuffing boots with straw, and never falling asleep during darkness when the temperature was lowest and the wind most lethal. The wind was the real killer. By day, sheltered from the wind, it was quite possible to sleep on the sunlit snow for three to four hours. The German soldiers who survived those terrible weeks of winter formed an exclusive club; they were very proud of themselves and, Lambrecht went on to say, they in general survived all the ordeals which they had to face during the rest of the war, either on the Russian front or in Normandy. Such men, he said, were like iron which had been tempered in the white heat of a furnace. As always in groups of soldiers, it was the most unexpected man who rose to the occasion and showed his true worth, while many others just gave up and died or had to be sent away.

To protect the Observers on Winter Shield from the mud and cold, the US Army Quartermasters at Vilseck made sets of military winter clothing available to us, and John Waldron and I noticed with some satisfaction that the British and German visitors alone stuck to their own national uniforms and declined to be seen with the words US ARMY written across their chests in yellow letters.

After six days of watching guns fire, aircraft drop bombs and examining the procedures and the kit of the Seventh Army, Brigadier Waldron, Colonel Lambrecht and I decided we had seen enough. I myself was beginning to find communal life in the American Mess a bit of a trial. Surrounded by huge men, all with almost shaven heads, dressed exactly alike even down to the army issue vests and pants which they seemed not to take off by day or night, I was particularly intrigued by the absence of doors on the lavatory cubicles. The sight each morning of rows of Americans defecating in full view of anybody who passed through the building was very odd, and I have often wondered what undesirable habits Uncle Sam was seeking to curb in his Officers by depriving them of that privacy. On duty the Americans were keen as mustard and professionally knowledgeable, but off duty in the barracks the young Officers appeared to us to do little but drink and gamble until the small hours.

I slept in a double-tiered bunk next to an Artillery Captain, a very soft spoken and most likeable chap. He was a Negro of huge physique. I greatly enjoyed talking to him but not a single one of the dozens of his fellow Americans in that dormitory, all white, ever addressed a word to him.

I also found that a diet of US Army rations was beginning to gum up my innards, so we left Vilseck and after an interesting day looking at Nurnberg, a fine city shattered by wartime bombing but already being lovingly and skilfully restored, we were invited by General Challe to return to France in his aircraft.

Our impression of what the US Seventh Army had laid on for us was one of extreme friendliness, marvellous hospitality and efficiency at most levels. Theirs was, we reflected, a great war machine, splendidly equipped and impaired only by a lack of maturity and education in their Junior Leaders. The American subalterns and captains were at that time noticeably less seasoned than their British and German equivalents.

My conversations with that black Officer at Vilseck reminded me of an experience I had had very soon after arriving in Fontainebleau. I was sent off to Soissons to look at some possible sites for war-time Headquarters, so ordered a car and driver from the Motor Pool. As there were only the two of us in the vehicle I had an enjoyable journey chatting to my chauffeur who was a smart, intelligent young American soldier. To open the conversation I said to him: 'You are from the AFCENT Motor Pool, aren't you? Is the Motor Pool manned only by US personnel or is it, like the Headquarters Staff, fully international and manned by chaps from all the eight AFCENT nations?'.

'Yes, it is fully international in its personnel.'

'Is it an efficient, and equally important, a happy outfit?'

'We think we do our work OK; there are few complaints about us and we all get along pretty well together.'

'But surely, out of such a mixed bunch of men from different nations there must be some group or some individual who is different and fits in less well than the others?'

My American driver thought for a moment before replying:

'Well seeing that you've mentioned it, Sir, there is one fellow in the Motor Pool who doesn't really fit in and who none of us get along with at all easily. But what do you expect?' he went on to say: 'The fellow's only a poor black bastard from South Carolina!'

That statement staggered me, for the man who made it was as black as ink – but he came from New York.

With the poor impression we got from observing French troops on Winter Shield in mind, I tactfully asked Robert de Grandmaison for his opinion about the morale and effectiveness of the French Army and in particular to explain the tragedy of their defeat in Indo-China. He summarised the reasons thus:

—The French High Command and the Rank & File alike refused to admit the possibility of the Viet Minh enemy putting into the field a large force of efficient and competently led units: the French suffered through a misplaced contempt for their opponents.

—The French totally underestimated the Viets' ability to move artillery and stores in great quantities over concealed and poor jungle tracks; much of their motor transport was supplied by Red China, but huge amounts of ammunition and so on were carried on the backs of human convoys.

—The Dien Binh Phu position had to be held for political reasons as it lay astride the route to Laos, which, though the most backward, was the most loyal to France of the colonies which made up French Indo-China. But the defending force was never strong enough to hold the surrounding heights. Once those heights were taken by the enemy and his artillery established there in strength, the fate of the garrison below was sealed.

—The lack of grip and drive by the C-in-C, General de Castries.

—The effect on the French troops of the climate, and of their distrust of the politicians in Paris.

—Tactical indiscipline, carelessness, lack of security precautions and a general notion that panache in action was more important than disciplined and meticulous preparation.

Having just read André Maurois' *History of France*, I was struck by the closeness of de Grandmaison's analysis with Maurois' description of the French character of two thousand years earlier: 'Energy in superiority, disunity in defeat; capable of heroism but not of discipline or long-continued effort'.

General Challe had on 24 January visited General Norstad and Prime Minister Debré and asked to be allowed to retire as soon as possible. The reasons given out officially in the French Press and within the Headquarters were 'purely personal', but Colonel Sengès told de Grandmaison, Bill, Hubert and me that Challe's decision stemmed from Algeria. When he was out there as Commander-in-Chief he was obliged to take many actions and to make many statements in which he sincerely believed at the time, and he did so in the name of the French government in Paris and in furtherance of its policies.

But the views and policies concerning Algeria of General de Gaulle changed; they were no longer in accord with those which Challe had striven to implement and to which he had persuaded many Algerians, French and Muslim, to pledge their loyalty. Thus he now felt that he could rightly be accused of hypocrisy by those who had trusted him. The poor man seemed to feel this deeply. The next day General Challe called in the three Subordinate Commanders (Speidel, Broadhurst and van Erkel) and told them of his decision.

France: A Coup That Failed

On 17 February I accompanied him to München-Gladbach, the Headquarters of the Northern Army Group, for a farewell parade in his honour and for him to say goodbye personally to General Cassels. The parade was well carried out, all the NORTHAG nations being represented. CINCENT remarked to me on the way back how relaxed and happy an atmosphere existed at that HQ, a tribute to Jim Cassels; and how young British Officers, when giving orders on parade, 'always shout them out at the tops of their voices as if they were commanding an Army Corps rather than the small group of soldiers formed up behind them'.

The next week we had a small ceremony in the office at which Challe presented the medal of an Officer of the Legion of Honour to Captain Barbieri, his ADC for many years, and we, his Assistants, presented CINCENT with a new pipe and an album of photographs. He made a short speech in reply, pleading for more unity within NATO and especially within Western Europe. He stressed: 'unless we sink our differences and "particularismes", Europe will be sovietised within twelve years'. To the assembled French Officers at AFCENT he explained why he felt unable to remain at his post; he had to leave rather than perjure himself by supporting a policy different to the one he had worked for and had believed in while C-in-C in Algeria, and to which he had persuaded so many Algerians to commit themselves also. On 24 February, after our own private *pot d'adieu* in the Cabinet Office, General Challe said goodbye to each of us individually, gave us a signed photograph, walked through a Guard of Honour of French Military Police and Sailors and was driven to his house in Paris. It was a sad parting. We all, I believe, respected him for quitting the service of a State which had, in his view, deceived him and, through him, many others.

An Army General, Pierre-Elie Jacquot, was nominated to be the next CINCENT. Aged 59, he had had a distinguished career in the Resistance, as the last C-in-C of the French Forces in Indo-China, then in Germany and latterly as Inspector-General of the Land Forces. All the French at AFCENT seemed to be scared stiff of General Jacquot and were dreading his arrival at the beginning of March. A new Directeur du Cabinet arrived first to replace Colonel Sengès. Brigadier-General Costa de Beauregard we liked from the first moment. Gentle, cultured, married to an elegant and attractive countess and fluent in English, Costa, an Infantryman, had been an Instructor at the Royal Military Academy, Woolwich and more recently a member of Field Marshal Montgomery's staff at SHAPE. He was an ardent admirer of Britain.

He used to declare: 'there are only two civilisations'; and *à propos* some rather crummy arrangements the US Delegation had made for their 4th of July party which contrasted ill with our own celebration of The Queen's Birthday the previous month: 'You are a Great Nation; you know how to do things properly'.

One Saturday while I was alone in the Office, Brigadier Costa came in holding a copy of *Le Monde* in which there was a photograph of President and Madame de Gaulle standing on the steps of the Elysée Palace with between them a black man and a black woman.

'Do you know who that black African is who's standing with General de Gaulle?'

'No, Brigadier, I do not recognise him.'

'Well, he is Monsieur M'ba, the President of the newly independent French colony of Gabon. He and Madame M'ba are on an official visit to Paris. But do you know *how* he became President of Gabon?'

'No, but please tell me.'

'He ate his first wife!'

'Good Lord, do tell me more.'

'Yes, M'ba was born into a tribe which had a curious custom. If someone died, before the burial, the next-of-kin was obliged to swallow a mouthful of flesh from the body of the deceased – in a strange way something rather like the Catholic Mass or your Protestant Holy Communion. Nevertheless, the French colonial Power took a dim view of this ritual and outlawed it. Alas, the first Madame M'ba died and her grieving husband, perhaps ignorant of French law, consumed his prescribed mouthful of spousal meat. But an enemy reported to the authorities what he had done and poor M'ba was arrested, charged and sentenced to many years in prison. While there he learned to read and write, became a Catholic and, being a model prisoner, was released after some ten years and returned to his homeland. At that time the wind of change was blowing through the African continent; independence was in the air. Furthermore M'ba got back to find that he was regarded as a hero for having fallen foul of the French for loyally observing a tribal convention. So when Gabon was edging towards independence Monsieur M'ba, popular and educated, was the obvious chap to lead the Gabonese and to be their first President.'

(Many years later I read M'ba's obituary in *The Times*. He died in his bed after a long, full life. The paper gave him three columns of print, but the reason for his imprisonment had been omitted.)

In the spring of 1961 South Africa was much in the news as the white Nationalist government of Dr Verwoerd, the apostle of apartheid, had found itself unable to remain a member of the Commonwealth and therefore resigned from that great global multiracial association of states. We Grahams, linked by sentiment with that beautiful land ever since John Graham, 13th Laird of Fintry and a Major in the 93rd Highlanders, landed at the Cape of Good Hope in 1805 – and for whom the city of Grahamstown was named – grieved particularly over this subjugation of English values by Boer bigotry. As a long article in *The Times* of 17 March stated '. . . South Africans should know that we in Britain regard this parting of the ways with the deepest regret, as a temporary measure and one that does not in the slightest affect our regard for men with whom we have had such a happy association for so long. Relief that the Commonwealth has stood an unprecedented strain must be coupled today with a message of heartfelt goodwill to the peoples of all colours in the Union of South Africa'.

That Boer intolerance was to prove far from temporary. It was to endure, despite the opprobrium of most of the human race, for thirty-three years, until May 1994 when another Afrikaner, F W de Klerk, instituted the first nation-wide elections through which a remarkable man, Nelson Mandela, was chosen to be the first black President of the Republic of South Africa. The demolition of the system of apartheid and the creation of full democracy in that country were, like the invention of the atomic weapon, of penicillin, the razing of the Berlin Wall and the collapse of the Communist Empire in Eastern Europe, milestones on mankind's hopeful but fitful trek through the bloodstained 20th century towards a better world. Or so it seemed to me as I wrote in 1994.

On the afternoon of 7 March General Jacquot's Ceremony of Installation as CINCENT was held in la Cour Henri IV with in attendance a company of French soldiers, one of Allied Servicemen, a military band, the flags of the Allies and all Lieutenant-Colonels upwards. After the top brass had met their new Chief – (Air Chief Marshal The Earl of Bandon, 'The Abandoned Earl', had recently taken over from Sir Harry Broadhurst as COMAIRCENT) – we members of the Cabinet were introduced to our new boss. Small, stocky, and fairhaired, General Jacquot made an excellent impression: direct, courteous, very quick-minded and endlessly amusing – he seldom drew breath – that initial impression was to grow the longer I worked for him.

During our first week together it became clear that we all agreed that the size of the Headquarters' staffs had become inflated and needed to be reduced, and that far too many expensive and pointless cocktail parties were getting into the NATO calendar. Also that Bill, Hubert and I should be fully employed as Staff Officers rather than as additional ADCs which had been a tendency in General Challe's time. To this end I was instructed to draw up a paper on the duties of the Military Assistants which was accepted and put into practice.

The new CINCENT, the son of a Sergeant-Major in the Gendarmerie, had been born in Vrécourt in the Vosges Mountains in 1902, and that had remained his family home. Unusually for a French Catholic couple, General Jacquot and his wife had only two children; a son, Philippe who was a subaltern in a Parachute Regiment serving in Algeria, and a daughter, Lise, married to Captain George, one of the two ADCs. The other ADC was a bright and charming Cavalryman from the Philipponnat family whose vines covered many hectares around Epernay, one of the great centres of champagne production.

General Jacquot, who had last visited England twenty-three years before, was keen to return at an early date to meet the UK Chiefs of Staff, the Minister of Defence and if possible to call on Field Marshal Montgomery, whom he greatly admired, at his home near Farnham. All this fell to me to arrange and CINCENT, Costa de Beauregard, Bernard Philipponnat and I took off from Orly early on 11 April in Lord Bandon's personal aircraft and landed at Northolt an hour later. The impressions we were to get from the Home Counties, from the London area and from the arrangements made for our reception by the British authorities were excellent. CINCENT was struck by the absence of litter on the streets, in the capital and in the villages alike, by the road system on which the signing was first-rate, and by the standard of road courtesy and traffic discipline which was noticeably better than in France.

While the Generals were taken to lunch at the Royal Automobile Club by the Chief of the Imperial General Staff, Field Marshal Sir Francis Festing, I took Bernard to the 'Senior', the United Services Club, to which I had belonged for many years. This visit to London gave me a welcome opportunity to see my Mother and Brothers again, the first time we had been together since my Father's funeral in 1957. We met up at Jane's Chelsea flat in Cheyne Court and had a most enjoyable twelve hours together. After breakfast, Moray drove me to the Park Lane Hotel to pick up my French colleagues for the drive in a plush Humber limousine provided by the RASC down to Hampshire for lunch with Monty.

During the afternoon the Field Marshal spent an hour showing us his two battle caravans, the operations lorry and other trophies which he kept in a barn beside his house, Isington Mill, built with a variety of timbers donated by the Dominion governments. The great warrior had the clearest blue eyes I had ever seen; his hair was turning white but his energy and alertness and his sense of humour belied his 73 years.

He introduced us to his driver, the famous Sergeant Parker, who had known Costa de Beauregard several years previously and who greeted him with the words: 'I see that you're a General now'. At this Monty chipped in with: 'What Parker really means is that you wouldn't be one in the British Army!'. But any sting in this quip was wholly removed by the Field Marshal and the Sergeant throwing up big salutes to the bemused Frenchman. Monty had been particularly diverting on the subject of American visitors to the Mill, some of whom offered him money for the under-clothes, fly-swatters and other personal articles which he had used during his battles and which he kept in the caravans as memorabilia. To keep the Yanks happy and to make some money for themselves he proposed sending Parker into the local Woolworth's to buy up quantities of those items into which they would then rub dust and sand to give them a wartime-vintage appearance, ready for sale to the next bunch of gullible Americans who called on him.

We drove back to Northolt by way of Aldershot and Windsor, and arrived back at Orly in bright evening sunshine after two days which had clearly given much pleasure to my French charges, and respect for the quality of life they had glimpsed in southern England.

In addition to CINCENT's expeditions, conferences and briefings, we Assistants were kept busy arranging the visits to Fontainebleau of senior officials from NATO countries. A fairly continuous stream of Ministers, Ambassadors, Generals and other VIPs descended on us. From London came the Minister of Defence, Mr Harold Watkinson, Lord Mountbatten of Burma, Mr Julian Amery, the Secretary-of-State for Air (and a sincere friend of the Sultanate of Oman). And one day General Jacquot introduced me to Edouard Daladier, the French Prime Minister at the time of the Munich 'Betrayal' of Czechoslovakia in 1938. He spoke warmly of Neville Chamberlain and of the debt France owed to England. Parliamentarians took up much of our time as they usually arrived with preconceived notions but little accurate knowledge of NATO's structure and of the problems we in AFCENT were grappling with in planning the defence of the Central European front. They therefore required detailed briefings, and with practice these became polished performances by the Staff.

One party of MPs from Westminster included the Labour Member for a part of Glasgow from which a high proportion of Argyll & Sutherland Highlanders was recruited. Looking at my uniform he enquired which regiment I was in and whether the Scottish Regiments were affected in any way by the latest reorganisation of the British Infantry. His ignorance disappointed me.

Each delegation that comprised the multi-national and tri-service Staffs at the four Fontainebleau Headquarters was administered by its own National Support Unit. The British unit was housed in a nearby barracks and looked after our pay, housing, documentation and so on very competently. One of the pillars of that unit, Captain Mike Jordan, an efficient, portly and generous RASC Officer Rosemary and I got to know well and our friendship with him and his amusing wife, Elizabeth, was to last for many years.

That year spring came in mid-February and much of Europe enjoyed a spell of hot, dry weather which lasted in our bit of France until early April. Bulbs, blossom, flowers and butterflies came out in glorious profusion, and during the lunch-breaks Rosemary and I would take Lisa and the children out into the Arbonne Forest for a succession of memorable picnics; and one February evening we stood listening for ten minutes to a nightingale singing in the birch tree in our garden.

Pinky had by then completed some weeks at Madame Pelletier's Jardin d'Enfants day school. Her first report read: 'Jacqueline s'habitue très bien a l'école. C'est une petite fille douce et obéissante; elle est déjà très attentive et essaye de bien travailler. Dans le jardin elle aime surtout la balançoire'. In March we all went up to see the fine new buildings recently opened by de Gaulle at Orly Airport. There were great crowds of people watching like us the succession of jet airliners taking off and landing. Pinky and Christopher enjoyed it so much that people stopped to laugh with them, and when some young Frenchmen waved at her Pinky announced proudly 'Those men like me'. This was a splendidly happy period in our family life. We were making new and lasting friendships, old friends and relatives came from Britain and Lemgo to stay with us and, for me, work in the new CINCENT's Cabinet was thoroughly enjoyable and worthwhile. Our only anxiety continued to be money; the overdraft had now reached £1,300 and the National Provincial Bank in Ryde had cried 'Halt'. Nevertheless Rosemary and I decided to pass the next three weeks on leave touring round a slice of the continent in our Peugeot 403 car. We took Pinky with us but left baby Christopher, now generally called Didi, in the care of Lisa, who adored him almost as much as we did, in her parents' house in Lemgo.

Two events had recently hit the headlines in the world's media. The USSR had beaten the Americans in the race to put the first man into space; thus Major Gagarin ranks with Sir Edmund Hillary and Sherpa Tenzing in the pantheon of the great explorers of our time. In Jerusalem the trial had opened of the SS Colonel Adolf Eichmann, the infamous executive in the Nazi 'Final Solution to the Jewish Problem'. There was considerable anti-Israeli comment about the way Eichmann had been kidnapped in the Argentine by Israeli agents and about the presumed partiality of his judges. But his crimes were so dreadful that he had to be tried in the sight of all mankind by those who had suffered the most from his actions and by them be condemned. He was hanged.

We set off in bright sunshine but by the time we reached Grenoble it was raining heavily. As we approached the Mediterranean, driving in reverse down the route Napoleon Bonaparte had taken in 1815 on his return from Elba three months before his defeat at Waterloo, the weather cleared marvellously and we gawped at the opulence of Cannes and Nice and watched the changing of the Guard on the Palace in Monaco of Prince Rainier and his beautiful wife, the former actress Grace Kelly. We spent our second night on a heath surrounded by the scent of wild thyme, sleeping in a hired tent on camp beds, and Rosemary fed us from a paraffin cooker. We continued down the lower corniche road to the frontier at Ventimiglia, and thence on towards Rome via industrial Genoa, exquisite Portofino, La Spezia with her associations with the Italian navy and Shelley's death in 1822, Pisa and her tower, and Orbitello. We found Italy very undeveloped.

It is, General Jacquot had explained to me, 'basically an Arab country, not at all a proper part of Europe'; and the inhabitants were drably clothed, plain looking but warm-hearted and kind, especially when they caught sight of Pinky. 'O la bella bambina,' they laughed as they brought us sweets or flowers or just charming gestures of welcome. That girl of ours while moving around in the car, exclaimed, 'Damn, I've hurt my foot!'. When her Mother choked her off for using such a word, she, aged 3½, replied in astonishment: 'Why you scold me? I not say Bloody'.

The nearer we got to Rome the worse the driving conditions became, with rain and long traffic hold-ups caused by 'Lavori in corso'. There were a lot of tourists around, mainly German, but we met up also with Americans, all compulsive sight-seers but delightful people to chat with at the various camp sites. One such family of six, devout Catholics, had gone without meat for the four weeks of Lent. They were trying to cram as many churches and museums as possible into their itinerary, and their Father, an artist, told us their ambition on returning to North America was to spend the rest of their lives in Canada in a log cabin beside a lake, isolated from all other human beings. The three girls, all about Pinky's age, were named after birds: Robin, Piper and Lark. A delightfully relaxed and unfettered sextet, but they must have been terribly squashed inside that small Volkswagen.

The Italian military whom we could see from the roads on sentry duty or out on training looked fit and well turned out, but those we passed, wandering about in the towns, were nearly all scruffy with dirty boots and belts. Those close glimpses of Italy's Servicemen reminded me of something else General Jacquot had told me. Before the outbreak of the Second World War Maurice Gamelin, the French Generalissimo, was asked how many divisions he would need to defend the Franco-Italian frontier. He replied: 'If the Italians come into the war against us, two; if on our side, four'. He remembered what had happened at Caporetto in 1917.

On the seventh day of our tour, a Sunday, we drove into Rome, parked in St Peter's Square and walked past the Papal Guards into the huge basilica with its wonderful paintings and statues. We were much impressed both by the choirs singing Mass and by the conduct of the multitude of worshippers who surrounded us. It was raining when we came out and I bought a copy of *The Sunday Times* for us to read in the car. We saw at once that the previous day a coup d'état had been launched in Algeria; furthermore that my ex-boss at Fontainebleau, General Challe, was its leader. My first reaction was that Challe had gone off his head; physically unfit, mentally tired and out of touch with what the bulk of the French nation had come to feel about Algeria. But on reflection I judged that, after his departure from Fontainebleau, he must have been approached by his three accomplices, Generals Salan, Jouhaud and Zeller, who assured him that their plan could not fail but required only a respected and popular man to head it. Maurice Challe had foolishly allowed himself to be persuaded to provide in his own person a point around whom all who sought to keep Algeria French could rally. (Had not Hughie Stockwell told me of his 'extraordinary vanity'?) Everything we read in the papers that day, and in the leaflets which began to appear on the streets of Italy warning 'La Francia è minacciata dal fascismo' and such like, made us fear for France, for the cohesion of her Armed Forces and by extension for the NATO alliance.

Rosemary and I decided however that there was no point in our returning directly to Fontainebleau and so we continued with our holiday, spending a day in enchanting Florence and then driving on to Como along the excellent autostrada via Bologna and Milan. We were joined in the camp site at Como by a caravan load of French people. From what they told us it seemed that Challe's coup was already a lost cause. As the St Gotthard Pass over the Alps was still blocked by snow, we put the car onto a train and were carried for half an hour through the pitch dark tunnel then on to Basel and Freiburg in clean, orderly and well signed Germany. We had a bit of a crisis about money for buying petrol for the rest of the journey and I expected to have to sell my camera, but all was well and we arrived in Lemgo ten days after setting out from Fontainebleau. We went straight to the Schraders' house and found Didi and Lisa in a very good form, and then to the Macphersons where Tim and Mouse put us up for three nights. It was great fun to be back with the Regiment for a short spell, and we were splendidly entertained by many friends, from Hugh and Mary Spens down to the Jocks in the Band and my old D Company. I got the impression that the Battalion was bored. That year there was less money in the BAOR kitty for training exercises and sporting expeditions, and in consequence some of the troops had rampaged around Lemgo. The 91st was not alone in this; the Cameronians stationed in Minden were soon to misbehave badly and acquire the name 'The Poison Dwarfs'. All our friends in Lemgo knew about Challe's coup and I got asked many questions about the affair and quizzed about when I too would be arrested as one of his accomplices.

We reached Fontainebleau safely very late on 2 May having covered 4,360 kms. Back in the AFCENT office I learned the details of what had occurred in Algeria. The coup had failed ignominiously after a mere four days. The President of the Republic had taken an unwavering firm line, and in this had been supported by the majority of the French nation. In Algeria itself none of the Navy and few of the Air Force or the Police had rallied to Challe. Although a number of Army units, following the lead taken by their COs, joined the rebels, de Gaulle appealed by radio to the conscripts over the heads of their commanders, ordering them to crush the rebellion, if necessary by force. It worked and Challe to his credit soon saw that the game was up and surrendered. He was put in arrest and flown to France to be tried together with Zeller by a special court which was to convene at the end of May. It was believed that Generals Salan and Jouhaud had fled to Spain, rather shamefully deserting those they had seduced onto the rebel side.

I found Brigadier Costa de Beauregard in a most depressed state. He had just lost a close friend in an aeroplane crash in Africa and he was extremely upset by the recent events in Algeria. He regarded Challe's actions as being criminally wrong and stupid, and was appalled at the effect all that would have on the French Army, its morale, discipline and reputation. I had not expected Costa to think otherwise, but as the days passed I was astounded to perceive how few of the French Officers at Fontainebleau thought as he did. Some openly supported Challe and deplored the fact that he had failed; others with remarkably woolly reasoning declared that de Gaulle, who had set himself up in London in opposition to the French government in 1940, had no right to punish Challe for doing exactly the same thing in Algiers in 1961. And at his trial it became alarmingly clear that many senior Officers, though ardent supporters of the concept of Algérie Française, had hung back from joining Challe not from conviction but through irresolution: *loyaux par lâcheté*.

De Gaulle by all accounts had conducted himself magnificently, though some of his Ministers seemed to have rather lost their heads. The panic assembling and equipping of a sort of Home Guard to defend Paris 'against the expected assault by parachutists from Algiers' was said to have angered the President more than anything else. The alarm given, aircraft were forbidden to overfly French territory, and guards were positioned on airfields, some with anti-aircraft guns. These developments caused some brief consternation in the German delegation at AFCENT as two Boche parachute units were already airborne en route to a long-planned exercise in France.

General Jacquot, like de Beauregard, declared himself completely against Challe's action. Nevertheless he decided to refuse all social invitations (except those from SACEUR personally) until Challe's trial ended, thereby going into a state of semi-mourning. Costa, to my surprise, tried to persuade the French committee responsible for arranging Le Bal des Huit Nations billed for 2 June to cancel the function as 'that will be the day on which ex-General Challe will be shot'. Rosemary and I were greatly looking forward to this SHAPE Ball, so when he asked my opinion on the matter I replied, a. the Ball is a NATO celebration; we should not be too influenced by purely French considerations; b. Challe had broken the law and acted in a criminal manner, and c. he had left AFCENT and gone into retirement three months earlier.

General Jacquot himself was affected by the disciplinary action being taken against those who had backed the rebellion. The principal offenders had been the Parachute and Foreign Legion regiments and some of these were already being broken up, the Officers placed in Fortress Arrest and the Rank and File dispersed among other parts of the Army. One young man in gaol for having obeyed the orders of his Commanding Officer, who had rallied to Challe, was Lieutenant Philippe Jacquot, CINCENT's only son. In Algeria, according to a *Times* report, 220 Army Officers had been relieved of their commands and two hundred civil servants moved from their posts as an early consequence of the attempted coup. The trial by the special court ended with Challe and Zeller being sentenced to fifteen years' imprisonment at hard labour. Other conspirators were to receive lesser sentences. Some regarded these punishments as being unwisely light, no real deterrent to anyone considering launching future coups. But most people seemed to think that de Gaulle had got it about right. He truly towered over France and the pygmies on whom he had to rely for her administration. But while he continued along the path he had chosen towards early independence for Algeria, the OAS, the secret army organisation, was mounting a campaign of propaganda, bombings and attempted assassination against de Gaulle. Living near Paris during that period we were to find ourselves rivetted onlookers in that underground war so evocatively depicted in the novel and the film *The Day of the Jackal*.

At that moment in her history de Gaulle was France. As was written in *The Economist* of 20 May: 'It was not the constitution, it was not the majesty of the French Republic that outfaced Challe and his allies. It was the majesty, the legend, the character, the height and the nose of General de Gaulle . . .'

Maurice Challe was pardoned by de Gaulle in 1966 having served five and a half years of his sentence. He died in January 1979, aged 73. General Jacquot decided to stay away from the office for most of June; he wanted to take the leave granted to senior French officials to 'flush out their kidneys at a spa', in his case at Vittel near his home in Vrécourt. Also he had much work to do for the French government in connection with the ongoing purge of the Officer Corps. So on 8 June Costa, Bernard and I accompanied him to NORTHAG HQ, a visit which went extremely well – as Jacquot's relations with General Cassels and Air Marshal Sir John Grandy (COMTWOATAF) were from the start excellent. We then dropped him off at an airfield near Vittel and made our way back to Fontainebleau.

During the flight Costa told me that even if he had not resigned, Challe would have been removed from AFCENT at an early date, so numerous were the complaints about him to their governments by senior German, British and American Commanders. Two items from our latest NORTHAG meeting seemed worth recording. It was depressing to hear the briefing staff recite the list of major concerns which had for many years been regularly brought to the attention of CINCENT's Headquarters and yet over which little or no action had been taken. This probably was more the fault of our political masters than of the military. Secondly, Jacquot's insistence on the scientists of the western nations finding soon an antidote to the effects on the human body of nuclear radiation. Without such protection NATO could not employ any nuclear weapon over German territory. The Soviet attackers would thus be at a significant advantage. Jacquot was convinced that a pill or injected drug could be invented to that end.

One morning my colleague Robert de Grandmaison spent an hour giving me his personal views on the political situation in France. The main points he stressed were the continuing opposition to de Gaulle's Algerian policy, his unpopularity with some sections of the population, particularly the farmers and fishermen, and the extent to which the French Communist Party was benefitting from these. In the Army this political instability and conflict, combined with the purges (*épurations*) to which the Armed Forces had been subjected after the war, and more recently as a consequence of Challe's attempted coup, had led to a disturbing lowering of morale and widespread indiscipline. Soldiers' Committees displaying Red Flags were now, he told me, being set up in some units. An indication of the extent to which the conduct of senior French Officers was influenced by their political attitudes was even revealed by our own boss, General Jacquot.

The President of the Republic had promoted him to the grade of Grand Cross of the Legion of Honour. When so informed, Jacquot wrote to the Elysée Palace asking to be excused from attending the formal investiture and that the emblem be sent to him through the post. Jacquot regarded himself as a 'pillar of the Left' and did not wish his political reputation to be compromised in public by being seen to receive from de Gaulle in person either the emblem or the presidential embrace. This singular request was turned down and CINCENT and eleven other notables were invested shortly afterwards at a formal ceremony. On that occasion, however, the lunch which customarily followed the investiture was omitted from the programme; moreover de Gaulle had given orders that no foreigners were to be present. This was further proof of de Gaulle's reluctance to recognise the presence on French soil of NATO installations and personalities (five years later he was to order their complete removal from France), and in particular, of his hostility towards the German General Speidel. But for their specific exclusion by de Gaulle, CINCENT would have invited Speidel, the Earl of Bandon and Admiral van Erkel to be present as his guests. General Jacquot was distinctly put out and instructed me to explain tactfully to each of these senior Commanders in person why they could not be invited. General Speidel appreciated Jacquot's courtesy in sending me to speak to him on the matter – a courtesy he would not have been shown by Challe – but he was clearly resigned to never being included in any occasion over which de Gaulle had a say. He told me in a sad tone: 'You know, we Germans are never invited to the 14th July Parade, nor is NATO ever included'. The Admiral showed no surprise whatever but spent twenty minutes telling me how bad the labour conditions were in France compared with those the Dutch workers were enjoying. Lord Bandon's reaction was to spell out his concern for the state of the UK's Armed Forces in view of the ending by 1963 of national service, when the UK would be the only European nation without conscription. Even the figure of 180,000, laid down by the government as a target for the strength of the Army, was then being regarded as too low in view of all the tensions in the world and our nation's defence commitments; but almost certainly unattainable by voluntary recruiting alone. Moreover COMAIRCENT was worried because a recent major BAOR exercise had given rise to widely held doubts about the capabilities of the British contribution to NATO.

BAOR's exposed and predictably multiplying deficiencies could in an emergency only be corrected by reinforcing that Army with many more Reservists from the UK and by the early use of tactical nuclear weapons. The hazards in resorting to these measures were apparent to all who studied the problems of the defence of Europe against a Warsaw Pact attack, and the whole matter was becoming a major topic for analysis and controversy in the UK media and at Westminister. Our NATO Allies, it seemed to me, were more reticent; they had their own defence problems. But Lord Bandon wondered, as many of us younger Officers were doing, how much longer the UK would be justified in retaining in the NATO structure so many senior command appointments. His view, he told me, was that Britain should commit fewer resources to Imperial defence – did Hong Kong really need two brigades? – and more to BAOR where the principal Red threat lay.

One day when Brigadier Costa and I were alone in the office the conversation turned, as it often did, to Field Marshal Montgomery. I asked him where in his opinion Monty's loyalty principally lay: to NATO, to Britain or to himself? I put this latter impertinent question to him because of the allegations, made chiefly by Americans, that Monty was *au fond* a self-centred and bumptious man. Costa's immediate reply was: 'Completely to his Sovereign and his country. He was the most patriotic man I've ever met. He would dive naked into that lake,' he continued, pointing in the direction of the Carp Pond, 'if he thought it be for the good of Britain'. I said that I thought Monty and General Jacquot had much in common: austerity in their private lives, quick brains and the ability to get straight to the root of a problem; and interest in the young. He agreed and added that Monty, who really had very little time for foreigners, had a high opinion of Jacquot and valued his opinion.

We then talked about the French Marshal de Lattre de Tassigny for whom Costa had also worked and whose reputation in England was high. 'Brilliantly clever . . . but evil. Completely unscrupulous and immoral, and entirely self-seeking. But a great actor . . . he'd have made a fortune on the stage, and he got people to follow him blindly. For that reason he can be classed as a great General – except that he never had a real enemy to be a General against!'

Whereas the loyalty to our Sovereign, and to the governments elected to run our national affairs, of the Armed Forces of Britain is taken for granted, the events in France of which we were the interested spectators, and memories of the bomb plot of July 1944 against Hitler, had made some of us think deeply about the meaning of loyalty and about the Serviceman's obligation to serve with undeviating and total dedication a leader or government which was embarking on wrong or wholly evil policies. In France, although many in the Armed Forces sympathised with or had actively supported the Algiers putsch of General Challe and his three colleagues, this sympathy soon turned to derision in all except the most ardent disciples of the Algérie Française creed; and the violent but ineffective tactics of the OAS in the end quenched the remaining embers of hatred for de Gaulle and his policies. De Gaulle triumphed. Challe and company had vastly over-estimated their own esteem in the eyes of the conscript *'contingent'* and of the working class, and had under-estimated the response of most French men and women to de Gaulle's majestic appeal for their support; and his remarkably sound judgement. In France by 1962 the wages of disloyalty were contempt and professional disgrace.

As regards the plot against Hitler at the height of the fighting in Normandy, my discussions with Germans over the years have left me with two differing conclusions. The attitude of Germans of my own generation seems to be that, as every member of the Wehrmacht had taken an oath of loyalty to Hitler personally, to break that oath was wrong. To break that oath at a time when German soldiers were facing a desperate situation on the battlefield was doubly wrong. To break that oath under those circumstances and then fail to achieve the plot's aim, the elimination of Hitler's leadership, damned the plotters three-fold. Failure brought contempt onto their heads in addition to barbaric punishment; moreover it convinced some Germans that Adolf Hitler was indeed a superman. Certainly there was no lessening of the fighting spirit in the German Army we confronted in north-west Europe in the second half of 1944; and I am not convinced that even if the conspirators had removed Hitler and the leading Nazis from power, all members of the German Armed Forces would have obeyed the orders of a successor government and meekly accepted the Unconditional Surrender terms which the Allies had already proclaimed as a principal War Aim. But when talking to Germans born after the war I have found that they hold rather different views. They seem to regard an oath of loyalty as something which cannot be binding in all circumstances; some circumstances could nullify its legitimacy, and that above all, Germans must never again be asked to swear allegiance to a single mortal individual. Although the conspirators of 20 July 1944 made a deadly botch of the affair, they are now, I am told, regarded as heroes for having made the attempt, and their executions as martyrdoms.

All my adult life I have counted myself lucky not to have been put to this test as were the French and German Officers of my generation. When in 1970 I had to decide precisely where my loyalty as a senior commander lay, the question was swiftly answered in my own mind because my allegiance to one Sovereign in no way conflicted with my duty to the nation of another. Moreover the line of action I took had a successful ending; the consequences were wholly beneficial. But I realised at the time that if my decision proved wrong or the enterprise failed, no one would have uttered a word of sympathy. I would have been universally condemned; for ineptitude as well as for treason. Verily, treason doth never prosper; for if it does, none dare call it treason.

Notes

1. Of the central circle of conspirators (in the plot to get rid of Hitler) Lieutenant-General Dr Hans Speidel was the sole survivor. On 20 July the members of the Army Group Staff loyal to the regime and Field Marshal von Kluge did not suspect him of having been one of the conspirators. This was partially due to the fact that Speidel on this day was totally occupied with his duties as Chief of Staff of the Army Group, for crucial battles were being fought near Caen and St Lo. Partially it was attributable to his circumspection and caution . . . In front of the uninitiated he acted the role of the passive observer. Fundamentally he had fulfilled his function within the conspiracy during the planning of the coup, namely attempting to persuade Rommel and making contacts for the conspiracy in the west. His caution, though, did not save him from arrest and interrogation by the Gestapo after his name had been mentioned by some conspirators already detained. Hitler himself ordered his arrest. However, the Army Court of Honour refused to expel him from the Army, though Keitel stressed that the Führer was convinced of Speidel's guilt. Thus he was spared public prosecution. But until the end of the war he was dragged from prison to confinement in a fortress. Ultimately, before the SS were able to liquidate him and other prominent detainees, he was freed by Allied troops in Bavaria.

(from *Hitler's Generals*, edited by Correlli Barnett, Part 2 by Klaus-Jürgen Müller, published by Phoenix Giants)

CHAPTER VIII
1961–1962

HQ AFCENT (cont'd)
A Medley of Memories

During the summer of 1961 Nikita Khrushchev, the Chairman of the Council of Ministers of the USSR, made provocative statements about resuming tests of Soviet nuclear weapons and about his intention to sign a separate treaty with the German Democratic Republic. In September the Russians detonated three nuclear devices in four days, and in October a thirty megaton weapon in the upper atmosphere. This was disturbing, as the international community had high hopes of the forthcoming nuclear disarmament conference. But more alarming was the sealing by Herr Ulbricht's East German government of the borders within Berlin between the Russian sector of the city and the American, British and French sectors which made up the western half. Ulbricht could not have taken this drastic step without Moscow's blessing even though he had been driven to it by the need to staunch the westward haemorrhage of disillusioned citizens, the workforce of the GDR. The rapid construction by the East Germans of a high wall and the bricking up of windows in buildings adjacent to the border to prevent movement between the two halves of Berlin, and the continuous patrols by Border Guards with orders to shoot anyone attempting to cross this barrier, were evidence that the Communists did not regard this sealing off of GDR territory as a temporary expedient. It was a symbol of a dissatisfied population; but it was proof too of the Communist Party's determination to suppress it. The Berlin Wall remained a formidable and grim reminder of Communist callousness until 1989 when it was torn down during that sudden East European upheaval when 'the Evil Empire' of the Soviet System, as President Reagan was to call it, disintegrated. During the twenty-eight years of its existence eighty people were killed trying to cross that wall.

Not only was this action by the GDR and the USSR a contravention of the agreements signed by the four victorious Allied Powers at the end of World War Two, by recognising the GDR the USSR handed over to the East German authorities control of the surface and air routes into and from Berlin which the Russians themselves had guaranteed. In 1948 they deliberately attempted to sever those routes and that Soviet blockade had alerted the world to the fundamentally hostile attitude of the Russians to the Western democracies, their former allies. The subsistence of not only the Allied garrisons in the city but of the two million plus souls who made up the civilian population had only been ensured by the Berlin Airlift, the *Luftbrücke*, which British and United States air power sustained for fifteen months at great financial cost and with the loss of sixty-eight aircrew who perished on that unique humanitarian mission. The possibility of a new blockade being imposed by East Germany, and more effectively than in 1948-9, was taken very seriously by the Western governments and in the newspapers of the NATO countries.

A major crisis was upon us: the Cold War was in everyone's mind. The West European leaders all professed to be standing firm. President Kennedy was determined to prevent a war breaking out through miscalculation or false readings of the signals given out by the other side. He also sought to restore the reputation of a US government whose fingers had been burnt a few months earlier in the Cuban Bay of Pigs debacle. The Pentagon therefore prepared a number of drastic measures such as the evacuation from the continent of all US Service families and a significant reinforcement of USAREUR, the American Army in Europe.

The British Prime Minister, MacMillan, took a calmer view of the situation but pressed for an international conference to remove the tension. His government's action, however, in lowering the manpower ceiling for the Army to 165,000, and the proposal to remove a complete division from BAOR to save money, vexed our NATO partners just when the Americans were increasing the strength of the US Army by 125,000 and the French were moving a division to Europe from North Africa. Some commentators were making acid references to Britain as 'a spineless and reluctant ally'. De Gaulle pronounced himself against a large multi-national conference: 'They only boost the ego of the Communist rulers and end with the West giving things away unnecessarily to demonstrate our good intentions'.

On both sides of the Iron Curtain the question was being asked: 'To what extent is the other side bluffing?' In the West a further question was posed: 'To what extent is Red China encouraging the USSR in this new East-West confrontation?'

Khrushchev looked the embodiment of bold, thrusting Bolshevism, and the Russian Major Titov's feat in making the longest journey hitherto in space, seventeen orbits of Earth, had plainly increased the self-confidence of his countrymen.

At AFCENT all remained calm. I was instructed to stay close at hand during one weekend in case an emergency arose; Air Marshal Bandon and Admiral van Erkel stayed on leave. General Jacquot was certain that the crisis would be resolved by diplomacy and that there would be 'no shooting unless someone on one side or the other goes totally mad'. His chief anxiety was that inaccurate intelligence reports would cause a major rise in the temperature. 'Our national Intelligence Services can not be trusted; they always predict the worst in order to cover themselves. Moreover they still have not learned to understand the history of Russia or the Russian mind. They apply the same methods against the Russians as against other European nations. Russia is different.'

In October he, Costa and I spent ten days in Germany initially watching a phase of the BAOR annual exercise, Spearpoint, directed by the Corps Commander General 'Splosh' Jones who had been Commandant of the Staff College when I was a student there. We were accompanied by two young Officers, Captain Loic Éon-Duval and CINCENT's son, Philippe. Both had been in units whose COs went over to Challe in the April coup and both had been in arrest for forty days until cleared by a Court of Enquiry. General Jacquot had taken them onto his personal staff for a period of moral convalescence.

Our expedition started with an excellent dinner in the home near Thionville of a distant cousin of Costa's and her husband, Count Jean de Selancy. Both spoke perfect English although neither had visited Britain; they attributed their fluency to the English governesses of their childhood. The house was very large, fairly old and filled with beautiful tapestries, paintings, books and furniture; and the impression of luxury was heightened by the perfume of joss-sticks. The de Selancy were plainly a wealthy couple, and since the Countess had been the Mayoress of Thionville for many years, an active and intelligent one too. The meal was served by a butler aged about 19 in a white uniform and white gloves. The conversation was animated and to begin with concerned the well-known figures who had visited the house. The ex-King of Italy was the last royal to call; the most dramatic visitor was the Grand Duchess of Luxembourg who in 1940 arrived in her nightdress ahead of the German invaders. De Gaulle had not been for some years 'as the Countess loathes him'. When the conversation turned to French affairs it was dominated by lamentations about the iniquities of the President, hopes for his early demise and a change of government. No one, however, could tell me, a diffident but intensely interested listener, who was likely to form the successor government to de Gaulle for which they were all praying.

Spearpoint was held in the area of Germany I knew best, and while the senior members of our party lodged in a hotel in Detmold, the French drivers, Pujol and Roux, and I were put up in the barracks of a Royal Artillery regiment who looked after us admirably. The Gunner orderlies were loud, however, in their complaints against the Cameronians, the 'Poison Dwarfs', whose bad behaviour had caused Minden to be put Out of Bounds to British troops. I also had a very happy interlude back in Lemgo seeing again the wives and children of my Argyll friends – the men of the battalion being out on the exercise – and the Rear Party under Gerald Hadow whom I had known since 5 PARA days. CINCENT spent two days in the exercise area. Apart from some helicopter-borne attacks by US troops – which the umpires adjudged to have failed because the bridges were defended by tanks and the landing zones had been 'mined' – we saw very little of the 'battles'. This was entirely proper and proof of good camouflage and movement discipline by the British units. I should have liked to see the 91st in action and CINCENT was a bit peeved that no senior British Officer came near him. Our guide was a most uninspiring Captain in the Education Corps, with nauseatingly bad breath and in a state of great anxiety as he had just mislaid his wallet containing three hundred deutsch marks. He compared very badly with the young American who had 'bear-led' me so well in Bavaria the previous February.

So we left the British Army to its mock battles and headed east through the magnificent scenery of the Oberharz to Goslar and thence down the line of the frontier with the GDR to Kassel. The West German Frontier Guards (*Bundesgrenzschütz*) were out in strength and their alertness and bearing were impressive. In that sector the Iron Curtain consisted then merely of some rusty barbed wire through which groups of tourists gawped at the East German Guards who could be seen high up in the watch-towers or patrolling with dogs the frontier belt. Apart from these uniformed sentinels the landscape beyond the frontier looked denuded of life, human or animal.

A long bash followed, down past Karlsruhe to Herrenalb in the French zone where we stayed the night in a hotel well-known to CINCENT and where we had excellent food and log-like sleep. General Jacquot had generously brought us down to that part of Germany to introduce us to Baden-Baden where he had been based when C-in-C of the French Army; also to visit some of the places through which he had fought in 1944 when second-in-command to André Malraux, a brigade commander, in the drive to liberate Strasbourg. Baden-Baden and its surroundings were strikingly beautiful; the countryside lush, varied and well kept, and the buildings used by the French for Headquarters and families' accommodation looked modern and comfortable but unused, for so much of the French Army was at that time in North Africa. Jacquot told me that evening how the French employed Germans to go round the empty barracks and offices turning the lights on and off to mislead Russian spies. And when General Heusinger, the Inspector-General of the Bundeswehr, was searching for additional buildings for the expanding West German Army, Jacquot told him he could immediately let him have accommodation for sixty thousand men if Paris authorised the transfer.

Re-crossing the Rhine at Kehl we found ourselves back in a land of dilapidated buildings, cow dung, rusting farm machinery and cigarettes drooping from the lips of indolent men. As Costa exclaimed, it was perfectly understandable that Montgomery, when sailing down the Rhine with him, had pointed out the contrast between Germany and France. 'On one bank were men, everywhere working like ants; on the other men just sitting fishing.'

Our drive through the wine country of Alsace and the lunch which followed in a restaurant, owned by an old comrade of Jacquot's from the Resistance, in the enchanting hill village of Riquewihr were most enjoyable; as was the route over the Vosges Mountains which reminded me of Cyprus's Troodos Range. We arrived at the Jacquot family house in Vrécourt after dark to find all the electricity in the district out of order. We were greeted by candlelight by the General's wife, his very pregnant daughter, Lise, her husband the ADC, various servants and a dog. The house was quite ordinary, in atmosphere and decor similar to his Paris flat; no pictures on the walls, potted plants, a tricolor flag and every window tightly shut against the fresh country air. The floors all being of highly polished wood, we were at once instructed by Madame Jacquot to remove our shoes and to walk around with special pieces of felt material on our feet. All this conformed quite naturally with the frugal, rural background from which the Jacquots had sprung. And it explained why, when Bill Wildman had driven up to the Jacquot home early one morning, he was confronted by CINCENT's wife in her nightdress emptying a chamber-pot into the gutter in front of the house.

We left CINCENT with his family and headed back to Fontainebleau spending the night at Neufchateau where we slept badly, I on account of the continuous noise of heavy lorries at the traffic lights outside; Costa because of the antics of the two couples sharing the adjoining room.

The next month President de Gaulle addressed some three thousand of the cream of the French Officer Corps assembled in Strasbourg. Wearing his two-star General's uniform he spoke to an army he knew well. He understood its two major complaints of recent years; that it had received no clear directives from government, and that it had been called on to 'implement a policy of abandon in France's colonial empire'. He praised the Army for having fulfilled its task in Algeria, whether engaged in combat or pacification, with courage and honour; but he made it clear that Algeria was finished as a battleground and that the Army must 'henceforth adapt itself to the threats of nuclear war'. The chief purpose of his magisterial address, however, was to bring the Army back to the path of duty: it must forget the bitter memories of lost causes and assume its role as the guardian of French renewal. 'When State and Nation have chosen the way, military duty is made clear once and for all. Outside these rules there can only be doomed soldiers.' The OAS detonated a number of bombs in Strasbourg and elsewhere to coincide with de Gaulle's arrival in the city. He ignored them.

This campaign of violence by the OAS continued well into the next year and on two occasions, driving back down the autoroute from Paris by night, Rosemary and I had the tyres of our car punctured by metal devices scattered over the carriageway. Several attempts to kill the President failed through ineptitude. Cynics said that the attempts were bogus, mounted by de Gaulle's supporters to enhance his prestige; for 'ineptitude is not characteristic of the OAS in action'.

For me 1961 ended on a pleasing note. I had been selected to attend the next course at the Joint Services Staff College. This was a prestigious course with places on it much sought after, and it advanced the career prospects of those who were lucky enough to get there. Rosemary and I however heard the news with mixed feelings. To be selected was a professional compliment, but it meant leaving Fontainebleau, CINCENT and all our friends six months earlier than planned; and a premature return to England meant a reduced income and paying out a large sum in customs duty to import our car. General Jacquot was delighted for me; he seemed to take it as a compliment to himself that a member of his personal staff had been selected for this preferment. He insisted moreover that I be replaced, not by an RAF Officer as scheduled, but by a British soldier who spoke French and was staff trained. In the event my successor was a Lieutenant-Colonel in the Scots Guards.

At the beginning of December I succeeded in getting the Pipes and Drums and Military Band of my regiment sent down from Lemgo. In that long-hoped-for venture I was warmly supported by the CO, Hugh Spens, by the Command Secretary who would have to foot the bill, and by our Support Unit at Fontainebleau who would have to house and feed the Argyll contingent. The Pipers, Dancers and Bandsmen spent nine days with me and were worked pretty hard on a programme of engagements at AFCENT and at SHAPE for General Norstad and his staff. They were acclaimed everywhere they performed and hosted generously.

After their public performance on the Place d'Armes the Mayor asked me to accept on the regiment's behalf the Gold Medal of Fontainebleau. The last recipient had been the King of the Belgians. There was a memorable moment during the British Army Guest Night when the Band played the march of the Royal Württemberg Grenadiers in which our chief guest, General Hans Speidel, had begun his military career. He was visibly moved by this British gesture. The bearing and musical and dancing skills of the Scots was excellent, as was their conduct in their brief spells of free time. I had arranged for them to be given guided tours of Paris and of the palaces in Fontainebleau and Versailles, and the SHAPE staff laid on a briefing about NATO and why the alliance existed. One young musician from Argyllshire confessed to me afterwards that he and his parents strongly disapproved of the stationing near his home of US submarines armed with Polaris missiles; indeed, he told me, his family had taken part in public demonstrations to get the vessels removed. 'But,' he said to me, 'now that I have heard that lecture I understand what NATO is all about, and I think we are wrong to protest. But why couldn't I, my family and people like us have been told more about NATO and its aims both at home in Scotland and as part of our army training?'

As I wrote to RHQ, I doubt that the regiment's bands had ever before played for audiences with such a high density of multinational brass. I considered that their visit was taxpayers' money well spent, for their colourful, skilled performances and good manners made a fine impression at a time when Britain's commitment to the European ideal and to the continent's defence was being widely doubted. But in assessing the relative strengths of the Armed Forces of NATO and of the Warsaw Pact, bagpipes and feather bonnets count for little compared with machine guns and entrenching tools; and watching our displays were some who were quietly calculating the dividend to be reaped if defence spending were directed less towards musical panoply and more to battlefield essentials.

My Brother, Moray had just announced his engagement and Jane was very keen that we should all be together for a 'last family Christmas'; so she, Moray and Alastair came over to us and we all had a thoroughly good five days; Christmas at its best.

1961 had been a happy year, and for me, a British soldier in a French setting, an instructive one.

I knew little about nuclear weapons, their characteristics and possible employment on the battlefield, so I asked for a vacancy on the NATO Special Weapons course run by the US Army in Bavaria. I had planned to go by car taking Rosemary and our two children but so much snow fell during the night before our departure that we took the overnight Orient Express to Munich and from there went on in an electric train thronged with happy young German skiers for the forty-five miles to Oberammergau where we stayed in the Hotel Boeld run by friends of General Speidel. Sunshine and thick snow covered everything, for that winter was an unusually severe one in Europe. We were enchanted by the village with its houses attractively painted with Biblical and local, rural scenes, and by the courtesy and kindness of the people, most of whom bore the surname Lang, and who perform every ten years the famous Passion Play. That tradition dates back to 1634 when, during the Thirty Years War, a terrible plague swept through Bavaria, mercifully sparing Oberammergau. We had a great time tobogganing with the kids and the US Army ran a bus into Garmisch where we went to their

Services' Recreation Center, a large modern building with restaurants, bars, bowling alleys and two novel features: a retractable dance-floor over an ice-rink and in the wash-rooms machines dispensing contraceptives at ten cents a packet.

Alas poor Rosemary developed a very sore throat and high temperature and had to spend five days in bed. But the problem of looking after Pinky and Didi all day while I was at school was solved by the kindness of two people living in the hotel, an elderly widow from Hamburg, Frau Weser, and Shirley Hahn whose US Navy husband was on the course with me. A local doctor named Lang (what else?) came and filled Rosemary up with penicillin. That got her back on her feet but in a very weak state. She had been having too many bouts of quinsy and we decided that her tonsils would have to come out when we got back to England.

The course was held in Hawkins Barracks, a US Army establishment commanded by a Colonel Chapman, and the administration and instruction were a wholly American effort of the highest quality. There were fifty-two Officers on my course from twelve of the fifteen NATO nations, only Portugal, Iceland and Luxembourg not being represented.

Apart from registering mentally the excellence of the US Army's arrangements, I came away in some confusion about the subject we had been studying. Firstly, the high degree of secrecy surrounding the whole field of nuclear weapons and their relevance to the battlefield. During lectures all the windows were shut and blacked out – thereby greatly adding to the heat and 'fug' in the room – and any notes we took were removed from our possession, though we could apply for access to them later while serving in NATO posts. If combat officers, NCOs and private soldiers were going to encounter nuclear weapons and the heat, blast and radiation they produce, the whole subject would have to be brought more into the open and treated as a terrifying but endurable aspect of warfare. Knowledge dispels fear; but the dissemination of knowledge at platoon level would not be possible while such strict secrecy rules remained extant.

Secondly, the immense organisation needed to produce a weapon like the Polaris missile and to train its operators must for many decades limit the number of countries capable of joining the Nuclear Club. Thirdly, the degree of exactness necessary in calculating the effects of a nuclear detonation likely to be suffered by our own troops, by the enemy and by civilians and their property. These effects would be significantly modified by the weapon yield, the terrain, weather, height of burst and by the protective measures troops could take during the warning period. I wondered whether the factors of fatigue, stress, haste, imperfect communications and the fog of war which bedevil the commander in the field might not make those calculations, through error, either extremely hazardous to our own side, or deemed so unreliable and dangerous that the optimum moment for their employment against the enemy might be allowed to pass through over-caution on our part. And how were our friendly forces, widely dispersed and in contact with a watchful enemy going to be adequately warned of an impending nuclear explosion? The whole subject, then still in its infancy, was complicated, expensive, daunting and not wholly comprehensible even to those whose native tongue is English. Our Greek and Turkish fellow-students looked lost most of the time. (Five months earlier the Turks had hanged Prime Minister Menderes and two of his ministers, but my colleagues on the course from that robust nation were unable or unwilling to explain the reasons for that drastic treatment of well-known politicians.)

The French students, although many spoke English well, tiresomely adhered to their national policy of insisting that everything be translated into French; for rather like King Cnut and the waves, General de Gaulle was trying to delay the supplanting of French as the traditional world-language of diplomacy and professional intercourse by Anglo-Saxon/American English.

Our departure from Oberammergau was marred by a rumour which had filtered through from Fontainebleau. CINCENT's only son, Lieutenant Philippe Jacquot, had been killed in action in Algeria three days before. I knew him quite well as he used to come into the office when on leave and he had accompanied us on our autumn visit to Spearpoint and along the Iron Curtain. On leaving St Cyr he had been posted to the 18th RCP (Colonial Parachute Regiment) under the command of a Colonel Masselot. The Colonel took his regiment over to General Challe in the April 1961 coup: for this folly he was sentenced to ten years in prison and the regiment was disbanded. At that point young Jacquot came to live with his parents in Paris for a spell before being posted back to Algeria.

The recent crescendo of bomb outrages by the OAS in Algeria had increased the tension between European and Muslim communities. It was a deliberate tactic of the OAS to try to destroy the accord which was developing between the French and Algerian negotiators. Philippe was acting as Commander of No 2 Company of the 21st Infantry Regiment in Oran. When the curfew was lifted at 7am on 14 February the Muslims started to get worked up about the latest OAS bomb explosions of which there had been forty-four in the area during the night; and agitators and terrorists began to infiltrate the crowd. Between eleven o'clock and noon an FNL member shot at and wounded one of Jacquot's platoon commanders. The building from which the shot was fired was immediately sealed off, and Lieutenant Jacquot ran into the building at the head of a squad of his men. They searched the ground floor, then ran up the narrow staircase to the first floor where a number of doors led off a landing. As Jacquot opened one door the gunman in the room fired, hitting him in the liver and knocking him backwards down the stairs. He never regained consciousness and died in hospital some two hours later. The Company Sergeant-Major and the squad killed the gunman and six other terrorists found hiding in the building. The news of Philippe's death was phoned through to Fontainebleau via Paris on the French Army Chaplains' 'net' and by the Corps Commander in Oran direct to Brigadier Costa. That evening General Jacquot and his wife flew to Oran, kept watch all night over the body of their son, and attended the funeral the next day.

His body was later brought back to France for a private burial at the family home in Vrécourt. Philippe was without doubt a good young Officer with a promising career ahead of him. He had done well at St Cyr and was already highly regarded in his new unit, the 21st RI. This personal tragedy for General Jacquot and his wife, the more grievous for losing their only son, was made even more poignant by the fact that when he died the Algerian war was almost at an end. A cease-fire was declared within a month. With Philippe's death General Jacquot became the tenth of the *Grands Chefs* of the French Army who had lost sons in the service of France in Indo-China and North Africa. We three foreign members of CINCENT's personal Cabinet were greatly saddened by this cruel blow to a man whom we admired and for whom we felt much affection.

By March the expected cease-fire had been agreed by the French government and the FNL, and in a referendum held in France on 8 April, 90.7% of the voters approved de Gaulle's policy over Algeria and for the exercise by him of special powers. That was a triumph for him and proof that public support for the OAS in metropolitan France was virtually nil. General Jacquot was particularly scathing about the OAS leaders and their claim to respect and honour. 'Not one has even got himself killed! They allow themselves to be arrested without putting up the slightest resistance! If you have a cause at least be prepared to die for it. The Communards got themselves slaughtered in 1871, and the Swiss Guards died defending the monarchy on the steps of the Tuileries – but not these people.' Ex-Generals Salan and Jouhaud were eventually sentenced to life imprisonment; only Colonel Bastien-Thierry, who had tried to assassinate the President, was executed.

The Ministry of Defence in Paris had just published the figures of casualties in the Algerian war up to the end of 1961. I reproduce them here as those relating to accidental deaths and injuries are, as de Grandmaison agreed, an indictment of the training methods and discipline in the French conscript army.

* * *

	Killed in action	Wounded in action	Killed accidentally	Wounded accidentally
French (pure)	9,000	18,500	4,300	22,000
Foreign Legion	1,200	2,600	600	2,000
French (North (African)	1,250	2,800	900	3,900
Others	2,500	3,500	?	?
Totals (75,050)	13,950	27,400	5,800	27,900
Approx % of total casualties	19%	36%	8%	37%

The total dead in the seven-year-long war was estimated at 141,000.

Bill Wildman, Hubert Jeschke and I being the foreign members of CINCENT's Cabinet and therefore members of the Jacquot family, attended Philippe's funeral in Vrécourt on 14 March. We put up for the night in Contrexéville after calling in to pay our respects to the family. The General was composed but his wife was still very upset. The service was held in a very old and small village church; luckily it was heated for the wind was bitter. The church was packed, with men sitting on the right of the aisle and women on the left. The singing by the village choir was excellent and the service was conducted with great dignity and beauty by two Padres, one of whom had been Jacquot's chaplain in the Resistance. The pall bearers and the Guard of Honour were from the 1st Parachute Regiment wearing camouflage overalls and red berets. Sturdy, smart and polished they, like the male villagers, gave a better impression of French manhood than we had been accustomed to seeing around Fontainebleau. Of those in the church and at the Jacquot house afterwards, the man who interested me the most was General Massu. He became famous in 1958 when he and his parachute soldiers successfully cleaned up the Algiers kasbah. But soon after that he fell foul of '*Le Pouvoir*' and was sacked. In 1961 de Gaulle brought him out of disgrace and appointed him Governor of Metz, in which capacity he attended the funeral. Tall, broad, with dark hair *coupé en brosse*, he had an unusually craggy face and a great beak of a nose. I got the impression that he was very full of Massu; on arrival at his place in the church he remained standing for a good ten minutes – presumably to ensure that everyone saw him.

In mid-April I had just finished reading Georges Blond's book, *Verdun*, and during a quiet spell in the office Bill Wildman and I went off to study the ground where that dreadful long battle in 1916, the 'mincing machine to bleed France white' the German C-in-C had termed it, had been fought. We drove via Bar-le-Duc and up La Voie Sacrée to get an idea of the logistic problems the French faced, but the single-track railway Pétain laid had long been lifted. At Souilly where the French Second Army HQ was established in the Town Hall, I compared the 1962 scene with a photograph in Blond's book taken from the identical spot in 1916. The only change after forty-six years was the addition of a bus shelter and a petrol filling-station. I was amazed by the small size of the Town Hall and wondered how the Staff managed to work in such cramped conditions and with the incessant noise of motor transport and marching columns passing by the front door. In Verdun itself we thought the cathedral rather ugly, but the Citadel, built by Vauban, impressive; its four kilometres of underground galleries had sheltered thousands of troops and civilians during the city's ordeal.

The next morning Bill and I visited all the well-known landmarks on the battleground: Fort de Tavannes; de Vaux; Souville, the high watermark of the German advance; Douaumont with its moonscape of cratered fields, the cemetery and the ossuaire with the skulls and bones of thousands recovered from the battlefields and all displayed, German and French together. Then on to Le Ravin de la Mort, la Tranchée des Baionettes and Colonel Driant's Battle HQ in the Bois des Caures. The countryside has not been reclaimed; it has been left to Nature as a memorial to the buildings, forests, woods, animals and human lives destroyed during that terrible year. More poignantly even than Flanders or the Somme, the Verdun battlefield evokes today the horror of the fighting in the Great War and the endurance of the soldiers engaged. According to a calculation I made there, the ground fought over in 1916 covers 140 map squares: a conservative estimate of the total casualties on both sides in the battle for Verdun is 500,000 killed and 800,000 crippled. That means 9,300 lives lost or wrecked per map square. And some people cannot comprehend why France capitulated in 1940!

Ever since childhood I had wanted to visit the battlefields where the British Army had fought in the Great War of 1914-18. I had done a lot of reading and collected a useful series of maps and sketches, so in August 1961 I set off for Flanders taking Rosemary and Pinky with me. Not, I thought, a very amusing holiday expedition for them but they were reluctant to stay behind. We went first to Ypres, to the Cloth Hall which had been most lovingly rebuilt after destruction by the Germans; and then to the Menin Gate, the superb memorial to the British Empire's 54,896 dead of the Ypres Salient who have no known grave and where every evening the Belgian Police halt the traffic and two buglers of the Fire Brigade sound the Last Post. This memorial inscribed with regiment, rank and name of every fallen man, the sunset ceremony performed since 1927 without interruption, save during the German occupation of 1940-4, and the immaculate way in which the War Graves Commission tends the 174 British and Imperial cemeteries in the Ypres area moved us greatly.

The men who tend the graves were all young Englishmen, some of whom had married local girls and would live out their lives in France and Belgium. Several told us that as the years pass the number and variety of visitors increases; and all remark on the beauty and perfect order in the cemeteries, on the quality of the headstones and the glorious Cross of Sacrifice which are standard wherever in the world British Servicemen lie buried. So different, I found, to the sombre and rather uncouth stones which mark the resting places of so many of the German dead. Go and compare our great Tyne Cot cemetery, centred on the site of the principal German blockhouse (where I found the names of fourteen Officers and 300 Other Ranks of an Argyll battalion on plaques 141-143 on the east wall) with the largest German cemetery at Langemarck!! Other key features we visited were Passchendaele, the village on the ridge captured at last by the Canadians in November 1917 in the Third Battle of Ypres after five months' fighting through flooded ground and deep mud. Even on a summer's day in peacetime, those Flanders fields have a drab, uninviting look. Only God and those who fought there know what they were like under autumn rain and winter snow. Nearby is the Canadian memorial at St Julien, the scene of the first gas attack in April 1915. Then down to the Messines Ridge with Hill 60 and the huge crater at Lone Tree, now water-filled. That crater is from a mine, one of nineteen blown at 3.10 a.m. on 7 June 1917 under the German front line at the start of General Plumer's successful attack. It took our Sappers six months to dig it, the tunnel reaching 1,730 feet from behind our lines to the point of detonation, and it contained 91,000 pounds of ammonal explosive. It is recorded that on that June morning the Prime Minister of England, awake in No 10 Downing Street, felt the earth under London shudder as the nineteen mines were set off.

Then to Gheluvelt, the scene of Haig's hour of crisis on 29 October 1914 when the German breakthrough was only prevented by a gallant counter-attack by the Worcestershire Regiment under Major Hankey. (Does the British Infantry salute the Worcesters on the anniversary each year of that action? We observe Minden Day and the Battle of Waterloo, but was not Gheluvelt equally remarkable and decisive?) And lastly to Mount Kemmel, a prominent feature which like the Salient itself, was only lost briefly to the great German offensive of 1918. The foreign tactician will say that the British were foolish to have stubbornly clung for over three years onto Ypres and the low lying salient our trenches formed beyond the town. So many lives could have been saved if we had pulled back to the higher ground overlooking Ypres and thus put the Germans at the disadvantage from which we suffered all through the war. But Ypres – 'Wipers' – was where in 1914 the incomparable little British Regular

Army had died. Its soil was therefore sacred and had to be held whatever the cost. And until 1918 it was.

Waterloo is a gift for the tourist industry with an uninterrupted view of the battlefield from the top of La Butte, three hundred steps up which Pinky climbed unaided. The many exhibits, waxworks of Napoleon and his generals and the fine panorama depicting the situation at six o'clock in the evening of 18 June 1815 are interesting and well displayed. The whole impression given to us, though, was that the Prussians won tactically, the French morally and the English, apart from Wellington, took little part. The contribution to the Allied victory as shown to posterity is directly related to the proportion of tourists from each nation engaged in the battle; or so it seemed to us. Certainly the relics of British participation were hard to locate and even the Guards' Chapel at Hougomont (Goumont now) was bare and poorly maintained when we were there in 1962.

The battlefields of the Somme which we visited next are set in country quite different to wretched, flattish, wet Flanders with its gloomy poplars and hideous brick houses. Here it was rather like Sussex; open rolling cornfields with thick woods set like tiaras on the crests of the main features which bear well-known names such as Combles, Leuze Wood, Guillemont, Delville Wood, Bazentin, Pozières and Beaumont Hamel. At Thiepval stands the huge memorial to the 73,357 British and Empire dead who have no known grave. Around it the land was still desolate and scarred though becoming overgrown with weeds, brambles and young trees. About two miles away in Newfoundland Park we saw the memorials to the Newfoundlanders and to the 29th and 51st (Highland) Divisions; and some lengths of British and German trenches, at one point separated only by a few metres, had been preserved and labelled. The death toll on 1 July 1916, the first day of the Battle of the Somme, was appalling and has continued to appal the people of Britain more even than the thousands who died in the mud and squalor of Flanders. The reason is that so much had been expected from that Somme attack; also the soldiers who died there were not Regulars but the cream of British manhood who had enlisted voluntarily out of patriotism. Despite the heavy and prolonged bombardment by our artillery of the enemy trenches – ('By the time the barrage lifts,' Tommy Carew-Hunt had been told, 'there won't be a black beetle alive in the Jerry lines.') – the Germans had time to emerge from the safety of their deep protective *'Stollen'*, set up their machine-guns and pour fire into the rows of heavy-laden British Infantry as they plodded across the open fields. I have frequently asked myself if my generation would have stood the strain of trench warfare and fearful casualty lists as did the generation of 1914-18. Our attitudes to death, victory and defeat, and to patriotism too, have changed since 1918. So have the skills of our leaders and their means of waging war. But I do not believe that our men, though more educated and questioning, and more sceptical now than their Fathers and Grandfathers, would do their duty less staunchly. The endurance of our soldiers in Burma, in Japanese captivity and in the Italian winter, of our merchant seamen in the Arctic convoys, was remarkable. And the fortitude of the German soldier on the Russian front and of the sailor in the U-boat fleet indicate to me that European fighting men, if well led in a cause they consider just, will conduct themselves no less impressively than earlier generations.

With Rosemary at the wheel we drove slowly along the country lanes looking from side to side lest we missed something of interest. Just ahead of us, right in the middle of the road, was a middle-aged man riding on a moped, a motor-assisted bicycle, and hanging from the handlebars he had a radio blaring out music. That must have concealed from him the sound of our car for as we entered the village of Guillemont he, catching sight of a friend mending the roof of his house, stopped without warning. Rosemary braked hard but could not prevent the car from bumping into his rear wheel and causing him to somersault gracefully over the front of his machine. The man was not amused and made off at a good pace through the village towards a telephone kiosk. While he was away summoning the police, quite a crowd of villagers gathered round us, attracted by Pinky and intrigued by the presence of us foreigners. I explained that we 'had come to see where my Grandfathers had fought for France in the war of fourteen-eighteen', and the whole proceedings became very jolly and good natured. We must have won the villagers over for when the cyclist reappeared they pointed at him: '*Cochon*, we saw you run to the telephone; now you have put on a limp pretending that these nice people have done you an injury'. He was not injured but his bicycle had a bent wheel and burst tyre. In due course the Law arrived; no uniformed gendarme but the local Huissier de Justice, a very tall, pale man with drooping moustaches, and his short, fat and florid Assistant. Measurements were taken and recorded in a notebook and details of identity exchanged in the happiest of atmospheres. When all was done we bade farewell to the good people of Guillemont and took Monsieur Renard and his damaged moped to a blacksmith for repair. When we reached the Renard residence, an ugly house surrounded by acres of wasteland and rubbish, we were greeted by his family: his wife and eleven dirty and unkempt children. Thank Heavens we had not killed him, the breadwinner of that tribe! I had eventually to pay a small sum for the services of the Huissier, but all other loose ends were tidied up for me by my admirable friend Captain Dicharry, the energetic and efficient commander of the French Military Police Detachment at AFCENT Headquarters.

Dicharry and I got along very well together. We had first met over the incident of the drunken Major. One morning he came into my office wearing a long face.

'O you Britanniques, you did a terrible thing last night!' I asked him to explain.

'Yes, last night your newly arrived British Major left the Officers' Club at a late hour, drove his car straight onto the autoroute and hit a police motorcyclist who was badly injured.'

'I *am* sorry. Was the Major hurt?'

'No, not hurt at all but we had to detain him.'

'Good Lord why?'

'Because he, while driving the car, was drunk.'

'What made you think he was drunk?' 'Oh, his speech: it was obvious from the way he talked that he'd had far too much to drink.'

It so happened that I had been in the Club the previous evening and had spent some time in that Major's company and had walked with him to his car when he left. In my judgement he was perfectly sober, but he had an Irish brogue which made his English sound like an outlandish tongue.

'May I suggest that you go and speak to him again now, and you will find his speech just as incomprehensible as it was last night. You see, he is from an Irish regiment and some of them talk like that all the time.'

The senior British Officer at AFCENT was Major-General TBL Churchill. Fontainebleau was his last posting as he was to retire late in 1962. He had a sweet wife, Jane, whom we all adored but she was already ill with the cancer which was to kill her within a year. The way the British Army was being 'messed about' by the government's defence policy at a time when NATO needed military strengthening and firm, united political direction saddened him and he told me how glad he was that his son was not joining any of the Services.

Originally in the Manchester Regiment, Tom Churchill had a Brother Jack, a Seaforth; both had been in the Commandos during the war. Jack I had met years before in Perham Down when I first joined the Scottish Parachute Battalion and, knowing this, General Tom kindly arranged, a few weeks before I left France, a small dinner party for his Brother to meet me again; and more interestingly, to meet Brigadier Freiherr von Varnbuehler, the new Chief of Intelligence at LANDCENT who in the war had been for a period an Intelligence Officer with the German forces in Yugoslavia.

The Germans dropped a parachute battalion in an attempt, which very nearly came off, to capture the Yugoslav partisan leader, Tito, and the British Mission attached to him which included amongst others Fitzroy Maclean and Randolph Churchill. The Commando Brigade commanded by Tom Churchill was based on an island in the Adriatic and was ordered by Allied Headquarters in Algiers to mount without delay an attack to divert some of the German effort from their valuable quarry. But Tom Churchill was temporarily in London and Jack was acting brigade commander. All the officers of his own unit were on a parachute course in Italy, so the best the brigade could do to comply with the urgent Algiers order was to attack with two Royal Marine commandos led by Jack. The operation achieved little and Jack Churchill was captured along with thirteen Marines. All this was recounted by Tom and Jack with a wealth of detail and very jovially, and I could see that the German Brigadier, a charming bachelor with a great mane of white hair, was even more rivetted than I. The reason became clear. Because they were Commandos Jack and his fellow captives should have been shot in accordance with the notorious *Führerbefehl*; but the staff of the enemy formation holding them, the 118th Infantry Division, disregarded the Execution Order and, after a number of adventures such as setting fire to the aircraft taking him to Germany, Jack ended up in Berlin where he was well treated by the Army authorities who concealed him from the SS and the Gestapo in the belief that he, Jack, was actually Tom, the brigade commander and that there was some family connection with the Prime Minister, Winston. Jack was put into the Sachsenhausen concentration camp where he met a number of the European '*Prominente*'; the Austrian Chancellor Schuschnigg; Léon Blum, the French Prime Minister; General Papagos, the Greek C-in-C, and various German generals who had incurred the distrust of Adolf Hitler. Also in the camp were Peter Churchill, later the husband of Odette Sansom, also an SOE agent, and four RAF Officers who had survived the massacre at Stalag Luft III. Jack and these four airmen got out of Sachsenhausen by digging a tunnel with a knife. All were recaptured, though Jack got as far as Rostock where he planned to stowaway on a boat bound for Sweden. It was an enthralling tale of 'cops and robbers'; not least because of the evident pleasure shown by the German guest that it was the British 'robbers' who won. On a more sober note I asked Jack Churchill his advice for Prisoners of War planning to escape. He stressed four things:

1. Learn how to navigate without a map or compass
2. Have proper boots
3. Make food hot whenever possible; cold raw vegetables make one rapidly ill
4. Patience

Ten days before my departure from AFCENT General Jacquot devoted three days to showing me the area of the Massif Central where he had fought in the Maquis, the French Resistance movement. We set out in two cars accompanied by two of the ADCs, George and Eon-Duval. I sat next to the General who freely answered all my questions.

I have grouped the main points I learnt from him under headings as follows:

1. <u>Jacquot's Resistance Group</u> After commanding a battalion in the 109th

Infantry Regiment in 1940 followed by a spell on the staff of the 'Armistice Army', Major Jacquot went to the area Corrèze-Lot-Dordogne, and in this impoverished and wild region of hills and forests he formed a Resistance group. The region was noticeably under-populated and the village war memorials bear tragically long lists of names; far, far longer than would be found in English villages of comparable size. This, General Jacquot explained, is because the standard of education, particularly of technical training, was so low that the young men were in the main drafted into the infantry and artillery where the casualties were highest. The members of Jacquot's group were Frenchmen, military and civilian, and the nucleus was provided by the weapons, equipment and leaders from the 41st Infantry Regiment with which Jacquot had been in close touch. The area where the group was formed was initially in Unoccupied France but after November 1942, when the Germans took over the whole country, the Resistance was confronted by both the Wehrmacht and the pro-German Milice.

By 1944 Jacquot had three 'battalions' each of about 3,500 men, a total force of some 11,000. Up until June 1944 recruiting was difficult; men were reluctant to join and those who did were often seeking escape from the police or tiresome wives. But some were dedicated Communists. Once it became clear that the Allied invasion of Normandy had succeeded, the waverers, pro-Vichy types and other self-seekers, sought to jump on the bandwagon before the war came to an end. Resistance groups were nominally under the control of the National Resistance Committee in Paris but in fact had a great deal of autonomy.

2. Supply Arranged through the Allied Liaison Officers with the group by radio. Arms, cash, and ammunition were delivered by air. Ammunition and explosives were in short supply but weapons were plentiful. In July 1944 Jacquot received 400 tons dropped in three hours. The problem was not demanding and receiving the deliveries, but moving the consignments off the Dropping Zones and concealing them.

3. Their Task The main task of Jacquot's group was to delay the movement towards Normandy of the German division stationed in southern France once the Allied invasion was launched. To achieve this required surprise, a good state of training in ambush and rail sabotage operations, and discipline. Jacquot had set up a training centre in a pretty inaccessible area between the rivers Céré and Dordogne, but so as to avoid premature losses, waste of equipment and alarming the enemy, Jacquot permitted his men to carry out before 6 June 1944 very few hostile actions. Other groups such as those in the Haute Savoie got themselves embroiled with the Germans long before D-Day, with the result that when they really were needed they had ceased to exist.

4. The Enemy The garrison troops of the Wehrmacht consisted of mixed battalions of infantry and artillery in the large towns, with about one

battalion per 100 kilometres; a large mobile central reserve was held in the Bordeaux region. The battalion-sized units were usually from formations withdrawn from more active fronts for rest and re-fitting, and it was obvious that their commanders had no desire to meddle with the local Resistance forces or even to send alarming reports about their potential threat for fear of being criticised for lack of zeal and sent to Russia as a punishment. As well as the Wehrmacht, the Resistance Forces had to contend with the Vichy pro-German militia, the normal French Police and the Gestapo. Further, there were Communist Resistance Forces which, though not pro-German, were anti-de Gaulle and whose aims and methods hindered rather than helped Jacquot's operations. I got a very clear impression from the General's accounts during the three days of our tour that the main dangers to him and his force came from the following:

a. Rashness and the indiscipline of his subordinates.
b. Treachery: people talked too much. Also Leaders got involved with women who gave them away; and treachery for money. Jacquot himself was nearly caught on three occasions on which his planned meetings with professional men were reported by their wives who had lovers in the German occupation forces, the Milice or the Police. 'Sex is a very dangerous and almost universal weapon,' he told me.
c. Trying to take on Germans with orthodox tactics. Pitched battles always ended badly. 'Go for ambushes: fire three or four magazines then beat it quick.'

5. Tactics and Results Achieved Warning of the Allied invasion was received on 5 June and orders for a General Rising the next day. The local railways were cut every five kilometres or so and trains were brought to a standstill, yielding several hundred Boche prisoners. (The blowing of bridges was not allowed.) The move north through Jacquot's operational area of SS Division 'Das Reich' up the N20 and N140 was reduced to a speed of 2 kph and the division, General Jacquot claimed, lost six hundred casualties. Of these four hundred were inflicted north of Souillac when the German column, without taking any precautions, drove quite unsuspecting into well-sited ambush. Subsequently the Germans lost two hundred, but in every engagement inflicted a greater number of losses on the French. Of the fifteen principal leaders in Jacquot's group only he and two others were still in action at the end of June.

6. Jacquot's Rules for Resistance Operations were:
– Fight no pitched battles: 'Shoot and Scoot'.
– Keep unit camps quite separate from supply dumps.
– Brief the minimum number of leaders: 'need to know' principle.
– Never move in parties of more than thirty men.

– Do not waste ammunition; save it for really big occasions.
– Go for transport rather than enemy personnel.

7. The Main Requirements for Partisan Forces

a. Hope for the future i.e. proof of tangible help from outside (LOs, air drops, radio contact, etc.), and likelihood of eventual liberation by UK/US forces, or in the Balkans, etc. by the Red Army.
b. Discipline (Jacquot had three of his men shot for looting).
c. Skill at moving and operating by night.
d. Sufficient manpower to ensure numerous detachments of adequate strength.
e. Gain friendship and support of local population: behave justly, pay for everything and avoid needlessly giving the enemy grounds for reprisals.
f. Suitably inaccessible terrain for base and training areas.
g. For communications use couriers and the railway telephone network (which was never monitored).
h. Command. Jacquot wished to have a civilian as a commander of his large group so as to ease relationships with the returning French civil administration and Regular Army commanders. He therefore nominated André Malraux (Colonel Berger) as the 'brigade commander' and himself as Malraux's 2IC. Malraux, on the wanted list, drove his car into a ditch and was captured by the Germans. He admitted his identity but the Gestapo did not believe him and he was released. He played a leading role in the liberation of Strasbourg and in 1962 was Minister of Culture.

8. <u>Terror</u> General Jacquot was adamant that terror does not pay. The exactions and cruelties of the Occupying Forces, particularly of the SS and Slav elements in the Wehrmacht, were the greatest stimulants to the Partisans. After the Souillac ambush and subsequent activities carried out by the Resistance against units of 2nd SS Panzer Division 'Das Reich' during their 450-mile move from Montauban in southern France to the Normandy battlefields had imposed delays and further losses on the Germans, General Lammerding, the SS Divisional Commander, had ninety-nine citizens of Tulle hanged from the town's lampposts and balconies, and their bodies thrown onto the municipal rubbish dump. They and the 101 other Tullois who died in German camps are commemorated by the Champ des Martyrs outside the town on the Brive road. When I asked Jacquot if after the war he had given evidence at Lammerding's War Crimes Trial, his reply indicated that he thought my question extremely naive. Jacquot himself, I was told by one who had served with him in the war, had a boatload of Vichy militiamen put to death in 1945 by having the vessel sunk in which they were crossing a lake on the Swiss frontier.

(Note: General Jacquot, like many other participants in the French

Resistance, exaggerated the losses inflicted on the Germans and underplayed the paralysing effects on the population of both German reprisal actions and the depredations of the Communist Resistance bands, the Francs-Tireurs et Partisans (FTP). The events which occurred during the march through France in June 1944 of the 2nd SS Panzer Division have been thoroughly researched and recorded by Max Hastings in his book, *Das Reich* (Pan Books, 1983) which should be studied by anyone interested in the activities of that Division and the punitive actions inflicted by its units in Tulle, Oradour-sur-Glane and other villages in that region of France. His book also puts into proper perspective the contributions made to the French Resistance movement there by the Armée Secrète (AS) to which General Jacquot's group belonged, by the Communist FTP and the British organisations, the SOE and the SAS. General Heinz Lammerding died in 1971 at his home in Düsseldorf, prosperous and unpunished after reverting to his career as an engineer.)

The three questions which have I most constantly asked myself since 1945 are:

– If the Germans had invaded the United Kingdom in 1940 and occupied, say, the southern half of England, how would we who were living there have conducted ourselves?
– If during their occupation the Germans had carried out reprisals and atrocities such as those at Tulle (and at Oradour-sur-Glane where all the women and children were massacred in a church and the men shot in barns), how would English men and women have behaved towards the Occupying Powers and to each other?
– Have we grounds for supposing that our conduct, individual and collective, would have been significantly different to that of West Europeans living just across the Channel? This matter of national character and conduct after defeat and occupation still intrigues me, but I shall never find conclusive answers to my queries. Few conversations however on this subject have surprised me more than what my German colleague in CINCENT's Cabinet, Hubert Jeschke, told me.

I said to him one day: 'When you were not at sea in your U-boat, but living on shore in Brest or some other naval base in France, did you not have to be very careful when going outside the base lest some French patriot tried to kill you; or when going home to Germany on leave did you not worry about the train being blown up by the Maquis? And then, in Germany on leave, the chances of being bombed in an air raid must have made the whole period of your leave a bit of an ordeal, didn't they?'

Hubert looked at me as if I was mad. 'My dear chap, ashore in France was the best time I've ever had in my life. We in the German U-boat fleet were the toast of the local population, particularly of our age-group, and anything we wanted, girls, champagne, hospitality, hunting, you name it, was ours for the asking. It seemed that in us German sailors the French girls found something that their young men lacked. It was GREAT! As regards your point about the dangers of rail travel, that the train would be delayed, let alone derailed, never entered our heads; the continental railway system worked almost as in peacetime until shortly before the Allied invasion of Normandy. The air raids on Germany luckily did not affect my parents or me; they had been evacuated to the Black Forest area and I doubt if they heard an enemy bomber during the whole of the war. No, life in France was marvellous. But, my friend, when we put to sea it was a different story; especially after your ships and aircraft had been equipped with radar and Asdic and so on. Then it became terrible and our losses were horrendous.[1] I am so very, very lucky to have come through it in one piece.'

Admittedly this is the story of the war as experienced by a single German; but it is at variance with the reports we were given before D-Day about the fortitude of the French population and how they sabotaged and paralysed and ostracised everything and everybody in the hated German Occupation Forces.

One thing which my advancing years has taught me is that in life nothing is purely black or white; the predominating colour of human activity is a shade of grey. Moreover nothing stays the same; change is constant. And some changes are bewildering as the following anecdote published in *The Economist* proves.

> There is a nice story of a political prophet in Munich in 1928, who was asked to prophesy what would be happening to the burghers of his city in five, fifteen, twenty and forty years' time.
>
> He began: 'I prophesy that in five years' time, in 1933, Munich will be part of a Germany that has just suffered 5 million unemployed and that is ruled by a dictator with a certifiable mental illness who will proceed to murder 6 million Jews'.
>
> His audience said: 'Ah, then you must think that in fifteen years' time we shall be in a sad plight'.
>
> 'No,' replied the prophet, 'I prophesy that in 1943 Munich will be part of a Greater Germany whose flag will fly from the Volga to Bordeaux, from northern Norway to the Sahara'.
>
> 'Ah, then you must think that in twenty years' time we will be mighty indeed.'
>
> 'No, my guess is that in 1948 Munich will be part of a Germany

that stretches only from the Elbe to the Rhine, and whose ruined cities will recently have seen production down to only 10 per cent of the 1928 level.'

'So you think we face black ruin in forty years' time.'

'No, by 1968 I prophesy that real income per head in Munich will be four times greater than now, and that in the year after that 90 per cent of German adults will sit looking at a box in a corner of their drawing rooms, which will show live pictures of a man walking upon the moon.'

They locked him up as a madman, of course.

On 10 May, the anniversary of the German *Blitzkrieg* in 1940 which overwhelmed France and the British Expeditionary Force, I started the lengthy process of form-filling to obtain release from NATO and introducing my successor, Lieutenant-Colonel Anthony Readman, to the personalities he would have to deal with most regularly. I gave a champagne *pot d'adieu* at mid-day for all the members of the Cabinet and they presented me with a most attractive book, signed by each of them, of photographs of France. I made a little speech of appreciation for the innumerable kindnesses the General and all of them had shown me during my eighteen months in the Cabinet. I was truly very sad to be leaving. We all went off then to the Club where General Jacquot gave a lunch for his personal staff and our wives during which the dear man said some heart-warming things. I feared I would return to earth with a bang when I got back to the British Army with its distaste for hyperbole. But I would not have missed those experiences in Fontainebleau for the world.

That evening we dined with the Jeschkes, Hubert and Marie-Madelène. They had married a couple of weeks before and Rosemary and I were their first guests. It was an enjoyable note on which to end a memorable day; and with it a year-and-a-half of interest, variety, astonishment and fun, in the company of some men and women of the highest quality. I had been very fortunate.

A few years later I ran into a young Argyll who had been with us in Lemgo. He said to me: 'Didn't you leave the battalion in Germany and go off to work in France?'.

'Yes, I was sent to the NATO Headquarters in Fontainebleau.'

'What was your appointment there?'

'I was the Military Assistant to the Commander-in-Chief of Allied Forces Central Europe.'

'What did that involve; what did you have to do?'

'Well, in broad terms my job was to make all the arrangements for CINCENT's personal meetings with subordinate commanders and politicians and for his visits to the Land Forces of the Alliance'.

'And did you do it well?' the young man asked me. I was able to reply: 'It is not for me to say whether I did it well or badly, but I can tell you one thing about my work there. On one occasion that the Commander-in-Chief did something on land without first discussing it with me, he was sent to prison for fifteen years!' I doubt that there is another British Major who can say that.

*   *   *

Course No 26 at the Joint Services Staff College lasted from May to November 1962. It was an excellent period of professional education, analysing the state of the world and debating how to structure and deploy our Armed Forces so as to cope best with the demands placed on them. The programme of lectures, discussions and demonstrations was presented to us most expertly: it was the British Services performing at their best. Furthermore the six months were enriched by an atmosphere of friendship and fun. The Directing Staff was headed by the Commandant. We had two Commandants; Rear Admiral Jack Scatchard was with us for most of the course and left to become No 2 in the Far East Fleet. His successor was a Guardsman, Major-General CMF Deakin. These two 'Headmasters' set the tone for all our activities. Some of the work was actually quite taxing. Getting a consensus out of the disparate chaps in a syndicate and drafting papers against a very tight deadline was not easy, but it was good practice for later life. Rosemary was a special boon to the syndicates I was in, for by rattling off our papers on her typewriter she gave us an advantage over our competitors.

Latimer House is a lovely old building in Buckinghamshire, not far from Amersham. Set in glorious country it had been an Interrogation Centre for senior Prisoners of War. In it were the Mess facilities and bedrooms for 'grass-widowers', but the lectures and discussion periods were held in a collection of huts around the grounds. Each day began with a short service of worship in the Latimer church conducted by us Student Officers in turn. It was a fitting start to the day's work and I think it is a pity that this custom is not more widely observed in Army units. There were hiccups such as those which caused the Naval DS, Captain Splash Carver, to refer to 'Trevor Alexander struggling every morning with his recalcitrant organ'. That organ has since been replaced with money subscribed by the grateful graduates of the JSSC. One of the many valuable features of the course was the participation of Officers from Commonwealth countries and the United States. There were eighty-four students in all; fifty-eight from Britain, the remainder from the US, Australia, New Zealand, Canada, Malaya, Rhodesia, India, Pakistan and Nigeria. Major Emeka Ojukwu from this last country was destined to become the most notorious of our lot. An Old Boy of Epsom and Oxford, fluent in English and with a sense of humour he was a popular fellow. But on returning to his country he led the Ibo people of the Eastern Region into seceding from Nigeria which was then ruled by a military government headed by General Jakabu Gowon. When in 1967 Ojukwu declared Biafra to be a republic independent of the Federation, a bitter civil war broke out. By the following year Gowon's Federal forces had confined the Biafrans to a shrinking area of the interior and by 1970 Biafra had ceased to exist. Ojukwu escaped, to the Ivory Coast I believe, by which time he seemed from his TV appearances to have gone slightly mad.

A conclusion we had been driven to by listening to our colleagues in the Royal Navy and the RAF, and by our individual experiences on the continent was that the structure, terminology and some of the attitudes of the British Army were outdated. As General Stockwell, Deputy SACEUR, declared in a lecture on 'The Problems of NATO', the British Army 'now needed to emulate the US Army in Europe and develop the professional outlook and dedication that our great Ally is demonstrating'. This reminded me at once of Lord Bandon's lament the year before about the UK's defence policy and our country's flagging resolve in the defence of Europe.

The capricious system by which the careers of British Officers were being prescribed was brought home to me personally when I received a letter from the new Colonel of the Argylls, Freddie Graham, telling me that I would not get command of the 91st. This was a blow for I had hoped to command the regiment in which I had served since 1941 and for which I had turned down the offer of a career outside the Armed Forces. Rosemary took this news very badly, blaming herself for General Freddie's decision. Providence however is remarkably kind, for soon after getting his letter I was invited by the Colonel of The Parachute Regiment, Graham Mills, to return to Airborne Forces.

I agreed and looking back I can say that it was one of the most rewarding decisions I have ever taken. Before the next six years ended I was to become 2IC of 2 PARA, CO of 1 PARA and Regimental Colonel, and to find myself in the company of the warriors of our 1st and 6th Airborne Divisions, serving with their successors in our peacetime forces and being introduced to the Persian Gulf region which was to play in my later life an important role. By his decision, set out in that mortifying letter, Freddie Graham no doubt did the Argylls a service for they came to be commanded by a fine Officer in The Black Watch. But the service he did me, quite unwittingly, was immense. The family and I lived in the wing of a charming house called 'Croyland' near Great Missenden and owned by a Mr and Mrs Savidge. We were very comfortable and happy there, and although my diary contains many references to rain and 'wretched weather', my memories of our six months in Buckinghamshire are of sunshine and laughter, country walks en famille, stimulating days at work and many excellent parties.

Soon after our arrival in England I took Rosemary into the RAF hospital at Halton where she had her tonsils removed and a much deserved rest in that well-run establishment. The kids during her absence were looked after by a sensible and amusing lady named Mrs Courage whom Jane, who had also found Croyland for us, acquired through Universal Aunts. She was an excellent find; for two weeks of looking after our off-spring she charged £17. Now a char would demand that for just a few hours of hoovering.

The Party of the Year was the one we gave with Adrian and Valerie Rouse in their house. The theme was The Common Market which Britain was then seeking to join. Everyone had to come dressed so as to represent one of the Six (France, West Germany, Belgium, The Netherlands, Luxembourg or Italy). Trevor Alexander came as a stuffed olive, several echoed Luxembourg's radio station or Lux soap powder; I hired a French gendarme's uniform, Ian Burrow that of a German soldier, while Rosemary and Valerie, a most attractive girl and a good friend, dressed very saucily as French waitresses. The most difficult thing about that evening was compiling the invitation list. Space limited the number we could ask, but everyone on the course was such a congenial companion that the task of separating the uninvited from the chosen was highly invidious. Sadly our festivities proved to be premature. Britain's entry into the European Community was vetoed by President de Gaulle and our country did not sign the Treaty of Rome until Edward Heath's premiership twelve years later.

Latimer parties ran on alcohol, not continuously and not excessively, but the first hours of many days were got through thanks only to Alka-Seltzer. As the end of the course drew near the pace of social life increased, and with it the tests inflicted on our stamina. I, a committed European and advocate for keeping BAOR strong, was detailed off at short notice to speak in the final discussion on 'The Case AGAINST the UK having a major Involvement in Europe'. This went against the grain of all I believed in, but I jotted down some points about our global experience and how, by keeping forces in the Persian Gulf, Far East and so on, we were protecting the interests of our continental neighbours as well as our own. That indeed had been our Army's traditional role. Pursuing my bogus argument against keeping strong forces in Germany, I voiced the fear that 'Making our Soldiers ride around the North German Plain in armoured vehicles will only result in them getting hard arses and soft feet – exactly the opposite of what is required'. That statement brought the house down and was, I like to believe, my most useful contribution to the course.

We were living through anxious times in 1962 for that autumn the

Cuban missile crisis blew up. The danger of a nuclear war between the USA and the USSR was averted by President Kennedy's exemplary calmness and the skill with which he outfaced Khrushchev and manoeuvred him into a humiliating withdrawal from a situation he had rashly got into. In the north-eastern corner of India an age-old border dispute escalated into a major Chinese attack from which the Indians suffered a chastening defeat and loss of face. Our course ended with the Latimer Loons' Revue 'Outward Bound', produced by Major Roy Redgrave of The Royal Horse Guards (who was to retire as a Knight, a Major-General and C-in-C Hong-Kong), followed by a cracking good Guest Night with speeches, songs and promises to keep in touch.

The next day we all dispersed to our new assignments. It had been a memorable six months.

Thanks to hard work by Rosemary and Mrs Ware, our 'daily', we handed our rooms back in good order to a grateful Mrs Savidge, and with the car as usual grossly over-loaded we set off for the Thames Valley. In the small village of South Stoke, lying between Wallingford and Goring, stood Elm House, a large brick structure with a sizeable garden which Tim and Mouse Macpherson had bought when he left the Army and started a new career as a maltster. These two excellent friends had most generously let us rent the top floor of their new home. This was a particular blessing for us, as at that time we did not own a house and as 2 PARA, which I was to join, was to return for another year to Bahrain with very few families, this offer of a nest for Rosemary and the two kids during my absence was Heaven-sent. Nice also for Mouse who was about to produce her first child. Our arrival at Elm House coincided with the onset of one of the severest winters England experienced during this century and which was to last almost without a break until 31 March. The snow and frost made the countryside and the branches and twigs on the trees extraordinarily beautiful, but as always in the UK the days of below-zero temperatures dislocated traffic on the roads and railways, blocked water-pipes in most houses and, typical of labour discipline in the UK from the end of the Second World War up to the Premiership of Margaret Thatcher, the nation's power workers started a 'Go Slow' at the height of the cold spell.

I went off to RAF Abingdon, to the Parachute School, for a spell of refresher training. I found myself quite fit enough to get through all the drills and exertions, and had no difficulty in completing the series of jumps from Hastings and Beverley aircraft. The bad weather, however, delayed the whole process badly, and we had many early reveilles, cancelled drops and much hanging about. But we got away eventually in good time for Christmas. We had an excellent time with the Macphersons in Elm House and also with Jane in her flat at No 46 Cheyne Court in

Chelsea. The snow gave the season an unusual, continental feel; and we amused ourselves by crossing the frozen Thames on foot at several points. The village carol service was enlivened by the boys and girls of the South Stoke school which Pinky had joined.

In mid-January I reported to Guillemont Barracks in Cove, near Aldershot, a collection of wooden huts erected for the Canadian Army during the war and which was now the home of the 2nd Battalion The Parachute Regiment, my new outfit. The CO was Neale Gordon-Wilson, a nice man but one who never seemed really happy with his lot. Neale was under a certain disadvantage in having taken over from a remarkably gifted and popular leader of men, Frank King. To my chagrin I was appointed to command Headquarter Company – the clerks, drivers, signallers and such like – and to take over the unit's accounts. This was something I rather dreaded but had half-expected seeing that I came to 2 PARA as a strange and unknown Highlander. Like all Officers seconded to Airborne Forces I wore the uniforms of the Argylls but with the red beret on my head. The tartan kilt and the badger-head sporran caused some merriment among the onlookers when the Battalion carried out its farewell march through the streets of Aldershot, a town which had honoured The Parachute Regiment with the Freedom of the Borough.

I had found the Officers of 2 PARA a mixed bunch; fit, keen, welcoming but in administrative matters pretty untutored. The Rank & File impressed me greatly: in January not one came before the CO for punishment. Some attributed this good discipline to Scottish influence; 2 PARA was the offspring born in 1948 of the Scottish parachute battalion in which I had served so happily. The whole unit went off on block leave during March in preparation for the move to Bahrain, and I took the opportunity to see as much of my family as possible. Parting from those I love I never find easy, be it to go back to school, to duty or even when going away on a short military exercise. Once away the heartache vanishes and one gets caught up in the activities of the new place, the new interests and scenes. But the great tonic always are the Soldiers; human, witty, loyal and responsive to proper leadership.

Note

1. Doenitz's U-boat crews totalled no more than 40,900 from the war's beginning to the war's end. Of these 28,000 had gone down with their boats; a casualty rate of 70 per cent, unapproached by that of any branch of any other service in any country (Keegan, *The Price of Admiralty*, page 265).

CHAPTER IX
1963–1964

With 2 PARA I am introduced to the Persian Gulf; and Episodes in Normandy and the Congo

On the last day of March Rosemary drove the kids and me to Cove where we parted miserably. With about a hundred chaps of 2 PARA I travelled to Heathrow in a convoy of RASC lorries; we were the first 'chalk' of the battalion group and were due to fly to Bahrain that evening in a Britannia chartered from Cunard-Eagle. We were unarmed and wearing mufti, and described in our passports as 'Government Officials' so as to reduce unpleasantness in the event of having to land in an unfriendly country. The plane developed some mechanical fault so we were put into buses and put up in hotels in West London for the night. This delay must have cost the charter company a tidy sum, but I was glad that the 'Toms' (our Soldiers) were being properly looked after. In the morning I rang Rosemary before being taken back to the airport; my call out of the blue and on 1 April was a happy surprise for her. There were further delays and it was early evening before the aircraft was ready for take-off, so we had a tedious day confined to the Departure Lounge watching the multitude of travellers passing through the terminal. I was surprised to learn that despite its size and resemblance, due to the continuous activity going on, to an ant-hill, London ranked only eighth in the list of the world's busiest airports.

But we got away eventually and had a good flight, passing over the snow-covered Alps in bright moonlight, then on down over mist-covered Yugoslavia and Greece to Istanbul where we refuelled at a grotty terminal full of sleeping officials and smelling of tobacco and unwashed feet. Over eastern Turkey and the Caspian it got cold, but as the darkness gave way to daylight we could see Iran as we flew southwards changing from snow-capped mountains to endless bare brown ridges until we reached the oil town of Abadan where the Shatt al Arab river flows into the northern end of the Persian Gulf. Quite soon we got our first sight of Bahrain. From the air it looked like a piece of dried-up sewage floating on a shallow green lake, and this uninviting impression was confirmed when we drove the twenty or so miles to Hamala Camp in the southern half of the island.

We had been sent out to relieve the First Battalion of the Regiment, commanded by a friend and contemporary of mine at Cheltenham, the popular and uncommonly good-looking Pat Thursby. During their year in Bahrain 1 PARA had built on a bare desert ridge a superb village of Twynham huts, made largely of aluminium and air-conditioned, including a NAAFI, a Church, messes, a swimming pool, even a squash court – the lot. Fit, bronzed, alert and helpful the men of Thursby's battalion impressed me that day as being the finest body of British soldiers I had ever come across; beside them my 2 PARA party of new arrivals, white-faced and wearing a scruffy miscellany of civilian garbs, looked distinctly second-rate. But all that would change within a week as we settled down to make the most of our year in the sunshine and open spaces of our desert island.

Joe Starling, Pat Thursby's 2IC, had greeted me at Muharraq airfield with the news that King Hussein of Jordan had just been assassinated. This grievous report was soon proved false – to our great relief, for the King was much admired in Britain and regarded as a loyal ally and a calming influence in the volatile Middle East. Moreover he was particularly popular with all ranks of the 16th Parachute Brigade which had been despatched to Jordan in 1958 to counter the hostile attitude of the revolutionary regime in Iraq. Iraq was the principal reason for our presence in Bahrain. In 1961 it was believed that the Iraqis were about to invade and annex the small but wealthy oil-state of Kuwait. When the Ruler appealed for help Britain responded promptly, and a military force which included 2 PARA arrived and quickly dug in on the Mutla Ridge to block the approaches to Kuwait City. Though no Iraqi invasion occurred then, the threat to Kuwait remained, and from 1961 until 1967 a strong British force, including a parachute battalion group, was retained in Bahrain three hundred miles to the south. The region was also important to Britain for reasons other than the preservation of the sovereignty of Kuwait; the free flow of oil from the head of the Gulf through the narrow Strait of Hormuz, our communications with our bases in Aden, East Africa and the Far East and our obligations to our friends and allies in the Middle East. The latter were mostly pro-western monarchs who like HMG were apprehensive about the rising tides of Arab socialism, Marxism and communist-inspired insurgency that were seeking to undermine the existing order. The policies and sentiments of the Rulers who looked to Britain for counsel, support and protection differed from the sentiments of many of their subjects, notably the younger generation, who regarded western military bases and influence as intrusions; foreign in religion, offensive in behaviour and imperialist in purpose. Many rejoiced at the Egyptian leader Colonel Nasser's triumph over the British and French in the Suez crisis of 1956. It was therefore evidence of his courage and faith in Britain when Sheikh Isa bin Sulman Al Khalifa, the Ruler of Bahrain and its Dependencies, gave permission for the establishment on

With 2 Para

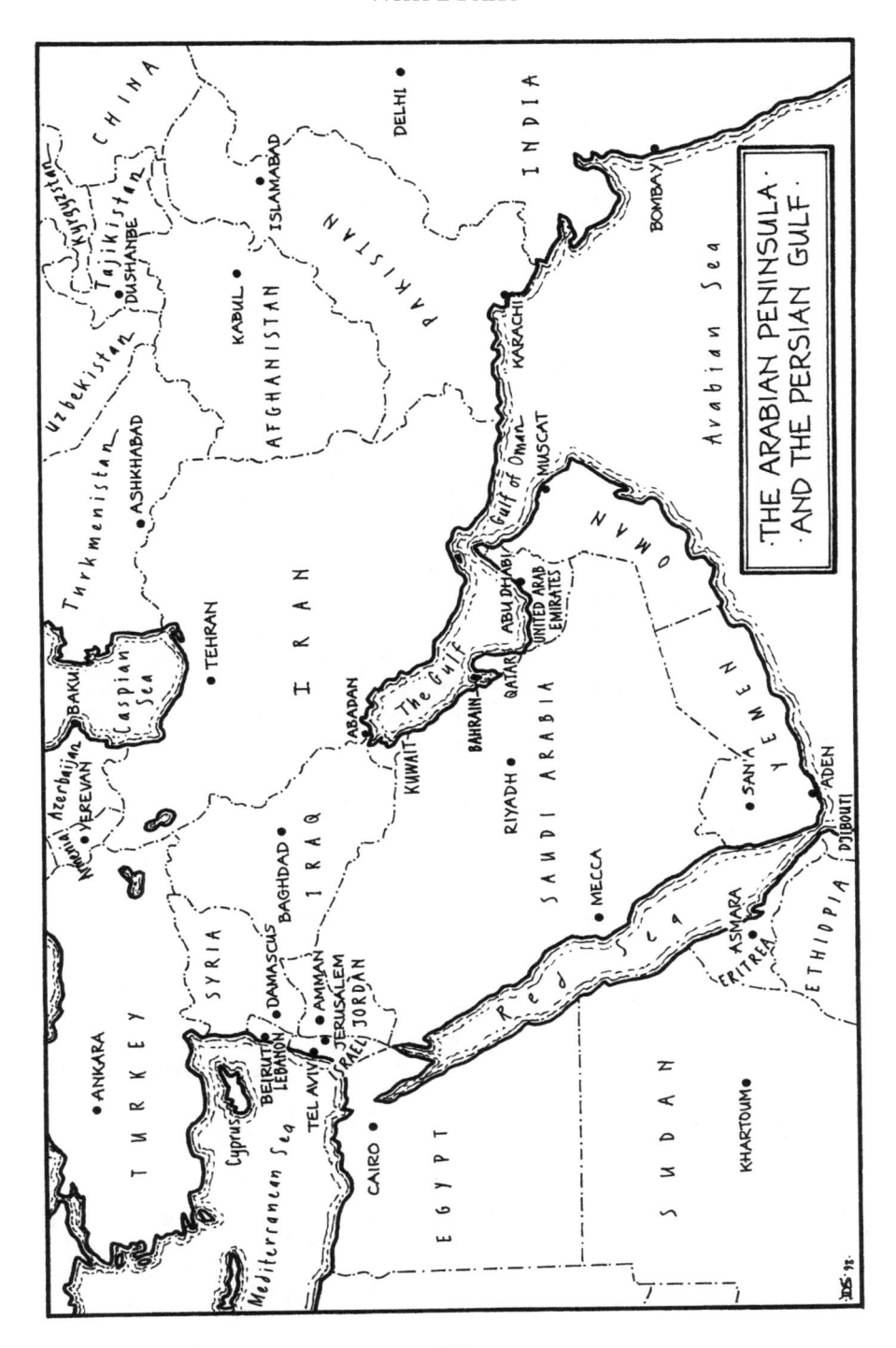

THE ARABIAN PENINSULA AND THE PERSIAN GULF

his territory of a British garrison and airfield complex in addition to the facilities which the Royal Navy had long enjoyed in Bahrain.

2 PARA was the first battalion to be accompanied by some wives and children; forty-four families in 1963 but this number was doubled two years later. The 'marrieds' were housed in Manama in accommodation rented by the Army and were well equipped with refrigerators, air-conditioners and the extra money to pay for the electricity and so on. Out of deference to the feelings of the Moslem population, a number of restrictions were imposed on our activities, dress and behaviour in public. With one exception these restrictions were not irksome: everybody obeyed the rules sensibly to the extent that when in 1966 Sir William Luce retired as Political Resident Persian Gulf he made the following reference to The Parachute Regiment in his final report to the Foreign Secretary: 'I feel that I must put on record my very high opinion of the Regiment, all three of whose Battalions I have come to know well, and the very important part it has played in the Gulf since the days of the Kuwait crisis in 1961. What I am particularly concerned with here is not the military prowess and efficiency of the Regiment, which are of course well-known to all, but with the very considerable contribution it has made to good relations between ourselves and the Bahrainis and also with some of the Trucial States. Their excellent behaviour in Bahrain and the trouble to which they have gone to gain the confidence and friendship of the Bahrainis from the Ruler downwards have been quite outstanding and I for one am deeply appreciative of the efforts they have made to support the policies of Her Majesty's Government in the Persian Gulf'.

The one exceptionally irksome restriction was that we were not allowed to carry out any military training outside the perimeter of Hamala Camp. In consequence parachute and tactical training had to be conducted on the mainland, chiefly in the Sharjah area.

The rule that all the 'unmarrieds' had to be back in camp before nightfall each evening meant that considerable energy and imagination had to be expended by the Officers, and above all by the PRI (myself), in laying on entertainment and recreational activities for the Soldiers. This labour was increased by the CO's decision that 2 PARA's daily routine would adhere to 'Indian hours' – starting work soon after sunrise and finishing around 2 pm. Thus from lunch-time onwards little military training was undertaken, the troops being left free for sports or swimming. In practice, however, many of them spent the time lying on their beds (an activity the British Army terms 'doing Egyptian PT'), as Michael Forrester, our Parachute Brigade Commander discovered when, on a visit from Aldershot, he asked two of the 'Toms' what they did during their leisure hours. The reply was: 'Mostly, Sir, we just play with each other'.

I already knew quite a lot about Bahrain and the Gulf because Cosmo Graham had in the first years of the Second World War been the Senior

Naval Officer Persian Gulf. This, a Commodore's appointment, was abbreviated to SNOPG, which caused one General Officer who was about to be introduced to Cosmo to query his nationality. Was he Czech or Yugoslav? After his death his widow published his letters from war-time Bahrain in a book entitled *A Space for Delight*. One of Cosmo Graham's first actions had been to move the Royal Navy's Headquarters, HMS *Jufair*, from Bushire to a green and leafy compound on the main island of Bahrain, which in 1963 it shared with HQ Land Forces Persian Gulf and the British Political Residency.

From early in the 19th century until 1971 Britain undertook at the request of the local Rulers the responsibility for their defence and relations with other countries. Britain's obligations to the six Trucial States, Qatar and Bahrain[1] were long established and of proven benefit to the inhabitants and British interests alike. Their significance was reflected in the status of the Political Resident Persian Gulf who ranked fifth in the ambassadorial pecking order in the Diplomatic Service. Sir William Luce, universally admired and trusted, was PRPG during my two tours in Bahrain. Subordinate to him were the Political Agents in the individual States. In Bahrain Mr Peter Tripp and his successor, Anthony Parsons, and their wives were generous to my colleagues and myself with counsel and hospitality. Our military affairs were supervised by the Commander Land Forces Persian Gulf (CLFPG); in 1963 Brigadier Dick Bryers. He and his wife, Phyllis, were tireless in promoting 2 PARA's contentment and effectiveness.

Because of the demands of the Kuwait commitment the battalion of parachute infantry stationed in Bahrain had been augmented from within 16th Parachute Brigade with elements of the Airborne Arms and Services. The resultant parachute battalion group was unique in the British Army of the era and undoubtedly the most stimulating Lieutenant-Colonel's command in the Order of Battle. I summarize here for the record 2 PARA Group's deployment.

HAMALA CAMP	Headquarters 2 PARA Gp
	Headquarter and Support Companies
	Two Rifle Companies
	F (Sphinx) Battery of 7th Para Royal Horse Artillery
	2 Troop of 9th Para Squadron Royal Engineers
	Section, Para Field Ambulance RAMC
	Air Contact Team, Royal Signals
	Detachment, RAF Para Jumping Instructors
RAF STATION MUHARRAQ	One Rifle Company
	16 Heavy Drop Platoon RAOC
JEBEL ALI (SHARJAH)	One Rifle Company

The prospect of spending my second tour with Airborne Forces administering the clerks, drivers and signallers of 2 PARA and keeping the unit accounts did not excite me at all, but as a newcomer to the battalion I had no right to expect to walk into a more eminent appointment. A merciful Providence, however, acted swiftly to get me out of that rut. During our first week in the Gulf Geoffrey Cox's Company parachuted into the desert near Sharjah to establish themselves in the tented camp which 1 PARA had set up at Jebel Ali. Our 2IC, Jack Lloyd, decided to jump in with them, had a bad landing and sustained a severe head injury. He was sent back to England to recover and was away for several months. The CO, Neale Gordon-Wilson, immediately elevated me to fill Jack's shoes; furthermore, because Neale was called away from Bahrain periodically for conferences, exercises or leave, I found myself acting as the CO of 2 PARA Group during much of the summer of 1963. This was an extraordinary stroke of good fortune at a crucial point in my career. I saw the opportunities for progressive and imaginative training which service in the Gulf offered despite the local restrictions imposed in Bahrain.

I personally was very fit in body and exhilarated in spirit: my cup, which had in April been so unexpectedly replenished, overflowed in mid-July when it was announced that I had been picked by the War Office's No 3 Selection Board to be the next CO of 1 PARA after Pat Thursby. It was a fine compliment and for Rosemary a vindication of our marriage which had so irked my superiors in the Highland Brigade.

An institution which did much to make our life within Hamala Camp congenial and our public image polished was the Unit Contractor who, with his team of tailors, barbers, cobblers, tea-makers and laundrymen, catered to the needs of every Officer and Soldier with zest and good humour. To have all one's uniform and clothing, soiled by the sweat and toil of the previous day, returned that evening neatly folded, impeccably laundered, ironed and starched, was a great boon, and we lamented its loss when back in Aldershot. Ghulam Hassan and his fellow Pakistanis looked after each of our battalion groups as they came to Bahrain on rotation for eleven-month tours, and I like to believe that we matched his devotion with friendship and consideration – and by ensuring that the bills which the Toms ran up with him were settled promptly.

The following year, when I was back in Hamala in command of 1 PARA Group, I sought the help of Ghulam Hassan in the matter of our military headgear. At that time every member of Airborne Forces was issued with one steel helmet (to protect the head while jumping and in combat) and two red berets; one for everyday wear and one for 'best dress' occasions. We were proud of The Red Beret but in the glare and humidity of Arabia it quickly lost its colour and shape, and it was expensive to replace. I decided that we badly needed a uniform headdress which was far less conspicuous, more effective in protecting the eyes, neck and head from the sun's rays, and cheaper. The German troops in the North African campaign seemed to have got the right solution, so working from photographs and a rough sketch Ghulam's nimble-fingered tailors set to, and within two weeks had produced from sturdy material, light khaki in colour, over nine hundred peaked caps, individually fitted to each member of the Group, with neck-cloth and embroidered symbol to show the wearer's sub-unit. Because we had borrowed the idea from Rommel's Afrika Korps, we christened our 'invention' The Hat AK. It proved to be effective and popular, and it so impressed the Staff at GHQ Middle East that Ghulam Hassan's bill was paid in full from Command funds.

Local shopkeepers did well out of British Servicemen and their families, especially those who sold jewellery and objects made in gold, silver, copper or onyx; much cheaper than in England and easy to pack into luggage. In the Sharjah souk was an Arab jeweller whose speciality was producing regimental and suchlike badges in gold. They were much sought after as gifts for wives and girl-friends. The jeweller's real name was Sheikh Na'eem, but the name by which he was known throughout the Gulf – and in which he exulted because, he said, 'it made him feel English' – was Robin Bastard. The two airmen from RAF Sharjah whose meanness is alleged to have named him thus did Sheikh Na'eem an injustice for his craftmanship was excellent and his prices most reasonable.

The Royal Navy also employed 'locals' to relieve British seamen of routine housekeeping chores and domestic duties. One evening I was a guest at a cocktail party on board the Frigate HMS *Nubian* which had recently come out to relieve her sister-ship HMS *Zulu*. The food and drinks were being handed round by *Nubian*'s stewards, dark-skinned men who seemed to be neither English nor Arab, so I asked one of our hosts, a young Midshipman:

'These stewards of yours who are looking after us so well, what nationality are they?'

'Oh, they are from India; they are Goanese who have enlisted to serve in the Royal Navy for a term of years. It's a good arrangement really.'

'Do they remain in one ship throughout their service and move around the world in it, to the UK, Far East, South Atlantic or wherever?'

'No, they spend their service in one theatre, normally the one closest to their homes, and they are passed from ship to ship as naval vessels arrive and leave. These men will only serve in the Gulf and Indian Ocean area.'

'So these here in *Nubian* are *Zulu's*?'

'No Sir, I've just told you, they are Goanese.' One Infantry Officer deflated!! . . .

I got to know quite well the chaps in the Jufair naval offices and those in the frigates and ships of the Amphibious Warfare Squadron, and I welcomed the invitation from the Captain of HMS *Ashanti* (Commander David Hepworth, RN) to sail in his ship which was to take the Flag Officer Middle East, Rear Admiral John Scotland, on a courtesy visit to the Imperial Iranian Navy. *Ashanti* was the first of the new Tribal Class of General Purpose Frigates of 2,000 tons and with a complement of fifteen Officers and 240 men, built by Messrs Yarrow and Co. of Glasgow and accepted for service in November 1961. Everything in the ship was of the most modern and labour-saving design and of an almost hospital-like sterility. The propulsion machinery of linked steam and gas turbines was quite unlike any I had seen before in a ship, being controlled by two men in a small office over the engine room seated at consoles reading dials and working the engines' throttles by hand.

We were away from Bahrain for eight days during which we went ashore at Abadan, a hot place reeking of oil fumes, and the Persian naval base at Khorramshah. It was at Khorramshah during the 'Rashid Ali' pro-German revolt in 1941 that Cosmo Graham had the task of landing British troops to secure the base for the Allies. One of the few casualties in the operation, for Persian resistance was purely token, was the local Admiral whom Cosmo knew and whose death he deplored. I was taken to see his tomb just outside the naval HQ.

Many of the young Persian Officers I met at the numerous parties laid on for us were accompanied by their wives, nearly all foreign women they had picked up while on training courses in Europe. I was introduced to two Italians, a Greek, a Turk, a German, an Austrian, a Swiss, and a girl from Plymouth. I had a long talk with the latter and that night wrote in my diary: 'Not a good specimen of English womanhood so she may be better off materially out here married to a Moslem naval Officer than if she had stayed in Devon; but she made it quite plain to me that she regrets the whole affair.'

The plight of the English women we were to encounter in later years in remote mountain villages on the Yemeni frontier, married to Moslem shopkeepers or farmers whom they had believed to be wealthy Arab princes, was more disturbing than the lamentations of that girl from Plymouth in 1963. There was nothing we could do to lighten their self-imposed afflictions, alas.

Apart from some useful shopping in the Abadan bazaar, where by robust haggling I persuaded myself that I got £10 worth of silver ware for an outlay of £6, our time was spent in parties; especially sumptuous were those hosted by the European big-wheels of the oil companies whose vodka, caviar and strawberries flown down from the Caspian outclassed the more pedestrian fare provided at the parties hosted by naval Officers, Royal or Imperial. As we sailed back to Bahrain I noted in my diary: 'The cost of all this official, obligatory entertaining hits *Ashanti*'s Officers pretty hard, and having an Admiral and his Flag Lieutenant on board, as well as outsiders like me, means a lot of extra work in addition and cramped accommodation. I shall not recommend the Navy to Christopher as a career; very little variety in day-to-day life, restricted space, having to get up at odd hours for watch-keeping, endless drinking on these flag-showing missions, and the feeling which several of the Officers have expressed to me, that their seniors and the Admiralty staff are not to be relied on to promote wisely the careers of those more junior.' This lack of faith in the Top was, I wrote, striking; but no doubt many Army Officers would make the same comment about career planning in my Service.

Persia used to be the paramount State in the Gulf, occupying for many years Bahrain, other islands in those waters and the littoral of the Arabian Sea in the Sultanate of Muscat and Oman. On land and at sea she was an important Power, Shia Moslem by religion. Despite her decline in the 18th century her Rulers periodically renewed their claims for Iran's sovereign rights over territories whose defence had become a British commitment. Thus our diplomats and Service chiefs in the 1960s watched developments in Iran as carefully as those in Iraq. One of the benefits of the British presence in the Gulf (which endured from 1820 until the withdrawal of our naval, military and air force units in December 1971) was the Persian Gulf Lighting Service, an organisation responsible for the maintenance of the numerous lighthouses and beacons on the islands and sandbanks. This useful mission was carried out by a vessel, the *Relume*, which regularly sailed round the Gulf to top up the lights with oil and to make any repairs needed. In the autumn of 1963 *Relume* returned to Jufair from her latest topping-up sortie but shortly afterwards had to be despatched in haste because an important light on an island off the northern shore-line had been extinguished. The report of this vexed the Officers of the Lighting Service, for that light should have remained functioning for very much longer. When *Relume* reached the place the cause of the breakdown became immediately clear. On the island was a body of Iranian troops whose Officer explained to Commander Sutcliffe, *Relume*'s Captain: 'We were sent here three weeks ago with orders to occupy this island as evidence of the Imperial Government's claims to it and to other similar islands around here. They sent us with food and water for two weeks but they have forgotten to come back with more. Our food and water ran out days ago, no one came to rescue us and the island is uninhabited. We decided that the only way to get help was to extinguish the light for we were confident that you English would come immediately to see what was wrong. And here you are, God be Praised!'

Flag-showing visits by naval vessels are more often than not welcomed both by the ship's company and the community on land. In time of war they were a cost-effective way of sustaining British influence and the confidence of local leaders in the Allies' eventual victory. Such visits were an important part of Cosmo Graham's activities as Senior Naval Officer

Persian Gulf in the Second World War; and some were memorable as the following episode which he used to relate shows.

One day in 1940 Cosmo anchored his ship off a small Gulf State and, as arranged through the local political Agent, made his formal courtesy call on the Ruler in his Palace, and he was pleased that the Ruler had decided to respond personally by calling on him in his ship. This visit had gone quite well, and the young Ruler showed interest in the weapons, engines and so on. It was a very hot day and Cosmo had wisely cut short the business of inspecting the ship and took the first opportunity to lead his guest into his cabin which, though not air-conditioned, contained a good array of glasses and cool drinks. There Cosmo and the Ruler sat alone killing time – for conversation was beginning to flag – until the launch came to take the latter back to his Palace on shore. It was late coming and Cosmo was racking his brains for further topics which might interest or amuse his young Arab guest. Just then the Ruler saw the picture on the writing desk: it was a large framed photograph of King George VI wearing naval uniform with beside him his Queen, Elizabeth. Both were in full ceremonial attire with medals and orders galore. The Arab's eyes lit up and hastening to the desk he exclaimed: 'To have so many medals is very good, but my knowledge of English ones is alas small. What please, Commodore, is that ribbon?' he asked; 'And what does that star mean? And why does she have that jewel over her heart?' Cosmo's forebears had long served Britain with distinction and medals and orders were things about which he had from his youth absorbed a fair knowledge, so he had no difficulty in answering the flow of questions as the brown finger stabbed in turn at each decoration in the photograph, and the conversation only ended when the arrival of the launch was announced. As Cosmo stood to see him off the Ruler shook his hand and said' I thank you, Commodore Graham, for a most happy visit to your ship; especially for the answers you gave to my many questions about medals and orders; for that, as you will have noticed, is a matter in which I am much interested. But, pray tell me, who is the pretty lady in the photograph?'

As I got to know Bahrain I realized that my first impressions had been quite wrong. Every excursion was to reveal sights and sounds that quickened the senses and encouraged further exploration. I was fortunate in having my own Landrover; the Toms who had fewer opportunities to get outside the camp left Bahrain with rather jaundiced memories of the place.

The houses of the merchants and senior expatriates had pleasant, well established gardens with green lawns, bright shrubs flowering all the year round, and shade. The CO resolved to beautify Hamala Camp likewise and appointed me Landscape Officer. This was a congenial task, for the

Government Agricultural Centre at Budaiya produced the plants which would grow best on our bare ridge, and friends were generous with encouragement and cuttings. Nevertheless expert advice about matters horticultural was hard to find for there were no professional Arab garden specialists, or large commercial garden centres as in Britain. In the Gulf gardening, like all manual work, was done by the many labourers imported from India, Pakistan or South Arabia. PRPG's wife, Margaret Luce, one morning pointed out to her gardener a flowering shrub she had not noticed before in the Residency grounds. 'O Bashir, look at this pretty bush growing here! Do you know what it is called?' 'No, Memsahib, I do not know, but I will find out.' Some days later an excited Bashir, clutching a cutting from the anonymous bush, exclaimed to Lady Luce. 'Memsahib, I now know the name of the flower you showed me. It is called Hedge.'

Our project at Hamala progressed well. There were plenty of willing hands for the planting and no shortage of water; and I managed to get a supply of manure from the royal stables in the nearby Rifa'a Palace. The small trees and bushes we planted round the camp perimeter and alongside the internal roads required a lot of watering and care, but smaller plants such as zinnias and morning glory flourished if placed where the moisture from the air conditioners in the Twynham huts dripped continuously onto the sandy ground. Our chief difficulties in this beautification project were the sand blown by the fierce winds which lashed the young trees, and the bitter cold in December and January. This was a real surprise. To create a lawn outside the Officers' Mess we acquired grass sprigs from Budaiya, planted them in rows in well prepared ground, and set up a sprinkler-hose to keep them moist. On 20 January 1964 we awoke to find the sprinkler frozen solid (as were the pipes in some of our huts), and when I drove down to the beach that afternoon I found a barrier some two feet wide of seaweed, fish, crabs and other creatures of the sea-shore all killed by the cold. I had six blankets on my bed and needed them; to the poorer sections of the Arab population the exceptionally low temperatures brought great discomfort, influenza and pneumonia.

My driver at this time was Private Saville, a soldier with an unusual range of interests – he read *The Financial Times* each day – and plenty of energy. He and I spent many of our free afternoons snorkelling in the shallow sea off the west coast and marvelling at the variety of brightly coloured fish which loitered around us in the clear water. Saville's enthusiasm for helping me in my landscaping task sometimes took him off alone into the ridges and valleys far beyond the camp's bounds, into an area which seemed to be inhabited solely by goats and the occasional bird; and the odd sapling growing wild which he from time to time dug up and replanted in Hamala. On one such expedition, however, he was spotted by hidden eyes, intercepted by a State Police patrol, charged with theft and taken before the Ruler himself for summary punishment. We did not discover whether Sheikh Isa was that day feeling particularly benevolent towards the British Army or whether he was won over by Saville's charm. The outcome of the encounter was that the Ruler kept my soldier for a long and amicable discussion about the wild life in Bahrain and our Hamala Camp gardening project in particular, before dismissing him with an injunction to refrain from digging up any more State property. As the much relieved Saville was about to drive away a Palace servant handed him an envelope containing rupees to the value of seventy pounds. Not a bad fee for one hour's conversation.

The Regiment became fond of Sheikh Isa, and as the months passed we were to enjoy his generosity and hospitality almost to an embarrassing extent, for there was little we could do to repay him. But there were other Bahraini personages whose entertainment was intimately provided by female members of the transient British community. Espied at the swimming pool or on the beach, they would be engaged with smiles and relaxing chatter. In due course there would be an invitation to a private meeting *à deux*, the customary reward for which was the gift of a Sunbeam Alpine sports car; and as they drove past envious comments could be heard: 'There goes . . . I wonder who had her for a sunbeam'.

Bahrain's significance to the global petroleum industry chiefly lay in her refinery at Sitra on the east coast, where an American-managed organisation BAPCO (The Bahrain Petroleum Company) operated a large installation from which the refined products were pumped out into the waiting oil tanker ships. The Company's operations were run from Awali, a township built on the desert not far from Hamala Camp. There the large expatriate community of managers and supervisory staff lived in some style with clubs, cinemas, swimming pools, tennis courts and air-conditioned bungalows set in neat colourful gardens. Near Awali was the field covering most of the southern half of the island out of which Bahraini oil was extracted and pumped to Sitra for refining along with the greater quantity (75%:25%) brought in from Saudi Arabia. By 1963 a few of the white collar posts in BAPCO had been filled by Arabs, and the number was to grow in the next decade while the number of expatriates declined accordingly. Oil companies exerted a powerful influence over the policies and actions of the Gulf Rulers whose income was largely – and in some cases almost wholly – derived from oil revenues.

The impressions I gained during my years in Bahrain, the Trucial States and Oman was that the European and American General Managers of the oil companies built up and sustained good relationships with the local Rulers; they were in general distinguished, mature men, tactful and perceptive by nature as well as being highly skilled in the administration of a great industry. But there were exceptions. The Head Man at Awali, Mr Braun (not his real name) was one of these. Though efficient and respected by his colleagues he had for some reason incurred Sheikh Isa's displeasure. In 1964 he was transferred to another refinery in West Germany having been replaced in Bahrain by an elegant and high-grade American named Jefferson. I first met Jefferson at the Palace: it was his first meeting with His Highness. He and I were shown to seats on either side of Sheikh Isa and after some minutes of coffee and conversation – the Ruler spoke excellent English – Jefferson was asked: 'What happened to your predecessor Mr Braun? Did he go back to the States?'

'No, Your Highness, he is in Europe running one of our company's installations in West Germany.'

'Is that the one where there was a bad accident recently?' (This was a reference to an explosion widely reported in the newspapers and on the radio.)

'Yes. It was quite a serious accident; two men were killed and a number injured.'

'Was Mr Braun one of the casualties?'

'No. His office is some distance from the explosion and he was unharmed.'

'That's a pity,' whispered the Ruler.

Later, in 1964, Rosemary and I were guests at a BAPCO banquet arranged in honour of the company's Vice-President visiting from the USA. The oil companies were being pressed to increase the revenues they paid to Arab Rulers who were themselves under mounting pressure to strengthen their nations' economies and satisfy the expectations of their subjects. A flat rejection of any oil price increase was the key-note of this V-P's speech at the banquet. 'If any oil producer in the Arab world is so foolish as to believe that people in the West are going to accept the price of oil going up by two dollars a barrel, he should get his head examined.' The many Bahraini guests present kept silent, but I recalled that speech with some mirth when, nine years later, the Arabs put the price per barrel up to more than thirty dollars.

It was assumed that Bahrain had been too far from the battlefields to have experienced any fighting during the Second World War.

This assumption was wrong, for in his letters from Jufair to Elspeth in England, Cosmo Graham had mentioned in some detail an air raid on Sitra. The gist of his description is as follows.

'In 1941 the Italians sent three aircraft to bomb the refinery at Sitra. [Whether the raid was mounted in an Italian colony in the Horn of Africa or from a pro-Axis base in Iraq, Cosmo had not stated. Either would have entailed a mighty long flight, remarkable for that era.] The Italian fliers arrived over Bahrain in darkness and were astonished to find the whole island lit up; for no blackout was deemed necessary in that undisturbed part of the world. After a careful search they located Sitra and its extensive illuminated refinery complex, in the middle of which was a large unlit area. "That dark area," they must have said to themselves, "is the most important part of the refinery, for that is the bit the English have blacked out." So they dropped their bombs with great accuracy, almost all falling within the darkened area. The Italians then flew off. In fact the damage done by the raid was negligible for the unlit target selected by the enemy bomb-aimers was the Sitra coal dump,[2] and being a soft target some of the bombs had failed to detonate.'

A post-war sequel to this little known episode was that when the refinery's system of power generation was in due course changed from solid fuel to oil, the company auctioned off its surplus coal. It was the Italians who bought the whole lot and thereby got their unexploded bombs back.

We all acknowledged that our skills in night-fighting were not good enough, and claimed that in England it was too difficult to practise them. In fact this was an excuse made to cover up a lack of resolve and an unwillingness to disrupt the domestic routine of our many married members. But in Bahrain we were presented with an opportunity to remedy this weakness and at the same time to avoid working in the heat of a Gulf mid-summer day. July and August were very trying months, and by the time autumn came most of us felt a bit jaded and mentally slower than when we arrived on the island.

So, with the CO's blessing, I got 2 PARA Group launched into spending the second half of July working by night with the minimum of chaps on duty during daylight. Everyone paraded at 1930 hours and carried on with training activities, the emphasis being on outdoor tactical exercises and weapon handling, until 0400 hours when we slept until lunch-time. Afternoons were kept free, as usual, for recreation, and at sunset the night routine began again. The rifle companies and the Supporting Arms enjoyed and benefitted from this unorthodox programme, and we would have gone on longer if The Ruler had relaxed his ban on our use of the island's desert area for military purposes. The administrative departments who had to keep in contact with the outside world worked in shifts round the clock, and since they were seldom disturbed by telephone calls during the ten hours of darkness each day, they got a lot of work done.

In August I took a mixed bag of our more sedentary soldiers from HQ Company and from Dan Putt's RAOC Heavy Drop Platoon off to our training camp at Jebel Ali. We parachuted in. (I twisted one ankle in a patch of soft sand so limped around for a week. This was the only embarrassment I ever experienced in my years with Airborne Forces.) We slept in tents within a few feet of the sea which teemed with sardine-like fish and whose breaking waves by night glowed with a startling phosphorescence. Despite the drenching humidity, this period near Sharjah was one of great good humour and valuable training; the former due to the excellent spirit in the Mess Tent which the Sergeants shared with Daniel Putt, Nicky Thompson and me; the latter thanks to the personality and skill of the senior instructor, Drum Major John Williams of 2 PARA. He set the tone and we had a ball. Two years later, during the Borneo campaign, he was CSM in 2 PARA when an Indonesian battalion attacked his company position. For his part in repelling the enemy (who lost fifty killed) Williams got the DCM, but he lost an eye in the battle. He ended his service in 1990 in the rank of Lieutenant-Colonel and in the plum appointment of quartermaster of the Staff College at Camberley.

For the last week of September and the whole of October I was back in Sharjah in charge of arrangements for Exercise BILTONG. This was an event for which the command and staff elements of Brigadier David Lloyd-Owen's 24th Infantry Brigade Group was flown up from Kenya. (David L-O was one of a remarkable trio from The Queen's Regiment highly decorated for gallantry during the war. He had been in the Long Range Desert Group. Our own Brigade Commander, Michael Forrester, was another: his conduct in the fighting round the Cretan village of Galatas is still well remembered.) The brigade came to Sharjah to carry out a large-scale command post exercise in which the commanders and their Staff Officers are put through a series of battle situations but with no troops on the ground. The absence of troops means that the pace of the exercise can be speeded up; it also makes for easier administration and is of course much less expensive to organise.

My job was to set up, run and dismantle a base camp from which 24 Brigade and the umpires, etc. would operate. I was given D Company of 2 PARA, some specialists from HQ Company and from the Services, and a group of Officers and Soldiers from the Royal Scots Greys, embarked with their tanks in landing craft of the Navy's Amphibious Warfare Squadron, and kept in Bahraini waters as part of the Kuwait Contingency Force. We set the camp up in an area of desert sand and scrub near the edge of the RAF airfield at Sharjah, and we named it Bruneval Camp after the exploits of C Company of 2 PARA who stole a German radar from the north coast of France in February 1942 under the leadership of the legendary John Frost. Exercise BILTONG I remember well for a number of reasons.

First, the whole enterprise was a success. The chaps from Kenya and the many visitors who came from the UK, Aden and Bahrain to see them, were provided with a service and facilities which made the exercise run smoothly and in an ambiance of high morale. It was clear from the many letters and signals that flowed in afterwards that our contribution had earned our Battalion some pretty high marks. This was important because, with the Army's strength being progressively reduced and its organisation, particularly the structure of the Infantry component, being constantly reviewed, the young Parachute Regiment was always a target for sniping and disparagement by jealous fellows in older regiments who claimed precedence over us in the battle for unit survival. (It was pleasing to note in 1999 that the three battalions of The Parachute Regiment and the one battalion of the Argylls have emerged intact from the long series of reorganisation and change and been retained in the Order of Battle of the Regular Army. Merit tells.)

Secondly, my BILTONG team worked without exception quite splendidly. In the final paragraph of my full post-exercise report I wrote: 'Lastly, I must pay tribute to the soldiers of The Royal Scots Greys and of D and HQ Companies of 2 PARA. I have no hesitation in stating that they formed the most cheerful, helpful, dependable, self-disciplined and energetic team of young men with whom it has ever been my good fortune to serve.' And not only these soldiers. I decided that the most helpful thing for everyone concerned would be if all the camp rules, instructions, bits of advice and information that people needed to know were issued in pamphlet form. So I drafted the whole thing and took it into Dubai to get it printed as cheaply as possible. I found a small printing outfit and left the draft with them but with no confidence that the work would be done either quickly or adequately. The proof-reading took me hours as the printers were a Persian and a Pakistani with little knowledge of written English and no machines for type-setting: every letter and punctuation mark had to be picked up with tweezers and set individually by hand. But the results were impeccable; those two men in that Dubai alley served the British Army well that week.

Thirdly, living for a month in the outskirts of Sharjah brought me into contact with the Trucial Oman Scouts (the TOS), the efficient, smart and cost-effective gendarmerie-type force which kept the peace along the south coast of the Gulf, led by British and some Arab Officers, with Pakistani technicians and Arab Rank and File. Their Commander in 1963, Colonel HJ Bartholomew and his Quartermaster, George Cook, were especially helpful to my team and me. At the invitation of the former, I went on a fishing expedition to Abu Musa, the purple-coloured island formed of iron oxide, and with George on several long and instructive journeys round that great expanse of desert and mountain in what is now the territory of the Union of Arab Emirates which in 1963 was the domain of the TOS.

The Middle East Correspondent of *The Times* wrote on 4 February 1964 about the TOS in the following terms: 'In the TOS are some 39 British Officers and 90 British NCOs, having, it seems, the happiest time of their lives. Their uniform is Arab head-dress (shemargs), grey shirts enclosed by red belts and worn hanging outside sand-coloured trousers and the popular desert boots (irreverently known throughout the Army as Brothel Creepers). They have five mobile squadrons operating from Sharjah and from points inland and along the coast. The force is a British creation and its upkeep a charge on Britain. To see it arouses sentiments both affectionate and critical, for it is the last image of imperialism or paternalism. Nevertheless, imperialism or no, it is a back-bone of stability in an oil area which has none of its own . . . Already Britain has no direct power, and more responsibility is passing to some rulers. But if there is a lesson rampant in the world today it is that to make changes merely because they are fashionable often causes all government hereafter to crumble to the ground.'

My BILTONG team and I enjoyed our association with the 24 Brigade chaps and were much indebted to the TOS staff for many kindnesses, so the evening before the former flew back to Kenya, we gave a supper and roulette party in our tented Mess which the soldiers decorated with remarkable energy and imagination. James Craig, the PA in Dubai, and his wife came together with a number of British bankers and such like. The food was excellent and Private Cuddihy ran the roulette with a good grip, though many of our guests won handsomely and the 'Bank' would have lost about £30 if a Gunner Captain from 148 Battery had not generously refused to accept his winnings. The 2 PARA Band played well and looked very smart sitting in the middle of the desert surrounded by hurricane lamps. It was a happy episode in a very happy period.

Closing down the camp and returning all the stores and vehicles to Aden and Bahrain by sea (1,066 crates and sixty-two vehicles) kept us busy until the end of October but we managed to go swimming and fishing most afternoons in a creek opposite Khan village. There were masses of fish but I was not clever at catching them. However I was given a special treat by the RAF, a four-hour flight in a Canberra aircraft of No 73 Squadron on detachment to Sharjah from RAF Akrotiri (Cyprus). The crew consisted of an Australian, a Trinidadian and an Anglo-Indian. I sat on the 'rumble seat' beside the pilot and had a good view as we flew very low over the desert towards Buraimi and over the sea off Abu Dhabi. The aim of the mission was to practise rocket attacks onto a target area marked out near Jebel Ali, involving steep dives and sudden pull-ups. I was surprised by the inaccuracy of the strikes, but they would doubtless have frightened those on the receiving end.

The airfield at Sharjah has a long history. It was first built as a staging post for Imperial Airways in 1930 and formed the last refuelling point for aircraft before reaching India. In those days the passengers were housed in the nearby fort which was secured against marauding tribesmen. During the Second World War the station was run by the US Army Air Force but had RAF squadrons operating from it. By 1963 it had the capacity for handling the largest aircraft and was equipped with the most modern ground systems. On the mainland and in Bahrain we got on very well with the RAF aircrew and, of course, with our PJIs. But certain elements in the air force community at Sharjah and Muharraq we found consistently unreliable and unhelpful. I wrote in my diary in late October 1963:

'I am having a "hate" against the RAF Movements Staff here. They really are bloody; unkempt, dirty, ignorant, unhelpful and discourteous. The trouble is that they are low-grade people commanded by the most junior and inexperienced Officers. They cause us endless vexations and much anger which is a pity as the Services are very dependent on having a good Movements organisation. Everyone curses this Sharjah bunch and holds them in great contempt. The alarming thing is that the more senior RAF Officers do nothing to put matters right.'

We made a point of inviting the Officers of RAF Muharraq and their wives to all our ceremonies and festivities at Hamala Camp and sometimes got invited back to their Mess or homes. In 1965, when I was back in Bahrain commanding 1 PARA Group, a number of my Officers and I had been invited to the Muharraq Mess for the annual Battle of Britain party starting, according to the note on the invitation card, at 6pm and finishing at 8pm. I was standing with the Group Captain commanding and one of his Wing Commanders; my glass was empty so the Wing Commander signalled one of the waiters to refill it for me. By this time it was about 8 o'clock. When the waiter returned from the bar with my fresh glass he said to me: 'That will be five rupees please'. I replied: 'I think you are making a mistake; I am a guest, here by invitation'. 'But it is now one minute after 8 o'clock and the drinks are no longer free,' he said. So I handed my glass to the Group Captain, our host, and said, 'Please hold this while I get my money out of my wallet'. He did, I paid and neither of those two Officers thought there was anything odd about the episode.

Since early summer the subject of our conversations in the Mess, stimulated by the coverage in all the UK papers and the BBC, had been the Profumo scandal. Following on directly after the sordid Argyll divorce case, this latest example of disgraceful behaviour in the upper echelons of our Conservative government shocked and angered millions of those Britons who form the Silent Majority in the electorate. If Denis Wheatley had written a novel revolving round a Cabinet Minister, a call-girl, two negro criminals, the Soviet naval attaché, drugs, VD and a Harley Street doctor, it would have been declared too preposterous for belief. But it had happened; in London and at the heart of the Tory Party. Profumo's conduct was made trebly reprehensible by his lying statement to Parliament. If he had got up and said openly and without shame words to the effect: 'Yes, I must tell the House that Miss Keeler, who is a remarkably attractive girl, and I have had a sexual relationship for many weeks now, a relationship which has brought much pleasure to us both, done no harm whatsoever to the nation's security and which my dear wife has accepted with total compassion', he would probably have been applauded. The whole episode reflected banefully on the competence of Prime Minister Macmillan, about to play host at Birch Grove to President

Kennedy of the United States. As *The Sunday Telegraph* wrote: 'Kennedy will come to a country deeply ashamed of the spectacle presented to the world by the Profumo scandal; a Prime Minister whose stock is even lower with the people than that of his party and an Opposition which if it came to power would give up the last shreds of Britain's military independence by falling in with American ideas on nuclear weapons. Our post-war spree had to end one day. It is distressing and mortifying that it should end like this: in scandal, weakness and mendacity'.

One of the tabloid papers added this snippet of verse (Selwyn Lloyd being then Chairman of the Conservative Party):

C3 AT LLOYD'S
No wonder Macmillan's annoyed:
He's heard from his pal, Selwyn Lloyd
The Party machine
Doesn't need a spring-clean;
What it needs is a session with Freud!

Alas, though well remembered, the Profumo scandal, far from being a turning point in the decline in the standards of behaviour of our leaders, seemed to be forerunner to an unfolding series of shocking incidents of corruption, treachery, perversion and immorality. The British nation was badly let down in the last four decades of the twentieth century by those who hitherto had by tradition and merit been respected, revered and often loved. The deepest wounds to our national pride were inflicted by an iconoclastic press gloating in the discomfiture of the Queen and her ill-starred sons as the century approached its end. The national scene, our self-esteem and our status in the eyes of the world belied the noble expectations that so many people had had of our victorious country fifty years earlier. A dismal observation: but could chaps like me have averted the rot?

Neale Gordon-Wilson did me a considerable kindness in November; he arranged for me to get back to England for six weeks to attend a course at the Joint Warfare Establishment and as a bonus to have Christmas with my family. So after a happy session in the Sergeants' Mess, and a concert in a bitterly cold Hamala Camp, I had a smooth and swift journey in a Comet IV aircraft of BOAC, and arrived at Heathrow at dawn to be greeted there on our Wedding Anniversary by my beloved Rosemary before driving down to South Stoke for a glorious reunion with Pinky, Didi and the Macphersons. All very well, though Rosemary had lost too much weight, caused in part by worry about the overdraft; for she had bought some furniture and pictures which we badly needed and which have served us very well ever since. She spends money liberally but very wisely. In fact, she had run the family exceedingly wisely while I was away. I was most proud of her but liked to think that with my promotion now decreed we would be together on most future overseas postings. The kids and she had fitted into the Berkshire village well and made many friends. We were getting ready to dine with a couple down the road when we learned of the assassination in Dallas of young President Kennedy, a tragic act which begot universal grief of an unprecedented degree. JFK had caught the imagination and secured the confidence of millions. Each of us became intimately involved through television with that American tragedy and with the Kennedy family members. We mourned the killing of an American idol, who with his wife, Jacqueline, had created in their trans-Atlantic Camelot a quasi-royal court.

But as seems to happen in liberal societies, where adulation and reverence are replaced by denigration and censure as surely as night follows day, the Camelot idyll was destroyed as tales of Kennedy's sexual adventures, his wife's extravagances and the improprieties of kinsmen were dragged up and multiplied on paper and film. The fatal blow to the Kennedy legend was surely struck by his widow herself; by her marriage to an exceedingly ugly Greek millionaire she debased herself and humiliated the American nation.

Most of December I spent at RAF Old Sarum, near Salisbury, on No 1 Joint Warfare Course; interesting and well run. Old Sarum was one of the original flying stations having been associated with the Royal Flying Corps since 1917. We were addressed early on in the course by the Chief of the Defence Staff, Earl Mountbatten, the creator of the modern Ministry of Defence with its Central Staff and reduced power vested in the three single Services subordinated to it. A fine looking achiever who talked amusingly about the history – an erratic one – of British Joint Warfare (muddled at Gallipoli in 1915, admirable in 1944 in Normandy and muddled again in 1956 at Suez), and about his Father's relations with Kitchener before the outbreak of the Great War in 1914. Mountbatten reminded us on that 1963 December day that since 1945 the British Army had been called on to take part in forty-six operations of varying magnitude and each time, he said, we had been taken by surprise and the machine had creaked. The Army had become so small that it could only tackle one crisis at a time. I was increasingly querying the wisdom of the current regimental system. It seemed to me to be failing in practice; a Grenadier was being brought in to command the Welch Regiment, Black Watch Officers to the Worcesters and the Argylls; a Colonel on the course with me had just completed two and a half years as CO of his county regiment in Minden with a total strength of less than 300! But whatever the weaknesses that were becoming apparent in our Army, largely the consequences of government policy, we still adhered to certain standards of behaviour, courtesy and care for our men which the rest of the nation seemed to have cast aside.

Christmas was super; our run-up to the 25th was in South Stoke where we had bonfires, fireworks, a school pantomime in which Pinky was a very pretty fairy, glühwein, visits from Argyll friends and our dear Fontainebleau couple, Richard and Maureen Willey, and the traditional Service of Nine Lessons and Carols in the village church, conducted by the Parson, Roy Price, a former Padre in 6th Airborne Division. Although the population of South Stoke is a mere four hundred, they raised £6,000 that year for church renovation. Christmas and Boxing Days we spent in London with Jane in her Cheyne Court flat which she was in the process of improving and where my two Brothers and Margaret, Moray's wife, joined us. The grub and the presents at Jane's were splendid. They always were. All her life Jane made a big thing of our family Christmases and birthdays and never failed to amaze us with her menus and the profusion of gifts she wrapped up for us to open on Christmas afternoon, as soon as the Royal Message to the Commonwealth had been broadcast.

My leave was up on 30 December, so I caught a Britannia aircraft of BUA and landed in Aden the next morning. I was feeling pretty depressed at leaving Rosemary and the kids and Aden seemed seedy under a drab sky, but I fell into the hands of a former colleague from Fontainebleau days; actually the man I had saved with Dicharry's help from the accusation of driving while drunk. People on the Staff in Aden, HQ Middle East Command, were by now pessimistic about the future of the Aden Federation and of our bases in that corner of Arabia. Also the Greek and Turkish populations in Cyprus had started to fight each other again, and to keep the two sides apart, our 16 Parachute Brigade HQ under Brigadier Roly Gibbs together with 1 PARA had been sent out there at very short notice – and in the middle of Christmas-New Year leave. Furthermore the continuing Indonesian threat to Malaysia added to a general anxiety about overstretch in the Army, and raised again the need for Britain to reintroduce some form of compulsory military service.

Late on 2 January 1964 I got back to Hamala having flown in an Argosy via Salalah and Sharjah. I never dreamt that Salalah would in the next decade play such a significant part in my life, or that I would there on a July day in 1970 grasp a nettle and thereby help to transform the lives of the million inhabitants of the Sultanate of Muscat and Oman.

2 PARA was in excellent heart having had a splendid Christmas and Hogmanay with lashings of beer and zero indiscipline, but Bahrain was exceptionally cold; four degrees colder than London. The Battalion had formed a mountaineering club when we first got to Bahrain, and many afternoons Jon Fleming, the Adjutant and formerly a Royal Berkshire, used to disappear with them towards the south of the island to practise their skills. Bahrain is a pretty flat place, some hillocks are to be found but nothing that can be termed a mountain. One day I came across Jon and his stalwarts performing on the face of a cliff perhaps twenty feet high, which

was fine for beginners but inadequate for the more experienced climbers. So I managed to fix the Club up with a flight to Cyprus and a spell among the more challenging peaks of the Pentadaktylos Range. I was glad to do this, for Jon was a first-class Officer and his colleagues some of the cream of the battalion. By mid-January the Advance Party was getting ready to fly to Aldershot to prepare for the battalion's return in April. As 2IC it was my job to head the party. I shall always think kindly of the CO, Neale G-W. He was not everyone's cup of tea and I do not believe that he enjoyed being CO of 2 PARA, as his forte was as a Staff Officer rather than a Leader and Inspirer of men. But he was consistently helpful and generous to me, and my promotion to command 1 PARA was very largely due to what he had said and written about me to our superiors during the short time we had been together.

Bahrain during the first weeks of 1964 remained an exceedingly cold place, and the heavy rains which turned the desert around our camp green with a mass of hitherto invisible vegetation also produced a sea of mud. Thus we were quite glad to get away again to the mainland, this time to the Sultanate of Muscat and Oman. The Ruler of this large and picturesque land with its wide stretches of gravel or sand desert and a range of mountains, the Jebel al Akhdar, rising to ten thousand feet, rarely permitted our Forces to exercise on his territory and seldom allowed entry to individuals from the West such as journalists or businessmen. Tourists were forbidden to enter this closed country which Sultan Said bin Taimur governed by radio telephone from his distant Palace in Salalah, and in which the population was denied the basic facilities of medical care and education which were already commonplace in neighbouring States. The Sultanate was strikingly backward but the Omanis whom we came across were charming, polite and fine of feature. We knew this because we had the previous year been allowed to carry out an amphibious and parachute exercise in the Sohar area; and from time to time we sent at the Ruler's request small patrols led by Officers to 'show the flag' in the mountainous area which had been the battleground in the campaign of 1957-9 against Saudi-sponsored rebels, and which was still in 1964 experiencing some sniping and furtive mine-laying. These patrols served also to boost the confidence of the Sultan's own armed forces, two infantry battalions, a Gendarmerie unit and small artillery and air force components. The whole lot were commanded by British Officers seconded to the Sultanate or on contract.

   The exercise which started on 10 January took place west of Muscat and took the form of an advance to contact by 2 PARA Group and tanks of 16/5th Lancers landed from the navy's AW Squadron on the Batinah coast just north of Azaiba. The planning had been done by me with the Commander of SAF, Colonel Hugh Oldman. Our advance through the foothills of the Jebel Akhdar from Rusayl towards Fanjah and BidBid was resisted by two units of the Sultan's Forces, Muscat Regiment and Northern Frontier Regiment. My personal task was to observe, note and report for after-exercise action. This gave me an agreeable and productive four days. 2 PARA Group went in by parachute from Beverley and Argosy aircraft in two lifts. I was on the second lift with a P-hour of 0730. That meant no sleep as we had to report to Muharraq airfield by 0230 for a take-off two hours later. However the flight was smooth, we were well handled in the air by our PJIs, and I had a good landing on the soft DZ. The Gunner next to me got his container entangled with mine and broke his ankle on hitting the ground. We were 'shot up' on the DZ by 'hostile' aircraft but soon got away heading for Rusayl whence our advance was along two separate tracks, lasting about two and a half days of marching, mounting company attacks supported by Hunter aircraft against the SAF defenders and more marching. Not a particularly exciting exercise for our men but memorable for the Arab and Baluch soldiers opposing us who were impressed by the Lancers' tanks and the skill of the Hunter pilots doing their ground attacks in those mountain valleys.

I noted a number of things which needed to be put right before the battalion went on exercise in the more critical environment of England: our Battalion HQ procedures in particular had collected a lot of rust in Bahrain. The Soldiers as usual were excellent, but it appeared to me that not all our Officers were as professional as their men deserved and had a right to expect. If the battle had been for real we would, I believe, have suffered a rather bloody nose fighting those Sultanate soldiers in their bare, broken, taxing terrain. But for me Exercise AZAIBA was to have important consequences. I got to know and respect some of the SAF 'enemy', and was impressed by their high morale and the evident good relations that existed between the races and ranks: they had an air of 'zing'. I found too the country glorious to see: high mountains divided by deep wadis, patches of lush greenery wherever water abounded, and in January an excellent climate – just like a perfect English summer. But beyond all these stirring sensations I had the opportunity to talk at length with Colonel Oldman, the Commander of SAF. Tall, elegant with a small moustache and an MC from the war, this former Officer of the Durham Light Infantry had, I found, an outlook on matters military, about our nation's role in the Middle East and about the standards expected of British officials which was almost identical to my own. Furthermore he told me a lot about his life in the Sultanate and the joys of commanding the Sultan's Forces. The more I listened to Hugh Oldman the more I liked him; and the more I began to reflect on the pleasant challenges and the scope for helping a friendly and deserving nation which a period of secondment, away from the orthodoxy of the British Army proper, might present. A return to Oman was definitely something to contrive providing it would not impair one's career or distress one's family. As I used to advise young Officers seeking to plot to the best advantage the course of their careers: 'Don't fuss about the future. Leave it to God and the Military Secretary; together they will contrive for you a more satisfying professional life than you could devise for yourself'. In my own case that injunction was to prove one hundred percent accurate.

The Advance Party and I flew back at the end of February to Stansted where Rosemary met me, although I had besought her not to drive so far so early in a winter morning, and in no time I was back in South Stoke with my two sprogs and the Macphersons. Rosemary had not had an easy time for the kids had had several colds; Christopher was quite ill until he was put on penicillin. The damp of the Thames Valley had a bad effect on many people but on him particularly, poor little chap.

RQMS Gillies, the soldiers and I started the business of taking over the accommodation and stores in Blenheim Barracks. 2 PARA would return there to find them pretty squalid as we were to be the last occupants before the whole complex was demolished as part of the Aldershot Re-build. Aldershot we found almost denuded of troops as 3 PARA were on leave prior to replacing us in Bahrain, and Brigade HQ and 1 PARA were in Cyprus as part of a United Nations peace-keeping Force. I sorted out our family quarter, a semi-detached house in Wakeford's Copse, Crookham; but not ours for long as we would move into a larger and more fitting house when the time came for me to assume command of the First Battalion that autumn.

Those weeks on the Advance Party gave me plenty of time to make my number with the Regimental Headquarters of The Parachute Regiment in Maida Barracks (the barracks from which Max had taken The Berkshires to war in August 1914), and to look up with Rosemary a number of old friends from our Fontainebleau and Lemgo days; also to get to know our way around Military Aldershot with which we were to become intimately associated as it was the Home of my new Regiment.

The Regimental Colonel at this time was Bob Flood on whose Staff were my old friend from 5 PARA at Perham Down in 1947, Bill Corbould, and a most distinguished soldier, John Lord. Regimental Sergeant-Major Lord had been captured at Arnhem with 1 PARA, and on arrival at the Prison Camp in Germany was appalled by the slovenly state into which the inmates, British and other Allied troops, had slumped. He at once set about raising the whole tone of the place, to the very great good of the prisoners and to the astonishment of the German garrison who had never witnessed the grandeur and the grip embodied in a British Warrant Officer reared in The Brigade of Guards. When the camp was liberated at the end of the war, the first Officer to reach the place was greeted by a Guard of Honour of 1 PARA men whose bearing and turn-out under Lord's influence were impeccable. He was later the Academy Sergeant-Major at Sandhurst, and he died alas of cancer soon after I met him; greatly revered, and much loved too for he was a fine Christian gentleman as well as an outstanding soldier.

Because Neale Gordon-Wilson was required back in England for a conference ahead of the departure from Bahrain of the Battalion, the new Brigadier, Michael Holme, who had taken over from Dick Bryers in September, insisted that I return there for two weeks to command 2 PARA in case the Kuwait operation 'GOODWOOD' had to be carried out. So, on Good Friday, I flew back to Bahrain to find the 3 PARA Advance Party already in Hamala and in time to enjoy the new cabaret show 'Love in a Turnip Field', excellently contrived and produced by Michael Bowden of Sphinx Battery and based on Dylan Thomas' 'Under Milk Wood'. The proceeds from the show were donated to Private Chadwick, a 2 PARA soldier in the Stoke Mandeville paraplegic hospital as a result of a crippling gymnastic accident ten months earlier.

In January 1964 I wrote in my diary: 'I cannot remember a year in peacetime which has opened with so many "crises"': East Africa was particularly in the headlines. A revolt broke out in Zanzibar and one of 2 PARA's companies was flown to Aden for a possible parachute operation onto Pemba or Zanzibar island. The black battalions in Tanganyka, Kenya and Uganda went on strike and put their British Officers and NCOs under arrest; 'mutiny' is too strong a term for those acts of indiscipline which were *au fond* protests against conditions of service, pay and the slow rate of Africanisation. Nevertheless the harm was done, and those incidents demonstrated the inherent instability of those countries. British Army and Royal Marine units moved in quickly and settled the troubles with good sense and humanity, earning the gratitude of the black politicians. The misbehaviour of the battalion of the King's African Rifles was especially disturbing and gave rise to some talk about Chinese or Cuban communist conspiracies. Above all these episodes posed the question: 'What will happen when the British leave as we are committed to doing?' The continuing massacres in the Congo were not a reassuring portent.

On 2 April, at ten minutes to four in the morning, Peter Hamer, the GSO2 at HQ LFPG walked into my bedroom with a batch of signals putting 2 PARA Group at immediate notice to carry out Operation BORIS. This operation was one of several planned to restore peace in Zanzibar, independent only since 1963, where communist subversion was causing fears of an imminent breakdown of law and order and the risk to the lives of the large Arab population and of the pro-British Sultan. It was quite clear to me what had to be done and done quickly, for as Brigadier Michael Holme exclaimed: 'You are almost certain to go'. But there were two problems. One was that we had only two maps of Zanzibar – one of the island and one street plan of the town. All planning and briefing had to be done from these. The more interesting problem was that the relief of our battalion by 3 PARA had already begun. Two companies of the incoming group were in Bahrain; one at Muharraq and one in Hamala, and an equivalent number of our chaps and their families were on their way to England. So I had to plan the show with a mixed force of 2 and 3 PARA, and to avoid confusion referred to the sub-units by the names of their commanders: Daniel, Burke, Walsh and Walters.

By ten o'clock a Beverley aircraft was on its way to Aden with our Heavy Drop teams and equipment for rigging the platforms on which guns, vehicles and other heavy loads would be delivered to the battle zone by parachute, and a Royal Marine Commando had arrived from Aden and taken over the commitments at Muharraq of Mike Walsh's newly arrived company. The urgency of the operation meant that the staff and I held Orders Groups in the Hamala Officers' Mess with our two solitary maps pinned to a blackboard, and that the troops drew the ammunition, ration packs, medical kits, weapons and everything else needed for a parachute assault into a hostile environment and had packed these into their personal containers. By lunch-time we were all ready to go and waiting only for the long-range transport planes to arrive to lift us to Kenya where we were to transfer into parachute-roled aircraft.

All this planning and preparation of course disrupted the hand-over plans of Quartermaster George Ferguson and the detailed fly-out tables that Morton Pollock, our Air Adjutant, had made for 2 PARA. But everyone put their shoulders to the wheel and, stimulated by the prospect of being launched imminently into an operation in a distant country, made light of all the difficulties. The families accepted stoically the prospect of having suddenly to return to England without their menfolk. It was a hectic day and a good test of our flexibility and professionalism.

But alas the effort and the excitement were wasted. As the afternoon wore on and the LRT aircraft failed to arrive, I began to suspect that we had been ordered to prepare for Operation BORIS prematurely; before the British government had finally agreed that a military intervention by us was essential and given the green light. The military staffs in Aden and Whitehall had based their orders on a worst case scenario and alerted 2 PARA Group ahead of the politicians' decisions. The Stand Down was a disappointment and I did my best to soften the blow to the deflated Soldiers in a speech the next day. We learned in due course that the Foreign Office had ruled against BORIS being launched. It also became clear that by our failure to intervene in Zanzibar many hundreds of lives were lost in the spate of inter-racial butchery which erupted.

The rest of 3 PARA came out to Bahrain and we returned to the UK rather glad to be shot of the restricted life and demanding Gulf climate. 3 PARA was commanded by an outstanding man, Tony Farrar-Hockley. Very experienced in war and peace, he had joined 6 PARA, our Welsh battalion, from The Glosters which was his parent regiment at a young age, had been Adjutant of that regiment in their fine action on the Imjin River in the Korean campaign, been taken prisoner and suffered greatly at the hands of his North Korean and Chinese captors. I first met him when we were fellow-students at Camberley in 1955, and like everyone on that course sat enthralled as he lectured to the assembled college about his Korean experiences and the lessons to be learned from them, recorded also in his book, *The Edge of the Sword*.

It was obvious that Tony would rise to the top of the profession of arms; it was only in later years, however, when he and I served together in 16 PARA Brigade, that I realised his abilities as a cook, as a writer, and as a military historian. He is also an exceedingly nice man. To have rubbed shoulders with him and with so many other distinguished wearers of the Red Beret has been a privilege. I regret that Tony had the bother of accounting for all the ration packs and other expendable items which 2 PARA had broken down or consumed when preparing for BORIS; an episode regarded by the financial auditors as an expensive false alarm.

Nor did 3 PARA ever get to Zanzibar. But within a month of arriving in Bahrain they were deployed in the Radfan area north of Aden where the tribesmen, influenced by the Arab nationalist movement, took up arms to force the British to withdraw from the small protectorate on the southern tip of Arabia. In the spring of 1964 the main Radfan tribe, backed with Egyptian and Yemeni weapons, mined the roads and began regular ambushes. Their activities provoked a swift response by the Marines of 45 Commando and 3 PARA Group; the latter in an operation conducted by TF-H captured a vital ridge and brought to the area a period of peace. This achievement was all the more valued because the tribesmen had put to death two soldiers of the SAS whom they had captured early on, and stuck their heads on poles outside the town of Taiz. Unfairly in our view, the politicians in London blamed the local GOC, Major General John Cubbon, for this atrocity.

The situation in and around Aden grew steadily worse, and British plans for handing over power to a stable government were increasingly frustrated by traditional antagonisms, subversion from outside the Colony, and vacillation in Whitehall. 1 PARA was to be drawn into the area when I brought them back to the Gulf in the following year, and again in 1967 when, under the command of Mike Walsh, they played the major role in securing the vital Sheikh Othman suburb of Aden against frequent guerilla attacks and covering the evacuation when we withdrew in November 1967 after 128 years of British rule.

As 6 June 1964 was the 20th anniversary of the Allied invasion of Normandy, Operation OVERLORD, the occasion was to be celebrated in some style, and we assumed that the Regiment would be included in the British contingent. In the middle of May I was sent with George Morrison, our head PJI, on a reconnaissance of the Ranville area, to the north-east of Caen, where 6th Airborne Division had landed in the early hours of D-Day. We crossed by the Newhaven-Dieppe ferry and were picked up on landing by a car from the Paris embassy. This was a considerable convenience as it enabled me to show George the Norman villages where the airborne soldiers had fought, and also the places through which we in 15th Scottish Division had advanced on Operation EPSOM. I had not been in Normandy since the Staff College Battlefield tour in 1955, and although the roads had been improved, the hedges had grown higher and new buildings had replaced the many destroyed in the fighting, I had no trouble in finding all the spots which had impressed themselves on my memory; even the outlines of our slit trenches overlooking the River Odon at Gavrus were visible.

We also visited the French Air Force base at Carpiquet (where the Canadians had such difficulty in overcoming the ferocious resistance of Kurt Meyer's Hitler Jugend Division, 12 SS Panzer) to see if it would provide a suitable DZ, but it was too restricted. Then to Cabourg to arrange with the Mairie for the Retreat Programme on 6 June, to the Ranville Mairie to make outline plans for our reception and billetting, and finally to the US Air Force base at Evreux in case our RAF planes had to be diverted on account of bad weather. The base Officers at Carpiquet and Evreux were exceedingly helpful, and I again realised how very much I like France and the French; the rich Norman countryside looked glorious, the weather was superb, and I was especially moved by the skill and dedication with which Caen, largely destroyed by our bombers in July 1944, had been restored using the original stone and architectural styles. On the way back to Dieppe we stopped at Bayeux to see the AD 1066 Tapestry, stretching the length of the four walls of the gallery; the colours were a bit faded but the expressions on the depicted faces are amusing. We, by chance, went round with a party of gendarmes guided by a charming woman who was clearly the No 1 authority on William the Conqueror and his activities, so enjoyed a particularly informative morning. At Arromanches quite a lot of the original Mulberry artificial harbour could be seen; caissons and blockships and numerous German blockhouses and bunkers too. In the museum there is a fine working model of that historic anchorage.

In the event 2 PARA's contingent to the anniversary celebrations consisted of the Band, Drums and men from three companies. I took the musicians, administrative party and the vehicles over in the landing craft HMS *Rampart* (Lt Cdr Tindale). After a comfortable night in Seaton Barracks looked after by The King's Shropshire Light Infantry, we sailed from Plymouth for Cherbourg where we arrived just before midnight. The next morning, having disembarked, we set off for the Caen area escorted by most helpful and efficient police motorcyclists. The weather was still beautiful and the countryside even lusher than in May, and we were given a great welcome by the French farmers and motorists as we sped through the US battlefields on the Cotentin Peninsula and along the coast road through the former beach-heads Omaha, Gold, Juno and Sword. On arrival at the Ranville Mairie I found my farmer friend, Monsieur Joyeux, who had made the arrangements for dispersing our 160-strong party among six farms. Seemingly we were the first British soldiers the villagers had seen since 1945 and we were enthusiastically received. The Bandsmen were a bit put out at having to sleep in barns, but the novel experience gave them something to talk about when they got home. We all slept exceedingly well in fact, thanks to the fresh air and the circulating bottles of calvados, and despite a heavy bombardment of our sleeping bags from the pigeons on the rafters above us. Before turning in Colour Sergeant Cannon and I spent a couple of hours in the village bar where a visiting team of salesmen from Maison Pernod put on a hilarious impromptu cabaret with conjuring, acrobatics and clowning. In the meantime some of the troops, digging a latrine behind our farm, came across an unexploded German shell; and my driver, Private Kirke from Argyllshire, delivered a calf out of one of Joyeux's cows.

The next day I went over to Carpiquet to meet the remainder of our chaps arriving in two Argosy aircraft. I was pleased by their appearance and good order on deplaning; this high standard of discipline and turn-out they maintained during the whole of their time in France. Major Jock Daniel and I took them to their various billets where we were all plied with wine and calvados. In spite of appearances and the rather ordinary contents of their houses, these Norman farmers were wealthy indeed. They held little animosity against the Germans. Joyeux told me that those billetted in Ranville were really very ordinary and well-behaved people who caused little trouble, helping with the farm-work when off-duty and paying promptly and in full for whatever they bought. These Frenchmen also (out of politeness?) paid tribute to the bravery and discipline of the 6th Airborne men who had been in the thick of the fighting round Ranville during June and July of 1944, but, we were told, the Scottish troops (presumably of 51st Highland Division) who moved in later conducted themselves badly; *'pire que les Boches'*.

The following day I took the opportunity to tell the troops about the achievements of their Fathers in 6th Airborne and to take them on a tour of the most historic battlefields in that bit of Normandy, such as 9 PARA's Merville Battery and the Bois de Bavent – that wide, wooded feature on the east flank of the Allied landings which Alastair Pearson's 8 PARA, by incessant aggressive patrolling, completely dominated during those crucial first weeks of the campaign. The high spot of the tour was naturally the bridge over the Caen canal, Pegasus Bridge, which was seized intact by a company of the 2nd Battalion The Oxfordshire and Buckinghamshire

Light Infantry (the immortal 52nd L.I), who led by Major John Howard landed in gliders in the dark within a few yards of the bridge and the German defences. It was a notable feat of arms. For my 2 PARA party the tour that day was made memorable quite unexpectedly. As we drove into the field next to the bridge I recognised John Howard and one of his former subalterns, David Wood. I had no idea they were in France, had come across them quite fortuitously, and had no difficulty in getting them to relate to my rivetted soldiers how the capture of that vital bridge, and a second one nearby over the River Orne, had been planned, rehearsed and accomplished.

The next day, 6 June, was fine but windy. Colonel Neale, Bob Flood, General Napier Crookenden and I went from the Château de Ranville where they were staying with the Mayor, Count Rohan de Chabot, to La Place du 6 Juin for the annual ceremony in front of the 13 PARA plaque. There we were joined by the Pilgrims led by General Sir Richard Gale who commanded 6th Airborne Division in the invasion, Brigadiers Flavell and Poett, Colonel Luard and their wives; the latter very smart in new hats and regimental brooches. The Sous-Prefet of Calvados, the Mayors, Standard Bearers from the villages around and a French military band were all there and greeted the Pilgrims with fervour and affection. We had speeches, exchanges of flags and the two national anthems, much saluting and some tears. It was very Gallic and wholly sincere.

We then walked up to the Ranville church, packed for the Service which was conducted by an Airborne RC Padre, and later on to the military cemetery, the route lined by my 2 PARA chaps in No 2 Dress. In the cemetery, impeccably kept by the Commonwealth War Graves Commission as they all are, lie some two thousand men, mostly of 6th Airborne together with a number of German dead. The two Buglers from our Junior Parachute Company played 'The Last Post' and 'Reveille' but the display by a team of French Army parachutists had to be cancelled because of the high wind. Lunch on the Ranville village green took place in a large marquee while Bandmaster Best and his men played selections of French and British music outside. The food and drink, provided by the community for us British visitors, were excellent, and the Pilgrims were soon all giggles and repartee; and hilarity too when the roof of the tent started to collapse. I sat beside a engaging octogenarian who had walked fifteen kilometres from his house that morning 'to pay homage to our British liberators'. The oration by the Sous-Prefet was listened to, however, with proper respect and our Band was loudly acclaimed.

I spent some of the afternoon back at our farm with M. Joyeux who gave me a bottle of calvados in exchange for my whisky and a regimental plaque to hang on his wall.

The Beating of Retreat ceremony at Cabourg went well, Napier Crookenden taking the salute as Richard Gale could not be found, after which we all went into the Mairie for a *vin d'honneur*. As that memorable day drew to an end, Napier, Bob Flood, Neale G-W and I motored to Carpiquet and flew back to England by helicopter while Jock Daniel prepared to return the sea-party to Cherbourg and eventually Plymouth in my place. We had a dreary stop at Thorney Island for customs' clearance, then flew on to Odiham whence I drove home to Rosemary who, as always, was delighted to have me back.

The Congo basin was unknown territory until the explorations during the 1870s of Livingstone and Stanley. The King of the Belgians, Leopold II, who had financed Stanley's journeys, established personal rule over the country, recognized in 1885 as the Congo Free State, and subjected the inhabitants to a good deal of brutal exploitation. The scandal caused by Leopold's maladminstration and the huge fortune he had personally derived from the place resulted in its annexation as a Belgian colony in 1908. It was generally believed that the Belgian Congo became one of the best administered colonies in Africa, but the granting of independence in 1960 revealed that its people had been given no preparation whatsoever for self-rule. Old tribal antagonisms revived, many of the Belgian settlers were driven out, and the province of Katanga, very rich in copper and uranium, sought to break away from the new republic. A United Nations force was sent to damp down the bloodshed in that huge (900,000 square miles), productive country of fifteen million natives, the majority of Bantu stock, but was withdrawn in 1964. The bloodshed continued. As John Bulloch, *The Daily Telegraph*'s experienced writer on African and Middle East affairs, wrote that year: 'After four years of fighting, four years in which the United Nations expended millions of pounds and hundreds of men, the Congo is now worse off than when it was granted precipitate independence. Worse off because this is a war incomprehensible by Western standards ... The spear-carrying warriors of Pierre Mulele and Gaston Soumialot are rebels without any cause but that of the witchdoctors who work them up to battle pitch. Now this brush fire of revolt has spread over a third of the Congo – and the Congo is the size of Western Europe. It threatens the rich investments in Katanga; the diamond mines and pastures of Kasai; the commerce of Equateur, and even the primitive life of the pygmies in the rain forest in the north. The Congolese National Army, 30,000-strong but ill-trained, has proved itself unable to cope with the outbreak, and M. Tshombe, the head of the government has been forced to call in outside help. The people he has called on are Les Mercénaires, the rootless, ill-balanced men of many nationalities willing to fight for £100 a month and £90 danger money.'

The situation, which was expected to worsen, had placed the lives of the Europeans who were still working in the Republic of Congo in real peril, and several countries began to make contingency plans for the evacuation of their nationals. Britain was one of these countries and I was suddenly extracted from the 2 PARA Camp at Westdown, briefed by HQ Southern Command and the Foreign Office, and flown out to Leopoldville (now Kinshasa), the capital of Congo together with another 2 PARA Officer, Major Brian Barnes of the Irish Guards, and an airman, Wing Commander Sid Oliver. Our task was to report to Ambassador Rose at the British Embassy and his Military Attaché, Colonel John Stevens, and in collaboration with them to make a plan for the evacuation by air in an emergency of British and Commonwealth nationals. I can no longer remember the details of the plan, and I do not think it had to be put into operation that year, but during our week in the Republic we were able to get a feel for the immensity of the territory and for the depth of the natives' hatred of the Belgians. The very size of the country really caused us the most anxiety, for the crux of the problem was how to assemble rapidly and securely at an airhead or river port the individuals and families living far distant in the mining and other installations, or in church missions. The Belgians had good reason to fear for their lives, and I did not meet one who expressed any optimism about the future of their former colony. John Bulloch's article which I referred to above was entitled 'Civilisation v. Savagery in the Congo'. It was an apt title as the following episode, which had occurred just before my team reached Leopoldville, shows.

Up country, far from the city, a Belgian missionary had lived for most of his adult life expending his energy on the well-being of his large African flock and on bringing them into the Roman Catholic faith. In his life of devotion and charity he had been for many years loyally assisted by a Congolese convert to Christianity, his house boy whose name was Philippe. As the situation got worse this good man was advised by his superiors to make arrangements for handing over his Mission and his work of service and to return to Belgium. He accepted this official advice with sadness and he entrusted Philippe with the task of carrying on the good work after his departure. He said to Philippe: 'You have served me very well for many, many years and I am confident that you will, as I have tried to do, work for your people to the best of your ability. As proof of my trust in you and in gratitude for all that you have done for me and with me during our many years together in this Mission, I am going to leave to you the house and all its contents. This is a large gift and because it may fill other people of your tribe with jealousy so that they may try to take it away from you, I am going to drive you into the town to get my gift to you set out on paper by a lawyer so that you will have lasting proof that you are truly the legal owner henceforth of these my possessions.'

Philippe was delighted and expressed his gratitude fervently as they drove together into town for the meeting with the lawyer, who duly recorded in proper form the details of the good Belgian's bequest to his house boy. As they made their way back to the Mission-house Philippe asked: 'What will happen to this car?'. 'I have long ago promised it to our friend and superior, the Bishop of this province. He is of your tribe and the car will enable him to visit all the people and to look after them even better than I have tried to do'.

'But I am your special friend; I want the car also.'

'I am very sorry, Philippe; I've left you everything else, but the car I have promised to the Bishop; he needs it for his work and I cannot break my word.'

During the rest of the drive back Philippe never uttered, but when the Belgian had lain down to rest after the journey the house boy took a knife from the kitchen and stabbed him to death.

Notes

1. An exception was the Sultanate of Muscat & Oman which, although closely linked with Britain, remained fully independent.
2. The reference to the coal dump is an amusing fiction. The bombs had in fact exploded harmlessly in the desert between Awali and Sitra.

CHAPTER X
1964–1967

Commanding 1 PARA Group in Aldershot, Bahrain, Aden and Aldershot again

In the first week of October one of the best English summers I had known was transformed into a splendid autumn of golden leaves, bright sun and brisk days; one of those periods when it is good to be alive. Wearing my new badges I was driven from Blenheim House to Guillemont Barracks in Cove by my new driver, Private Garroway. He was a well built young parachutist with a pretty Welsh wife. She was a qualified nurse so Garroway was in exceptionally good hands. So was I; for Garroway's hobby was buying elderly, run-down cars for small financial outlays, doing them up and selling them at a good profit. His car at that time was an elegant Jaguar, a far more imposing vehicle than the rather crummy little staff car provided by the War Department for CO 1 PARA. Thus, early in my tour of command, Garroway and I came to the sensible arrangement that if I had to go on duty to a place where first impressions were important, he drove me in his Jaguar, I paid for the petrol and the staff car remained unused. This tactic was especially fruitful when visiting the Ministry of Defence; the police found without delay a space for us in the Horse Guards car park, men took their hats off and sentries saluted. And, I like to think, the standing of The Regiment was raised a notch.

The majority of the Battalion had recently returned home from Cyprus where their service in the United Nations Force had earned them a special medal. By holding a series of 'investitures' at which I handed out the medals, I was able to meet every Officer and Man in the space of a few days, question them briefly and get the 'feel' of the unit. Two questions in particular I wanted their views on. Firstly, how would they view another tour of duty in Bahrain if we were sent back there? Secondly, would they prefer to stay in Cove for the few weeks before we went overseas again or accept the upheaval and fuss of moving for a brief spell into the new barracks in Aldershot, Montgomery Lines, which were nearing completion? Their replies were convincing. To move from Cove would be an upheaval, but with winter coming on they would much rather be housed within walking distance of Aldershot than remain in the outfields of Farnborough at the mercy of an unreliable bus service. Such a move for a short period of occupation would give my excellent Quartermaster, Charles Storey, an Arnhem veteran, and his staff much extra work but they accepted the inconvenience, and having moved everyone smoothly into Normandy Barracks we held a short service on 30 November on the square to bless the buildings and us their occupants. That date I chose expressly for it was St Andrew's Day; also the 90th birthday of Sir Winston Churchill whose inspiration in 1940 had called for the Raising of our Airborne Forces.

The Soldiers' answers to my other question pleased me. Few grumbled about the prospect of leaving England again; many said they were positively looking forward to the chance to save some money out there, to get away from the garrison atmosphere of Aldershot, and to get back into the sunshine. Their chief anxiety was that they would get bored, with not enough to do and much time, valuable in their young lives, being frittered away to little purpose. This fear entirely matched my memories of my own tour in Bahrain; and I decided that if we had to go back to Hamala Camp, 1 PARA would work English hours, 8am to 5pm, irrespective of the climate – for the day's activities could be tailored sensibly to take account of the perils of heat exhaustion and heat stroke; also that each man would be given, long before we left Aldershot, a list of thirty-two activities, hobbies and pastimes from which he could choose and which we would do our best to lay on for him. In the event this worked pretty well and was appreciated. My own contribution was to teach French and German to a small group of beginners.

But all this was for the future. My days between assuming command and the opening of 1965 were kept fully busy; varied and interesting. And for Rosemary also, for apart from an increase in the tempo of entertainment – giving and receiving – she had the business of looking after our two sprogs under the daily instruction of Miss Seed, getting to know the Battalion's wives and keeping our quarter, Blenheim House, reasonably welcoming and warm for ourselves and our many visitors. This was not easy for the building was old and rambling. Built many years before, and designed for a large domestic staff, it had in the Second World War housed a wing of the Camberley Staff College. Living in it in 1964 the four Grahams, with no living-in staff, felt distinctly lost. Pointing the children past the kitchen and the various pantries and larders, we used to say to them: 'Be good now and go down that corridor to play; but do be certain to make your way back by the end of the week'. The house was also exceedingly ill-equipped to keep out the cold, and by November the winter had arrived with a bite. The windows did not fit properly, draughts abounded and, apart from the gas water-heater in the bathroom and a solitary radiator in our bedroom, the only way to keep the building warm was to light coal fires in the open grates. This was not practicable and so the four of us in the really cold weather used to hibernate under the blankets in our double bed; and for entertainment mounted the black-and-white television set on a table at the foot of the bed.

During that bitter winter the BBC produced an excellent series, lasting many weeks, about The Great War. It was a document of unique historical importance and being keen on military history, I was also keen that my young Officers should, if possible, watch the programme and thus learn something about that tragic conflict. When 'The Battle of the Somme' was being shown, the weather turned especially cold, and so Rosemary, Ted Loden and Birdie Martin (two of the subalterns) and I lay on our large bed with eiderdowns up to our chins. In some regiments, I know, young Officers were from time to time found in bed with their CO's wife; but only in 1 PARA was the CO himself in the bed too! Blenheim House and all those like it were pulled down in the Aldershot Rebuild of the late 1960s and 1970s. But the grounds were extensive, good for the children and our rabbits, and we have happy memories of our months in that spacious residence.

In the General Election held in October the Conservatives led by Sir Alec Douglas-Home were defeated by Harold Wilson's Labour Party; but narrowly for Labour had a majority in the House of only four votes. Ten days later the newly appointed Minister of Defence (Army), Mr Frederick Mulley, was brought to see 1 PARA in our Guillemont Camp. A former Sergeant in the Worcestershire Regiment, he was taken prisoner in 1940, and during his five years in German hands he studied economics and qualified as a Chartered Secretary, becoming a barrister in 1954. I took him into my office for a short briefing, a light-hearted session in which he showed himself to be relaxed and charming, with no pretensions to knowing the answers to the Army's problems but interested in everything and genuinely seeking knowledge. I then took him to meet as many of the soldiers as time allowed. He stayed an hour longer than planned, we parted very amicably and the next day I received from him a very nice letter.

Fred Mulley, rather unfairly, will be remembered by my generation of Servicemen for falling fast asleep beside the Queen when, as Minister of Defence, he accompanied her to Germany for the Rhine Army Silver Jubilee Review. The poor chap was exhausted, but the photographers mercilessly captured him slumped in his chair on the royal dais, out for the count.

Throughout my long association with the British Army, the general attitude of the Officer caste towards Labour politicians was one of disrespect. It was believed that Socialists when in office neglected the Armed Forces, undermined discipline and tried to interfere with our traditional ways of life and operating. It was rare to meet an Officer who gave ungrudging credit to our Labour Ministers. I have never forgotten the day when Clement Attlee, that shrewd, quiet and effective Prime Minister, appointed in 1947 as War Minister Emanuel Shinwell. Member for Seaham, a Jew and rumoured to have been imprisoned during the Great War for refusing to serve, Shinwell's arrival at the War Office was marked by universal tooth-sucking, dire predictions, and from the other two Services caustic comments and considerable sympathy. The newspaper cartoonists of that era had a field day. Shinwell went on to be Minister of Defence in the early fifties and, long before his death at a great age, was recognised as having been perhaps the best politician the Services had had at their head in this century. Montgomery, Chief of the Imperial General Staff at the time and no admirer of the political world, thought very highly of Shinwell. To name but four, Denis Healey and Margaret Thatcher protected the interests of our Servicemen and Women very well; James Callaghan and Tom King less so. There was not much to choose between their policies which were in truth based more on the financial imperatives of the time than on Party dogma.

Soon after taking over command I had the whole battalion assembled to give them a chance to see me and for me to put a number of points across to them, the principal ones being:

1. My insistence on professional efficiency at all levels, and on good behaviour especially when in the public eye.
2. Family spirit; try to be good soldiers but also better citizens, husbands and fathers too.
3. Pride in team work and in achieving the highest standards in everything.
4. We would, I knew, have to overcome a situation into which the Army, and 16 PARA Brigade especially, had been pushed trying to do too much

in a short time-frame, inadequately prepared, and with too little stability at most levels of command. We must get away from the practice of doing things off the cuff. For, I emphasised, cuffmanship in peacetime works OK because our Soldiers seldom let the side down and achieve results superior to those in other units. But cuffmanship on the battlefield will endanger us all. Thus all of us in the Battalion Group were to set about honing our professional skills and military knowledge to a fine edge. And we had a year ahead of us in the Persian Gulf to do all these things.

(I was able to make that last statement as it had just been confirmed that we were to return to Bahrain in early March, in five months' time, but accompanied by eighty-eight families; double the number that 2 PARA Group had taken.) Although it is jumping ahead in this narrative, I can truly state that these rather ambitious aims were realised. Every single chap in the large 1 PARA Group whom I took to the Persian Gulf worked hard, played hard and made the most of that year. As a result 1965 was for me personally a true *annus mirabilis*; and from what many of my comrades have told me since, it was for them also a year of rare achievement and unit pride.

For many years the Records of all our Soldiers had been maintained, along with those of certain other regiments, at Exeter, and every six months a conference was held for the Regimental and Battalion commanders and the Records Office Staff to plan the promotions, postings and other steps up the military ladder important to the development of the soldier's career and for the flow of qualified leaders between the three regular battalions, the TA units and the Depot. No one liked the turbulence within units which these cross-postings caused, but they were unavoidable in those days when an Officer or NCO expected to change jobs every eighteen months to two years. For the young Officer the turbulence was worst. Between leaving Sandhurst and getting promoted to captain (at about 28 years of age), he had to fit in at least a year in command of a rifle platoon, junior staff courses, a spell as an ADC or some such mind-broadening experience, a parachute course, maybe a language course, a spell in charge of a specialist platoon (signals, mortar, anti-tank, etc.), having first completed the relevant course at the Army School, and also completed a spell teaching recruits at the Regimental Depot. This schedule of steps up the first rungs of his career ladder limited the depth of knowledge a subaltern could absorb on each rung and was bewildering to the young Soldiers whose platoon Officers arrived and all too soon departed. The harm done to the unit was however lessened by the Warrant Officers and senior NCOs who stayed longer and constituted a stabilising influence in the ranks.

I got back to Aldershot from Exeter to find that the Brigade Commander had spent most of the day at the Ministry of Defence and wanted to see me without delay. There were rumours about some contingency plan for Africa, for the Sudan had been in the news, but it was on the Congo that our attention was now fixed. The situation was that rebels had seized and were holding hostage about a thousand whites whom they threatened to massacre if the Congolese government forces attacked. A plan being worked out was for my 1 PARA, reinforced by an RHA battery and accompanied by a skeleton staff from Para Brigade HQ, to fly to Leopoldville and from there carry out a parachute assault onto Stanleyville to rescue the hostages. Few of us believed that our operation would come off; it was going to take the RAF six days to get us all into Leopoldville, whereas the Belgian Paras could be there within thirty-six hours. Nevertheless planning and briefing went on continuously throughout the weekend until being officially cancelled on 17 November, our eighth wedding anniversary.

Instead of fighting in central Africa, 1 PARA was given the task of finding the ceremonial guard on Windsor Castle thereby relieving The Household Troops who needed to get away for a couple of weeks' field training. This duty was a prestigious one, and for the Regiment a novel commitment calling for faultless turn-out, arms drill and bearing under the eyes of the daily legion of tourists and critical Britons. As the Parachute Soldier was not issued with the standard Army greatcoat, the first thing we had to do was draw a greatcoat for each man, get it tailored to fit him and replace the buttons with those of The Regiment. And the Officers and Soldiers had to master the special drills and procedures long practised by The Household Brigade. The whole thing went off well and the troops' hard work and their determination to at least match the traditional high standards of The Foot Guards earned the Battalion many compliments and me an enjoyable hour with the Governor of the Castle, Field Marshal Lord Slim, rated by many as the most outstanding British General of the 1939-45 war, and Father of John Slim, my colleague in the 91st Highlanders.

At the beginning of December my new Adjutant arrived. I had seen a lot of James Emson out in Bahrain, for as ADC to the GOC, Middle East Land Forces he used to accompany General John Cubbon on his tours of the area. James had charm, great energy, an engaging sense of fun and seemed to be blessed by Fortune. Whenever horse-racing or roulette was set up in the Mess, Emson walked away with the prizes; girls liked him, the 'Toms' thought the world of him, he was a popular Mess member, and he had a nice streak of irreverence, being a gentle deflater of the pompous. RHQ had given me the choice as Adjutant of Emson or another chap, more orthodox in outlook and cleverer in intellect, but I saw in James the personality we needed to get us efficiently but happily through another year in the Gulf.

Commanding 1 Para

A year or so later James injured his feet and had to leave The Regiment, but he got picked up by The Life Guards whom he went on to command before ending up as Assistant Commandant at Sandhurst in the rank of Brigadier.

Another charmer and a soldier of unusual promise was James's close friend, Colin Thomson. He was my Battalion Intelligence Officer, later commanded 2 PARA who suffered grievously from a road-side bomb in Northern Ireland, soon after which Colin died of cancer. The Good, it is said, die young; the Excellent alas seem to die even younger.

Four days after settling into our new barracks we set off on a memorable exercise (CROSS MED) in North Africa. On parade in the pitch dark at 3 am, we were taken by bus to Lyneham where we emplaned in Britannia aircraft arriving in Malta four hours later. When the Battalion, our affiliated Gunner Battery, Mercer's Troop of 7th Parachute RHA commanded by David Archibald, and the Umpire and Control organisation had all assembled, we prepared for our insertion by night into the Libyan hinterland. Colin Thomson and his section had made a couple of excellent map enlargements off which I briefed all the Officers and NCOs down to Lance Corporal level. This was unusual, but my experience in the war and afterwards had taught me that it pays to put all Leaders, irrespective of rank, into 'the same picture'. Corporals do find themselves suddenly filling a Captain's shoes. The GOC Malta and Libya, General Johnny Frost, came to see us. A former Cameronian, he had commanded C Company 2 PARA on their famous Bruneval raid in February 1942, led the battalion on a long, testing withdrawal through enemy lines in North Africa, and at Arnhem in September 1944, still in command of 2 PARA, reached and held one end of the great bridge over the Rhine against strong German armoured forces. John Frost and Alastair Pearson were the most famous of the Regiment's galaxy of wartime heroes. John Dutton Frost died in 1993 after a long illness. The Aldershot Royal Garrison Church was packed to overflowing for the Service of Thanksgiving for his Life, and the Address by the Burgomaster of Arnhem, Mr Paul Scholten, was composed with the most elegant of phrases and delivered in flawless English. A fine and fitting tribute and, we asked ourselves, how many of us could have given such an address in a foreign tongue?

Another senior chap who came to see us off was Sir Kenneth Cross, the AOC-in-C of the RAF's Transport Command. It was clear that his airmen were going to give us their best shot, to atone perhaps for their poor showing on recent parachute exercises in the UK. At sunset we moved off in a long convoy to Luqa airfield and emplaned in the assembled Hastings, Argosy and Beverley aircraft. I flew in the leading Hastings, and after a smooth two-hour flight, we were despatched into total darkness and, suspended from PX 1 parachutes, recently introduced to replace the smaller, wartime X-type, descended rapidly onto the hard, dry soil of the Libyan jebel to the south of Tripoli. When the Battalion had rallied at the sub-unit RVs I found that out of six company commanders, four had become casualties in the drop. In all we suffered thirty-five injured, including Brigadier Roly Gibbs, but none was seriously hurt. Nevertheless it led to a certain amount of correspondence in the British press. This was not unwelcome as it strengthened the Army's case for the retention of Parachute Pay in the annual squabbling with the Treasury. The bitter cold dark night gave way to a clear bright morning and the exercise got off to a good start. And so it continued; everything went with a swing. The Battalion Group earned good marks from the Umpires and I was pleased with what I found in my new 'family'. The temporary removal to hospital of the four company commanders meant that command devolved suddenly onto the shoulders of much younger Officers who seized the opportunity to show what they were made of, and that gave added zest to 1 PARA's performance during those seven days and nights on that jebel plateau 800 metres above sea-level.

In the field, as part of David Archibald's Battery, was an American artillery captain, Carl Vuono, the US Exchange Officer with 16 Para Brigade. Thirty years later he was back in England for a reunion with his 7 RHA friends, unchanged in looks or manner but now Chief of Staff of the United States Army.

After a long drive down to the coast via Gasr Garian and Kassala we cleaned ourselves up and slept for hours at the HQ Tripoli Mess, and eventually straggled back to a fog-bound Lyneham in time for Christmas with our families. While I had been away Rosemary had spent a lot of time getting to know the Soldiers' wives, shipping our heavy baggage off to Bahrain, and helping Didi to get over measles.

Rosemary and I saw in the New Year at Hermitage, the Royal Engineer Survey School, where Dick Scott was an Instructor. He and his attractive wife, Jill, were to become two of our closest friends. We drove home at 5am on icy roads, but the day turned out cold and clear, an ideal start to 1965. I was relieved to find the electricity bill for our rambling Blenheim House was only £13 for the past quarter; less than I had expected and due perhaps to my vigorous campaign of switching off the lights when not essential; a discipline which I enforced on my long-suffering family and our house-guests.

The command of 2 PARA was now in the hands of Ted Eberhardie, Neale G-W having gone off to a Staff appointment. Ted had made a great name for himself as a company commander and was to end up as a Major-General at SHAPE. His introduction to life as a CO was memorable. 2 PARA was away on Christmas-New Year leave. On 31 December the whole unit was recalled to Aldershot by telegrams containing the single code-word 'Bruneval', and on 2 January without a single absentee 2 PARA started to fly out to Malaya, for a six-month emergency tour as part of the measures being taken to counter the threat from Indonesia. While there was no certainty yet of a major Indonesian assault on the Malayan mainland, this and other British and Australian moves were being taken to deter President Soekarno from an act of international folly of which he was thought quite capable. While the Commonwealth forces in the Far East were being thus strengthened the whole situation in that theatre was becoming graver. As *The Sunday Times* reported: 'South Vietnamese forces were said to have recently suffered heavily at the hands of the Vietcong guerillas. Behind it all looms Communist China which, US experts are forecasting, will be able to launch short-range nuclear missiles within five years. The US is expected to build up a fleet of six or eight Polaris-carrying submarines in the Pacific to counter the Chinese threat. And in India the Government's mass-arrest of pro-Peking Communists appears to have nipped in the bud a Chinese attempt to undermine Indian morale in advance of a renewal of military pressure in the north'. The swift and impressive performance by Ted and 2 PARA got a lot of TV and Press publicity, and we wished that 1 PARA rather than they were going out East, but given the current state of the world we knew that we would be granted only a brief respite before some other new crisis blew up.

Just before the end of my own leave Rosemary and I went up to Cheyne Court for an excellent family reunion and dinner. We knew it was to be, for us with Bahrain again on the immediate horizon, a farewell occasion, but at the back of all our minds was the prediction made to Jane, born in 1900, by an Indian soothsayer in Naini Tal that she was to die at the age of 65. Her early demise seemed unlikely for she was fit, active and happy; living comfortably after grim years of financial struggle and marital disappointment. (She was in fact to live into her 88th year.)

In mid-January the Battalion and I were put through one of the principal yearly tests; the Annual Administrative Inspection, to be carried out by our Brigade Commander Roly Gibbs[1] and his Staff. Because the format of such tests was to change towards the end of the century, I record here for the possible interest of future generations of soldiers some of my recollections of that event. The Battalion at all levels had been preparing hard for the Brigadier's visit, and shortly before the Great Day I carried out my own 'pre-admin' inspection. I started with Headquarter Company at 0915 hours. By 1215 I was so angered by the lack of administrative grip and what the Army termed sound 'Interior Economy' that I gave the company commander until the evening to get matters put right. At 6 pm I returned and went on until nine-thirty. The Men were in good heart and rather amused, but the poor Major, his Officers and the senior NCOs were distinctly boot-faced. I had determined that as Administration was disdained by the typical 'gung-ho' Parachute Officer I would try to reverse this trend; not only for my own peace of mind but chiefly because it involved Public Money. I had long since learned that in peacetime the cruellest snares lying in the path of an unwary Commanding Officer were the loss of weapons and ammunition, misuse of public monies and stores, and (to a lesser extent) sexual misconduct.

Two days later Brigadier Gibbs and his team arrived. I really enjoyed the morning and was confident that no real horrors would be revealed. The skeletons in our battalion closet – surplus kit, broken items and things we did not want disclosed – we locked up in the darkness of the Miniature Shooting Range. The companies were all put through their paces in different Orders of Dress; PT kit, Drill Order, Battle Order and so on. It was a good opportunity too for Brigadier Roly to look closely at the fittings in our newly built barracks. Although the concept was good and the Soldiers were happy, the space was cramped, the drainage and ventilation were poor, there was too much glass (easily broken, dangerous and expensive to replace), and the workmanship was generally inferior in quality. Many of the married Soldiers' quarters also suffered from the same hasty construction and false economies in the materials used. At 1230 we all went off to the Dining Hall for the Troops' belated Christmas Dinner. The Band played; Private Lee, a splendidly bewhiskered armourer, proposed Roly's health, the Officers and Sergeants served, as is traditional, the food to the Men and everyone was in excellent form. The Brigadier was pleased, said some nice things about the Battalion and gave the Toms a half-holiday. It was a good day.

On 24 January I wrote in my diary: 'At 8 am this morning the greatest heart in England ceased to beat, and a great sadness has fallen on the land. After being in a coma for a week Sir Winston Churchill died to-day at his London home, 28 Hyde Park Gate.' The television and newspapers of the next days reminded us of his unique greatness and the remarkable course of his life which had run from 30 November 1874 to 24 January 1965; spanning the reigns of six Monarchs (Victoria, Edward VII, George V, Edward VIII, George VI and Elizabeth II). It was a privilege to have lived under his leadership and to have learned from his books so much about the events he witnessed or shaped. 'Of the war-time Greats,' I wrote, 'only de Gaulle remains!'

The day of Winston's funeral dawned dry but very cold. I got up at 5 am to see our Detachment of Colour Party, four Officers and 120 soldiers leave by coach for London and the State Funeral. They had to line part of the route in the area of Blackfriars' Bridge and had spent three days rehearsing in the snow. The rest of us watched the ceremonies and the Service in St Paul's Cathedral on TV; the family and I as usual in our bedroom in Blenheim House. The whole thing was admirably planned and carried out. My cousin John James Graham (the 17th Laird of Fintry) who was a Major in the Queen's Royal Irish Hussars, recently amalgamated with Churchill's old Regiment the 4th Hussars, carried Winston's Cinque Ports Banner in the procession. The most touching of all the tributes paid to him was the long line of cranes on the South Bank lowering their jibs in salute as the coffin of the Great Man was borne upstream to Waterloo Station and thence to his final resting-place in the churchyard of the Oxfordshire village of Bladon. The Parachute Brigade held our own Memorial Service the next day in the Royal Garrison Church.

A few days later General John Nelson, the GOC of London District who had commanded 1 PARA in Palestine, came to lunch with us in Aldershot. He naturally had had much to do with the arrangements for the State Funeral for which, he said, the planning file had been opened fifteen years earlier and in which Churchill took a close interest, adding many notes and instructions in his own hand. The Bearer Party found by 2nd Battalion The Grenadier Guards had to carry the coffin which weighed 10 cwt down and up steps, to and from the river-launch and then onto the train. It was a stiff test of stamina and devotion, but they did it faultlessly throughout and had refused at the outset to share the task with a relief party. My troops had already told me that the administrative arrangements for everyone taking part in the Procession and the Route Lining had been excellent.

The next evening I dined with the Chaplain-General, Ivor Neill, and the resident Padres over in Bagshot Park, a fine house given by Queen Victoria to the Duke of Connaught on his marriage, and later the Home of the Royal Army Chaplains' Department. I was shown some fine Indian carvings done by students in a school in Lahore run by Rudyard Kipling's father, and the Padres' excellent museum. I was amused when at the end of the dinner the Chaplain-General proposed the Queen's health himself, whereas in our Infantry Messes the PMC first tells the Vice-President to propose the toast. 'But we are Padres, we like to believe we have no vices so we dispense with a Vice-President in our Mess,' Ivor explained to me.

As the date of our departure for Bahrain approached, the social whirl increased in tempo; we gave and went to a succession of farewell parties and dances. We Officers gave a champagne party and supper for two hundred people in the Mess which was much enjoyed, especially as the whole expense was met from accumulated funds. The Dance Band and the Mess Staff under the direction of the good Colour-Sergeant Thorne did well, and the dancing went on until 3am. Rosemary looked super, but I thought that the girls invited by some of my subalterns were distinctly tartish; and the next day I said so. Later in the week the Warrant Officers and Sergeants gave a Ball in our new gymnasium, really excellently done in every respect with many guests from the local civic and Army community, including our own subalterns whose partners that evening were exceptionally attractive and a pronounced cut above those they'd brought to our own Mess party.

During the same month General Sir Gerald Lathbury, who was going off to be the Governor of Gibraltar, handed over the appointment of Colonel Commandant of the Regiment to someone whom I had got to know and admire out in Cyprus during the EOKA campaign, General Sir Kenneth Darling. Ken Darling was also the Colonel of the Royal Fusiliers whose First Battalion is given each year from long-established regimental funds the useful sum of £1,500. He was surprised when I told him that we could expect nothing from our RHQ for The Parachute Regiment had only been in existence for twenty years. Money was again a worry for Rosemary and me also as the Bank Manager had written about the rising overdraft. Although I was drawing £200 per month as a Lieutenant-Colonel, the standing orders, garage bills and household and entertainment expenses seemed to eat it up long before the months ended: and we still had no school fees to pay. Perhaps I could have cut down a bit; I had made a practice of giving to each of the 1 PARA sports teams a bottle of champagne every time they won a major competition, the theory being that when they lost they would give me a bottle. But they hardly ever lost! Our Cross-Country team won the Army Championship again – for the fifth time in a row – thanks to the experience and dedication of Colour-Sergeant Gordon Burt who ran a hundred miles every week to keep in training; we beat the Irish Guards at boxing, but just lost in the finals to The King's Regiment, whose team included several coloured chaps, which was quite a novelty in that era and caused that regiment to be referred to as The King's African Regiment. I forgot to claim my champagne too after that nail-biting contest!

In our spare time Rosemary, the children and I set off to say goodbye to various relations and friends: the Macphersons and Willeys and our village friends in South Stoke, Jane and the Brothers in London, John and Betty Hewitt in Limpsfield (he was the Appointments Secretary to the Prime Minister), dear Elspeth Graham in her new flat in lovely Bath, and Neil and Mirren Campbell-Baldwin, friends from Husum and Guiana. Somehow we managed to fit into this busy schedule enough time for packing up all our things for removal into storage and for handing the quarter back to the Barrack Office. Moving was always hell; tiring and expensive, and unsettling for the kids too, but the Garroways and Mrs Jefferies, our 'daily', could not have been more helpful and kind. We were sad to part from them. David and Margaret O'Morchoe put us up for our last two nights in England in their Wakefords Copse quarter. The O'Morchoe (an Irish title, pronounced O'Mara), was the senior administrative Staff Officer at Brigade HQ and after commanding the Parachute Brigade went on to command the Sultan's Armed Forces six years after I had left Oman. He and his wife retired to his estate in southern Ireland but did not have a peaceful life, for his links with the British Army condemned him in the eyes of the Irish Republicans and during the long years of unrest in Ulster David and Margaret had to put up with harassment and anxiety.

I managed to get Rosemary, Pinks and Didi and all the baggage into the staff car and into Normandy Barracks on time despite the foot of snow on the ground. David O'Morchoe and the Brigade Major, David Alexander, saw us off; us being seventy-nine men, including the Adjutant, James Emson and RSM Cole, eight wives and sixteen assorted children, heading for Gatwick Airport in three unheated buses. The events of the next three days did not bring credit to the Service Movements Organisation. We were scheduled to fly in Britannia aircraft of BUA (British United Airways); BUA alas was in the middle of a labour dispute over pay, and to keep the planes operating the managerial staff were doing all the work on the ground such as booking in passengers and supervising the catering. This was regarded as strike-breaking by trade unions who declared BUA to be 'black' – ostracised, excommunicated. This meant that instead of taking off at 3pm we did not get airborne until six. Shortly after take-off the aircraft flew into a flock of birds and lost the use of one engine so after jettisoning fuel over the Channel we landed back in England, at Heathrow Airport. Because BUA was 'black', the workers there would not handle either the baggage or us passengers. We were stranded in a remote corner of a hostile airfield on a bitterly cold and pitch-dark night. The wives and kids in my party were by now tired and hungry. RSM Cole and I went off in search of any helpful official who happened to be around, while James Emson got a party of our soldiers together, marched out to the empty plane and somehow got all our baggage out of the hold. We managed to locate a switched-on Royal Navy Petty Officer who eventually procured some buses into which we piled, with our baggage, and driven with bad grace by members of the Transport and General Workers' Union we arrived at the Services' Transit Centre at Hendon. This establishment was run by the RAF who gave us some poor food, scruffily served by a thoroughly unimpressive staff. There was no running water so we all had to wash in the fire buckets; the water-heating system had been out of action, I was told, for several weeks. However we slept well. The next afternoon we were driven, in different buses, to the excellent Route Hotel at RAF Station Lyneham in Wiltshire where we had first-rate food, rooms and bags of hot water, and where the long-suffering wives and kids recovered from their experiences at Gatwick, Heathrow and Hendon. Sleep was cut short though as we had to get up at 4am for a take-off at dawn in a Britannia of RAF Transport Command. We landed at RAF Akrotiri in Cyprus in time for lunch in the bright warm sunshine of early March, waited on by fit, bronzed airmen. Morale soared as memories of snow-covered, strike-ridden England were replaced by the anticipation of sea, sun, sand and servants in Bahrain. But contentment was premature. While we were at lunch mechanics found that a propellor shaft on our plane had a fault. To repair it a torque-wrench was required for the loosening of certain nuts. The wrenches at RAF Akrotiri were unserviceable that day, an embarrassed Engineer Officer told me, and we were obliged to hang around in Cyprus until a fresh wrench was flown in from elsewhere. But our saga did not end then, for when the fault had been repaired, some of the vital nuts could not be found. In due course fresh nuts were obtained and, after several strained sessions with the RAF ground staff, I got my 102 fellow-travellers back into the plane and we took off at 10pm. By this time we were all tired, hungry and very vexed. John Weeks, the RSM, and I did what we could to amuse the children while the mothers got a bit of rest.

We arrived in Bahrain at 4 o'clock in the morning to be greeted by a little RAF Movements Officer who bounded up the steps with the words, 'Good afternoon and welcome to Muharraq!' Our flight had taken 61½ hours instead of the planned fourteen. We had not been the only persons inconvenienced: our waiting friends in 3 PARA had been mucked about also by our erratic journey. But they were at Muharraq to meet us, with their courteous and thoughtful Commanding Officer, Tony Farrar-Hockley,[2] first in the Reception Line. He could not have been kinder, for he then guided us to our new quarter, Churchill House in the Jufair district, where he had stocked up the larder, fridge and bar for our arrival; and that evening after some hand-over chat he took Rosemary, James Emson and me out for a meal in the Airport Hotel. We were back again in the Regimental Family: it was a great feeling.

Only a few days after our relief of 3 PARA had been completed, troubles broke out in Bahrain. Crowds of young men gathered in Manama and Muharraq, stoning shops and houses and burning cars, while a strike by the BAPCO oil workers continued into its fifth day. There was a lot of intimidation of shopkeepers and taxi drivers, and the normal life of the islanders was disrupted for a week. The State Police did well and contained the situation, shooting four rioters, and we were not called on to intervene. Nevertheless I had to move Ric Oddie's A Company to Jufair and set up my own tactical HQ beside him in case the police lost control. It was a useful exercise for the Battalion Group and its timing was perfect, as only the previous week I had assembled every Officer and Soldier in the Hamala Camp cinema and briefed them in detail about the local situation and the Internal Security procedures we were to adopt, and got the sub-units to brush up their IS drills. Our families in their Manama hirings were the most affected; all had to stay indoors for several days and some had their windows broken. But the demonstrations did not seem to be anti-British, though if we had been deployed overtly in support of the police, they would undoubtedly have turned that way, for behind this unrest the hand of the Egyptian President Nasser could be felt and his portrait and slogans were flourished by the demonstrators. The whole outbreak had been planned, we were told, several weeks earlier at an

Arab Nationalist meeting in Kuwait, and some of the arrested leaders of the Bahraini crowds turned out to be Egyptian school-teachers. The Ruler, Sheikh Isa, got a bit of a shock and some accused him of weakness when he pardoned a number of the trouble-makers his police had picked up; but he was, I still believe, wholly right in the way he handled this minor crisis, for there was no repeat of the troubles until long after we had quitted the island.

But although this storm in the Bahraini tea-cup was quickly calmed, the situation in Aden and in its hinterland was deteriorating. Terrorist activity in Aden town and guerilla fighting in the mountainous area between Aden and the Yemeni frontier were on the increase, backed by Egyptian and Algerian money, arms, training and propaganda. This was orchestrated by Arab Nationalists with the aim of forcing the British government to speed up the granting of independence to the area, thereby creating a power vacuum which Nasser was to fill. Thus the focus of military attention soon swung away from Bahrain and Kuwait and onto Aden where it was to remain until November 1967 when Britain pulled out of the place. The consequences for 1 PARA Group were stimulating, for during the rest of our year in the Gulf I was called on to keep one company group down in Aden. Each rifle company did two tours down there, the first month up-country near the Yemeni frontier engaged in anti-guerilla operations, and the second month down in Aden in the anti-terrorist role. In the spring of 1965 I also had to send a platoon to protect the RAF Station at Salalah in the southern Omani province of Dhofar where a tribal rebellion against the repressive rule of the Sultan, Said bin Taimur, had flared up. This fledgling revolt in fact posed no threat then to the RAF base, but badly handled by the Sultan and sustained by communist forces in South Arabia, China and the USSR, the Dhofar rebellion developed into a minor war which was to last ten years and in which British forces were to become closely and effectively involved. Little did I realise, when I visited my platoon in Salalah in June 1965, that that small town on the edge of the Indian Ocean, and the whole province of which it was the capital, would play a most memorable part in my own professional life.

The report written by Major Richard Dawnay when he returned to Bahrain with his D Company describes well the experiences which each company group enjoyed during their spell in the Western Aden Protectorate. He wrote: 'Looking fit, bronzed and on average weighing seven pounds lighter, we got back to the Battalion after a month under active service conditions. My Group which included a section each of mortars and machine guns and a troop from Mercer's [Battery] arrived in Aden on 3rd April and moved upcountry to the airstrip at Ath Thumayr where we spent ten days under command of 2nd Battalion Coldstream Guards. This period was most useful for acclimatisation and getting the feel of the area. Picquets were manned on the high ground dominating the airstrip and patrols and ambushing parties were sent out nightly, the guns and mortars having ranged each afternoon onto their night DF [defensive fire] tasks. On 12th April we relieved a company of the Coldstream at the village of Ad Dimnah, right up at the "sharp end" about five miles from Dhala, and close to the Yemeni border. Ad Dimnah is perched on the sides and top of a steep hill overlooking a vital stretch of the Aden-Dhala road which we had by constant patrolling to keep open and free of mines. As Ad Dimnah village seemed to be built on camel dung accumulated over centuries, the smells were overpowering but we got used to them and contributed a few of our own. We turned the place into a defensive stronghold with sangars, wire and grenade necklaces for it had previously been attacked on several occasions by dissidents armed with mortars, rocket launchers and small arms. We were attacked three times, on each occasion after dark, fortunately suffering only three minor casualties. We learned a great deal during our month in the WAP and are keen to return there.' Richard Dawnay's company was relieved in May by Norrie Giles' C Company. They were also attacked on several occasions during one of which Private HR Alexander was killed.

Major Ric Oddie's A Company had a most active six weeks in that Radfan area during August and early September. Ric and his Company Headquarters party were blown up by a mine while returning from a patrol north of Dhala, eight chaps being injured, though none seriously, even though their convoy came under fire after the explosion. The victims wrote an account of their experiences, an account valuable because of the points it highlighted. The mine was a British Mark VII anti-tank mine, one of many acquired by the dissidents from friends in countries traditionally armed by the UK. It was a powerful weapon. The reason why so few serious injuries occurred was that the floor of the lorry had been covered by a thick layer of sandbags; furthermore the sand in them had been sodden by a recent rain storm. A hazard just as significant as the blast of the detonation was 'the shower of equipment, weapons, stores, etc. which descended around the victims, having been blown out of their hands or from the vehicle to a considerable height.'

Ric Oddie's company had another, sadder, incident in late August. The Company Group had left Dhala at first light to march to Habilayn, a distance of about fifteen miles as the crow flies but across rocky, bare, mountainous terrain; they moved widely dispersed, anticipating opposition, deployed tactically and avoiding low ground. As the rear-most platoon was moving along a track high up the face of a deep wadi [valley or canyon], a single shot was fired from the other side at a range of 600–700 yards with a stiff wind blowing. The bullet struck Private Robert Gray in the back of his head, emerged near his right eye and subsequently lodged in the back of the soldier a few yards in front of him. Gray died almost immediately. Robert Gray was an excellent and popular young man from Ayr. He had insisted on leaving his job in our Officers' Mess in order to accompany his friends in A Company on active service in the Radfan. Like many British soldiers who died doing their duty in that inhospitable but majestic corner of the Arabian Peninsula, Gray was buried in the Silent Valley Military Cemetery in Little Aden. Ric Oddie and his boys got their reward at the end of the year for they had a successful tour of duty in Aden, starting with the capture of two members of a murder gang. As Brigadier Louis Hargroves wrote to me about them: 'they have consistently made their presence felt to the detriment of the opposition and to the delight of the Europeans in Aden'. A Company's early success enabled the Security Forces to have a minor breakthrough and to pick up a quantity of arms, ammunition and wanted people. As a result Aden had a more peaceful Christmas than expected.

While not in the Aden area my various sub-units were able to get around the Gulf on different tasks such as the OMEX patrols in the Jebel Akhdar mountains of Oman, live firing in the Trucial States, and exercising with the navy on Yas Island. Some went farther afield. One of our Doctors, Captain Aitken, led a climbing expedition to Kenya on which alas Private Parry of the Orderly Room Staff died of pneumonia. An excellent facility for the Forces existed in the Silver Sands Leave Centre run by NAAFI just outside Mombasa to which All Ranks and their families, jaded by the oppressive heat and humidity of the Persian Gulf, could go for two weeks at little cost. Pinky and Christopher had enrolled in a convent school in Bahrain, which did them no harm and gave them also the opportunity to learn swimming, diving and life-saving. Christopher gained his Bronze Survival badge there; no mean feat for a 5-year-old. During the long summer holidays Rosemary and I took them off on the Kenya leave scheme. Flown by the RAF to Aden and thence to Mombasa we had a splendid fortnight at Silver Sands where the first joy was to be able to drink glass after glass of fresh milk, unobtainable at that time in Bahrain. We hired a car and toured the Tsavo Game Park, crossed into Tanzania (where the pre-1918 German influence was still evident), and explored the great Portuguese fort in Mombasa. All this was a gift for my ciné camera and to this day I have a fine record of the places and the animals we saw during our two weeks. But perhaps the most surprising thing was the cost: rather less than one hundred pounds for the whole expedition.

Being keen on military history and the marking of the anniversaries of great events in our nation's past, I made sure that Waterloo Day (18 June 1815) was fittingly celebrated at Hamala Camp; especially important as our G Battery RHA had played a notable part in the battle as the Troop commanded by Captain Mercer. As the account printed by David Archibald on this the 150th anniversary of the battle described: 'When the fighting was over, of two hundred horses, one hundred and forty were dead or dying and the Gunners who were left were so exhausted they could not work the guns but threw themselves down in the wet and blood-stained mud beside the carriages'. 18 June 1965 was celebrated by 1 PARA Group with a church service, a carnival and a dance; and to the lecture which I got David Archibald to give to All Ranks in the Awali Cinema, borrowed from BAPCO, I in time added four more military history productions: Gallipoli, Crete, the Battle of Britain and Arnhem. Captain Michael Benjamin helped me with the research and by getting the large maps made; Ghulam Hassan and his tailors ran up proper uniforms as required by the actors, and the Soldiers (whose attendance was obligatory) appreciated this, to them, novel form of education.

All this engendered in the Group a wonderful spirit and sense of pride. All manner of big-wigs came to visit us in Hamala Camp; five-star Admirals, Generals, politicians and journalists, British, American and Bahraini. Almost all of them remarked on the morale and zing of the Officers and Men, and I made a point of passing on to All Ranks the gist of what those visitors said or wrote about our unit. This was done in the Part One Orders issued daily or in Special Orders. One of the aspects of our training in 1965 was to identify those soldiers who had the special aptitudes necessary for service with the SAS (Special Air Service Regiment) or in the Special Patrol Companies which were about to be formed by each of the regular parachute battalions. One of these aptitudes was the ability to send and read transmissions in the morse code. To make everyone more familiar with that jumble of dots and dashes I got the Chief Clerk, Warrant Officer Whitfield, to have a portion of each Part One Order printed in that code; sometimes in the form of a simple question to which the first chap to report with the correct answer got a small prize. By such novelties did we keep the interest of the Toms geared up and helped the days to pass quickly and without tedium.

We were proud of ourselves, very fit and keen to show the civilian community in Bahrain more of our separate components and our manifold and varied skills: also to repay in some measure those Bahrainis and expatriates who had gone out of their way to entertain us Officers and our soldiers. Not least the Ruler himself, for Sheikh Isa during our year on his island had by many acts of kindness or generosity demonstrated his interest in our Group's well-being.

When I was in Bahrain with 2 PARA in 1963 I had produced a Military Tattoo which many from the civilian community had enjoyed. In July 1965 Norrie Giles and his C Company got together an excellent Tattoo while stationed at Muharraq, largely for the entertainment of the Royal Air Force. It went down well and I resolved to produce at Hamala later in the year a similar military spectacle but, of course, on a far bigger and more ambitious scale. I chose 15 October as at that time the Regimental

Commanding 1 Para

Free Fall Parachute Team, the Army champions, General Ken Darling, our Colonel Commandant, and my Mother would be in Bahrain. There is no point here in listing the participants and their activities, but I want to mention a few of the aspects of that ambitious production which remain engraved in my memory. Everyone worked hard at their own acts, but when I attended the Dress Rehearsal I was alarmed by the listlessness of the performers and the mundane commentary. I was disheartened and said so. I need not have worried; the public performances in October went off marvellously in every respect. The public address system broke down in the first minutes during the Free Fall display, but a young Signalman on his own initiative traced the fault, cured it and we had no more worry on that score; or on any other. The weather was perfect, the performers did their stuff with skill and verve and the audience of many hundreds was enthralled. The Ruler afterwards sent me thirty-three gold watches with the instruction that I hand them out on his behalf to those who had made the biggest contribution to the evening's success; and very many people wrote letters of warm thanks. I have many of them still and in moments of low morale I re-read them to good effect.

To round off the Tattoo performance we had decided that the guests should be invited to drinks, light food and dancing in the three Messes; and the Officers, Warrant Officers and Sergeants, and the Corporals and Privates had gone to much trouble to decorate their premises and generally give each guest a good time. A problem, however, manifested itself at an early stage in the planning: the separation of sheep and goats – who was to be invited to each of the Messes and by what criteria selected? It was quite clear that most expected to be classed as guests of the Officers' Mess; not many regarded themselves as equals of our Sergeants, and virtually none on a level with the junior NCOs and Privates. Thus when the tickets were sent out steering individuals to the separate Messes to which we had allocated them, there was any amount of toothsucking and pleas (fruitless) for upgrading. But on the night they all seemed to have gone off quite contentedly, following the trails of coloured lights to their separate parties, and wherever they ended up they had a rollicking good time.

Throughout that happy year in Bahrain, Rosemary and I and our 1 PARA Group team were greatly blessed by the friendship and encouragement of our seniors; from the Foreign and Commonwealth Office Sir William Luce, Peter Tripp and Tony Parsons; Captain 'Splash' Carver, a naval aviator whom we had first met at Latimer, and at the head of the Royal Air Force in the Gulf Air Commodore Geoffrey Millington and Group Captain Brian Frow, both of whom were accompanied by uncommonly pretty wives and daughters. My immediate superior, the Brigadier commanding the Land Forces Persian Gulf (CLFPG), was initially the excellent Dick Bryers who was relieved by an equally excellent friend of the Regiment,

Michael Holme. Tall, athletic, relaxed, with a Military Cross, Mike was an experienced Infantryman from the Essex Regiment whom I had first come across as an Instructor at Camberley in 1955. Like Dick and Phyllis Bryers, Mike and Sally Holme were tireless in the hospitality and kindness which they lavished on Rosemary and me; and also on those Officers in 1 PARA who had not been able to bring their wives out to Bahrain. Brigadier Holme's Staff was headed by two Officers who went out of their way to smooth our path, Peter Hamer, the GSO2 from the 11th Hussars, and Donald Hildick-Smith, a Sapper and the senior administrative Officer. I have retained very many happy memories of 1965 and one of the foremost constituents of that period was the remarkable comradeship and two-way loyalty which existed in Bahrain between CLFPG's staff and my own.

Within 1 PARA Group, Mercer's Troop of the Royal Horse Artillery was an outstanding sub-unit. Commanded by David Archibald and his team of exceptional young Officers, the personnel of this battery set the highest standards in everything they did and thus raised the tone in every aspect of our Group's life. It was a pleasure to have such a high-class body of men in my Group, men whose professional gunnery skills were matched by sporting prowess, excellent discipline and impeccable manners under all circumstances.

Our days and nights were very full, for as always in the British peacetime Army we were continuously required to keep a variety of balls in the air simultaneously; operational balls, ceremonial commitments, sporting fixtures, leave rosters, detachments and duties which the other Services were unwilling to do or less capable of carrying out.

One commitment which came our way I had to put onto the plate of poor Richard Dawnay. The Army's scientists decided that they needed to know more about the soldier's anatomy, how it functioned in the heat and humidity of the Gulf, and how it could be made to perform better through more expert planning of its daily food and liquid intake. Dawnay's D Company was therefore banished to a remote part of the island, put under canvas and subjected to a two-week-long regime during which everything that each soldier ate and drank throughout the period was weighed, measured and recorded. Everything that his body produced as waste products was likewise measured and recorded, and his daily physical and mental efficiency was gauged and recorded also. This was an uncongenial exercise for Richard and his fellow guinea-pigs; moreover we were never told whether the data obtained by the scientists turned out to have the slightest practical value to our country's Defence Planners.

The Gulf climate made exceptional demands on the physique of the Soldier who was expected to be able to operate strenuously at any time and in any season, avoiding sunburn, heat stroke and heat exhaustion. These hazards put a particular onus on commanders and staff Officers to ensure that proper preventative training, resupply and medical arrangements were on hand. The first requirement was to teach All Ranks the basic rules for prevention; the second was to see that all new arrivals became properly acclimatised. The first was easily accomplished for it was a matter of discipline and supervision that every man should comply with the rules. The second was less easy for it took two to three weeks for a man out from the UK for the first time to get adapted to the heat and humidity. Newly joined youngsters were, I found, the most vulnerable for they were keen to impress their Leaders and therefore tended to over-work, whereas the older chaps took things at a calmer pace. The young had to be watched and restrained. I noticed too that a man who had already served in the Middle East required only a day or two before he was again fully fit to operate. He not only knew the rules, his anatomy had remained prepared for the climate's demands. It thus became apparent that to fly a unit of Gulf-seasoned troops out from Britain in an emergency should cause through climate-change only a small drop in their fitness to operate on arrival. The principal cause of any drop would more likely be fatigue caused by the turmoil of preparing for the move and by the vexations of being mishandled by an inefficient Movements Organisation.

Water was the key to fitness. Body fluid-loss through sweating was constant and substantial, and it had to be replaced. Adding salt tablets to the contents of the water-bottle helped greatly, but a ready supply of drinking water was vital, and in the heat of a Gulf summer we took as a yardstick, when planning the water resupply for exercises and operations, thirty-three pints per man per day. This was a major challenge for the Quartermasters, Sappers, Logisticians and helicopter crews, but it had to be done. But long discarded were the pith helmets, the cholera belts and the spine pads which soldiers of the pre-1940 Army were compelled to wear out of doors when in the tropics. And gone too was the use of the dreaded 'umbrella' in the treatment of venereal disease.

Visitors took up a lot of our time for they were inevitably steered by Headquarters towards Hamala Camp where we had to brief, feed, bear-lead and generally keep them interested and amused for half a day or more. Actually most of these people were welcome for the Toms enjoyed showing off their skills, the visitors brought news of the world outside the Gulf and inklings of policy changes being mooted in the MoD, and without exception they wrote in appreciative terms about their impressions of 1 PARA Group. Some visitors were unforgettable.

My wife, Rosemary, has never been, thank God, a truly military woman; it took me some months to teach her the difference between a Lieutenant and a Lance-Corporal. This pleasing lacuna in her military awareness, however, got her into a scrape about which we still giggle, though at the time I feared that my career was on her account right up against the buffers; terminated. The circumstances were these. During the autumn of 1965 the Quartermaster-General visited the Army in the Gulf. A most eminent Sapper with a brilliant war record, he was a member of the Army Board; important, influential and a real military heavy-weight. General Sir Charles Richardson was a self-made man, rather shy and exceptionally taciturn. Rosemary and I met him at various parties laid on for him in Bahrain and found conversation with him fairly heavy going. Everyone was therefore rather relieved when the time came for the QMG's departure from the island. On the final evening of his visit the telephone rang in our quarter, Churchill House. It was the ADC to Sir William Luce. 'Sir Charles' aircraft has gone unserviceable and he has to spend an extra day in Bahrain. Sir William realises that 1 PARA are away tomorrow on an exercise in the Trucial States but he would be awfully grateful if Mrs Graham could be so kind as to take the QMG under her wing for the morning and look after him until his 'plane leaves after lunch.' There was no ready reason to decline this request, so after a brief discussion with Rosemary, it was agreed that she would escort Sir Charles during the next morning in a car provided by the Residency. I left early the next day for Sharjah. When I returned that evening I asked Rosemary how her job escorting the QMG went. Her reply was memorable. 'I sat in the back with Sir Charles, with the ADC and the driver in the front. But before we had gone far along the road to Zallaq beach – for I thought that the best place to take him to for an enjoyable morning – our conversation rather dried up, for as you know Sir Charles is not a very talkative man. So racking my brains for some topic I said to him: "You are the Quartermaster-General to the Forces, aren't you?" "Yes, that is why I've come on this visit to Bahrain."

"Well then, which regiment were you Quartermaster of before you became a General?" My young innocent Rosemary went on:

'I thought that to be a very natural question but Sir Charles looked at me oddly as if I was pulling his leg, and it was only when I saw that the ADC was cringing down in his seat, his shoulders shaking with mirth, that I realised that I'd made a *faux pas*. What, my darling husband, had I said that was wrong?'

For nearly twenty years Rosemary had been soldiering at my side without learning that the appointment of Quartermaster in our Army was reserved for men who had risen through the Corporals' and Sergeants' Messes and whose long, devoted service was rewarded by a QM's Commission. Many years later when I was the General Officer Commanding in Wales, the Royal Monmouthshire Royal Engineers celebrated their 300th birthday with a parade and banquet. When she heard that Sir Charles Richardson was to be present as head of the Corps of Royal Engineers, Rosemary, anxious lest he remembered her gaffe in 1965, developed diplomatic 'flu and sent me to Monmouth on my own.

Our wives, the fortunate minority who were allowed to accompany their husbands to Bahrain, made a sterling contribution to the unit's morale, and I have to this day marvelled at the way in which my own wife rose to meet the challenges of life in the Gulf, encouraged the younger wives, invented pantomimes and concerts for the Toms and their families, and bore the brunt of entertaining on behalf of the Group. The parties Rosemary planned for the great range of people we had to host, and the skill with which she transformed the flat roof of Churchill House into an exotic banqueting area, won for her true admiration just as her attractive personality had won many friends. Those were unusually busy and rewarding days and nights. When the time came to return to England my engagement book showed that during our eleven months in Bahrain Rosemary and I had had seventeen evenings off duty and free for our own diversions. The experience of our colleagues in diplomatic posts and in command of the other Services in Bahrain at that time was no different; such a schedule of commitments was part of the job, and by and large a most enjoyable and rewarding obligation. We were all helped by the abundance of servants, mostly Indian or Pakistani, and the dependable climate; but the expense far outweighed the small allowances granted to unit commanders, and I also regretted that those professional commitments at weekends and in so many evenings deprived us of the companionship of our children.

The sense of duty, concept of care for our subordinates and the general attitude to other human beings exhibited by members of Britain's uniformed Services seemed totally at variance with the behaviour of the civilian expatriate community. The Gymkhana Club with its swimming pool and restaurant and cinema was a popular meeting place for British and European men and women. It was the Bahraini version of an English pub, and the clientele were in general of the artisan class. A regulation drawn up by the committee of management and strongly supported by the membership barred all non-whites from the premises. This hang-over from pre-war custom was in 1965 resented by the Bahrainis and infuriated the senior British officials on the island. It took a very firm Political Agent, Tony Parsons, many weeks of cajoling followed by threats of closure to get this obnoxious regulation rescinded. As we Service onlookers predicted, rescindment did not result in an immediate influx of Asians: few non-whites wished to belong to such a Club. What was intolerable in the 1960s was their exclusion by foreigners from facilities built by Bahrainis on Bahraini soil. Alas, too many of our civilian compatriots abroad had failed to recognise that obvious fact until damage had been done to our country's reputation.

I like to believe that the Ruler, Sheikh Isa, had a better opinion of British Servicemen than some of our civilian compatriots merited. He was invariably courteous to us and our wives, and very hospitable. His Highness, unlike some Arab monarchs, was seldom seen personally to be distributing gifts. Thus, when I was invited with one or other of my

Officers, together with our wives, to an audience at the Rifa'a Palace and we were driving away at the end of the ceremony, our cars would be stopped at the Palace gate and an elderly servant would hand to each of us men a small plain brown paper bag, stapled at the top for security, which we would open discreetly when out of sight. In it was an assortment of gifts; a watch perhaps, pearls for our wives, brooches and ornaments with the insignia of the State of Bahrain. My 1 PARA Group was exceptionally honoured, for just before we departed for the UK, Sheikh Isa presented me with a beautiful bejewelled curved sword, elegantly mounted in an inscribed case. When a year later I handed over command of the Battalion, I decided to donate this fine token of regal regard to the Officers' Mess of the First Battalion. When, long after retirement from the Army, I returned to Aldershot to work on a regimental project, I was dismayed to learn that the sword had been stolen and never retrieved. I now wish that I had kept it for my family. That, however, would have vexed my colleagues in the Foreign Service whose regulations decreed that such personal gifts, though never to be declined, must not be retained but handed over to the Department.

The Advance Party of 2 PARA came out in early February 1966 and we started to leave for England two weeks later. Our months in Bahrain had for me, and I believe for most of the Officers and Men and our wives, been an exceptionally rewarding, constructive and memorable period. We were very fit, professionally in good shape and rather proud of ourselves. Every member of that fine Battalion Group had given of his best and had won for the unit and the Army an enviable reputation. As a gesture of thanks I had a letter handed to each chap as he left Bahrain; a letter which I had addressed and signed individually in my own hand. There were nine hundred and thirty-two of them. It was the least I could have done for those splendid comrades-in-arms.

The family and I and our 'chalk' arrived back at Gatwick to be met by Pat Thursby and David O'Morchoe, a kindness typical of those two airborne friends. A number of my Officers and Soldiers had permission to make their own ways home from Bahrain; some motored, some bought and equipped a sailing boat, others trusted to 'airborne initiative' and the hazards of hitch-hiking. But all went well and the Battalion re-mustered in Bruneval Barracks, Aldershot on 12 April. I was allotted a comfortable quarter in Kitchener Road named Sedgemoor, and we were able to move straight in as our friend, the beautiful Valerie Rouse, had off her own bat cleaned the place up ahead of our arrival. Pinky and Didi returned to Miss Seed for daily education and Rosemary and I settled back into garrison life. The months that followed were not as enjoyable as our time in Bahrain had been; every unit prefers to be away from the immediate supervision of senior Officers and the Royal Military Police.

Commanding 1 Para

In Aldershot we at once got caught up in the many varied commitments, and the routine chores, inseparable from life in a big garrison. Red letter days in the annual calendar of Airborne Forces are the anniversaries of the Rhine Crossing (24 March 1945), of the Normandy Landings (6 June 1944) and Arnhem Day (17 September 1944). These are celebrated by units of The Parachute Regiment wherever they happen to be in the world; in Aldershot there was the great annual summer regimental Reunion, Airborne Forces Day, with its hectic programme of ceremonial parades, lunches, side-shows, dinner dances and much drinking. ABF Day was entirely a regimental event for which the planning was done by the Depot, the chief burden falling on that Quartermaster, and on the Regimental Colonel and the small team in Maida Barracks who existed to run the Regimental Association, the PRA. The principal major Service commitments in which we got involved at the whim of the Ministry of Defence, of Southern Command or of Aldershot District HQ, were the Farnborough Air Show, the Army Equipment Exhibition, helping to run the Bisley Rifle Meeting, demonstrations for overseas politicians and military observers, the Royal Tournament in London, guards, running annual camps for Cadet Forces, acting as 'enemy' on Territorial Army exercises, and Keeping the Army in the Public Eye (KAPE). This latter commitment took up a lot of time, took companies away from the Battalion on recruiting drives all over the Kingdom, and was essential as the Regular Army's inflow of suitable young volunteers seldom matched the continuous drain of trained men whose period of service with the Colours had expired.

Amongst all these activities, units had to fit in the crucial business of the annual training cycle; the training of the individual soldier and Officer, many of whom had joined the battalion only on its return from abroad, junior leaders' training, platoon and company exercises and the larger exercises to test complete units and formations. In 1966 1 PARA took part in two unusually prolonged and large-scale manoeuvres. Exercise LIFE LINE was planned by 3rd Division and was intended to be a spectacular occasion for showing off the chief components of the Armed Forces in the UK and a number of their new assets such as the Navy's assault landing ship, *Fearless*, helicopters and 38 Group of the RAF. LIFE LINE started a week after my battalion returned from leave but that caused no problems. The opening phase consisted of a parachute assault by 1 PARA and other elements of the Brigade into the Thetford training area in Norfolk. That went well and was rather enjoyable. For the second phase the whole caboodle was switched to the south west. By that time the weather had turned cold and exceedingly wet – and when it rains few parts of the United Kingdom experience the rainfall of South Wales. We carried out a second parachute drop during a short break in the bad weather onto the Castlemartin tank ranges in Dyfed. The rain then fell heavier than before and continued for about a week. The landing on the Welsh coast by Marine Commandos from *Fearless* had to be postponed, and as 1 PARA Group was required at Sennybridge for the third exercise phase, we handed over our lodgement area overlooking the shore to a company of Bersaglieri, a corps d'élite of the Italian Army. I have an enduring memory of standing on a headland as the Italians prepared to take over from my blokes. Huddled together against the driving rain they looked totally bewildered, and their misery was made more apparent by the black feathers drooping from their head-dress glued by the rain to their faces. We had to leave them to cope as best they could and moved by lorry up into the bare expanse of the Sennybridge Training Area. There our orders were to seek out and engage the enemy with especial skill and vigour for the benefit of the Soviet Military Attaché and his Red Army colleagues, the most important of all the many observers invited to participate in LIFE LINE. This was not easy. The rain did not let up, the whole countryside became a bog, no reinforcements could join us in that dreary sodden wilderness, and moreover 10 PARA, the enemy whom we were supposed to engage, had not yet arrived from London. I fear that the Soviet Officers were not taken in by my briefings on non-existent engagements in distant fields and bogus descriptions of our defences and patrol activities. The Military Attaché scoured the horizon through his binoculars, looking in vain for signs of the battles I had described. I never really believed that 'skill in moving undetected and good camouflage' were convincing explanations for his inability to detect any activity whatsoever. Those were uncomfortable and profitless hours, above all for the commanders and staff Officers who had had high hopes of LIFE LINE as valuable large-scale manoeuvres and a shop window for our Services. We, marooned on Sennybridge, learned to appreciate our new waterproofed sleeping bags and the consolation of the 24-hour ration-pack meals accompanied, because of the climate, by a tot of the QM's rum.

Exercise LINK WEST in the autumn turned out to be quite a different affair. Fast moving and stimulating it covered much of Yorkshire, East Anglia and Salisbury Plain; and we never once got wet. 16 PARA Brigade started by clearing up pockets of 'rebels' in the Catterick area where 'Jones' Force, commanded by my new 2IC, Martin Jones, who had replaced Maurice Tugwell, was alleged to have freed the wrong prisoners in an attack on an ill-defined jail. Having sorted out Catterick, we moved to two RAF airfields and from there mounted an air-landed move to West Raynham prior to moving onto the Stanford training area to close with the main body of enemy operating in East Anglia from their base in Tottington village. No sooner were local Police authority and civilian morale restored, than 1 PARA was withdrawn from Stanford to West Raynham and warned for a parachute assault onto the New Zealand

Farm sector of Salisbury Plain. Within six hours of quitting Tottington I had the Battalion manifested, fed, rested and briefed. The briefing I did myself; initially to All Ranks, then when the Privates had fallen out, to every Leader from Lance Corporal upwards in order to emphasize certain points of detail. It was as well that I did so. We emplaned in Hastings, Argosy and Beverley aircraft at RAF West Raynham and RAF Leconfield at around 0400 hours, but after about thirty minutes in the air the whole aircraft stream ran into thick fog which had unexpectedly descended over southern England. The drop was cancelled and the RAF controllers dispersed our aircraft to a variety of airfields in eastern England and the Midlands. No one was able to tell me, the Commander, where the scattered elements of my parachute force ended up; nor did I have any means of contacting them or they me. There was no point in hanging around in the hope of regaining some control. The correct action, it seemed to me, was to stick to the plan and the orders I had issued a few hours earlier and to trust the Officers and Soldiers to do likewise. They did. Although widely dispersed far from Salisbury Plain, the chaps in 1 PARA Group made their own way in various forms of transport – military, public and private – over many miles of fog-bound England to the Battalion Assembly Area near Salisbury Plain. From there we at mid-day set out to attack as planned the objective at New Zealand Farm. 1 PARA was complete when it crossed the Start Line; Ian Chapman's platoon was the last to catch up with us having travelling down from the Midlands in a 'borrowed' ten-ton lorry. They arrived four minutes before we started the attack.

Another testimony to the quality of the men of 1 PARA in that era arises from the performance of the Battalion's Transport Platoon, that body of oil-begrimed drivers and mechanics on whose skills and self-discipline our mobility and safety depended; and by whom, because drivers are constantly in the public eye, the reputation of the Regiment among the civil community could be marred or enhanced. Commanded by Geoffrey Banks, a former RSM of the Airborne Forces Depot at Maida Barracks, our vehicles and their supervision was, I knew, in excellent hands. Indeed, the MT Platoon was the only sub-unit in the Battalion Group which I never formally inspected during our year in Bahrain: my confidence was justified by their record. During the many thousands of miles that the Platoon had driven our vehicles around the camp, through the crowded streets of Jufair, Manama and Muharraq, and over the long tracks in the mainland deserts where we so often exercised, they had been involved in only one traffic accident, the cost of which to the British taxpayer was less than three pounds. My deliberate unconcern with Banks's Boys was however a reflection of a fact of military life which, I am sure, many other unit commanders regretted. Our days and nights were very busy; the things that had to be done outnumbered the hours available for their completion. Some actions, however desirable, had to yield to the more pressing. Thus in the matter of a CO's acquaintance with the individual Private Soldier, he got to know best the malefactors (the small element routinely brought before him for punishment), the outstanding (those whom he wished to reward or groom for promotion), and the weaker brethren whose domestic affairs so often got into a muddle. One had therefore to create opportunities to talk to the Toms who constituted the majority, the host of good, dependable, self-disciplined and engaging young men whom it was a true privilege to lead. I wish I had made more opportunities for relaxed and rewarding conversations with these.

Though sport or free-fall parachuting is a pretty safe activity, military parachuting has always been hazardous. The military parachutist is called on to emplane heavily laden and usually tired by the hours of preparation, packing, briefing and travel to the mounting airfield, and after an uncomfortable flight to throw himself and his burden out of the aircraft in the midst of his many comrades, tired and laden as himself, at a low altitude, and in daylight or darkness to control his brief descent so as to avoid collision and to land correctly. Consequently minor injuries such as sprains and fractures were common. Fatalities in peacetime were mercifully rare. Those which did occur were often due to navigation errors by the aircrew, such as the despatch of a number of TA parachutists over the Kiel Canal in which a number drowned, or the aircraft itself crashing as happened at the PTS in the 1960s. When a man lost his life in the act of parachuting the circumstances were rigorously investigated.

My Battalion Group suffered a most grievous loss in the summer of 1966. One of the companies, including men from other units in the brigade, carried out a routine night parachuting exercise onto the Fox Covert Dropping Zone on Salisbury Plain. When the drop was completed one man was found on the ground dead. His parachute had opened correctly but it was deduced that he died through some million-to-one chance of entanglement of his static line around his neck as he went through the side door of his Hastings aircraft. Everyone in Airborne Forces grieved over every fatal or serious accident. This death was a particular blow, for the victim was Captain George Morgan of Mercer's Troop. George had been in Bahrain with us, was very popular and rated as an exceptionally fine Officer destined for a successful career in the Royal Artillery, or the SAS in which he had already served. Moreover George was the only son of a most eminent Gunner General, Sir Frederick Morgan, who in 1943 as Chief of Staff to the Supreme Allied Commander (designate) had prepared the initial plan for the invasion of Normandy. George Morgan lies buried in the military cemetery in Bulford.

My personal experience in Airborne Forces indicates that Officers seem to suffer a proportionately higher casualty rate than the NCOs and Privates. This I put down to their greater preoccupations during the planning stage of an operation or exercise, a tendency to skimp on the essential preliminary synthetic refresher training, and their older age. Certainly these were factors which led to the Officer casualties on the Libyan exercise 'Cross Med' in 1964; and ten years later Brigadier Pat O'Kane, the commander of the TA Parachute Brigade, died of the injuries he sustained parachuting shortly before taking up a NATO staff appointment. (One consequence of this tragedy was that I, recently returned from India, was sent at short notice to take his place in Holland.)

In October I got the whole battalion parachuted into the Sennybridge area where, left to ourselves for two weeks, we had a valuable spell of varied training; in reasonably good weather too. This training was necessary in order to weld into the 1 PARA team the many chaps who had joined us during the summer. There had been a substantial outflow of friends who had been with me in Bahrain, and although I was to leave the Battalion myself at the end of 1966, it was important to prepare the new team for whatever emergency or overseas commitment might arise. The main event was an exercise in which the whole unit advanced over fifty-five miles of desolate Welsh countryside to destroy a 'rebel' force in the Sennybridge area. We moved on foot, manpacking all the weapons and equipment (except the anti-tank guns and the heavy cooking kit), with Joe Starling's newly formed Patrol Company operating some miles ahead of the main body. In spite of the very bad going, deliberately chosen to provide a stiff challenge, the heavy loads and the cold, only six men fell out, four through injury and two for urgent family reasons. Exercise 'CHINDIT COLUMN' culminated in a splendidly noisy battle for Quarry Ridge following a night minefield breaching operation. It had been a profitable and enjoyable (in hindsight) fortnight. It had also been a period of sadness. One morning we heard on the radio that disaster had befallen the small mining village of Aberfan, near Merthyr Tydfil. An avalanche of coalmine waste, loosened by the recent heavy rains, had overwhelmed the village school and some houses, burying 144 people including 116 children. I at once sent off our Medical Officer, Alex Rosser, and the new Padre, John McNaughton, with an offer of help. They returned later in the day reporting that the civilian authorities and Police were coping well and had declined the assistance of 1 PARA. The reasons given were that the local men, professional miners, were more skilled than soldiers at digging away the mountain of mud and debris which had covered the site of the disaster and that 'outsiders would only get in the way and obstruct the rescue operations'. My two Officers also formed the opinion that military help was being rejected for historical reasons: Winston Churchill, when Home Secretary at the beginning of the century, had sent troops into the Mining Valleys during a pit strike. That event had never been forgotten and antipathy to the Army remained part of the local culture. While we got on with the carefully planned exercise programme, the Welsh soon found that military assistance had become indispensable and an Infantry unit was sent from Devon to Aberfan.

We returned to Aldershot by train and I prepared to hand over my 1 PARA to a distinguished former Greenjacket, Mike Walsh. The dismal process of extracting myself from the Battalion at Christmas-time was much eased by the farewell parties our friends laid on for us in their different Messes, in the Wives' Club and in Camberley's Civic Hall which the Warrant Officers and Sergeants hired for a splendid evening in our honour.

At times I had questioned my perception of 1 PARA Group; were my swans in reality mere geese? The answer to this self-doubt was made plain by others in better positions than I to judge our professional competence and standing in the Service. But when Tony Farrar-Hockley telephoned me at home in late December with the news that I was to be awarded the OBE in the New Year Honours, I was surprised – but also exceedingly pleased; in particular for Rosemary who had been such a gem of a CO's wife and for my two children who had had to put up with their Father's distractions and regimental preoccupations for so much of their young lives.

Now, in January 1967, we could look forward to at least two years of stability and undisturbed family life, for I had been appointed an Instructor at the Army Staff College in Camberley. At Rosemary's urging we bought a house, Tamarisk, on Diamond Ridge about a mile from the Staff College. Modern, convenient and with space for creating a pleasant garden, we settled in excitedly having acquired an 80% mortgage on the purchase price of £8,950. This was a very fair price indeed for the house had charm and potential, but the monthly repayments of this (by modern standards minuscule) mortgage were to give us much anxiety until I was promoted Brigadier and sent to Oman three years later. Actually, I personally played little part in the moving into our home. Knowing that teaching during the first term of the Staff College year required Instructors to work until well past midnight on most weekdays, I selfishly slept in the College for the first three months, returning to Tamarisk only for weekends, by which time Rosemary, helped again by Valerie Rouse, had got our home into a happy and comfortable state. Owning one's own home was in those days seldom attempted by Army Officers; I was the first member of my immediate family to have done so, for renting or taking an Army quarter was the custom; but as the years passed and house prices in Britain soared, those who left the Services without having acquired a house found themselves in trouble. Thus in 1967, as so often in the years that lay ahead, our children and I came to profit hugely from the clear thinking, determination and good sense of Rosemary Graham. Christopher we sent to the local State school each day, though we soon learned that he often failed to turn up, preferring to play in the woods with a friend. Pinky we enrolled in the well-known Camberley ballet school, Elmhurst. This turned out to be another of those decisions that alter for the better the course of a family's life and lead to unimagined experiences and joys. Through our association with Elmhurst, Rosemary and Pinky soon became friends with the Hartongs, a wealthy American family living in Camberley who also rented a house in Austria, in the Tirolean village of Kirchberg. Frank and Lan Hartong were to be our closest friends until their deaths twenty years later, and with their five children our family has remained linked by affection and many shared memories.

Notes

1. Later Field Marshal Sir Roland Gibbs, GCB, CBE, DSO, MC
2. Later General Sir Anthony Farrar-Hockley, GBE, KCB, DSO, MC

CHAPTER XI
1967–1970

Staff College, RHQ The Parachute Regiment and Beaconsfield

The Staff College course which I had been on in 1955, a year late on account of Colonel Jim Church's marital problem, differed from that which I now joined as a member of the Directing Staff in two important respects. In 1955 the students had all served in the Second World War and the campaigns which followed. We were experienced soldiers; and the inclusion of Officers whose service in the Korean War had exempted them from the competitive Entrance Examination to Camberley brought into our midst a group of colleagues whose experiences and gallantry evoked our admiration and interest.

The other significant difference between the curricula of 1955 and 1967 was the hydrogen bomb. By 1967 nuclear warfare, though never waged, had been studied in theory with the help of much detailed data and the writings of some of the keenest intellects in the Western World. Nuclear war by 1967 had ceased to be 'unthinkable'. It was being thought about, introduced routinely in War Games, tactical exercises and in the training of the individual Serviceman; and a whole branch of government had been set up in the countries of the Warsaw Pact and of NATO to plan for the survival of civilian populations during and after the nuclear exchange. Nuclear war had become, like conventional war, an aspect of modern warfare. Indeed the fact that the Cold War did not turn Hot during the second half of the 20th century is chiefly due to the validity of the Nuclear Deterrent and its influence on East and West. That validity was sustained in part by the high place it was consistently accorded in the training, equipment and doctrines of the Armed Forces.

Nevertheless, much of the detailed study of nuclear weapons, their employment and the measures to mitigate their effects was classified Secret or higher. This meant that at Camberley nuclear studies were relegated to the final term of the year's course, and the non-British students were sent away at the end of the fifth term. This was rather bad luck on them for one of the traditional highlights of the Camberley year was the Pantomine put on by the students during the last week. When I had been a student the highlight of the Staff College year was the expedition to Normandy for the Battlefield Tour where we studied on the ground and in detail three operations of the campaign of 1944. In 1955 men who had played prominent roles in the fighting were invited to return as Guest Speakers and describe to us their experiences in those dramatic and bloody weeks in the lush Norman countryside. Furthermore, the records of the German defenders had by then been analysed. We students were rivetted by the accounts, graphic and fluent, of the veterans of the battles: OVERLORD, the operations of the British Sixth Airborne Division; GOODWOOD, the advance towards the Bourguebus Ridge on the east of Caen of the three armoured divisions (Guards, 7th and 11th), and Operation EPSOM, the crossing of the River Odon by my own 15th Scottish Division. The star turn of the Epsom Guest Speakers was the history master from Stowe, Bill McElwee, who had won the MC for the spirited way he had conducted the defence of the 93rd's bridgehead at Gavrus (described earlier in Chapter III). I had no difficulty in recognising, eleven years after the battle, the landmarks, woods and hedgerows which had been so important to the Infantryman of 1944; and the site of my slit-trench in the Battalion HQ position overlooking the north bank of the Odon was easy to make out. It was all very evocative and of the greatest professional value. Two things struck me most forcibly during this meticulously researched study. One, how little I had known during the actual battle of what was going on around 2A&SH. Even though I was the Adjutant manning the Brigade Rear-Link wireless set, I had learned little of the tribulations of the HLI and the Gordons, sister units in 227 Brigade, and virtually nothing of the rest of the Division. One's comprehension of the progress of the operation was limited to what one could see or hear amid the noise and confusion. In reality knowledge was confined to a single field surrounded by those high Norman hedges or to the nearest crest-line. Thus it was surprising to hear from McElwee and the other speakers, former battalion and brigade commanders, of epic or tragic events which had occurred within a mile or so of 2A&SH

of which I at least had at the time been totally unaware. Also – rather mortifyingly – this 1955 study of the EPSOM battle revealed that the grief and pain suffered by our Scottish Division in our advance from Bretteville l'Orgueilleuse to Tourmauville and Gavrus had in the main been inflicted by a German engineer unit and a battery of artillery, both led by and composed of resolute fighting men.

Though I had learned a lot and had come to admire the way in which the Staff College was run, 1955 had been for me over-clouded by the antagonisms I was encountering over my engagement to Rosemary Adamson. She, poor soul, got the backlash and must have found me during our weekends together a depressed companion. But we were comforted by the kindness of a number of friends in particular, two Argyll colleagues, Duncan Darroch whose Mother-in-law, Mrs Seidl, put Rosemary up in her Camberley house when she came down for the Staff College Ball and other parties; and Colin Mitchell, my one-time subaltern in Palestine and lasting friend who announced his engagement to Sue Phillips during the Camberley course and whose wedding in Perth Rosemary and I attended the following spring.

I had been therefore quite glad to get away when the course ended at Christmas-time and to enter the New Year, 1956, with a course at the Amphibious Warfare School at Fremington, an agreeable three months at the Army's Technical Staff College at Shrivenham, a move to Edinburgh Castle to take up an undemanding staff appointment – and marriage.

In 1967 I was one of the first Instructors posted to the Staff College after having commanded a battalion. Hitherto the Directing Staff had been found from the brightest Majors in the Army, granted while acting as Instructors the temporary rank of Lieutenant-Colonel. Bringing in people like me, post command, did I suppose bring an element of realism and practical experience into the Syndicate Rooms, but I have always suspected that the students were more inhibited in discussion than if they had been guided by a younger Instructor; also that I personally pontificated to excess. That excellent component of the Camberley year, the 'Bottlefield' Tour, continued but with difficulty, as those who had taken part in the battles were dying off and we younger chaps had to act the part of the traditional Guest Speakers. Also the financiers in the MoD had set their sights on the Normandy expedition in the continuous search for economies. I understand that this valuable method of professional instruction has now been abandoned. The new methods are doubtless very good and enjoy the latest technical devices, but I am exceedingly glad that soldiers of my generation were able to 'walk the ground' in France rather than study the operations from film and cassette in a Surrey classroom.

The Commandant of the Staff College during my second time there was

Major-General Mervyn Butler, much loved, with outstanding powers of leadership, a great sense of humour and a remarkable capacity for whisky. Known throughout the Service as 'Tubby', he and his wife, Bunzie, made the Camberley ambiance a particularly happy one. I was only there for a year, however; my tour as an Instructor was cut short as General Tubby selected me for the job of Regimental Colonel of The Parachute Regiment of which he had become the Colonel-Commandant. Promotion to Colonel and the prospect of continuing to work and live in the Camberley-Aldershot area were welcome developments in our family life, and we were able to plan our domestic affairs with a confidence unusual in the Armed Forces of that era. Pinky was to remain at Elmhurst for six more years, amid girls, some of whom became life-long friends, boarding in the periods when Rosemary and I were out of England.

The local state school to which Christopher was despatched each morning through the pine woods which stood between Tamarisk and the school was clearly not the right environment for him, a consistent truant, and on the recommendation of Geoffrey and Barbara Hill, a stalwart couple who had been with us in Bahrain in 1 PARA, we entered Christopher for the Blue Coat School in Birmingham. This proved to be a happy decision, for the school was set in an attractive and surprisingly rural quarter of that great industrial city, with spacious buildings and grounds and clean air; and in the Headmaster, Mr Faulds, and the Master of St Philip's House, Mr Smith, Christopher found two sterling mentors, guardians and friends. Rosemary and I much enjoyed our periodic visits to Harbourne to see him doing his stuff on the running track, the cricket pitch or in the choir, surrounded by smiling faces and bright eyes – for Christopher has the personality which makes friends easily and enables him to retain their friendship and goodwill. Christopher is fortunate in having inherited his principal characteristics from his Mother and the Adamsons. His Sister seems to have been saddled by Nature with some of the traits which came out in me, but I rejoice that Pinky's good qualities far outweigh those inherited inhibitions and have gained for her many good friends and a life-style which matches the hopes we, her parents, have since September 1957 nourished for her.

Regimental Headquarters had recently moved from Maida Barracks into a brand new complex situated beside the main Farnborough-Farnham road and the Basingstoke Canal, at the southern end of that broad expanse of grass, the Queen's Parade. The chap from whom I took over as Regimental Colonel was the fellow-Cheltonian, Pat Thursby, from whom I had inherited 1 PARA. I did not, however, take over the nice quarter which went with the job as Rosemary and I were determined to live in our own newly-bought house. Paying the mortgage plus school fees in addition to our entertainment commitments – obligatory but very enjoyable, for Rosemary was by now an excellent and experienced hostess – took up most of my pay. While I was at the Staff College she had taken a full-time job to make ends meet. For her, our first three years in Camberley were a most testing period; but she brought us through it and kept the family and our home on an even keel and helped me tremendously in my work. In those days it was regarded as improper for a Lieutenant-Colonel's wife to take paid employment, but as I was away at the Staff College for long hours during the whole of 1967, how she passed her days went largely unnoticed. But a working full-Colonel's wife was a novelty which raised some eyebrows in the higher military echelons of the District. But she persisted for we financially had no option, and her example encouraged a number of younger Officers' wives, understretched during their husbands' duty absences and struggling with a meagre income, to launch themselves onto the job market thereby gaining both satisfaction and profit.

I inherited from Pat an experienced and competent staff, headed in the post of Regimental Adjutant by my friend from 1 PARA, Norrie Giles. A former Coldstream Guardsman, his knowledge and easy charm were to be of great help when the Regiment was called on to carry out Public Duties in London. The function of RHQ was to run the affairs of The Parachute Regiment and of its individual members, serving and retired. The latter comprised a great body of men living throughout the United Kingdom and in several parts of the Commonwealth. This body, the Parachute Regimental Association, was administered by RHQ through a galaxy of Branches and the membership was even two decades after the end of the Second World War motivated and bound together by remarkably deep and enduring memories of shared experiences and by pride. The prime founder and sustainer of this splendid Association was Claude Milman who had fought with the 6th Airborne Division. We were all responsible to the Colonel-Commandant, Tubby Butler, now promoted to Lieutenant-General, knighted and in Germany in command of the 1st British Corps.

The recruiting of Officers and Men was handled by Peter Cockcroft, a former Royal Berkshire, who deployed round the country on publicity drives our well-equipped and motivated Recruiting Teams. These like the Free-Fall Team, The Red Devils, were popular at the great public gatherings such as the Bath & West Show, and in the late 1960s we had no shortage of applicants to join The Regiment. Many, however, failed to match up to our standards of physical fitness and mental robustness; these were either rejected at an early stage or opted to quit the Service after only a few weeks. The shortage of good Officer material was more serious, and the regular battalions for several years had to manage with serious deficiencies in their subalterns and captains. This was a further reason why The Parachute Regiment was already paying the closest attention to the selection and training of our Junior Leaders, the Lance-Corporals and Corporals. Bob Flood, a previous Regimental Colonel had set up, in Dering Lines on the outskirts of the Welsh town of Brecon, a Parachute Regimental Battle School. Through this establishment every NCO in the Regiment passed; attendance and success on the courses there were obligatory qualifications for promotion. The benefits of this training were plain to see and, as they became recognized throughout the Service, we expanded our resources and accepted into the Battle School students from other Infantry units. Initially a significant proportion of these failed to meet the standards The Parachute Regiment demanded from its own members, and many a CO protested when one of his blue-eyed NCOs returned from Brecon with 'Failed' written on his report. But the merits of the scheme were so evident that after several years Dering Lines and these courses were taken over by the School of Infantry. This raised the standard of junior leadership throughout the Army and reduced for The Parachute Regiment the burden of providing the essential high-class administrative staff and instructors.

The personal administration and career planning for our Regiment's Officers and Soldiers was done by another retired Officer, David Mayfield. He worked in collaboration with, in the case of Officers, the Military Secretary and the Adjutant-General whose departments were located at Stanmore in Middlesex. The careers and interests of the Warrant Officers and below were monitored by the Records Office in Exeter. Thus RHQ and these higher authorities worked together closely and continuously. Turbulence was perhaps the most unsettling aspect of Service life, especially for our married Officers and Men. I had come to RHQ resolved to give to each Officer and Warrant Officer a helpful indication of the path his career would take over the following six years or so. This would, I hoped, at least make it easier for him and his wife to take important domestic decisions about house-purchase, childrens' schooling and so on. After some six months I realised that the attempt was vain: the postings of each chap were so interwoven with the vicissitudes of others, and so influenced by the unforeseeable demands of the Service, that forecasting what lay ahead for an individual was not only unreliable, it did more harm than good. Ignorance of the future, I decided, did less injury to a man's morale than dashed hopes. The Army has for many years tried to grapple with this problem of turbulence and instability but it seems to me (writing in 1999) that for the Infantry in particular the situation has not improved. The succession of unforeseen emergencies in the Far East, Arabia and the Persian Gulf, in Ulster, the Falklands and the Balkans during the last four decades of the 20th century, combined with the upheavals inflicted on the Armed Forces by strength reductions and reorganisations, consequences of the dissolution of the Soviet Empire, have aggravated the problem. The Army since the victories of 1945 has been unable to settle down. But if it did, the attraction of Service life would lessen; our young men still thirst for adventure, and for challenge and purposeful work in stimulating surroundings. A predictable existence of humdrum routine, though comfortable for the mature marrieds, is not what young men join up for; and as the Duke of Wellington observed before Waterloo, it is on the sufficiency of our young Thomas Atkins that the business of the British Army depends.

An important part of our work at RHQ, and a major cause of the frequent postings and moves that affected our Officers and senior NCOs, was keeping the parachute elements of the Territorial Army supplied with the good commanders and instructors indispensable to these units of part-time citizen-soldiers. There were four of these: 10 PARA based on London and covering the Home Counties; 4 PARA in the Midlands and the North of England; 15 PARA, our Scottish battalion with Headquarters in Glasgow; and the Independent Company with a pathfinder role in Lincoln. We also had some responsibilities for those contingents of the Combined Cadet Force and the Army Cadet Force which were affiliated to The Parachute Regiment and wore our cap-badge.

Our main concern, of course, was for the three regular battalions which in 1968 were deployed thus: 1 PARA under Mike Walsh was in Aldershot having returned from Aden where it played an important role in the last months of British rule in that troubled area; 2 PARA, commanded by John Roberts, an ebullient Welsh Guardsman with a Victorian-sized family, was in Malaysia. (They were to go in 1969 on an emergency tour to the destablised Caribbean island of Anguilla, led by Richard Dawnay and Norrie Giles and for which they were awarded the Wilkinson Sword of Peace.) 3 PARA was in Malta where Peter Chiswell had taken over command from Tony Ward-Booth.

Although RHQ and the Depot had already moved into the new barrack complex it had not been formally opened. The name chosen for it was Browning Barracks, after General Sir Frederick ('Boy') Browning, the Father of British Airborne Forces. His widow, the author Daphne du Maurier, came on 6 June (the anniversary of D-Day in 1944) and performed the Opening Ceremony. She was accompanied by her daughter, Tessa. In March the next year, 1969, on the anniversary of the Rhine Crossing operation, Field Marshal Lord Montgomery opened the Museum of Airborne Forces, whose premises had been incorporated in the design of the barracks and where the good Colour-Sergeant Fitch had amassed a unique array of airborne memorabilia. This Museum has grown with the passage of time and is a major attraction. I greatly enjoyed planning these memorable ceremonies, especially the visit to Lady Browning in her Cornish home and to Isington Mill near Farnham where the Field Marshal was quietly living out his life. Invited to tea for one of our discussions, I asked if I could bring with me my old friend Colin Mitchell. Monty of course agreed at once and we had a spirited tea party, and Colin and I left the Mill each bearing copies of his book, *A History of Warfare*, dedicated to us personally in the author's handwriting.

The Field Marshal was 80 years of age and was becoming visibly frailer, to the extent that when on the day of the Museum opening I arrived at the Mill to escort him to Aldershot, he had to be helped to put on his uniform and get into the limousine. But as soon as we got near to the barracks and were passing through the lines of cheering Airborne Soldiers, he shed many years and became the animated and stimulating Commander whom we remembered from his days of glory in 1944. The day went off very well, and after a convivial lunch in the Regimental Mess, we returned to Isington Mill. On this trip Pinky, at Monty's invitation, came with us. In reply to his question 'Which subject at school do you most enjoy?' she replied, 'English'. This pleased Monty very much: 'Quite right. To think, speak and write English clearly and properly is the most important achievement for a young person these days'. On parting he kissed her; and several days later she received from him a handwritten letter saying how much he had enjoyed her company. I never saw him again for I was abroad when he died.

The tabloid newpapers called it a mutiny but as far as military insurrections go it was pretty small beer. The Junior Parachute Company was a sub-unit of the Depot in which were concentrated The Regiment's Boy Soldiers, volunteers too young to enter adult service. It was a good outfit, the seed-bed of a high proportion of our Junior Leaders, had a good reputation, and was a contented and well-managed part of the Regiment. This was due in great measure to the personality and sound judgement of the Company Commander, a former school master but also an experienced soldier. The JPC was housed in a separate camp and enjoyed being insulated from the direct gaze of the Depot hierarchy and of RHQ. The experienced Company Commander, however, retired in 1967 and was replaced by a well respected Officer whose background and temperament were very different. A former Guardsman who rose to be a Regimental Sergeant-Major and thereafter Quartermaster, he was brought in, I understand, to raise the military tone of the JPC and to bring its attitudes more into conformity with those of the Depot with which it was henceforth to be co-located.

In 1968 the JPC moved into Browning Barracks. The transition went smoothly and, spending half a day with the Boys and their Instructors, I was pleased by their high morale and good standards, and by the sensible way in which the new Company Commander was handling his youthful subordinates. The ambiance and the performance of the JPC in its new surroundings seemed perfectly satisfactory. But youngsters, even those in uniform, are volatile. The Company returned from summer leave to find that some dignitaries, Members of Parliament I believe, were visiting them the next day. Having been long away from their rooms the Boys had much to do to bring the place up to the standard required by their Commander; and to homesickness was added resentment at being obliged to devote much energy and long hours to unwelcome and unexpected chores. It would seem that some of their Instructors, instead of cajoling the youngsters by good humour and example away from petulance, inflamed their resentment to the extent that a number quitted the barracks and their duty.

This created for the Commanders of the Depot and the JPC an embarrassment and loss of face. The affair could have been handled discreetly and solved easily and sensibly through regimental channels; the bulk of the Boy Soldiers remained in barracks and did what was required of them. Those who had gone absent would, we knew, soon return to us or be sent back by their parents. I do not remember how the press got to know of the incident; I suppose that one of the Boys, called on to explain his absence from Aldershot, spoke about his grievances. The press got hold of his account, inflated it into a sensational story, the tabloid papers came out with headlines in which the word 'Mutiny' caught the eye, and for several days the Depot Commander and his Adjutant were badgered by journalists and telephone calls from people who thought they had a right to know what the rumpus was all about. Naturally these press reports excited our seniors in the Service; this was understandable for there had recently been incidents of unrest in several other Junior Soldiers' units. But it took much time and effort to bring the affair down to a sensible level of interest – into proper perspective – and to get our agitated seniors to comprehend the facts and their causes. I inevitably got involved in this process. It was interesting to note the different attitudes of those I had to brief. Some belonged to the segment of the Army who disliked or envied The Parachute Regiment; their jealousy led them to see in the JPC 'mutiny' an opportunity to bring about the disbandment of the Regiment. Others openly relished our discomfiture (for *Schadenfreude* is a common emotion), but the majority of our Infantry sister-regiments expressed sympathy for us while no doubt saying to themselves 'But for the Grace of God . . .'.

Vexed and initially hostile, the C-in-C of Southern Command and the acting District Commander (Charles Stainforth was away) accepted my explanation of the causes of the incident, and I found myself a few days later addressing the assembled Boy Soldiers in phrases both stern and forbearing. The episode ended in applause and smiles, and life in Browning Barracks returned almost to normal; not entirely for it was thought wise to replace the Company Commander, also one of his subaltern Officers whose man-management qualities had been found defective. The Depot Commander, to whom neglible blame attached, took the incident ill and left the Service believing that his career had been hurt. This was sad, for he was an excellent Officer.

* * *

In the early winter of 1968 the Regiment was ordered to relieve the Foot Guards for several weeks of their London Duties. We had to take over the ceremonial guarding of the two palaces, Buckingham and St James's, the Tower and the Bank of England. This involved, as it had when 1 PARA provided the Windsor Castle Guard, a major blitz on drill and turnout, much liaison with the Brigade of Guards and detailed rehearsal of the traditional procedures. Having Norrie Giles as Regimental Adjutant was a great boon and the Regiment did well in this unusual role. The whole period of the London commitment was a good experience for our Officers and the Toms, and for our musicians, and provided us with some pleasant memories. I took the opportunity to arrange a special Regimental Dinner in the apartments in St James's Palace set aside for the Officers of the Guard, and to this banquet came our most senior and eminent personalities; Tubby Butler and several previous Colonel Commandants, Richard Gale who had led 6th Airborne Division in Normandy, Sir John Hackett of Arnhem fame and others. It was an evening unique in our annals. Norrie added up the stars[1] seated round the table; they came to forty-two – not bad, we thought, for a regiment raised only twenty-eight years before.

We also gave in the same premises a Cocktail Party for the Outward Bound Trust with which the Regiment was associated and to which our wives were invited. I was in London all that day so Rosemary had to drive up from Camberley after work and join me in St James's Palace. It was a wet, foggy November evening. She reached London safely but a bit late, parked the car and joined the throng of smartly dressed people who were slowly making their way into the hall, via the cloakroom and up the staircase to the receiving line. There, somewhat to her surprise, she was greeted by Denis Healey, the Minister of Defence and his aides, and on passing through into the large room was even more surprised not to see me or any close regimental friends. She soon spotted Sir Charles Harington, a former CO of 1 PARA, talking to General Tony Deane-Drummond, both of whom she knew, and after a brief chat asked: 'Have you seen John?' They shook their heads adding 'Should he be here?' 'Yes, we are giving a party for Outward Bound and I was to meet him here.'

'But this is not the Outward Bound party; this is the Minister of Defence's annual reception for all the defence attachés. Are you sure you've come to the right place?' My poor wife, agitated by the drive through the fog in the dark and by her delayed arrival, had found herself in Lancaster House, which is close by St James's Palace.

Before I took over the RHQ appointment from Pat Thursby, The Parachute Regiment had been nominated by the Ministry of Defence for the task of organising and conducting a British Army Tattoo which was scheduled to tour North America for three months in the autumn of the next year, 1969. The Tattoo Contingent, drawn from several corps and regiments and including young Servicewomen, was to number over four hundred. It was made clear to us from the onset that the MoD, while giving advice, would play no part in the organisation: the whole business was the responsibility of The Parachute Regiment and of whichever American sponsor we decided to adopt. From the Regiment only the small RHQ staff had a fixed abode and could undertake such a prolonged commitment; and for a number of reasons it became clear that the detailed work could only be done by the newly appointed Regimental Colonel, JDCG. Furthermore as the secretary, dedicated to this project and found for me by Brigade HQ, could only attend after normal working hours, I was to have during the next year or so some long days in the office; and some moments of anxiety also.

Two impresarios had got in touch with The Regiment to seek the sponsorship of the 1969 Tattoo (several having been sent in earlier years to the USA, though smaller in size, and these had proved popular and profitable). Pat Thursby gave me the correspondence, and after reading it, I could only agree with his conclusion that the terms offered by Columbia Festivals were far more satisfactory than those presented by Mr Sol Hurok. The Ministry of Defence and General Tubby in Germany were of the same opinion. So my first action in this matter was to write formally to both impresarios committing The Parachute Regiment to collaborate solely with Columbia Festivals Inc.

The next weekend I was weeding our front garden in Camberley when the telegraph boy arrived bearing a long cable addressed to me from New York. It was from Sol Hurok personally. He was perhaps the most famous impresario of the age. In it he expressed his surprise and displeasure that on this occasion the British Army had declined his services and disregarded his experience; and guessing that Columbia's terms were better, he laid out for my urgent consideration conditions and guaranteed profits which far exceeded anything we had been offered before. Financially and in other ways what Mr Hurok now proposed was too good to reject, so playing the callow amateur inexperienced in such matters, I was obliged to inform Columbia that my original undertaking was cancelled and Hurok was informed that his new terms were accepted. I spent the next days in a highly nervous state with fears of breach of contract charges descending on me from Columbia Festivals or at the least a refusal to accept my changed decision. In fact I need not have worried; their head man in London was very understanding about it all. So in cooperation with the Hurok team I began the business of building up the Tattoo contingent and planning their various acts. We were lucky to get from the Sappers as our Director of Music Lieutenant-Colonel Basil Brown. This was a key appointment as the performances were to have a sizeable musical content, with the Pipes and Drums of the Royal Scots Greys and the Bands and Corps of Drums of 1 and 2 PARA. I cannot now remember all the units that took part, but I do remember the versatility of the Royal Signals Motorcycle Display Team, the White Helmets, and the tireless performances of the young men and women in our gymnastic team as they made their way round the major cities in Canada and the United States between late August and the end of November, travelling in Greyhound buses, accommodated by Hurok in hotels, and well gripped throughout by Bill Corbould, whom I had persuaded on his return from the High Commission in Canberra, to take charge of the contingent. Bill was the ideal man for this job, and as his wife Edna was a trained nurse immediate medical cover was assured.

The contingent very nearly did not leave England. At the beginning of the planning stage Hurok had agreed to pay the large sum demanded by the MoD as insurance cover for every Serviceman and woman in the Tattoo. About four weeks before their departure the Treasury increased the sum very greatly. I was appalled when the MoD told me the new figure and, as I anticipated, the Hurok team in their vexation seriously considered cancelling the entire project. I briefed General Tubby who personally got in touch with Denis Healey, the Minister of Defence, and the matter got sorted out; though at Hurok's expense for the Treasury did not agree much of a reduction in the sum demanded. Rosemary and I joined the contingent in Montreal and remained with them for about ten days. I got us across the Atlantic on indulgence passages in an RAF aircraft flying out to the great training area at Suffield in Alberta. The trip cost me five pounds for each of us.

After breakfast in a grey, damp Gander we flew on to Quebec. Rosemary and I got off there and, as it is a city of considerable historical and political importance, we had thought it proper to arrive dressed for the occasion; she in a hat and high-heeled shoes and I in a suit. But the pilot put the plane down on no recognised aerodrome. He landed the Britannia on a large expanse of grass. When the aircraft came to a stop the Steward lowered the steps, indicated that we should alight and handed down our luggage. Within two minutes the plane had disappeared over the horizon and we were left surrounded by long grass and many attractive wild flowers. A road ran alongside the field so we walked towards it, suitcases in hand, climbed the wire fence and waited. Quite soon a bus drove up, we paid and after a few miles found ourselves in the centre of the beautiful old city which we enjoyed exploring until long after night fell.

We had to take a train to Ottawa to join up with the Corboulds & Co and found that we had the choice of travelling from the same station and for the identical fare by two railroad companies. The man in the ticket office told us that the food was better on the Canadian Pacific line, so we climbed in and had a superbly colourful journey along the valley of the St Lawrence river with on either side the reds, golds, greens and browns of the North American autumn. These were even more striking when, the next day Bill and Edna took us into the Gatineau Park. After performing in Ottawa and Montreal we all moved down into New England. Rosemary and I stayed with the Tattoo party until they left Philadelphia, marvelling at the versatility of our Soldiers, called on to perform in some towns in small arenas such as college gymnasiums and in the cities in huge stadiums.

When the Tattoo tour ended it was obvious that it had not been the money-spinner that Sol Hurok and his minions had anticipated. The expense of conveying and accommodating such a large party so far for so long was great; the audiences had been enthusiastic but in the USA had seldom filled the seats to capacity. The reasons were twofold; in the New York area public attention was rivetted on the unwonted success in the baseball championship of the local team, the Mets, and elsewhere public antipathy to the war in Vietnam, and by extension to the military, was becoming conspicuous. Nevertheless Mr Hurok honoured to the letter the revised terms he had put to me, and the MoD and the units which provided the Tattoo performers picked up some welcome income from the sales of the recordings and souvenir programmes as well as from the generous guaranteed sums he had himself proposed in that cable of early 1968. Columbia Festivals must have rejoiced that I had slid out of that initial commitment to them.

One day during the autumn General Charles Stainforth, the GOC of Aldershot District, dropped into my office in Browning Barracks with the news that I had been selected for promotion to Brigadier. Furthermore, he said, I had a choice of job in my new rank. It was probable that I would be given command of a brigade in Europe unless I preferred to take up the appointment, which was soon to fall vacant, of Commander of the Sultan's Armed Forces – 'a small outfit in a part of the Persian Gulf which I believe you already know'. I did know the area and the Sultan's Forces, but recognised at once that, although I would be able to take my wife with me to Muscat and Oman, it was an environment which from the career or domestic perspective certainly did not appeal to everyone. Rosemary and I had been happy in Bahrain, the extra allowances for service in SAF would be helpful and the living expenses less than in Europe, and the job would present a challenge not unlike those which had lured our military forefathers to India, Africa and Egypt in the previous century. To command SAF for two or three years would not advance one's career but it should be fun, novel and add a colourful patch to the 'rich tapestry of life'. What I had seen of SAF in 1963-5 I had liked; moreover the chap from whom I would be taking over, Corran Purdon, an Ulster Rifleman with a Military Cross from war service with the Commandos, had been a fellow-student at Camberley in 1955. The thing which clinched the decision for me was hearing that Colonel Hugh Oldman, who had so impressed me during the 2 PARA versus SAF exercise in 1964, was about to return to the Sultanate as Defence Secretary. I knew that in Hugh I would find a congenial and wise partner. Rosemary did not hesitate; she gave me her full backing in opting for the Muscat job, and it only remained for my nomination to receive the approval of the Ruler, Sultan Said bin Taimur. This came through fairly quickly and I started the process of handing over the regimental colonelcy to Ken Came and getting myself a place on the Arabic course at the Army School of Languages in Beaconsfield.

A grounding in colloquial Arabic was essential for those going on secondment to the various armies in the Gulf area, the Trucial Oman Scouts, the Abu Dhabi Defence Force, the Saudi and Kuwaiti Armed Forces and to SAF. In 1970 these forces were still looking to Britain for suitable volunteers to fill command and staff posts and to assist in training their nationals. There were about twelve Officers on my course; the junior ones were Captains, I was the senior and the oldest and for that reason was put into the senior Officer's suite in the Mess. (Although Beaconsfield is not far from Camberley, it would have been foolish to commute daily in winter from Tamarisk; also we had all been warned that learning Arabic would involve much tedious study in the evenings. Beside these considerations, we only had one car and Rosemary needed it for getting to work. So I stayed in the Mess from Sunday nights until Friday afternoons.) I soon discovered that being in that suite had a drawback: it was on the fifteenth floor of a skycraper. The views on a fine day were splendid but I was to live in it during eleven weeks of a cold English winter. Furthermore the two lifts were frequently out of order and, it seemed to me, could only be repaired by one man who lived in Nottingham and travelled by bicycle. Thus I made much use of the staircase but got fit in the process. The school was run by the Royal Army Education Corps and existed primarily to teach Russian to a large body of Servicemen. Our Arabic class was small and our usual teachers were two Palestinian Arabs. They taught us well. One day my sister-in-law, Penelope, had wanted to speak to me on the telephone, but not knowing the number of the extension to my room she asked the operator on the School's switchboard to look it up. But to no avail. The operator told her that he had a School telephone directory in front of him but that he couldn't help her as he had not yet learned to read. I have to admit that I found learning this language hard going. The grammar was not difficult to grasp for the underlying structure of sentences and the derivation of words follow fixed rules. The problem was that the nouns, adjectives and verbs bear no relation to those in the European languages I had learnt at school or since. It was a hard slog for the memory, harder perhaps for mine than for my youthful fellow-pupil's, and I rather dreaded the final exam. This was an oral affair conducted by an Englishman and an Arab; it lasted all day, we students going in one by one to be tested. I knew that the other chaps wanted to get away early; also that Rosemary could not pick me up until she left work, so I elected to go in last. My turn did not come until tea-time but by keeping my ears open during the coffee break, during lunch and in the brief chats with my colleagues as we parted, I acquired a pretty accurate idea of what the questions were going to be. They gave me the top marks!

These three years of living in our own house in Camberley, though very testing financially and hard work for Rosemary, were a novelty for this member of the Graham tribe. Neither my parents nor my Grandfathers had owned houses. To rent other peoples' had been the custom. Rosemary's family in South America had a better understanding of the importance of land and property, and she, thank Heavens, had insisted that I break with the unadventurous Graham attitude and thus we bought Tamarisk at a price which was to increase greatly in the property boom before we sold it in 1978. Those years saw the children develop well in various particulars, and they had notable introductions into the world of film-making and popular songs, having small parts in the comedy film 'Chitty Chitty Bang-Bang' and singing with a well-known and thoroughly respectable group 'The Seekers' on BBC television on Christmas Eve. Pinky and Didi earned a nice bit of pocket money thereby, and Rosemary and I for several weeks basked in the warmth of the compliments that flowed in by post and telephone.

To the business of creating a home within the four walls of Tamarisk, a business which brought out all my wife's excellent taste, foresight and her nose for bargains in the sales and antique shops, there of course was linked the task of carving a reasonable garden out of our half-acre of sandy soil which nourished little except rhododendrons and some sixty young fir trees.

One of the joys of my job as Regimental Colonel was the use of a Staff Car with a full-time uniformed driver from the Regiment. Corporal Tait was a charmer. Sensible, totally reliable, and devoted to our children he really became one of our family. He had a pretty blond wife and a baby with whom he lived in an army quarter in Aldershot, but she brought him increasing unhappiness and Tait came to spend more and more of his spare hours over in Camberley with us. Short, broad-chested and immensely strong, Tait had the ideal physique for a parachutist; and for a landscape gardener. The forest of unwanted fir trees he felled with ease, and the ingenuity with which he extracted the great roots from the ground and dug sunken heather plots and laid paved patios was remarkable. Long before we sold Tamarisk we had together made there a most attractive and colourful garden. I hope that those who occupy that house in future years will tend that garden with care and imagination. For to us, that garden is a memorial to Corporal Tait of The Parachute Regiment; a first-rate soldier, an excellent man and a friend. He died a few years later while we were overseas.

The versatility of the Parachute soldier is well-known; that of his Officer is less publicised – taken rather for granted. However some incidents are writ large in the book of human achievement and The Regiment, together with the Nation, rejoices. One such achievement occurred in 1968 when Captain John Ridgway and Sergeant Chay Blyth successfully rowed across the Atlantic Ocean. The excitement and lavish publicity that greeted their arrival reminded one of the arrival at the summit of Everest in 1953 of Edmund Hillary and Sherpa Tensing. I did ask myself whether we and the national press had gone overboard in the fanfares for Ridgway and Blyth, for at about the same time two members of our Parachute Brigade had broken the record for crossing the North American continent on foot; an achievement that passed unremarked save within our brigade in Aldershot. And when several months later Trooper Tom McClean of the Special Air Service Regiment rowed himself across the Atlantic Ocean singlehanded, his feat was proclaimed in a mere three lines of small print in *The Telegraph*.

Note

1. The US system of denoting the grade of General Officers by stars had been adopted throughout NATO; it was:—
   * Brigadier, ** Major General, *** Lieutenant General, **** General.

CHAPTER XII

1970: Muscat and Oman

A Dismal Situation

The Sultanate of Muscat and Oman (as Oman was called until 1970) lies in the south-east part of the Arabian peninsula, flanked by the waters of the Indian Ocean and the Gulf of Oman, to the north and west by the United Arab Emirates (UAE) and Saudi Arabia, and in the south-west corner by the Peoples' Democratic Republic of Yemen (PDRY). The northern tip of Sultanate territory, the Musandam, barren, mountainous and sparsely populated, projects into the narrowest part of the sea-route between the Persian Gulf and the open sea and through this waterway, the Straits of Hormuz, are carried more than half of the EEC's oil imports, a third of the USA's and almost the whole of Japan's. In its strategic position at the choke point on a vital shipping route lies Oman's singular importance to the world's most industrialised nations.

The British first became involved with Oman when the East India Company began to trade in the Gulf in the early 17th century and relations were formalised by treaties in 1798 and 1800. These treaties were forerunners of a series under which Britain acquired an increasingly dominant position in the region, and on account of her Imperial responsibilities on the Indian sub-continent she came to assume a growing influence over, and became accountable for, the affairs of the Sultanate. Nevertheless Oman has remained a wholly independent and sovereign state, ruled since 1744 by members of the Al Bu Said dynasty.

During the early 19th century British naval and military forces supported the Sultan on operations to stamp out piracy, to subdue dissident tribesmen or to suppress the slave trade; and in 1915 when the tribes of the Interior, discontented by their economic conditions, united in arms against the Sultan and advanced on Muscat, it was by seven hundred sepoys of the British-Indian army that they were heavily defeated near Bait al Falaj. In 1955 the British-led Trucial Oman Scouts cooperated with Sultanate forces in putting an end to the Saudi occupation of the Buraimi Oasis, and in defeating the tribes which under the Imam Ghalib were trying to seize full control of the Interior. In June 1957, however, Ghalib returned with more guerrillas armed, trained and backed by Saudi Arabia, and they routed the Sultan's forces. Sultan Said bin Taimur appealed for help, and despite Arab League opposition, British forces intervened and the rebels were driven into the fastnesses of the Jebel Akhdar from which they were not dislodged until January 1959 when two squadrons of the SAS led an assault onto the summit of that mountain. By that time an Agreement had been reached between the British government and Sultan Said under the terms of which Britain undertook to strengthen the Sultan's forces and to second Officers to command and train them. It also extended the arrangements by which the RAF used the airfields at Salalah and Masirah. The first commander of the reorganised Sultan's Armed Forces (SAF) was Colonel David Smiley. I was the fifth. But while northern Oman was being made safe for the Sultanate, the seeds of rebellion were being sown in the southern province of Dhofar.

Dhofar is sharply different from the rest of Oman in climate, fertility and in its people. The latter, thought to number about 50,000, are more volatile, darker in complexion and finer-featured than the northern Omanis. The mountain people of Dhofar, the Jebalis, are descended mainly from the aboriginal inhabitants, speak their own language and live out their lives closely linked with their numerous cattle. The population of the coastal villages has a strong negro element. The coastal plain is some forty miles long but nowhere more than ten miles deep; and behind it the hills and mountains rise in a great arc to a height of about 4,000 feet. Coconut palms abound along the shore of the Indian Ocean, and the areas around Salalah, the provincial capital, and other settlements were once rich in crops, fruits and vegetables to the extent that, during the campaigns in Mesopotamia during the Great War, much of the fodder for the Imperial Cavalry was supplied from there. By 1970 alas most of this agricultural abundance had been allowed to decay, though the outlines of the former fields could be plainly seen from the air.

Dhofar from 1879 remained continously under the Sultans' rule. But rebellions were frequent, the most serious being put down only when an Anglo-Omani force was sent by sea in 1897. Faisal bin Turki was the first Sultan to visit Dhofar, his son Taimur spent more time there than in Muscat, and his grandson, Said bin Taimur became a permanent resident, marrying a Dhofari, the mother of the present Sultan Qaboos. When in 1932 Said succeeded his father, he inherited an almost insolvent country. He asserted his authority throughout the province, but his mediaeval restrictions, his refusal to acknowledge Dhofari grievances and his bitter reaction to expressions of discontent led to a rebellion which was to become the Dhofar War. Said's rule was harsh and reactionary; he was out of his time and should be compared with despots of a past age. In debt for most of his reign, he set his face against development and he sought to keep the modern world out of Oman. Although he belatedly started to modernise northern Oman, he regarded Dhofar as his personal feudal estate. It remained undeveloped with few amenities, roads, schools or medical facilities. The Dhofaris had genuine grievances, and when they became aware of the development in the 1950s in the oil-rich Gulf states their disillusionment was deepened.

Hostility to the rule of Said bin Taimur was fanned by two movements which in the early 1960s were sweeping the Middle East; Pan-Arabism and scientific socialism. The former was anti-colonialist and therefore anti-British; the latter, often termed Marxist-Leninism, was disseminated and fostered by the Communist powers, the Peoples' Republic of China, the USSR and her European satellites.

Where these movements penetrated unchecked, disorder intended to precipitate change arose. A Dhofar Liberation Front (DLF) emerged, and in December 1962 some of the Bait Kathir tribe led by a disgruntled Dhofari, Mussalim bin Nufl, carried out some minor sabotage against RAF Salalah and four months later attacked some oil company vehicles. Bin Nufl fled to Saudi Arabia but returned accompanied by others who had been trained and equipped in Iraq. Towards the end of 1964 dissident activity increased significantly, and for the first time an SAF force was sent down to Dhofar. In territorial terms this was a tiny force in a country as big as Great Britain, sent to tackle a rebellion in a hostile province, previously unvisited, the size of Wales. The SAF company withdrew after a month

First Months in Oman

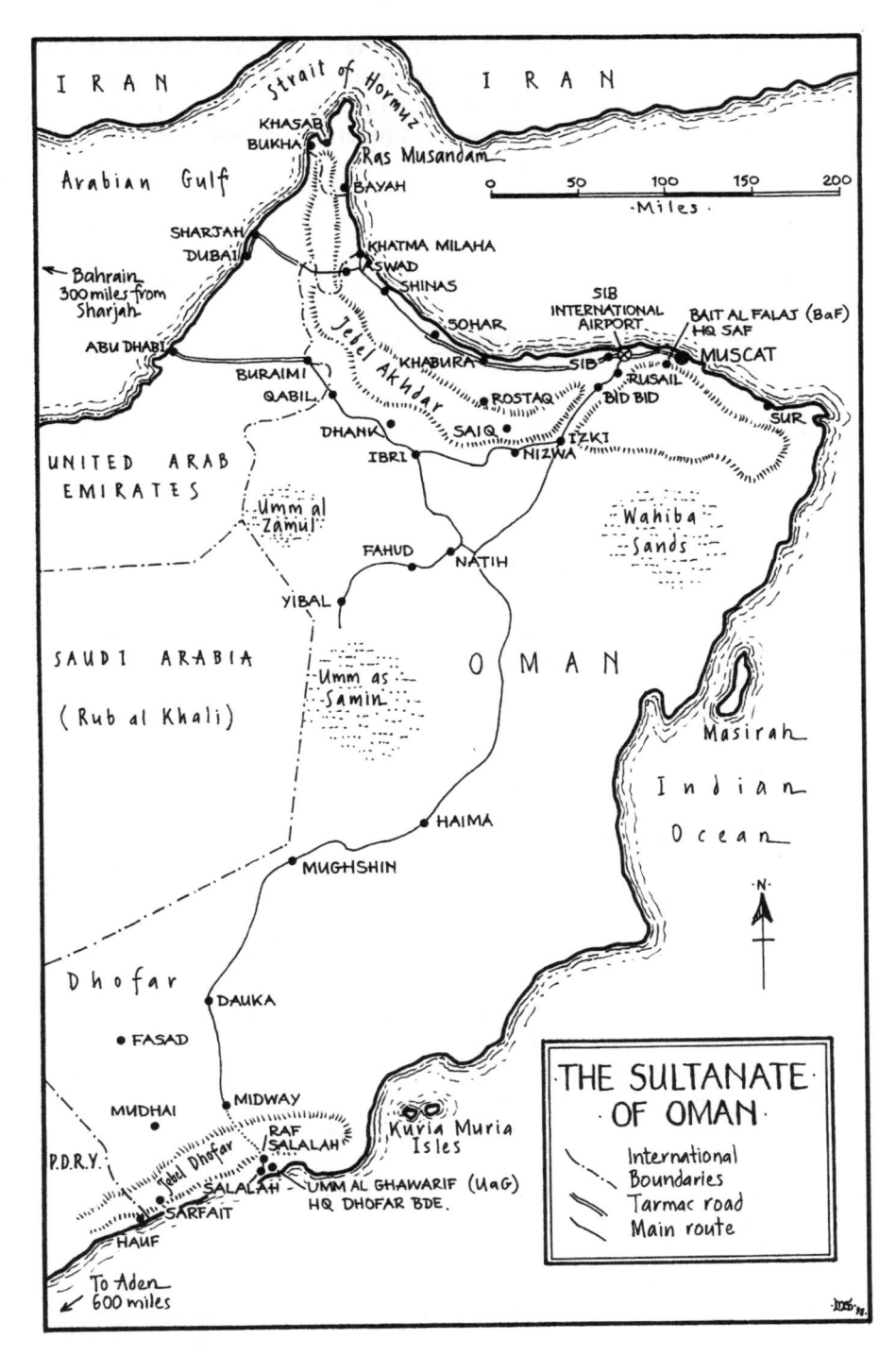

without encountering any rebels, but having produced from this initial armed reconnaissance the valuable first map of Dhofar. Several months of apparent calm followed until June 1965 when the DLF convened their first Congress, elected an eighteen-man executive and issued a Manifesto which declared:

1. The poor classes, the farmers, workers, soldiers and revolutionary intellectuals will form the backbone of the organisation.
2. The imperialist presence will be destroyed in all its forms – military, economic and political.
3. The hireling regime under its ruler, Said bin Taimur, will be destroyed.

Their first armed action occurred on 9 June 1965, and this date is recognised as being the start of the Dhofar War. Other actions followed extending across the Jebel area as far as Midway, Taqa and Marbat, and the oil company's vehicles continued to be targets for mines and ambushes. All this prompted the Sultan to raise a third infantry battalion, the Desert Regiment, and to keep a small force permanently in Dhofar based on a tented camp at Umm al Ghawarif.

Despite the increasing numbers of incidents and casualties, the campaign had hitherto gone rather better for SAF than it had for the rebels. By the spring of 1967 Dhofar had become quiet to the extent that the local SAF commander considered that 'the DLF is virtually finished . . . our difficulty was to find any *adoo* [enemy].' The situation was in reality one of stalemate. SAF was too strong for the tribesmen of the DLF to destroy; but because of manpower and equipment shortages, and the dearth of intelligence, SAF was unable to crush the rebel movement. Furthermore, Said bin Taimur rejected all advice that the rebels be shown some leniency and be encouraged to surrender: he vetoed political concessions and insisted on harsher tactics. 1967 was to be the last time when he could have ended the war by making concessions from a position of strength.

The newly formed but not fully trained Desert Regiment was sent to garrison Dhofar from September 1967 to April 1968. In this period the whole situation changed in the enemy's favour, although the effects were not to be felt for many months.

[Note: I am indebted to Lieutenant-Colonel John McKeown, RE for his Dissertation 'Britain and Oman; The Dhofar War and its Significance' from which I have summarised the events outlined above.]

As a consequence of the British withdrawal in August 1967 from the East Aden Protectorate, and three months later from Aden itself, committed Marxist-Leninists took power in PDRY and began to supply bases, equipment, training and direction for the Dhofar rebellion. From early 1968 the rebels received resupplies from Hauf and the incident rate and casualties rose. The CO of DR, at the end of his tour in Dhofar, was able to state that his battalion had 'done a workmanlike job of containment but without materially shortening the war which,' [he predicted], 'would go on for a long time'. The time for concessions had passed; the DLF was becoming politicised as trained Communist commanders supplanted the Dhofari tribal leaders, and men trained as political commissars at the Anti-Imperialist Academy in Peking arrived in Dhofar. The rebels were also getting more effective militarily as arms, ammunition and instructors reached them from overseas. By late 1969 the worsening situation was causing disquiet in London and discussions were held about Britain giving the direct assistance for which CSAF, Brigadier Corran Purdon, was appealing, and which some other experts advocated. Such appeals were, however, unwelcome at that time, particularly to the Labour government which had decided to withdraw all British forces from the Gulf by the end of 1971. Thus the proposals were shelved: the direct involvement of British units to help Said bin Taimur was ruled out.

To the wider world Oman and what was happening there remained unknown. The country produced no newspaper, had no radio broadcast system, and foreign official presence was limited to two consulates, a British and an Indian, both in Muscat. Sultan Said personally controlled the issue of entry permits and ensured that inquisitive reporters and their like did not set foot on his territory.

Soldiering in the south of England for four years before my appointment to command SAF, I had been aware that the SAS had driven the rebels off the Jebel Akhdar in 1959, and that some skirmishes and mining incidents still occurred in northern Oman. Indeed, some of my parachute soldiers had been sent on routine patrols there from our base in Bahrain. As regards Dhofar, we heard from time to time that tribal guerrillas used to come down from the Jebel to raid the coastal villages or to probe the perimeter of the RAF station outside Salalah. These tales reminded us of the adventures of our predecessors on the North-West frontier of India in the 1930s.

My personal distant and very limited perception of Sultan Said was of a beleaguered and stubborn old autocrat whose little army, run by his traditional ally Britain, was striving to protect Oman from the evils of Communism. If there was serious anxiety in Whitehall about the march of events in Oman, it was concealed from me by the experts in the Foreign Office and the MoD who briefed me before I left England. Moreover, at the end of my final interview, with the Vice-Chief of the General Staff, Sir Victor FitzGeorge-Balfour, his parting instructions to me were clear: 'When you get to Muscat you will find that among the British Officers there is a sizeable element that goes around saying that the problems facing that country are all the fault of the Sultan, Said bin Taimur, and that he should be removed. It is your duty to hammer anybody who expresses such views. You are to remind them that Oman is his country and that he knows better than anyone how it should be governed.'

Leaving Rosemary and the children to follow when the schools' term ended, I flew out to Muscat at the end of March, breaking my journey in Bahrain and Sharjah for briefing, to renew old friendships, and to dispel the pallor of an English winter. As the little aircraft lined up for its descent onto the airstrip at Bait al Falaj, its wings almost brushed the rock walls of the narrow entrance to the Ruwi valley. Little had changed since my last visit five years before. There were the same welcoming faces: Colin Maxwell, Malcolm Dennison, Bob Warner and Richard Anderson, all veterans in the Sultan's service; Hugh Oldman, now the Defence Secretary, and Corran Purdon, the staunch and energetic Commander of the Forces from whom I took over a day or two later. The Sultan had sent word from his palace in Salalah that I need not call on him until I had been round the units and made an assessment of the situation.

The SAF which I took over was a single entity commanded and administered from the Fort at Bait al Falaj. I was responsible to His Highness the Sultan through Hugh Oldman, a former CSAF and Infantryman who had replaced Pat Waterfield as Defence Secretary three months before I arrived. Hugh and I were to work in the greatest harmony and our friendship continued until his death eighteen years later.

The largest component of SAF, the Army, consisted mainly of three Infantry battalions, Muscat Regiment (MR), Northern Frontier Regiment (NFR) and Desert Regiment (DR). Each battalion was deployed in turn to Dhofar on a nine-month tour. The soldiers in most of the rifle sections were mixed Arab and Baluch, the latter slightly outnumbering the former. The Baluch were indispensable. They were eager to find employment and Sultan Said had retained the recruiting rights in the impoverished Makran area of Baluchistan when it joined Pakistan in 1948. He also rated their reliability higher than his Omani troops, and for that reason insisted that the rank and file in the Artillery Battery should all be Baluch. (This meant that the British Gunner Officers went on a Baluch language course before joining SAF.) There was also a battalion-sized unit, the Oman Gendarmerie (OG), whose soldiers were solely Arab. Lightly armed and trained principally for patrolling the long coast-line and the tracks leading into the Interior the OG did not serve in Dhofar.

Because of the extreme dearth of educated Omanis the junior administrative and technical posts were filled by Pakistanis. The Regimental Medical Officers, like the Force Dentist, were Indian, though the senior doctor, Ian Hynd, was a Scot. SAF's medical capabilities were limited to what could be done for our sick and wounded in the regimental aid posts (RAPs) or in the sick-bay at Bait al Falaj. Any SAF personnel needing more advanced treatment or surgery had to be flown at the Sultanate's expense by RAF aircraft to Bahrain.

All the Officers commanding above platoon level and on the HQ staff were British. Those employed by the Sultan on contract came from a variety of backgrounds. Most had been in the British or British-Indian Army or in colonial police forces, and therefore had experienced Service life; but not all had. SAF really was obliged to accept almost everyone willing to join on contract. The seconded element were professionals, stimulated perhaps by the prospect of active service and sunshine, who had volunteered for duty in Oman and had managed to persuade their Service superiors to release them for a couple of years or so. (Some did not succeed in this; the Scottish Division and the RAF were reluctant to let their young men deviate from the orthodox career patterns mapped out for them.) Those of us above the rank of Major came to SAF for two-and-a-half to three years; those in more junior command and staff appointments for nineteen months. These younger men were normally given a rank in SAF higher than the one they held in British units; but what they lacked in qualifications they made up for with keenness and good sense.

Each rifle company had an establishment of three British Officers, but leave, sickness and wounds meant that often only two were available for operations. Consequently companies tended to operate in two halves, each commanded by a single British chap who, amongst his other preoccupations, had to control the mortar and artillery fire and the air strikes. There were a number of Omani and Baluch subalterns of great combat experience and proven bravery, but Sultan Said would not allow them to receive formal officer training or hold any rank above Lieutenant.

The battalion weapons were the Belgian FN rifle which had largely replaced the Mark 4 rifle by the end of 1969, the Bren light machine gun (LMG), and 3-inch mortars. These last two weapons were already obsolete in the British Army. In terms of range and weight of fire, the enemy in Dhofar – the *adoo* – armed with Soviet and Chinese weapons, was better equipped than was our Infantry.

The air component of SAF, the Sultan of Oman's Air Force (SOAF), commanded by Squadron Leader Alan Bridges seconded from the Royal Air Force, was a small but excellent force of Strikemasters, Beavers and two aged Dakotas. An element of SOAF, together with essential mechanics from Airwork Services Ltd, an English civilian organisation, was based within the perimeter of the RAF station at Salalah where it was dependent on the expertise and goodwill of the RAF personnel. The importance of RAF Salalah to SOAF, and thus to SAF's ability to continue the war, was crucial. The protection of this indispensable air base was to remain a cardinal factor in determining the deployment in Dhofar of SAF's limited resources.

The Sultan's navy, the Coastal Patrol, consisted of two armed dhows, *Nasr al Bahr* and *Muntassir*, commanded with zest by a bearded sea-dog, Lieutenant-Commander Jeremy Raybould. In addition to the minor, ill-equipped Transport, Ordnance and Signals units and the Mechanical Engineers, SAF included a company-sized Oil Installation Police unit of Pakistanis and Baluch under a British contract Officer. The only civil police in the whole country were the squads in Muttrah and Muscat.

In June 1970 the total strength of the Sultan's Armed Forces was 3,800. The rank and file were indifferently housed and fed, and in comparison with local forces elsewhere in the Gulf, poorly paid even though Colonel Oldman and the senior administrative staff Officer, Lieutenant-Colonel John Moore, prevailed upon the Sultan soon after I arrived to authorise some improvements. Throughout SAF discipline and turn-out were in general remarkably good.

Bait al Falaj in 1970 was solely a military cantonment which, with its concrete airstrip, had grown up around the picturesque white Fort which housed the Headquarters. The cantonment was made up of living quarters, bungalows for the six British who were permitted to have their wives with them, the Messes (separate for each nationality), a few huts for the families of the Muscat Garrison soldiers, the SOAF/Airwork complex, SAF's workshops, sick bay and other technical installations and the British military cemetery. Air conditioners were not installed in offices until August 1970. The Force ammunition, after unloading in Muscat harbour, was kept stacked in a wadi beside the airstrip (and despite being open to the elements nothing blew up until it had been moved in 1973 into special new bunkers farther inland). The only hard-surfaced public road in the whole country ran from Bait al Falaj via Muttrah to Muscat.

The leisure time of the British inhabitants of Bait al Falaj was spent largely in an old Officers' Mess building, The Muskateer, or on the beaches at Blackpool or Qurm. To get to these we had to drive by Land Rover to the big tree in Ruwi village, turn right and bump our way over sand, gravel and rock past the Customs Post with its good-natured, one-armed warden, through the oil company's camp, the PD(O) complex, and down to Blackpool with its charming little cove, slipway and SAF Sailing Club hut, or on to the deserted sands of Qurm with its marshes and prominent wrecked steamship, half-submerged half a mile off-shore. The highlights of life in my first months there were the thrice-weekly arrival of the Gulf Air Fokker Friendship bringing mail, new arrivals and chums back from leave; and the open-air cinema. As Rosemary found when she joined me, life for the few European wives was particularly limited. None was permitted to travel more than twenty-five miles from Bait al Falaj without special dispensation from the Sultan; and he was permanently remote for he had not left Salalah since 1957 nor set foot outside his palace there since 1967. And those couples who ventured out from Muscat for supper with

SAF or the Oil Company could not get back home through the closed gates of the capital unless their hosts had remembered to furnish them with the obligatory permit from the Governor. We were of necessity a close-knit community, and we were proud of our soldiers. We were aware too that, although Said bin Taimur remained many hundreds of miles from our community, reports of our activities and utterances reached his ears with remarkable swiftness. His most zealous informants, we were to find out, were those Omanis who went out of their way to befriend us, creatures newly arrived in a place as primitive and remote, it seemed to Rosemary, as the moon.

By the middle of April I had made my first visits to the OG at Sib and in their outlying posts, to NFR at BidBid, and to MR just outside Nizwa, the capital of the Interior and formerly of the Imamate. Standards in the Force were better than I had expected in view of the poor conditions in which everyone lived and the limited facilities for military training. The soldiers' morale too seemed pretty good – though I was soon to learn that the Arabs, Baluch, Indians and Pakistanis tended to say what they believed would give me pleasure rather than reveal their true anxieties or deepest thoughts. The depressing consequences of the Sultan's parsimony were somewhat mitigated by the British Officers on whom the soldiery knew they could rely for caring leadership, food and regular pay. And among those Officers I found a general contentment with their lot, an affection for their subordinates (while recognising their limitations), and a genuine desire somehow to help the Omani nation.

I suppose that the thing which struck me most during my early experiences in Oman, in the sixties when I used to come across from Bahrain, and now in the spring of 1970, was the emptiness of the country; it seemed largely devoid of life, human or animal. The male inhabitants whom we encountered in the villages had fine features and excellent manners. Courtesy is a hallmark of the Omani but the Army, Baluch-manned and British-led, was set apart from the population; respected but not loved. The other impression I have retained of the Oman of Said bin Taimur is of the natural grandeur of the country, be it amid the mountains of the Jebel Akhdar massif or on the gravel plain of the Batinah coast. It all looked unspoilt by human activity, apart from the occasional dwelling place erected near a grove of date palms or an ancient watch tower built for the protection of a remote settlement. The land had altered little since the Creation. It was marvellous to behold and in no way repellent. I felt serene and very privileged to be there; a tiny being on the face of a beautiful, majestic, and secret segment of Planet Earth.

Only when I got down to Dhofar did I become aware of the extent to which the situation had changed in the enemy's favour. Corran Purdon, a contemporary of mine at Camberley and a Royal Ulster Rifleman who

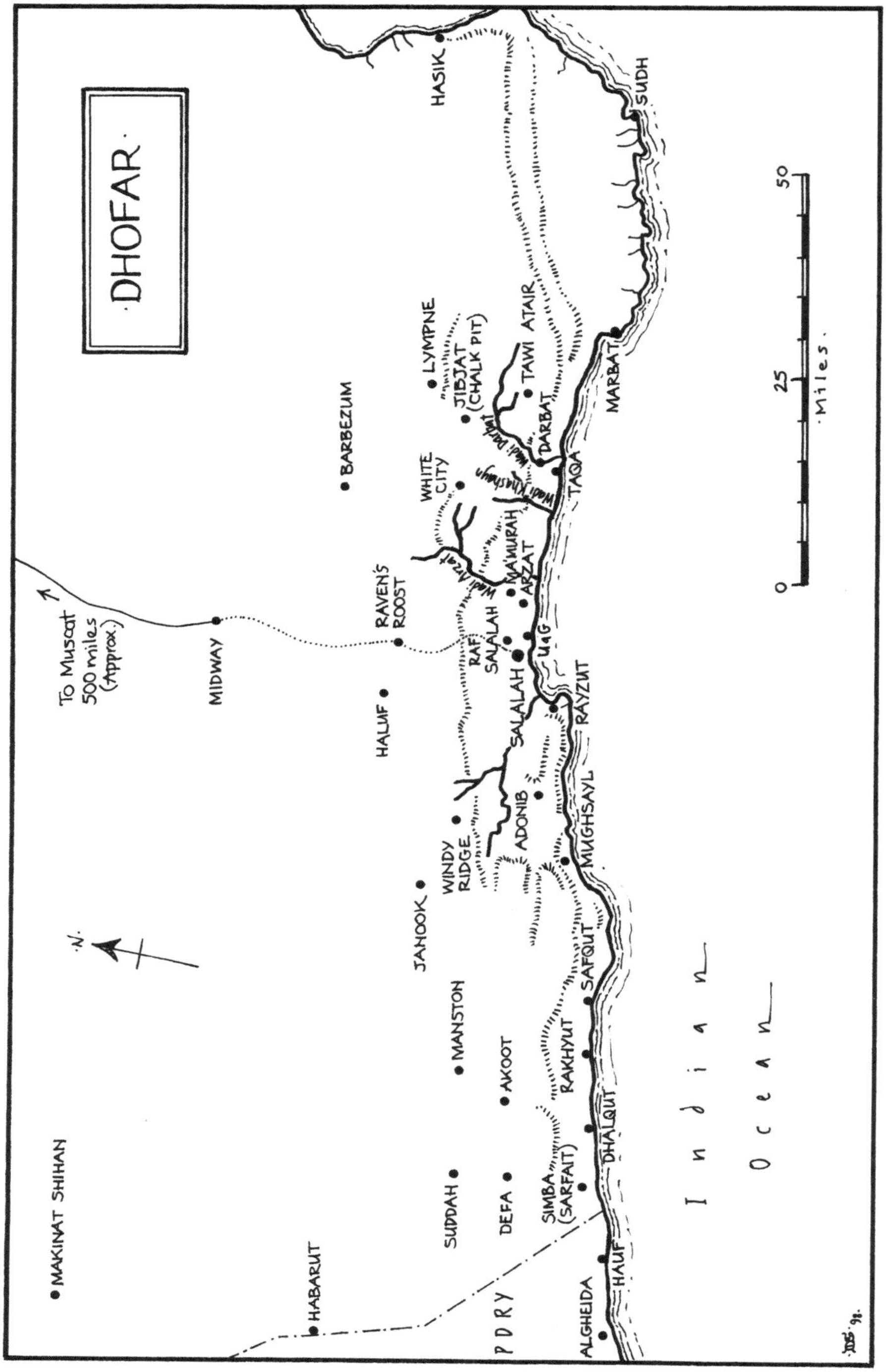
DHOFAR
HASIK
SUDH
LYMPNE
JIBJAT
(CHALK PIT)
TAWI ATAIR
MARBAT
DARBAT
Wadi Darbat
BARBEZUM
WHITE CITY
TAQA
Wadi Khashayn
MA'MURAH
ARZAT
Wadi Arzat
RAVEN'S ROOST
RAF SALALAH
UAG
SALALAH
RAYZUT
To Muscat
500 miles
(Approx.)
MIDWAY
HALUF
ADONIB
WINDY RIDGE
MUGHSAYL
JANOOK
N
SAFQUT
MANSTON
AKOOT
RAKHYUT
DHALQUT
SIMBA
(SARFAIT)
SUDDAH
DEFA
MAKINAT SHIHAN
HABARUT
HAUF
ALGHEIDA
PDRY
Indian
Ocean
0
25
50
Miles

had won a Military Cross with the Commandos, had arrived as CSAF in April 1967. He was determined to prosecute the war with vigour, and when NFR, under its experienced and aggressive CO, Mike Harvey, relieved DR in Dhofar they carried the war deep into *adoo*-held territory, with companies operating even in the rugged country astride the Wadi Saiq, overlooking the PDRY frontier town of Hauf, and on the coast at Rakhyut.

Mike's strategy was to establish bases in areas such as Defa and Janook, which the enemy could not ignore, and having brought them to battle, fragment the enemy into smaller and less effective groups. The weakness of these bases was that their occupants were dependent for resupply, especially for water, on the convoys of lorries which routinely ground their way over the long sandy and rocky tracks from NFR's main base on the plain, or on what could be flown in by Beaver aircraft on to a rough airstrip. The carriage to safety of the wounded could at times bring to those involved the quality of a nightmare; the exertion of bearing stretchers over the Jebel terrain while fighting off the *adoo* gangs pursuing, or trying to head off the struggling SAF troops, meant that it at times took one hundred men six hours to bring a single wounded comrade out of danger. Casualties thus caused several operations to be terminated prematurely. Moreover, the fact that a SAF position on the *adoo*-held Jebel could only be maintained for a brief period and at some cost was quickly discerned by both sides – and by the civilian population who soon realised they could no longer look to SAF for lasting protection (a SAF which the Jebalis had accurately come to regard as an alien force of Baluchis led by Englishmen).

Purdon pleaded with Waterfield and Said bin Taimur for the two essentials if the *adoo* were to be defeated; more Infantry and helicopters. But the Sultan was not willing to spend the money; it was not until October 1969 that he authorised the raising of a fourth battalion, Jebel Regiment, or the placing of the first order for helicopters.

The political aspect of the war had changed dramatically in August 1968. In that month the enemy held another Congress at which a General Command was set up to direct the war. The leadership now included only three of the original Dhofari chiefs; the name Dhofar Liberation Front was changed to Popular Front for the Liberation of Oman and the Arabian Gulf (PFLOAG); the ideology changed from nationalism to Marxism-Leninism, and the target area was extended to embrace the whole Gulf. Thus was the simple rebellion of disgruntled Dhofari tribesmen grimly transformed into a Communist revolution. The revolutionary transformation of Dhofar commenced with the political instruction of the armed units, the organisation of the Jebali men (and women also for under Communism they were granted rights and privileges hitherto denied to their sex) into the Militia, some 3,000 Jebali armed men, and the smaller but better equipped and motivated Hard Core units of 'PFLOAG Fighters'. These were estimated to number 2,000. Many Jebalis objected to the transformation being imposed on their way of life and to the denial of God demanded of them. The objectors were put to death or brutally tortured; the nature of life on the Dhofar Jebel changed savagely. In the weeks following the 1968 monsoon the *adoo* launched their first attacks against Salalah and with mortars and rocket-launchers (RCLs) against the RAF station and the SAF Hedgehogs erected for its defence. NFR continued a series of aggressive operations, some accompanied by CSAF in person, against the coastal settlements in the west, against Marbat and onto key areas of the Jebel, and in these encounters SAF inflicted significantly more casualties on the enemy than it suffered. But although SAF was coming off best in the individual battles, PFLOAG was winning the war. The Front's numbers and equipment, and the degree of collaboration coerced from the population, were increasing steadily: but SAF's strength and equipment were static and her credit was ebbing. Furthermore the contacts, previously one or two a week, were in early 1969 running at two or three a day.

Mike Harvey and NFR went back to Oman rightly feeling that they had completed a successful tour of active service, that they had proved themselves better at fighting than the *adoo*, and that they had proved from hard-won experience how the enemy could be defeated.

The Muscat Regiment that relieved NFR had a new CO; those in MR who had served in Dhofar in earlier years found the situation facing them dramatically different; and in the weeks taken up by the process of roulement (the change-over of battalions between Dhofar and the Omani garrison towns of BidBid and Nizwa, a journey of nearly a thousand kilometres over rough desert tracks in the Force's inadequate and clapped-out 3-ton lorries), the impetus of SAF operations was lost. Nevertheless MR began a series of operations in the west, emulating NFR, based on Defa and Janook, and taking the war to the very citadel of *adoo* resistance, the Sherishitti cave complex. But enemy fire-power and tactical skill had increased (the latter operation has been recorded as 'a sobering experience') and MR's bases for these operations were being subjected to heavier fire than hitherto. Moreover the mines and ambushes on the tracks and airstrips were inflicting unacceptable losses on SAF's transport resources. The Colonel commanding MR decided that he could no longer maintain forces in the west and withdrew to the western end of the Salalah Plain. The abandonment of all Dhofar lying between Mughsayl and the PDRY frontier was inevitable given the reluctance of Said bin Taimur to grant Corran Purdon the extra men, the modern weapons and helicopters, and the intervention of men and materiel from Britain, for which he had pleaded. The occupation of western Dhofar was a significant prize for the Front who named it 'Liberated Dhofar' and executed the representatives of the Sultan's rule they found there. In 1967 SAF could perhaps have suppressed the rebellion; by the end of 1969 SAF in Dhofar was merely capable of holding Salalah, some coastal settlements and the RAF station, and of undertaking small offensive actions of at most two days' duration. Purdon's strategy was reduced to one of containment.

Of all the British Commanders of the Sultan's Armed Forces since David Smiley handed over to Hugh Oldman in 1962, Corran Purdon had, in my opinion, quite the hardest row to hoe. Ill-supported by his superiors in Muscat and London, dependent for the scope of his military operations on the blinkered judgement and penurious nature of a despotic Monarch, Corran was denied the professional satisfaction of bringing the Dhofar rebellion to an end, and he had a particular misfortune in that this denial was the legacy of that same Monarch who, rejecting all counsels of compassion and leniency, drove into the alien arms of Communist revolutionaries thousands of his subjects.

By the spring of 1970 the enemy had established themselves over the whole of the Dhofari Jebel, and of especial significance, they dominated and cratered the Midway road, the only overland route between Salalah and Oman proper. In consequence the units operating south of the Jebel could only be supplied by air or by sea. As no harbour nor even a simple jetty existed, everything had to be brought ashore by barge; moreover this slow, cumbersome procedure could only be carried out when the sea was calm. During the monsoon months of May to October it was too rough. Thus there were severe limitations on the size of the force which could be maintained on the Salalah Plain.

Desert Regiment, commanded by Lieutenant-Colonel Teddy Turnill, from the Royal Anglian Regiment, was based on Umm al Ghawarif camp and reinforced by a company of NFR and Z Company of the Muscat Guard Unit. This last outfit was led by a dynamic warrior from Rhodesia, Major Spike Powell. DR was supported by a troop from the Artillery Battery consisting of four 25-pounder field guns and one 5.5-inch medium gun and by the flight of SOAF Strikemasters and Beaver aircraft which operated out of the RAF station. Turnill's paramount tasks were to control Salalah town, which was totally enclosed by a thick belt of barbed wire with Control Posts manned by the Sultan's askars at the few gates, and to protect the RAF station. This latter task he carried out by manning the Hedgehogs, platoon bases strongly constructed out of sand-filled oil drums, rock and timber about four hundred yards to the flanks and north of the air base, and by establishing a prohibited zone within which anything moving by night could be freely fired upon. There was one DR company dug in on the Jebel just to the east of the Midway road. It was difficult to resupply, drew quite a lot of fire and served no purpose other than to sustain the fiction that SAF still dominated a slice of the Jebel. My first action was to bring it down to the Plain where it could be of greater use. Along the coast Arzat, Taqa and Marbat were still under government control, garrisoned by parties of the Sultan's askars and armed inhabitants supervised by the local Wali or his deputy. Taqa and Marbat, like Rayzut to the west, could only be reached after deliberate road-opening operations – for the tracks were frequently mined and for stretches lay under aimed fire – or by Beaver aircraft using rough landing strips on the shore.

At Arzat was located the Dhofar Force. This was a private army which had been set up, under Pakistani Officers, by Sultan Said as his personal reserve. It was not part of SAF, we were not permitted to test it, and its members at that time played no part in the campaign. I got myself flown to Taqa accompanied by Captain Tim Landon, a young Hussar who had left the British Army to come on contract as the Dhofar Intelligence Officer. The men of Taqa, and the elderly Naib Wali in charge of the place, were beyond question the most miserable, hand-wringing bunch of humanity I had ever encountered. The mud walls of many houses were holed by bullets or rocket projectiles and, according to Landon, the *adoo* had such a grip on the place that they came and went at will. The Wali and his retinue were scared stiff of *adoo* retribution if they defended themselves and terrified of the Sultan's punishment if they did not. Thus they did nothing, and I could see the many coils of barbed wire sent for the town's protection still lying about unused. When the Wali urged me to have more rifles and ammunition issued to his men I refused saying: 'Not until you have made proper use of the wire and weapons you already have will I allow SAF to hand over more to Taqa'. Landon and I suspected that any we sent would surely end up in *adoo* hands. My visit to Taqa was a sobering experience.

Teddy Turnill was a robust but sensitive and deeply reflective man; a good, sound and wholly reliable chap to direct the defence of the Salalah Plain. Although his Desert Regiment Group was holding its own from Adonib to Marbat, the outlook was not encouraging. The morale of the civilian population was low, or even abysmal as I had seen in Taqa, and with the exception of a few splendid men such as Baraik bin Hamood, the son of the bed-ridden Wali of Salalah, the population was unsympathetic to SAF. By night the enemy were coming down onto the Plain for minelaying or ambushes, probing the defences of the RAF station or engaging DR's Hedgehogs with mortar and RCL fire. Our knowledge of PFLOAG's organisation and plans was exceedingly meagre. Not surprisingly, for, whereas young Dhofaris were creeping away from Salalah – some drowning in the sea – in the hope of reaching the Jebel and thereafter Aden, only a handful of enemy had been captured or come across to the Sultan's side.

Teddy Turnill and his colleagues were confident that they would hold the line for as long as required, but none expressed any hope that SAF would get back onto the Jebel and stay there to defeat the Communist enemy without major assistance from outside Oman.

First Months in Oman

* * *

In the evening of my visit to Taqa I had my first audience of Sultan Said. He was shorter in stature than I had expected and his white beard and distinctive turban gave him a truly regal air. For an elderly man who never set foot outside his palace, he looked remarkably healthy and he was throughout our hour alone in the small Audience Chamber vigorous in movement and agile in mind. He began by asking about my family and my past experiences. Many minutes passed with these civilities – for His Highness was a most courteous questioner and fluent in English – before he touched on more serious matters. As we spoke of these, certain impressions built up in my mind. He had a surprisingly accurate knowledge of what was happening hundreds of miles away in Muscat or Nizwa or Sohar – his informants were obviously doing their stuff – but of the true situation five miles away on the Dhofar Jebel he appeared exceedingly ignorant. This ignorance he combined with an astonishing complacency. He expressed no appreciation of the toil and hardships that Corran Purdon and his forces had undergone, but rather resentment that western Dhofar had been yielded to the enemy. And when he reminded me that he had given permission for a fourth battalion to be raised, he indicated that that decision alone would suffice to bring about the collapse of his enemies. He said to me: 'Just be patient, for one day soon the *adoo* will just give up, go away and disappear'. I got him to agree in principle to reviewing again with Hugh Oldman the poor pay and conditions under which his soldiers served, but when I broached the matter of a political approach to the jebalis, a hearts-and-minds approach aimed at seducing some of the waverers away from Communist rule, he became almost vehement. His last words before I left the room were: 'Those people on the Jebel are very bad. Brigadier, I want you to kill them all'. Earlier in our conversation I had felt that I was talking to a dignified, tenacious Hanoverian monarch who was attempting unaided to govern England from a beleaguered Balmoral Castle. But that final injunction left me with a bleaker image of Said bin Taimur; and with much food for thought. Nevertheless I kept these sentiments to myself, and when Colonel Turnill asked how I had got on with the Sultan, I replied: 'He seems a nice old boy with firm ideas about how to run his country, and optimistic about the way the war is going'. I knew from the despairing glance that Teddy gave Landon that they were thinking: 'Here is another naive fellow straight out from England who has been captivated by the Sultan's charm and obstinacy'.

Back home in Bait al Falaj the stark scenery of the Ruwi valley was wonderfully softened by the setting sun, and to sit on the patio of Flagstaff House surveying our private military enclave was balm to the soul. But in those moments of solitude we reflected with growing unease on the abyss to which Said bin Taimur's policies were driving the people of that majestic land for which we British soldiers had a great affection.

Whereas the information we had about the PFLOAG enemy in Dhofar was almost zero, the little we had gleaned about the National Democratic Front (NDFLOAG), our Iraqi-backed principal threat in the north was positively misleading.

As the Head of our Intelligence Staff, Major John McFrederick, was shortly to leave Oman, I convened a meeting of all Intelligence Officers in the Sultanate at which they were to report on the situation in their areas of responsibility and to state how they thought events would develop. This meeting would usefully round off McFrederick's service with SAF and enable him to speak with up-to-date authority at his debriefing in London. It would also be of particular interest to me personally as I had not yet had an opportunity to be briefed by all the members of our far-flung Intelligence family assembled in one room

The conference which lasted all day was held on Thursday 11 June 1970 at Bait al Falaj in the Muskateer, the long, dark, cool building which was the hub of the corporate life of the British element at HQ SAF.

What these Officers had to say to me on that June day merited unusual credence, since only the previous month they had supervised the issue of the new Sultanate currency, the Rial Saidi, in exchange for the long-used Indian rupee and the Maria Theresa dollar. This operation had taken SAF to pretty well every village in Oman and had presented us with a rare opportunity to read the pulse of the population.

In their reports the Officers mentioned the universal public complaints about the Sultan's continuing seclusion in Salalah, about his refusal to spend the oil revenues, accruing since 1967, for the benefit of his subjects, and about the indifference or incompetence of some of the Walis. They also confirmed what we already knew; that SAF with its British leadership and a largely Baluch Rank and File was generally now regarded as the sole institution keeping Said bin Taimur in power and the Omani nation deprived. The population in consequence was becoming increasingly reluctant to cooperate with us or to allow their young men to enlist in SAF. To us none of this was new or unexpected. What was surprising was the fact that none of the Intelligence Officers produced evidence that subversion was growing or that the arms-smuggling, about which we knew quite a lot, was to be translated into more violent actions. After all, only six months earlier the Wadi Jizzi had been the scene of a rebel incursion and there was no reason to conclude that the incident would be the last. Nevertheless in Oman on 11 June 1970 all seemed quiet. Thus when I summed up at the end of the day I could only describe the military situation as follows: 'In Dhofar the *adoo* now controls nine-tenths of that Province; SAF however is holding its own on the vital Salalah Plain and there is no reason to fear that our grip there will be broken. If however

First Months in Oman

SAF was faced with new outbreaks of revolutionary activity in Central or Northern Oman our ability to continue the campaign in the South would be imperilled. But after listening all day to the reports of you Intelligence Officers I conclude that such new outbreaks are not to be expected in the near future. There is some clandestine activity, and public sympathy for the rebel movements is undoubtedly growing; but no explosion is imminent. Thus,' I said, 'we must concentrate on helping Teddy Turnill and his Desert Regiment Group in their task of defending the Salalah Plain.' Everyone nodded in agreement, the meeting dispersed and we at HQ SAF turned our thoughts to the morrow, the weekly juma'a holiday, and to our preoccupations with Dhofar.

It was not long before we were made to realise how superficial was our knowledge about what was really going on around us.

Soon after first light the next day, 12 June, the Brigade Major, Andrew Shelley, rang me with the news that during the night machine guns and a rocket launcher had been fired into the camp at Izki of B Company The Northern Frontier Regiment. This fusillade had miraculously caused no casualties and no great damage. Nor had the explosive charges which had been placed round the Muscat Regiment's petrol dump at Nizwa.

At Izki the attackers had made no attempt to enter the camp but had moved off at speed into the darkness towards the broken and sparsely inhabited terrain which lies at the eastern foot of the Jebel Akhdar massif. Karl Beale's NFR, based at BidBid, gave chase with B Company in the van and by daybreak had tracked the enemy gang, eleven-strong, into the Wadi Mahram where the 'going' and the cover would greatly increase the odds against NFR catching up with them. I told Shelley to get SOAF to put up a Beaver aircraft with instructions to circle continuously the whole area through which the enemy might be moving. Shelley sensibly replied: 'But the country is so broken and the undergrowth so dense that the pilot will see little on the ground'. I said: 'Yes, but the enemy may not realise this; fear of being spotted from the air will make them cautious, slow them up and thus give NFR a chance – the only chance – of catching up with them before nightfall'. And that is what happened. Around midday the leading platoons of NFR, led by Captain Charles Hepworth, came under fire from a party of enemy hidden in the wadi bottom. Three of his soldiers were hit at once, but after some delay Hepworth and his troops attacked and dealt with the enemy group. Other elements of NFR took over the lead and by the end of that day, 12 June, all but one of the Izki gang were dead or made prisoner: the man who got away was arrested the following month.

When later that day I called in at Izki Camp to see Hepworth his shirt and trousers were stained, torn and holed. This young Officer of The King's Regiment had been on the same Arabic language course as I immediately before coming out to Oman. He described to me how he and his men had suddenly bumped the enemy and come under fierce fire. Charles, having worked out his plan of attack shouted out, in Arabic, the orders for his soldiers and then charged into the midst of the enemy. There he found himself quite alone; not one of his men had moved forward with him. He somehow made his way back, still under fire, to his troops' position, repeated his orders and for the second time charged the enemy. This time he was not alone. When he later berated his men for having let him go forward alone they said to him: 'Sahib, we could hear you shouting but couldn't understand a word of what you were saying. But the second time, after you had shown us, we understood and we came with you'. Charles Hepworth was a very plucky – and lucky – young man. His conduct that day earned him the Sultan's Bravery Medal.

If the Izki gang had eluded NFR the situation in Oman could have become extremely serious. How serious I was to learn some two months later in a conversation with Seyyid Tariq bin Taimur after he had returned to Oman to become Prime Minister. Tariq while abroad had been an influential supporter of NDFLOAG and an active campaigner for the liberation of Muscat and Oman from the repressive rule of his Brother, Sultan Said. Tariq said to me: 'You were more lucky that you realise in having that success after the attack on Izki Camp'. 'Yes,' I replied, 'Things turned out well for us, but to attribute that success solely to luck would be unfair to the Northern Frontier Regiment.' He went on: 'What you did not know is that those incidents at Izki and Nizwa were planned to be just the first in a whole series of actions, actions designed to get SAF dispersed in small groups over a wide area of Central Oman'. He continued: 'And I must tell you that when SAF had become split up in that way, a number of British Officers were to be killed by certain of their soldiers. You see,' he said, 'we had come to realise that only when their British leaders were put out of action would the Sultan's Forces lose their cohesion and effectiveness. Until that happened the Omani and Baluch soldiers would continue to serve Sultan Said. Without SAF to protect him Sultan Said could be swiftly overthrown; but with SAF intact he would remain invulnerable and the peoples of the Sultanate would continue to suffer.'

This conversation with Tariq deepened my conviction that the cardinal role in preserving the security and unity of the Sultanate would continue for many years to fall to SAF; and that the crucial element in sustaining the effectiveness of the three Services would be the leadership qualities of the British.

During the first half of 1970 the Rank and File of SAF, particularly the Omani Arabs, had been under great strain, torn between a desire to see their country modernised under a more enlightened Ruler and their loyalty to their British commanders in the service of Sultan Said. Many were being taunted by their relatives and civilian friends who accused them of keeping Sultan Said in power and thus prolonging Oman's unhappy state. That SAF emerged intact from that testing period reflects credit on the Sultanate's Servicemen of that era, as it does on the Force Commanders of earlier years and their subordinates on secondment or contract. They built well and Britain can be proud of them.

In June we had two Officers murdered. A Pakistani subaltern was killed by a Baluch Private Soldier: the latter was tried and executed. Earlier Captain Eddie Vutirakis of Desert Regiment was shot while asleep in Dhofar by an NCO of his company who immediately fled to the *adoo* lines. A former member of the British Special Air Service Regiment, Eddie had joined SAF on contract in September 1969 and shortly thereafter was awarded the Sultan's Bravery Medal for rescuing from a minefield a seriously wounded soldier. He had developed with the Corporal who became his murderer a particularly close relationship; and it became clear to us that these murders were wholly unpolitical but were due to personal relationships going sour at a time when All Ranks were under stress in combat in Dhofar, and furthermore seemingly on the losing side.

But to return to the immediate aftermath of NFR's success in the Wadi Mahram . . . Towards evening the bodies of those killed were flown to BidBid for burial. As I looked at the enemy dead a number of thoughts passed through my mind. How sad that they, young and vigorous, had been driven to take up arms in order to win for their country a government and standard of living which other people in the region had long enjoyed. How foolish too that they had taken up arms against SAF, vastly more powerful in weapons and skilled in their use. But looking at the formidable armament they had been carrying I asked myself how much more weaponry was lying concealed throughout the country awaiting a more favourable moment to be used against us. And of course in the minds of us all was the question 'Would SAF be as lucky next time as NFR had been today?' A matter which gave us much food for thought was the large amounts of money, in the new Omani currency, found on the corpses. Introduced only four weeks before, how had they obtained it? And from whom? Whatever the deficiencies in their tactical skills, this gang was clearly well equipped and supported.

Many of our questions were answered during the following weeks. The interrogation of those taken prisoner led to the identification and arrest of others implicated in the rebel movements. As we pursued our investigations the net became more and more widely cast. The interrogations were carried out in the basement of the fort at Bait al Falaj and were conducted, since the Sultanate had no one trained to do this, by a team of specialists in the Intelligence Corps sent out from England. As information flowed in from a growing variety of sources, we became aware of the great number of people both in the coastal towns and in the Interior who had come to support by word or deed the aims and activities of NDFLOAG and the lesser rebel movements. Many were openly dismayed that SAF by its success in the Wadi Mahram had thwarted the overthrow of Said bin Taimur; and we were left in no doubt that other patriots were waiting for further opportunities to strike with greater skill and effectiveness. Each day that passed since the Izki incident made us realise the size of the problem facing the Sultan's Armed Forces, already heavily engaged eight hundred kilometres away in Dhofar against our principal adversary PFLOAG.

The reports of these new threats, in the heartland of Oman, to the rule of Sultan Said had set the alarm bells ringing at Bait al Falaj, where we prepared defensive positions against possible ground attack or sabotage attempts, and in Bahrain. There the British Political Residency and the Headquarters of British Forces Gulf were already committed to the withdrawal from the region of all UK forces by the end of 1971, and to them any increase in instability in the Gulf would be highly unwelcome. Our situation in Oman was also watched with concern in London where a Conservative government, headed by Mr Edward Heath, had on 18 June – and contrary to what the BBC had led us to expect – replaced Harold Wilson's Labour administration. The result of the 1970 UK election turned out to be a boon for Oman and for us in her service. Had Labour remained in office the course of events in Oman would not have been so happy for both countries as they have. The Conservatives were to support us in our exertions in Dhofar and throughout the Sultanate to an extent which the left-wing of the Labour Party could not have permitted to their Ministers.

An early consequence of our recent experiences was the visit of two Officers from London, a Colonel and a Wing Commander. They had been sent to prepare in secrecy with the Consul-General and me a contingency plan for the evacuation of British personnel in the event that the security situation in Oman got beyond the control of SAF. When discussing the numbers of people they had calculated for evacuation I stressed that there could be no question of any British seconded personnel being removed from the Sultanate unless all our British contract colleagues came too. Furthermore that no British Officer or NCO could leave until equally protective measures and safe passage had been arranged and guaranteed for our subordinates from Pakistan, India, Zanzibar and other places outside Oman whence they had been recruited into the Sultan's service. This obligation had been overlooked in the draft plan and the two Officers seemed a bit taken aback so I said to them. 'Don't worry. The Sultanate is not going to fall apart. SAF will remain in control out here, so there is no need to regard the evacuation contingency as anything other than academic'. Thereafter I heard no more of the matter.

For Qaboos, the Sultan's only son, living in semi-isolation in a modest house outside the Palace walls in Salalah, the events of May and June were proof of the worsening situation in his country; and combined with his own assessment of the conditions in Dhofar, they convinced him that if the Al Bu Said dynasty and the Sultanate were to be saved, his Father's rule would have be terminated.

I had met Qaboos on my initial visit to Dhofar; he had kindly come out to greet me at the airfield. In early June I returned to Salalah for a week and with the Sultan's permission he invited me to tea in his house. Qaboos and I already had in common a rather unusual association. After leaving the Royal Military Academy Sandhurst, Qaboos was attached to a regular battalion of the British Army. The Regiment selected by Sultan Said for his son's attachment was the Cameronians, who had been flown in from Kenya to assist the Sultan during the early phase of the Jebel Akhdar campaign of 1957-9. The Cameronians, raised in 1794 by an ancestor of mine, Thomas Graham of Balgowan, as the Perthshire Light Volunteers or 'Graham's Greybreeks', was a Lowland Scottish Rifle Regiment with a reputation for red-blooded conduct on and off the battlefield. They were a rough lot, so many years later I asked Qaboos how he had enjoyed his eight months with them in the Army of the Rhine. He replied: 'Very much indeed. Colonel Reggie Kettles and his chaps were good to me, not only in deepening my military knowledge but also in arranging for me to see much of West Germany and other parts of Europe. That was for me a most valuable experience'. He added: 'You see, the only education I ever had to prepare me for the real world was what I received at Sandhurst and with the Cameronians'. That Regiment was disbanded in 1968: their memory, however, continues to be honoured in Oman in the headdress of the Muscat Regiment and in the Douglas tartan worn by the Sultan's Pipers.

Qaboos looked older than his 28 years due to his long straggling beard, but the two things which struck me – as they have many others – were the extraordinary size and beauty of his eyes and the quality of his voice whether speaking Arabic, or English which he did faultlessly. We were alone during tea apart from a servant who kept popping in and out of the room. I had been warned that Said bin Taimur had probably had Qaboos' quarters 'bugged'; moreover, at that time, I had no evidence that Qaboos was other than a devoted and supportive son of the Sultan. I was therefore on my guard. Thus when towards the end of our meeting Qaboos asked me what action SAF would take if a move was made to depose Sultan Said, the words I used in reply were: 'I am confident that the Armed Forces will do whatever is best for the country'.

The lack of success achieved by HMG and their emissary, Sir Stewart Crawford, the Political Resident in the Persian Gulf, in persuading the Sultan to amend his repressive and unpopular policies – they had tried again in May – and the evidence of growing instability in Central Oman, were viewed with particular dismay by the Directors of Shell, the oil company which had invested a very great deal of money in successfully locating and extracting oil in the Fahud area and pumping it via the Sumail Gap to the coastal terminal just west of Muscat. Petroleum Development (Oman) – PD(O) for short – would be a rich prize for any revolutionary movement that won power in the Sultanate. I was therefore not at all surprised to note the increasingly frequent meetings of Hugh Oldman, the Defence Secretary, with the robust and shrewd General Manager of PD(O), Francis Hughes. Nor was I surprised when, while we were swimming alone off Blackpool Beach in the PD(O) compound, Hugh said to me: 'What would your reaction be if Said bin Taimur was deposed?'

'I'd give three cheers.'

'And how do you think SAF would react?'

'I'm sure that the majority of the Soldiers would be greatly relieved. The British Officers in the main would likewise welcome such a change, but I am doubtful about the older, senior contract Officers who have served Sultan Said for many years and whose loyalty to and respect for him are sincere and must be admired.'

'That is undoubtedly true.'

I continued: 'I assume that Qaboos wishes to take over himself as Sultan.'

'Yes, Qaboos has indicated that he is resolved to take over to save the Sultanate, and that he has the means and the following to achieve that.'

'And what,' I asked, 'is the role, if any, of SAF in all this to be?'

'To hold the position in Dhofar against the *adoo*, to maintain law and order in the rest of the country and not to get involved in Qaboos' activities until after he has taken over from his Father.'

'And if he fails?'

'In that case Said bin Taimur remains the Ruler and SAF will have to go on serving him loyally, as now.'

'Have you any idea as to how Qaboos proposes to bring about his Father's removal from power?'

'No, none at all. All I know is that Qaboos has told Francis Hughes that he has some reliable followers who have sworn to support him in this venture.'

'And is the attitude of the new government in London known?'[1]

'No.' But he added: 'Great changes for better or worse in this country are now inevitable and cannot be long delayed, and it seems to be generally agreed that the replacement of Said bin Taimur by his son would be in the best interests of Oman and Britain.'

Hugh and I parted. I returned home to Flagstaff House and my excellent Bearer from Gwadur, Mohammed Shareef; Rosemary having gone back to England for our childrens' half-term holiday.

First Months in Oman

I was heartened by the knowledge that the replacement of Said bin Taimur was imminent, but I did not believe that SAF could long be kept uninvolved. And I foresaw dire problems if Qaboos' move failed and SAF was called on to sustain Said bin Taimur on the throne, for that would test, probably to breaking point, the discipline of our Arab soldiers. I was also worried by Hugh Oldman's intimation that Qaboos intended to carry out his coup d'état virtually single-handed. My knowledge, admittedly limited, of his restricted life, of the strength of the Palace garrison, of the Sultan's fear of assassination – a consequence of the attempt on his life in 1967 – and the inability of the Arab to keep a secret, all this led me to fear that the chances of Qaboos succeeding in his plan or even remaining alive were slim.

By early July I was perfectly clear in my own mind that the best hope, not only for the cohesion of SAF but also for the salvation of the peoples of the Sultanate, lay in Qaboos' hands. I therefore resolved that the best contribution I could make to these ends was to ensure, if called upon, that the transfer of power would be as smooth and bloodless as possible.[2]

I had become aware that two of my colleagues, both contract Officers in SAF, knew of Qaboos' intention to depose his Father. These were Major Malcolm Dennison, the Force Intelligence Officer, and Captain Tim Landon, the Intelligence Officer in Dhofar Province. Tim Landon had been a cadet at Sandhurst at about the same time as Qaboos and he was important as he was the sole British Officer to whom the Sultan permitted regular access to Qaboos and to certain other dignitaries in Salalah. Furthermore Landon had, properly and in strict confidence, alerted his Commanding Officer, Colonel Turnill, to Qaboos' intention. All three welcomed it but none of them up to that point had known the line which I, the Force Commander, would take in the matter.

However, all we knew about Qaboos' plans was that he had resolved to remove his Father and that two young sheikhs, Buraik the son of the Wali, and Hilal bin Sultan Al Hosni, were pledged to support him in the deed. Hilal was important as he commanded the Hawasini contingent which formed half of the guards outside the Palace; the other half being Baluch askars recruited by a cautious Sultan as a counter-weight to Hilal's lot who were Omani.

In mid-July there was still no hint as to when Qaboos would act, so I decided to go down to Salalah for a week on an overdue inspection of the units in Dhofar. Teddy Turnill and Tim Landon were awaiting me at Umm al Ghawarif Camp, the HQ of Desert Regiment. It struck Teddy and me simultaneously that the date, 20 July, was the anniversary of the ill-fated plot in 1944 against Adolf Hitler and we made a silent prayer that Providence would be kinder to Qaboos. But we were not encouraged by the state of affairs that day. There was evidence that the armed forces of PDRY (South Yemen) were now actively supporting the PFLOAG units in the Habarut area of north-west Dhofar, and the *adoo* probes around the RAF station were becoming bolder. A Gulf radio station had announced that a bomb had exploded in the palace of the Ruler of Sharjah, and from the transcript of a British television programme we had learned that 'a palace coup is imminent in Muscat'. All this, we had to assume, would increase Said bin Taimur's fears for his own position and his surveillance over Qaboos. Sultan Said, though permanently immured inside his Salalah Palace, was known to be remarkably well informed about what went on and he rapidly saw or heard of most events, important or trivial, which occurred within the perimeter of Salalah town. Furthermore, Landon reported that Buraik and Hilal had become pessimistic about the whole venture and fearful too of the Sultan's retribution against themselves and Qaboos if reports of what was afoot reached the ears of Said bin Taimur.[3]

Early the next day, 21 July, I went out with a mobile patrol to the east end of the Salalah Plain where I made a point of chatting up members of the Dhofar Force exercising near their Ma'amura barracks. This unit of some 250 men had been raised in 1954 by Said bin Taimur as his personal protection force. They had Pakistani officers, were well armed and unlike SAF had some armoured vehicles. Dhofar Force was not part of SAF, we had no responsibility for its efficiency or discipline and were not permitted to enter its barracks. The Sultan was known to have direct telephone and radio links with its commander, and despite the fact that it had been members of Dhofar Force who had tried to assassinate him in 1967, Sultan Said retained this unit under his own control primarily, it was rumoured, to preserve him from a mutinous SAF. Dhofar Force had no role in the campaign being fought in the province other than to protect themselves and, if summoned, the person of the Sultan. Thus Dhofar Force could not be regarded as friendly to Qaboos; nor could the Baluch askars or the Palace garrison. Qaboos could rely solely on Sheikh Hilal's Hawasini.[4]

That evening there was a sharp engagement to the north-east of RAF Salalah between a strong *adoo* patrol and one of our platoons. DR had two men wounded but they wounded one of the enemy and killed two, one of whom was identified as 'a known hard-core group leader'. This was gratifying but served to remind us that, whatever our immediate preoccupations with the occupancy of the Palace, the campaign with all its perils and strains was the principal and permanent backcloth to SAF's service to the people of Dhofar and the Sultanate in general.

The following day, Wednesday, when I returned from visiting the DR's Hedgehog positions, I found waiting for me a letter from Said bin Taimur. He had heard that I was in Dhofar and requested me to call on him in the evening of the next day. For Turnill, Landon and me those were days of yearning expectancy overclouded by acute and growing anxiety for the safety of Qaboos and the success of his cause. But all was to come right.

Thursday 23 July dawned dull and wet, real monsoon weather. But as rain is precious in Arabia I took this as a good omen, as I did the knowledge that that day was the birthday of my Brother, Alastair, then a Housemaster at Eton. For Oman it was a date to be recorded in letters of gold.

Around mid-day a letter was brought to Teddy Turnill. It was a long letter, in English, written in Qaboos' own hand. In it Qaboos expressed his dismay and anger at the course of events in the Sultanate and at the deprivations being suffered by the people, and he declared his decision to remove his Father from power, and for the sake of his country and all its people, to assume himself the government of Muscat and Oman. In order to minimize bloodshed and to maintain law and order, he called on Colonel Turnill to rally with his troops to his side without delay. Turnill handed it to me to read. It was a forceful letter which left no doubt about its authenticity or its purpose. We could not have asked for a clearer call. I told him to comply and he at once commenced the series of activities necessary to ensure his regiment's smooth deployment inside Salalah town.

As Turnill's Orders Group was assembling I asked him to send in to me the three senior local Officers, the representative in Desert Regiment of the Omani Arabs, of the Oman-born Baluch and of the Makran (overseas)-born Baluch. When they were seated I told them that an historic moment had arrived. Qaboos Bin Said, I said, acting in the interests of his country had decided to depose the Sultan and assume power himself. I read out to them some of the more stirring sentences from his letter to Colonel Turnill and told them that Qaboos had appealed for the immediate help of SAF. I explained that this presented Turnill, me and our British colleagues, foreigners in their country, with a conflict of loyalties. But there was, I said, no time for me to consult with my superiors in Muscat or London. Moreover, I told them, the action being taken by Qaboos was in my view wholly in the best interests of Oman. I stated that I was not going to ask for their advice but that, having told Colonel Turnill to comply with Qaboos' request, I ordered them as good soldiers to go back to their men and to obey all the instructions of their Commanding Officer. I added that I had sent for them because of their special status in the regiment, as I wished them to learn from me in person why I had taken this decision. At this the three men leapt to their feet, shook me warmly by the hand, one with tears in his eyes, and ran off to rejoin their platoons.

Aircraft would be useful, I had decided, in two ways: as an addition to the show of strength about to be mounted by DR, and to keep us informed about the movement of crowds within the straggling town of Salalah and of any hostile movement down from the Jebel. As I left Umm al Ghawarif Camp I could see DR preparing for action with some sub-units beginning to thin out from their positions round the airfield. On arrival at RAF Salalah I briefed two pilots on the actions they were to take in support of DR's movements. I then called on the Station Commander, Squadron Leader Phil Crawshaw. I said that I had an exceptional request to make to him, the reasons for which would soon become clear. My request was that for the rest of the day he should place the facilities of his Station in support of SAF, and that he be good enough to carry out any instructions which Colonel Turnill or I might give him. Although neither I nor any member of the Sultan's Forces had any jurisdiction over members of the Royal Air Force stationed there, Crawshaw readily agreed. This ensured that the Station's medical and flying facilities would be available to us during the unpredictable hours that lay ahead. I then returned to Umm al Ghawarif and sat by the radio control set until I heard that Said bin Taimur had been taken under the protection of Desert Regiment. I then drove into the town and rejoined Teddy Turnill who briefed me on the events of the past hour.

The DR column arrived without incident in the town. On seeing them approach Sheikh Hilal's men rushed out to surround the Palace and to cut the electricity supply to its communications room. Large crowds started to gather in silence but did not interfere; neither did the Baluch askars. Meanwhile Sheikh Buraik and a group of friends made their way into the Palace. The main gates were firmly closed but they had found a small door through which a man could pass stooping. This door was not locked but was guarded on the inside by an armed slave. Close behind Buraik's group was a party of DR soldiers led by Lieutenant Said Salem Al Wahaibi. They over-powered those slaves who attempted to resist and disarmed them all. One slave was killed in the process. Buraik and his men passed through two more guarded doors before vanishing into the interior of the Palace in search of the Sultan. They eventually found him and called on him to surrender. Said bin Taimur retorted by shooting Buraik in the stomach before running off deeper into the building firing wildly at anyone in his path.

Sporadic but heavy firing broke out as Buraik's friends pursued the Sultan. They eventually located him in an upper room at the end of a long corridor where they were pinned down by the bursts of fire coming at them from behind the closed door. The fire was returned wounding, it transpired, both the Sultan and one of his two companions. Lieutenant Said Salem and some of his men had run through the labyrinth of corridors towards the shooting and they were soon joined by more of DR. They too were fired upon before the Sultan's voice was heard saying, 'I have shot myself by accident. I wish to surrender but I will not surrender to anyone except a senior British Officer.' When asked if he would give himself up to Colonel Turnill he replied: 'Yes'. While Turnill was being fetched up from the courtyard, the SAF Officers put a stop to all further shooting, and began the process of clearing all the corridors and the adjoining rooms and disarming the Palace garrison. The whole Palace complex was then placed under armed guard. Teddy Turnill described to me how, when he entered the room, the Sultan levelled a machine pistol at him. Turnill said: 'Sir, put that gun down; I have come to save you'. The Sultan complied; at the same time the unwounded bodyguard put down his rifle.

Turnill found that the Sultan was wounded in five places and sent at once for his Regimental Doctor and medical team. While his wounds were being dressed Said bin Taimur clung with both hands to Turnill's shirt crying: 'Don't leave me, don't leave me; the people will kill me'. He was terrified for his life. I could see that Teddy Turnill was deeply moved by what had passed between him and the Sultan in that upstairs room.

All this time Qaboos had stayed in his house out of sight of the multitude in the streets. I made my way there on foot and was greeted by him. We sat down in his small drawing-room and I told him what had happened during the afternoon. I said that I much regretted that his Father had started the shooting and had ended up getting wounded himself. Qaboos replied saying: 'The sheikhs who helped me plan this had warned me that that might happen'. I was curious as to how DR would get the wounded Sultan discreetly out of the Palace, safely through the crowded streets and into the medical centre at the RAF base. So I excused myself from Qaboos with the suggestion that as soon as he heard that his Father and his escort were well clear of the Palace area, he might like to step outside his house and be seen by the people. I learned later that on seeing him emerge the crowd neither moved nor cried out; total silence reigned for some seconds. Then the penny dropped. The people now realised the significance of all that had been happening that afternoon. Their joy and relief were extraordinary; exuberant, continuous and marvellous to hear. I could hear it growing and spreading as I walked with the DR party escorting the Sultan out towards the RAF station.

Said bin Taimur had been placed on a stretcher and carried slowly down to one of the lesser Palace doors and there concealed in a covered Land Rover ambulance vehicle. We then moved cautiously at walking pace through the crowds. They were totally unaware that Said bin Taimur, their Ruler since 1932, was passing through their midst and out of their country for ever. I myself had been taken aback by the subdued, almost sullen attitude, of the population. I now understood why this was. When Desert Regiment arrived at the Palace they assumed that the soldiers had come to crush Hilal and his Hawasini, and to protect the Sultan. To them it was inconceivable that SAF should play a part in dethroning the Ruler; and their glum faces expressed this disbelief.

I accompanied the ambulance and its escort as far as the town's perimeter wire where I got back into my vehicle and drove to Umm al Ghawarif Camp and sent a brief report to Bait al Falaj. At about seven o'clock in the evening Qaboos sent for me to join him in the Palace and to stay overnight. Halfway across the plain I met Teddy Turnill returning from RAF Salalah where he had earlier placed Said bin Taimur under the protection of the Station Commander. Buraik, wounded in the stomach by the Sultan, had had his wound dressed by the RAF medics and had been put to bed in the sick-bay. When Said bin Taimur was admitted the orderlies put him in the bed next to Buraik! This arrangement was soon changed.

It had transpired that through some oversight an incorrect version of an abdication document had been presented to Said bin Taimur for his signature, and to put this right Qaboos had asked Turnill to return to the RAF station and get him to sign the correct one. As I drove through the massive wire fences which enclosed Salalah town, I saw bonfires blazing and men and children crowded round my vehicle clapping and shouting 'Long live Qaboos; Long live the Army'. To see these people hitherto withdrawn and deprived now so ecstatically happy made all our anxieties of the past month seem hugely worthwhile.

I was shown into a room in the Palace Guest Wing. Tim Landon was in the next room and the corridors were guarded by smart and smiling soldiers from DR. After a relaxed conversation Qaboos led us into the dining room where we had an excellent meal and a wide-ranging discussion. After dinner Qaboos went back to his own house.

Landon and I made a tour of the private apartments in the Palace, rooms seen by few Europeans and which Qaboos had never been allowed by his Father to enter. There were rooms filled with perfumes, cinematograph equipment, radios, expensive books and bedding. Piles of state documents, neatly stacked, were on tables, on windowsills, in cupboards, on chairs and on the floor alongside bundles of glossy American magazines. Bundles too of the new currency notes; watches and clocks were on all sides. It was rather like walking through Harrods.

But more sinister was the extensive arsenal which our searching soldiers revealed. In the entrance hall stood eight crates of searchlight equipment awaiting installation on the palace walls. In cupboards and cellars, on chairs and beds, and hanging from pegs on the walls of every room were weapons and tear gas devices of the most modern types, loaded and ready for use. Landon and I had difficulty in believing our eyes; and it made us reflect on the blood which would have been shed if SAF had not taken control of the situation inside the Palace[5]. No wonder Said bin Taimur had petulantly exclaimed to Teddy Turnill: 'Why did they have to come then? At any other time we would have killed them all!'

The assembling and transportation of this armament out to Umm al Ghawarif took four days and thirty-three lorry loads to complete; and to this haul were subsequently added two Belgian-made howitzers and three US-made armoured cars which had been concealed in out-houses.

After this unforgettable day I went to bed with the sound of the Indian Ocean pounding the sandy shore just outside the windows; and no matter where I have found myself in all the years since the Salalah coup, that sound of waves breaking on sand has never failed to recapture for me the thankfulness I felt as 23 July 1970 drew to its close.

On that day, and on other occasions during my time in command in the Sultanate, when things could have gone wrong and calamity could have befallen the Sultan's cause, I felt that our Father in Heaven was saying to me: 'The Omanis are good people, they have suffered enough. I now plan to give them a reward for their privations and a better life for them and their children. You British, do your best for Oman and I shall see that all will come out right'.

The next day, Friday, we were awakened early by the cheers and shouts of crowds surging towards the Palace. This enthusiasm for the accession of Qaboos increased as the hours passed. I saw Teddy Turnill carried shoulder-high by a group of excited townsfolk; never had the Army been so popular; the morale of our Arab soldiers was sky-high and the more stolid Baluch were no less pleased with themselves. Tim Landon took on the task of screening the prisoners in the jail and releasing those who had been unjustly incarcerated. Three bad officials of the Sultan were arrested and jailed. This was done in an orderly, civilised way.

Technically Said bin Taimur was still the lawful Ruler for there had been another hitch over the abdication document. When presented with the correct text the previous evening Said bin Taimur had signed with a shortened version of his name and style; not with the correct full signature. Qaboos would not accept this, so the busy Colonel Turnill was once again despatched to the royal bedside. This time the formalities were completed properly. Said bin Taimur made no complaint but merely asked Turnill to pass on to Qaboos the following requests: that he be allowed to keep certain personal effects left to him by his Mother; that he would receive medical treatment only in the United Kingdom, and that his personal servants be cared for and treated generously. These requests were, I know, honoured. That morning an RAF aircraft conveyed Said bin Taimur and three servants to Bahrain and thence to England, and there the ex-Sultan remained in safety and comfort until he died of a heart attack while watching television in a five-star London hotel on 19 October 1972. He was 62 years of age. He was buried the next day in the Brookwood cemetery, near Woking, in a brief ceremony at which I was present.

Qaboos could not be confirmed as Sultan until the members of the Royal Family in Muscat gave their agreement. This procedure was launched by Hugh Oldman once he got my signal confirming Sultan Said's abdication.

There was a pressing need to organise some sort of government so that the reforms which Qaboos wished to introduce without delay could be discussed and promulgated; and also so that the war could be more effectively prosecuted with the Ruler, the Dhofar provincial officials and SAF working more closely together. I therefore with Qaboos' approval spent the morning setting up the first meeting of a Dhofar Council. This new body met after lunch. Qaboos presided and round the table were:

> Sheikh Hilal, acting for the bed-ridden Wali
> Hamed bin Hamood, Secretary to the Sultan
> Haj Mohammed Ibrahim Khan, Under-Secretary
> Lieutenant Said Salem Al Wahaibi, representing Colonel Turnill
> Captain Tim Landon, Intelligence Officer Dhofar
> Myself, Commander the Sultan's Armed Forces.

We achieved a great deal. Hamed bin Hamood told me with pride the next day how he had sat up until 2am typing out the minutes and preparing the proclamations about food, freedom of movement, smoking, schools, medical care, etc., etc., which Sultan Qaboos wanted his people to enjoy. The announcement to the public of these reforms led to rejoicings even more exuberant than those we had witnessed the previous days.

After lunch on Saturday 25 July I left for Muscat to make arrangements for the new Ruler's arrival in the capital five days later, and to brief David Crawford, the Consul-General, on what had been happening in Salalah. Driving out to the airfield it took me twenty minutes to get through the Palace gates so great was the crowd of citizens who wanted to embrace me or shake my hand.

While I was still in Salalah, Oldman and Dennison had composed a letter to all SAF unit commanders informing them that Sultan Said had abdicated, that Qaboos had taken over, and instructing them on how to impart this news to their troops. It was, I must emphasise, by no means certain that all the varied nationalities, tribes and age-groups which were serving together in SAF would greet the enforced exile of Sultan Said with equal enthusiasm. Exceeding disgruntlement, bewilderment or even a mutiny by some were not impossible. At most places the news was greeted by the troops with surprise and unfeigned pleasure; but not immediately everywhere. At Sib, facing Tony Best, the Commandant of the Oman Gendarmerie, an all-Arab battalion, the soldiers remained totally impassive, stood quite still and appeared, if anything, to be unhappy with the news being broken to them. A worried Tony Best dismissed the Officers, told the (Arab) RSM to take over and took refuge in his office. But all was well. The RSM gave the order 'Fall Out!' on which

40 JDCG, Rosemary, Pinky and Christopher, Oxford, 1962

41 Our Latimer Common Market party, 1962, JDCG, Rosemary, Valerie and Adrian Rouse

42 On exercise near Sharjah, 1965, showing our 'Hats Afrika Korps'

43 Hamala Camp, Bahrain, 1965. JDCG (CO 1 PARA), and RSM Cole with our contractor, Ghulam Hassan and his team

44 Sheikh Isa bin Sulman Al Khalifa, Ruler of Bahrain, at the 1 PARA Tattoo in Hamala Camp, October 1965. Behind HH are General Sir Kenneth Darling (Colonel Commandant of The Parachute Regiment) and my Mother, Jane Graham

45 With Colour-Sergeant Gordon Burt and the 1 PARA Cross Country Team, 1966

46 Rosemary on our first visit to Kirchberg, 1967

47 Colin Mitchell and Field Marshal The Viscount Montgomery of Alamein ('Monty') at Isington Mill, near Farnham, 1969

48 *Above left:* His Highness Said bin Taimur, Sultan of Muscat & Oman

49 *Above right:* Colonel Hugh Oldman, Sultanate Defence Secretary, with reporter from Radio Dubai, July 1970

50 Lieut-Colonel Teddy Turnill, CO Desert Regiment, and 2nd Lieut Miran Sabil, Salalah, 1970

this page:

51 *Left:* Sultan Qaboos bin Said being greeted by JDCG on arrival at Bait al Falaj on 30 July 1970.

52 *Below:* Sultan Qaboos inspects Guard of Honour, commanded by Major John Cooper, prior to the Accession Ceremony at Bait al Falaj, 30 July 1970

opposite page:

53 *Left:* His Majesty Qaboos bin Said, Sultan of Oman and Commander-in-Chief of the Armed Forces, 1972

54 *Right:* HE Lieut-Colonel Said Salem Al Wahaibi, Minister of Royal Court Affairs, 1985

55 *Below:* Said bin Geyr, an early defector from the communist enemy ranks, with local colleagues, Salalah, early 1970

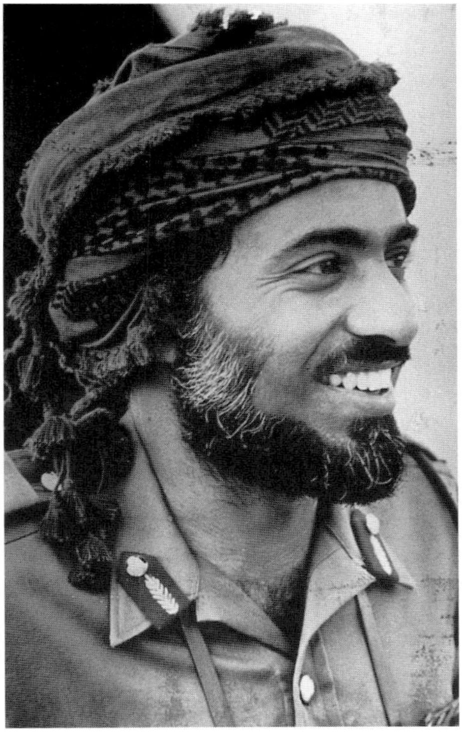
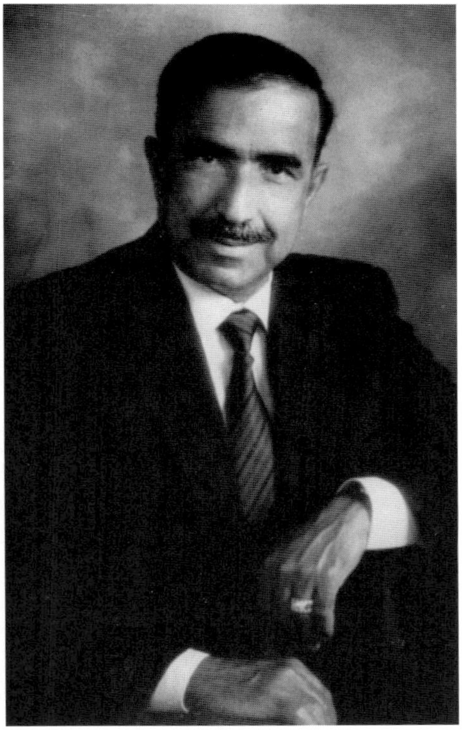
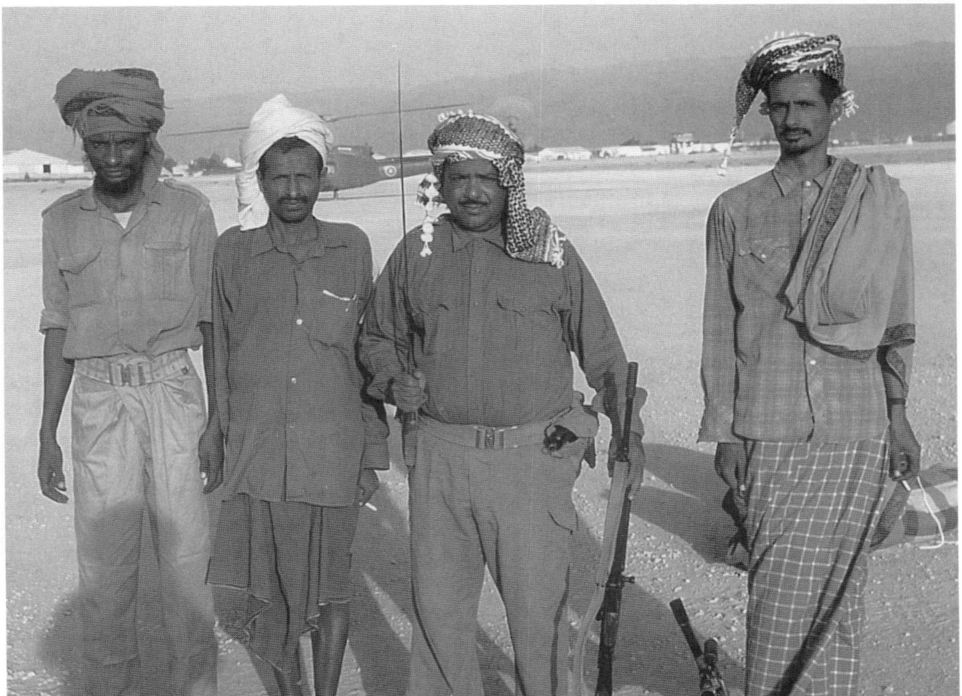

56 Major Spike Powell with Major Vyvyan Robinson in rear

57 Colonel Mike Harvey (Comd Dhofar Brigade) with Lieut-Colonel David Glazebrook (Senior Administrative Staff Officer, HQ SAF)

58 Major Vyvyan Robinson (OC Baluch recruit training centre at Rayzut) and David Glazebrook

59 Mr Donald Hawley, the first British Ambassador to the Sultanate, with Major-General Roland Gibbs (Comd British Forces Gulf) 1971

60 Muscat harbour; Fort Mirani, and in foreground, the sole quay

61 Major Paul Wright (Jebel Regt) and Colonel Courtney Welch (British Defence Attaché) 1972

62 Former SAF colleagues at a lunch hosted by JDCG in Browning Barracks, Aldershot on 23 July 1990 to celebrate the 20th anniversary of the Accession of HM Sultan Qaboos

From left, Top row: Hugh Colley, John Moore, Donal Douglas, Peter Walton, Tony Molesworth, Bob Tomlinson
Centre row: Alastair Morrison, Bill Goodfellow, Richard John, John Shipman, Ted Ashley, Tony Hazeldine, John Westing
Bottom row: Fergus MacKain-Bremner, Jeremy Phipps, Malcolm Dennison, Sir Donald Hawley, John Graham, Francis Hughes, Salim bin Hilal Al-Barwani, Peter Worthy

63 At the Taj Mahal in Agra, India, 1973

64 General Ernst Ferber (CINCENT), Brunssum, The Netherlands

65 Air Chief Marshal Sir Lewis Hodges (Comd Air Forces Central Europe), General Alexander Haig (SACEUR), General Dr Karl Schnell (CINCENT on retirement of General Ferber) and Major-General Zwyner (NL Military Representative of Supreme Headquarters) 1975

66 The Silver Jubilee of The Queen, Cardiff, 1977. Her Majesty inspecting the Guard of Honour found by The Royal Regiment of Wales outside the City Hall

67 The Queen with JDCG (GOC Wales)

68 Chevening, view from the south-west

69 Jacqueline (Pinky) with Roland Dane on their wedding day, Chevening, 5 June 1982

70 Sir Geoffrey Howe (S-of-S for Foreign & Commonwealth Affairs), Lady Howe and 'Budget', Chevening, 1986

71 Rosemary and JDCG in Kirchberg, summer 1985

72 The 50th anniversary of the Raising of British Airborne Forces, London, 22 June 1990. The March from St Paul's Cathedral to Guildhall after the Service of Thanksgiving

73 Contingents of serving and retired members of The Parachute Regiment march past The Prince of Wales, our Colonel-in-Chief, the Lord Mayor, Sir Hugh Bidwell, the Aldermen, Commoners and Sheriffs, St Paul's Churchyard

74 The wedding of Christopher (Didi) and Cynthia (Tia) Brus, 26 October 1996. St James's Parish Church, Barbados

75 JDCG, 1948 (5th [Scottish] Bn, The Parachute Regiment)

76 JDCG, 1963 (2nd Bn The Parachute Regiment) outside the lines of F (Sphinx) Battery, 7th Royal Horse Artillery, Hamala Camp, Bahrain

77 JDCG, 1972 (Comd The Sultan's Armed Forces), Bait al Falaj, Oman

78 Rosemary Graham, née Adamson, 1970

79 HM Sultan Qaboos bin Said, 1998

command the troops turned to the right and took three paces as laid down in the Drill Book. At that point, and only then, did they react. They turned to each other, threw their hands in the air, embraced and began a period of rejoicing that the whole of Oman was to share in until the end of the month. For the men of the Gendarmerie to have cheered or even smiled while still 'On Parade' would have been bad discipline.

On 30 July Sultan Qaboos arrived at Bait al Falaj in a chartered aircraft accompanied by Lieutenant Said Salem, now his ADC[6]. I greeted His Highness as he stepped on to the ground and escorted him to the SOAF hangar which had been superbly prepared and decorated at short notice by my Staff headed by Lieutenant-Colonel John Moore and Major John Martyn-Fisher.

After inspecting a Guard of Honour drawn from almost every unit, Qaboos was seated on a throne – a large chair mounted on a dais – in front of a crowd of dignitaries and local onlookers. Seyyid Shihab, an uncle, made a speech in his ugly, rasping voice. Qaboos replied. I believe that all who heard it will remember for ever the sound of his voice, speaking in classical Arabic and clearly winning the hearts of his subjects. When this, the Accession ceremony, was over, the new Sultan was driven slowly along the road to Muscat through Muttrah, a journey he had never before made in his life. The route was lined by some eleven hundred assorted SAF servicemen and hundreds of excited citizens, with acres of red bunting and improvised flags draped over trees, telegraph poles and the windows of houses and shops. As an English newspaper was to record, Muscat had never before seen anything like it.

It was an exhilarating and unforgettable privilege to be in Oman during those momentous days; and with my comrades-in-arms to have made a contribution to the happiness, security and dawning prosperity of that majestic and deserving country. But we had no illusions about the magnitude of the problems which lay ahead of the young Sultan or of the work which would have to be done – and which at that time could only be done – by the sole cohesive, disciplined, literate, country-wide organisation existing in the Sultanate in 1970; the Armed Forces, with their Arab, Baluch, Pakistani, Indian and British members working side by side in the service of His Highness Qaboos bin Said Al Bu Saidi, Sultan of Muscat and Oman.

Notes

1. I put this last question to Hugh because, although we British were sent to Oman to serve the Sultan, the seconded element were serving members of the British Armed Forces and in consequence we had to ensure that our activities in that country did not conflict with the interests of our own country; or with our country's reputation. As, for example, when

Said bin Taimur, having decided as a punishment to destroy a tribal water source, ordered that the task be carried out by SAF, their British commander refused to comply and the work was done instead by the Sultan's askars.
2. I foresaw that any clash between Qaboos' supporters and the Palace guards would be a bloody affair which could result in the killing of either the Sultan or Qaboos or both of them. Such an outcome would be for the Sultanate a calamity.
3. A senior member of Said bin Taimur's Household Staff later told me that informants had warned Said bin Taimur on several occasions during July that a plot was being mounted to kill him. These warnings the Sultan brushed aside exclaiming that 'his enemies were too feeble and his protective measures outside and within the Palace too strong'. In his Palace he believed himself to be invulnerable.
4. Qaboos' first action on becoming Sultan was to order the incorporation of Dhofar Force into SAF, renamed the Dhofar Gendarmerie, with its commander replaced by a British major.
5. The ribbon of the Accession Medal which Sultan Qaboos awarded to every person serving in the Armed Forces on 23 July 1970 has, in recognition of Desert Regiment's good work on that day, as its primary colour that of DR's beret: the colour of sand.
6. At Appendix IV I have included a summary of Said Salem's career as it describes the experiences of one of Oman's veteran soldiers and, briefly, the early years of the Sultan's Armed Forces as seen through his eyes.

CHAPTER XIII
1970–72: The Sultanate of Oman
From Darkness into Light

For SAF the aftermath of the change of Ruler was marked by a proliferation of novel activities. Some contributions which we were able to make in that euphoric period of national rebirth were the setting up and running, by a young RAOC Captain on my Staff, Peter Walton, and Mrs Pauline Searle in a hut near the Fort, of the first Oman Radio Broadcast station; the printing and distribution by my Headquarters of a weekly news sheet in Arabic, Urdu and English, and the winning by Flight Lieutenant Bill Goodfellow, SOAF's Administrative Officer, of the competition for the design of a new Sultanate flag. I knew vaguely that Qaboos had launched the competition but was surprised when Bill came to my house one afternoon bearing a large sheet of paper. He asked me: 'Have I your permission to enter the competition, and if so, which of these six designs for the new flag should I submit?'. I pointed at the two which seemed to me to be the most attractive and fitting. The nicer one was selected and has been Oman's flag ever since. Bill collected the prize, one hundred rials, but I foolishly neglected to charge him a slice of his winnings as my consultation fee. Soon afterwards Qaboos changed both the official title of the country from Muscat and Oman and his own title from His Highness to His Majesty the Sultan of Oman.

A new dawn had indeed broken over Oman. But the problems, economic and political, social and medical, military and diplomatic which confronted the young new Sultan and his nation were formidable. As Seyyid Tariq exclaimed soon after his return from abroad to be appointed Prime Minister: 'In Oman we are having to start from less than scratch'.

The problems were indeed formidable. To begin with, Qaboos' accession produced in his people an upsurge of expectations which needed to be met early and convincingly by him and those he selected to help him govern the country. Even though a number of Omanis returned from abroad to fill posts in the embryonic government, the creation of an effective nation-wide civil administration was severely hampered by the appalling dearth of educated men and women. It was to take many years, and even where qualified men were appointed, the time and energy of some were to be devoted more to personal gain than to good governance. 'I despair,' Qaboos declared on one occasion in 1971 to Malcolm Dennison and me, 'I can seldom get anyone to work properly for me unless I first give him a large financial inducement.' Thus during the first years of his reign it was inevitable that the advances made by SAF in the military field far outstripped the ability of Oman's civilian agencies to keep pace with them. This became exceedingly frustrating, particularly in Dhofar where we, the military commanders, knew that the battle for hearts and minds was at least as important as the physical defeat of the *adoo*; and our energy and time had frequently to be diverted to reinforcing the slender resources of Robin Young's newly created Development Department and elsewhere of the fledgling ministries and local walis.

Similarly the nation's infrastructure – roads, ports, schools, hospitals, electricity supply and so on – could not be built up without massive technical help from outside. This, however, was speedily marshalled, and from the autumn of 1970 onwards numerous contracting firms, together with a large labour force imported mostly from India, flowed into Oman to set about their varied construction tasks. They made remarkable progress. For obvious reasons the coastal areas around Muscat and Salalah were the first to benefit, to the chagrin of the inhabitants of the less-favoured places.

The pace of this development had repercussions also on the Armed Forces. In Dhofar the contractors' personnel and plant had to be protected by an already over-stretched DR Group, while up north as the number of vehicles grew dramatically so did the number of traffic accidents. In the second half of 1970 SAF's casualties from this cause exceeded those from enemy action. More worrying, however, was the effect on SAF recruiting. The opportunities now open to Omanis for a wide range of well-paid jobs with construction firms or the burgeoning government agencies led to a sharp decline in the number of volunteers for the hazards of military service and concurrently to a flood of requests to quit SAF from our valuable battle-experienced junior leaders. We managed to overcome this problem with Qaboos' help. He put pressure on the walis and community leaders by appealing to their loyalty and by having service in his Forces extolled as the highest form of patriotism. We for our part widely publicised the benefits that service in our ranks conferred on young men; education, technical skills and improved health.

One of Qaboos' first actions was to approve the recommendations which Hugh Oldman and I put to him for the substantial expansion of his Armed Forces. He confirmed his Father's decision to raise a fourth Infantry battalion and agreed its title, the Jebel Regiment (JR). The navy was to be modernised by the purchase of patrol boats, a Logistic Ship and an armed Flagship, SNV *Al Said*. Even more impressive was the enlargement of the SOAF squadron to the wing organisation of four squadrons which Alan Bridges bequeathed to his successor as CSOAF, Curly Hirst, and for which the first helicopters and Caribou transport aircraft, already ordered by Said bin Taimur, arrived in September 1970. Further aircraft followed, including an invaluable fleet of Skyvans, together with the trained aircrew and mechanics to operate and service them. On land the raising of JR – their first CO was Peter Worthy – was accompanied by the formation of an Armoured Car squadron (Major Tim Cornwell) equipped with Saladins and Ferret scout cars, the gradual expansion of Major Hugh Colley's artillery battery to regimental size, and some essential increases to the Force Medical Unit. The procurement in such a short period of all this additional equipment, weapons, spares and personnel was made possible basically by three things: the fact that Said bin Taimur, though guilty of scorning his peoples' welfare, had husbanded the oil revenues accruing since March 1967; the willingness of the young Sultan to take bold financial decisions, and the dedicated work of Colonel Oldman and his small staff at the Defence Department. SAF has many reasons for remembering Hugh Oldman with gratitude, but perhaps above all else for the skill and energy with which he acquired the men and the materiel which enabled SAF to accomplish so much in 1971 and 1972. Large though the defence budget was – alarmingly large, we recognised, in the light of the multitude of other pressing national needs – it could not stretch to providing then more than the minimum essential increases to SAF's strength and firepower. SAF in consequence had to function for several more years without a combat engineer unit, with inadequate motor transport, ordnance and repair services, and lacking the establishment of qualified Officers necessary for the command and management of a fighting force of ten thousand All Ranks which SAF was to become by the autumn of 1972. All this expansion, including the extra buildings which had to be put up to accommodate it, put a heavy load on my administrative staff headed by the able and selfless David Glazebrook. We were not to know that after we had left the Omani scene, the massive oil price hike of 1973 would enable our successors to obtain many of the assets denied in our time to SAF and the nation; and we rejoice for them.

In addition to his workload, Hugh Oldman had a difficult time while Tariq was Prime Minister. Qaboos and Oldman worked closely together in matters of defence and the Dhofar war – the campaign was after all being fought over Qaboos' home territory – and Tariq felt excluded. Moreover, when the Sultan attempted to involve him in defence counsels, Tariq refused: he openly washed his hands of the whole subject. Some of us believed at the time that he had resolved to steer clear of all responsibility for military affairs so that if the Dhofar war went badly, he could justly cry 'You can't blame me!', but I subsequently came to the conclusion that he was *au fond* both lazy and unwell; he resigned his office in 1971 and died several years later. When Qaboos became his own Prime Minister things became easier for Hugh and me, but during 1970 and the first half of 1971 the prosecution of the war was complicated by our having to act for a Sultan who was frequently away from Muscat without being able to consult the head of the government on any matter affecting the Forces or the war.

In training the many extra men recruited into SAF we were helped by the Royal Marines and the British Infantry battalions stationed in Bahrain, Sharjah and Cyprus. They generously detached instructors for periods of four months to boost the resources of our Training Regiment at Ghalla. They could only instruct in English through interpreters; we therefore needed to obtain people qualified to teach in Arabic (which was now the medium of instruction for our Baluch recruits), and to replace the British chaps who anyway would not be available after the British withdrew from the Gulf in December 1971. At the same time we drew up a long-term programme to select and fit Omanis for promotion to progressively higher ranks. I asked Colonel Colin Maxwell, Deputy CSAF and the wise and beloved 'Father of the Force', to supervise this Omanisation plan, and in this most important project he was enthusiastically supported by our British colleagues; though less so by the Pakistanis who foresaw their early replacement by Omani Arabs looming. As part of the project we set up at Ghalla an Officers' Training Wing, run by Captain David Baxter under pretty austere conditions. It worked so well that by late 1972 nearly a hundred Arabs and Baluch had passed out as commissioned Officers or moved on to the more renowned academies in the UK, Jordan or India.

In its support of the new government SAF found itself with other novel commitments. MR did good work in coping with a bad outbreak of cholera in the Rostaq area; OG had the task of making arrangements in their Sib camp for the Sultan's first meetings with the Rulers of Abu Dhabi, Dubai and Sharjah; and the decision to change the rule of the road to driving on the right was put into effect and policed country-wide by SAF.

A constant preoccupation was the protection of His Majesty, not only from the actions of evil or deranged men, but also from the perils of road and air travel. With the help of a team from the British SAS Regiment led by Captain Jeremy Phipps, a small Royal Bodyguard Unit was selected, largely from OG, and trained together with a cadre of chauffeurs, pilots and aides for personal attendance on the Sultan. This selection was not at all easy. Many of the Arabs lacked the qualities required; others were unwilling to assume a responsibility for guarding anybody against an occurrence which Allah Himself might have preordained. Nevertheless this platoon-sized bodyguard was to grow in effectiveness and numbers and was the seed from which the Royal Guard Brigade was to spring. It escorted His Majesty when he undertook his visits into the Interior, such as in September 1970 when he inspected MR at Nizwa, held an investiture, and watched a fire-power demonstration the battalion laid on at his command for the enlightenment of the local Sheikhs and many other tribal leaders.

In the first year of his reign Qaboos was noticeably hesitant about meeting his people, and when faced with crowds of ordinary folk was patently ill at ease and in his manner reserved and very formal. He lacked, or at least seldom demonstrated to his civilian subjects, the warmth and sympathetic character that was to make him beloved by so many in the years to come. By contrast, when he was in uniform in the midst of a gathering of his soldiers or in an Officers' Mess, he was totally different: relaxed, smiling and joining in the flow of conversation be it in Arabic or English. None of this was at all surprising, for in his life hitherto Qaboos' only uninhibited contact with mankind had been with Servicemen during his time at Sandhurst or in the Cameronians. For the young Sultan the hours with his Forces were manifestly happy ones, and we much enjoyed his visits to our lines.

The travel arrangements of the palace staff, government officials and the growing swarm of businessmen put an added daily burden on SAF's small Movements team and on SOAF's aircraft hours. But they coped. These varied commitments underscored the fact that at that time SAF was the sole organisation in the Sultanate which had the means and the disciplined flexibility to cover the whole country and to play fast balls. It was to us that everyone turned when a problem arose, however divorced from a military context or remote from our encampments. We met these challenges with ingenuity, and usually with a smile, and thereby helped to bring the benefits of the new reign to the dispersed population of Oman.

The Musandam Peninsula had been particularly neglected. Indeed until August 1970 this strategically important area of Sultanate territory, aptly described as 'a hot Norway' on account of its fjord-like inlets and mountain ridges, had long been off limits to SAF. There was no military presence or government interest. OG formed a further squadron and troop bases were set up at Bukha, Bayah and Khassab where Major Sandy Gordon established himself as the first Commander Peninsular Sector – to the evident surprise of the Shihu and other inhabitants. They had grown to believe that they were subjects of the Ruler of Abu Dhabi whose portrait and flag were displayed on the few public buildings. There were few visible signs of Sultanate sovereignty over the peninsula.

SAF's presence in the Musandam, albeit sparse and of little initial effectiveness, did not go unchallenged. Border skirmishes broke out spasmodically calling for vigilance and restraint on the part of the OG garrison; on two occasions for a sharper response. In December 1970 an Arab Action Party cell was discovered near Bukha. This was considered by the British authorities to be a potential threat to the stability of the Gulf from which they were committed to withdraw within twelve months. HQ British Forces Gulf therefore mounted an operation employing British units, the TOS and the one company of Peter Worthy's JR which had completed its basic training. The operation was a success in that the AAP gang was evicted, but the leaders whose identity and whereabouts were known with some precision, evaded capture. Eleven months later an incursion of armed men from Ras al Khaima had to be seen off by a sub-unit of MR flown up to Bayah who after a brisk action in which they killed two and captured one man drove the intruders back over the border.

The destruction by SAF in July 1970 of the NDFLOAG organisation in the aftermath of the Izki incident had led to a greatly increased flow of intelligence in central Oman. Searches in the Fanjah-Izki-Nizwa area during the next two months uncovered large well-concealed caches of weapons, mines and explosives, mostly of Soviet origin. Many other weapons had already been dispersed among the population, and as an inducement to the possessors to hand these in, the Sultan decreed a weapons amnesty coupled with substantial financial rewards. The implementation of this policy fell to Tony Molesworth, Malcolm Dennison and the Intelligence staff, and before the year was out the remnants of the discredited NDFLOAG were absorbed into PFLOAG, our principal enemy in the south.

While all these things had been going on in central and northern Oman, much had been happening in Dhofar. A radio station was set up in Salalah and a psyops[1] campaign by leaflets (many designed by Tim Landon) and wireless programmes was mounted to persuade the Jebalis to desert their Communist masters and to declare themselves openly for the Sultan. At the same time the Sultan ordered a period of restraint during which Teddy Turnill's DR Group and SOAF were stopped from engaging in offensive operations on the Jebel. The respite thus given to the enemy was not however reciprocated, nor did it meet with the response Qaboos had hoped for, for the following reasons. Firstly, our radio broadcasts and leaflets could only reach a tiny proportion of the Jebel population, whose chief source of information was the hostile and more powerful Radio Aden. Secondly, the Jebalis were still unconvinced of the significance – and in some cases even of the reality – of Qaboos' accession. Thirdly, those individuals who toyed with the idea of coming across to the government's side were so scared of *adoo* reprisals against their cattle and families that they stayed put.

It was in fact Communist brutality rather than the Sultan's inducements which led to the first significant split between the *adoo* and the Jebalis. Some anti-Marxist dissention broke out in the Eastern Area which the *adoo*, using hard-core squads brought in from farther west, punished with unusual ferocity. Tribal leaders whose loyalty to the rebel cause was suspect were put to death, conscription into the Militia was imposed on young men, camels were confiscated for resupply convoys and shortly afterwards, children started to be removed from their families for an alien education in Hauf and to serve as hostages. These vicious acts, coupled with the *adoo* losses in their continuing attacks on our positions on the Plain, caused the Jebalis increasingly to look to the Sultan for salvation. Thus, though only one man surrendered to the government forces in September 1970, by March 1971 the total of Surrendered Enemy Persons (SEPs) had risen to over a hundred. Among these was Musallim bin Nufl, the leader of the original Dhofari rebellion against Said bin Taimur.

The employment in Dhofar of the Special Air Service Regiment had been mooted in 1969 but rejected by London. Soon after Qaboos' accession, however, elements of this remarkable unit came out to the Sultanate in secrecy, subject to stringent operational constraints and calling themselves the British Army Training Team (BATT). BATT's first invaluable contribution to the campaign was the compilation in November 1970 by their Intelligence cell in Umm al Ghawarif camp of an enemy Order of Battle showing unit names, boundaries, personalities and resupply routes in unprecedented detail. This was a significant development for us, and as the number of SEPs grew, so did the depth of our knowledge of the enemy.

The next breakthrough was the proposal by the SAS squadron commander, Major Tony Jeapes, that BATT teams be used to recruit, train and control Dhofari fighting men as they defected down to the Plain. After a brief discussion in my office in the Fort, I saw that the potential in Jeapes' idea far outweighed those minus factors which first sprang to mind; and that if brought to fruition, such a role for BATT could produce for SAF in Dhofar a weapon of a quality it had never before possessed: Jebalis armed but supervised, and motivated to fight on our side on ground they knew intimately and against an enemy among whom they had lived. There was one other, though less weighty, plus factor. The lorry-loads of weapons and kit we had removed from Said bin Taimur's rooms in July were to hand and suitable for the initial arming of these warriors. That day I discussed the idea with David Crawford at the Consulate. He was receptive and must have relayed our ideas convincingly in his telegrams, for Jeapes' proposal was quickly and courageously supported in Whitehall and Hereford. The creation of the resultant Firqa Force was to be a campaign-winning factor of cardinal importance. The equipping, management and leading of the Firqas were tasks for which SAF quite simply had neither the resources nor the expertise to take on at that time. It proved to be a most demanding commitment. The SAS's tribulations and successes, frustrations and rewards have been well described by Tony Jeapes in his *SAS Operation Oman*, a book which is also valuable for his account of the part played by the SAS Civil Action Teams (CATs) in giving medical cover, leadership and confidence to the people of the remoter parts of government-held territory.

Military help from the UK also came in other forms. It eased our problems and increased the confidence of our soldiers: they could see that they were no longer fighting in a world uninterested in the fate of Dhofar. The provision by the Royal Corps of Transport of a Uniflote in a cove at Rayzut (the plan for a harbour there was still only on the drawing-board) made it possible at last to bring vehicles and great quantities of stores into Dhofar by sea, and the defence of the RAF/SOAF airbase was strengthened by RAF Regiment mortar detachments and, the next year, by Royal Artillery teams (the 'Cracker Battery') operating ground radars and acting as extra fire controllers for our SAF guns. British Sappers supervised the building of schools and clinics in Salalah and Taqa, and operated a number of well-drilling devices on the now more secure Plain; and, of immense value, Field Surgical Teams from the RAF and 16 Parachute Brigade in rotation set themselves up in Salalah to deal with battle casualties and to help in the new civilian hospital.

By the beginning of 1971 I was able to state with confidence that 'the enemy will not succeed in conquering the whole of Dhofar by military means. They had missed their chance during the previous summer'. But the fact remained that nine-tenths of the province was under Communist control and could not be liberated unless the Sultan's forces, military and civilian working together, established a firm, permanent and expanding presence on the Jebel. This, however, was out of the question until we got more Infantry and sufficient helicopters and tactical transport aircraft, plus some reliable civilian agencies to help the Armed Forces in the vital Hearts and Minds aspects of the campaign.

An SAF offensive on the Jebel before the autumn of 1971 was therefore ruled out but detailed planning for a major operation as soon as the monsoon ended was begun in secrecy.

Much though had to be done in the interim to improve the government's grip on the coastal villages, to prepare SAF and the Firqas for the coming offensive and, more immediately, to break down the enemy units deployed throughout the Jebel from the PDRY frontier in the west to Sudh in the east. Their tactical and weapon-handling skills had at the end of 1970 been noticeably improved by the return of *adoo* junior leaders from training in the USSR and China, and by the addition to the enemy ranks of Dhofari soldiers in the Trucial Oman Scouts. These men, aware that their service in the TOS would probably end when the British left the Gulf, ignorant of Qaboos' hopes for Dhofar and infected by PFLOAG propaganda when at home on leave, were beginning to desert in worrying numbers and join the *adoo* against us. DR was therefore ordered to recommence short-duration offensive operations onto the jebel between the Midway Road and Taqa, and we concurrently achieved some heartening successes with SOAF and medium artillery strikes against rebel headquarters, stores dumps and resupply convoys pointed out to us by SEPs taken aloft to act as 'Flying Fingers'.

In January 1971 NFR moved down from BidBid to a new base at Haluf, on the north side of the Jebel, from which Karl Beale launched his HORNET series of operations in the Central Area with the aim of fragmenting the enemy 'Guevara' unit.

In February Fergus Mackain-Bremner brought his MR down from Nizwa and relieved DR in their positions south of the Jebel. This relief was for the first time carried out in RAF aircraft and completed in four days; Salalah to Firq in one-and-a-half hours! This was a most welcome improvement on the tedious and expensive overland journey our troops had been forced to endure on roulement up to that time. MR soon engaged in a number of operations north of Taqa, around the Wadi Darbat and as far west as Ashoq, against *adoo* units calling themselves 'Lenin', 'Ho Chi Minh' and 'Red'. A good augury was Operation EVEREST at the end of February by which Firqa Salahadin, our first Firqa to go into battle, supported by their SAS team and a company of MR, recaptured Sudh.

To command the now larger forces in the south a miniscule Brigade Headquarters was formed in Umm al Ghawarif camp with, as the first Commander Dhofar Area, Mike Harvey who not long before had commanded NFR with conspicuous zest and ability and who had returned to Oman in the rank of Colonel. His right-hand man at 'HQ Army Group South' was Captain David Venn on secondment from the Intelligence Corps as the Ops/Int Staff Officer. In February also the Navy's Coastal

Patrol and SOAF bombarded enemy installations near Rakhyut. Radio Aden put out a report that *Nasr al Bahr* had been sunk and her crew captured during this foray; this caused great mirth in Salalah where that vessel had already returned unscathed. About this time a patrol of the Armoured Car Squadron had its first brisk engagement with a party of *adoo* near Rayzut and the occupants of the hitherto untried Ferrets were relieved to find that the armour really did keep the enemy bullets out.

The intensity of all these operations was greater than that previously experienced in Dhofar: in the first ten days of February 1971 SAF suffered more casualties than in the whole of the preceding year. Enemy losses were however consistently greater; for the period 1 January to 4 May they were to be confirmed as killed and wounded 180, captured 9 and SEPs 185.

What was accomplished throughout the Sultanate between August 1970 and May 1971 was of fundamental importance both to the eventual liberation of Dhofar and to the building of Oman as a unified, secure, modern state. Those were memorable and extremely busy days; the SAF elastic was stretched mighty taut. But it did not break. Those of us who were intimately involved with the variety of daily challenges were often asked how it was that so much was accomplished by so few in such a short period. The explanation is simple. Everyone gave of his best; all shoulders were applied to the same wheel. Decisions were taken not by ponderous committees but by a small group of people in Bait al Falaj acting largely by instinct, with no time for prolonged cogitation or second thoughts. Furthermore, everyone was so engrossed in the work-load of each day that little energy remained for belly-aching. To state that the burden was chiefly borne by the seconded element in SAF is not to belittle the work of our contract colleagues. They had chosen to spend the greater part of their working lives in the climate and environment of Oman; to remain reasonably fit they, like our brown-faced assistants in the Headquarters, took to their beds every afternoon. We, however, who were to serve there for at the most three years were content to work from dawn to sunset, stopping only for breakfast and tiffin.

The sudden visible inflow of military aid from the UK was a great fillip to a long beleaguered SAF, whose members should never forget the debt Oman owes to David Crawford, the British Consul-General, whose advocacy on our behalf stiffened Whitehall's inclination to help Sultan Qaboos and his Armed Forces and whose work on SAF's behalf was to be admirably sustained by his successor as Ambassador, Donald Hawley.[2]

The British Services, however, quite apart from their impending withdrawal from the Gulf, were having to face at home harsh political and financial constraints, and the growing burden of Ulster. MoD London made it consistently clear to Hugh Oldman and me that any form of assistance they provided to SAF was to be of short duration, for months rather than years; and that its continuance depended on SAF proving by its actions on the battlefield that Oman was 'a horse worth backing'. That some officials in London in 1971 and 1972 had unrealistic notions of Oman's capabilities in that era was apparent from their repeated exhortations that, for example, Sultanate doctors replace the SAS CATs and the Field Surgical teams in Dhofar, that SAF personnel relieve the SAS of the burden of training and controlling the Firqas, and that SOAF take over the running of the Salalah air force base.

Thus it was certain that the British Armed Forces would not be permitted to sustain for long this novel level of support for SAF, let alone increase it. But if Dhofar, the size of Wales, was to be cleared of enemy and kept secure, more troops and more materiel would be needed than the weak brigade and their Firqa colleagues which was the most that Oman could produce from its own resources.

One of the distressing legacies of the rule of Said bin Taimur was that by 1970 Oman had become isolated and bereft of friends. This state of affairs was improved by the personality and skill of Sultan Qaboos who, during the latter months of 1970 and in 1971, established close relations with his neighbours, notably the Rulers of Abu Dhabi, Jordan, Saudi Arabia and Iran. This was to gain for Oman significant political rewards gratifyingly early. But concrete rewards in the form of much needed military help were slower to materialise.

I came to see clearly that the Sultanate had to win over other allies; not from Europe but from those Islamic states which were prepared, like Oman, to resist the advance of Communist power. SAF's ability to influence constructively the attitude of the Sultanate's neighbours from that time on therefore became an important factor in my concept of operations.

As the 1971 monsoon season approached there was a rush, hectic for the logistic staff, to assemble and embark the supplies needed to see the Dhofar units through the next five months. We were not helped when the coolies and stevedores in Muscat refused to load the chartered ship, but Captain Peter Felton, our subtle Movements Officer, got them to change their minds and the last 650 tons were off-loaded in Rayzut cove just in time. SOAF too did sterling work; in May they lifted an unprecedented 2,135 passengers and over a million pounds of freight. The government's grip on the Salalah area was also tightened by Wali Baraik enforcing stricter controls on the movement in and out of the town of food, firewood and currency.

As the khareef came down, MR, the Plains battalion, pulled their company back from Adonib to Rayzut, strengthened the Hedgehogs around the RAF station and made plans for harrying the *adoo* on the mist-covered Jebel.

BATT had already learned through hard experience a number of lessons about the motivation, management and organisation of the Firqa Force: principally that a Firqa should be recruited only from one tribe and its strength limited to about seventy. By the summer of 1971 six Firqas had been raised and under the patient guidance of their SAS teams they had reached varying degrees of effectiveness and reliability. These six Firqas were:

F. Salahadin (Central area tribes)
F. Al Asifat (Eastern area)
F. Al Nasr (Bait Kathir)
F. Khalid bin Walid (Bait Masheni)
F. Gamal Abdul Nasser (from Sudh area)
F. Tariq bin Ziad (from Western area)

The Firqa Al Umri was raised during the summer of 1971 in Marbat. Some serious early problems of Firqa motivation and indiscipline were eased by the chastening spur which the Sultan personally applied to their leaders after the exasperated BATT Officers put HM in the picture during one of his sojourns in Salalah.

Most of the Firqa members were ex-*adoo*: thus the sincerity of their recent adherence to the Sultan's cause could not be taken for granted at this early stage. Our suspicions were deepened when one SEP defected back to the enemy, taking with him from Arzat one of the armoured cars of the Dhofar Gendarmerie (DG), the new title of the former Dhofar Force. It has to be stated, however, that this defection was unique. Furthermore the chap returned to our lines three months later, exclaiming that, after all, life under the Sultan's banner was to be preferred to eventual death at the hands of his distrustful Communist commanders.

The contributions of some SEPs were heartening as well as helpful. One senior *adoo* leader came across in September, bringing with him the notebooks and manuals from his guerrilla training course in China. He told us frankly that he found his experiences in that country entertaining and interesting, and he was grateful to his Chinese hosts for their generosity to himself and his Dhofari fellow-travellers. But as to the military value of the knowledge he had absorbed while there, he declared that he had learned far more from his British instructors when he enlisted in the Trucial Oman Scouts in Sharjah.

The operations of NFR out of their Haluf position had undoubtedly weakened the enemy in the Central Area, but Haluf was too far from the enemy resupply routes (about which we now had a clearer picture) for that good battalion to operate to full effect. Colonel Harvey therefore moved NFR farther west, to Akoot, a monsoon-free location near Janook which he knew well from his earlier and successful years at the head of the same battalion. From Akoot they were able to engage the enemy more closely, provide a base for Firqa operations and draw unto themselves *adoo* manpower and ammunition which otherwise would probably have been employed against us in the more sensitive Salalah area.

From Akoot NFR mounted their VIPER series of operations and, like DR who later relieved them there, increasingly successful patrols and ambushes, inflicting a disproportionate number of casualties and causing the *adoo* to squander large amounts of ordnance. This period was alas marred by tragedy when a Caribou transport aircraft crashed, its load of burmails having shifted when the pilot was suddenly waved off from landing under fire. Flight Lieutenants Mac MacDonald and Jack Wynne and their Omani Air Quartermaster lost their lives that day. 1971 was a bad year for British Officer casualties; six others were to die before the year ended, three from enemy action, the others from accidents but no less grievous for that:

Major TEF Taylor, Royal Green Jackets (DR)
Captain MRA Campbell, Coldstream Guards (MR)
Captain SJ Rae, Royal Marines (NFR)
Major THC Lomas, (SIO Buraimi)
Captain RG Mawle, (DG)
Flight Lieutenant DE Moore, RAF (SOAF)

Despite the khareef, MR and the Firqas carried out a number of testing and useful probes onto the Jebel north of Salalah and Taqa. For their part the *adoo* limited their operations in the Central and Eastern Areas mainly to stand-off attacks by RCL and mortars and the spasmodic mining of tracks and airstrips. But they celebrated the anniversary of the rebellion (9 June) with a flurry of fire around RAF Salalah just as the Commander RAF Persian Gulf arrived there on a visit from Bahrain. Safeguarding the airbase and the morale of the RAF personnel in it was a persistent problem for Harvey and me, for had our enemy inflicted casualties on them the repercussions in Westminster would have been distinctly unhelpful for the Sultanate. One quite senior British Officer told me that he considered it 'entirely wrong that RAF boys should be placed in danger in Dhofar on account of a quirk of British foreign policy', and we knew from sources in London that some of the RAF lower ranks used to write home complaining about the hazards and privations of life in that RAF station. Morale was brittle; but I noted with interest, though with no surprise, that the amount of belly-aching by the RAF personnel decreased significantly when the Station Commander personally displayed a robust outlook. Several of those in charge of the Salalah air base in my years in Oman were excellent; by their attitude and common sense they helped us to prosecute the war against the Communists more singlemindedly than when the station was in weaker hands.

To the accumulating evidence that PFLOAG in Dhofar was feeling the strain were added rumours of anti-Marxist unrest among the Mahra people on the other side of the border in PDRY territory. The element of truth in these rumours became more evident when the PDRY fort at Habarut, just across the wadi which marked the border and opposite the Sultanate fort, was attacked. This was for us a most unwelcome development. Though in no way involved in the incident, the Sultanate government and SAF had no wish to encourage increased support for PFLOAG from the government in Aden or to incur misdirected retaliation from either quarter. This distant event was to have significant consequences in 1972.

The principal evidence of *adoo* discomfiture, however, was revealed in the proceedings of a high-level PFLOAG conference held in June which included inter alia a directive that in order to relieve the pressure on the Front's units in Dhofar, the 'forces of revolution in Oman and the Gulf states were to be unified and strengthened'. This intelligence was supported by reports that a team of terrorists was en route to the Gulf and it was to be borne out by the outbreaks of civil unrest in the Muscat area in September.

Meanwhile up north, Peter Worthy's JR continued to form at Ibri and at Nizwa; the latter place could now, thanks to PD(O) having graded the road, be reached by Land Rover from Bait al Falaj in three-and-a-half hours. OG continued their good work in bringing, despite inadequate backing from government, security and medical care to the inhabitants of the Musandam peninsula. May brought a change of command to DR at BidBid. Teddy Turnill, who had played such a stalwart role in holding the line in Dhofar during the critical first half of 1970, handed over to Nigel Knocker, was awarded an OBE, and took up a satisfying appointment in NATO after marrying a charming Irish doctor. He was alas to die of cancer before the next decade ended.

Changes also had to be made at HQ SAF. Tony Best left OG to become my GSO1, thereby releasing Major Ted Ashley to boost Mike Harvey's minuscule staff at HQ Dhofar where Major Peter Boxhall had already arrived to be his senior administrative assistant. Two notable SAF characters left Bait al Falaj during this period. Captain Aziz-Ur-Rahman, our first Pakistani to be promoted to that rank, was seen off in great style in August; a fitting end to his nineteen years of service in Oman after many earlier years in the British-Indian Army. The next month we lost, his tour ended, Victor Seely, an irrepressibly enthusiastic Royal Hussar who had made time, in addition to his job as Staff Captain 'A', to act as the Sultanate's Chief Traffic Cop, Provost Marshal and Master of the Royal Horse.

Although the inflow of seconded and contract Officers from the UK was still just about adequate, the elastic remained extremely stretched, a situation which leave, wounds and sickness made more precarious. One evening I was discussing this matter with Seyyid Tariq and suggested that if the supply from the UK faltered, Oman should consider recruiting experienced military men from other countries such as France or the USA. He would not hear of it. 'No,' he replied at once; 'We will not change; we know the British and get on well with them. Furthermore they lead from the front.' Because Colonel Harvey had no deputy, when he went on leave I had to transfer myself down to Umm al Ghawarif camp and run the military affairs of the Sultanate from there. This was an enjoyable break in a better climate and enabled me to become intimately acquainted with the terrain and problems of Dhofar. I almost got written off by a large chunk of metal which, thrown up by a vehicle passing at speed, was hurtling straight for my head. My left arm was upright and it got broken by the missile. That was preferable to a fractured skull, although I had to spend the next six weeks in heavy plaster and a sling. I could still jump around and write with my right hand, and people such as my Bearer Shareef were helpful about tying up shoe laces, cutting up my food and so on. Rosemary at this time was with the children visiting her Mother in Guyana. In the very hour of my injury a telegram reached me from her saying: 'Am worried. What is wrong?'

Although the units in Dhofar were on active service in a combat zone, Hugh Oldman and I had agreed that the whole of SAF should be administered in accordance with the strict rules of peacetime accountancy. This was essential if the country's slender financial resources were to be safeguarded and SAF's Officers shielded from accusations of wastefulness or peculation. We did our best to be vigilant and prudent managers of Oman's money and stores, but during the hot summer of 1971 there were occasional regrettable lapses. The losses of equipment and cash that occurred through theft, carelessness or pure accident all had to be investigated and the expenditure of time and energy by the Boards of Enquiry set up to probe each incident was an unwelcome additional imposition on my colleagues and me who had our hands full enough with operational matters.

Losses to our twelve Strikemaster aircraft became a particular worry. In September one was brought down by enemy fire though its pilot, Barry Williams, ejected and made a good recovery from his injuries. This was the first aircraft in SOAF's history to be lost through hostile action (even though Radio Aden was to claim two months later that 'the losses inflicted on the Sultan's forces in Dhofar since 1968 total 3,808 killed, 54 aircraft destroyed and ten Sultanate naval vessels sunk'). During the last months of 1971 three others were written off from accidental causes including that piloted by Del Moore who crashed near Mudhai. The replacement of these expensive aircraft and the purchase of all the extra kit and ammunition needed to sustain our operations post-monsoon, and of almost equal importance, to improve the food, clothing and accommodation of our Servicemen, all this was suddenly imperilled by the government's decision to cut the 1972 Defence Budget by £2 million to £18 million (equivalent).

The United Kingdom was still the chief source from which Oman obtained its weapons, munitions and expatriate Officers. This caused problems. Firstly, because some of our equipments, once in general use throughout the British Forces, were now obsolete and no longer in production. We were thereby faced with the difficulty of obtaining replacements and spare parts. The other problem was cost; for despite the pleas of the Ambassador, Donald Hawley, and the Service chiefs in London, the price demanded by the financial authorities in Whitehall remained heavy. This attitude seemed especially vexatious to us seconded chaps whose pay remained taxed in the UK, and unfair too to Oman, the country whose interests were uppermost in our minds. As Sir Michael Carver, the Chief of the General Staff, told me: 'The impediments to support for Oman do not come from the military side in London but wholly from the politicians, and they are ruled by the Treasury'. I have a poignant memory of Hugh Oldman on his return in mid-June 1972 from London where he had again argued the case for easing Oman's financial burden. He exclaimed, almost in tears: 'Bloody British! They all show interest in Oman, but there is NO plan to help financially – not even by a reduction in the capitation charges[3]. He went on to say: 'It is disgraceful. The Arab nations must help Oman but the UK and the US should take the lead. The British after all started the rot here when they left Aden!'

As the summer of 1971 drew to a close, the anticipated upsurge of unrest in Central Oman began. The first manifestation was an outburst of anti-Baluch feeling. As far as the Armed Forces were concerned this took the form of violence, stimulated by PFLOAG agitprops (promoters of Communist-style agitation and propaganda) whom we later identified, against the Baluch recruits at SAFTR. This was calmed, luckily before blood was shed, by the combined efforts of the British and Omani Officers and Cadets, but it had a deplorable effect on the morale of the young Baluch. It also had two lasting consequences. It persuaded Qaboos that the recruitment of Baluch into his Forces must cease, and that SAF be reorganised as a matter of urgency so as to separate those then serving into distinct Baluch and Arab units. When he told me of these decisions I replied that, although the business of separating the nationalities so soon before the launch of our Dhofar offensive was 'like the drivers of a car trying to change places while the vehicle was speeding down a motorway', we would implement the change as early as possible and in each battalion at the time that best fitted in with its commitments. But I had to remind him that if real and lasting progress was to be made in liberating Dhofar the chief requirement would be for more Infantry, and that the only source from which these men could be obtained in quantity and speedily was Oman's traditional recruiting areas in Baluchistan. Qaboos was quick to appreciate the truth of this, and after a moment of reflection, told me to raise a new, purely Baluch unit, that I was to do this very discreetly, and that its personnel were to be trained and employed solely in Dhofar. Major Vyvyan Robinson and Lieutenant Khuda Bux were therefore despatched across the waters of the Gulf and in due course returned with a large contingent of very young, impoverished but mustard-keen volunteers for whom they set up a training camp at Rayzut. These two Officers and their stalwart protégés settled down well, and the products of this hasty recruiting expedition, together with the Baluch askars already enlisted, were to play an invaluable part in the liberation of Dhofar and its security in the post-war years. Thus began the history of the Baluch Guard, later renamed The Frontier Force.

More serious disturbances broke out on 1 September when a general strike of the workers, many non-Omani, was organised in Muscat, Muttrah and Ruwi. This was accompanied by the gathering of noisy mobs spurred on by agitators, hooliganism and the smashing of car and house windows. By mid-morning the situation was getting out of the control of the small Police Force and SAF was ordered to intervene. I brought elements of DR and OG by lorry and helicopter into the capital area where they set up road blocks and formed a reserve. Despite the great disparity in the strengths and experience of the civil Police and Armed Forces, I was determined that the affair should be handled in such a way as to set a precedent for the future and that, as a demonstration of national policy, SAF should act in support of the Police rather than the other way round. A small joint Headquarters was set up and the whole operation was run by the Police Commandant, Major Felix da Silva, with myself or my representative sitting beside him. A curfew was imposed and maintained for forty-eight hours by Police and SAF patrols, being relaxed once for three hours so as to allow the citizens to emerge from their houses to get water. This break also gave the tiny CID an opportunity to detect the ringleaders, some twenty of whom were arrested and brought before a special tribunal. One curfew breaker was shot while trying to seize a constable's rifle. This was the sole fatality. By the morning of 4 September, after a further night of curfew, the situation had returned to normal and everybody went back to work in total peace, clearly relieved that their uncomfortable enforced confinement had ended.

This episode had been a salutary experience for the population. Any sympathy they might have had for the agitators who incited the unrest rapidly vanished, and their respect for the effectiveness and disciplined restraint of the Police and SAF was enhanced. The events of early

September 1971 were also a milestone for the Police, who emerged from that novel test with credit, for they were soon very greatly expanded so as to cover the whole country, well equipped and with Felix da Silva, promoted to General's rank, in command of the Royal Oman Police.

It would be unjust not to record also the part which Sultan Qaboos played amid the turbulence which surrounded him in his Muscat residence. I saw a lot of him during those four days and was struck particularly by his calmness and sense of humour; as, for example, when our conversation was interrupted by an excited woman shouting down the telephone to His Majesty that 'the mob are about to attack the laundry-women; will you please send help!' By his calm and clear orders, his firm attitude towards the law-breakers and his understanding of the real feelings of his Omani subjects, he made the job of his military and Police commanders easier and averted the evil consequences hoped for by the instigators of the troubles.

It was in the evening of the first day that I recognised in Qaboos the voice of Said bin Taimur. I was called from my bath to answer the telephone. It was the Sultan himself: 'If any people should break through the cordon at Ruwi and try to reach the oil company's complex, you are to shoot them all'.

It is possible that a reader of the story of the Sultan's Armed Forces during the first years of the reign of Qaboos bin Said may wonder about the extent to which the situation in Dhofar impinged on the life and thoughts of the people in the rest of Oman. It hardly did. The vast majority of Omanis, it seemed to us, regarded Dhofar as a remote area inhabited by quarrelsome, grasping, alien tribes who did not deserve the salvation which Qaboos and SAF were striving to bring them. There was much perceived truth in the Omani saying: 'If in your path you meet a snake and a Dhofari, first kill the Dhofari'.

The war in Dhofar was unpopular, its drain on the Sultanate's blood and treasure was resented and SAF's problems, when mentioned, were in general dismissed or viewed with impatience. Even at Bait al Falaj there were many times when Dhofar preoccupied us less than did events in the heartland of Oman, where each week there seemed to arise a fresh challenge and new commitments. This was understandable, for in Dhofar the military initiative was passing from the *adoo* to SAF, and in Mike Harvey we had a resolute commander who knew the terrain and the enemy well. The course of events in the south had become more predictable than elsewhere in Oman. Also the date was fast approaching when SAF with our SAS and Firqa colleagues would move onto the Dhofar Jebel in strength and remain there permanently. The months of the 1971 khareef, now nearing its end, were the last in which there was no continuous SAF presence on the jebel. Operation JAGUAR, the first phase in the coming battles to rid Dhofar of its Communist oppressors, was to be a landmark in the history of the campaign. The seizure of a secure base on the Jebel was the essential first step.

The planning and logistic build up by air for JAGUAR had continued throughout the monsoon, as had the training of SAF units in the use of the new assault helicopters. My initial concept had been for this base to be established in the Central Area, to the north-west of Salalah, so as both to block the passage of *adoo* resupply convoys to their units east of the Midway road and to reduce significantly the threat to the RAF station. This last factor had an especial appeal for the British authorities who were sensitive about the security of their personnel there, and for Mike Harvey and me who were obliged to retain around the airfield for their protection SAF units and guns which could profitably have been employed elsewhere.

This concept had to be discarded at an early stage in favour of a lodgement area much farther east. The Eastern Area was more suitable for several reasons. It was there that the anti-Marxist rising had taken place during the previous autumn; the greatest number of the SEPs to date had come from that area, and it was the homeland of the strongest tribal Firqas formed so far. Further, the local people had a particular bond with Sultan Qaboos through his Mother. The terrain also offered some important advantages; relatively little dense scrub, good fields of fire, observation over considerable distances and an abundance of sites for the speedy development of airstrips for SOAF's Skyvan and Caribou aircraft. Indeed the countryside was to remind one of Salisbury Plain at the end of a long dry summer. But above all other considerations, it was in the east that the SAS wanted to attack first. It was there that they had gained the most experience since coming to Dhofar and it had long been recognised that the SAS and their Firqas would play the major role in hunting down the *adoo* gangs and in winning over the Jebali population. I appointed as Tactical Commander of the JAGUAR Force Lieutenant-Colonel John Watts, the CO of 22 SAS Regiment whose presence in Dhofar had been increased in September to two squadrons (commanded by Majors Alastair Morrison and Richard Pirie) and elements of RHQ. Also under Watts' command were placed two companies of SAF (one each from MR and JR), JR's pioneer platoon, a platoon of Baluch askars, five Firqas and two 75-mm mountain guns, with in support one 5.5-inch medium gun plus the bulk of the SOAF strike and transport aircraft and helicopters based at RAF Salalah.

Viewed against the background of previous operations in Dhofar this was a large force: it was however tiny in the light of the task and the geographical challenge it faced. But as the SAS's participation at this strength was authorised by London only up to the end of 1971, this force was the largest that could be produced from the combined British and Omani resources in the foreseeable future.

The timing of the operation was critical. It had to be launched as soon as possible after the end of the khareef and yet guarantee continuous good flying weather and visibility. The consensus of opinion of the RAF meteorologists and local inhabitants was that the desired conditions could be expected that year in the last week in September or the first in October. I selected as J-Day Saturday 2 October – a Saturday so as to enable our final preparations for battle to be carried out on a juma'a[4] and thus free from the eyes of civilian workers in the airbase and at Umm al Ghawarif. For security I had drafted the Operation Order and all its annexes and had them typed and run off by Sergeant Davies inside the guest room in my bungalow at Bait al Falaj. We took special measures too to deceive the enemy about the location and timing of the assault; rumours were started, leaflets dropped and overt military moves made to mislead the adoo into expecting our attack to be directed just to the north of Taqa.

The real plan was for a squadron of SAS, two Firqas and the Baluch askars to march by night from Barbezum and to secure by first light on J-Day a former air strip known as Lympne, four miles to the east of Jibjat, to which the remainder of the force would be flown in from Salalah.

On J-Day minus 1, the Friday, the sky was still clouded over and the Jebel was alarmingly obscured by monsoon mists; the dawn of J-Day, however, brought a cloudless sky and perfect visibility. As I watched Neville Baker, the OC of the Helicopter Squadron, set off in his 206 in the fading darkness to check on the situation at Lympne, I reflected on how good the other auguries were too for this, our most important enterprise. Two days earlier we had heard via the BBC that Oman had been accepted, very much quicker than expected, into the Arab League, and shortly afterwards came confirmation that the Security Council had recommended the admission of Oman into the United Nations Organisation. These events, which were of great political significance to the Sultanate and a marked rebuff for PDRY, were personal triumphs for Sultan Qaboos.

The contingent from Barbezum had a most gruelling march on a hot, humid night across taxing country, but they reached Lympne in sufficient strength to secure it before first light and without encountering either *adoo* or mines. Our deception plan was successful and there was no enemy reaction in the Lympne area on the critical first day. The airlift began on Neville Baker's return and by mid-afternoon the helicopters and Skyvans – a rough airstrip had been cleared by noon – had brought in the remainder of the force. SOAF, as usual, had come up trumps and the smoothness of the fly-in had been greatly helped by the zest and good discipline of the MR and JR soldiers for whom this was their first experience of going into battle by air. The chief credit must, I believe, be given to Captain Sean Brogan who, with his SAS troop and Al Umri Firqa, had drawn onto themselves on the Jebel far to the south the attention of the enemy.

During the next seven days Johnny Watts, having moved his base farther west to Jibjat, split his force into two groups and moved down both sides of the formidable Wadi Darbat in which strong *adoo* gangs were known to have their bases. Enemy reaction, negligible at first, soon became extremely fierce and casualties mounted on both sides. The outcome was that by 9 October the enemy had withdrawn into their wadi fastnesses. They would eventually have to be winkled out and destroyed there in a slow and exacting operation, but for the moment we could claim that JAGUAR had got off to an encouraging start.

The initial defeat thus inflicted on the enemy enabled the Firqa Khalid bin Walid, who had fought like tigers with Watts' group on the west side of the Darbat, to establish in their own Bait Maasheni territory an ideal operational base and, of particular long-term importance, a government Centre to which Jebali could come for safety, food, grazing and medical care. The erection of this centre, initially called the White City but later renamed Medinat al Haq, was the first evidence visible to the Jebalis of the government's resolve to remain on the jebel and to bring to them the facilities they had for so long been denied.

By the middle of October some 100 square kilometres of the Eastern Area were dominated by our forces. Nevertheless the Jebali, although increasingly willing to give information about *adoo* movements, were still reluctant to seek refuge within our lines. There were several reasons for this. Firstly, some of the Firqas had proved themselves less than wholly disciplined even on the first day of JAGUAR. To lighten their loads on the approach march to Lympne, many had thrown away their rations, yet demanded more from their SAS colleagues when the next day came. They now refused to fight during Ramadan despite the specific dispensation to this end that the Sultan and the Qadi had given them. This was a most vexing and untimely set-back, and one which infuriated Colonel Watts; for not only did it cause our offensive to slacken at the very moment when the enemy in the Eastern Area were severely shaken, but it also temporarily removed from the scene most of those Firqamen who were best fitted to contact, persuade and bring over to our side their Jebali kinsmen. Secondly, the movements of the Jebali are dictated by the supply of water for their goats and cattle, and at that early stage before government had acquired well-drilling equipment, and while SAF's positions were dependent on air supply, we could not guarantee the quantities of water they and their flocks required. This problem was partly solved by Wali Buraik's astuteness. He arranged with Mike Harvey and Johnny Watts that as many goats as possible and six hundred head of cattle were to be rounded up and moved off the Jebel down onto the Plain where government, would buy them up. This was done – we called it Operation TAURUS – under the noses of the enemy and it proved to be both spectacular and effective, though government was to be fleeced of much money by the grasping cattle owners.

But the fact remained that the timetable for our offensive in the east had slipped. The *adoo* had been given the opportunity to recover from his initial defeat, the Wadi Darbat had still not been cleared, and reinforcements, despite the activities of DR at Akoot, were reaching the enemy on the JAGUAR front. Some of the hardest fighting of this phase of the campaign occurred during November. Inevitably that further evidence of Firqa unreliability dismayed their SAS controllers and those of us who realised the magnitude of the problem facing SAF and the government in Dhofar and the cardinal role which the Firqas would have to play in its liberation. Moreover, despite the success of the cattle drive and the setting up of White City, the Dhofar Development Department though admirably staffed in the persons of Robin Young and that splendid married couple, Mike and Robin Butler, was still expected to operate with only the most rudimentary material resources. Getting the government in Muscat to take an interest in Dhofar was well-nigh impossible. The ministries gave other areas in the Sultanate a higher priority and the Sultan, who had special links with Dhofar, was away from Oman a lot during the first year of his reign; also he may have felt diffident about being seen to favour Dhofar over the rest of his long deprived country. Thus, despite Watts' success in defeating the enemy so far encountered in battle, the government side was still distressingly ill-equipped to win the vital and more lasting contest for the hearts and minds of the Jebali. Many months were to pass before the civilian agencies in Dhofar were geared to exploit SAF's successes – even to replacing our Civil Action Teams (CATs) with qualified recruits, many from India. His Majesty visited the White City on 7 December; that was a memorable event for his soldiers and showed that he at least appreciated what we were trying to do for the Jebali in such havens.

In November Mike Harvey and Johnny Watts decided that more needed to be done to hinder the passage of *adoo* reinforcements and heavy weapons, which according to intelligence reports were being despatched from the far west, to counter-attack our thinly held positions in the east, and they came to the conclusion that the best place to do this at that juncture was where the sea, the coastal plain and the mountains converge just to the west of Adonib. Accordingly Operations LEOPARD and PUMA were mounted by which three positions were established by DR, JR, the SAS and the Firqa Al Nasr along a line running north from Mughsayl via Al's Place (named after Alastair Morrison, the OC of G Sqn of the SAS), the Jebel Khaftawt to Windy Ridge. These positions, known collectively as the Leopard Line, did not form a continuous barrier, and the enemy soon learned how to pass between them; furthermore they could not be held during the monsoon months. But their value was proved by the violence of the *adoo* reaction; and the creation of permanent obstacle belts was from then on viewed at Bait al Falaj as a long-term requirement. I was especially interested in this as an effective contribution to ending the war, as the C-in-C in 1961 when I was serving at a NATO HQ in France, General Maurice Challe, had as C-in-C Algeria had a great belt of wire and mines (the Meurice Line) constructed at great cost in money, materials and manpower to patrol it, to stop the passage into Algeria of FNL reinforcements from Tunisia. In 1971 SAF's budget allowed us no engineers, little wire and only a few mines. Nevertheless Harvey's Leopard Line was replaced in 1972 by his Hornbeam Line, and other barrier lines were to follow, each more effective as the resources needed to construct and man them were acquired by our successors.

December 1971 brought the withdrawal from the Persian Gulf of the British forces in consequence of decisions taken by the Labour government three years earlier. The removal of the Royal Navy ships and the Army and Air Force units from Bahrain and Sharjah ended a military presence which for over a century had kept the peace in the Trucial States and Gulf waters pretty consistently, cost effectively and to the benefit of the indigenous populations. The period of their withdrawal, and the concurrent formation of the United Arab Emirates (UAE) with its own defence force, was not wholly tranquil. The Bayah incident in late November when I sent elements of MR and OG to deal with an armed incursion from Ras Al Khaima onto Sultanate territory has been mentioned earlier, and the seizure by Iran of the Tumbs Islands and an attempted coup d'état in Sharjah also led to bloodshed and some ripples of anti-British feeling. The outbreak of war between India and Pakistan saddened us and brought new worries to our colleagues from those two countries, but to their credit it resulted in no lessening of their service to Oman or to their mutual comradeship within SAF.

The departure from the Gulf of the British forces was felt by many of us in Oman as a personal loss – a bereavement almost – for with them went that fine team who from their Bahrain Headquarters and Political Residency had watched over and encouraged our efforts with wisdom, sympathy and generosity. The Sultanate and SAF had uncommonly staunch friends in Sir Geoffrey Arthur, General Roly Gibbs, Brigadier Philip Ward and their colleagues in the FCO and Armed Forces. Thereafter our affairs, personal and collective, would be the concern of a Headquarters in Cyprus, remoter and inevitably less well acquainted with Gulf and Sultanate problems. This worried me and in a document I wrote for circulation in Whitehall I pleaded for a proper degree of consideration to be shown to the seconded element in SAF, particularly in the matter of recognising the background against which I and my successors wrote confidential reports and citations for awards for bravery and distinguished conduct. However, the addition to Mr

Donald Hawley's staff at the Embassy in Muscat of Colonel Courtney Welch as Defence Attaché was a great boon; and the visit which the Chief of the General Staff, General Sir Michael Carver, paid to Dhofar in October ensured that SAF's achievements, hopes and needs were well understood in London. Especially welcome was his decision that the SAS could remain in Dhofar at two-squadron strength until April 1972. This extension of their commitment to Oman, albeit only for four extra months, confirmed the conviction that had been forming in the minds of Mike Harvey and myself that 1972 was going to be for SAF in Dhofar the year of decision; of a 'shit or bust' effort to be made while some British help was still in place. This effort must, we concluded, have the overriding aim of convincing the rulers of other states in the region that Oman, in its fight against revolutionary forces, both urgently needed and fully deserved military and financial help: that it was a horse worth backing.

Military help from Jordan first came to us in the persons of four Officers. They were a useful, Arabic-speaking addition to the instructional staff at SAFTR, and in late 1971 Colin Maxwell and John Cooper bought back the news that the Jordanians had reserved vacancies for our Arab soldiers on their military training courses and such like. This was excellent news for the improvement of SAF's training and educational standards and for broadening the horizons of our Omanis, but it did nothing to address our principal need, the ungrudging provision to Oman of military manpower, weapons and all the stuff classed by Quartermasters as 'warlike stores'.

1971 had been a year of striking advances for the Sultanate on the diplomatic and military fronts, and in the building-up of the nation's infrastructure, and we entered 1972 deeply grateful for the efforts, human and divine, which had brought Oman so far so quickly. But we were all the time conscious of the immense problems which remained to be solved before all Dhofar could be liberated and Oman made secure. By now the Sultanate's resources were severely stretched and there was no evidence that help from outside would be forthcoming soon or in adequate form and quantity.

The early weeks of 1972 brought an unusually heavy rainfall. This delayed the work of the construction firms, but to those living in flimsy dwellings it caused great hardship, and to help our Servicemen's families an SAF Flood Relief Fund was set up supported by some public monies and generous donations from Officers. A more welcome event was the acceptance by government of our budget proposals for improved welfare services in SAF and higher ration allowances. The latter made possible the long hoped for establishment of multi-national Officers' and Sergeants' Messes. By now too much better accommodation was being provided for our troops. In the Musandam the OG could at last move out of their tents, and work had already started on the new SAF/SOAF complex and the international airport at Sib which would free the Bait al Falaj and Ruwi areas for massive civil development.

Before 1971 ended John Watts left us to go as an Instructor to the Army Staff College in Camberley, his place as CO of 22 SAS Regiment being taken by Lieutenant-Colonel Peter de la Billière. February saw the departure of Karl Beale from NFR which he had cared for with a single-minded and reciprocated devotion, and the arrival of Bryan Ray as the new CO. Tony Molesworth left too, replaced by Ray Nightingale. Tony's tour as GSO2 Intelligence had been one of unrelenting hard work and responsibility. The contribution which the whole Intelligence team made to the Sultanate during those anxious years was quite splendid. In March Bill Kerr from the Royal Highland Fusiliers took over MR from Fergus Mackain-Bremner who had led his regiment with unflagging good humour and panache. In camp and on the battlefield our units were blessed with sound, sensitive and selfless Commanding Officers.

In Dhofar Peter Worthy's JR, Nigel Knocker's DR, the SAS and Firqas continued to hunt the enemy in the Eastern Area, along the Leopard Line and from Akoot. DR's position at Akoot was important to the overall operational plan for against it, as Mike Harvey had predicted, the *adoo* continued to fight a conventional type of battle using large groups and wasting themselves in the process. JR Group's long slog around and in the Wadi Darbat on Operations PANTHER, AMATOL and CYCLOPS was crowned with success in March when they linked up at the Darbat Falls, that large and extraordinary geological feature, and Land Rovers were able to drive for the first time in almost three years along the length of that great valley.

Now a substantial portion of east Dhofar was clear of all save small pockets of enemy. But it had taken the six months since the launching of JAGUAR to achieve even this. Farther west the Leopard Line, despite its imperfections, was frustrating *adoo* resupply. Some small camel convoys were undoubtedly getting through, but they were having to resort to manpacking ammunition, and thanks to the tightened restrictions on food taken out of the coastal villages, rations also. The number of occasions on which the *adoo* fired at the Salalah air base had dropped off, whereas DR's base at Akoot, visited by His Majesty on 23 March, became the target for an even heavier weight of machine-gun, mortar and RCL fire.

From early 1972 our attention was being increasingly drawn to the Habarut area in the north-west of Dhofar, where soldiers of the PDRY garrison had taken to crossing over onto Sultanate territory and generally making a nuisance of themselves, provoking the inhabitants and pinching the dates and such like. Although there had been some shooting, relations between the commanders of the two opposing forts had remained reasonably courteous. In late February, however, it became known to us that the PDRY military forces in the 6th (Eastern) Province of the Republic had been increased. We did not know why. It could have been in preparation for a move against us at Habarut, or to take over PFLOAG's 'Liberated Zone' in Western Dhofar, or it could have been in response to some threat from Saudi Arabia with whom the Aden government was on bad terms. As a precaution Mike Harvey reinforced the askars in our fort with a troop of DG. Not long afterwards the bulk of the PDRY forces there moved away, but those that remained were joined by elements of PFLOAG. The consequences were to be seen some two months later.

Despite Dhofar Brigade's encouraging tactical successes, particularly in ambush operations, my colleagues and I at Bait al Falaj were coming more and more to question the ability of the government forces to continue the war at this intensity and to liberate the remaining larger areas of Dhofar with our existing resources. Oman could not without compulsion produce more indigenous manpower for SAF, nor afford without greatly increased oil revenues to buy the great amounts of weaponry, ammunition and spares a prolonged campaign would consume. The prospect of an infinite succession of operational tours in Dhofar was beginning to strain the motivation of our veteran Servicemen and their families, and the cost of the war was resented by the Omani public. And as I have already indicated, the British were making it very clear to Hugh Oldman and me that their material support for the Sultanate would from mid-1972 gradually decrease. Not only was the indispensible SAS contingent under Peter de la Billière to be reduced in April from its peak JAGUAR strength, but Whitehall was seeking an early withdrawal of the British presence at Salalah. Also with its military commitments in Northern Ireland, Europe and elsewhere it could not be guaranteed that the UK would continue to supply the numbers of seconded and contract Officers Oman needed to train, administer and lead her overstretched forces.

Happily Oman's relations with Saudi Arabia, Jordan and Iran had grown much closer after the earlier years of estrangement, but with the exceptions of the contribution from Jordan I referred to earlier and a consignment of Sura rockets for SOAF and rifles for SAF from the Ruler of Abu Dhabi, little in the way of military hardware or personnel had been offered. Although the men of our Armoured Car Squadron were allowed to train in Abu Dhabi using the facilities of the Union Defence Force, my proposal that UDF units should be temporarily stationed in Central Oman for training, thereby releasing more SAF units for deployment to Dhofar, was in the end vetoed by the UAE Rulers.

The situation was clear. Time was still on the side of the forces of revolution. PFLOAG and its affiliates in disruption, backed by the USSR and China, even if halted in Dhofar, were elsewhere in the ascendant and motivated to fill in the Gulf region the vacuum left by the departed British. SAF in 1971 and 1972 was capable of fighting on one front; it could not have competed successfully with a fresh, major, outbreak of communist aggression somewhere else in Oman.

Although we were heartened by the progress made in Dhofar since JAGUAR was launched, Hugh Oldman, I and our closest confidants at Bait al Falaj as we contemplated the developing situation in the Gulf, came to recognise that unless outside help was forthcoming soon the Sultan's Forces might be compelled by the march of events elsewhere to abandon Dhofar. To prevent that calamity was our first duty. What was needed was some incisive act designed to focus the attention of the leaders of the conservative, monarchist Arab world on the struggle in Dhofar and to convince them that SAF, even though long engaged in a solitary battle, was still robust and resolute. But we had to make them also realise that without outside help SAF might conceivably become exhausted and fold.

Our primary, but unspoken, task during the summer of 1972 must, I decided, be to spur Oman's newly won friends into providing her with the sinews of war, just as aid from Roosevelt's America kept Churchill's beleaguered Britain in the field in 1940. Hugh Oldman agreed; he was actually quite pessimistic about the Sultanate's fate if the forces of revolution prospered significantly after the British left the area.

We came to see that a bold, startling stroke by SAF might rivet the attention of the region and beyond, increase awareness of Qaboos' lone stand against the Marxist tide, and hopefully win from some new source an early commitment to intervene alongside his forces with military material, manpower or money. Such intervention would be a major set-back for our enemies, and could in time prove decisive in the Dhofar war. A decision there would have a profound influence throughout the region. But how could SAF make a stroke, sufficiently bold to gain and hold the attention of the wider world and sufficiently hard to weaken the enemy, yet avoid hazarding Qaboos' greatest asset at that time, his Armed Forces?

To remain in the east rounding up the remnants of the *adoo* gangs and securing the area for good government, although an essential sequel to JAGUAR, would hardly inspire foreign interest any more than had our operations there hitherto. A bold move against the Central Area had to be ruled out for many reasons, not least the nature of the terrain and the inadequacy of the force we could muster and sustain in action against the *adoo* units long in occupation. We were in consequence drawn to the conclusion that the west was where we would have to make this very important move. Ever since 1968 when SAF was operating as far west as the PDRY frontier, it had been universally recognised that the war would not be won until the *adoo* supply routes were blocked and their arsenals in the Western Approaches destroyed. There stood the citadel which the enemy had to hold at all costs; only there could the

Sultanate Forces, fighting alone and unaided, make an enduring impact on the Marxists' ability to sustain the rebellion and by the same stroke make on Oman's friends and other bystanders a powerful impression.

The place selected was in the south-west corner of the Western Area, at Sarfait. By seizing and holding this high and broad mountain feature, about four miles from the PDRY frontier town of Hauf, SAF would be in an unassailable position overlooking the 'Chinese Road' where the *adoo* supply lines were funnelled into a narrow corridor between the sea and the escarpment which formed the southern face of Sarfait. Sarfait had been proposed in late 1971 by Nigel Knocker, the Commanding Officer of Desert Regiment, as the ideal location from which to insert 'the cork in the enemy bottleneck' which that narrow corridor created. Mike Harvey, who was ever keen to strike where it would hurt the enemy the most, had long advocated an early return by SAF to the west. I too was impressed for I saw in Sarfait the setting for that bold, startling blow so necessary to transform the perspective of the war. The concept was audacious; it was also strategically compelling. The tactical arguments for it were however questionable, for the force on Sarfait would be far from Salalah and wholly dependent on air supply, and that could be imperilled if the *adoo* obtained ground-to-air missiles. Also the operation to block the corridor – to put the cork in the bottleneck – would not be fully effective unless Capstan, a prominent feature on the coastal strip, was captured and held. An important source of water was reported to exist near Capstan but its location was not known with precision. Also to be really effective the 'cork' would have to take the form of a permanent barrier of wire and mines, constantly patrolled by our Infantry. At that time we had little wire, few mines and no combat engineers. Furthermore, as well as being logistically hazardous and of uncertain tactical fulfilment, this Sarfait enterprise would demand of our soldiers marooned there an exceptional level of moral fortitude. Nevertheless the concept was examined during November and after the SAF and SAS commanders in Dhofar had signified their agreement, the Defence Secretary's approval was obtained and planning for Operation SIMBA was put in hand.

Mike Harvey and the Battalion Commanders knew the risks involved but were confident that SAF could never be driven off the Sarfait feature except by a total failure of the resupply system, in which unlikely case, as Mike Harvey said: 'We can always walk out on foot'. They were also confident that the descent down the escarpment to the coast and the seizing of Capstan could be carried out; and the SOAF stalwarts on whom the responsibility for the aerial lifeline would fall were positive in their response to orders.

I personally remained convinced that if the prospects for the war were to be transformed in Oman's favour, a bold operation like SIMBA was indispensable, and that Sarfait was the place to strike. But the hazards were very great, and even if SAF was able to 'walk out' if a logistical crisis arose, to abandon such a key frontier position would inflict immense harm on the reputation of Sultan Qaboos and his British advisers. During the weeks of April and May 1972 the security of the Officers and men on Sarfait and the possibility that the enemy might produce some novel weapon or new tactic to imperil them caused me more anxiety than at any other period of my life. But my overriding fear was that all the effort to mount SIMBA, all the risks run in the east and elsewhere to maintain such a large proportion of SAF's manpower on Sarfait, would in the end prove to be fruitless. Fruitless because it was not possible to place a permanent block on the coastal corridor; fruitless because the enemy might chose merely to isolate our force; fruitless because the impact on foreign observers of our Sarfait blow might turn out to be negligible.

The detailed orders were written by Nigel Knocker whose DR Group carried out the helicopter assault with skill on the night of 17 April, the landing zone having been secured by the Firqa Tariq bin Ziad the previous night. No enemy were encountered, but the consolidation of the positions on the features Yardarm and Mainbrace, and the move down to seize the key Capstan feature, were delayed by freak storms and torrential rains: one NCO was killed by lightning. Nevertheless the airstrip was open two days later for Caribous and Skyvans, and the Firqas had already engaged the *adoo* on the coastal strip. Two companies of NFR were then flown in to reinforce Nigel's force and a subsidiary operation VULTURE was mounted to block the *adoo* supply routes to the north of Sarfait.

But the move down onto Capstan was too slow; it did not occur for ten days. That feature was held for a further ten days against strong opposition which soon broke up into small groups under the weight of our GPMG and mortar fire. And the water source, known to be there, could not be found. There then occurred an event which was to have a unique influence on the outcome of the war in Dhofar.

On Friday 5 May heavy and accurate fire was opened from the PDRY side of the frontier on to our positions at Habarut, and despite the dropping by SOAF of leaflets carrying an ultimatum from the Sultanate government, this fire was kept up for thirty-six hours. Only then did the Sultan permit SOAF to intervene with bomb and rocket attacks against the hostile positions; and Mike Harvey reinforced the SAF garrison until ordered for political reasons to withdraw the whole garrison temporarily. The enemy then moved across and blew up the Sultanate fort. This sudden and violent ordeal in which our small force lost eight dead and four wounded will be remembered also for the admirable leadership and personal bravery of its commander, 2nd Lieutenant Hassan Ehsan of the Dhofar Gendarmerie, which was recognised by the award to him of the Sultan's Gallantry Medal, the Omani equivalent of the Victoria Cross. We learned later that this attack on Habarut had been conceived and led by the leader of the PFLOAG Ho Chi Minh unit and it was rumoured that he, like many of his comrades, was killed there by our aerial retribution.

This episode caused a most unwelcome diversion of effort from the planned operations of DR and NFR, and was a principal reason why the extension of the Sarfait position down to the sea was not completed. By their action at Habarut the *adoo* gang had served the PFLOAG cause well; but only in the short term. It was also a considerable vexation to my wife and me. We were due to go on leave on 6 May and an Arab benefactor had arranged for us a splendid trip to and around the Far East, which we had never visited, and we were enormously looking forward to that stimulating and much needed holiday. As the crisis over Habarut developed during the 5th and the morning of the 6th, it became clear that I could not leave Oman. That was a great disappointment, and a considerable annoyance to our generous Arab friend.

The wider consequences for PFLOAG and the PDRY government of these developments at Sarfait and Habarut were to prove far less happy. In fact, as the next weeks were to show, the PFLOAG action at Habarut and the events which flowed from it were to attract to Oman international sympathy and the onset of a flow of military aid which in April we could only dream of, and which was to exceed in quantity and speed of delivery my personal expectations when SIMBA was launched. Quite apart from the other benefits which the occupation of Sarfait was to confer on SAF during the three remaining years of the war, this upsurge of interest and assistance from outside fully justified our move into the extreme west in April 1972.

That very satisfactory outcome was not, however, immediately apparent. In fact the Sultan and his advisers had some anxious days in early May when the representatives at the United Nations of the PDRY government accused Oman of having been the aggressor at Habarut, and the PDRY false account of the affair initially gained general acceptance. The failure of the novice Omani delegation to counter the PDRY allegations made Sultan Qaboos extremely angry and he asked me to draft for him a paper giving the 'Case for Oman'. This I did, dictating the sentences to my typists, Sergeants Davis and Page. The Sultan had the paper translated into Arabic and eventually circulated by the fledgling Ministry of Foreign Affairs, and by June the whole diplomatic situation had been reversed as the weight of international opinion swung against the Aden government.

Their attack on 5 May and the sporadic aggression which continued at Habarut throughout that month convinced Qaboos that firm retaliatory action had to be taken against PFLOAG and their PDRY sponsors, and that this should be directed onto the PFLOAG base, hitherto immune on PDRY territory, at Hauf. On the afternoon of 23 May I was summoned by telephone to the Sultan's side. I took the GSO1, Tony Best, with me. Qaboos told us that ever since the attack on Habarut he had wanted to strike directly at Hauf but that his advisers had urged him not to. Their arguments, he said, were based on the need to avoid provoking the Aden government further and thereby leading those people to increase their support for PFLOAG, and also on the dangers of incurring criticism from nations whose sympathies lay with Oman, now recognised as the innocent victim in the Habarut affair. Qaboos told us that he had heeded their advice reluctantly, but the more he considered the matter, the more he believed their arguments to be unconvincing, especially since he was now receiving from important Arab countries 'strong messages of support'. His Majesty asked me for my opinion. This put me on a bit of a spot as I knew Qaboos' principal advisers and I had no wish to be disloyal to them. Nevertheless Qaboos had asked me for advice in my capacity as his senior military Officer, and as I had already come to certain conclusions about the matter under discussion I decided to speak frankly.

I said that since the situation at Habarut was quieter – for our forces had been withdrawn and our fort destroyed – there was no military necessity to strike at Hauf at that time. We were fully engaged in taxing operations around Sarfait and did not wish to increase our difficulties or add to our commitments, particularly not against PDRY forces and territory. I added that any attack on Hauf must, by the nature of our weapons and relative paucity of our information on that place, be of short duration and of only fleeting military consequence. From the purely military stand-point there was not much to be gained by an attack on Hauf but much to lose. But I went on to say: 'In this matter the political factors are at least as weighty as the military, and no one is better able to assess the political side than Your Majesty. If you decide that the political grounds for striking at Hauf outweigh the military disadvantages to which I have referred, I for one would be very pleased, as would everyone in your Forces. Moreover my colleagues in SAF and SOAF would do our utmost to carry out an effective strike and do our best also to protect the Sultanate from any hostile retaliation'. His Majesty confirmed that he understood what I had been saying and declared that he was 'resolved on Hauf'.

I then asked whether he wished us to make a Token or a Maximum Destruction attack. He came out firmly for the latter, saying again that he had weighed up all the factors before arriving at this decision. Thus the die was cast. I was very glad about this and knew that the chaps in SAF and most of the Omani nation would welcome this most positive and courageous act of leadership by their Ruler. Before I left to start the planning for this operation which was to add a new dimension to the Dhofar war, I asked Qaboos to inform HMG through Donald Hawley of his decision as it could have significant consequences for RAF Salalah and the many British in Dhofar. His Majesty promised to do so without delay.

Late in the day I went to the Embassy, staying until after midnight with

Donald Hawley. He was personally sympathetic to the Sultan's decision and to SAF who had to carry it out. He was more worried about the reaction in Parliament and in the UK papers than that in the Arab world. He gave me to read a secret directive from Whitehall about the employment of seconded Officers on offensive operations outside Oman. Its contents did not surprise me, and I had already arranged matters so that while I and the seconded staff Officers did the detailed planning, briefing and wrote the orders, the latter were signed and executed solely by contract personnel. Thus I got Colin Maxwell, my Deputy and the senior contract Officer in the Sultanate, to sign six sheets of blank paper which I then took down to Salalah for Sergeant Simcock to type out the orders as I dictated them.

The operation named AQOOBA (Punishment) was launched against Hauf at 0835 hours on 25 May. It took the form of bomb and rocket attacks by SOAF and artillery fire from Sarfait onto known or suspected PFLOAG buildings in and around the town. That evening Curly Hirst reported to me that 'to-day's six strikes were satisfactory. Some vehicles, stores, radios, tents, etc. were identified in the target areas. 25 x 540 lb bombs were dropped (8 fell in the sea) and 180 Sura rockets fired'. The air sorties were led by Peter Hulme, the ex-RAF Commander of SOAF Tac; his aircraft collected four bullet holes. The 25-pounder guns and the single 5.5-inch medium gun on the Sarfait feature also fired deliberately at targets requiring greater accuracy of engagement than the air weapons could guarantee, for we strove in selecting the targets to avoid damaging innocent premises.

The news that Oman had at last retaliated against the *adoo* base in Hauf was greeted with relief within the Armed Forces and, as far as we could tell, with the greatest joy throughout the nation, and the broadcast speech by Sultan Qaboos four days later in which he explained his reasons and his policies towards the Dhofaris and his other enemies made an excellent impression both on his subjects and on listeners in other lands.

Late on 25 May Curly Hirst sought my agreement to SOAF putting in two more strikes early the next day 'to complete properly the job we have started'. They did this at 0920 hours. Foolishly I had not weighed up all the likely consequences of the first day's sorties. I failed to foresee that the *adoo* would reposition and maybe augment their anti-aircraft defences during the night. They did, and the last two strikes against Hauf met very heavy fire, two of the Strikemasters being damaged. Peter Hulme's was very badly hit, but with great courage he ignored his companions' pleas to eject, remained in his fume-filled and crippled aircraft and somehow landed it back at Salalah. For this remarkable act of bravery and flying skill the Sultan awarded Peter the Gallantry Medal; he was the first European to win that supreme Sultanate decoration.

Apart from the physical damage inflicted on Hauf, Operation AQOOBA caused consternation to the PFLOAG leadership and to the Aden government whose verbal assaults on Sultan Qaboos and the British, so strident after our earlier retaliation at Hauf, softened markedly. We learned from sources in Saudi Arabia that in Hauf we had inflicted many casualties and so much damage that the authorities there were calling on Aden for urgent help. PDRY moved reinforcements into Hauf and additional Soviet-manned aircraft up to their airhead at Al Gheida.

By our attack on Hauf we had extended the Dhofar war into a new dimension: as I wrote in my diary 'from volley ball to rugger' and we fully expected that the PDRY and PFLOAG forces would combine to intensify their activities against Oman. We rather hurriedly set about improving our camouflage techniques and putting into practice basic anti-aircraft drills, for we took it for granted that the PDRY airforce would be ordered to attack our positions on the exposed Sarfait feature, or even the Salalah airbase. But apart from the alleged sighting of three MIG 17s high over the RAF station, nothing happened. The opposition at that stage seemed more preoccupied with sorting out the damage at Hauf, where even Radio Aden admitted that PFLOAG casualties had been heavy.

The most pleasing consequence of the operations in April and May 1972 was the extent to which other Islamic nations declared their support for Qaboos. Even as our first strikes were going in on Hauf, messages of encouragement and firm support were reaching him from Saudi Arabia, the Gulf States, Jordan, North Yemen, Tunisia and Syria, and Egypt and Libya too. Only Iraq and (naturally) PDRY remained hostile. And not only messages of support arrived in Muscat. The first of several helpful and rather charming delegations from Saudi Arabia flew in, and from Jordan and Iran the first Ambassadors, General Mohammed Khalil and Mr Zand. I got to know both very well; the former accompanying me on many visits to our far-flung SAF positions and taking a most heart-warming interest in our soldiers and what we British were seeking to do for them and their country. In June Jordan delivered to SAF twelve 25-pounder guns and an Omani-Iranian conference which I chaired in Salalah in August was followed by the airlift into Dhofar by sixty C130 aircraft sorties of the Imperial Iranian Airforce (on what I named Operation CAVIAR) of weapons, ammunition and invaluable equipment, a gift from the Shah to Qaboos and his Armed Forces. At the same time the Imperial government made the first tentative proposal that Iranian Special Forces be employed in Dhofar.

This influx of support and material aid was heartening beyond my expectations, and was a deserved tribute from abroad to the personality and leadership qualities of Oman's Ruler. It was also judged by many in the region to be a total justification of the effort we had devoted in April to the Sarfait enterprise: 'Sarfait was the turning-point in the war', it is still averred by Omanis. While it cannot be proved beyond argument that the PFLOAG aggression at Habarut was a direct response to our SIMBA stroke, the Sultan's AQOOBA action against Hauf was a specific act of punishment for what PFLOAG had done at Habarut; and the result of these blows and counter-blows was a splendid transformation of Oman's political and military stature. Furthermore, the intervention in the following years of strong military units from the Royal Jordanian Army and from the Special Forces of Iran to fight alongside SAF and the Firqas, plus the extraordinary hike in the price of oil in 1973, ensured the eventual defeat, in December 1975, of the rebel movement.

Not everyone saw the events of spring 1972 in that light. Some of the SAS Officers in Dhofar and Hereford and many military experts in London, watching the war from afar, declared that SIMBA was launched prematurely, that Sarfait consumed too early too great a proportion of SAF's limited resources. They were unable to convince us, however, that the alternative strategy they advocated, of totally cleansing the Eastern Area of all *adoo* and setting up good government there before launching operations farther west, would have won for Oman so much material and moral support in such short order, nor brought such discomfiture on PFLOAG and its PDRY sponsors.

In June MR relieved DR on Sarfait. During their nine-month tour in Dhofar DR had lost eleven men killed and forty wounded, mercifully few in comparison with the casualties they had inflicted on the enemy and viewed against the weight of ammunition thrown at them. The Sarfait position was in the months ahead to absorb many more tons of enemy ordnance. This was a most useful contribution to our strategy, for otherwise much of that ammunition would undoubtedly have been fired at our most sensitive points, RAF Salalah and the static units manning the developing barrier lines. One Front member when interviewed after capture was positive about the significance of the Sarfait feature. 'Sarfait was the most important position to us. Even though we could get supplies past the position, it stopped us moving freely. It was like having someone's hands around your throat.' Also the final enemy collapse came when three years later a secure line was seized and held from Sarfait to the sea. During the summer of 1972 the enemy continued to mine the tracks leading down from that great feature, and random minelaying elsewhere continued to cause casualties to our vehicles and men – and to careless *adoo* minelayers also. But as more hard-surfaced roads were built this threat decreased.

On the eve of the anniversary of the revolution, 9 June, the enemy fired their annual celebratory salvo at RAF Salalah. One shell landed on the Officers' Mess patio where, despite Harvey's warning, a barbecue was being held. Eight people were wounded, the most grievously being Peter Hulme, the hero of the Hauf attacks only twelve days earlier. Operations

JAGUAR, SIMBA and AQOOBA and the establishment of the Leopard Line had been milestones in the campaign. In July came another in which the *adoo* suffered their bloodiest defeat.

The PFLOAG enemy had lost the military initiative and had to do something to regain it. Mike Harvey and I had appreciated that they would attempt a spectacular 'prestige' attack on a softer target on the coastal plain while the main body of Dhofar Brigade was engaging them on the Jebel. Sudh and Taqa were for several reasons judged to be the more likely targets. The enemy leadership decided on Taqa but at a late stage and in the mistaken belief that the garrison at Marbat had been withdrawn, changed the objective to that latter town. With stealth and skill they assembled from over a wide area of Dhofar a well equipped and eager force some three hundred strong which attacked Marbat early on 19 July. Their plan was simple: take the place by storm, execute a number of government supporters, terrify the population and then move triumphantly back to the Jebel. Marbat was garrisoned by a platoon of DG, a Firqa and an eight-man SAS team led by Captain Mike Kealy. When the enemy attack started, late because of the heavy monsoon mist, fierce fire was directed onto the SAS's and the Wali's houses on the northern edge of the town and onto a fort 300 yards away to the north-east near the corner of the perimeter wire. About 200 enemy closed in and started to scramble over the wire. Kealy called for air strikes and a helicopter to evacuate the wounded, and then ran under heavy fire to the 25-pounder gun emplacement near the fort. The gun was being fired over open sights, two SAS men were shot down beside him, but Kealy and another SAS trooper continued to fight off the enemy who were coming round the fort inside which the small garrison was pinned down. It was at this stage that the delayed start of the *adoo* attack brought them to grief. In the daylight three Strikemasters led by Squadron Leader Bill Stoker were able to fly in along the shoreline only a few feet above the surface and under the low cloud base. With rocket and machine gun fire they caught the enemy in the open along the town's perimeter wire and the attack on the fort was halted.

By chance, the SAS squadron in Dhofar was about to be relieved, and the new squadron was rapidly taken by helicopter to Marbat and landed close to the town which they then fought through while SOAF and a platoon of NFR dealt with the enemy support weapons firing onto Marbat from the feature above it, Jebel Ali. The scene after the battle was horrifying. Thirty-eight enemy dead lay within the perimeter wire while other corpses and wounded had been carried away, and a number of the attackers were made prisoner. It was a severe defeat for PFLOAG who, it is reckoned, lost a third of the force engaged, and who never again risked a major attack off the Jebel; and when their battered force reassembled, recriminations started, executions followed and other *adoo* members defected to the government side. The conduct of the SAS was truly heroic – Kealy was most deservedly awarded a DSO – and aided by the swift response and flying skills of the SOAF pilots made Marbat for PFLOAG a catastrophe and for our side the place of an almost miraculous deliverance.

The flow from the Jebel of *adoo* fighters, disillusioned by their set-backs or fearful for their lives at the hands of the 'hard core' leadership, grew as the weeks passed. One man came in on his own. He had been sent by his commander to carry a message to a neighbouring unit. The journey was long and the day hot so he sat down to rest. Out of interest he unfolded the message he was carrying and read it. The message was: 'The bearer of this letter is unreliable. When he arrives at your location, put him to death'. The last defector whom I personally met came over to our lines carrying two AK47 assault rifles and the sight mechanism from a Chinese artillery equipment. He explained that the extra Kalashnikov weapon he carried had belonged to his section commander. That man had some time before killed the Brother of the defector who before coming over to us killed him in revenge.

I was not in Oman at the time of the Marbat victory but I heard about it almost immediately as Peter de la Billière was good enough to telephone me in London with an account of his regiment's great feat of arms. I was in London on leave. The summer in Muscat had been exceptionally hot, Rosemary was in England to be nearer to the children – sensibly to avoid the heat and my frequent spells away from Bait al Falaj – and I had been getting increasingly run down and exhausted. On 17 June I passed out in my office, was found by John Lewis, the Gunner GSO3, lying on the floor and after a few days in bed with Ian Hynd's drugs inside me, was despatched home for a month of rest and recuperation. I was thoroughly ashamed but did not feel up to arguing with our SMO.

After four weeks with Rosemary during which she took me to the Hartong's house in Kirchberg, an excellent base from which to revisit our favourite spots in the Tirol and South Germany, I returned alone to Muscat, arriving on the second anniversary of the Salalah coup; alone because Rosemary was about to set off with the children on a long-planned cultural trip through France and Spain, driving all the way in our Volkswagen Minibus. It was a formidable undertaking and I was relieved that Dick and Jill Scott would be accompanying her for some of the time.

After their bloody nose at Marbat the *adoo* in Dhofar had been keeping pretty quiet.

The PFLOAG threats to the Gulf remained unchecked however. The

Head of our Intelligence Branch, Ray Nightingale, came to breakfast on the morrow of my return. He was depressed about the lack of government in Oman, the weakness of our Intelligence set-up and the evidence of increasing subversion within SAF. He described the 'remorseless Soviet and PDRY activities aimed at escalating the war in Dhofar', and the PFLOAG infiltration into Oman and the former Trucial States. 'Blood chilling' was the term he used.

Some Dhofaris had remained loyal to the Al Said dynasty. I got to know one of them very well, and he and his family were to become close friends of Rosemary and myself. Abdul Hafidh Rajab was born and raised on the Dhofar Jebel whence he eventually made his way to Russia where he was admitted to Kiev University. He was not at all happy there, for his Russian hosts openly despised coloured Asiatics, and Abdul Hafidh is as black as they come, but he got a degree in economics and married Anna, a charming and intelligent Ukrainian doctor. I met the two of them when Abdul Hafidh was Minister of Finance in Qaboos' fledgling government in 1972. At that time he was best known because of his Father, then aged 115 years. One of the first questions I, like so many others, put to the Minister was: 'How do you account for your Father's remarkably long life and good health?'. 'There are three reasons. Every day he walks at least ten kilometres; his diet throughout his life has consisted largely of dates and honey, and he has always had many women.'

During the monsoon, throughout which the SAF positions at White City and Sarfait had been fully maintained, a new team of commanders, fresh in mind and body, came out to Oman. In August Mike Harvey, who had served the Sultanate on two tours with great distinction, handed over his Dhofar Brigade to Jack Fletcher and returned to Britain to promotion and the award of the CBE. Jack Fletcher (like Teddy Turnill and my own successor, Tim Creasey), was alas to die of cancer at an early age; his wife, Mary, then married Bryan Ray, the successor to Karl Beale in command of NFR. It had already been agreed that I would hand over command of SAF in mid-September so as to allow the next CSAF time to plan, before the monsoon ended, the next phase of operations. My final weeks were mostly taken up by lengthy visits to all the sub-units of the Forces including a memorable voyage to the Musandam in *Al Said*. The Jordanian Ambassador accompanied me on several of these trips. Not only was he good company – for he was extremely pro-British and had a wide military background – these expeditions enabled him to see the strengths and weaknesses of the Omani soldier and the backward state to which Said bin Taimur had reduced the nation; and all his impressions he reported to Amman to the eventual great good of SAF and Sultan Qaboos. He was a nice man and a good friend.

The Iranian Ambassador had problems when he first came to Muscat. Most people did, as accommodation was scarce, the roads were few and the utilities such as electricity, water and the information media were not at all geared to cope with the sudden influx of officials and businessmen from the developed countries. When His Majesty provided a Datsun saloon and a Range Rover, both airconditioned, for my use I was able to lend my clapped out Land Rover to Mr Zand. In return he quietly arranged an official invitation for Rosemary and me to visit Iran for ten days at the expense of the Imperial government before we returned to Britain. To this fine surprise present was shortly added a similar invitation from the Chief of Staff of the Royal Jordanian Army to visit his country for a week[5]. The rapprochement of Qaboos with the Shah and King Hussain was not welcomed by everyone. Sheikh Zaid of Abu Dhabi was particularly suspicious of Iranian intentions towards the Gulf, and many people feared that close relations with Jordan would entangle Oman in the Palestine imbroglio. But Qaboos has proved to be a master of statecraft.

The Officers and Men of all the Service units gave me a superb send-off (which I was so glad Rosemary returned to share in after the children went back to school in September), as did Hugh Oldman and the Staff at the Embassy. His Majesty had already conferred on me the Order of Oman and had sought to promote me to the honorary rank of Major-General in the Omani forces 'in perpetuity'. British regulations, however, did not permit this sort of reward to a serving soldier, so Whitehall advised the Sultan to drop the idea.

On 15 September Major-General Tim Creasey arrived to take over from me and to begin an association with SAF and Oman which was to win him promotion, a knighthood and deserved fame; but also an early death, after a long struggle, from cancer. His rank and that of Brigadier Jack Fletcher reflected the transformation which had been brought about in SAF since 1970. Until 1971 Dhofar Brigade did not exist. SAF, which in early 1970 had totalled fewer than four thousand, was now ten thousand-strong, with a powerful air force of nearly fifty aircraft, a modernised and growing navy, a large Firqa force; and the SEPs, virtually nil before Sultan Qaboos' accession, had swelled to just under a thousand.

The Communist conquest of Dhofar, in June 1970 seemingly inevitable, had been averted and the means were now being acquired and the pattern set for their eventual defeat. Izki in June 1970, JAGUAR in 1971 and the Leopard Line, SIMBA, AQOOBA and Marbat in 1972 had indeed been milestones in the Sultanate's successful crusade to halt the wave of revolution and anti-western plots. But the critical milestone, the one of supreme importance, had been reached on 23

July 1970. Without the abdication of Said bin Taimur and the accession of his son, Qaboos, the cohesion and loyalty to the dynasty of the Armed Forces could not have been sustained. And had SAF fallen into disarray Dhofar would have been lost. But SAF did not fall into disarray.

On 17 September, Arnhem Day, we got up early, tipped the servants and gave them their testimonials. These were well deserved, especially by our Head Bearer Shareef who had looked after us and our many guests so very well. After a final trip round the offices in the Fort I headed for the Mess where all the Officers had assembled to give Rosemary and me a champagne breakfast and a large, engraved, silver salver. While Rosemary was escorted to the airstrip I was invited to mount the bonnet of a Land Rover and be driven all the way from the Mess through the ranks of soldiers, from every unit and with their flags, all clapping and waving, and with the signallers buzzing their morse-key buzzers. Naturally I jumped off to shake hands as my vehicle reached each new detachment, and before the end of the ride this energetic behaviour had split open my uniform trousers. This necessitated a further delay at SOAF HQ where someone mended my embarrassment with an office stapler. Waiting beside the aircraft, the Sultan's own Viscount, were a Guard of Honour, Bugler and the Dhofar Gendarmerie Pipers in their plaids in the Douglas tartan of the Cameronians and a great number of VIPs assembled to see us off. The sun was very hot and I fear they had an uncomfortable time waiting for me to arrive. It was good of them. The last thing I did before emplaning with Rosemary was to pin a Sergeant's stripes onto the sleeve of my trusted and careful driver, Abdullah. It was a great event in our lives which John Lewis managed to film using my ciné camera.

We soon reached Sharjah where we were met by Tony Teague, 2IC of the UDF, who put us up in his house and helped us to unwind after the hectic and emotional programme of the past week and to prepare for our odyssey to Iran and Jordan. My commitment to Oman had not however ended. On 20 October, two weeks after we settled back in our house in Camberley, an official rang me from London to say: 'Said bin Taimur died last night in London and is to be buried this afternoon at Brookwood. Do you wish to attend?'. I drove over to the large multi-national cemetery near Working after lunch. The ceremony was extremely brief, largely perhaps on account of the bitter wind. The coffin was lifted out of the hearse, lowered into the grave and covered over. Two quick prayers by a beturbanned Mullah and finish. They did not even wait until 3.30pm, the announced time of the service, nor for the arrival of Anthony Kershaw from the FCO bearing a wreath from Julian Amery. There were only twelve people present: Seyyid Shabib bin Taimur, Tariq, Wali Buraik, an Omani student, some servants, Sir David Scott-Fox, representing Sir Alec Douglas-Home, and me. Tariq was vexed because UK regulations did not permit the ex-Sultan to be buried in Ibadi fashion but the Omanis seemed pleased that I was present. His Highness's grave was, I noted, in a pleasantly elevated position under pine trees in the Muslim section of the cemetery. Shabib told me that Said had been happy and active the day before, and that he died suddenly and painlessly watching television in his London hotel.

But I was distressed by the hasty and ill-attended burial of this former Ruler and life-long friend of Britain; a man of great charm and strong personality, even though his policies latterly almost destroyed his country, and I consoled myself with the knowledge that his abdication had made it possible for him to enjoy two years of peace and freedom from anxiety, a serenity he could not have experienced if he had remained immured in that palace in Salalah. Nevertheless, I resolved to do something to make his burial more fitting. So the following Monday I bought a large vase of growing yellow chrysanthemums, the most suitable flowers on sale in Camberley that day, and planted them on the grave together with an inscribed card from the SAF Association and myself; a final salute to our former Commander-in-Chief. That same night I wrote to Sultan Qaboos[6] and to Hugh Oldman.

Many more problems and hazards had still to be surmounted in Dhofar in the three years that followed my departure. And not only in Dhofar. Even as I left Oman there were signs that the Sultan's enemies were plotting a new campaign of infiltration, subversion and murder more clandestine and sophisticated than their earlier attempts had been. The plotters were by good fortune unmasked and a number ended up before a firing squad.

So much has happened to Oman so rapidly during the reign of Sultan Qaboos that one can only marvel. None can appreciate the wondrous transformation that he has wrought in his country better than my generation of expatriates who, after service among perhaps the most deprived people in the Middle East, have watched that majestic country ascend to its current pinnacle of esteem and well-being. Since 1970 Qaboos, the former Sandhurst Cadet and Cameronian, has brought his country out of the Middle Ages onto the threshold of the 21st century. The contribution made by the Armed Forces to that transformation is inestimable. To have been at the head of those Armed Forces during the decisive years 1970–72 was a rare privilege, and to each man who served under me during my thirty months as CSAF, I send warm greetings and express my deep gratitude for great things greatly done. For our brothers-in-arms from Britain, Arabia and the Indian sub-continent who died to make possible the Oman we see today, the most fitting epitaph must surely be, like Wren's in St Paul's Cathedral, 'Si monumentum requiris, circumspice'.

Notes

1. Psychological (warfare) operations
2. Like many of Britain's distinguished colonial administrators and diplomats, Donald (now Sir Donald) Hawley began his career in the elite Sudan Service. He and his wife, Ruth, made an outstanding contribution to Anglo-Omani relations. They are remembered also for their books on the history and culture of Oman.
3. Capitation charges were the fees that the Sultan had to pay to HMG for the services of us, the seconded British personnel. We considered the scale exorbitant.
4. Juma'a = Friday, equivalent to the Christian Sunday, the day of rest.
5. Our days in Iran and Jordan on these official visits were so interesting, enjoyable and, I like to believe, helpful for Oman, that I have included at Appendix V the entries I made in my diary each day.
6. Sultan Qaboos never lost his respect for his Father, and after the abdication their relations became increasingly warm. His Majesty has stressed to me consistently that he had taken the decision to depose Said bin Taimur with reluctance and solely in the interests of his country.

CHAPTER XIV
1973

With the Indian National Defence College, and in parts of South-East Asia

I had been recommended for promotion and was in line for a vacancy at the Royal College of Defence Studies (the RCDS), formerly the Imperial Defence College, in London's Belgravia. I was nevertheless glad when the Military Secretary asked me if I would be willing to go instead to India to spend 1973 at the National Defence College in New Delhi, to which Britain sent each year one senior serving Officer in exchange for two Indians who went to the RCDS. I was glad because having had Indians and Pakistanis under me in SAF I was keen to learn more about their backgrounds and the Armed Forces from which they had come to Oman. Also I believed that my recent experiences in the Gulf area might be a useful source of information for the government of India who, it was rumoured, were lamenting the fact that affairs in Arabia and the Gulf were better understood when that region was controlled by the British from Calcutta and New Delhi than later when independent India was represented by her own consular and diplomatic personnel. Furthermore, since the family had gone out to India without me in 1933, I was keen to see for myself the land and the people who had given my parents many happy memories. I flew out in mid-January leaving Rosemary and the kids to follow when the school term ended in late March. Christopher, well coached by Mr Faulds and his colleagues, had passed the Entrance Exam into Wellington and he (naturally) joined Lynedoch House shortly before I left England. I remember our parting vividly. The little chap, dwarfed by the senior boys who were milling around, struggled to hold back his tears as he ran down the drive behind my car. I left him with a heavy heart for I had not forgotten the misery of my own initiation into English public school life, and like Rosemary I knew that our son, a small boy of racially mixed parentage, would even in 1973 be the target of malicious harassment by his fellow-pupils.

I arrived in Delhi just in time for the annual Independence Day holiday and watched the long colourful parade along Rajpath, that fine imperial avenue conceived by Lutyens, with proud cohorts of marching Servicemen and women, jingling horsemen, richly garbed, lumbering elephants, many excellent bands, lorries, armoured cars, tanks (some designed and built in India), teams of dancers from the various regions and tribes of the sub-continent, and aircraft in formations flying overhead. The whole show took up most of the morning and getting to and from one's seat through the immense crowds of onlookers had added to the interest of my first week in India, a republic within the Commonwealth populated by some 680 million humans. One of the star-turns in the procession was a series of floats depicting incidents in India's Struggle for Independence. Mahatma Gandhi and his fasts, his campaign of non-violence and his imprisonments featured largely, as did the executions of those few who had murdered British officials during the past century; but I remember being astonished by the shallowness of the enacted fight to rid India of British rule, and by the paucity of episodes staged in 1973 to glorify her Freedom Fighters. When I had settled into the Defence College I broached this to my new Indian colleagues. They did not disagree with my observation; their general comment was to the effect that the Fight for Independence should be spelt with a very small 'f'; much had to be made out of rather insignificant incidents to dramatize the struggle, and that only Britain would have relinquished sovereignty so lightly: 'Any other country,' they told me, 'would have mounted machine-guns in the main streets and put an end to the matter for a number of years.' Throughout my twelve months in the sub-continent, working beside proud and highly intelligent men, I was to meet only rare personal antagonism or disparagement of those British who before 1947 had devoted their lives to India.

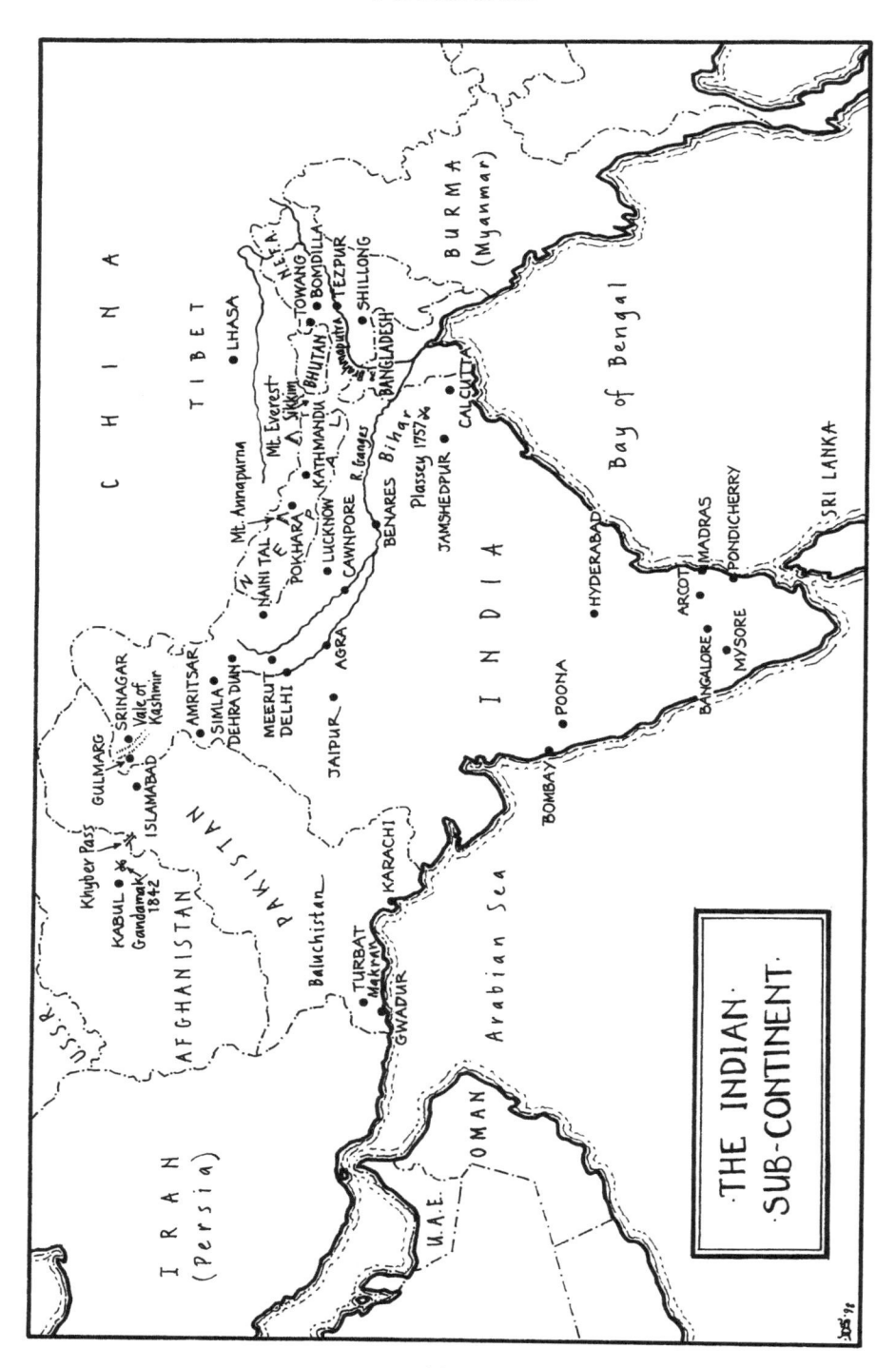

THE INDIAN SUB-CONTINENT

India

At that time the British student at the National Defence College (NDC) and his wife were housed in Claridges Hotel, only a few minutes' walk from the College, and one of New Delhi's best addresses. It had a tennis court and a swimming pool, the latter much used by the East European advisers, traders and specialists who thronged the capital, for in 1973 India was closely, but reluctantly, linked to the industries and armament-producers of the Soviet Union and her satellites. The hotel restaurant served food from three menus: European, Indian and Chinese. The contents never altered from January to December, but the monotony of the meals was enlivened at breakfast by the reading of the morning newspaper and in the evening by the melodies of Mollie and Mervyn Fernandes, a Goanese musical couple whose good nature and versatility had wisely been engaged by the hotel's management. Except on Sunday, I lunched at the NDC. Lunch was really a misnomer, for the fare provided seemed to consist mostly of spiced chips, birdseed and vegetables washed down with water. I was warned by the High Commission that my mail from England would from time to time be opened and read, and Rosemary and I were certain that our bedroom was electronically bugged; but these occurrences did not disturb us for we understood the reasons for Indian sensitivity during that era of close relations with the USSR; and a war with Pakistan had ended not long before our arrival.

The National Defence College was housed in Tees January Marg, close by the place where Gandhi had been assassinated on 30 January 1948, in a large building which had once held the British High Commission. The Commandant was a Lieutenant-General with a Signal Corps background, MN Batra commonly known as Bim, tall, good-looking and by his compatriots respected rather than liked. The Directing Staff were senior Officers from the three Services and one high-powered civil servant. I was on Course No 13 and my fellow-students numbered forty-four of which six were from outside India. The Indian students, all of Brigadier or Colonel rank or civilian equivalent, were reckoned to be high-fliers. Many of those from the Army and Air Force had recently distinguished themselves in the short victorious war to liberate East Pakistan and enable it to secede and become independent as Bangladesh. The six foreigners, apart from myself, were a tall, very likeable Brigadier from the Iraqi Army, Abdul Munim Lafta; Colonel Perera from Sri Lanka; a Kenyan Colonel, pleasant, uncomprehending and whose contribution to our studies was almost zero; John McDonagh, an Royal Australian Engineer who had served in Vietnam and graduated from Latimer; and Fred Akuffo, a Colonel from the Ghana Army, amusing, fluent and popular; as was his wife, Emily, a bonny, plump lady shaped like an 'S'. On his return to Ghana Fred was made Chief of Staff, Head of the Army, and in due course Head of State. Unfortunately he was induced to enter politics. Soldiers rarely succeed in making for themselves good reputations in two such disparate fields, and for Fred Akuffo the transition proved fatal. There was a coup d'état led by Flight Lieutenant Jerry Rawlings; Rawlings won and had Fred put to death by firing squad. I was sad to hear how the life of my good-natured friend was prematurely ended; I also reflected on the humiliation that punctilious and senior soldier must have felt at being toppled from power by a junior Officer of the junior Service. Rawlings however seems to have made good; at the time of writing (October 1998) he is still the Leader of his nation.

The British now reproach themselves for colour prejudice, and the critics of Empire go on about the practice of barring clubs, offices, marriage to whites and a whole range of privileges, to people of colour in condemnation of our Imperial tradition. That practice undoubtedly did in the past cause resentment, but by the second half of the 20th century it had been largely eliminated throughout the British Commonwealth. That was my belief until I found myself reading *The Sunday Times of India*, of which page two was devoted each week to columns of entries placed by men seeking marriage partners. Most of the entries emphasised the educational levels required in their prospective mates; a few stated 'caste no bar', but rare were those which stated 'colour no bar'. The majority that I read throughout 1973 gave a clear indication of the preferred skin colour; 'wheat-' or 'honey-coloured' being the standard adjectives. As my Australian colleague was frequently to observe, he and I, the only white men at the NDC, conversed more freely with the dark-skinned students than did those Indian Officers whose lightly tanned complexions belied their nationality. The very dark-skinned, albeit of high rank and with successful careers behind them, seemed to have an in-built shyness and a reluctance to thrust themselves forward in debate or in our collective activities, and their lights, though some of the brightest, were habitually kept hidden under bushels. During the year much time was devoted to studying the relations between India and Pakistan. Despite the notable Hindu victories over their Muslim foe and the self-esteem, won on the battlefield, which our Indian class-mates rightly enjoyed, John McDonagh and I were left with the feeling that the deep-thinking Indian Officer rated the individual Pakistani soldier as equal to three Indians. This was perhaps an expression of the respect which Lowlanders universally have for the Highlander?

The manner in which the NDC was run reflected the government's decree outlawing 'conspicuous consumption' in the public service. Thus, economy was the basic facet of the College housekeeping, and meant that many facilities taken for granted in European institutions were skimped or not provided at all. This affected our working ambiance, from the cleanliness of the lavatories, the appeal of the lunch menu to the efficiency of the clerical staff. The standard of the lectures given to us by the many Indian experts was however excellent; well composed and in general delivered in impeccable English. So was our introduction to the European Economic Community by the French and German Ambassadors. Alas the man to whom we looked for the most informative talk on this novel and important subject disappointed us shamefully. The British High Commissioner read without enthusiasm from a bland script and failed to answer any questions. His performance greatly discomfited me, the only Briton in the audience. But I must not be too hard on the fellow; I am told that he was very skilled on paper.

My principal dealings with the High Commission were with the Service Attachés. Major-General Logan Scott-Bowden was a large, jovial former Sapper who was the image of Punch. He had played a significant role in the preparations for D-Day 1944 as he was one of those brave men who examined the Normandy beaches in darkness under the noses of the Germans and brought back samples of the sand and gravel and other data essential to the planning of the assault from the sea. Logan and his wife, Jocelyn, loved India, knew it well and their affection was reciprocated. They were also very kind to my family and me, as was our Naval Attache. Sadly his return to England was marred by tragedy.[1]

An aspect of life in India which repels many visitors from the western world is the hordes of beggars who surrounded one as we drove or walked through city streets. Revulsion grew with learning that many of the begging children had been crippled deliberately by their parents in order to gain greater sympathy from tourists. Also distasteful was the sight of young Europeans and Americans squatting on the crowded pavements, often stupefied by drugs, begging for money or food. The desire of many Indians to emigrate to Britain gave our consular staff a lot of work, and in view of the tightening UK immigration laws, many problems. In the spring of 1973 two Australian youths decided to travel round India by rail at minimal expense. This meant riding, along with a legion of native travellers, on the carriage roofs. This they did without hindrance until one of the pair, unaware that the train was about to enter a tunnel, stood up. He fell to the ground dead. His stalwart companion, determined to retrieve the body and escort it to the Australian authorities in New Delhi, encountered from the Indian railway officials little help but much embuggerance: 'Your friend is dead; he is not entitled to a seat'; 'Where is his ticket?', and after the first day, 'He has a bad smell and cannot come into my train', and such like. I have always been surprised by the invisibility of dead things. Considering the number of insects, birds and mammals that expire each day, it is remarkable how Nature leaves little evidence of their end. And even in 'teeming India' it was rare to see corpses being taken away for cremation. Cremation is carried out at the burning ghats, often open spaces on the banks of rivers into which the ashes are finally scattered. A sad consequence of this cremation process is the deforestation of wide areas. In February we drove out to Meerut, a city about an hour's drive from Delhi and the place where the Great Mutiny broke out in 1857. That part of the Gangetic Plain was in 1973 almost denuded of trees, yet the Viceroy, I read, on hunting expeditions before the Second World War needed to drive only a few miles from Delhi before he entered forests and jungle. I personally saw no evidence of efforts to restore the countryside by tree replanting, but human concern for the environment and its conservation was less marked then than it is now, so maybe something is at last being done to rehabilitate that bit of India.

But a bit farther down the great plain there is a wonderful place, a nature reserve named after Jim Corbett, a man exceptionally wise in forest lore, a skilled hunter and lover of animals. In this broad protected area live tigers, pumas and many animals in danger of extinction. Rosemary took the children to the Park during the Easter holidays. Mounted on an elephant in the care of a wiry little native guide, they glimpsed creatures normally seen only in zoos. Christopher's attempt to photograph a tiger at short range was spoilt by Rosemary in her excitement plonking her bottom on his hand as he reached for his camera.

I was in Calcutta when the family arrived in Delhi as the NDC had been taken east to look at various aspects of industry including a coalmine in Bihar. This mine was not especially deep, but the working conditions and the inadequate safety precautions were alarming to western eyes. Calcutta was for me memorable for three reasons. The poverty here was more apparent than in Delhi and was encapsulated vividly by the sight of whole families living out their lives in the bus shelters erected along the main streets. Elsewhere in that great city were some magnificent buildings and monuments to the British monarchs and their subjects who had done fine things in Bengal. I also spent half-an-hour in the principal English cemetery in, I believe, West Park Street. There stand headstones, tombs and sepulchres dating back to the early 17th century when the first English trading post was set up. What surprised me most from my inspection of the inscriptions was not the number of English who died in childhood in that implacable climate, but how many of our forebears, dressed in garments more suitable for temperate zones and drinking claret in place of polluted water, survived into three score years and more.

Rosemary and I, and the children when out with us for the Easter and summer holidays, got away from Delhi whenever the NDC programme permitted, for there was so much to see in that vast, varied sub-continent. Because my Parents and Brothers had lived before the Second World War in Naini Tal I was keen to make an early pilgrimage to that lakeside hill station some 150 miles (as the crow flies) to the north-east of Delhi and about fifty miles from the Nepalese frontier. We hired a rather clapped-out taxi with a driver who spoke good English. Most taxis in India were clapped-out. Called 'Ambassadors' they were locally made versions of the famous Morris Oxford. Not particularly comfortable for long journeys, they got us there without breaking down and they were cheap. It was a long climb up from the Plain of the Ganges to that little town with its military buildings, cathedral and bungalows situated around the lake on terraces carved out of the steeply sloping land. The air was cool and invigorating and the eye, accustomed to the city bustle of humans, vehicles and the ubiquitous sacred cows, rejoiced at the sight of the distant Himalayan mountains and at the green ocean of hillsides, covered with pines and rhododendrons, which lay between Naini Tal and their snow-covered summits. Naini was exactly as the photographs taken by my Father in 1934 described. Apart from the absence of white faces nothing seemed to have changed. Rosemary and I spent one night there before returning to Delhi in, I reckoned, the same hotel as my family had slept on the eve of their move to Dehra Dun in 1935 and in which the rooms seemed not to have been cleaned since. Perhaps the most disagreeable aspect of India is the lack of cleanliness. Streets, rivers, buildings, vehicles and the people's clothing – except for the uniformed members of the Armed Forces – all were dirty. It was an enormous contrast with litter-free Oman and the spotless garments of her citizens. The sheets on our hotel bed had not, it seemed, been changed since the last occupant departed, leaving behind hairs, pubic and other. We slept fully dressed, Rosemary with her head wrapped in a towel, as protection against the dust, dirt and unseen vermin.

Kashmir was different, for we put up not in buildings on land but in house-boats on the two lakes, Dal or Naguin. These boats were extremely comfortable, roomy and well-equipped, each having a small staff to cook, clean and run errands. They lived in a separate boat. The experience was idyllic, one of the charming features being the rows of brightly coloured kingfishers which flew in to line the gunwale of our floating home. The native-born inhabitants too were quite different to the darker-skinned people who surrounded us in Delhi, and I remain convinced that Hindu rule over those light-skinned Muslim Kashmiris is an anomaly and will remain a source of friction for many years between India and Pakistan. This friction arose in 1947 when the Hindu maharajah acceded to India without seeking the consent of his Muslim subjects, an event in stark contrast to that which occurred in the State of Hyderabad whose Muslim ruler, the Nizam, was compelled by the government in Delhi, newly independent from Britain, to join the republican Union of India. Nevertheless the people we saw around us in Srinagar, on the banks of the lakes and in the hill villages, seemed very content, good humoured and helpful. How could they be otherwise?; for life in the Vale of Kashmir with its gardens, waterlilies, snow-capped peaks, pure air and well nourished oxen is enviable; and of all the sights we enjoyed during our months in India none were more beautiful or more memorable than the mountains and hills surrounding our lakes, and the views of the distant Himalayas from Yusmarg and Gulmarg which we visited on horseback. Apart from memories and ciné film we have several mementos of that happy interlude in Kashmir acquired from engaging shopkeepers in Srinagar, chief of whom went by the name 'Suffering Moses'.

We did not fail to visit the Taj Mahal, built on the bank of the Jumna river in 1650 by the Emperor Shah Jehan as a tomb for his wife, Mumtaz Mahal. We four, for the children had joined us for the school holidays, sat in wonderment as the sun set over that jewel of architecture, as the full moon rose, and as the dawn of a new day changed into the glare and heat of an Indian summer morning. I personally was even more impressed by that other great building near Agra, Fatepur Sikri, a huge red and white palace constructed for a Mogul emperor at enormous cost in money and lives but almost immediately deserted through lack of water. In the autumn of 1973, after Rosemary had gone back with the kids at the end of the summer holidays, I was taken by a retired Indian General to Lucknow, principally to inspect the ruins of the Residency in which British women and children, who had taken shelter on the outbreak of the Great Mutiny in 1857, were defended by a small garrison of British and Indian troops under the command of Sir Henry Lawrence. The siege lasted from 2 July until 16 November when a relieving column under Sir Colin Campbell broke through the besieging force – though too late to save Lawrence who was mortally wounded on the first day of the siege and is buried in the grounds. The saga of the siege is well documented and explained on notice boards around the ruins. When I asked my Indian host: 'How was it that such a small, beleaguered garrison of British and loyal Indian troops withstood for so long the assaults and bombardments of the vastly greater army of Mutineers?', he replied without hesitation: 'Leadership. The British Officers set a wonderful example to their men, and the men did not let them down'.

The business of getting the children out of England for their school holidays and back again for the new terms was well handled by friends who escorted them to the airport and by the airlines' cabin staff. Each child was entitled to two journeys by air each year at public expense to the place overseas where his or her Father was stationed. This meant that for one of the three annual school holidays arrangements had to be made by the childrens' family or guardian. The staff work was initiated by the Father's unit and then finalised by the Movements Branch of the Armed Services. At the British end it invariably worked smoothly and the passage of legions of school children between the UK and the overseas theatres became a matter of normal routine Service business. As we were to discover in July 1973, the confidence we placed in British arrangements was seriously misplaced at the Indian end. The morning that Pinky and Christopher were due to arrive was windless but overcast with a heavy mist. Rosemary and I drove out to Palam Airport, on the outskirts of Delhi, to await the arrival of their Qantas flight. Although we could not see everything that occurred, it was obvious that something had gone amiss with their plane's landing, for instead of touching down on the ground the aircraft roared up into a steep climb away from Palam, went round and belatedly landed properly and smoothly. What had happened was that the Indian air traffic controller had talked the pilot down through the mist and fog, not accurately onto the runway but about a mile short of the runway into the middle of a village. By the Grace of God the Australian pilot realised the catastrophe into which he was being led, climbed away and, disregarding the Palam controller, brought the aircraft down safely, using his own judgement and thereby saving the lives of everyone on board. It was a very angry Australian who stormed into the Palam control tower; and our vexation was compounded by the excuse given by the Indians for their controller's gross error. The ground approach radar set was not working that day so the plane had to be talked down by eye and voice. The set was not working because a spare part was not available; it had not been working for over two weeks and there was no money to enable the Palam Airport Authority to obtain the essential spare part. So many things were hampered in India in the 1970s by a lack of funds, above all by a shortage of foreign currencies.

West Bengal with a population of 35 million adjoins a Bangladesh created out of East Pakistan by the Indian victory in the 1972 war, a war which simplified India's military problem in her continuing confrontation with Pakistan. West Bengal is economically important to India being the centre of the jute and steel-making industries. It was also of interest in 1973 as it was one of the few States in the Union ruled by a Communist administration. It was an informative visit for there was much to admire in the Tata installations whose products were varied and impressive, especially in the range of vehicles and earth-moving equipments designed for the commercial and military markets. The great steel-rolling mills which we were shown in detail resembled, like the Bihar coal mines, scenes from a Brueghel painting; filthy, noisy and deliberately overmanned to employ Bengalis whose motivations were expressed in the pernicious Marxist slogans crudely painted on the factory walls and ceilings. Labour indiscipline was rife but management, we gathered, could do little to improve the situation bar the wringing of hands and bribing the workers with various incentives. Nevertheless, as I noted above, the products were impressive in quality; with a more disciplined, motivated and educated work force the quantity of the Tata products could be greatly increased to the nation's benefit. This was the gist of the lamentations intimated to us, the NDC visitors, by management at various levels in the different plants.

We had arrived in Jamshedpur on a Saturday and settled ourselves in the Company Guest House, a modern, well-equipped facility with a large garden filled with colourful shrubs, manicured lawns and neat flowerbeds; a scene evocative of southern Europe but exceptional, in our experience, in the India of 1973. My Australian colleague, John McDonagh, suggested that we stretch our legs after the long coach journey, so in the cool of the late afternoon we went for a stroll past the neat bungalows and trim gardens of the Tata Company's residential cantonment. It was a peaceful and uplifting amble.

On the outskirts of the cantonment we came across a church. It was set back a bit from the roadside, at the end of a short path leading from the gate beside which stood a noticeboard. The board was headed by the words, writ large: Church of Syria, and beneath in smaller letters were set out the weekly services and their timings; all in English. The board and its setting so resembled the entrance to a church in an English village that John and I decided on the spot to attend the service scheduled for the following morning. We told no one of our intention and we took our seats in a rear-most pew shortly before the service began. The congregation pretty well filled the church; middle-aged men and women mostly, some youths and a few children. All were black or brown. The Australian McDonagh and the Scottish Graham were the only whites in the building. The service, conducted in English, followed the rubric of the Anglican Church; we knew the hymns, and in that House of God in West Bengal felt as much at home as in Surrey or New South Wales. But it was the sermon which made the occasion unforgettable. The Indian Preacher mounted the pulpit and declared that the date of that Sunday was of particular significance to the people of that part of India for it is the date on which, one hundred years earlier in 1873, there had arrived from Britain a new man to join the officials administering, under the Viceroy and in the name of the Empress of India, that District. The sermon consisted largely of a summary of all the good works which this British official – the Preacher called him Reid or Reeve (I could not hear distinctly) – and his colleagues had done, their hardships and vexations and the benefits which their governance had brought to the District. The relevance to the congregation that day, he stated, was this:

'Almighty God does His work in mysterious ways, and truly it is a most wonderful thing that He should bring from a mist-covered island far distant from Jamshedpur men such as this Englishman, who was content to devote his working life to improving the lot of this congregation's forebears and who, when his work was done, quietly departed back across the ocean. We citizens of independent India,' he said, 'must hold in honour these long-dead benefactors from far away and never cease to give thanks to God for having brought to our people the blessing of that Englishman, of the many like him and of the good things they had wrought, often without recognition, in those parts of India where they had been called by God to serve.'

Some weeks earlier I had been on a journey through the countryside to the west of Delhi in a hired taxi. We stopped for petrol in a large village and I asked the attendant, a young man who spoke English: 'Today and on other days I have seen standing alongside the main roads in this area concrete pillars. They are triangular in shape but have flat tops and have been erected about three miles apart. Can you please tell me their purpose?'

'Yes, I can tell you about them. Many years ago one of the British officials responsible for the administration here was a young military engineer. In those days the roads were few and, this being a poor district, not many farmers had carts or animals to pull them. Most therefore had to carry their produce to the markets on their backs, loaded onto a wooden frame. This young engineer noticed that the farmers had to stop often to rest, but that to lift those heavy loads back onto their shoulders took a great effort and to the older men sometimes caused injury. So he designed these stone pillars, had them set up about one hour's travel apart, and gave them flat tops so that the farmers could rest their burdens without taking the frames off their shoulders.'

We foreign students were not to be allowed to visit southern India, an embarrassed Commandant informed John McDonagh and me. Although he did not divulge the reason, I had already been warned by the High Commission that this ban was to be expected: a consequence of India's close relations with the USSR and of certain military installations where Soviet personnel and equipment were alleged to be operating. I therefore opted to be included in the contingent going on a tour of South-East Asia. I am very glad I did so for the tour was extremely well laid on; generously too, for on this occasion government had not stinted the NDC's travel budget; and although we spent less than a week in each country on our schedule, we met the right people and acquired a comprehensive understanding of its structure, problems, affiliations and potential. We travelled by air using several of the regional air lines. On checking in at the Delhi airport I drew the attention of the Customs officials to my ciné camera which I was determined to take on the tour. I had been advised to do this in order to avoid having to pay a large importation charge on return to India. The temporary export of this camera kept two officials busy for nearly half-an-hour. The article had to be inscribed on forms and in my passport and I was admonished not to sell it abroad in exchange for foreign currency, at that time an offence. I was not as surprised by the time and paperwork that had to be devoted to the passage of my camera, for the Indian clerical multitude was notorious for its pedantry, as I was by the evident singularity of my owning a ciné camera and of my wish to take it on my travels. In truth many items which we in the West acquire as a matter of course for our comfort, to save time or to add colour – or prestige – to our personal identity were spurned by my Indian colleagues as superfluous, extravagant or inordinately expensive. This self-denial was matched, I came to realise, by a sincere compassion on the part of the better-off, educated, privileged Indians for the great mass of their compatriots who through caste, illiteracy or disability were condemned to the lower strata of the social pile. Those at the top expressed, it seemed to me, in their words and deeds an unfeigned professional intention to add to the cohesion and stability of their country; and as citizens of that great democracy to seek a fairer distribution of the national wealth.

We went first to Nepal. The air was cool and pure after the stifling heat and dust of mid-summer in Delhi, and the scenery magnificent, our stop-overs having as a backcloth the snow-covered peaks of the Himalayas, chief of which is Everest, named after Sir George Everest, Surveyor General of India in the 19th century, which we saw from the air standing near the border with Tibet. The continuing tension between India and the People's Republic of China, and the Chinese occupation of Tibet, had heightened Indian concern for events in Nepal where Communist influence was strong, and a major project had been initatiated by India with the USA, the building of a 650 mile-long east-west highway, in a bid to counter that unwelcome trend. Most Nepalese live in villages perched on the sides of hills and mountains, and we saw at once the problems the villagers had in carving terraces for their crops, in obtaining water, which had to be fetched from often distant wells or streams, or electricity supplied by a community-owned generator or not at all. We motored from Katmandu to Pokhara expressly to attend a reunion of Ex-Servicemen of the Indian Army during which they were paid their pensions. The event with its assembly of upright, bemedalled veterans, reminded me of Airborne Forces Day in Aldershot in miniature, except that the towering peaks of Annapurna and her lesser sisters dominate the scene more impressively than does the Farnborough skyline. The capital Katmandu was a disappointment after the dignity and bracing air of rural Nepal and its hardy people. There were few interesting buildings and the streets were sullied by the scruffy young Europeans and Americans on drugs or begging for money to buy them.

It was therefore a relief to emplane for our next port of call, Bangkok. Siam, named since 1939 Thailand (a translation of Muang T'ai or Land of the Free People), rather resembles a reed. No matter from which direction it is buffeted by wind or floodwaters, it does not break but bends, yielding unharmed to every onslaught. This gift of accommodation got the country through Japanese occupation and a declaration of war against Britain and the USA in 1941, without lingering post-war rancour on the part of the Allies; a gift which is sustained by the nation's deeply rooted Buddhism and by the monarchy which originated in the 14th century. Thailand's natural wealth combines with this traditional sense of stability to give her thirty-five-odd million people a good living by Asian standards. Water abounds and with it rice in plenty; the forests produce precious stones, tin, wolfram and much timber: sugar, tobacco and cotton are grown, and pigs and oxen raised in quantities.

The national wealth was already being visibly augmented by a generous in-flow of foreign currency. This came from two principal sources. The United States was in 1973 supplying the Thai Army with military advisers and material aid in the campaign to suppress the Communist guerillas active in the areas where Thailand borders Malaysia and Laos. (Thailand was one of the dominoes in South-East Asia which could not be allowed to fall; this Domino Theory was the fundamental rationalisation for Washington's ill-starred intervention in Vietnam.)

The other source was tourism, for by 1973 Bangkok had already become notorious as the Sex Capital of the world; a consequence, it was claimed, of large numbers of American servicemen, randy and well-paid, on R&R from Vietnam continuously descending onto a city where the young girls are extraordinarily pretty, seductive and uninhibited. Apart, however, from the lures of the brothels and sex shows, there was much to see in Bangkok that was appealing, such as the architecture of the Palace and the traditional dancers who put on an entertaining show for us at a banquet which the Chief of the Army Staff hosted. I left Thailand feeling that I had glimpsed a country uniquely fortunate in its stability, cultural and religious convictions and natural resources, but vulnerable to the corrupting influences of the permissive liberal Western societies: intolerable traffic congestion in the capital city, air pollution and Aids.

The Federation of Malaysia was formed within the Commonwealth in 1963 by the linking of Malaya, Sarawak, North Borneo (Sabah) and Singapore. Singapore seceded two years later and Indonesian hostility, which had taken the form of militant confrontation, petered out in 1966 thanks in part to the competence of the British Forces deployed to defend Malaysian territory and interests. Malaysian fears of Indonesian hostility lessened when the unstable Soekarno was ousted by General Suharto. The major preoccupations of the government officials whom we met in Kuala Lumpur were Communism – for they had not forgotten the long campaign fought two decades earlier under British leadership and by a sizeable part of Britain's national service Army against the resolute Chinese Communist gangs – and anxiety lest the Chinese segment of the population, smaller but cleverer and more industrious than the indigenous Malays, secured the dominant power in the nation's political, financial and military structures. The country gave us the impression that it had developed rapidly since 1963 and that its economy was sound with good potential for growth. The major problem was that of national cohesion. The loss to the Federation of Singapore no longer rankled but the rivalry of the two races remained an inhibiting factor. Kuala Lumpur has some impressive buildings – the main railway station was especially striking – but on the whole I personally found Malaysia less interesting than the other countries on our tour, for I had arrived better acquainted with the place on account of the publicity the military journals and newspapers in Britain had devoted to Malaya during the campaign so brilliantly directed by General Templer in 1952-4. A happy interlude in our visit however was meeting again General Ungku Nazaruddin, Chief of the Federation's General Staff who, known then as 'Bruno,' had been a popular fellow student on my Latimer course eleven years previously.

Singapore was an eye-opener. This island state of 220 square miles and two million citizens, predominantly Chinese, and an independent republic within the Commonwealth, was admired and envied on many counts. The feature which immediately impressed my Indian colleagues as we strolled on our first evening through the streets was its cleanliness. Not a weed nor a cigarette-end was to be seen. 'One could eat a meal off the pavement,' they declared in wonderment. It reminded me of Muscat where a multitude of labourers imported from the sub-continent keep the public places spotless, the lawns manicured and the flowers watered for the benefit of their Arab employers. In Singapore this remarkable quality of Good Order stemmed from a national pride sustained by a stern code of civic discipline. The Chief Minister, Lee Kuan Yew, ran the island on a tight rein, imposing the death sentence on all caught trafficking in drugs and denying entrance to Singapore to young men arriving at the airport whose hair was deemed too long. This draconian rule did not please everyone, but we soldiers with a professional veneration of good order and discipline envied the Singaporeans for the authoritarian leadership under which they manifestly flourished; a leadership lacking in our own countries. They had much to be proud of. The modern buildings crammed into the confined area of dry land, and those planned for areas yet to be claimed from the sea, merged well with the majestic hotels, churches and business houses erected during the 140 years of British colonial rule. Trade and industry was prospering, for Singapore with its fine harbour and airport is ideally situated at the confluence of the Indian and Pacific Oceans. But it is above all the quality of her people which has enabled this small island to set standards which the world admires (and which her commercial competitors fear). The potential for commercial dominance, for military power and for global influence of the Chinese race is formidable to judge by the achievements of the Chinese in Singapore. Two questions that arise are: – when will the people of China, whose population is the biggest in the world, be released from the straitjacket of Communist ideology to reap likewise the benefits of a free economy? And what will be the consequences for the world of that release? When we regretfully left that remarkable island we could discern on its horizon only two possible clouds. Firstly, with the rising standard and cost of living could the island's labour force remain a low-wage one and thereby a most profitable factor in terms of international competitiveness? Secondly, might hostility on the part of Indonesia, that huge and unstable nation lying so close beyond the narrow Malacca Straits, endanger the orderly development of Singapore and her mercantile prosperity? We set off for Djakarta eager to learn about that land of fifteen thousand islands (only eleven thousand had in 1973 been named) and over one hundred million inhabitants. Of all the nations that live in South-East Asia Indonesia is the giant.

During our tour of South-East Asia I cannot recall any of our hosts mentioning the Japanese occupation of their countries during the Second World War; an occupation which, though initially welcomed as a by-product of the humiliating defeat of the white colonial powers, became increasingly oppressive as the war went on. Nevertheless the officials who briefed us did not conceal their unease at the prospect of Japanese economic supremacy evolving into political domination of the region. They did not believe that United States' influence over the Japanese would for long restrict the latter's military capability to the existing small Self-Defence Force. The distaste of the American public for the war in Vietnam, unconcealed by 1973, would, it was assumed, lead to an eventual US withdrawal from Asian affairs just as isolationism had detached America from Europe after the First World War.

The Indonesians made it quite plain to us that they viewed Dutch colonial rule over their former empire in the East Indies as oppressive and cruel, and they were eloquent on the subject of the heroic War of Liberation which they had fought and won in 1945 against the returning Dutch Forces and against the British. Although I knew that we had sent a number of units to keep order in the wake of the Japanese surrender, I had not known that they had been involved in heavy prolonged fighting as the Indonesians were claiming. But I suppose that if a country has no martyrs to extol, its liberation would be spelt with a very small 'l'. I suppose too that Indonesian pride had been dented by the humbling experiences that Soekarno's confrontation policy had inflicted on his Armed Forces. But Indonesian dislike of those bygone European intrusions was small beer compared with the hatred and fear they expressed towards the Indonesian Communist Party. That organisation had attempted to seize power in a coup a few years previously and in the attempt had committed some vile acts. (We were taken to see a place where a number of leading civilian and military personalities, opponents of the Communists, had been butchered and their bodies thrown down a well.) The coup was crushed and in the sequel Communists, many of them ethnic Chinese, were hunted down and slaughtered in great numbers.

The Indonesian people whom we observed in 1973 appeared docile and rather lazy. Indeed in a climate and soil where a bean planted, it is said, on Monday has by Friday grown into a mature tree, there is less incentive to labour than in temperate zones and the major challenge facing the government in Djakarta is that of energizing a large and rapidly expanding population spread over three quarters of a million square miles of territory astride the Equator. But, perhaps unduly influenced by the bloody events of the earlier decade, I have never lost the conviction that to have to face a hostile Indonesian mob must be a most frightening ordeal.

The richness of the land and the innate intelligence of the people ensure for the Indonesian nation not only an increasingly comfortable standard of living but also growing influence and importance in the region. The Australians had already recognised this trend, and their increasing reference to 'the Near North' denotes above all Indonesia. The manner in which that nation develops and the smoothness with which economic prosperity is attained will depend on the quality of its leadership. This, to an extent we had not seen elsewhere, was military. Generals were numerous, powerful and had wide responsibilities beyond their narrow professional duties. That seemed to ensure social stability and discipline but would inhibit rapid development, foreign investment and economic freedom. Or so we judged.

It was a curious thing that during our many days in this influential, dynamic, populous region of the Asian continent nothing had been said by our hosts or our informants to indicate a high regard for India. After all, India was the first nation to win independence, her population is second in size only to that of China, she is a democracy and in the East-West confrontation claimed to be non-aligned; and her people include some of the cleverest and most skilled in the fields of human activity. Did her association with the USSR condemn her to a second-rate significance? Perhaps the massive burden of her poor and largely illiterate population was presumed to absorb all her energies? Certainly she was not regarded as a fruitful source of financial investment. India's continuing tensions with Pakistan undoubtedly alienated the Muslim countries, and despite her recent military success in Bangladesh, the memory of India's humiliation in 1962 on the Tibetan border had dented her prestige. Delhi's significance in the post-independence era did not, some lamented, match her status in the years of the Raj: China ruled by the Communist Mao Tse-Tung was now the Asian country in the international limelight.

In September we were taken to northern Assam. I was especially interested to see something of the terrain to which units of the Indian Army had been rashly committed at short notice with orders to evict the larger Chinese force which had crossed the Thagla Ridge, the Indo-Tibetan frontier (the McMahon Line) in 1962.

The problems confronting the Indian units were daunting: the great distances between Headquarters and the forward units[2], non-existent road and rail communications in the North-East Frontier Area (NEFA) forward of Tezpur; shortage of equipment, radios, ammunition and winter clothing; the difficulty of operating at altitudes of around 16,000 feet without prior acclimatisation; scarcity in that precipitous terrain on the Indian side of the frontier of dropping zones for parachute resupply. But the fundamental weaknesses under which the Army was obliged to fight were essentially political. The professionalism of the Army and the status of the senior Officer had for many years been deliberately eroded, and few Generals had had the courage to try to halt the decay. Neither the Prime Minister, Jawaharlal Nehru, nor the Defence Minister, Krishna Menon, would accept that a threat to the NEFA by Chinese forces was credible, and in consequence no contingency plans had been drawn up; and both Menon and the professional head of the Army, General Kaul, when the crisis arose on the Border, handled their subordinates arrogantly and the situation disastrously. The upshot of this 'Himalayan Blunder', as the episode is termed by Brigadier Jack Dalvi[3], was that the battalions in Dalvi's 7th Brigade[4] were attacked on 20 October 1962 along a twelve-mile front by two divisions of Chinese infantry backed with artillery. Within a few hours almost all the Officers and men of 7th Brigade were dead, wounded or prisoners. The Chinese force pushed south unopposed and reached the bank of the great Brahmaputra River on 20 November. There they halted for one night before marching back over the mountains to Tibet. They had made their point[5] to a chastened India and to an incredulous world. The same month they returned the captives to India, and to emphasise their professional excellence, handed back all the weapons taken on the battlefield; every one accounted for, cleaned and listed by serial number. The latter gesture had impressed my NDC colleagues mightily; they were still talking about it eleven years later.

This very black month in the annals of the proud Indian Army had some constructive results. Nehru and his government reversed the policy of non-alignment and appealed to the West for diplomatic and material help; Nehru died the following year, broken-hearted it was said. The neglect of the Armed Forces was reversed and pride restored, and many of the factors which had so handicapped the soldiers in 1962 were put right. These we were able to see on our 1973 visit. The road communications from the Plain up via Bomdilla into the mountains at the Sela Pass had been transformed by the construction of a military dual-carriage highway. This was a fine feat of engineering and had cost many lives. Along the highway staging posts had been set up, permanent camps such as 'Shangri-La', in which troops entering the

NEFA could get acclimatised to the altitude and thinner air, and money had been spent to equip the units at least adequately for operations in that great tree-covered expanse of hills and mountains. It was impressive and heartening. Northern Assam though was very sparsely populated; the few people we saw were mongoloid with round faces, pink cheeks and slit eyes. In NEFA the Indian soldier looks as foreign to these hillmen as he does in Muslim Kashmir. It is questionable how deep is the loyalty and devotion to India of the inhabitants; police and military protection can only be sparse and thus there is almost unlimited scope for hostile infiltration. The principal lessons we learnt during our visit to the NEFA are these. The Chinese in Tibet enjoy substantial strategic advantages: airfields and roadheads near the Border, a plateau over which to approach the Border and ground which falls steeply away once the Border is crossed. Geography is not on the side of the Indian defenders. The improved Indian defences and the heightened political resolve behind them may deter future Border infringements and minor skirmishes, but if the Chinese decide to repeat the operation of 1962 the outcome on the ground will probably be little different. The defence of the NEFA cannot be assured by military means; only by diplomatic and political measures.

Rosemary had brought Pinky and Christopher out at the beginning of the Easter holidays and she stayed with me until the beginning of the school autumn term. She made many friends and, as usual, allowed little grass to grow under her feet, taking every opportunity to explore her new surroundings and to add to the family's store of experiences and possessions. She spent much time in the dark back streets of Old Delhi, and got to know the shops and booths where real treasures could be picked up for the proverbial song. Several of the Indian Officers' wives marvelled at her nerve; they would not set foot in that part of the city for fear of being mugged or killed. Rosemary's greatest coup was tracking down Mr Barmi. This elderly Indian ran a carpentry and joinery business, and at my wife's direction produced pieces of hand-made furniture of excellent quality, including an oval dining table to seat twelve persons and a dozen matching chairs, copied from a Chippendale catalogue, with seats exquisitely embroidered by the women of a nearby village. These and the other pieces he made for her cost £400 only (in 1973 £1 sterling bought Rupees 18), a Chinese firm produced a sturdy lead-lined container and carefully packed our possessions into it. The filled container left Delhi by train at the end of August and was shipped from Bombay arriving at the English port of Tilbury in October. To our consternation British Rail then lost all track of it for two months, and thanks entirely to one compassionate female clerk in that organisation who pledged herself to find it, our container was eventually delivered to us in Camberley in the middle of a still, bright, frosty January afternoon. Everything inside was in perfect order. I could not have had a more welcome birthday present.

Our closest friends at the NDC were the two Australians, John and Helen McDonagh and a charming Sikh family, Brigadier Narindar Singh, his wife, Indu, son 'TV' and daughter, Shabnam ('Dewdrop'). We enjoyed their company, wrote frequently to each other after the NDC course dispersed and when Narindar, by now a Major-General and Head of India's Sports Council, came to England we looked him up again. But Indian security fears intervened; Narindar asked me to write to him no more; his mail was censored and intimacy with non-Indians was for chaps like him *verboten*.

My year at the NDC was interesting, informative and valuable; also pretty carefree as we foreigners were well looked after by the College and in my case by the British High Commission too. I kept fit by playing tennis with the McDonaghs, though Rosemary had some dreadful bouts of squitters (she claims that her innards have never recovered from her six months in India), and I had some tiresome correspondence with the UK Inland Revenue people over a trifling sum which Rosemary in England had deposited in a bank and which I in India had not known of and therefore not declared. After that episode I looked more kindly on the maligned local bureaucrats.

I had to make several visits to a dentist and a Dr Sahni was recommended to me. I mention him because in the years that followed every dentist I have been to has remarked on the excellence of Sahni's work. The most tiresome aspect of life in India, I concluded, are those infernal holy cows which roam at will, disrupt the traffic on the roads and defecate where they please. Standing at the entrance to our hotel in some town we were visiting, I was vexed to feel my best uniform trousers being soiled by a cow which had wandered behind me.

In my experience, the visitor from the developed, industrialised world leaves India shocked by the universal dirt, the seething crowds, by the armies of beggars, the obstructive meanderings of unbridled holy cows, the pedantry of Indian officialdom and by the gross disparities of wealth and education. Such a kaleidoscope of jaundiced impressions eclipses any recollections of the grandeur of the scenery, of the ancient buildings and of acts of kindness received from individual citizens. And these negative impressions are carried away and narrated to listeners in their own societies, often with awe but seldom with compassion. How can it be otherwise for a man or woman from Europe or the New World? Their acquaintance with the sub-continent is limited to days in an hotel in a city or tourist resort which they seldom leave save to journey out into the countryside by coach or taxi expressly to be shown those temples and palaces considered to be of special interest to foreigners. The real India they never see.

The real India is rural; the soul of India lies in the hearts and minds of her millions of peasant-farmers and villagers. They constitute a segment of humanity rarely glimpsed by outsiders but to which we of the National Defence College were introduced deliberately. A peasant's life is one of incessant labour; for the men, their womenfolk and their offspring, and for the beasts on whom they depend above all for motive-power at the well or before the plough. Accident, disease or the death of an animal or male member brings to a family calamity and distress, as do abnormal floods and prolonged drought. But Nature is not alone in oppressing the villager. Taxed by government, neglected by indolent or corrupt local administration and cheated by merchants, the lot of the Indian peasant is perhaps little different to that of the small farmer in other parts of the Third World. The Indian, however, is additionally afflicted by the caste system which cramps his ambition and the Hindu religion which extols submissiveness during this transitory life on earth; and by the money-lender. Few escape having to deal with the village usurer to see them through lean years. Weddings too are a natural part of life and even in the poorest families it is a matter of pride that the ceremony is accompanied by expenditures which can saddle the family for many years with heavy debts. The Central government was seeking to curb this ruinous tradition just as it was striving to reduce the nation's birth rate. The latter was essential, for the benefits of higher productivity in field and factory and the rising revenue into the national exchequer were being vitiated by the unchecked fertility of Indian couplings. The government of Mrs Gandhi had already launched a nation-wide campaign to encourage birth control when I arrived in early 1973, and walls, TV screens and newspapers were displaying large images of a happy family; the smiling faces of Dad, Mum and two kids with the message 'Four is good, more is bad'. This propaganda was backed up by groups of men and women equipped with a variety of contraceptive devices despatched into the villages to instruct the people, for the most part illiterates, on the merits and methods of family planning. In the towns special clinics were being set up, often in the railway stations, where teams of surgeons performed a swift vasectomy on any man patriotic enough to make this sacrifice while waiting for his train. In return the patient was presented with a transistor radio as a mark of his country's appreciation. During our first term at the NDC we were invited to devote much time and thought to the subject of population control, and as the weeks passed we came to realise that despite occasional short-term successes, family planning by coercion or exhortation alone achieves little. Indeed the pressures on men to submit to vasectomy were a significant cause of the unpopularity which was to undo Mrs Gandhi and her political son, Sanjay. The common-sense reasoning of the peasant-farmer explained why. 'When we are old,' the villagers told us, 'my wife and I will need two sons to look after us, our land and our animals. That means that we shall have to beget four sons; four because one will die and one will go away to live in a town. Furthermore, one or more of our offspring will alas be girls. So you see, to guarantee a modicum of security in our old age I must father many children. What nonsense the government talks with its slogan "Four is good".'

After seeing more of India and visiting some of the other developing countries in Asia we, all of us I think, had come to the conclusion that population control can effectively be brought about in a free democratic society only by raising the standard of the peoples' living. Material benefits once acquired are cherished by their possessors, and the down-to-earth peasant will understand the folly of jeopardising his improving lot by careless breeding. Education, especially of the women, is indispensable to sustain that attitude and bring it to general fulfilment. All this, we reckoned, would take many years. 'In the meantime,' we muttered to each other, 'an effective way to control the birth rate might be to bring electricity into every village and a television set into every sleeping place, thereby banishing those long hours of darkness fitted only for copulation and sleep.' (As I write this in 1998 I am told that the Green Revolution and other advances have significantly improved the conditions of life in rural India.)

In the final weeks of our course we were entertained by the President of the Republic, Shri Giri, in the cavernous former Viceregal House, by the members of the Lower House of Parliament, the Lok Sabha, and by the Prime Minister. The MPs seemed to be an unruly lot judging by their behaviour on the day we attended their proceedings. Corpulent and loud-mouthed, many gave the Speaker a hard time, and little worthwhile debate was possible as individuals slanged each other across the floor or lounged asleep in their pews.

Mrs Gandhi, our hostess at a garden party, was physically much smaller than I had expected; so small that when I stepped backwards after chatting with a group of friends I almost trod on her foot. She had approached us alone and unseen. But her smile was enchanting. Born in 1917 the daughter of the great Jawaharlal Nehru, she had been imprisoned by the British during the struggle for independence. Indira Gandhi was not related to the Mahatma but had taken her name from her husband Feroz Gandhi who had died in 1964. In 1966 she was elected Prime Minister and Leader of the Congress Party and in 1973 was at the zenith of her powers and fame, glowing like her compatriots in the aftermath of the defeat of Pakistan and the creation of Bangladesh. But the complexities of governing almost seven hundred million people inhabiting over a million square miles through Party colleagues who were in many cases corrupt and entirely self-seeking had become almost overwhelming. By 1975 she was being accused of electoral malpractices and intolerance, and she countered the rising opposition to her rule by declaring a State of Emergency and giving her government a distinctly authoritarian character. This may have been what the Indian nation needed; it was not, however, what the Indian electorate wanted, and in 1977 she was turned out of office until becoming Prime Minister again in 1980. The final years of her life cannot have been smooth or happy. The political turmoil in India was exacerbated for her by the conduct of her favourite son, Sanjay, who made himself unpopular, widely feared and accused of corruption, a reputation which continued to harm his Mother even after his death in an aeroplane accident in 1980. Four years later Indira Gandhi herself met her death, murdered by her Sikh personal bodyguard. Her mantle fell on her second son, Rajiv, a gentle, unassuming businessman who had, it was said, no desire to enter the political fray but who as a matter of patriotic duty assumed the leadership of the Party and of the nation, and who in a short time won the respect of many people in India and beyond her shores. I met Rajiv Gandhi briefly in Muscat in 1990 in a great gathering of rulers and friends of Oman celebrating the 20th anniversary of the Accession of Sultan Qaboos. From his bearing, his manner of speaking and from what others were saying and writing about him, I formed the impression that India was in the hands of an uncommonly good man. But some evil men and women saw Rajiv Gandhi in a different light, and he too was assassinated while at an election rally near Madras in 1991. The garland of welcome which they had placed around his neck concealed a bomb. This wicked deed distressed me a lot. Although I had been only a very distant admirer of him, I addressed a brief letter of condolence to the Commandant of the National Defence College with the request that he pass my letter on as he might consider appropriate. I was touched to receive some weeks later in Barbados an acknowledgement signed by Rajiv's Italian-born widow, Sonia.

After the end-of-course parties and speeches I stayed on for a week or so, having an agreeable stay in Agra with the Brigadier commanding the 50th Parachute Brigade and his English wife, and a trip to Jaipur with John and Helen McDonagh. The Jaipur City Palace, built in glowing pink stone by Raja Jai Singh in the 1730s, became the richest and most magnificent of the many palaces of the Rajputs, and the ruling house of Jaipur was reputed to have the second finest collection of precious jewels; surpassed only by that of the Nizam of Hyderabad. The Jaipur treasures were said to be hidden under a fort perched high above the family's ancestral home of Amber, clinging to the side of a mountain on the edge of the Jaipur plain, and approachable only by a long, very steep path up which the McDonaghs and I were carried by an elephant. The prosperity and influence of the Hindu Maharajas of Jaipur had been assured when in 1556 the Mughal Emperor Akbar wed the daughter of that family. John, Helen and I were ushered into the Palace on the occasion of the annual blessing by the Ruler of the horses, oxen and elephants of the Household

Transport Department. The Maharaja sat in the midst of his court officials and armed retainers quietly greeting each animal as it was led up to him. Dressed in traditional robes and ornate headdress, His Highness and his Court gave us a glimpse of the colour, dignity, pride and pomp of the princely rule which the British had in 1858 undertaken to respect and which ended only when the Congress Party finally abolished the Princely Order, their privileges and privy purses.

I am exceedingly glad that I lived in New Delhi for a year where I got to know many Indians, to admire the many achievements of the Independent Republic, and of individual citizens of that country. (It is said, probably rightly, that in every field of human expertise one will find an Indian in the top twenty.) The year had given me too a much better understanding of the manifold problems facing that nation and sympathy for those who are elected to lead and govern her.

Concurrently I had come to revere the legacy bequeathed to the sub-continent by those Administrators and Soldiers from my own country who had served what is now India, Pakistan and Bangladesh as the Founders and Guardians of the Raj.

The prospect of being back home with my family in Camberley, of Christmas and of the challenge and interest of a fresh posting stifled any regrets I may have had on leaving India in December 1973. But the longer I am away from India, the more I find myself thinking about episodes in her history and in my own months there, and yearning to go back: but on a longer visit so as to see more of that huge, gifted, resilient, extraordinary, disparate and ancient segment of the human race.

What I have set out above are my personal reflections from 1973. After a mere twelve months in that continent of fabulous contrasts, I felt able to write sensitively but not shrewdly. Moreover it is indisputable that since then the Republic of India has made remarkable advances. The Green and Technological Revolutions are transforming her economy, her self-esteem and her status on the world stage. India progresses, a juggernaut of contradictory realities or, as Professor John Kenneth Galbraith has written, a Functioning Anarchy. Nevertheless, when Silicon Valley in California sleeps, Indian scientists wake up in the Silicon Valley of Asia, the Indian city of Bangalore, to address the same problems that their sleeping American colleagues tried to solve the previous day.[6] And those scientists have made India a nuclear power; and India is one sixth of the human race.

Notes

1. His daughter was raped in London and his wife committed suicide.
2. Thagla Ridge (FDL) to Towang (HQ 7 Brigade) five days' march,

Towang to Tezpur (Divisional HQ) 200 miles,
Tezpur to Shillong (Corps HQ) 200 miles,
Shillong to Lucknow (Command HQ) 600 miles,
Lucknow to Delhi 250 miles.
3. *Himalayan Blunder* by Brigadier JP Dalvi, published by Hind Pocket Books in Delhi.
4. 2nd Rajputs, 9th Punjabis, 1st/9th Gorkhas, 4th Grenadiers.
5. 'India, do not provoke China again on the Border; learn from this lesson.'
6. An observation of Gita Mehta in her book *Snakes and Ladders, a View of Modern India*, published in Great Britain in 1997 by Martin Secker & Warburg Ltd.

CHAPTER XV
1974–1978

Back to HQ AFCENT, Wales as GOC, and Retirement

After my return from India I remained on leave awaiting my next posting. I spent the time rewardingly; gardening, having an extension built onto our Camberley home and visiting family and friends. Rosemary's Mother came over from Guyana and we all spent Easter with Dick and Jill Scott in the New Forest where Christopher and I hired horses and rode over miles of heathland and woods. At the end of one long day in the saddle he found that his wallet had at some point fallen out of his pocket. Moreover it contained eight pounds – a large sum for a boy of fifteen to possess. Vexed, we gave it up for lost. A week later the postman delivered to Christopher a packet; in it was the wallet intact with the eight pounds and a letter from a young woman describing how she had chanced upon the wallet lying in the undergrowth and from it she had discovered his address. Just like that honest German labourer who had retrieved from the waters of a Schleswig lake my expensive uniform and items stolen from me in 1948, this English girl's kindness reminded me of Mankind's prevailing but underrated goodness.

Of the senior members of the Parachute Regiment one whom I knew only slightly was Pat O'Kane. He was coming to the end of his tour in command of Britain's Reserve Army airborne formation, the 44th Parachute Brigade (TA), was due to take up a NATO appointment but was fatally injured on a parachute exercise. I was sent to NATO in his place.

I had served in the same Headquarters twelve years earlier. In those days HQ Allied Forces Central Europe was located in Fontainebleau and I had greatly enjoyed the experience. But when President Charles de Gaulle expelled NATO establishments from French soil, HQ AFCENT moved to the Netherlands and occupied a disused coalmine in Brunssum, a small town on the bit of Dutch territory lying between Belgium and Germany, the so-called Maastricht Appendix. Apart from the exchange of the attractive forests and rivers of Seine-et-Marne for the less elegant architecture and sandy heaths of Limburg, I found that much had changed in the working atmosphere in that large international Headquarters. The appointment I had been sent to fill in Pat's place was that of Assistant Chief of Staff (Exercises). In this capacity I headed a multinational team of Officers each of whom was responsible for composing AFCENT's input into one of the many exercises and competitions designed to practise NATO forces in wartime procedures. My team included some bright young colonels; one of them, Jörg Schönbohm, rose to the top of the Bundeswehr and later of Germany's Defence Ministry. I therefore had little to do apart from shielding them from the irritating interjections of our immediate superior, an excitable American two-star air force General of Italianate parentage. The United States filled many of the principal operational posts and they worked, it seemed to us from other nations, rather unjoyously. But we had not endured the trauma of Vietnam and our personal and professional sympathies reached out to our American colleagues, so many of whom were sterling characters and dedicated champions of the North Atlantic Alliance.[1]

The Red Threat continued to constitute the background for our planning and exercises, and developments within the Group of Soviet Forces in East Germany (GSFG) and in the Warsaw Pact nations were continously analysed, our assessments formulated and AFCENT's proposed countermeasures submitted to the Supreme Allied Commander, General Alexander Haig. Compared with those anxious years when I had in the sixties served in BAOR and AFCENT, the self-confidence of NATO's forces in their ability to hold and defeat an assault on Central Europe was now markedly greater; and for sound reasons. In 1974 the danger of war, we judged, lay in an attack launched by an infirm, ageing Kremlin leadership, dismayed by the technological advances being made in the West, by the faltering Soviet economy and by the dissatisfaction of their East European satellite states. There was a danger, we believed, that that leadership would see in the military might of the USSR the sole means of reversing the accelerating decline of their country and of the Communist creed.

The senior British Officer in the Headquarters was the Commander of the AFCENT air forces, Air Chief Marshal Sir Lewis Hodges, a distinguished airman whose experience and personality did much to keep our thinking and plans in touch with the realities of modern warfare, and British prestige upheld. Our Commander-in-Chief, CINCENT for short, was a German whom we all admired. General Ernst Ferber was a fine man whose military life had begun in the 19th Infantry Regiment (Bavaria's oldest) and he was an admirable leader of our international team. His personality also succeeded in dispelling the hostility which the Dutch population still felt towards Germans, the hated 'Moffe' who had invaded and occupied their country during the Second World War. Rosemary and I enjoyed a warm relationship with him and with his wife, Mette, long crippled in a motor-car accident; and by an extraordinary coincidence we found that his birthday was the same as my wife's, and Frau Ferber's the same as that of Rosemary's Brother, Mark. One of the occasions in their time in Brunssum which many were to remember with especial pleasure was the banquet which we British Army Officers gave in the Ferbers' honour; and I myself was delighted to be asked to organise the ceremonial parades, in which all our nations participated, to mark General Ferber's retirement and the arrival of his successor, General Dr Karl Schnell.

The local Dutch, whose fluency in English is remarkable, were particularly kind to us British. The sincerity of their gratitude for the liberation of their province by British units, and their respect for the memory of our Servicemen fallen in those operations, was movingly demonstrated annually on Remembrance Sunday.

To be with soldiers is truly the best part of soldiering. Thus the most congenial aspect of my work in Brunssum was managing the men of the British Element. These were in the main members of the Royal Signals squadrons responsible for the complex AFCENT communications networks. Aided by an outstandingly competent RAOC major, Ray Holland, I much enjoyed my days with those skilled operators and technicians, easing some of the problems of their families and organising some realistic combat training for them and their Bundeswehr colleagues down in the Allgäu area of south Germany.

This Brunssum period, though unstimulating for me personally after the excitements and dramas of Oman and the interests of India, had its compensations for Rosemary and the kids. We were able to escape from our little concrete hiring in Schaesberg and visited Venice, Amsterdam and other cities, Kirchberg as often as possible, and the colourful Dutch bulb-fields at Keukenhof. Christopher, now sixteen, made the most of his holidays from Wellington in the company of boys of his own age at AFCENT. Pinky had left Elmhurst, and to perfect her French we got her into a lycée in Liège as a weekly boarder. She chose rather to idle her time away with an English girl-student but nevertheless did achieve some fame – and kudos for the British – when she was elected the AFCENT photographic model of the year.

Rosemary and I made many new friends and were able to develop a friendship with a family we had first met in Aldershot in our 16 Parachute Brigade days. David Budd, a Horse Gunner who had commanded Bull's Troop (I Battery) in 7 RHA and the Royal Artillery Boys' Regiment, had come to AFCENT as head of the Special Projects Division. He, his beautiful and talented wife, Janet, and their offspring, Sarah and Jonathan, enlivened the months in Limburg of many of our compatriots and they were to play a lasting part in our own lives. Thus it was especially grievous for us Grahams when young Jonathan fell ill with Hodgkin's disease and, despite a long and exacting course of treatment, died in October 1978 in his third year at Winchester College.

My own tour of duty at AFCENT was cut short – like my first one in Fontainebleau. Out of the blue I was selected for promotion to Major-General. I like to believe that kind colleagues in the MoD had sympathised with my disenchantment with the Brunssum job and had decided to rescue me from that dreariness. Appointed to be the General Officer Commanding Wales I soon found myself in Brecon. It was to be a congenial place in which to end my career on the Active List, and I was not surprised to learn that soon after my departure the job of ACOS Exercises at HQ AFCENT was abolished.

In military circles Wales was regarded as a backwater. The number of Regular Army units stationed there was small, and of the Reserve Army units, most were earmarked for Home Defence rather than for the more prestigious role of reinforcing BAOR. Wales, it seemed to me, felt neglected. She outwardly lacked Scotland's self-esteem and the recognition which that country had won for herself from Westminster and the people of England. Whereas Scotland's senior resident soldier was a three-star General invariably invested with a knighthood, Wales had to make do with a two-star Major-General. But such disparities appeared to stem as much from the reticence with which the people of the Principality treated their history and military virtues as from English disdain. Proposals in Whitehall that Scottish regiments should be amalgamated or axed were regarded as an affront by that nation and evoked loud protests and stubborn campaigns got up by vocal ex-Servicemen, sustained by the Scottish media and by much of the electorate too. Scottish reaction was well illustrated by the almighty fuss preceding the amalgamation of the Royal Scots Fusiliers with the Highland Light Infantry and by the crusade to reprieve from disbandment the Argyll & Sutherland Highlanders.

The campaign to reprieve the Argylls was widespread, popular and clamorous: it was in the end successful. Among a variety of eye-catching propaganda methods used were large coloured posters of the Glengarrie cap with its red and white dicing and the regimental badge prominently displayed over the slogan 'Save the Argylls!'[2] By contrast few Welsh voices were raised in 1969 to save the Welch Regiment, yet Wales's contribution to the greatness of the British Army is striking and dates from 1689 when that fine regiment the 23rd Foot was raised, later to become the Royal Welch Fusiliers; and there can be few in the United

Kingdom who are unaware of the gallantry of the 24th Regiment, the South Wales Borderers, whose epic defence of Rorke's Drift in 1879 is thrillingly portrayed in the film 'Zulu'.[3]

Welsh pride did cause one journalist to challenge my appointment. At my first meeting with the local press he asked in a distinctly disgruntled tone: 'Why is it that London has selected to be the General Officer Commanding in Wales you, born in Kent, schooled in Gloucestershire and raised in the Isle of Wight? Do you think that is right?'. I was able to reply: 'The MoD may appear to you to have made an error in picking me for Brecon, but I can tell you that when they were appointing us recently promoted Generals to jobs – striving to fit round pegs into round holes – they saw that with my Scottish family background, my service with a Highland regiment, in East Europe, Northern India and the Arabian Jebel, coupled with my travels in the Alps and the Himalayas, I have more experience of hill tribes than any of my competitors. Thus they chose me for Wales and mighty happy I am with their choice!'.

Although few units were stationed in Wales the military facilities in that country were important and much used by the British and NATO armies; in particular the extensive Sennybridge Training Area, the anti-aircraft firing area at Manobier, and the tank gunnery ranges on the Castlemartin peninsula. The remoteness of these places and their sparse populations were of great advantage for the exercising of bodies of troops and the firing of live ammunition, but the weather, there always fickle and often exceedingly wet and cold, lessened their popularity somewhat. From March to October annually during the years 1961-1996 Castlemartin was taken over by the Bundeswehr for low-level tank training, and of the 84,000 German soldiers who used the range during those thirty-five years (during which they claim to have fired 270,000 shells) some 150 married local girls.

Headquarters Wales (Pencadlys Cymru) was in Brecon, a small cathedral town in Powys lying at the junction of the Usk and Honddhu rivers. Long before its castle was built in the 10th century the Romans had appreciated the strategic importance of the place and had stationed there a wing (*ala*) of the Second (Augusta) Legion which from AD 75 until the middle of the 3rd century was based at Caerleon (Isca Silurum), near Newport.

The Headquarters occupied the former Depot and home of the South Wales Borderers, the 24th Regiment, for whom twenty-four trees had been planted around the parade ground and whose museum lay alongside our complex. We were thirty-five Officers in all. Nine were 'retreads' – retired chaps re-employed, eight were civilians headed by the District Secretary who was our Financial Director, and three were women. My staff team was headed by a Grade One Staff Officer of Lieutenant-Colonel's rank, initially Charles Taylor, a cavalry veteran of the Korean War, and latterly Tony Laurie-Chiswell whose brother Peter, like me a member of the

Parachute Regiment, was to be GOC Wales a few years after my own retirement from that post.

When I took over in January 1976 there was a Deputy Commander. Brigadier Gordon McDonald was a robust Gunner who knew the country and the Territorial Army far better than I did, and I found his advice as valuable as his company was fun. After we had been working together for about six months he came to me with a request. He said: 'As you know, I was at one time our Defence Attaché in Pakistan and while there worked closely with chaps in the Foreign and Commonwealth Office. We got on well together and they seem to have liked what I did out there'. He went on: 'I have just been approached by the MoD on behalf of the FCO who are offering me the job of Governor of Ascension Island, an FCO appointment commonly filled by someone recently retired from the Armed Forces. I am very keen to take up the offer for I have been told by the Military Secretary that I shall not be promoted further in the Army, whereas if I took the job I should be employed for five years longer, I would get an additional pension and of course the prospect of living on that island with a Governor's perks very much appeals to my wife, Barbara, and me. As I've just mentioned, the Foreign Office are keen for me to take the job and the MoD have no objection. But, 'Gordon continued,' MS have told me to warn you that if you agree to let me go, they will not be able to replace me for at least a year. Barbara and I do want very much to take the FCO job but will quite understand if you are not prepared to do without a Deputy Commander for such a long period'. The inability of the Service to produce another Brigadier for Wales in less than twelve months surprised me, but I had resolved that Gordon must take the job. I had no wish to deny him and Barbara such a fine opportunity for extended service, extra financial reward and the benefices of governorship, and I was confident that with the help of my staff I would manage OK with no Brigadier at my side.

Not long afterwards Gordon left Brecon, retired from the Army, was transferred onto the FCO books and in late 1976 took up his appointment. Alas he did not enjoy it for long. By the April of the following year he was back in England, in the Aldershot Military Hospital; and two months later we buried him in his home village near Devizes. A large florid man and a heavy smoker, cigarettes had killed him. In 1977 the perils of smoking and the links between cigarettes and lung cancer were not so convincingly publicised as they are today.

Nevertheless we were shocked that his fatal illness had developed so rapidly and so soon after he had been passed fit by the medical boards which examined him on leaving the Army and on joining the Foreign Office.

The house we had taken over from Peter and Jill Leuchars stood on a hill just to the north of Brecon, in grounds of about an acre flanked by the extensive sports field of a comprehensive school and with superb views to the south over the Brecon Beacons and their most prominent feature, the almost 3,000-foot-high Pen-y-Fan. Penbryn had not long been the official residence of the GOC. Most of my predecessors had been quartered in a house on the Builth Wells road rented from a senior British diplomat who for most of the time was working overseas. But when he retired he wanted his house back, so the MoD had to do a hasty search for another residence. The sum allotted for the purpose fell short of the prices for which properties in the area were then being sold, but it was sufficient for the Ministry to purchase Penbryn, for that house was in a sad state. We were told the story soon after arriving in Brecon. The previous owner had been an elderly spinster whose two Brothers were killed in the First World War, and ever since their deaths she had kept their rooms cleaned but otherwise untouched. With the passage of time she became increasingly eccentric to the extent that she ended her life sharing the house with a horse. The horse lies buried in the garden, she in the local cemetery. After her death Penbryn remained neglected, occupied periodically only by ruinous squatters, and in that state it was acquired by the MoD who by the time we moved in had spent a very large sum of public money replacing the roof and putting right other major structural faults. 'If only,' the citizens of Brecon lamented to us, 'the Ministry had spent just a bit more money when first buying a house for the General, so much more would have been saved in the long run.' Although our son, Christopher, had proof that the house was haunted, Rosemary and I were happy in Penbryn and we like to think that our tenure there brought pleasure to others. Apart from family members and personal friends we had a great number of officials from Whitehall and the other Commands to put up, and civilian and Service colleagues from within the Principality also. Having them under our roof was an obligatory part of command, and to help Rosemary and me to do it properly we were given a house-staff; all on the Army's payroll. The House Manager was Corporal Lewis from my own regiment, the cook was a chef from the Army Catering Corps and there were two daily cleaning women and a gardener; all locals. The size of the house and our hospitality commitment necessitated a staff of this size. In addition of course I had a driver from the Royal Corps of Transport and an ADC, for the first year Hamish Fletcher from The Parachute Regiment and for the second Ian Tritton from the Royal Welch Fusiliers.

In 1976 the Labour government became anxious about the public image of the Armed Forces and sensitive to imputations that the standard of living of Servicemen, above all of senior Officers, was unacceptably lavish and above the level which most of the civilian population was having to put up with in a Britain in severe economic straits. In consequence the MoD issued an order to the effect that the frequency and standard of hospitality given in Service residencies and messes were to be significantly reduced. It struck me that this edict was based on a false premise.

I pointed out that far from the Services entertaining more lavishly than our civilian counterparts, our experience in Wales was that we and our wives were being entertained by corporations, industrial enterprises and even private houses more extravagantly than any Service establishment could match; moreover this hospitality had to be reciprocated. But to do this was becoming difficult, for the burden of reciprocation was falling on an ever smaller number of us. This state of affairs had arisen because MoD policy was to allow married Officers to leave their wives and children living in their own homes and themselves to live Monday to Friday at their place of duty unaccompanied. There were financial benefits in doing this and a growing number of Officers were taking advantage of this novel concession. But the natural consequence was that the duty of keeping the Service's hospitality flag flying was being carried out by the diminishing group of chaps whose wives were living with them. Only the most senior Officers received an allowance towards the cost of official entertainment and that money nowhere near met the costs incurred. The expense of duty entertaining was a constant worry to those who had no private means, and as I also wrote in my response to the MoD: 'We (senior Officers), as a duty to the Service and as is expected of us by our subordinates, shall have to bear personally this continuing financial burden, and in so doing hope that our individual Bank Managers will view with understanding and sympathy our private bank overdrafts'.

The expenses thus incurred were a principal reason why when I retired from the Active List two years later, my overdraft with the National Westminster Bank was over £12,000. Paying off this debt was to absorb much of my Retirement Terminal Grant; furthermore this indebtedness, incurred *pro bono publico*, made it impossible, Rosemary and I concluded, to avail ourselves of the scheme by which I could have purchased the upgrading of her widow's pension from one third to one half of mine. The generation of British Servicemen to which I belong has been deplorably penalised by government, and by none more than the Labour government of James Callaghan whose treatment of Armed Forces pensioners was immoral and the consequences, perhaps at the time not fully foreseen, are unlikely ever to be put right. Those who are the most penalised are the chaps who left the Services in 1976, 1977 and 1978 – in the so-called 'trough years' – the very chaps whose careers started during the Second World War.

Just as central and south Wales differ in scenery, resources and culture from the more mountainous and Welsh-speaking north, so the differences reflected in the two Welsh Infantry regiments were displayed for me in the Ceremony of Eating the Leek. When I was initiated into the Wrexham Mess of the Royal Welch Fusiliers their leek was presented to me on a silver salver, clean and delicately sliced. The one I was obliged to eat at

Llanelli when dining with Royal Regiment of Wales looked as if it had come straight out of the ground, albeit washed. Both vegetables however turned out to be quite palatable; I'd go through the ceremony again without demur. The ceremony which really dished me – and doubtless others who fell into the hands of the RRW – was the drinking of the Regimental Cocktail. This concoction was served up in a glass filled, so as to depict the regiment's colours, with three layers of liqueurs: red cherry brandy, white cointreau and green crème de menthe. One such initiation in a lifetime is enough! I owe much to the makers of Alka-Seltzer.

My introductions to the civic authorities in the Principality were thoroughly enjoyable. The buildings in the centre of Cardiff and the City Hall are exceptionally fine, and Rosemary and I were to have a happy relationship with the two Lord Mayors, Councillors Iowerth Jones and John Purnell, and our two years at Brecon were brightened by the encouragement and hospitality of the Lords Lieutenant and other dignitaries among whom were Sir Cennidd Trehearne, John Corbett-Winder, Mervyn Bourdillon and Alastair Graesser, with lunches at the Cardiff Club and afternoons at the Arms Park, the home of Welsh rugby. And in my dealings with the Territorial Army I was greatly helped by the two TA Colonels, Peter Howells and Philip Morris.

I spent as much time as I could with that section of the Army which has a good influence on the young. The Combined Cadet Force and the Army Cadet Force units, based in the leading schools and in the counties respectively, were in general run by keen and energetic adults, mostly school teachers and retired policemen; and if their affiliated Regular and TA units had been able to support them better, the Cadets would have enjoyed a more varied and inspiring curriculum. The Army Apprentices College at Chepstow I got to know well; one of three well-founded establishments designed to prepare youngsters for long service and rewarding careers in the technical corps: and I often and happily visited the Training Centre of the regiments of the Prince of Wales's Division at Crickhowell, just down the road from my Brecon office.

The Infantry Battle School nearby in Brecon's Dering Lines gave me a special interest as that excellent unit had originally been set up by The Parachute Regiment for the training of our own NCOs, but it had proved to be such an asset that it had been absorbed as a wing of the School of Infantry located at Warminster, and expanded to cater for NCOs from all regiments.

On the Order of Battle of the Reserve Army was a Royal Army Medical Corps unit. 203 (Welsh) General Hospital was a large outfit designed to set up and run in the event of war a static hospital in West Germany. In its ranks were nurses, matrons, surgeons, GPs, dentists and other high-grade members of the medical profession who, after busy days and nights, voluntarily devoted weekly evenings, monthly weekends and a fortnight every summer to preparing 203 for that wartime role. These specialists were supported by a number of essential orderlies, drivers, cooks, stretcher bearers – hewers of wood and drawers of water – many from the ranks of the unemployed, and it was the skills and motivation of these people which initially interested me the most.

I therefore decided to spend some days with 203 while it was at summer camp, and to get a real feel of the unit I inserted myself into the casualty chain on one of their test exercises. The umpires and make-up artists set me up as a stretcher-case, suffering from a fractured thigh, loss of blood and shock. With my right leg in a Thomas splint I joined the ambulance convoy delivering casualties to the Reception Post. The first thing that gave me doubts about them was that the orderlies whose job it was to lift the wounded out of the ambulances did not know how to release the clips by which the stretchers were secured in the vehicle. Eventually someone came and showed them how to do it. After being processed through Reception I was carried into a ward laid out with many beds and with a plasma drip into my arm I enjoyed being horizontal and cared for by engaging young nurses. But my enjoyment was short-lived, for the Exercise Director declared that the hospital had been attacked from the air and set on fire. We patients were thereupon lifted back onto stretchers and carried at great speed to a safer area. As I was being rushed into a new hut the doorhandle, unnoticed by those carrying me, got trapped under the metal ring of the splint, my injured leg got jerked up high over my head, the drip bottle went flying and there was great embarrassment all round. Though unharmed, I concluded that 203's expertise and general fitness for war needed closer scrutiny. Indeed at the end of that particular exercise I remarked that the only part of the hospital that seemed to my layman's eyes to be running smoothly was the mortuary. (But perhaps I was biased for the name of the Corporal in charge was Graham.) For the rest of my time as GOC I took an especial interest in that baffled body of stalwart volunteers, and when I retired I, an Infantryman, was invited to become the Honorary Colonel of that medical unit and in that capacity I enjoyed eight years with them on exercises in the UK, Belgium and Germany and at social events. Command of the unit was soon given to one of Wales's foremost dentists and it thrived under new leadership.

Two traditional events in our annual training calendar were the Welsh Three Thousands and the Cambrian March. The former was a team race along a route linking ten peaks in Snowdonia, all over 3,000 feet high. It was expensive to organise and its value limited to the few sturdy gladiators who took part, and it was soon significantly modified. By contrast the Cambrian March was an excellent competition, varied each year in content and popular with the British and NATO teams being tested.

Like other Headquarters in the United Kingdom we kept our plans for nuclear war updated, attended the first-rate courses run at the Civil Defence College at Easingwold and took part in the exercises organised to test the nation's preparedness to meet the challenge of keeping our forces on the Continent supplied and the population at home warned, and as far as was possible, protected and administered. The survival of the people of the Principality was to be the responsibility of the Commissioner of No 8 Region, a government Minister, exercised from a well-protected bunker and assisted at the different levels of community life by chaps from the Armed Forces, Police and Local government. These plans and exercises were often derided by pessimists whom the contemplation of a nuclear conflict reduced to doomsday hand-wringing and predictions about the extinction of civilised life. They may have been right; but we did not believe so, for in reality those plans and procedures, if activated in time, would have enabled a significant proportion of the population to remain alive in the nuclear strike phase and during the subsequent longer and more insidious period of radio-active fall-out. We who were part of the Civil Defence Organisation had no doubts about the value of our labours.

Rosemary and I were fortunate to be in Wales in 1977, the year of the Queen's Silver Jubilee. Her Majesty was, as elsewhere in the Kingdom, greeted with affection and warmth, and the presence beside her of her husband, Prince Philip, Palace dignitaries and the Sovereign's Escort of the Household Cavalry, rarely seen in Wales, evoked great interest. Even the small group of Welsh nationalists, who from time to time set fire to the holiday homes of English owners, seemed to keep quiet during that period of national rejoicing and unity. We were invited to the major events in that royal week, a reception in the Royal Yacht *Britannia* off the north coast, a Service in Llandaff Cathedral, a banquet in Cardiff and a reception in the Orangerie in Swansea's Margham Park. Despite her long and repetitive programme of walk-abouts, hand-shaking, inspections and small talk with a myriad of her subjects, the Queen appeared to enjoy every public moment of her visit. The Royal Family in 1977 was truly loved and admired; the Queen and her Mother (the Queen Mum) being universally respected for their life-long devotion to the service of the nation; and to the Commonwealth, of which the Queen was, by the choice of its member states, the Head. Only the most cynical observers of that year of Jubilee pageantry could have foreseen the decline in the fortunes and popular esteem of the House of Windsor which was to be such a sad feature of the 1990s. I was not one of those cynics. That year strengthened my admiration for the Monarchy and I truly believed that only extreme foolishness on the part of the electorate could reduce the prestige of that revered institution. That the decline would be caused primarily by the personalities and domestic crises of some members of the Royal House was, in 1977, beyond my comprehension.

The Netherlands and Wales

The Services also made a colourful contribution to that year by producing in the grounds of Cardiff Castle a spectacular Tattoo. We organised it in collaboration with the City Fathers and we were determined that it would provide for the Welsh and their foreign visitors a really memorable event. Having been involved elsewhere in similar events I approached this Cardiff project with some misgivings, believing that no setting could match Edinburgh's castle. I was wrong. Guided by that experienced Producer, Major Aubrey Jackman from Bath, and Derek Taylor the Director of Music, Welsh Guards, we worked up a first-rate and slickly conducted show, and made money for Service charities. It was a fine opportunity for the soldiers, regular and TA, and the musicians in the impressively massed Bands, to show their mettle. Rosemary and I enjoyed the whole period for which we moved from Brecon into a house in Cardiff so as to entertain visitors and friends nightly after each performance, and where we could put up guests from far afield among whom was General Sir Edwin Bramall, the Commander-in-Chief of the UK Land Forces. Five years later he was, as head of the Army, to support Prime Minister Thatcher staunchly during the Falklands crisis and the hazardous campaign which brought renown to her and to all the British Servicemen who took part.

During my two years in Brecon I was able to keep in closer touch with developments in the Persian Gulf and Oman than had been possible in Brunssum. In May 1977 Seyyid Fahar bin Taimur, Sultan Qaboos' uncle and Deputy Prime Minister for Security and Defence, had organised a celebration in honour of Brigadier Colin Maxwell who had completed twenty-five years of devoted service on contract to the Sultanate. The former Commanders of the Sultan's Armed Forces were flown out from England, and in Muscat joined General David O'Morchoe, the current CSAF, in paying homage to our stalwart colleague whose counsel and friendship had been so valuable to us. This was the first time I had been back to Oman since late 1972, and I was astounded by the transformations to the country's infra-structure; the highways, harbours, schools, hospitals and new barracks. Our old HQ in the white fort at Bait al Falaj, the SAF complex and the SOAF airfield in the otherwise deserted Ruwi valley were already being submerged in a thriving commercial estate with shops, banks, hotels and offices, all established in the most modern buildings, some many stories high and designed with excellent taste; for Oman's architects had learned much from the errors made earlier in the cities of the Gulf Emirates. The satisfactory end to the Dhofar Campaign in December 1975 and the spectacular progress made by their country during the first seven years of Sultan Qaboos' rule had made the Omanis proud but without, it seemed, warping their innate charm.

Colin Maxwell I got to know even more intimately after his retirement from SAF. The Sultan gave him a fine house to live in on the shore of a little bay near Muscat and there Colin started to write the long-awaited History of the Sultan's Armed Forces. Alas, his health deteriorated and the final years of his life were spent in London in hospitals or in comfortable hotels, paid for by a generous Sultan. During those pain-filled months I made a point of visiting him or taking him out into the countryside at least once a week, and during those quiet sessions he told me about his birth, early years and career, facts about which he had until then been extraordinarily reticent. Colin died peacefully in the Wellington Hospital in St John's Wood on 17 August 1988 at the age of 73, and was buried in the Military Cemetery in Oman. At the request of his relatives I arranged his Memorial Service held two months later in the Grosvenor Chapel in South Audley Street and gave the Address reproduced as Appendix VII. These things I was very pleased to do for my old and close friend: not only because of our shared adventures during a tricky period in Oman's history but because Colin and I had both served in the Second World War in the renowned 15th (Scottish) Infantry Division; Colin in the 6th Battalion Royal Scots Fusiliers (which Winston Churchill had commanded on the Western Front in 1916) and I in the 2nd Battalion Argyll & Sutherland Highlanders.

Our daughter, Pinky, had left her Belgian lycée when we left Brunssum and she enrolled in a language and secretarial college before getting employed in London. At Wellington Christopher, having got over the hurdle of the 'O' level exam, became a bit of a pain to his Housemaster; careless of College rules, wayward and a keen pursuer of the female sex, principally of the damsels in nearby boarding schools. Inevitably the Goddess Nemesis struck him down: he got a severe attack of glandular fever during the important weeks just before the 'A' level exam, and he was sent home to Penbryn into his Mother's care. He really was pretty ill and our doctor in an attempt to get him fit to sit the exam put him onto strong medicine. Sandy Cavanagh had a fine reputation as a GP in the Brecon area; moreover he had been the RMO of 3 PARA in the Suez operation of 1956. Thus Rosemary and I had full confidence in his optimistic predictions for our son. But Sandy had not bargained for the blunder of the Brecon dispensary who, in supplying the two markedly differing drugs he had ordered, had muddled the Directions for Use labels on the bottles, and many days elapsed before the error was noticed. So Christopher's recovery was delayed. He was allowed to take the exam in the college sanitorium but his results were not good enough to secure him a place in a university of his choice. As it turned out, this set-back opened an avenue from which he has greatly benefited. His Mother caught sight of an advertisement in a Sunday newspaper announcing the establishment of a small selective business school in Canada, and having got him through the selection procedures she despatched him to Montreal in October 1977. Located at Ste Agathe in the Laurentian Mountains the school, Bransons, gave him and the handful of his fellow students a year of intensive personal tuition with skiing instruction thrown in, educational tours throughout North America and a period of work experience at the end of the course. Christopher returned to England with qualifications and a maturity which have won for him a progression of rewarding jobs. He had won a scholarship, so his months in Canada cost me no more than years at a university would have; moreover he was able to enter the job market ahead of his contemporaries and endowed by his Canadian mentors with a background which excited the interest of employers in Britain.

With the prospect of living indefinitely in Britain after my looming compulsory retirement, and with our two children away from home paddling their own canoes through life, Rosemary and I were able for the first time to enjoy the companionship of dogs. From a breeder in Bwlch, near Brecon, we bought two Labrador puppies; a black male called Jason and a yellow bitch we named Carrie – Cariad being the Welsh word for Darling. The relationship which Rosemary developed with these two animals was extraordinary, as was the care with which she nursed Carrie through her pregnancies and the early weeks of her succession of puppies. Jason, highly intelligent and with a marked sense of humour, was sadly headstrong and he ran away from Penbryn and was killed by a car. But Carrie survived and remained with us for fourteen years during our sojourns in Wales, Kent, London and Farnham until she and her daughter Barley became infirm and had to be put to sleep. On leaving Wales in 1978 we went to live on an estate, Chevening, in Kent. There Carrie fell in love with a standard Poodle owned by a retired judge, Michael Chavasse. Out walking her one day I carelessly allowed Carrie to escape from my grasp and she made a beeline for the place where the Chavasses lived. The result of that hasty union was Gemma, a 'Labradoodle' with the colouring of her Mother, the intelligence of her Father and a personality in which the best qualities of both combined. The companionship of these animals enormously enriched our lives and we remember with thankfulness those four-legged members of our family who lavished such devotion on us.

In 1986 my wife and I were guests at a dinner given for the diplomatic community in London at which I was placed beside the Pro Nuncio of the Papal See, the Pope's Ambassador. He spoke good English and during a (for me) interesting conversation I put to him the following question: 'If when I die I am lucky enough to go to Heaven, can I expect to meet there men and women of other races and religions, Hindus, Mohammedans, Buddhists and so on whom I have met and liked during my travels in many countries?' He replied: 'Yes indeed, if they have lived good lives they too will be welcomed into Heaven'. I then asked: 'But there are some other creatures who have brought into my life interest, pleasure and a gentle devotion seldom matched by any of my human acquaintances. I refer to our family of Labrador dogs; I hope to find them beside me there also. Will I?'. 'No,' he explained. 'Animals do not have the power of reasoning and on that account do not qualify for entrance to Heaven.' This response saddened me. It also made me reflect that Paradise, if it excludes animals of the quality of our Labradors, must likewise exclude birds, butterflies, trees and flowers. And what a dull place it must be if inhabited solely by the souls of wimpish humans, beings whose earthly conduct was beyond reproach.

Leaving the Army's Active List after thirty-seven years was a landmark experience which the kindness of colleagues, military and civilian, in Wales and elsewhere, helped to soften. The Minister of Defence, Mr Fred Mulley, sent me a letter of appreciation and best wishes and I was honoured by the award of a CB which I received from the hands of Prince Charles in Buckingham Palace. (My earlier awards I had received there from the hands of the Queen and the Queen Mother.) My last weeks as GOC Wales I actually spent in Aldershot for I had opted for training in Household Maintenance, one of the many courses run to prepare Servicemen for retirement. It was a congenial four weeks and a good choice for I subsequently saved quite a lot of money by applying the skills and techniques I had picked up there. By this time the MoD had at last sent to Brecon a new Deputy Commander. Brigadier John Parham, a Gunner, and I had been fellow instructors at Camberley and while I was away on my 'bricks and mortar' course the running of the Army in Wales fell on his shoulders. The period was interesting as the nation's firemen had engaged in a lengthy strike. In consequence the duty of responding to emergency calls and fighting fires fell on the Armed Forces. The Army units, regular and TA, were equipped with fire engines known as Green Goddesses, used during the Second World War by the Auxiliary Fire Service and brought out of mothballs for this present crisis. The good sense and motivation of our Servicemen as usual got the country through that tricky period, and that latest demonstration of traditional virtues brought to the Services good publicity and from the people of Britain expressions of appreciation. This was welcome for the Armed Forces were having a bad deal then at the hands of Callaghan's Labour government. Morale was low and too many good Officers and men, despondent about their career prospects and poor pay, and nagged by their wives, were quitting the Service. In an attempt to stem the disquiet and unhappiness in the ranks, I made a point of exhorting my listeners as I went round the units in Wales, not to despair. 'Be patient,' I urged them, calling to mind the grim days in the 1930s. 'Something will happen, probably quite unexpectedly and sooner than now seems possible, to make things better for everyone in our Armed Forces.' I made these statements more in hope than with confidence; my hope sprang from a belief that, as so often has happened in the past, some sudden crisis would arise out of the continuing Cold War or from an upsurge in terrorist activity causing, just as the belated awareness of the menace of Hitler's Germany had, an invigoration of our country's defences.

In the event invigoration came from Margaret Thatcher. Elected Prime Minister in 1979 her Conservative government introduced very substantial increases to the pay and pensions of Servicemen, and when in 1982 she called on them to repel the Argentinian invasion of the Falkland Islands, they and their leaders did not fail her. But those of us who had been retired before she took office did not benefit from her reforms; we have continued to suffer from the policy of wage restraint imposed by the earlier Labour government. In pay and therefore in pensions, we who left the Services in the 'trough years' (1976-8) have been disadvantaged in comparison with those who retired in earlier or later years. And as no government is prepared to bring in retrospective legislation to remedy this injustice, we and our widows will remain penalised and disgruntled. Nevertheless our terms of service, our pensions and other financial provisions are more generous than those doled out to earlier generations of Servicemen. When I reflect on the anxieties inflicted on my own parents by the pay and pension codes relating to those who had contributed so much to the victories of 1918 and 1945 I count myself fortunate.

Notes

1. As one American military historian was to write of that period: 'While it brought the end of America's direct involvement in the war in Vietnam, 1973 was a moment of reckoning for the US military. There were those in uniform who blamed the defeat solely on mistakes made by the nation's civilian leadership, and they saw little reason for dramatic change. Others believed that nothing short of radical reform was needed. Not an officer who persevered through those dismal days was untouched by that fundamental struggle over the soul of their service. For some officers, the battles joined during what was arguably the lowest point ever in the military's fortunes would help shape not only their services' future but their own'. (James Kitfield, *Prodigal Soldiers*, Simon & Schuster, 1995)
2. The links between the regiment and the Dukes of Argyll are traditional. During the period of the campaign the Duke and Duchess were living in France, deeply preoccupied with their own affairs: it was rumoured that they were in financial difficulties. That fact may explain why, when they were being driven through London while on a brief visit to Britain, the Duchess is alleged to have pointed to a bus displaying the 'Save the Argylls!' poster and exclaimed to her husband: 'Aren't people kind, they've heard of our problems!'.
3. Eleven Victoria Crosses were awarded for the Defence of Rorke's Drift on 22 January 1879; seven of these to members of the 2nd Battalion 24th Regiment.

Of these seven VCs, six are on display in the regimental museum in Brecon. One hundred years after Lieutenant Bromhead of the 24th Regiment won his VC in that action, his great grand-nephew, Brigadier David de G Bromhead, CBE, LVO, FRGS, was the Colonel of the Royal Regiment of Wales.

CHAPTER XVI
1978–1988

Foreign Affairs in Kent and Home Affairs in Barnes

When the 7th Earl Stanhope (who was also the 13th Earl of Chesterfield) died on 15 August 1967 in his 87th year, there ended two and a half centuries of the duty, service to the public and nobility of purpose expressed in his family's motto 'A Deo et Rege'. He, James Richard Stanhope, was a descendant of a Stanhope who lived in the 12th century; the family name had been taken from the township of Stanhope in County Durham. His ancestor, General James Stanhope, created 1st Earl Stanhope in 1718, had a notable career as a soldier and from 1712 as a statesman. He campaigned for the Hanoverian succession and as a reward King George I made him Secretary of State and Leader of the House of Commons; in 1717 he became the King's Chief Minister and his confidant.

A grandson of the Philip Stanhope whom Charles I had in 1628 created Earl of Chesterfield, General Stanhope in 1713 wed Lucy Pitt, daughter of Thomas Pitt, the Governor of Madras. This marriage was the first link between two families who were to play major roles in the political life of England, for Lucy Pitt was the aunt of William, 1st Earl of Chatham, and she became the great-aunt of his son, the famous Prime Minister, William Pitt the Younger. The second link was established by the marriage in 1774 of Chatham's daughter Hester Pitt to Charles, the 3rd Earl Stanhope.

The death in 1967 of the 7th Earl also brought to an end the links between the Stanhope family and Chevening. This house in Kent, standing some two miles from Sevenoaks and just below the North Downs, had been bought in 1717 by General James Stanhope, and during the subsequent 250 years the successive Earls occupied Chevening, adding in accordance with their tastes and interests to the shape and contents of the mansion, its gardens and the surrounding land. They preferred Chevening to their other estates in Ireland and England which they gradually sold off to finance its upkeep. The 7th Earl, whose wife died childless in 1940, arranged for Chevening to pass on his death to a trust and thus be preserved in perpetuity for the nation. This was accomplished in 1959 when Parliament passed the Chevening Estate Act which came into force on his death eight years later. Two principal provisions in the Act concern the management and the usage of the House and Estate.

Management became the responsibility of Administrative Trustees whose Chairman is the Lord Privy Seal and whose members include the Director of the Victoria and Albert Museum, one member appointed by the Minister for the Environment and other persons appointed by the Prime Minister. The Prime Minister has the duty of nominating the Occupant of the House. This person can be 'the Prime Minister, a minister who is a serving member of the Cabinet, the widow or a lineal descendant of King George VI or the spouse, widow or widower of such a descendant'. The Act goes on to state that if it should, after a number of years, be found impracticable to nominate the Occupant from the above category of persons, the House and the Estate must be offered firstly to the Canadian High Commissioner and secondly to the Ambassador of the United States. (Lord Stanhope had toured North America before the First World War and greatly admired these two countries.) Should neither accept, the House, contents and Estate pass to the National Trust.

My own association with Chevening came about thus. After my Grandfather, Tommy Carew-Hunt, took as his second wife Mida Dale-Glossop, her daughter, Betty, married a civil servant named John Francis Hewitt. He rose far in his career, and by the time I retired from the Army he was a Knight, Appointments Secretary to the Prime Minister and one of the Chevening Trustees. He and his colleagues were faced with difficult problems. How to secure by the prudent investment of the Stanhope monies an income for the upkeep of the House and Estate, and the urgent need to carry out major works to repair and restore the House whose structure had been severely weakened and its appearance damaged by the passage of years. This work was massive and lengthy but it was completed by 1973, and in recognition of their achievements the firm of consultants whom the Trustees employed, Donald W. Insall and Associates, received the European Architectural Heritage Award 'for a scheme of exceptional merit'. The whole of this work was financed from funds provided by Lord Stanhope's Will; no call whatever was made on public funds. Likewise the wages of the small staff employed by the Trustees for the management of the House and its contents, for providing household services for the Occupant and for the maintenance of the gardens and Estate properties have continued to be paid wholly from Estate funds.

These trusteeship responsibilities became an increasing burden on elderly busy men living far from Kent. Furthermore, when in 1974 the Prime Minister, Mr James Callaghan, persuaded Charles, Prince of Wales and heir to the throne, to accept the Occupancy of Chevening, the need for the Trustees to be represented on the estate by a resident agent had to be addressed. The initial arrangements they made to this end proved to be unsatisfactory and Sir John Hewitt,[1] wrote to me to ask if I would consider living at Chevening and working three days a week for a small salary in the appointment of Secretary to the Administrative Trustees.

Micawber-like I had given little thought to a second career, and after several visits to Kent it seemed to Rosemary and me that Chevening would be a congenial place to live in and the work both interesting and of some service to the nation; moreover that the terms of employment would give us time to pursue other interests and occupations. I accepted the Trustees' offer, they submitted my name to Prince Charles and the Prime Minister[2] and in April 1978 Rosemary and I arrived at a snow-covered Chevening under a brilliant blue sky to settle into The Lodge, a cottage attached to the Estate Office with minute rooms heated by open coal fires and a large unkempt garden.

We soon discovered that our new home had been known to Jane Austen. In the garden of The Lodge lay, overgrown by nettles, the foundations of an earlier building, the Parsonage in *Pride and Prejudice* of Mr Collins; the location and ambiance of Rosings is said to have been modelled on the Chevening of the 3rd Earl Stanhope, and the character of Lady Catherine de Bourgh on that of his Mother Grizel who died, aged 93, two years before the great novel was published.

Chevening, first recorded in a 12th-century list of Kentish churches, was in 1978 still an isolated hamlet. On the west side of the narrow road which runs from the village of Chipstead to the entrance to Chevening Park stand twelve small cottages, each with a garden, one larger house, Lennard Lodge (named after the family who from 1515 owned Chevening for eight generations), the Recreation Room and opposite it the Church of St Botolph with its square tower and several graveyards. These dwellings the Trustees let out to 'gentry of good reputation and reduced means'. We were a contented population of some thirty souls, individually disparate in background and personality but all conscious of the privilege of living in a charming rural hamlet steeped in the history of England yet remote from the noise and hassle of the 20th century. (That is, until the M25 motorway separating Chevening from Chipstead was built in 1979 to relieve the traffic congestion which had become such a disagreeable feature of the more distant and winding A25.)

I had a small team of estate employees. The gardens were kept in order by John Eaton; Bert Brain was our elderly and gentle forester who maintained the many acres of woodland; Jim Goatham the handyman kept the drains unblocked, repaired broken windows and burst pipes, and the Chevening Shoot, renowned for its numerous high-flying pheasants, was supervised by Clive Barker.

Of the 3,500 acres stretching between Bessels Green and Biggin Hill the Trustees retained forty acres as the gardens, private to the House, and the Park sloping down from the crest of the Downs through which meandered the splendid Ride, conceived by Lord Chatham and which bears his name. The bulk of the Estate lands were let out to farmers, and a local firm of professional agents, Messrs Cluttons, was engaged to negotiate farm rents, building contracts, valuations and so on. The entrances to the House and gardens were kept locked; the public were admitted to the latter only by special permission and that chiefly for fund-raising events: into the House itself never. In the Estate Office I inherited a secretary, Rosie Brewer, and two girls employed part-time as book-keepers. After a year or so Mrs Brewer moved to Derbyshire to work at Chatsworth, the Duke of Devonshire's home, and in her place I was fortunate enough to get Beryl Duncan, a recently widowed former Matron at Sevenoaks School, and by the purchase of more modern office equipment we were in time able to get by with a single book-keeper, June Miles, who lived with her husband in the village. Looking after the House and its contents and catering for the needs and comfort of Prince Charles on his rare, brief visits was the duty of Frank Ennis, an ex-NCO of the Irish Guards, and his wife, Joy. They lived in a wing of the House, kept themselves remote from the rest of the community and for many years had refused to take any holiday away from Chevening. They were totally dedicated to their responsibilities and resented interference or advice from any quarter. They were an eccentric couple, but they were indispensable to the Trustees and they served Chevening with a laudable and singleminded devotion.

But it was obvious that someone had to be brought in to understudy the Ennises, and I recruited a recently retired Sergeant-Major but he, an ex-Sapper, soon resigned in vexation at the attitude towards him of the ex-Guardsman. I then sought the help of the Chief Constable of Kent, Mr Barry Paine. He eventually produced a sergeant about to retire from his Force who seemed entirely suitable and of whom Frank Ennis approved. But after celebrating with colleagues his last day in the constabulary, the sergeant collided in the dark with another vehicle, unwisely failed to stop and was finally cornered after a long pursuit. My luck then changed and I found another policeman, who like his wife, Mary, became an admired and popular member of our tiny community.

Such incidents and the variety of matters, many trivial, which landed on my plate kept me busy each week for more hours than the Trustees had anticipated. Nevertheless I had more leisure than I had enjoyed in the Army and could thus embark on other commitments, including publishing the account of my years commanding the Forces in Oman which I dictated to my kind and tolerant assistant, Mrs Duncan.

The Lord Lieutenant, Gavin Astor, took a close interest in the St John Ambulance, and at his invitation I soon found myself involved in that ancient and charitable Order as Chairman of its Council for Kent, and at the same time I was honoured by the appointment of Honorary Colonel of the Kent County Cadet Force and Chairman of the County Cadet Committee. As mentioned earlier I had already accepted the Honorary Colonelcy of the Welsh General Hospital unit. All this meant that I was away from Rosemary a lot, but she was very supportive for she knew that I enjoyed these extramural activities.

Although Prince Charles was the nominated Occupant of Chevening he was rarely there. His public duties and service in the Royal Navy engaged him elsewhere and the centres of his interests and the circles of his family and of his friends lay outside Kent. Furthermore, as he was to tell me later on several occasions when we met (for we were both members of The Parachute Regiment, he being our Colonel-in-Chief) he did not enjoy the prospect of living free in a residence over whose management he had little control and where for any significant item of expenditure he was obliged to seek the approval of elderly Trustees. Although the Chevening community was saddened, it came as no surprise to us that he decided to give up the Occupancy. He drove down one afternoon in July 1980 to announce his decision to the assembled staff and to bid us farewell. It was a melancholy occasion and we retain the memory of an earnest, transparently honest and considerate young man; and when we read that he had bought Highgrove in Gloucestershire for his home and learnt of his engagement to Lady Diana Spencer we wished for him and his fiancée a future good in every way.

The matter now arose of finding a new Occupant for Chevening from a list of candidates narrowly circumscribed by the terms of the Act. The Trustees and I already knew from unofficial soundings that neither Canada nor the United States wished in the foreseeable future to make use of the place, and the National Trust was unwilling to incur the expense arising from the acquisition of Chevening which by statute would have to be opened to the public. But the Prime Minister, Mrs Margaret Thatcher, was required by the Act to look firstly at her own Cabinet.

Prime Ministers by tradition occupy Chequers, the country mansion in Buckinghamshire bequeathed to the nation soon after the First World War by Lord Lee of Fareham, and Dorneywood, the gift of Lord Courtauld Thomson, was used as the official country residence of the Foreign Secretary. Chevening however has certain advantages over Dorneywood; size, richness of the interior and accessability from London by car or helicopter coupled with its convenience for the Channel ferries and Gatwick Airport.

The Foreign Secretary, Lord Carrington, was willing to test the facilities at Chevening, and shortly before Christmas 1980 set up an evening meeting there with a French delegation. In laying on this, our first, ministerial function we were guided by the Protocol and Conference Department (PCD) of the Foreign and Commonwealth Office, headed then by Mr Douglas Gordon and his efficient and tireless Scottish colleague, Miss Anne Hutchison. (She later married Alastair Morrison, a former commander of the SAS's G Squadron in Oman during my time as CSAF.)

That first event was not a total success. The French team arrived late because their British escort missed the turning off the new motorway, and the dinner prepared and brought down from London by the Government Hospitality organisation so displeased Lord Carrington that, when it was quietly suggested to him that the culinary arrangements should be changed, he agreed 'to let the local girls have a go'. Thereafter the business of preparing and serving all meals was undertaken by my wife, Rosemary, and her team of Chevening amateurs, Beryl Duncan, Mary Gamble, June Miles, and Doreen Edwards, and, from Tunbridge Wells, Maureen Willey who had been the Chief Instructress in Cookery at the Winkfield Finishing School.

Having Maureen on our team was a blessing as she was a cordon bleu expert; and a joy too, for she and her Royal Air Force husband, Richard, had been friends of ours since the days when we served together in Fontainebleau two decades earlier. And our collaboration with Anne Hutchison of PCD worked splendidly during all the years Rosemary and I were at Chevening: happily for us and, judging by the letters people were kind enough to write after every function, no less enjoyably for the British hosts and their foreign guests. By the spring of 1981 Mrs Thatcher was able to confirm that Lord Carrington would accept the Occupancy. This delighted us for he was an amusing and stimulating person to work for.

Although the main reception rooms in the House had been restored by the Trustees, using the skills of Jane Churchill, only two bedrooms had been prepared for the Prince of Wales; the remainder were still in the same state as when Lord Stanhope died. Thus, when Lord Carrington was offered the Occupancy, he made it a condition of his acceptance that the Trustees got the whole building redecorated and in every respect ready for a conference being planned with the Foreign Ministers of France and West Germany – in four months' time! This redecoration task was undertaken by Jane Ross, from Offham near Maidstone, and the essential repairs to the fine pieces of antique furniture by John Marno, a retired soldier living nearby, and their handiwork has been admired by the many people who have visited Chevening as the guests of successive ministers. Nevertheless a great many items had to be purchased in addition to bring the amenities of the House up to modern standards. Frank Ennis, Beryl Duncan and I compiled long lists of what was needed which I took up to the principal stores in London for them to study and tender for the fitting-out of Chevening. The prices and ideas submitted by the Manager of Peter Jones, in Sloane Square, were accepted and we could not have been better served. For me, now employed full-time, this was an exciting period. In buying the more personal household items I was helped by a damsel from the Foreign Office well versed in the minutiae of diplomatic hospitality, such as the proportion of mattresses that had to be provided for the benefit of people with spinal ailments and of pillows manufactured specially for those with breathing problems. Peter Jones's lorries delivered everything on time except for those items which I bought in Sevenoaks, such as wastepaper baskets and the ornate table lamps for the magnificent Stanhope Library which was to be much used for major conferences and for the elegant Tapestry Room with its unique Huguenot wall-hangings which was used for more intimate discussions. All this made a significant hole in the Trust finances, and many things such as the upgrading of the obsolete heating system and the rewiring of the electrics had to be postponed.

This new role in an age of increasing crime and terrorist activity imposed on Chevening House and on our lives many new constraints. The Gatehouse was transformed into a police post manned by the Kent Constabulary, who also patrolled the grounds whenever the House was occupied, and teams from the SAS examined the House and its approaches and made recommendations for the protection of those inside. In consequence much work had to be put in hand under the supervision of the Security Services to provide havens inside and below the House, fortified as far as practicable against high velocity bullet and remote-controlled bomb. The cost of this specialist work was, fortunately for the Trust, borne by the public purse, and from the late summer of 1981 Chevening was equipped to make, in the words of one Foreign Secretary, 'a major contribution to the conduct of British foreign policy'.

Lord Carrington's conference with the French and Germans, led by Monsieur Cheysson and Herr Genscher – our first big test – went off well, although we behind the scenes had some fast balls to play. The catering arrangements were based on running, for such a big occasion, three messes. In the main ornate dining room the No 1 Mess for the VIPs; in the adjacent study No 2 Mess for the 'Helpers' – Anne Hutchison, the top Security Officer, Colonel Peter Durrant, the Personal Protection Officers (Bodyguards) and me. In a third room near the kitchen we set up a third mess for the chauffeurs, duty policemen and such like; about a dozen people in all.

The French and German Ministers required police escorts between Gatwick and Chevening, the escorts being found by the Police Force of each county through which the route passed. Gatwick Airport is in Sussex, Chevening in Kent; between the two lies Surrey. Thus there suddenly appeared in our midst groups of motorcycle policemen from the three counties, all determined to get in on the act and expecting to be fed. Our girls somehow managed to pull off an impromptu loaves and fishes miracle.

One Whitehall outfit of which I came to form a poor opinion was the Government Car Service. This provided the uniformed drivers of the official vehicles which conveyed VIPs to and from Chevening. Scruffy and unhelpful to their passengers I thought some of them were a disgrace to our nation, and I expressed surprise that the service was not manned by men who through experience in the Armed Forces or the Police had achieved a proper degree of self-discipline and courtesy.

Sadly Lord Carrington, misled by the evidence from the South Atlantic and true to his character and background, resigned when the Falkland Islands crisis broke. We missed him greatly for he had been a vivacious and rewarding Occupant. My family is especially in his debt. Knowing that our daughter's wedding was planned for 5 June 1982, he let us have the use of Chevening House since that date was also his birthday which he was content to celebrate in his own home at Bledlow. On that day, the hottest in a very hot summer, our guests from the Estate, the county, the kingdom and from overseas had a chance to enjoy the setting, the paintings and the furniture of a fine English country mansion and to admire the 'Flying' Staircase and the display of swords and muskets which are such remarkable features of the Entrance Hall. The next Occupant was Lord Carrington's successor at the Foreign Office, Mr Francis Pym. He was soon replaced by Sir Geoffrey Howe.

The period of Sir Geoffrey's occupancy were golden years for Chevening. He and his wife, Elspeth, loved the place, used it extensively and entered into the life of our community as much as their commitments in London permitted. Sir Geoffrey, an unruffled, softly spoken Welsh lawyer and politician – and before that an Officer in the Royal Signals – we came to regard as our Squire. He befriended the farming tenants, worshipped in our church and supported the local charities, and the frequent events he and his wife hosted in the House gave us a welcome sense of purpose. He was a 'natural' for the nomination, for Chevening lay close to the constituency of East Surrey which he had represented since 1974. His first acquaintance with us had been the year before when, as Chancellor of the Exchequer, he had borrowed Chevening for a weekend in January 1982 in order to plan with his Treasury team, quietly and undisturbed, the details of the budget he was soon to present to Parliament. We welcomed this engagement especially since Lady Howe and the wives of Sir Geoffrey's colleagues came too, bringing into the former Stanhope family home chatter and laughter; and the countryside, beautiful under thick snow, tempted them out for brisk walks led by Budget, the Howes' aptly named terrier. Our visitors seemed to like the ambiance of the place and the facilities we provided, and the practice of using Chevening for planning the budget was followed by Mr Nigel Lawson who became Chancellor when Sir Geoffrey took over the Foreign and Commonwealth Office in 1983. That appointment enabled him to use the House for conducting foreign affairs, for his constituency work and as his private country home. On his nomination he had said to a journalist: 'I have been there several times and found it an extremely agreeable place and a marvellous house. It is the best possible use that Chevening could be put to, although being available to a minister who has to spend most of his time in London it cannot be used more than occasionally. But it is a marvellous thing and I am very pleased to have the use of it'.

Sir Geoffrey, like Lord Chatham and Macaulay years before, prized the Library and took a lot of trouble in adding to it each year a selection of the recently published books which he considered worthy; and he took a close interest in the work of our librarian, John Fuller and of the local branch of NADFAS (The National Association of Decorative and Fine Art Societies) who were cleaning and repairing the collection of volumes and documents built up since 1717. Some of the volumes and bindings are extremely rare and Sir Geoffrey delighted in displaying these to his closest colleagues and friends such as, for example, Mr George Shultz, the United States Secretary of State who had a personal interest in our edition of Adam Smith's *Wealth of Nations*. At Sir Geoffrey's prompting I put together a brochure rich in coloured photographs about Chevening and the Stanhopes for which he paid the costs of publication.

Lady Howe has described their life at Chevening in these words. 'It was a fabulous period. I've always taken the view that if you were lucky enough to have a lovely house like Chevening and people running it, then you should make it work. We'd try to entertain a mix of guests, which we've done all our lives; politicians, diplomats, visitors from abroad. And certainly all the Cabinet came at some stage. People would arrive for a light lunch on Saturday and then we'd go for walks or play tennis. We'd have tea. There would be a lot of talking and quite often people would have work to do or an interview. Political and diplomatic activity went on the whole time. Geoffrey would do some boxes and then a group of us might play snooker. The women who played clearly had a very misspent youth because they were frightfully good at it. On Sundays we'd have a fairly leisurely breakfast and there would be a lot of desultory chat about what was in the papers. Then there was church and walks round the lake. We usually had eight or ten on Saturday and we'd make it up to about twenty for Sunday lunch. It was a most exciting time.'

My private records show that during the years that I ran Chevening we looked after over seven hundred officials from more than twenty countries, the majority coming during the Howes' Occupancy, and to this tally we can add their personal guests whom we might meet after Morning Service, conducted by the Rector, Maurice Hewitt, or over pre-lunch drinks. I was often called on to tell the story of Chevening and the Stanhopes and to take visitors on tours of the House. One morning when a conference had been set up between the British and the West Germans, the latter turned up punctually but of the British only the Head Man arrived. The remainder had been delayed in London where the discovery in the Thames of an unexploded wartime bomb had severely disrupted the traffic. To fill in time I was asked to take the Germans round the House onto which during the Second World War one of their aeroplanes had dropped a bomb. Mercifully it had failed to explode but it took a chunk out of the masonry and the scar has been kept on display. When showing it to our visitors I was able to say: 'The Luftwaffe's attempt to disrupt life in Chevening during the war failed, but it has certainly succeeded this morning with that bomb in London'.

An agreeable spirit united the Estate staff and villagers. Guy Fawkes' Night, Royal birthdays and weddings we celebrated together and Rosemary and I made a point of including everybody in our children's 21st birthday parties and on New Year's Eve. We could do this because we had moved out of the tiny Lodge into a larger Estate property, Grove House, whose tenant had just died. From the drawing room we removed all the furniture and had about ninety people in each time for Scottish dancing and a buffet supper in the next room. It was all great fun and a happy way to greet each New Year, made even more pleasant for us by that admirable couple Geoffrey and Esmé Walford who always arrived early on our doorstep to help us put all the furniture back and to do the washing up. Bill and Margaret Foss too, who lived in Lennard Lodge, always made a fine contribution to the Chevening spirit. Both were busy people, he with his business and she with her social work in Sevenoaks: they were wonderful examples of generosity of spirit and of purse.

While the Howes were enlivening our lives and Sir Geoffrey was rejuvenating the Library, Elizabeth Banks, a landscape gardening expert and the wife of one of the Trustees, embarked after meticulous research on a large-scale programme to restore the gardens; opening up vistas, renewing the maze, replanting the Spot Garden and recreating with hornbeam the long allees which had been a feature of Stanhope taste. The Trustees let me restock with trout the long oblong lake on the south side of the House, and we had some success in suppressing the blanket weed which disfigured so much of its surface, but our attempts to get swans to settle there and breed failed – at least in my time.

Although the Act gives the Prime Minister some responsibility for Chevening, the Trust receives no money from government. Indeed the Occupant, at that time a member of the government, was only expected to bear the cost of personal items such as the food, drink and the laundry for himself, his family and guests. Moreover the Act allows for the Trust funds to pay him up to £100 per month to meet such expenses. We used that to pay for his newspapers. The Trust's finances were running into choppy waters. Although income from rents had kept ahead of inflation, this could not be sustained; our farmers were already suffering from the recession in which the country found itself, and concurrently the income from investments was declining. Moreover our expenditure – on maintenance of the House and gardens, professional fees, wages, pensions and so on – had doubled during the same period. In 1985 the gap between income received and routine expenditure had jumped to over £16,000; and expenditure from capital in 1984 had exceeded £100,000. This state of affairs could not be allowed to continue.

A new team of Trustees had been formed soon after the death of Sir John Hewitt and the resignation of Lord Hirshfield, and we all met formally once a year under the Chairmanship of the Lord Privy Seal (holders of that office seemed to change with remarkable frequency). The effective supervision of Chevening affairs was henceforth carried out by an Executive Committee headed by Lord Cornwallis with, as members, Messrs Lawrence Banks, Robin Leigh-Pemberton (later Lord Kingsdown), Martin Pym and David Innes; men younger than their predecessors and who, with the exception of Lawrence Banks, lived in Kent. They set about grasping the nettle of the Trust's finances.

The Chevening Act in its original 1959 form imposed on the management of the Estate a number of restrictions which in the 1980s were no longer realistic or conducive to good administration. In particular it tied the Trustees' hands over the manner in which they could dispose of redundant cottages and outlying areas of land for which property developers were willing to pay large sums to acquire. It was clear that a first step in the process of improving the Trust's financial situation was to have the 1959 Act amended. We in the Estate Office worked on this with the help of legal experts and parliamentary draughtsmen and were present in the gallery when the amendments we sought were introduced in the House of Lords by Baroness Young. They were embodied in the new Chevening Estate Act which came into force on 1 September 1987.

The Trustees did not benefit from the easing of those restrictions as much or as quickly as we had hoped. The deepening recession caused the property developers to withdraw their interest in buying estate land and – a bitter blow – the Secretary of State for the Environment refused to grant planning permission for building development on an important slice of farmland between Chipstead and Bessels Green which had been rendered unworkable by the construction of a road interchange complex and for which the Trust would have received about £4 million. The Trustees were thus obliged to cut expenditure significantly even at the risk of deterioration in the fabric of some properties; they imposed a moratorium on other than essential maintenance work, installed a number of labour-and money-saving devices, and negotiated with Whitehall for the Trust to be relieved of some of the costs incurred whenever the House was used, as it was increasingly, by government departments other than the Nominated Person. These measures helped but could not provide more than a temporary expedient in the search for financial solace, and in 1993 the Trustees, who had hitherto been reluctant to do so, arranged for many items of furniture, crockery, silverware, porcelain and such like, to be sold; items which mainly had been brought to Chevening from Lord Stanhope's house in London, cluttering the attics and outhouses ever since his death. None of the items displayed or used in the House were included. As Lord Cornwallis explained to the Press: 'This auction is not the Government selling off the family silver. It is prudent Trustees disposing of surplus material'. The sale of the 811 lots was conducted by Sotheby's: it was expected to raise £250,000. In fact it raised over twice that sum.

I had left Chevening six years earlier. After the introduction to Parliament of the helpful amendments, Rosemary and I decided that it was a good moment to move on. We had both had spells in hospital; Rosemary for a major operation which though successful was followed by a painful viral eye infection which took many months to shake off. My widowed Mother, living alone in London, had developed the illness from which she died a year later, and we, who had sold our Camberley house on moving to Chevening in 1978, had to get back onto the property ladder before house prices leapt beyond our reach. So we bought a small house in south-west London overlooking the Thames, hoping to live in it and to commute from there to Kent as Chevening duties required. But the Trustees considered it essential that their Secretary should be based continuously on the estate. Also, after the birth of our first grandchild in 1985, we wanted to be able to spend more time with that baby and her parents. Rather than trying to explain these domestic considerations to the many people who enquired why on earth we were leaving such an interesting and worthwhile job, I used to say merely: 'If one climbs to the top of a mountain, there is no point in spending the rest of life looking around at the view – and getting a wet bottom; it is better to come down and look for another mountain to climb'.

Chevening was by then established as a place useful and convenient for a Cabinet minister and his colleagues, our working procedures with the PCD and our drill for receiving and looking after visitors were functioning smoothly, and the Trust's financial problems had in part been eased. We missed the stimulation and laughter which the Howes had brought to Chevening; we grieved when Sir Geoffrey in 1989, in a dramatic episode in the modern political life of England, lost the use of that home which suited him and Elspeth so admirably, and we rejoiced to learn in due course that his successor, Mr Douglas Hurd, was using Chevening regularly as a retreat or for official entertaining, and that he named after that fine place a scholarship fund which he launched several years later.

Parting from good friends in the village and farms, and from sympathetic Trustees, was one more sombre incident in a soldier's life of unpacking, doing one's best in new surroundings, before packing up again and moving on. In 1986, after eight rewarding years in Kent, the county of my birth in 1923, I handed over the running of Chevening House and the estate to a retired Royal Navy Captain, David Husband, and Rosemary and I settled into our new house in Barnes. We thought it would be for good.

My younger brother, Alastair and his wife, Penelope, had been dealt a grievous blow in June 1979. Their 6-year-old daughter, Olivia Graham, a gifted and extrovert child for whom everything in life was set fair, fell on her head while playing on a car parked in the drive of Alastair's boys-House at Eton. Penelope at once took her to a doctor and on his instructions to the modern hospital in nearby Slough. There the Casualty Officer examined her and, despite her vomiting over his feet, sent her home. Her condition then deteriorated alarmingly and an emergency operation had to be carried out to relieve a huge pressure of blood building up on her brain. But it was too late. If she had been treated immediately she would have recovered, but as her Counsel stated in the subsequent High Court action, the effects of her injuries – she walks with a pronounced limp, her speech is impaired and her right arm paralysed – have meant that the prospects of any career and of married life are tragically remote.

After eight years of litigation the Casualty Officer and the Area Health Authority admitted liability and the sum awarded to Olivia in damages was large. It remains to be doubted, however, whether it will, in an era of rising costs and declining returns on investments, suffice to afford her a reasonable quality of life during her remaining years. Her parents have coped magnificently with the manifold consequences of this domestic calamity, and Olivia is fortunate in having mature and intelligent parents who were able to secure the best possible legal and medical expertise in preparing the case for the High Court. Rosemary and I often ask ourselves how another child, similarly crippled, would have fared with parents living in humbler circumstances, with no influential friends and less fitted to cope with the legal processes of late-20th-century England.

My other Brother, James Moray, two years senior to Alastair, had problems of a different nature. After passing out of Dartmouth at the age of 17 he spent eleven years in the Royal Navy, but believing that he could find a more profitable outlet for his creative talents he left in 1959. After studying architecture he joined the export-import branch of Selfridges for whom he worked successfully and happily for two years, marrying Margaret Willcocks, the Secretary to the Headmaster of Westminster School, by whom he had three children.[3] In 1963 he set up his own business in London. It prospered, but after twelve years he was introduced to a commercial organisation in the Persian Gulf and, induced to establish a branch of his interior design business out there, he went off to Dubai. Alas, badly let down by the negligence of his English solicitor, he had to spend nine testing years far from his family, living on the breadline and attempting singlehandedly to keep his firm afloat. In 1985 he cut his losses and returned to England where he joined a group of consultants designing and operating specialist rehabilitation units in collaboration with the National Health Service. Unlike the more philistine members of the Graham clan, by tradition government servants or soldiers, he was elected a Fellow of the Royal Society of Arts and of the Association of Industrial Artists and Designers. In his working life Moray has had a rather unrewarding row to hoe, but his great solace throughout has been the admirable support of his wife and the Willcocks family and the undiminished affection of his children. Adversity never dampened his optimistic outlook nor his sense of humour; and it has welded his family into an uncommonly united quintet.

We loved our Barnes home. It was one of six houses newly built round a small courtyard. Standing tall and narrow, with the top floor opening out onto a roof garden, it was cheap to heat and easy to secure against burglars. This was an important factor as housebreaking and theft were becoming commonplace in England, and the cost of insurance kept going up all the time. Our terrace was separated from the edge of the Thames only by a road. During the thirteen years that our family owned it, the volume of the passing traffic swelled dramatically, and because our European governors kept altering the regulations to allow ever-larger lorries onto our roads, the vibrations caused by their passage and the pollution from their exhausts shook the buildings and dirtied the windowpanes deplorably. But the views over the river, looking north towards the green open space of Duke's Meadows and the Rowing Club were delightful; and the Thames, downstream near Hammersmith at high water in the dawn light or with the setting sun starkly silhouetting Barnes Bridge, looked truly beautiful.

Living a stone's throw from that bridge we had a grandstand view of the final stretch of the University Boat Races and an excuse for an annual gathering of friends. On the top floor I slept right through the hurricane which struck a heedless England in October 1987, unaware that the gale had torn away some of the lead roof lining, but Rosemary and Christopher who were away from London that night had frightening experiences. And the Chevening woodlands, when the storm passed, had the appearance of a battlefield. Although the destruction over the south of England was immense, a lot of over-mature timber which should have been felled earlier by Man was removed by Nature. Alas many trees had already been killed by an epidemic of Dutch Elm disease.

The rooms in No 1 Maltings Close were small, and Rosemary set about converting the dining area and kitchen into a more convenient and comfortable space. Throughout our life together I have marvelled at my wife's flair for turning geese into swans; for spotting in quite ordinary and unobtrusive articles and places the potential for turning them into lasting assets. At Chevening she demonstrated her culinary skills and while there she had also taken up silversmithing, crafting a variety of gifts for special friends. In Barnes she studied the art of cake decorating and her creations were much admired at many weddings, christenings and suchlike jollifications. By keeping her eyes open as we travelled around the country she built up a pretty collection of antique glass, and she became so hooked on glass that she launched out into engraving it; and in later years she became a keen painter in oils and watercolours, and she wrote in verse too a story for children about a monkey and, for our family, an account of episodes in her youth. Freed from the obligations of Service life she was thus able to give full rein to her creative talents; though this inevitably resulted in our home becoming more and more cluttered with the handbooks and tools of her diverse enthusiasms. Like most grandmothers, Rosemary reserved her deepest love and most generous energy for Alexandra, born in 1985, and for Jessica who arrived five years later.

Roland and Pinky had by this time bought a house near Farnham and we were able to visit the flatlet there and to earn our keep by babysitting and improving the garden; building rockeries, clearing the bracken and encouraging the rhododendrons and azaleas which thrive in Surrey's sandy soil.

My Mother, for whom following the careers of her sons had always been the chief delight, had gone on working in the City where she ran the catering for an eminent group of trustees (for she too was an excellent cook), but at the age of 82 she developed leukaemia and had to have blood transfusions with increasing frequency until May 1987 when she died peacefully in hospital in her 88th year. Her ashes were placed beside her parents, Tommy and Emily Carew-Hunt, who lie buried in Putney Vale. (See Appendix VI)

To my Brothers and me she had been an excellent Mother; as a Mother-in-Law she had displayed a different personality – censorious and often unfeeling.

When I was an instructor at the Camberley Staff College I got to know a student Officer named Toni Holt; twenty years later we ran into each other again, at a bus stop near Trafalgar Square. Toni had left the Army and with his dynamic wife, Valmai, had set up an organisation for guiding people round some of the battlefields of the two World Wars, and by a combination of careful research and procuring as lecturers chaps who had fought there, they gave their clients entralling insights into the realities of warfare, coupled with well ordered travel arrangements. Success soon enabled the Holts to enlarge their horizons and to cover much of the globe and most campaigns from mediaeval to modern times. I had fought in France in 1944 with the Argylls, and ever since 1941 had taken a particular interest in the German airborne assault which in that year had defeated the British and Imperial forces in Crete and captured that large island for the Axis powers. So I was glad when Toni enlisted me as a Guest Speaker and I have happily accompanied Holts' groups many times to Normandy and to Crete; also Rosemary and I went in a bitterly cold April to Flanders and once to Berlin, divided by the Cold War, where the Communist Border Guards at Check Point Charlie held up our coach for a disquieting half-hour, asserting that the photograph in my wife's passport did not match her appearance that day.

There can be few more congenial ways of taking a holiday than touring with Holts'. Once you've paid, all that is required of you is that you follow the guides' injunctions, enjoy the scenery, food and drink and are pleasant to your fellow-travellers. Holts' take care of everything: if you fall ill they place you in expert hands; if you die they bring you home. Moreover you are not compelled to attend the lectures. I reckon you get from Holts' good value for your money. The variety of folk who come on their tours is surprising. Some are veterans refreshing wartime memories; some are in their teens. Many come because they 'want to see where Grandfather fought' or to pay homage beside the grave of a fallen relative. Most are genuinely interested in history; some merely want a holiday which is different, carefree and in agreeable company. The success of these expeditions largely depends of course on the personality of those who lead them. In the Martins the Holts had a couple of leaders by experience and background admirably fitted for a task which is always demanding and on occasions gruelling. Mike Martin, a former CO of the Royal Hampshire Regiment and his wife, Patricia, a trained nurse, are also good companions and I have greatly enjoyed being part of the flocks they shepherd round blood-stained fields. And because to my eyes Mike bears a remarkable likeness to a German Field-Marshal of Second World War fame, I invariably address them as 'Kesselring' and 'Frau K'. They take it in very good part.

One August day in 1988 the first thing that caught the eyes of those people in Barnes and Mortlake who read the local paper was a map of south-west London across which were printed bold black lines. The Conservative government, searching for ways to improve the traffic flow on the capital's congested roads, had commissioned four firms of consultants to study the problem, already serious and predicted to get worse. Sir William Halcrow and Partners had been tasked to carry out the Assessment Study of West London and they had just published their recommended solutions, two of which specifically related to Barnes, and it was the map and article summarising these which covered the front page of the newspaper that day.

In brief, they recommended that the railway line between Barnes and Chiswick, which crossed the Thames over Barnes Bridge, should be replaced by a motorway or, if that rail link was deemed indispensable, that another bridge should be built beside it to carry motor traffic. The public was not aware that government had launched this consultative process; nor, it seemed, had Halcrows consulted anyone living in the districts being studied. Thus what was printed in the newspaper came as a total surprise; surprise which soon gave way to shock, and shock to anger and fear. Such a reaction was wholly to be expected for either solution would have severely damaged the charm and village atmosphere for which Barnes is renowned, and as the Halcrow document admitted, entailed the destruction of many residential properties there and in Roehampton. Moreover the whole district would have been blighted for many months; property values would have slumped and the buying and selling of houses and businesses been brought to a standstill. This blight was already affecting several parts of England where the construction of new railway or motorway routes was contemplated, and to thousands of men and women it was causing significant financial hardship and anxiety.

The first requirement was to obtain copies of the Assessment Study document so as to find out precisely what Halcrows were recommending to government. This was done and it was clear that what the newspaper had printed was substantially accurate. Within a few days some energetic citizens formed a committee and they decided that their first action must be to make everyone in the district aware of what was being proposed. The Kitson Hall was booked and people were invited by poster, word of mouth and through the press to come and be briefed on 'The Threat to Barnes'.

Rosemary and I were particularly alarmed because any alterations made to Barnes Bridge would inevitably degrade the quality of life and the value of property in Maltings Close. So I joined the committee and undertook to make a large map showing what changes were proposed and the probable consequences for everyone who lived in the area. The map was hung up over the stage in the hall, a public address system was hired and with my fellow-members on that fledgling committee I waited for the public to turn up. Similar meetings were often held throughout the British Isles to discuss environmental matters and suchlike, and we knew that they usually ended with the organisers being discouraged by the public's reluctance to get involved in matters of that sort. We were not optimistic. In the hall there were seats for fifty with room for another fifty or so standing behind, but by the time the meeting opened the place was filled to capacity; others were queueing in the road outside waiting to get in and for their benefit we had to give two 'performances'.

All who attended made their dismay and deep concern very obvious, and our committee was instructed to mount a campaign to avert the threats hanging over the district. More members joined and the enlarged committee, headed by Silvan Robinson and John Seekings, two respected residents experienced in negotiating with officialdom, called itself the Barnes and Mortlake Traffic Action Group, abbreviated to BAMTAG. The Group's campaign was conducted with skill, perseverance and tact. We became well known in that part of London; and farther afield too, for some of us were interviewed by journalists and appeared on television. We got up a petition to Parliament supported by long lists of signatures of people we stopped in the streets or called on in their homes.

A small group from the committee managed to procure a meeting with the Secretary of State for Transport, Mr Peter Bottomley, an unhelpful fellow; and I wrote twice to our Member of Parliament, Mr Jeremy Handley. His replies were prompt, sympathetic and encouraging, and his actions throughout our campaign were consistently supportive.

In a letter written to me in June 1989 he declared: 'I fully accept and recognise the depth of feeling locally about this issue. Naturally the effect electorally upon me would be dire, but it is not only for that reason that I am trying to do all I can. It is for the natural justice of the case'.

I joined a long column of fellow-citizens and, holding aloft placards and banners and shouting out apt slogans, we marched past the Department of Transport building in Marsham Street, on through SW1 into Hyde Park where we gathered under the lenses of television cameras and the eyes of Londoners strolling around in the sunshine. It was for me a novel experience and great fun.

Peter Bottomley was replaced for a brief spell by Paul Channon. He appeared to be acutely conscious of our strong feelings about the Halcrow proposals, and although there was now some evidence that their most damaging recommendations would be rejected by the government, we feared that their alternative solutions would be equally objectionable. We were right.

In December Halcrows released their final proposals. To the horror of the people of Barnes and Mortlake they now proposed in place of the Barnes Bridge scheme, a tunnel from Chiswick to Wandsworth with a major interchange at Barn Elms. This would have devastated Barn Elms, would have created major new traffic problems, and its construction process would have caused for residents and road users very great disturbance as well as being extremely expensive. BAMTAG had by now been joined by other community groups in London, all expressing their opinions of the recommendations submitted by the other consultants. Each group took pains to balance its well-founded objections with positive suggestions of its own which might be helpful to the officials responsible for trying to solve the complex traffic problems. The government admitted that it had not expected such a wave of protests; the Department of Transport and its consultants had 'literally been inundated by petitions and submissions' and they let it be known that the 'sheer problem of wading through all the paper would delay the announcement of the Government's decisions beyond the promised deadline'.

Eventually, in March 1990, a new Transport Secretary, Mr Cecil Parkinson, made a statement in the House of Commons. He announced that he had decided, in the face of the barrage of public opinion, to scrap all the major new road schemes proposed by the consultants, including the Barnes Bridge scheme and the tunnel under Barnes Village. In their place more limited measures were to be taken to improve the traffic flow on the existing South Circular road and money made available for improvements to the bus and rail services.

So we had won. It had taken nineteen months, a lot of work and over £3,000 subscribed by our anxious supporters, to get the government, through three Secretaries of State, to cancel schemes which from the start it ought to have realised were unacceptable to the residents.

BAMTAG did not fade away after this success. As the committee warned in its newsletter, published after Mr Parkinson's statement in the House: 'It will be easy to fall into the trap of thinking that the scrapping of the tunnel means that the blight is over. It is not.' BAMTAG's decision was wise, for although we had won from one Minister an undertaking to scrap schemes unacceptable to the public in 1990, we had no guarantee that a future government, backed by an overwhelming parliamentary majority and faced with the same problems of traffic congestion and poor transportation services, might not resurrect the very schemes we had with so much effort managed to get cancelled. The blight which had been placed over Barnes and Mortlake – and Chiswick, Roehampton and Wandsworth too – was not dead; only suppressed. Such were the thoughts of my colleagues in BAMTAG as the months of 1990 passed.

By that time I had become involved again in activities in Aldershot, the Home of the British Army. But before I describe my adventures there I must state a personal view. It is that of all the aspects of national administration for which government is responsible, the one which British governments have consistently and most lamentably mismanaged in my lifetime is transport. Whenever I drive down the motorways from London to Aldershot in Hampshire or to Chevening in Kent I see on the opposite carriageway endless columns of vehicles moving at an exasperatingly slow speed, with the occupants inhaling exhaust fumes and the drivers either slumped with resignation behind the steering wheel or with difficulty containing their vexation. The effect on working men and women, condemned to endure this twice a day, five days a week, must surely be bad; bad for their health, bad for their domestic lives, and for our environment bad also. And the sum of all this time, motor fuel and human energy squandered on the roads leading into and from London and other great cities must surely impose on our nation's economy and creativity, and on the quality of life of our compatriots, serious and avoidable impediments. They deserve better.[4]

Notes

1. Sir John Hewitt died in late 1979 aged 69, and at Betty Hewitt's request I made the arrangements for his Memorial Service held on 13 February 1980 in the Queen's Chapel of the Savoy (the Chapel of the Royal Victorian Order). Four Prime Ministers were present: Mr Harold Macmillan read the first Lesson and Mr Edward Heath gave the Address.
2. I later learnt from one of the Trustees, Lord Hirshfield, that they had half expected my nomination to be turned down on the grounds that my wife was West Indian by birth.
3. Stephen, Piers and Julia
4. With hindsight it might have been wiser if, in the 1960s, Dr Beeching had taken to the railways of Britain not an axe but a bag of gold.

CHAPTER XVII
1988–1999

Visits to Oman, PARA 90 and our move to Barbados

By 1985 Sultan Qaboos Bin Said had led his country out of 'the years of darkness' into the golden light of his peoples' affection and international esteem. Oman, in 1970 a mediaeval, embattled state, friendless save for its association with the United Kingdom, with a deprived and despondent population, had in the space of fifteen years been transformed into a thriving nation in whose Arab citizens of every class the innate qualities of dignity, love of country and unvarying courtesy are plain to see. In the cities of that majestic country the streets are now immaculately clean, the well-watered grass in the gardens and along the highways is always green, and the deportment of every Omani is admirable. Oman has been reborn. This renaissance, unique I believe in its pace and in its style, has been accomplished by the vision and leadership of a man born the only son of an autocratic and illiberal Ruler, schooled in private but hardened by exposure to the disciplines of the British Army.

Thereafter his years of enforced solitary leisure in a modest house outside the Palace in Salalah had given him time to reflect on the plight of his compatriots and what had to be done to bring salvation to them – and to the Al Bu Said dynasty.[1]

Those years of Oman's darkness and rebirth had been witnessed also by expatriates, British Servicemen mostly, who had shared with the Omanis the hazards, the anxieties and finally the exhilaration of that period. Their contribution was indispensable. It is remembered – but only in private. All testimony, for example, to the presence of British Soldiers and Airmen in the Dhofar war has been removed from public view in the Armed Forces Museum in our old Headquarters in the white fort in Bait al Falaj[2]. Nevertheless being numbered among that privileged body of expatriates, Rosemary and I, and our children too, have been the fortunate recipients of many quiet kindnesses and the generous hospitality both of Sultan Qaboos and of Omanis who have prospered as the Sultanate emerged into the bustle of the late 20th century, with all the scope that has given them for building up their country – and their personal fortunes also.

Over the years we have been invited to visit, at their expense, in their sumptuous new houses in Oman, Europe and the United States, many Omani friends and former comrades-in-arms. And when invited to the National Days in November to celebrate His Majesty's birthday, we have marvelled in company with the legions of other guests at the fantastic illuminations along the highways, the millions of red, white and green electric lights which drape every building, and the faultless arrangements made for our reception and comfort. Those of us who knew Oman before Qaboos came to the throne are astonished by the precision and the panache of the great military parades and of the brilliant Tattoos sponsored by the Royal Oman Police; no less by the enthusiasm of Oman's Youth in the spectacles organized each year in the fine stadiums at Wattayah and on the Maidan Al Fateh.

The rising generation will have some formidable challenges to surmount. An exceptionally high birth-rate conflicts increasingly with declining job opportunities and with diminishing sources of natural water; popular demands for a more democratic form of government and for a more equal distribution of wealth are likely to be exacerbated by unhelpful fluctuations in the oil revenues. Moreover Sultan Qaboos has no heir; whoever succeeds him will have a difficult act to follow. We who served the Sultanate love Oman; many of us regard her as our second home, and as the world moves from the 20th into the 21st century we wish for her and her peoples all that is good.

Having left Chevening to live in Barnes I willingly agreed to help in the affairs of the Anglo-Omani Society. This organisation, based in London, exists to sponsor Omanis studying in the United Kingdom and to enable those who served in Oman to keep in touch with each other and with developments in that country. The Society has an annual programme of lectures, film shows, receptions and such like which are well attended. In November 1990 we presented to His Majesty, our Patron, an elegant illuminated scroll of respectful appreciation and birthday congratulations. Four months earlier I had hosted in the Regimental Mess in Aldershot a lunch to mark the 20th anniversary of Sultan Qaboos' accession to which I had invited twenty colleagues from my years in command of the Sultan's Armed Forces. It was fitting that I should do that there because the previous year I had been asked to return to Aldershot to assist the Regimental Colonel and his small staff in Browning Barracks in planning a major event in our history, the celebration of the Golden Jubilee of the Airborne Forces of the British Army in which The Parachute Regiment had since 1942 been an important part. In the interlude between the expulsion of the British Expeditionary Force from the continent in June 1940 and the German aerial onslaught which was to be launched against our islands in August, Mr Winston Churchill, the Prime Minister, sent a memorandum to the Head of the Military Wing of the War Cabinet secretariat which included the following:

'We should have a corps of at least five thousand parachute troops ... Pray let me have a note on the subject.' This instruction written to General Hastings Ismay on 22 June 1940 was the instrument which brought into being the Airborne Forces of Britain, forces which were to win great renown and in whose ranks were to serve Officers and Men of outstanding quality. It was the fiftieth anniversary of this milestone in the military history of our nation which was to be celebrated in 1990; the whole programme being called for brevity PARA 90.

To the soldiers of all nations the parachute was a novel piece of equipment: to the British soldier it was the most novel. Apart from Leonardo da Vinci's design in 1485 for a 'Fall-breaker', the parachute did not arouse much attention until the time of the French Revolution. Ballooning had been made popular in France even before 1789, principally by the Montgolfier Brothers who used to drop from their balloons parachutes to which animals were attached. In 1797 however André-Jacques Garnerin made the first successful human parachute descent over Paris from a height of 3,000 feet. Two years later his wife became the first woman parachutist, and his niece between 1815 and 1836 made nearly forty descents. In England the first descent was made in 1802 from a balloon over Mayfair by the same Frenchman, Garnerin. Fatalities were frequent and one must marvel at the courage of those men and women who, seated in a crude seat slung beneath a parachute canopy, rode upwards into the sky until, at the desired altitude, they released the balloon and parachuted to earth.

During the 19th century little use was made of the parachute save for suspending flares fired from artillery pieces; but with the 20th century came the aeroplane – and with it flying accidents. In consequence the parachute became an important potential life-saver, and in 1912 an American, Albert Berry, made the first successful jump from an aircraft flying at full speed – 70 mph. In England William Newall accomplished the same feat just before the outbreak of the First World War. That war brought great advances to aviation but fewer to the parachute. A parachute had been issued to the occupants of observation balloons, but none were made available to the Royal Flying Corps even though the lives of German airmen were, from the summer of 1918 onwards, being saved by their own service parachute. There had also been instances of agents being set down by parachute behind enemy lines in France and on the Austro-Italian front.

The inter-war years were fruitful for the parachute designer, above all in the US and the USSR. In the UK a small RAF unit was established at Henlow and parachutes were issued to all service aircrew. Our nation will be forever indebted to three men; Leslie Irvin (an anglophile American), James Gregory and Raymond Quilter, for their unrivalled contribution to the development of parachutes during the next five decades.

Italy was the first nation to develop a military paratrooping capability; the French, Polish and United States armies followed but more modestly. In the Soviet Union however parachuting was becoming a popular sport, and by 1936 the Red Army was dropping units of a thousand men and more, together with light supporting weapons. These Soviet developments impressed the military leaders of Germany, and under the direction of General Kurt Student, the Wehrmacht's airborne arm was forged shortly before the outbreak of the Second World War. In April 1940 the Germans seized Denmark and Norway and by mid-June had conquered the Low Countries and France and evicted the British Army from the European mainland. The actions of the German glider-borne and parachute troops in this staggering chain of victories were everywhere viewed with awe, and it was this new and seemingly invincible force, preparing to spearhead the invasion of the British Isles, which inspired Churchill to send that note to General Ismay.

Rather than endure the daily congestion on the roads between London and Aldershot I took a room in the Browning Barracks Mess and lived there from Monday to Friday. It was a wise move for there was much to be done. The initial intention of the Regimental Elders was to stage as the highlight of our Jubilee year a Parachute Regiment Spectacular on the lines of the Aldershot Tattoo which had been so popular during the 1930s and the annual Royal Tournament in London, and a lot of planning had already been done. However, at a late stage, the local Headquarters, South East District, then commanded by Sir Peter de la Billière, ruled that it was not feasible to dedicate to such an enterprise the numbers of military policemen, cooks, signallers and all the other specialists that would be needed. The MoD supported his decision and the Spectacular had to be scrubbed. It was a great disappointment.

That turn of events was not surprising. Cost-saving measures demanded by the Treasury were being imposed on the Service Chiefs by the Conservative government and for the next five years 'Options for Change'

Para 90 and Paradise

overshadowed the activities of our Armed Forces and brought much anxiety into the lives of All Ranks. There were three main causes of this anxiety. Many good Officers and soldiers were declared redundant and sent out into a civilian population already suffering from high unemployment. This was especially worrying for those with wives and children to support and for the technically unskilled Infantrymen. Moreover the reduction in the Services' manpower was not accompanied by a reduction in commitments. Indeed the Army soon found its commitments increased as units were deployed to Bosnia and Central Africa, and the security measures imposed to counter the continuing IRA threat could not be relaxed. Thus the over-stretch which for years had plagued the Army, the 'teeth arms' in particular, intensified. It was not a happy period, and living again after an absence of eleven years in the Home of the British Army I was disturbed by much of what I saw and heard. The third cause of dissatisfaction was the gulf between the Service Chiefs and the chaps in the units. The latter felt strongly that their views and anxieties were being ignored; the former did too little to explain or reassure.

Other observations were also disturbing to those of us brought up in an earlier military era. The status of the Regimental Sergeant-Major seemed to have been degraded and with it the respect – the awe – which his presence, or his voice alone, wrought on any gathering of soldiers. In place of the pace-stick he was now more likely to be seen carrying a mill-board; no longer a mini-god but rather a uniformed clerical Officer of the middle grade. Perhaps this was inevitable since his traditional stage, the Parade Ground, was now little used except for parking the private cars which so many soldiers owned. Foot and Arms Drill was of course still taught to every recruit, and from time to time units found themselves committed to ceremonial parades for which rehearsals were essential. But the natural tendency in over-stretched units was to put off such rehearsals until the last possible moment in the hope that the soldiers would rise to the occasion and perform splendidly on the day. Ours always did. But that habit of doing so much 'off the cuff' was unfair to everybody.

I discovered too how wide-ranging were the constraints which the terrorist threat was imposing on the lives of all Service personnel. Identity checks, the careful examination of vehicles approaching military establishments, of postal packages and the rigorous checks on the safe custody of weapons and ammunition, all these essential measures slowed up the pace of unit activity and much of the Junior Ranks' time had to be devoted to guarding the entrance or patrolling the perimeter of his camp or barracks. And the monetary cost was also substantial, for every Service establishment was now protected by high, strong fences, perimeter lights and other anti-intruder devices.

The Parachute Brigade, based in Aldershot, had to take the IRA threat especially seriously for its members were a prime target for terrorists frustrated by the consistently good performance in Northern Ireland of the Parachute soldier and motivated by revenge for the actions of 1 PARA on the so-called 'Bloody Sunday'. In two grievous incidents the IRA had blown up one of the Brigade's Officers' Messes in Aldershot, and in Ulster with a single road-side bomb had killed a number of 2 PARA's men passing by in a lorry. Members of The Parachute Regiment were, individually and collectively, vulnerable to IRA attack and the danger naturally extended to all members of Airborne Forces, wearers of the Red Beret, and to members of the public associating with them. Thus in every event we planned for PARA 90 the security factor had to be given close attention.

Many thousands of former members of The Parachute Regiment and of the airborne Arms and Services had joined our ex-Servicemen's organisation, the Parachute Regimental Association (the PRA) which has many branches in the United Kingdom as well as some overseas. Many of these branches undertook to contribute to the PARA 90 celebrations by organising locally parades, displays, pageants and such like with the aim of reminding the public of what British Airborne Forces had achieved, and to raise money for the Security Fund which does such excellent work supporting our former comrades-in-arms, especially the disabled and the bereaved.

The task of coordinating all these local activities and of planning in detail the major national PARA 90 events fell to the staff at RHQ headed by Colonel Hamish McGregor. I knew Hamish well as he had been one of my subalterns in 1 PARA, winning a Military Cross in 1967 when serving with them in Aden.

The principal national events were planned for Manchester, London and Aldershot. Organising these was in truth beyond the capacity unaided of the RHQ staff, already over-stretched by having to cope with the turbulence arising from 'Options for Change' on top of the diverse operational and administrative matters which the management of four Regular and three Reserve Army major[3] units generated, together with the duty of presiding over the PRA. For this reason General Mike Gray, knowing that I had left Chevening and assuming that I was at a loose end, invited me to rejoin RHQ and to take some of the load off the shoulders of Hamish McGregor and his Adjutant, Godfrey McFall.

The Colonel Commandant of the Parachute Regiment in 1990 was General Sir Geoffrey Howlett. He had won an MC while serving with the Royal West Kent Regiment, and he had played a prominent part in planning the parachute assault onto the El Gamil airfield in the 1956 Suez operation. By virtue of his appointment and seniority he was the chap – the Paramount Chief – for whom we all worked on the PARA 90 programme; it was in his name that most of the invitations and so on were issued. Geoffrey Howlett was however in Norway, working at his NATO

Para 90 and Paradise

Headquarters near Oslo from which he commanded the forces allotted to Allied Forces Northern Europe (AFNORTH). He therefore delegated the job of getting PARA 90 off the ground to his Deputy, Lieutenant-General Sir Michael Gray. Mike, recruited as a Gunner, then a young Officer in the East Yorkshire Regiment before transferring into the permanent cadre of the Parachute Regiment had, like me, commanded 1 PARA before being promoted in due course to be the Chief of Staff of Rhine Army and eventually GOC-in-C South East District, the post from which he had just retired. Energetic, imaginative and highly motivated despite a wonky hip, Mike was the mainspring in the design and realisation of our national and provincial celebrations.

The Manchester ceremony was held at that city's airport, Ringway, as it was there that the first centre was established in the summer of 1940 and where the techniques of dropping people and equipment by parachute and of operating gliders were tried out and perfected. On that afternoon in 1990 we paid homage to the far-sighted and courageous men, Squadron Leader Louis Strange, Major John Rock of the Royal Engineers and their colleagues who had set up the Central Landing School. Only twenty-one days after Churchill issued his famous memorandum, parachute descents were started onto the nearby Tatton Park Dropping Zone. They were made by eight instructors dropping from the rear platform of a Whitley bomber. The next day, 14 July, their pupils, men from No 2 Commando billetted in the Knutsford area, began their descents. By the end of 1940 over two thousand descents had been made and the School, renamed the Central Landing Establishment, had been organised into a Parachute Squadron, a Glider Squadron and a Technical Development Unit. No 2 Commando, which soon changed its name to 11 Special Air Service Battalion, in September 1941 became the 1st Parachute Battalion; the first of twenty-one battalions of parachute troops which the British and British-Indian Armies raised during the Second World War, alongside their brothers-in-arms in the 1st Canadian Parachute Battalion and the 1st Polish Parachute Brigade. Over ten thousand members of the Special Operations Executive (SOE), people of many nationalities, were also trained at Ringway.

To meet the needs of our airborne formations overseas parachute schools were set up in Egypt, Palestine, Italy and India. The Ringway School, from 1941 under the command of Group Captain Maurice Newnham, continued to develop parachuting techniques until it moved to Upper Heyford in March 1946. By that time the number of descents made totalled 429,800. Of these forty-six resulted in fatal injuries.

During our busy anniversary summer of 1990 the Queen inspected 5 Airborne Brigade (as the former 16 Parachute Brigade Group was now called) on Salisbury Plain and watched a private demonstration of a large-scale parachute assault which the brigade staff had organised for Her Majesty. The weather was good and the event went off well.

The two major London events were held on 16 February and 22 June. On the latter day, selected expressly in honour of Churchill's inspired memo of 1940, there was held in St Paul's Cathedral – for two centuries the Parish Church of the British Empire – a Service of Thanksgiving for the Raising of Airborne Forces. It was held in the presence of the Prince of Wales, who read the Lesson, the Bishop of London, the Lord Mayor and the Sheriffs, Churchill's grandson Mr Winston S. Churchill and a capacity congregation of VIPs, colleagues and friends from many nations and a great assembly of our serving and retired members and their families.

After the Colours of the Regiment had been received at the High Altar the Dean, Eric Evans, in the Bidding reminded us that: 'We have come here to praise God and to thank him for the faithful and courageous service given by Airborne Forces, both in war and peace. We thank God for the inspiration of The Right Honourable Winston Churchill who, fifty years ago this very day, in London, ordered that a Force of at least five thousand Airborne Troops be raised. We thank God for our founder members both of the Army and the Royal Air Force, and for all who have served in Airborne Forces since that time. We remember those who have been injured in any way during their service, those who are no longer with us, and especially their dependents. We also ask his blessing on those who are serving now'.

The Bishop of Peterborough, the Right Reverend William Westwood, a former Airborne Soldier, in a concise and sharply worded Address (reproduced at Appendix VIII) drew attention to the steady decline in national attitudes and values since the victory of 1945 and challenged us to reverse that decline with the same resolution and patriotism Airborne Soldiers had demonstrated in time of war. The Service, memorable also on account of the exuberant singing of hymns chosen for their popularity and martial tempo, was followed by the March from the Cathedral to Guildhall. To march through the City with Drums beating, Colours flying and Bayonets fixed was a privilege which the Lord Mayor, Sir Hugh Bidwell, had accorded to The Parachute Regiment to mark the exceptional circumstances of 22 June.

Preceded by the City Marshal,[4] mounted on a horse, the Regimental Pony Mascot 'Sergeant Pegasus III' and the Pony Major, Corporal Soane, Hamish McGregor and Godfrey McFall led the marching column past Prince Charles who with the Lord Mayor, the Sheriffs and General Geoffrey Howlett beside him, took the salute. The column was impressively long. It comprised six Guards found by the regular and TA battalions, led by their Commanding Officers and escorting their Queen's and Regimental Colours, the two regimental Bands, eight Guards made up of members of the PRA and, in a splendid phalanx, the massed Standards of the Association's branches. Each PRA Guard was led by a retired Officer of the Regiment of General's or Brigadier's rank; in rear of the column walked the Disabled and our Chelsea Hospital In-Pensioners led by a former CO of 1 PARA, General Sir Charles Harington. Placed separately and prominently in the column were four men who in the Second World War had commanded parachute brigades and seven who had commanded parachute battalions.

The March was a rare parade of military achievement and devoted service to Crown and Country. The sun shone and the pavements and windows were thronged by citizens and tourists attracted to the unique procession. The March ended at Guildhall where, after placing their Colours and rifles under guard, the Officers, Soldiers and many of us with our wives had been invited to a luncheon given by the Lord Mayor, the Aldermen, Commoners and Sheriffs. It was a great day. The help and advice we had received from the Dean and his staff, and from the City of London Police and the Security Service who ensured our safety inside the Cathedral and along the March-route were unstinted and the results admirable.

Because of the generosity of our hosts, Rosemary and I were able to include on the guest lists for the Service and the lunch our Argyll friends of long standing, Sue Mitchell and her husband, Colin, the 'Mad Mitch' of Aden fame. It was good that they could be with us on that day for it was the last time I saw Colin; he died of cancer six years later.

Airborne Forces Day that year was held in the large Rushmoor arena, much used before the war but now run down and neglected. We tarted it up and a large gathering of Old Comrades and their families had an enjoyable day in the sunshine; and in the presence of our Colonel-in-Chief. Prince Charles came with his arm in a sling, the result of a fall on the polo field, but without Princess Diana. That was a disappointment; rumours of the deterioration in their personal relations had not yet reached us and four years were to pass before the world knew that their marriage had come to an end.

Our anniversary year had in fact been launched five months earlier, in Guildhall, when on the evening of 16 February the Officers of The Parachute Regiment and Airborne Forces held the Golden Jubilee Dinner. We numbered some eight hundred of whom one hundred were distinguished men invited because of their special association with us; representatives of the SAS and SOE, of our sister Services, of the County of Hampshire, commanders of Allied airborne forces, our new Honorary Major, Prince Henri of Luxembourg, dignitaries from France, and Prince Bernhard of the Netherlands – and to mark our close links with his country – the Mayors of Arnhem and Renkum. After passing through security screens we assembled in the Old Library for the unveiling of Terence Cuneo's picture *'The Paras are landing'*. This artist, known for his pictorial signature, a tiny mouse, had first painted for the Regiment in 1950 when he was commissioned to portray the Presentation of

Colours by King George VI to the three regular parachute battalions at Aldershot.

As the Lord Mayor of London entered the Great Hall to the fanfare of the trumpeters of the Household Cavalry, and led the principal guests to their places at the Top Table, we lesser mortals saluted their procession as tradition required by clapping our hands in time to the music of the band aloft in the gallery.

The number and status of those attending and the prime target offered to terrorist attack meant that the measures taken to control admission to Guildhall and for the security of the whole area had to be unusually stringent. The planning for this event fell to Major Jeremy Hickman and me. It took us many days of visits to London, detailed discussions and a lot of paperwork (not least to ensure that everyone knew where to find his seat, those of his friends and how to get there without difficulty). But it was a thoroughly enjoyable commitment, and we gratefully paid attention to the expert advice of the Remembrancer and his staff in Guildhall, of the Police and the caterers: and the fact that John Holland, the Honorary Colonel of 10 PARA, was a Big Wheel in Guildhall affairs and a colleague of the Lord Mayor greatly smoothed our activities in the City of London.

On that February evening the contrast between the embellished scarlet of the Mess uniforms and the bemedalled black dinner jackets, the historic setting, the efficient table service and the fine spirit of comradeship all combined to enhance the sense of privilege we felt at having been brought together there, in the heart of London. It was an occasion with many high-spots; crowned perhaps by the warmth of the Lord Mayor's speech of welcome and the wit and elegance of Geoffrey Howlett's response.

It was Mike Gray's idea that we produce a special postage stamp, so we approached the Postal & Courier Service of the Royal Engineers at Mill Hill, in the former depot of the Middlesex Regiment. Those helpful people introduced to us Group Captain Bill Randall, a highly decorated Bomber Command pilot and the leading light in the Joint Services Philatelic Society. The result of this happy collaboration was the production of an attractive and informative series of commemorative covers, on each of which the art-work of Tony Theobald, a gifted illustrator from Reading, depicted a major event in the history of British airborne forces. We produced the covers in four editions; the most expensive (at £5.25p) being a Special Edition limited to one thousand covers individually numbered and signed by a distinguished warrior; the first one was signed by Sir Winston Churchill's grandson. The complete series of twenty-six covers was issued during the next four years and was distributed by our Philatelic Retailer Sergeant, Graham Hutton. They sold well and we are confident that the whole series, especially the Special Limited Edition with its informative inserts, will be widely recognised as a unique presentation of our history and for collectors a rewarding asset.

The profits from this and other PARA 90 projects were donated to airborne charities. Our Golden Jubilee naturally presented an opportunity for energetic money-raising to boost the Airborne Forces Security Fund set up soon after the war for the benefit of our Old Comrades and their dependents, and we watched with admiration the drive and skill with which General Glyn Gilbert and his team of volunteers coaxed generous donations out of a British public at a time of financial pessimism when the national economy was in the doldrums.

In 1992 the Isle of Man Post Office Authority honoured The Parachute Regiment by producing a set of six stamps, also designed by Tony Theobald, illustrating the principal campaigns in which the Regiment had fought. If I have written at length about PARA 90, an anniversary significant only to a small and very young part of the British Army, I have done so because that was an enjoyable episode in my life; and a rewarding one too. In June 1992 I was admitted into the Freedom of the City of London in a brief and undemanding ceremony in Guildhall, after which my family took me out for a slap-up lunch in a famous restaurant in the Strand.

Rosemary and I had visited Spain during the spring break as we were keen to see the Moorish legacy in Andalucia. On the way south we spent a couple of nights with Betty Hewitt, Sir John's widow, who was living near Madrid with her son, Jonathan and his Spanish wife, Carmen. Cordoba and Grenada were spectacular, and Seville in particular made us aware of the strength and wealth of 16th-century Spain; and we marvelled at the impertinence of Queen Elizabeth's England in challenging the might of the empire of Charles V and Philip II – and winning.

We also remarked on our bus journey from Madrid to Andalucia through the province of Murcia on the sweep and emptiness of the landscape, and I could not but reflect on the scope it offered for the military training of NATO's forces in contrast to the difficulty of securing adequate space for manoeuvres and gunnery in Britain and West Germany.

In October 1990 Rosemary set off with a cousin to revisit briefly the land of her birth, Guyana. She so enjoyed her days back among her childhood surroundings that she went back again in January for three weeks and took me with her. We had to break the journey in Barbados where there was a muddle about our onward flight as the computer recording aircraft seat reservations had ceased to function, but we eventually arrived and headed straight for Shanklands, a settlement on the east bank of the wide Essequibo river about eighty miles inland from Georgetown.

Shanklands had been cleared out of the tropical jungle by a remarkable woman of Canadian parentage, Joanne Jardim. Her Father had bought the area for its quarrying potential but he died leaving to her that bit of dense jungle. Joanne and her husband, Max, an engineer employed in Georgetown, cut a trail up from the river bank and over a period of many years cleared a space about the size of a football field and on it built a house for themselves and a couple of guest houses. As Max was away except at weekends, Joanne worked on alone, sleeping in the jungle and taking care to avoid tarantula nests and snakes. It was hard, hard physical work and people spoke of her as 'the mad white woman on the hill', and she described to us how at the beginning the bush was so thick that there was no room for a tent, so she used to sling a hammock between two trees and cover herself with a sheet of plastic. Later she brought to the cleared area pieces of grass from her garden in Georgetown and planted them each week; and after the grass she planted fruit trees and flowers which she transplanted from the surrounding jungle. The resultant scene is one of great beauty and the buildings are well furnished and comfortable. To have done all this virtually singlehandedly is no mean achievement, but as Joanne tells everyone: 'I love the jungle, I love it'. There really is nothing like the tranquillity of Shanklands where we spent five very pleasant days before going to stay with my wife's relations near Mahaicony and in Georgetown on the low-lying coastal belt.

When we left England we had half-expected that we would find a nice house in Guyana and be able to settle down there in retirement. The climate is congenial, the country large and beautiful and richly endowed by Nature. Moreover, with the local currency, the Guyanese dollar, so weak one could live out there on a British Army pension in great style. We were rapidly disenchanted; the Republic of Guyana was in a deplorable state, slumped to the bottom of the Third World pile due to Marxism, the mass emigration of the educated and crime. It was a lamentable experience for those who had known the country as British Guiana.

Because the 91st had been stationed there in 1953-54 I wrote on my return in 1991 an article for the Regimental Magazine, 'The Thin Red Line', and I reprint it as Appendix IX to this book to show the sad state to which that country had sunk during her first twenty-five years of independence.

By erasing from our minds any notion of settling in Guyana, Providence did us a great kindness. On the way home we spent a week in Barbados in a flat lent to us by friends and on our first morning we were introduced to an English family who had just decided to sell their house in the parish of Christ Church. Size, position, contents, garden, view and price, it all constituted an opportunity far too good to pass up. Rosemary and I sat on the seawall outside Colonel Sanders' Fried Chicken restaurant and had a long discussion, a discussion in which I trotted out every negative argument I could think up against settling down outside Britain. After I had reduced my poor wife to tears we went back to the owners and made an offer which they accepted. Back in England I contacted my bank where Bob Stay put together for us a financial package. Within the month the house and its contents were ours. The vendors were an elderly couple, a farming family from Humberside who asked only one thing of us: 'Please do not take over the house before the middle of April because we would like to have a final holiday, with our offspring here, during that month'. 'No problem,' I replied, 'for I shall be with my regiment in Aldershot until the twelfth of April and we shall need a day or two for final packing and so on'. While I finished my stint at RHQ, Rosemary selected the stuff we needed out in our new home, engaged packers and persuaded our son to move into our Barnes house. I left Browning Barracks and on 18 April 1991 we emplaned at Gatwick and eight hours later landed at Grantley Adams Airport in Barbados. After a night in the Ocean View, the island's oldest hotel, we moved into 6 Sheraton Park (which we named Fintry after the village in West Stirlingshire from which our bit of the Graham clan sprang). Two days later we gave a party for some twenty people, mostly friends whom Rosemary and I had known forty years previously and who had quit republican Guyana for the more congenial surroundings of Barbados. The couple from whom we bought the house could not join us; Eric Godfrey had died ten days before we arrived of a heart attack while swimming at the Yacht Club, His wife died later that year in England.

Our arrival in 'Bimshire' coincided with the brief Gulf War and the eviction from Kuwait of the Iraqi invaders; also with the transmutation of the Soviet Union[5] into a Commonwealth of Independent States and the end of the Cold War. This, a bloodless victory of momentous significance, was a fine reward for the firmness of purpose sustained for more than four decades by the nations of the North Atlantic Treaty Organisation. The 20th century would surely have been less calamitous if the members of the League of Nations had acted with similar prudence and unity.

Rosemary and I have now been living in Barbados for eight years; the longest period of unbroken contentment and well-being in our lives. Our move to the Caribbean was no sudden impulsive act. I only realised this when, leafing through my diaries, I saw that I had written twenty years earlier as our ship sailed away from Bridgetown on 20 April 1971: 'After a morning tour of the island and a lunch on the west coast at the Discovery Bay Inn, about nine miles north of Bridgetown – quite excellent in every way with beach, pool, food and superb flowers and humming birds in the garden – we returned down the coast passing attractive villas. This is a wonderfully tempting place to retire to. I must try to make it possible for we have all quite fallen in love with Barbados'. We have not been disappointed; though we were taken aback when completing the formalities to be granted Permanent Residence. We were required to sign two forms; Rosemary's in which she undertook not to indulge in prostitution; mine that I would not attempt to overthrow the government by force. I could write a book about our first years in Barbados but the following observations must suffice here as evidence of our contentment in 'Little England, Bimshire, Paradise' – people call her by a variety of names.

It is natural that I should make a point of studying the contributions made by West Indians to Britain's Armed Forces in the two World Wars and in our country's earlier battles for supremacy in the Caribbean. Their loyalty to the land they called 'The Mother Country' and the price paid in lives by the Royal Navy and by our regiments are ignored in modern Britain. Moreover, whenever I arrive back at Gatwick Airport, it disturbs me to see passing smoothly through the channel marked 'European Community Passport Holders' citizens of states whose traditional hostility has cost my country much in blood and treasure, whereas citizens of Barbados, now independent but still members of our Commonwealth family, are obliged to queue for interrogation at the 'tradesman's entrance' to the United Kingdom.

In Barbados the welcome given to visitors from Britain stands in contrast to the cold, unChristian reception endured in English streets by the coloured West Indian men recruited to replenish the depleted UK labour force in the post-war decade, and by their wives who forsook their sunnier homes across the Atlantic to join them.

I am often asked two questions. One is: 'Don't you miss the Army?'. My regret on leaving Aldershot, the Home of the British Army, was soon eclipsed by the Barbados Defence Force whose Commander, Brigadier Rudyard Lewis, and his Officers welcomed us into their hospitable Mess and to the parades and ceremonies in which the BDF and the Cadet Corps by their bearing and élan enhance the pride of the Bajan population. The other question is: 'Do you have enough to fill your days?'. Of course, Rosemary and I now have to spend less time on household chores and weeding the garden, for we have two caring servants whose smiling faces complement the sunshine this island enjoys almost every day of the year. We have made some ambitious improvements to the house. This work is carried out by a remarkable craftsman, a self-taught Bajan (who also manages a cricket team). Working alone from first light until dusk, he seems never to pause in his labours to drink, eat or even to spend pennies. His workmanship is immaculate and his fees low. The world could do with more men of the calibre of Winston Hewitt. He, like Ophelia our maid and Vinny the gardener, are more than friends; members of the family really. Because the island is small – no bigger than the Isle of Wight – and hospitable, many evenings are filled with parties, film shows or the excellent cultural events such as the Opera Season run annually at Holders House by John and Wendy Kidd. Our days in fact pass too rapidly, for Rosemary with her painting and writing and, because the pension goes further here than in the UK, with planning the next entertainment or expedition. As for me, I have found myself roped willingly into local organisations such as the Barbados Legion[6], the Royal Commonwealth Society, setting up an Environmental Protection Trust,[7] researching Britain's military heritage in the Caribbean, and lecturing. And when the children come out to stay, the time passes even more quickly.

Barbados is in truth an agreeable place[8] in which to drop anchor after a full life of soldiering; and in which to get married . . . I write this because a high point in our time here was the wedding of our son, Christopher, to Tia Brus in St James's Parish Church, their Reception at 'Fathoms' with the Caribbean waves softly lapping the sandy shore under a full moon, and the party the next day at Coral Point, so different with the thunder of the Atlantic breaking against the east coast rocks. We are lucky to find ourselves in this happy, well administered island. Whatever changes lie in her future – and change is inevitable – nothing can take away from us our memories of our first eight years in Barbados[9], nor of past long years doing worthwhile things in interesting places in the company of splendid Service colleagues.

In an earlier chapter I have mentioned the continuity and the eccentricity of change. The first years of this twentieth century saw conflict and bloodshed in north and south Africa, in the Balkans, in eastern Turkey and in the Far East; and in Russia especially growing turmoil. The century's last years are witnessing wars in central and west Africa, in the Balkans, in the Persian Gulf and in central Asia; and in Russia confusion and despair anew. So perhaps little has changed.

Nevertheless the cataclysms of the two World Wars, brought about principally by the aggressive energies of a united German nation, have not been repeated. The fears of the peoples of western Europe and the resolute policies of their governments have ensured that. Thus the prayer of those of us who passed in the heat of August 1944 through the destruction, the carnage and the stench of Normandy, that such things never be allowed to happen again, is being answered; at least in our part of the globe.

In other parts alas, mass-murder, genocide and ethnic cleansing continue, directed by wicked men. (Why is humanity's destiny so often shaped, not by heroes but by monsters?) The practice of indicting before an international tribunal those at whose hands, or on whose orders, outrageous crimes are committed, is surely an essential step towards a better world.

Some changes are bewildering however. As far as my personal experience is relevant, the most striking changes have occurred in the matters of money and morality. Not long ago, if the banks were shut, one had the devil of a job to obtain cash to see one through, say, a long week-end; it usually involved searching for a friendly shop-keeper willing to cash a cheque for five pounds. But now everyone, even adolescents with no identifiable qualifications or employment, is able by inserting a plastic card into a hole in a wall, to acquire at will large sums of money. Formerly the display of the naked body on the beach, on paper or on the cinema screen was prohibited, and full-fronted nudity and the portrayal of sexual intercourse caused outrage. Nowadays these things are on universal exhibition; whole branches of literature, of commerce and of television are lawfully devoted specifically to pornography and erotic titillation. And by the means of a novel system of communication, the stark details of the sexual antics of a President, politically successful but morally disgraced, of the United States of America have been revealed world-wide; even to school-children. It is all a bit perplexing; nor is it possible to foresee the social consequences of these recent revolutionary changes.

Thanks to enormous advances made in medicine, electronics, communications, information technology and air travel, and in our ability to enjoy these, most human beings are now living longer and happier lives. In the developed countries we are vastly more prosperous than were our grand-parents and much of life's daily grind has been removed. But for how long will Mankind tolerate the growing gap between the wealth of our rich countries and the poverty of the undeveloped, the degradation of the Earth's resources and the pollution of our Planet? To our heirs will fall the duty of devising effective and just solutions to these challenges.

I believe they will. The auguries are encouraging. The Young to-day are more caring, better informed and less impelled by Convention, Class or Nation. In ordering the affairs of the world's diverse peoples, and Mankind's relationships with Planet Earth (and with other planets too), those who come after us will do a better job than we have. And in their erratic, fitful, frustrating but ever-upward march through the 21st century, most prominent among the Standard Bearers will be Women.

Notes

1. The dynasty was founded in 1744 by the revered Imam Ahmad bin Said. Sultan Qaboos is the eighth in direct line of succession.
2. This omission is not surprising. In Britain what do we teach the young to-day about the fine British-Indian Army of the Raj, about the West India Regiments or of the Allied contingents who fought under British command in Normandy?
3. 1, 2 and 3 PARA Battalions and the Depot; and in the TA, 4, 10 and 15 (Scottish) PARA.
4. Colonel John Howard.
5. Called by President Reagan 'The Evil Empire'.
6. In May 1999 the Barbados Legion hosted a memorably successful Conference of the British Commonwealth Ex-Services League under the Grand Presidency of HRH Prince Philip, Duke of Edinburgh.
7. The Future Centre Trust, a non-profit organisation committed to creating a permanent stimulus to enhance the quality of life in Barbados, and to establish the island as a role model of sustainable development.
8. Granted Independence by Britain in 1966, a member of the Commonwealth but (in 1999) about to declare herself a republic: a symptom of the natural transformation of Barbados from 'Little England' and 'Bimshire' to . . .?
9. In large measure thanks to the kindness of friends from our British Guiana days, Tony and Terry Foster and Hammond and Barbara Farmer.

Epilogue

To be born English is to win first prize in the lottery of life.
Cecil Rhodes 1853–1902

(Will our heirs think likewise of their Britain?)

There is no greater risk than matrimony, but there is nothing happier than a happy marriage.
Benjamin Disraeli, 1st Earl of Beaconsfield 1804–1881

(on the marriage of Princess Louise, the first Colonel-in-Chief of the Argyll & Sutherland Highlanders, with the Marquis of Lorne)

Appendix I
Military Government in the British Zone of Germany, 1945–6

(reproduced from *Changing Enemies* by Noel Annan, 1995, by kind permission of the publishers, HarperCollins)

The mood of the British in May 1945 was bitter. They felt that no country had done more than Britain, indeed had done too much at Munich, in trying to meet Germany halfway towards its legitimate aspirations. In the twenties both the middle-aged and the young had been pulled emotionally towards Germany. The war veterans had formed lively 'No More War' Associations with their former foes; the unsophisticated young enjoyed Bavarian heartiness and respected the famous athlete Dr Peltzer; intellectuals lived in Hamburg and Berlin and admired the Bauhaus, the Expressionists, Ufa movies and Brecht-Weill. And what had been the result? Hitler. When the British contemplated the ruined German cities they felt hardly a twinge: they remembered only too well Nazi leaders and the Luftwaffe gloating over Coventry and a dozen other English cities. The Americans whose own homeland was unscathed found the non-fraternisation policy impossible to follow – they were too generous and outgoing. The British did not find it all that hard. They entered Germany believing that the Germans had got what they deserved and that this time, unlike in 1918, they were going to be made to feel the yoke, to submit, to acknowledge that they had been militarily defeated. This time the legend, put about by the Freikorps after 1918, that the German army had not been defeated but had been betrayed by a stab in the back, must be buried. Had not the Germans started five wars within the space of a century? Did not the lesson of history teach us that Prussian *Junkertum* was the seat of German militarism? Prussia therefore should be destroyed.

There was another dimension to British anger: the Holocaust. The discovery of Belsen on 15 April showed how the Nazis had exterminated political prisoners and hostages. That was only the prelude to the discovery of what had occurred in the concentration camps in east Germany and Poland. It took some time, however, for the enormity of Germany's crimes against the Jews to sink in. In Intelligence we knew of the gas ovens, but not of the scale, the thoroughness, the bureaucratic efficiency with which Jews had been hunted down and slaughtered. No one at the end of the war, as I recollect, realised that the figure of Jewish dead ran into millions. Yet the knowledge of Belsen alone did not make it hard for soldiers to accept the policy of non-fraternisation in the early days of the occupation, even though it became impracticable within a few weeks.

It became impracticable because almost at once the British came up against the brute facts of those terrible days. What were they to do in the country they now were ruling? Millions of people were on the move. Millions of displaced persons from all the countries which Germany had enslaved were on their way home or had decided that under no circumstances would they return home. Russian and Polish prisoners of war roamed the countryside: some took to rape and murder in revenge. In mid-August I attended a Military Government summary court and saw a Pole condemned to death for possessing arms and belonging to a raiding party – though the Commander in Chief had power to commute the sentence. Our troops who at first considered the Germans were getting just deserts became ever more sympathetic to them and hostile to the DPs when they had to turn out night after night to stop some affray.

It was not only the displaced persons who were on the move – millions of Germans expelled from Silesia and Czechoslovakia – or indeed by the British who had commandeered their homes – were moving from east to west. Countess Dönhoff, later to be editor of *Die Zeit*, made the journey from East Prussia to Hamburg on a horse. The two great canals were blocked. Trains crept over improvised bridges: only 650 out of 8000 miles of track were operating. You drove along roads where every few miles you met a sign, '*Umleitung*', and you were diverted down tracks and side-roads. The devastation of the bombed cities beggared description. Three out of four houses were destroyed, seven out of eight damaged and shattered. Scarcely a city of any size and importance had escaped. In Berlin the trees in the Tiergarten were cut down for firewood, and a familiar sight was of some wizened old man hauling a little cart with a few sticks in it, and of chains of men and women passing chunks of rubble from hand to hand in an attempt to clear a site. The spectacle of misery pervaded one's life. Calloused as our sensibility has become since then by the images on television and in the press, year in year out, of millions of human beings in Asia and Africa murdered or dispossessed in our brutal and violent century, the memory of Germany in defeat has never faded from my mind. Particularly since we, the new lords of creation, swept by in our cars bound for some snug mess remote from hunger and cold.

West Germany had been cut off from its natural source of food supply in the Russian zone and the Soviet authorities had no intention of releasing a morsel. When P.J. Grigg, Secretary of State for War, saw the man whom Montgomery appointed to be the Military Governor of the British zone, he told him he must resign himself to the fact that two million people would die of starvation in Europe after the war. General Sir Gerald Templer had no intention of resigning himself to any such calamity. He was a ruthless, incisive, dynamic commander, biting or disarming as occasion demanded. His smile was ferocious: like a wolf. As soon as he took over he sacked the dug-outs and failures who had been shunted into Military Government. He organised at once an operation to feed the Dutch who were on the verge of starvation. Then he got medicine and food to the concentration camps. Helping two and a half million displaced persons was his next concern. By June 1946 1.8 million had been repatriated. He then set up Operation Barleycorn, in which half a million German prisoners of war and women got in the harvest. When that was achieved he got German staff officers in the prisoner of war camps to identify former miners and recruit others to raise coal production – despite protests from the Russians in the Kommendatura that he was keeping the German army in being. Then he moved to provide pit-props and so on.

Templer's energy transformed the British zone. Military Government officers, who had previously spent happy hours commandeering the best houses and stocking up the messes with wine and schnapps, found themselves working late hours reconstituting the German administration and putting Templer's emergency plans into operation. Horses were gathered at three centres and sent by train to the main agricultural areas; 800 railway bridges and 7000 miles of track were repaired by the end of the year. But the food crisis did not disappear, the black market raged, and people left work to deal in it or went to the farms to barter their possessions.

Who were these new rulers in Germany whom Templer galvanised? Some were senior officers, generals and brigadiers, who a few months earlier had been commanding military units. Indeed during 1945 most of the Military Government detachments were manned by army officers, some like myself waiting to be demobilised. (German officials used to lament that no sooner had they learnt to work with a Military Government officer than he departed to resume his civilian life in Britain.) Then there were the civilians, many wearing ill-fitting uniforms and somewhat despised by the regular officers. Some were civil servants. Ministries had been asked to release experienced administrators, but few were willing to let their best men and women go when Britain was converting from a war to a peacetime economy. Others came from the Colonial Service. Some were young idealists who hoped for a lifetime career in the Control Commission – described by Con O'Neill of the Foreign Office as 'low-level zealots'. Quite a few, singularly lacking in zeal, were there for the pickings. This was hardly surprising, since to the fury of Ivone Kirkpatrick, the senior officer at the Foreign Office responsible for Germany, the Treasury insisted on one-year contracts and inadequate salaries.

APPENDIX II
A BALLAD OF TWO TROPIC NIGHTS
Prologue

That tropic night was humid. The trees wore a shroud of gloom.
A night that might entice malevolent beings from their tombs.
There was no breeze to bless that night; no stars, no moon shone down.
Death stalked her prey, night's natural child in her mother's soft black gown.
Oh darkest night, oh silent night, you watch and wait to see
The fate of a pair of lovers craving anonymity.
You foolish trusting lovers, you think this night your friend,
But you will learn her treachery before her term shall end.
You do not see her secret smile – your arms, your legs entangle –
For she has seen it all before, that fated love triangle.
She knows that in her darkest folds a darker Shadow stands
Concentrated rage and jealousy, a long knife in his hand.
No mercy in you, cruel night, you will not lift your veil
To warn unsuspecting lovers of what your dark entails.

Jaimie
(James-Jim)

Now Jaimie was a happy man – two children and a wife;
To him life was for living and he made the most of life.
No one could call him handsome and his problem was his weight
But it didn't seem to bother him – it was a family trait.
His strong asset was his nature, and he had a gentle smile;
He was loved by everybody be it woman, man or child.
He had a male attraction which few women could resist:
They always wanted to get closer, they wanted always to be kissed.
How could he disappoint them? Why should he anyway?
He was flattered by their flirting and delighted by their play.
He did no harm to anyone as far as he could guess
For the girls were all quite single; he wanted no marital mess.
As for his wife, they'd reached a state of mutual understanding,
She thought her family complete – so he was undemanding.

She refused to be a victim of an uncertain family plan;
Far better to be quite sure and impose a total ban.
They thought fondly of each other, but each had their lives to live:
Their interests were separate, and their marriage take and give.
But their mistress was Convention for it was clearly understood
There were rules that she dictated and follow them they would.
To all his peccadilloes a blind eye would be turned,
If together and in public their marriage was not spurned.

Then with no warning James fell ill, he had a bone disease;
He was taken into hospital and was openly displeased
For he was bored and he was listless, time hung heavy on his hands.
Then The Shadow came to see him, he'd arrived from distant lands.
Since this man was Jaimie's friend, when he heard he went to see
If he could cheer James up with laughter and cameraderie.
'You really do not look too bad – you're skiving, nothing more.
But wait till you hear my secret, you'll take notice, that's for sure.
I've met a most amazing girl, a little sex machine;
Last night was quite exhausting . . .' then he described the scene.
The Shadow kept on boasting, Jaimie thought he'd never cease,
He soon wished that he would leave him so he'd get a little peace.
He was completely discontented by the time The Shadow left;
To accept this role reversal made him totally bereft,
For in the past it had been Jaimie who would tell of some new find:
This man could never match him, now he was leaving him behind.
So next time he came to visit James invited him to bring
This new girl that was so special – 'Man, she must be quite something;'.

It was in this way fair Bella came into Jaimie's life,
An ill-starred introduction which led to fatal strife.
When she entered Jaimie's room it was clear from the way he looked
As she walked across to speak to him that Jaimie's goose was cooked.
They were instantly attracted, you could see it in their eyes;
Then Bella smiled and faced The Shadow – it was not good to advertise:
For The Shadow was a hard man, and she would have to watch her step.
But at having more than one string to her bow she was adept.
She sat close behind The Shadow, her long fingers caused him thrills,
Though her eyes were fixed on Jaimie she knew The Shadow paid her bills.
Their visit was a short one, soon he made a move to stand;
James though knew that they would meet again from the pressure of her hand.
Some days elapsed, then she called James. She said 'He's gone at last:
I'm coming round to see you'. And the fatal die was cast.

PONDER ANEW

The Shadow

The Shadow was a man of power in each and every way,
A power which he relished and would wield from day to day.
His origins were humble, for he was a self-made man,
Determined from his childhood to be no 'also-ran'.
By the time that he met Jaimie he'd acquired a sailing ship:
He would sail between the islands finding firms to be equipped.
He got them what they wanted, they knew they could rely on him;
For he'd go to endless trouble, even risking life and limb.
He soon made himself a fortune, enough to buy a little fleet:
He had everything he wanted and he found that life was sweet.
There was power in his massive frame, being large and very tall:
No one ever dared to cross him for he towered over all.
No beauty in his swarthy face, his eyes were small and red
And though they never missed a thing they always seemed quite dead.
His effect on little children was to make them run and hide;
The moment he came into view they would be terrified.
Few women were attracted, for he loved to slap and maul,
But there was a girl in every port – he had the wherewithal.
His money brought him power too in each community:
He could get away with murder, for he could buy immunity.

It was at a large reception, while waiting for a drink,
That he heard a conversation which made him stop and think.
Two men referred to Jaimie, so he stood where he could hide,
One said: 'Jim's pretending that he's sick, but he's got a new girl on the side'.
'That man really is too much,' said the second man with laughter;
'This one's called Bella'. 'But I thought that it was Rose that he was after.'
'Rose is history,' said the first: 'Belle's got a hold of Jim.
Last time I went to visit she was sitting close to him.
They were embarrassed, and she left. I promised not to tell:
James said he couldn't help it – he'd just looked at her and fell.
He'd met her through a mutual friend – I think he is a sailor
Who is giving her financial help – but James says he's not her gaoler.'

They laughed, and then The Shadow left, with stealth he slipped away;
He knew that he had heard enough, there was little more to say.
The rage that grew within him made him shake and drip with sweat.
That pair had made a fool of him and he would repay that debt.
This was a new experience for he'd thought no one would dare
To 'invade his territory' when The Shadow was not there.
He gave the matter careful thought, then telephoned a man

Who was given detailed orders to initiate a plan.
This man was told to monitor each move the lovers made
With special need to be discreet; not to make them feel afraid.

The Shadow did not want to leave, but he knew he must set sail.
He felt apprehensive of this man in case he was blackmailed.
It was a risk that must be taken, for his feelings deep inside
Would lead to consequences which must be justified.
He made a point of phoning James to say a warm goodbye,
A thing he'd never done before. James vaguely wondered why.
Then off to visit Bella with a costly farewell gift
But as she waved goodbye to him she felt her spirits lift.
He'd told her it would be two months before he could return.
She wondered how he'd take it if by chance he ever learned.
The thought was but a fleeting one – replaced by the delight
Of anticipating what she would experience that night.

Bella

Bella as a young girl was fat and rather plain.
In a gesture that was positive her parents chose her name:
They hoped she might become that name and Belle was sure of this
And set about to organise her metamorphosis.
She worked hard to improve her looks in each and every way,
And by the time she reached her teens she saw her efforts pay.
Belle found she could attract the boys, they swarmed around like flies;
To her it was irrelevant that girls would ostracize.
Their jealousy would please her more than the conquests that she made.
They called her names like 'pro' and 'tart' and pretended to be staid.
Her stunning figure cried for sex – full breasts and hips to sway.
But it was a close friend of her father who first 'took her all the way'.
He had held her as a baby, watched her grow, her figure soften;
Then their usual games lost innocence and Belle flirted once too often.
Bella didn't miss her chance and quickly made it clear
Her father would be furious to learn what he'd been doing there.
Then with a smile she reassured him, Father didn't have to know,
But she badly needed a new dress and she simply could not sew.
The hint was duly taken, her dress was shocking pink
Which she plausibly explained before her family could think.
This was the start, and then she found each man was like the rest;
Soon payment was demanded for the thing that she did best.
There was very little pleasure in this immorality
And she longed to find a man to love in true totality.

Ponder Anew

As time went by she ceased to count the men she knew and used:
She found them all despicable and felt her ego bruised.
She dreamed about a man who would be wise and very rich
And handsome, strong and gentle – such a man she could bewitch.
But it was hardly likely that Prince Charming would be found,
And being now well over thirty it was time to settle down.
She considered her new suitor and recalled the deep disgust
That she had felt when she experienced his crude and cruel lust.
But he made her life so easy – he would grant her every wish –
A new house, expensive jewellery or some rare exotic dish
Would be hers for just the asking. But there was a price to pay
By forced enactment of his fantasies or some sordid new display.

Then one day he came to see her looking pleased and very smug:
'I've got a friend in hospital,' he said giving her a hug,
'And I'm taking you to see him – I want you to look your best
For we must leave him really jealous. Now hurry and get dressed!'
When Bella later thought of this she decided life was strange,
She'd wanted to refuse to go but feared he might become deranged
With his apoplectic temper, for to anger he was quick,
But the one thing that she hated was visiting the sick.
Her reward was meeting Jaimie: she had felt her senses reel,
The attraction had been mutual – and that couple's fate was sealed.
When The Shadow sailed that day his dark face wore a frown.
His men were fairly used to this but wondered what had got him down.
They decided to avoid him – he could be a violent man
And needed very little reason for him to find a hide to tan.
He must complete his business soon so that he could return,
The report would then be ready and he wondered just what he would learn.
He thought he knew what it would say, that thought made him incensed.
How did they DARE to cheat him: his entire body tensed.

Meanwhile the lovers were oblivious to all except each other;
Their meetings now were more relaxed, they felt they needn't bother.
Neither suspected they were watched, they met each time they could
And Jaimie was recovered: so life felt very good.

The Shadow quietly returned, this time he came by 'plane.
As he listened to his spy's report he felt he was insane
But he kept his eyes averted lest his feelings he impart
And the man did not suspect that there was murder in his heart.
Then The Shadow watched the lovers for perhaps a week or so;
He learnt the hour they chose to meet and knew where they would go.

Each night he watched their movements, though he kept well out of sight;
Each night his rage intensified, his stomach got more tight
Until he thought his head would burst. He knew he could take no more,
That he must stop this treachery he was absolutely sure.
On that final, tragic night he chose his blade with care;
His movements were mechanical – he was in his own nightmare.
The night was very dark and it was all as he had planned.
Then he thought it was too easy as he watched them on the sand.
When he was close enough to touch them he heard Bella give a sigh.
That was all his anger needed; and he let his cutlass fly.

The Shadow never could remember how he got home that night.
Next day he learned that James was dead, but Bella was all right.
That day Bella got a 'phone call which made her feel more weak;
The voice said, 'If you want to live, then Bella DO NOT SPEAK!'.
Consequently Belle saw nothing, it was dark and she was dazed;
What was the point of telling? for the dead could not be raised.
They found a former felon and they tried him just for show,
But there was nothing to convict him and they had to let him go.
Some friends had their suspicions but they minded what they said:
Better to suppress such thoughts and sleep safe in their beds.

Epilogue

Another black and starless night but now a different scene.
The Shadow fights to save his ship, that other night a dream.
The wind is now no blessing, it shrieks and howls and whips
Black storm clouds with their lashing rains that drench the tossing ship.
The sea is wild and angry with giant threatening waves
And illusions of dead sailors rising from their briny graves.
The Captain screams his orders at his scared and sullen crew,
He ignores their deep resentment which after all is nothing new.
Their cargo was too heavy, they had warned him from the start;
The ship sailed low in the water, and he knew this in his heart.
He'd insisted they accept the load for its value was immense;
The reward was great, the risk was slight, it seemed to make good sense.
On board there was a passenger – this man was a young priest.
Though his crew thought this unlucky he didn't worry in the least.
There had also been a warning of a fearsome hurricane
But The Shadow sailed regardless; he enjoyed a stormy main.

The Bosun gave the situation his deepest scrutiny;
He knew the men had had a meeting and were now talking mutiny.
The heavy load must be reduced or every man would drown;
He must approach the Captain; he would have to stand his ground.
But the Bosun's pleas for safety were instantly refused.
As he left the stubborn Captain he knew the man's power was abused,
So the crew removed that power. They took their Captain without a sound,
They tied him up, bore him below and there they nailed him down.
All pulled away in lifeboats far from the scooner's final dip;
They'd refused to take the priest with them as they abandoned ship.
By dawn the storm abated, the sea was calm and blue.
The ship had gone, her cargo lost, but the crew's boats had pulled through.

The story of The Shadow's death is whispered to this day,
How on another tropic night Retribution had her way.

REG
1993

Appendix III
A MULATTO'S PRAYER

Make me a bridge, O Lord my God, between the different races.
Help me to reach the hearts and minds of those with different faces.

From the first day that I knew myself I never could quite see
Why God had made me different, with no real identity.
Though other friends were like me there was no one quite the same;
We were the rainbow children and they called us many names:
Mulatto – coloured – half-caste, we came in every shade
From nearly black to nearly white, our racial mix displayed.
My parents and grandparents, and their parents too, were mixed.
But I longed to be a single race and have my colour fixed.
Why was I not a maiden fair, a girl from Camelot,
With porcelain skin and large round eyes like blue forget-me-nots?
But O my pale-skinned forebears from far off shores of mist,
Was the lure of King Cane's tropic gold just too hard to resist?
You came, you saw, you conquered, you spread the seed about
To leave behind a harvest of plantocracy fall-out.

Why was I not a beauty black whose dark eyes made reflections,
With body tall and slim and lithe; pure ebony perfection?
But O my dark-skinned forebears, the choice was never yours;
You were brought across the ocean from your distant sunlit shores.
Did you send your maids to Massa to ward off some mishap?
Or was a light-skinned pick'nee a feather in your cap?
So here I am, a sort of brown, not one thing or the other,
With curly hair that all my life has caused a lot of bother.
The names they used to call me are no longer infra dig:
Should I call myself a 'Nigger-Honk' or perhaps a 'Honky-Nig'?
Though words no longer have the power a lovely day to mar,
Did You have a special plan for us, Your people 'touched with tar'?
So
Make me a bridge, O Lord my God, between the different races.
Help me to reach the hearts and minds of those with different faces.

REG
Christ Church
May 1993

Appendix IV
LIEUTENANT-COLONEL SAID SALEM AL WAHAIBI: AN OUTLINE BIOGRAPHY

He was born on 1 May 1936 in the Wadi Assarain where his Father, a farmer, had about one acre of stony but well irrigated land on which he raised crops and goats to sustain his family. He died young, leaving a widow and two sons of whom Said, then aged 3½, was the elder. Two years after her husband's death, Said's Mother re-married and produced two more sons, Habib and Salem, and two daughters. One daughter died but the surviving one, Salmu, and her brothers are still (in 1998) living in Oman. The family was cared for by an uncle. From the age of six Said used to walk once a month with this uncle to Muscat. The journey took twelve hours and the boy stayed there, while his uncle worked in the fields, before making his way back to Assarain on foot. When Said was 12 his uncle died and Said became the bread-winner for the family.

In April 1952 Said, aged 16, left the family homestead and set out for Sohar, once a flourishing seaport and still an important centre of administration and commerce on the northern part of the Batinah coast. There he got a job working for an Indian contractor, Pardhan Singh, who was building a camp for the Sultan's army beside a fine residence, Kashmir House, which an uncle of the Sultan had earlier constructed. Pardhan Singh employed young Said as his labour foreman.

1952 brought the beginning of a period in which problems of increasing seriousness were to beset the Sultanate; a depressed economy and rebellions in the Interior, and later in the southern province of Dhofar, both fuelled by the repressive, autocratic rule of Sultan Said bin Taimur and stimulated and supported by regimes in neighbouring countries. Oman's 'period of darkness' – as Qaboos Bin Said was to call it – did not end until he took over from his father as Sultan eighteen years later. The Buraimi oasis, a fertile area divided between Oman and Abu Dhabi and an important trading centre, was coveted by the Saudis who occupied it illegally and installed, as Wali at Hamasa, Turki bin Atashan. In the Sultanate the Imam, based in the great round fort in Nizwa, the capital of the Interior, was at that time Mohammed Abdullah Al Khalili. The reaction to that incursion of Sultan Said bin Taimur, who spent most of his time far away in greener and cooler Dhofar, was to assemble some twenty thousand armed followers and a detachment from his tiny army, with the intention of driving the Saudis out of Buraimi. The British Political Resident in the Persian Gulf, Sir Rupert Hay, anxious lest the Sultan should be defeated in the imminent encounter, ordered the Consul-General in Muscat, Leslie Chauncy, to follow the Sultan and persuade him to call off all military action and to allow the problem to be settled by negotiation.

At the same time, October 1952, there also arrived in Sohar a British soldier who was to devote the rest of his life to the Sultanate and its armed forces. Colin Maxwell has left an account of his arrival in the camp of Said bin Taimur. 'Having flown from Bahrain to Sharjah, I was taken in a landrover of the Trucial Oman Levies to a wadi which lay on the way to Sohar. The area was packed with tribesmen on camels; Mohammed Muhanna was there with a detachment of the Abriyin and there were representatives of most of the other tribal groups. Also in Sohar were some Muscat Infantry from Bait al Falaj. They had screw-guns – something out of Kipling – a few landrovers and three-ton Bedford lorries. Colonel Boulter was in charge of this group. I was then taken to Kashmir House where there were three tents. Sultan Said was in one, Seyyid Ahmad Ibrahim was in the second and the third was reserved for me. Sheikh Shakhbut of Abu Dhabi was also in Sohar, having joined forces with Sultan Said. Soon after,' Maxwell's report continues,' Leslie Chauncy arrived with a letter from PRPG in Bahrain. He saw the Sultan. There was then a three-day pause . . . Delivering that letter must have been very hard on Chauncy; one of the criticisms levelled against him was that he was more Omani than was proper for a representative of HMG. The Sultan was bitter about the episode and unhappy at having to bow to force majeure'.

The next year, in February 1953, Colin Maxwell was instructed by the Sultan to raise a new unit for the army, the Batinah Force. He wrote thus about his activities. 'I was responsible for everything to do with the Batinah Force, including recruiting and training . . . The Sultan gave me a particular area from which I could recruit, the Wadi Jizzi to the Wadi Hawasina, both Arabs and indigenous Baluch. As guidance the Sultan had said to me: 'We cannot offer the recruits very much money, but I can provide you with letters to some of the sheikhs to assist you'. I went first to Sheikh Sultan bin Saif of the Hawasina, so a large number of that tribe joined the Force . . . St John Armitage who came to Oman about nine months after my own arrival was my second-in-command. We had to do everything from scratch'.

At that time the Sultan's army consisted of three separate units whose activities and administration were not coordinated. They were:

– The Muscat and Oman Field Force (MOFF) later renamed the Oman Regiment
– The Muscat Infantry, descended from the Muscat Levy Corps and which was to become The Muscat Regiment
– The Batinah Force for which recruiting began in June 1953 and which was to be renamed The Northern Frontier Regiment.

By now Said Salem Al Wahaibi had married a local girl, Sheikha, who was to bear him five sons: Abdul Aziz, Salem, Hamed, Khalid and Ibrahim. While working in the Sohar camp he took a close interest in the military activities around him, studied the recruits at drill and weapon training and he became keen to enlist. Colin Maxwell had noticed this young, sharp-eyed observer and was not surprised when Said Salem approached him and asked to be allowed to join up. Armitage however persuaded Maxwell that Said would be of greater service if left in charge of the labour force, so his request was denied. But not for long. In August Armitage went on leave and on 1 September 1953 the lad from the Wadi Assarain, aged 17, was enlisted with Maxwell's blessing, into the Batinah Force. His pay was forty rupees a month. In fact the Medical Orderly, Darwish, initially rejected him for being under-nourished but that hitch too was overcome. Two army posts were formed by Batinah Force at the start of 1954, at Shinas and in the Wadi Jizzi. Said served first at Shinas and then returned to Sohar where he helped to support St John Armitage who faced a mutiny in January 1954. The mutiny was overcome and in June 1954 Said went to the Wadi Jizzi. Armitage soon afterwards left to go down to Salalah where he raised a private army for the Sultan, The Dhofar Force.

Said had an aptitude for soldiering. This was noticed by his superiors and after two months he was promoted to the rank of Lance-Corporal, and eight weeks later to Corporal. After twelve months in that rank he was made Sergeant. These rapid promotions caused some jealousy among his Hawasina comrades and Said still recalls the bad attitude towards him of an NCO from that tribe, Said Mohammed Humaid. This NCO attempted to steal a rifle from Said when he was Guard Commander, but when he failed he took a rifle from the other NCO who was asleep, intending that the blame would fall on Said. Maxwell and Armitage realised that an attempt was being made to discredit Said and the Sergeant was reduced to the ranks.

At the end of 1954 the Sultan's army was organised as follows:

– The Muscat & Oman Field Force commanded by Lieutenant-Colonel Percy Coriat numbered about 150 all ranks
– The Muscat Infantry, under Pat Waterfield, about 200 all ranks
– The Batinah Force under Colin Maxwell about 100.

In 1954 Imam Mohammed died and was succeeded by Ghalib bin Ali of the Bani Hina tribe. Ghalib took the opportunity, while MOFF was away at Duqm in the south-east of the country, to attack Ibri and replace the Wali. Three Sheikhs there, Mohammed bin Abdulla Al Yakobi, Hamed bin Saif Al Kibani and Ali bin Halal Al Duri, ran away and sought refuge with Sheikh Zaid of Abu Dhabi. It soon became clear that the real leader of this insurrection was not Ghalib but his more dynamic and astute Brother, Talib. MOFF was moved back to the Ibri area in order to reestablish for the Sultan contact with the other local Sheikhs. Said bin Taimur's orders to Colonel Coriat, a decorated veteran of World War I, can be summarised as: 'Keep the army in the background but find out what the situation is'. His agents reported that the population would welcome the presence of the army.

It was decided to get rid of Ghalib and Talib and concurrently to oust the Saudis from Buraimi, and operations to this end were put in train. Sergeant Said Salem was on the spot when a rebel attack on the customs post in the Wadi Jizzi was repulsed; an attack which Maxwell attributed to a local tribe acting in support of the Saudis.

He has written: 'The Trucial Oman Levies drove the Saudis out of Buraimi with Richard Anderson's B Squadron of MOFF in support'. Farther south operations were launched to clear the Nizwa-Rostaq area of Talib's rebel bands. In December 1955 while MOFF moved against Nizwa, which they captured without a shot being fired, the Batinah Force had the diversionary task of advancing on Rostaq and Hazm in order to prevent Talib from going to help his Brother in Nizwa. Maxwell has written: 'We had about six weeks' notice for that operation. The Sultan gave no direct orders, there was no elaborate coordination with MOFF's move against Nizwa, but I got to know that something was in the works'. Batinah Force took Rostaq in an operation lasting three days in which Said Salem, now a Staff-Sergeant, has described how Talib's supporters kept up a sporadic fire from the high ground to the north of the town until that area too, the Qur'm al Araid, was occupied on the fourth day. Talib fled to Saudi Arabia while his Brother, Ghalib, driven out of Nizwa, took refuge in Balad Sait.

With the occupation of Buraimi, Nizwa and Rostaq the authority of Sultan Said bin Taimur was reestablished over the Interior. The Sultan's Brother, Seyyid Tariq bin Taimur, came to Rostaq and installed as Wali Sheikh Hilal bin Hamed al Sammar. The Sultanate of Muscat and Oman, (the official name of the country at that time), was then to enjoy a brief period of peace. Batinah Force was deployed to Sohar, where Said Salem went initially, and Buraimi; and it was shortly thereafter renamed The Northern Frontier Regiment. The army too was reorganised with Pat Waterfield becoming (in Maxwell's words) 'a sort of ground administrative commander', and a training centre was set up.

In June 1957 Said Salem was promoted Warrant Officer Class II and appointed CSM of A Company NFR, commanded by a former Royal Marine, Douglas Pope, with which he was to see much active service and enhance his reputation as one of Oman's outstanding soldiers. While he was in Buraimi, then also occupied by the Trucial Oman Scouts (formerly Levies), a fresh uprising in the Interior was being planned; one which was to have far-reaching consequences for the Sultanate and for the Sultan's sole ally, Britain.

Suleiman bin Himyar, the self-styled Lord of the Green Mountain and the paramount sheikh of the Bani Riyam, was a moody, brooding man in his fifties, frequently ill (from a mental disease or from alcohol Said Salem believes). Seduced perhaps by Saudi money he wrote to Ghalib and Talib, now reunited in Saudi Arabia, urging them 'to come back and defeat the Sultan'. Talib returned secretly to Oman with some two hundred men whom he had trained and equipped with the help of his Saudi hosts. When the news of his reappearance on Sultanate soil reached Said bin Taimur, he ordered MOFF to engage and defeat them. When it was confirmed that Talib had arrived in Balad Sait and was provoking the tribesmen to attack Nizwa, Bill Cheeseman, the CO of MOFF, decided to take the attack to Balad Sait. He had been led to believe that the Abriyin were loyal to the Sultan and could be relied on to hold the rocky pass through which MOFF would have to pass. But the opposition turned out to be more effective and determined than MOFF had bargained for.

Cheeseman's force consisted of two companies of MOFF with mortars and machine-guns and two 75-mm screw-guns, but without the support of the Abriyin he was outnumbered. After he and Talib had faced each other at Balad Sait for about a week, Cheeseman realised that the defenders were better armed and disciplined than expected; furthermore that the rebels were cutting him off from his base at Firq, the other side of Nizwa, and that the tracks between Al Hamra and Firq had been mined. As a young officer, Philip Allfree, was to relate: 'MOFF was trapped . . . quite clearly there was only one thing to do. They must fight their way out, back to their base. The story of this retreat was both frightful and magnificent. The distance was about twenty miles of mountainous defiles and boulder-strewn tracks, and streets winding through villages where every window, every garden wall was alive with Arabs, eyes screwed to their sights and fingers bent on the trigger. The temperature was about 120 degrees Fahrenheit, the force's trucks were ambushed and blown up on mines, drivers abandoned their vehicles and made for the hills . . . for the rest, some died in the waterless blistering rocks as they wandered away from the firing; others were taken by Talib'. Other accounts tell of how the retreat became increasingly disorganised as the soldiers came under fire from groups of Talib's men and the local tribesmen joining in the fighting on their side. Rumour and panic spread throughout the column and the cry went up: 'Everyone is against the Army', 'The whole country is fighting for the rebels', 'The enemy number many many thousands' and such like.

Out of this calamity few emerged with credit. The bravery displayed by Seyyid Tariq and Richard Anderson was however conspicuous and is still talked of with respect. Talib, Ghalib and Suleiman planned to follow up this signal victory by attacking Ibri, Nizwa and eventually Muscat. As he gathered his remnant at the base camp, Bill Cheeseman, an experienced soldier who had fought with distinction against the Italians in Eritrea, decided that he could not hold Nizwa with what was left of his force; nor could he trust his remaining troops not to desert. He therefore fell back to Fahud, to the land of the loyal Duru.

For Said Salem, stationed with NFR at Ibri, the news of the MOFF debacle was not confirmed until he met some of the survivors at Adam: and it was not known in Muscat, from where the army's operations were controlled over the No 19 radio net, until Richard Anderson was flown in to report personally to the Sultan.

The situation was so serious that British forces in the region had to become involved. While the Sultan's forces were preparing to meet this new and alarming challenge, Venom aircraft of the Royal Air Force flew over rebel-held areas dropping leaflets containing threats of retribution by the Sultan against his opponents. These planes were shot at. The RAF were then ordered to attack with bombs and rockets, after warning, a number of villages suspected of being centres of the rebellion, but these air strikes merely increased the resolve and the defiance of the enemy. Wali Nizwa ran away from his post and sought safety in Ibri where his father was Wali. The Sultan's forces, less the remnants of MOFF at Fahud, were deployed with NFR concentrated together with the TOS at Ibri, and Muscat Regiment in the Sumail area. Brigadier JAR Robertson,

APPENDICES

the commander of the British land forces, flew in from Bahrain to assess the situation and advise the Sultan and HMG on what needed to be done. The year was 1957 and the month, August, was extremely hot. After assembling at Fahud, Maxwell's NFR and the TOS moved into the Firq area and, camped beside the wadi at Qaarsha, made preparations for an attack on that village. The attack was preceded by machine-gun and rocket strikes by Shackleton and Venom aircraft and went in with NFR on the right and the TOS on the left, advancing over open ground in the heat and glare of mid-afternoon. It was driven by heavy fire back to the start-line. The Sultan's forces were clearly going to fail unless substantially reinforced from outside the country.

The next day one company of a Scottish regiment, the Cameronians, based in Kenya, was flown in onto a rough airstrip, and they greatly surprised their Arab and Baluch comrades-in-arms, and the local people, by bathing naked in the wadi waters. A troop of five Ferret armoured cars of the 13th/18th Hussars arrived also to support the enlarged force and they engaged the rebel positions in Firq village with their machine-guns. The next day a fresh attack was put in, over the same route but starting at 0500 hours. This time there was no opposition; the way to Nizwa fort was open. There is an old saying: 'He who holds Nizwa holds Oman'.

Brigadier Robertson urged that the enemy, defeated on the low ground at the foot of the mountains, should be pursued right to the summit of the Jebel Akhdar. Sultan Said forbade this saying: 'There is no need. They [the rebels] will soon come down'. Thus the enemy were free to dominate the high features of the massif; they did so for the next one and a half years! Before the British forces left, and on instructions from the Sultan, the rebel forts at Balad Sait and Tanuf were blown up. NFR and MR remained in the Nizwa area for about ten days. After this operation his company commander put Said Salem's name forward with a recommendation for a commission, but it was turned down. At that time the Sultan permitted no Arab or Baluch to rise beyond the rank of Warrant Officer.

During 1958 a number of important changes were made to the armed forces. The Sultan signed with HMG a Letter of Agreement by which Britain undertook to finance much of Oman's expenditure on defence and to provide officers to command and administer the expanded Omani services. Colonel David Smiley was seconded from the Household Cavalry to become the first Commander of the Sultan's Armed Forces (CSAF), an appointment which was held by a succession of British Officers until well into the 1980s when the leadership of the three services was Omanised. Pat Waterfield, formerly a gunner major, was appointed Defence Secretary to the Sultan (in the rank of brigadier, for he insisted on holding a rank higher than Smiley); Maxwell left NFR to become deputy to CSAF, an important appointment he was to hold for many years. The SAF Training Centre at Ghalla was enlarged and John Clarke put in command.

Clarke had been lucky. While he was in A Company, shortly before he took over as Company Commander, NFR was engaged in the operations around Nizwa and a number of sharp little actions were fought between A Company and rebel patrols in the foothills of the Jebel Akhdar. On one occasion Clarke became separated from his company, and although he had been seen by Philip Allfree and Jasper Coates at dusk, he failed to rejoin his soldiers. Alone in hostile territory, without water and food, Clarke was presumed to have been killed. Said Salem, ordered to go and search for him, set off with a vehicle patrol. Near Kamah he saw a stumbling, bent figure, an old man shuffling along with the aid of a stick; on driving nearer he realised that the figure was an exhausted, dehydrated John Clarke. When Clarke left NFR his place as A Company Commander was taken by Billy Winder, a young artillery officer: he and Said have remained friends to this day. Not long after his arrival A Company was fiercely attacked by a strong rebel band. The opposition was becoming bolder now, for despite SAF's presence around the base of the mountains, the area was so vast that it was impossible to prevent the infiltration of men and supplies to the rebels in their mountain fastness. Indeed reinforcements were reaching them, entering Oman by lorry from Dubai or by camel from the Ibri area. Thus SAF had to spend much time and effort on ambush operations to reduce enemy mining and those resupply activities. This period of low intensity operations demanded patience, vigilance and a high standard of discipline. It was a good training ground for the war that was to be fought down in Dhofar.

From August 1958 to February 1959 Said Salem was with his company at Tanuf. This period, one of virtual stalemate, was used by the Sultanate and British commanders to plan the assault onto the summit of the Jebel Akhdar which alone could ensure the defeat of the rebellion.

In the last week of January 1959 A Squadron of the SAS, commanded by Major John Cooper, with elements of the Muscat Regiment and the Trucial Oman Scouts, assaulted the Jebel starting from a base near Awabi. This was a diversion to attract the rebels away from the north side. Two days later, on 26 January, the main attack was started from Kamah. It was led by Major John Watt's D Squadron of 22 SAS, followed by A Squadron (who had been switched from the south side), the Life Guards, then C Coy Northern Frontier Regiment. On 1 February all resistance ended.

Many of the rebels fled and among those who got away were the leaders, Ghalib, Talib and 'The Lord of the Green Mountain'. They had made their way down towards Firq and thence to the Adam area where they sought shelter among the bedu until finally reaching Saudi territory and sanctuary.

The Jebel Akhdar campaign was over. It had at the beginning exposed many weaknesses in the structure and competence of the Sultan's army; these were put right as British professional influence took root.

One feature of those testing months that did not change was the curious complacency of the Sultan. Said bin Taimur's refusal to heed Brigadier Robertson's advice concerning the Jebel Akhdar had prolonged the campaign by many months. His unwillingness to recognise unpalatable facts was to be a significant emcumbrance to his military commanders in the long war in Dhofar which broke out five years later. His ill judgements and obstinacy then were to cost him his throne.

A happy and over-due result of the Sultan's victory was that Said Salem was promoted to the rank of 2nd Lieutenant: he was the first Omani to be commissioned and he received his 'pips' from the hand of the Force Commander, David Smiley; and from the Paymaster a monthly salary of two hundred rupees, double what he had been paid as a company sergeant-major.

As is usual in these circumstances, Said was transferred from his friends in A Company into NFR's C Company, then commanded by Captain Wright and later by John Cooper (who had left the SAS and joined SAF). Said Salem remained in C Company until early 1965 when he was sent to the Training Centre at Ghalla to instruct Arab and Baluch in the NCO training wing established and run by David Betley. During this attachment which lasted eighteen months he attended a two-month course at Bait al Falaj in advanced Arabic.

David Smiley had been replaced as CSAF in 1962 by Hugh Oldman. It was during Smiley's tour that the Sultanate's defence requirements were reviewed by the British Brigadier Tim Hope-Thomson and in consequence the artillery was enlarged and new units such as the Gendarmerie and a small air force were added to SAF's order of battle. By 1966 the rebellion in Dhofar had become sufficiently serious for an SAF unit to be stationed there permanently, and the military situation in that fertile but remote province became the chief preoccupation of the new CSAF, Colonel Tony Lewis. In the middle of 1966 Lewis asked 2nd Lieutenant Said Salem if he wished to go back to his regiment. The reply was unhesitating and in December, having handed over to Ali Rashid, Said, accompanied by his orderly Sardoon, was flown to Salalah via Masirah to rejoin C Company NFR.

The very next day the company commander put Said in charge of a half-company and sent them out onto the Dhofar Jebel, tactically more hazardous and demanding than the much higher, barren Jebel around Nizwa. On the edge of the Wadi Jarsees one of his subordinates, Nasib, spotted the enemy who opened a sustained fire on the SAF soldiers, badly wounding one man. Said radioed for air support and a Provost arrived, recognised the air panel he had displayed and made two passes over the enemy positions. It then flew away leaving Said and his troops pinned down until darkness fell. That night by the help of a little moon, the battalion 2IC came with donkeys to carry the wounded and led them down off the Jebel. An angry Said then discovered the reason for the aircraft's abrupt disappearance. The company commander had been the passenger, the flight had made him sick and he had ordered the pilot to head back to base! Said Salem was recommended for the Gallantry Medal but his CO, an alcoholic Australian, refused to send it forward.

There then came out from England to take over command of NFR, in Rostaq, a remarkable man. Lieutenant-Colonel Mike Harvey had fought in the Korean War of 1950-53 with 'the Glorious Gloucesters' of the Imjin river battle fame in which he had done conspicuously well; he was also a 'black belt' in the martial art of karate. Under his leadership, for he had studied guerilla warfare and had a flair for aggressive tactics, NFR had much success in Dhofar. Harvey returned to SAF in February 1971 to command all the forces deployed in Dhofar and he is the most highly decorated British officer to have served the Sultanate on secondment.

Said bin Taimur had narrowly missed being assassinated by members of his private army, Dhofar Force, in April 1967, but during the early years of the rebellion there the small SAF units were able to contain the threat: over the rebel bands of the Dhofar Liberation Front (DLF) the Sultan's forces maintained an encouraging superiority. This changed after the British withdrawal from Aden. The DLF, now supplied and supported by the Marxist government which won power in Aden, posed a much more serious threat to the Sultan's rule. And when the original leaders of the DLF were supplanted by experienced communists and the rebellion was openly supported with materiel and propaganda by the Peoples' Republic of China and the USSR, the outlook became increasingly dismal.

NFR's A Company was sent back to Dhofar where its commander was killed in an action in the Wadi Naheez, whereupon C Company was flown from Hazm to Salalah. While there Said Salem took two platoons by ship to Dhalqat and patrolled as far as the frontier with South Yemen at Ras Darbat Ali where the Mahri had been trespassing onto Sultanate territory. Scouts sent out by Said were shot at and one Mahri tribesman was killed in the exchange of fire. This incident was quickly reported by Said back to his company commander who, realising that Said would face a strong attack in retaliation, ordered him to return. Getting back to Dhalqat was extremely difficult and exhausting: it had to be done in darkness and as the tide was in, the beach was impassable.

In 1967 the Sultan was persuaded to raise a third infantry battalion for SAF. This was Desert Regiment whose first CO was an Irish Guardsman, Brian Barnes, and together with other experienced leaders from MR and NFR Said Salem was transferred in to form No 2 Company of the new regiment. But he was soon switched to run the motor transport platoon and he had an enjoyable spell as MTO. It is said that DR was sent to

Dhofar before it had found its feet; that it was not fully fit for operations against an increasingly strong and confident enemy: the Popular Front for the Liberation of Oman and the Arabian Gulf (PFLOAG) had by now usurped from the DLF the leadership of the rebellion. During 1969 SAF was obliged to pull out of western Dhofar, back to a line running from the seashore to the Jebel at the west end of the Salalah plain. Barnes was relieved at the end of his tour by a tough, shrewd officer from the Royal Anglian Regiment. Lieutenant-Colonel Teddy Turnill replaced Said Salem as MTO with a Pakistani; at that time most of the junior technical and administrative posts in SAF were held by Pakistanis recruited on contract as they had attained a level of literacy which Sultan Said denied to his own countrymen. Said Salem took over command of DR's reconnaissance platoon.

During 1969 he became worried and unhappy. The situation in Dhofar was grim; moreover it was becoming clear to observers inside and outside Oman that unless the Sultan changed his policy of repressing the Dhofaris – whom he had in truth driven into rebellion against him – and of denying to his Omani subjects even the most basic needs such as medical treatment and education, the whole country would inevitably fall into Marxist hands. Said, who had served the Sultan with distinction from the age of 17 and had sacrificed in that service the companionship of his wife and growing children, now decided that he must leave SAF, move to Abu Dhabi or another of the Gulf states and there start a new career and, of prime importance, enable his sons to be educated. But when he went to Bait al Falaj to talk to Colin Maxwell, SAF's Deputy Commander, about his fears and plans, Maxwell talked him out of resigning from the army. In doing so Maxwell undoubtedly had Said's best interests at heart, and although that kind elderly British colonel had no inkling of the dramatic changes which the next year would bring to the Sultanate and to the personal fortunes of its citizens, it is perhaps providential that Said Salem was persuaded, against his will, to remain a soldier.

The new CO of DR was more realistic in his judgement of how the wind was blowing in Oman and had no doubt that the first step in bringing about the country's salvation would have to be the replacement of the Sultan by his son Qaboos Bin Said. That young man was leading a solitary existence in a small house outside the walls of the Palace in Salalah, permitted by a suspicious Father few contacts with influential Omanis and even fewer with the British.

In early 1970 Said's recce platoon had five men killed by a mine as they drove back to Thumrait from Rakhyut. This incident brought Said into a closer relationship with his CO, and during the weeks that followed Said and Turnill had discreet conversations about the country's future and disclosed to each other their innermost thoughts concerning Sultan Said bin Taimur. That others had already turned their thoughts to removing him from power was revealed to Said Salem in April 1970 when it was arranged that he should meet in secret Hilal bin Sultan Al Hosni, whom Said already knew. They met in the isolated fort at Habarut where Hilal, after swearing Said Salem to secrecy, outlined his views on what needed to be done and how it might be accomplished.

At the beginning of April 1970 a new CSAF arrived to take over from Brigadier Corran Purdon. Brigadier John Graham knew the Gulf area quite well and had developed a particular affection for Oman and the Omanis during his visits from Bahrain where he had been stationed with the Parachute Regiment in 1963-65. He had left London with crisp unambiguous orders to support the Sultan to the full and 'to deal firmly with anyone who had any ideas about removing him'. 'It is his country and he knows best how to rule it' was Whitehall's attitude in early 1970. When Graham had been in the country long enough to assess the situation and the military and political outlook, he realised that those orders, though morally impeccable, were a recipe for greater calamities befalling both the Sultanate and British interests in the region.

Qaboos Bin Said, impelled by the need to save his country, had already decided to depose his Father and assume power himself, and on 23 July he called on Colonel Turnill, the CO of Desert Regiment, to rally swiftly to his side. Brigadier Graham, who was in Dhofar and in Umm al Ghawarif Camp at the time, felt entirely justified in ordering Turnill to comply with Qaboos' call. The intervention of SAF that afternoon ensured that the crowds in Salalah, attracted by the activity in the Palace area, remained passive, that little blood was shed and that Sultan Said, though wounded, remained alive.

The main gates of the Palace were firmly closed and locked but a small door was found through which Sheikh Buraik, the son of the Wali, and a group of his friends were able to enter the Palace complex to seek out and arrest the Sultan. Said Salem and eleven soldiers he had personally selected followed and quietly disarmed those members of the garrison who tried to resist. Buraik eventually located Said bin Taimur who shot him in the stomach. Buraik was now out of action; the Sultan then secured himself in an area near the Palace roof where a fierce exchange of gunfire developed. Said Salem and six of his men ran upstairs towards the sound of the firing and were soon joined by other members of Desert Regiment. In a pause in the shooting the Sultan's voice was heard stating that he had been wounded and wished to give himself up. While Colonel Turnill and the battalion's medical team were being fetched up from the courtyard, Said Salem and his colleagues put a stop to all further shooting, cleared the corridors and rooms, disarmed the Palace garrison and placed the whole complex under armed guard.

The following morning Said bin Taimur, in the safety of the hospital in the RAF station, formally abdicated and within a few hours was flown out of his country to a comfortable exile in Britain where he died in October 1972. Great was the jubilation as the news of Qaboos' accession spread throughout the land. The same afternoon, Friday 24 July, the young new Sultan presided over the first meeting of the Dhofar Council at which numerous measures which he wished to introduce for the benefit or enjoyment of his subjects were discussed and immediately promulgated. Said Salem attended that meeting as Colonel Turnill's representative: his presence marked the beginning of a long period in which he was to work in ever closer relationship with Sultan Qaboos and in appointments where he could exercise great influence over the manner in which Oman developed as Qaboos led the country 'out of the darkness into the light'. Sultan Qaboos selected Said Salem as his first Aide de Camp, and in that capacity Said accompanied Qaboos when he flew up to Bait al Falaj on 30 July for the Accession Ceremony and then by car into Muscat where a temporary royal residence had been prepared.

In due course Said Salem was transferred out of DR onto the Palace establishment; Captain Tim Landon, a young Briton on contract as the Dhofar Intelligence Officer, simultaneously joined as His Majesty's Equerry.

From the onset the Sultan kept the duties of these, his personal assistants, clearly separated. Whereas Hamed bin Hamood handled tribal affairs and Landon became a long-term adviser on political matters, Said Salem was entrusted with the essential and overdue task of reorganising the composition, modus operandi and the logistical support of the Royal Household staffs in Muscat, Salalah and the other residences that Sultan Qaboos acquired. At this time Diwan Affairs were supervised by the respected but aged Minister of the Interior, Seyyid Ahmed bin Ibrahim. In 1973 however Said Salem was promoted. The circumstances were as follows. While on a visit to London the Sultan, in his Brook Street flat, expressed to his ADC his vexation at the impediments being placed in his way; arguments and inactivity by people who sought to block the reforms he wanted to introduce. He thereupon appointed Said Salem to be the Director (later President) of Royal Court Affairs, the equivalent perhaps of a Lord Chamberlain. This was a demanding post and Said worked direct to Qaboos who in 1975 raised him to the rank of Minister, though without a seat in the Cabinet. Qaboos' confidence in Said Salem's ability was clearly growing, as was his dissatisfaction with the attitudes of some members of his government and with the ineffectiveness of certain ministries. However the direction of the country's finances had been taken over by Qais Zawawi and proper systems of budgets and ministerial accountability were being introduced. Moreover, thanks to the massive increase in the oil revenues, Oman was acquiring the resources to fund an impressive programme of civic development and modernisation. Nevertheless the Sultan was particularly distressed by the state of the

Capital Area which the responsible authorities had allowed to become litter-strewn and in parts squalid, and by their slowness to respond to his instructions that such blemishes be put right. In 1983 therefore the Sultan turned again to Said, and to his responsibilities added the task of administering the Muscat municipality. Under his direction a thousand houses were built, each with running water, electricity and sanitation, the roads, drainage and street lighting were vastly improved, and with the laying out of parks and public gardens, and the importation of a large labour force to tend them, Muscat became a city famed for its charm and cleanliness. This is a lasting monument to Said Salem's dynamism and powers of leadership; and in working long hours, in his insistence on punctuality, efficiency and discipline he set an example rare in the Arab world. All this came to him naturally, a consequence, as he has consistently stated, 'of my twenty years of education and service in the Army'. He had come far since leaving in 1952 his birthplace in the Wadi Assarain.

The years of major contribution to his country's renaissance had brought him at last financial security and the means, though not the leisure, to bring up his family in style. During this period he took as his second wife a young Dhofari girl Fatima, the daughter of Saleh Baabood. By her he was to have two daughters, Nawal and Omaimah, and two sons, Mohammed and Maazin.

The zenith of Said's career must surely have arrived in 1985. In that year, the fifteenth of Sultan Qaboos' reign, the National Day celebrations surpassed in variety, splendour and skilled performance all such previous occasions. Those of us who had known Oman in the 'years of darkness', and the many foreign dignitaries who had never before set foot in the Sultanate, marvelled at the efficiency of the arrangements, the precision of the parades and the pride manifested by the population in their country's prosperity and reputation. The spirit of the nation, we averred, was most strikingly expressed in the multi-coloured illuminations which, using forty-four million electric light bulbs, draped every building along the highway from Sib to the farthest point in Muscat. To have seen all this was an unforgettable privilege. The burden of conceiving, planning and supervising the preparations for this great period of national rejoicing had fallen mainly on the shoulders of Said Salem, so none of us were surprised when His Majesty in grateful recognition conferred on him the Sultanate's highest Order. Shortly thereafter he was dismissed from office.

Now for the first time in his life he had the leisure to work wholly for himself, to direct personally and with obvious success his varied business enterprises; and to keep himself in fine condition physically and mentally: the former by striding daily over many kilometres, the latter by meeting the challenges of commerce and by travels abroad.

The virtue for which Said Salem is chiefly famed is his extraordinary generosity. The members of his family, of his tribe and many of his former Army colleagues have had their quality of life enhanced by his remarkable memory and his munificence. And the lives of his closest comrades-in-arms from Britain he has enriched with hospitality and with friendship of a warmth rarely found between human beings. We share countless memories of kindnesses received and of rich experiences. One, especially memorable, was the gathering, for a week in December 1996, of a host of his friends, Omani and foreign, for the wedding ceremonies of three of his sons, Hamed, Khalid and Ibrahim. But there are many others; and we who have been befriended by this exceptional man know that we have been blessed by that same divine Providence who long ago led us to Oman. It is clear too that Lieutenant-Colonel Said Salem Al Wahaibi likewise recognises the true fount of the good things that have been bestowed on him.

Appendix V
My personal diary entries (unedited) made each evening during the official visits of Rosemary and myself to Iran and Jordan in late September – early October 1972

September 19. Smooth flight to Shiraz. Arrived in warm sun, dry air and lots of green grass and a long queue of deplaning passengers. Rosemary and I had really no idea of what the 'drill' was to be for our stay in Iran. All we knew when we left Oman was that the Imperial Government had invited us through Mr Zand, and we presumed that something good would transpire. It did! As we walked out of the airport wondering what we should do next, a cavalcade of outriders and military cars drove up full of apologies 'because our plane had arrived early' and whisked us off to the Cyrus Intercontinental Hotel; VIP suite, good views and all very impressive. The chief greeter was a Brigadier from Corps HQ who left us in the care of an ADC, Lieut Hassan Rassouli from the Public Relations Dept of MoD Teheran, a staff car and driver for our own use. To bazaar to look for carpet; hundreds to choose from of many types. A most interesting experience. After dinner we all went for a walk; splendid climate and all exhilarating; and Iranians so hospitable and courteous.

September 20. In uniform with Hassan to HQ Shiraz Corps in a large modern building. 45 minutes with the GOC, LtGen Zargham, short, stocky and with many medals. Chatted about the Arabs, problems of Musandam, Iranian schools, etc. After changing into mufti we drove out through barren hills and fertile valleys to Persepolis, where we were taken by a good guide round the palaces, pavilions and tents still in place from the 2,500th Imperial anniversary celebrations of last year. I was invited to test the beds used by The Queen of the Belgians, the Greek King and Queen and the president of Lesotho before the guide took us into the huge marquees erected for the receptions and the banquets. The sun's rays coming thru' the satin roof made a wonderful orange light. The whole jamboree must have been a marvellously planned affair-a logistical and culinary nightmare, I suspect, for those in charge- but all reports at the time said it was superb, though criticised by many in the West for ultra-lavish expenditure. I know Qaboos was glad to have attended; his presence had helped Oman too. Very good lunch in nearby hotel, then on to Pasargad? to see ruined palaces and the Tomb of Cyrus, the founder in ca 550 BC of the Persian Empire. To the Tombs of Kings and, at dusk, to Zoroaster's Fire Temple. Back to Persepolis to drop our guide, Eduard, who goes to Philadelphia University next month. Back to hotel for dinner to blaring band. A satisfying day. Hassan, Mahmoud and Mehdi the driver make it all so easy and pleasant.

September 21. Up early and by car to Pars Museum, built by the Zand family, as was the Vakil Mosque with its beautiful tiling which we next visited; to the bazaar for R to get a strap repaired for a case; to Mahmoud's house at Sarai Moshir and to museum in Ghavam's house (a former Governor). Then to see the Garden of Oranges (Narenjesbar) currently the house of the Crown Prince; a gem, with 2,000 orange trees. To the tomb of Sa'adi and to Shah-Cheragh (King of Light) to see fine dome and interior of silver and glass. To get in, R had to put on chador (black gown to cover head and body), in which I photoed her. Place full of devouts. Pretty dome also next door over Mohammed's shrine. All v. fine mirrors and glasswork marvellous. In pm to tomb of Hafez, the 14th century poet born in Shiraz, set in splendid garden, and to the Ghavam family tomb next door. Then to the Eram Garden, with wonderful cypress trees and a house for VIPs. They took us finally to the Hafif Garden, being rebuilt as an Officers' Club. Taken over by Colonel Dodvar, a most enthusiastic and energetic chap who is working wonders. The artistry of the hand-painting and of the garden layout is exquisite. It is encouraging to see such pride and care in manual skills; no expense spared. The Iranian is a good army to be an Officer in! Wrote to the Corps Comd, bath, dinner and bed to thunder and lightning.

September 22, Friday. To the airport; seen off by the Brigadier, et al. General Zargham also there, as former Chief of Staff, now retired, travelling with young wife to Teheran. R's luggage searched in detail so some delay. Arrived Isfahan after 45 minutes. Met by Colonel of Artillery and ADC and driven to Shah Abbas Hotel with Police Outriders. The Shah Abbas, in an old building, is one of the most luxurious hotels in the world. The Manager had placed a huge bowl of fruits and a large bunch of blood-red gladioli in our room: the fruits of victory in Oman? The Iranians are giving us a superb time in their country, which we are determined to enjoy to the full as a unique experience. ADC and escort picked us up at 4pm and took us to the Shaking Minarets, round Isfahan, seeing the bridges, park and riverside cafe and back to hotel bar for recital of Persian music. After dinner we sat outside in hotel garden looking at the famous illuminated dome of the building. A perfection of climate, light, scenery and emotion; a wonderful close to a memorable day of beautiful sights and marvelling at the inspirations and skills of the Persian people of past eras. The sensation of being in Paradise this evening was (slightly) marred by a large bottle of tomato ketchup left by a waiter in our full view on a garden table.

September 23. After late start taken by Gunner Captain Nadiri to District HQ at the School of Artillery to meet Maj-General Borudand. We chatted for over ½-hour but he did not seem to have many ideas of his own or knowledge of the Arabian Peninsula, but he was nice enough and very solicitous over our comfort etc. Much bowing and scraping; Colonels and above receive God-like treatment in the Imp. Iranian Army. Taken on a short tour of the HQ block; very modern and posh, but I couldn't get any of the shaven-headed conscript soldiers to talk; security training based perhaps on xenophobia. General B's wife is ill so R arranged to get flowers to her. After lunch off with bodyguard to centre of town: Chahel Sotoon (Palace of 40 pillars) with marvellous murals within (being restored). Then to Ali Qapu Palace overlooking the Maidan-e-Shah (King's Square), the Mosque of Sh. Lotfallah and the Masjid-e-Shah. All huge and wonderful to behold; I have never had such a feast of architectural beauty anywhere in the world. Pottered around the bazaar inconclusively; Best buys seem to be silver, miniatures, local dress material and the superb fruits. Excellent chicken à la Kiev for dinner. What a nice, gentle and helpful soul our ADC, Hassan Rassouli, is.

September 24. Many shops shut as religious festival, but not the bazaar where R bought some sheets and dressing gowns cheaply; also parlaki (sweets), silver goblets and individual cruet sets. Was able to pay for silverware with American Express card. It is extraordinary to find that facility in crummy little booths in a huge market in a distant asiatic town. After lunch taken to see the Shah's Mosque, enormous and superbly tiled and the Sheikh Lotfallah Mosque, rich, warm, brown inside. Finished up at the 'Friday Mosque' (Masjid Jomeh); very old and with cellars lit by sunlight coming thru' slabs of alabaster. All very attractive and I got some good filming done. Great wedding party in the room next to our's in hotel went on until all hours. The bride looked most unattractive-almost vulpine.

September 25. Warm and sunny again. Morning in the bazaar. Boring no doubt for our escorts, but we did buy some nice presents as their eventual rewards. I bought a miniature, signed by Ali Sajjari who also did a sketch of Saadi for me. My miniature is a scene of polo being played circa 1660 AD on the Maidan-e-Shah in Isfahan. Ali S, we are told, is a famous miniaturist who has done presentation miniatures for The Queen, Eisenhower, de Gaulle, et al. Saw many carpets but none here in the silk we want, other than two beauties but they were over a thousand dollars each. We shall try in Teheran. The back streets of the bazaar are fascinating: blacksmiths, copper- and silver-smiths; spices, carpenters- all manner of crafts and trades are carried on here; and by people who all seem busy, happy, well nourished and very friendly. Iran does seem to be a good country in good hands. It is noteworthy how many Iranians, ordinary people to whom Rosemary and I are total strangers, go out of their way to praise The Shah; 'Look what His Imperial Majesty has done for me/my family/my village/our country etc'. In the evening we took Hassan and Captain Mozafar Pournaderi out to one of the few night clubs open to both sexes; 'The Noble'. In fact very grotty and food and wine 4th- rate, but the Persian and Arabic dancing and music were good, as was the singing of a girl named 'Midnight'. (A friend of James Bond 007?). My bodyguard turned up from out of the shadows where he had concealed himself, without our knowledge, the whole evening. These guys do take their duties seriously.

September 26. Very warm. Took flowers to GOC's wife, now hospitalised. By car to village of Polkalley (literally Bridgehead) about 70 kms from Isfahan where we had Iranian food on banks of River Zayander Rud. Very peaceful and beautiful with many dragonflies and a water snake. The trees and green rice fields and flowing waters give an impression of being in France. The fertile valleys are a joy to behold and contrast so starkly with the arid barren brown hills which seem to be the dominant geographical feature of this large country. Around this village much building is going on, including a new steel mill put up by the Russians. Last quick visit to the bazaar where R bought a suitcase and cushion covers. Sadly had to leave this most ancient and attractive city of Isfahan. Driven to airport in style with Guard of Honour of Military Police and seen off by Colonel from the local HQ after we had given our gifts to our helpful and patient escort, Pournaderi and the driver and bodyguard. Flight to Teheran only 35 minutes. The capital looked from the air like fairyland. Met by Brigadier and his wife (he used to be Iranian Military Attaché in London) and Colonel Ahmed Bidabadi from the MoD Public Relations Dept; he is the boss of Hassan Rassouli, with us since Shiraz. To the Arya Sheraton Hotel; fine views from room on 15th floor.

September 27. Rosemary's birthday but alas she has flu and I have now got it too. But by use of codeine I got myself off OK on the round of official visits arranged for me. First to the GOC Ground Forces, General Narjimi;

to Chief of Air Staff, General Khartam, and finally to General Azhari, the Chief of Staff at Supreme HQ. They are all very charming and interested in Oman and said they were particularly 'impressed by what the British element in SAF has achieved'. My friend Mr Zand has obviously briefed them in advance. The Headquarters are pretty palatial with masses of aides, Military Police, coffee bearers etc. Everyone speaks good english and I had a most enjoyable morning. From my long session with Gen Azhari I believe I learned as much about Iran's capabilities and intentions as he learned from me about the Sultanate. The friendship of His Imperial Majesty (The Shah is currently in China) is of great importance to Sultan Qaboos and I hope I am able to do something while here to foster it. After lunch, R's flu being better, Hassan took us to see the Imperial Crown jewels; fabulous but also serve to back the nation's currency. Carpets varied and cheaper than in Shiraz or Isfahan. By 9 pm I was feeling sick with fever so early bed without supper. Not, alas, the best of birthdays for poor Rosemary.

September 28. Slept well and much fitter. Out at 10 am with Hassan. First to Gulestan Palace, former residence of the Shahs and where the present Shah was crowned. Very beautiful things and it is good to note that the gifts from Queen Victoria and from King George V were well up to scratch. The clocks from Queen V. particularly ornate and still working. Then to Shahyad Aryamehr, a huge erection near the airport containing a museum and treasury of Iranian history. The whole edifice extremely cleverly and imaginatively designed by young local architect; the interior's layout of 'The History of the Ages' done by a Czech team. We were lucky enough to be specially guided by the Director, M. Bouchehri, and a pretty red-head. A moving and most instructive morning. Found the carpet we liked and paid £260 (RI 48,000) after Hassan had beaten the price down. Got our hairs tarted up, changed and out to buffet supper at home of General Massoumi. About 20 others there, mostly with english. House pretty lush with fine meissen, rugs and furniture, and food excellent. A most enjoyable evening which I hope the Iranians enjoyed as much as we did. They do us honour.

September 29, Friday. With Hassan and the two Bidabadis to the Amir Kubir Dam, about 50 kms from Teheran. The dam is very large and a most interesting construction which supplies power and controlled water to villages below and to the Capital. Shown over by M. Taheri and his staff which was very civil of them to do on a juma'a. The dam has created a lake where Iranian naval and rich civilian types have seaside club and bungalows. We were taken by motorboat on a fun tour of the lake followed by super lunch at Navy Club where Admiral Farzi? joined our party. Drove back through green populated villages with contented-looking people. Kept the evening for ourselves to give escorts spell at home and to prepare ourselves for trip to Kuwait tomorrow.

September 30. Hotel forgot to lay on b'fasts so number of vexed clients. We taken to airport by Hassan Rassouli and escort, joined there by Brigadier Nicobunyard and his wife (ex London Embassy). We leave Iran and them with regret. If we were travelling tomorrow we could have flown direct to Amman, but are compelled to spend day in Kuwait. Eventually got someone to take us and baggage to Sahara Hotel. Grotty; Rosemary insisted that the bedlinen be changed; food quite good though, mainly Lebanese. Passed dull afternoon sleeping, window shopping and taxi-tour round this sprawling, modern, super-rich town which seems totally to lack all charm. Pinky's 15th birthday today.

October 1. To airport at 5 am. Nice climate and light at that hour. Bloody awful organisation again at the so-called International Airport; but for R's foresight we would have lost half our luggage. Bless her. After very thorough security searches, to guard against hi-jacking attempts, took off in 707 of Jordan Airlines, arriving Amman about two hours later; delighted to have got away from Kuwait which we wish never to see again. Met by various Brigadiers and Colonels, many of whom I knew from before. Police escort to Intercontinental Hotel; v. lux. After unpacking, by car to Town Centre. Amman is smaller and much hiller than I had expected. Reminds me a bit of a Welsh or Italian mountain village; hardly like a capital. Invited our ADC, a Sapper Major, to lunch with us on terrace. Wrote letters and supped in icy-cold restaurant. Bed at 10 pm in preparation for busy programme laid on for me. The schedule had left R high and dry for too long so I proposed some amendments and have got us a trip to Petra in place of less interesting event.

October 2. (First anniversary of Op JAGUAR in Eastern Dhofar). Escorted early to Army HQ. Brief courtesy sessions with ACOS Ops, BGS Int (Brig Abood), the Chief of Staff (Major-General Sherif Zeid bin Shaker) who had invited me to Jordan and to whom I presented a SAF silver statuette, and Field Marshal Habes Majaly. Then whisked away, late, to Artillery Centre (Col Fatteh Hamed) where I was given a good brief and tour. Their equipments are now mostly of US origin. The Soldiers seemed very keen and switched on; all had fresh, alert, look and spoke up splendidly. Moreover they all appeared to know who I am and why here, and where Oman is. Very late arriving at Sch of Infantry -the Commandant is a Gunner!-, given a quick tour then taken to meet all the chaps from SAF on the training course which recently, and so welcome, opened for Omani soldiers. The Commandant and Instructors said they were working hard, doing well but handicapped by lack of education. I took the opportunity to put them in the picture about recent events in the Sultanate and about their duty towards their country and the Sultan. Felt ashamed that I spoke in english, but after 2+ years in BaF Headquarters, arabic simply not up to high class public speaking. Lunch in Comdt's house. Dined with Sharif Zeid (he is cousin of King Hussein) in sumptuous house with charming and pretty wife. The Minister of Economics, his wife and various Brigadiers there. Also Moona Rifai, the very beautiful wife of the Jordanian Ambassador to London who was recently shot at and wounded in hand by Arab terrorists. A most agreeable evening. Very strict security measures on roads and around the house; the Jordanians, led by their courageous King, have taken strong measures against the Palestinian Commandos/Fedayeen/terrorists and have to be constantly on their guard. It is a ruthless struggle that is being played out. My personal sympathies are with the Palestinian Arabs who have been dealt a poor hand by the international community, with Britain surely bearing a major share of the blame (Balfour Declaration and confused policies in the thirties and, since WW2, surrender to US pressure inspired by that powerful Jewish lobby in the States). But no one can condone the Palestinians' current campaign of indiscriminate acts of terror.

October 3. A great day. From Amman Air Force Base by RJAF helicopter south for 120 miles to Petra. Petra is a ruined city carved out of the red rock on the eastern slopes of the Wadi al Araba, 56 miles south of the Dead Sea. An Edomite stronghold, later the capital of the Nabataens, it was captured by Trajan in AD 106 and wrecked by the Saracens in the 7th century. In 1812 Petra was rediscovered by the Swiss traveller, Burckhardt. Landed by the guest house and thence by Landrover, by special permission of the Minister which ensured we saw everything in one day. Petra is bigger than we had expected and with many more cave-dwellings. Also I was unprepared for the mile-long drive thru' the narrow, earthquake-created gorge which gave sole access to the city and which made the place almost impregnable. Came across the actress Anne Todd doing a series for BBC TV. Good guide and good lunch. Shot lots of film of this beautiful, ancient and fascinating place. On flight back we had good views of the varied terrain and Crusader forts, such as Kerak. Some soil looks good and the roads everywhere are fine. Jordan and the Jordanians are attractive; they deserve the help as well as the admiration of the West. Our pilots (Capt Misq and Lieut Hamed) good value, fluent in english and amusing. Misq told us (but not until we had landed back in Amman) that he had 'been court-martialled last year for crashing his plane into power lines'. (Unhurt and found Not Guilty). Diverted to Iranian Embassy to deliver my B&B letters for onward despatch to Teheran. A very happy and instructive day.

October 4. Off with Hani Fakhoury for brief visit to RAC Centre; a thriving outfit with zing and sensible improvisation. The usual small boy recruits doing drill and weapon training with zeal: a sunburnt Aldershot. They gave me a nice plaque. Met up with Rosemary and we all went off to the Military Academy for the Passing Out Parade. About 250 in this year's class; smart in blue uniforms. Just like RMAS except that these Cadets ended by doubling past the saluting base singing at top of their voices.

More stimulating to me than the more rigid British March-Off. While the Cadets were singing, their female relatives in the crowd called out to them and ululated to their sons, etc, out of pride. Quite right too, for this is a great day in the lives of the Cadets and their families and tribes. We had been given seats in the front row so had excellent view. Very pleased to find myself sitting next to General Mohd Khalil, the Ambassador to Oman, and, on the other side, to General Ali Amer, the GOC of the Saudi troops in Jordan. When I mentioned gratefully the recent interest being shown in Omani affairs by his country, Ali Amer said words to the effect: 'Do not get too excited about offers of help and support. Out of Saudi Arabia come very many more words than actions'. We all coffeed in the Club where I was introduced to His Majesty. Thicker-set than I had expected but charming and, of course, fluent. Thanked me for everything I had done for Oman and her Armed Forces. Met Glenn Balfour-Paul, the British Ambassador, and many others. Then I was taken to the RJE Centre to see the Corps museum and laboratory. There I was shown 4 of the 'Black September' terrorist organisation's letterbombs which the Jordanians had intercepted; was told only 11 had ever been found and neutralised worldwide. Stand-up lunch in RJE Mess hosted by CRE (Brigadier A.H.Al Magaly). In evening invited Samih and Kenneth Timbrell to dine in hotel and see floor show.

October 5. Off at 9 am by car to Jerash. Remarkable ruins, so well preserved because wholly covered by sand from XIIth until XIXth century. Very well guided round by Police Sergeant. I took lots of film and learned much from our well informed and patient Teacher. We then drove to the recently-opened national park, (looks a bit like Troodos in Cyprus), where the guerillas had set up their base when driven out of Amman. Then for excellent lunch in the Hussein Sports Centre which we toured. First-rate facilities paid for by public subscription and built by UK firm for £2½M. While R had her hair done, I went for walk and some shopping: flowers for Mme Sharif Zeid and Farida, and a Bohemian vase for Hani and Farida who have looked after us so wonderfully. Changed and went for quick drinks with Glenn B-P (whose crippled wife died recently) before Gen Khalil took us to dine at Zerqa Officers' Club together with his wife, his Sapper Officer son and the Governor of Amman, M. Tarhouni (?) who most patiently answered all my questions about local govt and moslem religious practices. General Khalil repeated some nice things about me said by the Omani troops here.

October 6, Friday. Hani took us to the airport where all was made smooth. Samih and Farida Malhas also there to see us off on Royal Jordanian aircraft after very strict baggage and personal search. We are sorry to be leaving Jordan, and we got the feeling that our hosts too regret our departure. Splendid flight to Istanbul where I watched a Jumbo-jet land. Fascinating to see how the legion of service vehicles gathered round, like cygnets round a Mother swan. On to Frankfurt; very modern and impressive but impersonal and antiseptic like a hospital. At 2030 hrs we got on a BEA Trident; very cramped and tourist class only which vexed us no end (coming down to earth after so long away from the standards of a Britain in decline). However, after some anxiety at Heathrow, got all our baggage intact and everything through Customs without difficulty or payment. Spent the night in the nearby Skyways Hotel; expensive but adequate.

October 7. A really lovely morning; still, sunny and warm. The fields are green and the leaves beginning to turn. To-day England really does look beautiful. By taxi to Alastair's at Eton to collect car. Battery flat but got new one put in by obliging local garage-hand, (ex-2 PARA!) Everyone pleasant and helpful, and our first impressions of the cars, houses, shops and air of affluence, in this part of England at least, totally belie the gloomy reports we have been reading in the papers about the parlous state of the UK economy.

Appendix VI

Constance Mary (Jane) Graham born 10 March 1900, died 21 May 1987

Funeral Service held at Putney Vale Crematorium, London SW15 on Thursday, 28 May 1987 at 12.30 p.m.

Address Given By her Eldest Son, John Graham

'Up to the last hour of her life Jane put up a great fight: she had immense courage. One moral from her life is, I believe, 'Never give up'. I would now like to share with you some of my recollections of her. Jane's life spanned six reigns for she was born while Queen Victoria was on the throne. She was the only child of Thomas Edward Carew-Hunt – (Tommy we called him) – and his wife Emily. They lie buried some 500 yards from this chapel and it is there that Jane's ashes will be interred. Tommy, a gentle, unassuming and essentially passive man, distinguished himself while commanding a company of the Royal Berkshire Regiment in the retreat from Mons in 1914 and subsequently on the Army Intelligence Staff. The Colonel commanding the Berkshires at that time was Max Graham – our other Grandfather-to-be. Though severely wounded in the First Battle of Ypres he recovered sufficiently to become Deputy Military Secretary at the War Office and ADC to King George V. Soon after the 1914-18 war however he settled in South Africa and was not seen again by his family.

Max, who had lost his wife after only a few years of marriage, was left with a five-year old son named John Alexander (Jack for short). This child was brought up by a spinster aunt, had a brilliant school career, became a first-class cricketer and a regular Officer in the Royal Engineers. He and Jane married in 1921 and in due course produced my Brothers and me.

I relate all this to highlight the fact, exceptional in that age when large families were the norm, that Jane and her husband were both only children brought up in restrictive circumstances and deprived of the support of parents whilst denied the companionship of brothers or sisters. I used even as a child to feel that they were a slightly waif-like couple, rather ill-prepared to cope with the problems and perils of a changing world. And problems there were to be for them:

– a perennial shortage of money, for Army pay was meagre
– costly doctors' bills in those days before the National Health Service was invented
– long periods of separation in peace and war due to Jack's postings to India and Egypt
– the outbreak of the Second World War with all its anxieties and strain, followed by early widowhood for Jane.

She however faced up to these tests with unfailing fortitude and from 1936 onwards singlehandedly brought up her three sons. She gave us in Sussex, Suffolk and Seaview a succession of warm houses with an assortment of fine contents, inherited or inexpensively acquired, excellent grub and a good public school education. I particularly remember the care and generosity with which she organised our birthdays, Christmases and other family red-letter days. She was an outstanding cook, a prolific knitter and sewer and a most regular composer of letters in her distinctive hand-writing and that invariable blue ink. Her possessions, wardrobe, documents and household impedimenta she kept immaculately; not only because that was the way she had been brought up but also to aid those to whom these things now pass. She was in so many ways a true product of the age and circle into which she was born. But it is nevertheless remarkable that during her 87 years she never sought to drive a car, ride a horse or a bicycle, play any outside sport or speak a word of a foreign language. Her happiest times were, I know, during her betrothal to Jack and their first six years together at the Sapper Depot in Chatham, her years in India, the war years in Seaview and her working years in Chelsea.

On behalf of all the family I most sincerely thank you and everyone else who cared for, entertained or encouraged her during her often solitary periods in the Isle of Wight, and at Cheyne Court during her last illness. Her long association with the Minster Trust brought her, and us, especial pleasure and deserved pride.

APPENDICES

But it was above all for Moray, Alastair and myself that she lived, struggled, worried and often, I am happy to say, rejoiced. Jane was indeed a devoted Mother and for this above all she was greatly admired. We were very lucky boys.'

Appendix VII
Address given by JDCG at the Memorial Service for Brigadier Colin Maxwell

It was entirely natural that Colin Maxwell should have been a Soldier, for the bulk of his life serving far from these islands. It was in the blood. His great-grandfather, a Bengal Gunner, served in India for 40 years rising to the rank of Major-General. His son, Colin's grandfather, spent his life in India, became a Lieutenant-Colonel of Infantry but transferred to the Political Service after being severely wounded in Northern Burma. Colin's Father Charles, after whom Colin was named, in his turn joined that Army and was a Captain in the 8th Gurkha Rifles.

It is also entirely apt that this service should be held in this fine Chapel, near to Colin's club, the Royal Overseas League, and to the hotels in which he rested in between those many spells in hospital this year and last.

There are two other reasons . . . A plaque on the north wall tells us that beneath this Chapel lie buried the parents of the great Duke of Wellington: Colin would have liked that for his two military heroes were Wellington and Lawrence of Arabia. And further along that wall is a memorial to a Captain Mackain[1] who was killed in action in Flanders while serving with the Indian Army Expeditionary Corps. He was killed on 23rd November 1914. Colin's Father, serving in the same Corps, was killed in the same action, at Festubert, the following day.

On that day, 24th November, Colin was with his Mother at Misoori, an Indian hill station. He was 16 days old. Thus he never saw his Father, but we do know that before he died Charles Maxwell had received the news of his son's arrival into this world.

Perhaps the most endearing of Colin's virtues was his extreme modesty; he seldom talked about his early years. However during our many days together in London during his last painful 17 months of life, he overcame that reluctance and I would like to tell you about him . . .

After his Father's death, Colin's Mother Ida remarried, became Mrs Russell and moved to Egypt where her new husband worked. From this union there was born a half-sister to Colin, Joan Russell who died this year only a few weeks before Colin. Those early days in Egypt introduced

Colin to sun, desert and to the Arabic language; but education demanded all too soon his removal to England, first to Edgeborough School near Guildford and then to Radley, a public school from which he retained very happy memories. School holidays were spent with relatives, some of whom are here today. After Radley Colin went up to Cambridge where he read history. But he was keen to get back to the area of his childhood and in 1936 went on a 3-year contract to the Palestine Police. Those were bitter years for Briton and Arab alike in Palestine and Colin's scrap-book from that period in his life makes grim reading.

Back in England on the outbreak of the Second World War Colin joined the Army. He started as a Trooper in the Royal Armoured Corps, learning at Tidworth how to drive a tank; but he hankered after the Infantry and got himself transferred to the Border Regt. In 1941 he was commissioned and was finally posted to the 6th Battalion Royal Scots Fusiliers. (This battalion incidentally was the one Winston Churchill commanded on the Western Front in 1916 when he was out of office.) Throughout the campaign from Normandy to the Baltic 6 RSF was part of the renowned 15th (Scottish) Infantry Division. There were three of us in 15th (Scottish) who were later to serve together in SAF. The third chap was the late Kingsley Gray from the Divisional Reconnaissance Regiment whom many will remember as 2IC of the Oman Gendarmerie.

Colin went to Normandy in June 1944 as Anti-tank Platoon Commander, but was switched to the Carrier Platoon when its commander was wounded. Colin came through the whole campaign without a scratch. He was exceptionally lucky: he was also much loved by his men. I know this because some three years ago while in Wapping I got into conversation with a docker who to my surprise and pleasure had been a Fusilier not only in 6RSF but actually in Colin's company. He remembered him with clarity and real affection.

When the war was over and the battalion was on the Baltic coast of Germany, Colin applied for a regular commission. The War Office however turned him down – he was already well over 30 – and after a short tour as Brigade Major he was demobilized in 1947. But he was determined somehow to go on soldiering and in 1948 went to Somalia and Eritrea as a member of the British Military Administration of those former Italian colonies. Colin served there with distinction and is to this day remembered by his former colleagues for his dedication, kindness and quiet good humour. Alas he became prone to illness and injury – some from comic causes – and in 1950 started to suffer from the arthritis which was to cause him much pain in later years. These infirmities never impaired his duty, but they did induce in him that prudent care for himself which led to jokes about Colin being 'a walking medicine chest'. All this time he was the Staff Officer to the Commissioner of Police, David Cracknell. He was best man at David's wedding and it is splendid that Mr and Mrs Cracknell are here today, together with their daughter to whom Colin was Godfather.

By 1952 the nature of the Force had changed and Colin began to look for new pastures. He read a Foreign Office leaflet about employment in Muscat & Oman, got a recommendation and set off for that little known land. In Bahrain he was interviewed by the British Commander, Brigadier Baird, who gave him his blessing and a packet of air photos addressed to Sultan Said bin Taimur. From Sharjah Colin was driven down to Oman by an Officer of the Trucial Oman Levies and reported to the Sultan outside Sohar. It was October 1952. The Sultan had assembled a large force of tribesmen at Sohar with the intention of marching up the Wadi Jizzi and driving the Saudis out of Buraimi. Within hours of meeting the Sultan Colin resolved to stay in his service, and so he was the first of that notable quintet of pioneer Contract Officers who were to contribute so much to the Armed Forces of the Sultanate and thereby to the Omani nation. Maxwell came first, followed by St John Armitage, Richard Anderson ('the Drum'), Malcolm Dennison and Bob Warner; in that order.

Sultan Said's march against Buraimi was called off but Colin remained at Sohar to raise the Batinah Force – armed with little money but with helpful royal letters to the sheikhs to stimulate recruitment.

One young boy who caught Colin's eye in those early days rose to be a Colonel in SAF and later a highly placed member of the Omani Government.

Batinah Force was soon renamed Northern Frontier Regiment and in December 1955 Colin led it in a successful attack on Rostaq as part of a general move against the dissident Imam and his brother Talib. These two fled to Saudi Arabia but two years later returned secretly to Oman and raised the standard of revolt against the Sultan. The Jebel Akhdar War of 1957-59 had begun. Northern Frontier Regiment, still under Maxwell's command, played a prominent role in the first phase of the operations, but in April 1958 Colin was moved to Bait al Falaj to become Deputy Commander of the Sultan's Armed Forces: a post he held until retirement in 1978. This appointment gave Colin endless opportunities to serve Oman and to influence the lives of countless people who live in that majestic land; from being Governor of the Jebel Akhdar after the war to becoming a friend and confidant of all manner of people, including Sultan Said whom he visited regularly.

Colin thought highly of Sultan Said but was by no means blind to his weaknesses. Like so many others however who were close to the Ruler he was unable to persuade him of the need to change his policies. The events of 23rd July 1970 took Maxwell by surprise: the replacement of Said bin Taimur by his son Qaboos shocked him and his first reaction was to quit Oman. But he soon saw the truth in what his friends at Bait al Falaj told him: if he loved Oman and its people he owed it to them – and to himself

– to stay and make an even greater contribution under the opportunities the new regime would open up. Many of you know far better than I the multiplicity of services and kindnesses Colin rendered to the people of the Sultanate individually or collectively. Shortly before he died I asked him what episodes in his life gave him the greatest feeling of pride. He said, 'Raising and commanding NFR and, in 1970, creating the scheme for the eventual Omanization of the Forces'. This scheme was to open to Oman's servicemen avenues, promotions and qualifications undreamt of in earlier decades. He truly was 'The Father of the Force', not only because of his uniquely long service in SAF but also because he was our trusted friend and counsellor. We seconded members owe a particular debt to our contract colleagues, and to Colin above all.

It is sad that he did not live to see the Official History of SAF completed, nor the Museum of The Armed Forces opened. But he will have many memorials elsewhere.

We should, I believe, not let today pass without expressing our sincere gratitude to His Majesty the Sultan and his Government for the most generous and careful way Colin was looked after ever since he retired. That splendid house by the sea beyond Sidab, with the good sergeant Darwish to watch over him, and during his prolonged illness the very best of medical attention and devoted nursing here in London; and when convalescing the most comfortable of Mayfair hotels to stay in. Some regret that in contrast to the honour and kindnesses conferred on him by the Sultanate, the British authorities have let Colin's life pass unrecognized save for the Mention in Despatches he was awarded in 1945. This omission perhaps merely highlights the fact that Colin's real home and the love of his life was Oman.

Everyone will remember him differently. I cannot recall him ever saying an unkind word about anybody, and even when he had cause to utter some criticism he straightway adjusted the balance with a complimentary phrase. He was totally without malice, and in return received none. His only vice, as far as I was concerned, were those foul-smelling French cigarettes of which he seemed to have an endless supply. 'A good, quiet, honest man'; 'A real gentleman'; 'The nicest man I've ever met' . . . these are just three of the tributes I heard at the time of his death. I suggest however that Fusilier Hammond of the London docks got it right when he recalled Colin to me as 'A proper Officer and a lovely Man'.

That surely is how Colin wishes to be remembered.

Note

1. Uncle of Lt Col Fergus Mackain-Bremner, OBE, CO, Muscat Regt, 1969–71

Appendix VIII
Sermon given by the Bishop of Peterborough 22 June 1990

Sermon Preached in St Paul's Cathedral at the Service of Thanksgiving on the Fiftieth Anniversary of the Raising of Airborne Forces: Friday, 22 June 1990.

Preacher: The Rt Rev William Westwood, Lord Bishop of Peterborough and formerly of the Sixth Airborne Division in time of War.

The text is taken from the first chapter of the book *Joshua* (verses 1-9) which was read as a lesson by His Royal Highness The Prince of Wales, Colonel-in-Chief.

I

Words from the first chapter of the book *Joshua*: 'Be strong and of a good courage. Be strong and very courageous'.

The voice of the Commanding Officer down the ages.

On the banks of the Rhine: on June 5th 1944: as the ships approached the Falklands; now in the streets of Belfast.

The voice said: you have been trained, you are fit, you are well equipped, you are as ready as you ever will be, the enemy is on the run – be strong and of good courage and go.

These words were said on the bank of another river. They had been wandering for 40 years and now they had lost their beloved leader but the voice said go. So they went. They crossed the river.

Naked courage gets you a long way but doesn't get you everywhere and the voice of the Commander said to them, 'The book of the law: you shall meditate therein day and night that you may do according to all that is written there. Then you shall have good success'. That was their equipment and their armament and then it was enough. In the history of the Airborne Forces and of the Parachute Regiment in their various manifestations, the equipment and the weapons were there, the meticulously maintained gliders, the exactly packed parachutes – even the hole in the floor of the Whitleys, even those hair-dryer style helmets, even the Sten gun which fired fingers instead of bullets – the equipment was there and the good courage was there, as we all remember.

Our memory stretches back a mere 50 years and those officers and men who responded to the Prime Minister's call 50 years ago today came from regiments with hundreds of years of memory and honour. Now we have our names in memory. Now we have our honours, and we remember how they were won.

But walking down memory lane can be dangerous.

II

In preparation for today I was generously invited to a Dining Out Night at Browning Barracks. In the afternoon the newest recruits were drilling and they kindly asked me to inspect them. After I had walked through their ranks I worked out that their parents had not been born when I left the Division in 1947. Even the red beret is no longer sacred. Now-a-days if you wear it they think you are some sort of Scout Master. Mark you, I have brought my last one with me today (Kangol 1945), thinking if I froze up I could put it on, salute the Colonel-in-Chief and make a discreet retreat, knowing that you would all understand.

Yes, as we look back we know that we needed the right equipment and the good courage 50 years ago and we were given them. We know that we have needed them down the years and we have been given them. We need them now.

As we step out from this service into the squalid streets of our capital city we take that squalor for granted. As we arrived, coming through the massive security because the murderers are among us, we take them for granted. We take the fact of the football hooligan for granted. We take for granted the fact that the resting places of the dead will be vandalised, that old people will be mocked and that women will be raped.

These things have always happened but we didn't take them for granted once. We expect them now because in our land we have seen the death of respect. Respect for God, respect for men and women, respect for property, self-respect.

I think that after a harsh war, a nation which had known privation and the limitation of liberties, wished for their children a better time without all the restrictions of war. So education became child-centred and we were glad to give our children what they wanted rather than what they needed for we had been denied these things. We created a society chiefly interested in itself and suddenly the new Jerusalem has dark streets and the bright and shining world has a shadow side. Suddenly we are aware that the squalor of our streets is reflected in a squalor of the spirit.

III

I remember a Battalion Commander in Germany saying to me how greatly he was worried by the contrast between what he knew his Regiment was about and the sort of world from which his recruits came.

He saw the contrast and held on to the values which he knew were important. But many don't see and many refuse to see. But we ought to see. From our backgrounds, with our traditions, we ought to see that there is still a war to fight. And where is the equipment with which we will fight it?

'The book of the law, you shall meditate therein, you shall do according to all that is written there'.

The historian J.R. Green said 'The people of Britain are the people of a book and that book is the Bible'. When he wrote those words long years ago the standards we value from our tradition were strong among us. We now need to restate those standards. The standards of the Bible, the standards of straight and honourable dealing, of dignity and respect, and we know that all the equipment in the world and all the high standards and hopes are worth nothing if they are not anchored to strength and courage. Our 50 years tells us that we, the people of Britain have the strength and courage to change and to change our nation. Voices say that the tempo of the times doesn't go this way. Voices say that the spirit of the age is against us. We have been surrounded before. We have broken out. Like Joshua we have crossed rivers before.

But I believe the tempo of the times is changing and the spirit of the age is moving in a new way. Be strong and of good courage. The nation needs us again.

Appendix IX
BRITISH GUIANA REVISITED, 1991

In October 1953, not long after the Queen had presented new Colours to us in Edinburgh, the First Battalion was ordered at short notice to move by sea to British Guiana, the only British colony on mainland South America. Widespread unrest and communal violence, allegedly planned by the Peoples' Progressive Party, was anticipated and the Constitution had been suspended by the Governor on the instructions of HMG. The Argylls were the first major unit to be stationed in the colony during this century. In the event we had little to do in the fields of Internal Security and Aid to the Civil Power: we had a pretty unexciting year spent largely on training, sport and showing the flag.

In early 1991, thirty-six years after the 91st was relieved by the 2nd Black Watch and returned to Scotland, the author and his wife revisited the Republic of Guyana, as British Guiana is now styled.

The first change that strikes the returning visitor is the dearth of white faces. Apart from the diplomatic community and itinerant businessmen, very few Europeans or people of European extraction are to be seen: they are mainly senior technicians or managers of the distilling and engineering enterprises which still operate there. Equally absent is the Chinese element which used to make such a notable contribution to the colony's commercial life. The driving force in the Guyanese business world now comes from the Indian community which comprises about 65% of the population. The Negro element however predominates in government, in the Police and the Defence Force, in the unemployed and the unemployable. Crime is widespread and increasing and citizens, to avoid the gangs who 'choke an' rob', are advised not to venture beyond the principal streets by day or night.

In Georgetown the Mariners' Club which housed our Officers' Mess and the Battalion Headquarters group of wooden buildings opposite looked intact, though seedy; but on the road which runs between them lay the putrifying carcass of a dog. This unappetizing sight seemed to symbolize the state of Guyana to-day.

Some of the buildings which line Main Street have been kept in good order. The Tower Hotel has been refurbished recently; Government House still stands in its large garden but is rarely used. The British High Commission works on the west side of Main Street in a building modest in comparison with the US and Soviet Embassies and the Georgetown Club has been well preserved, as has St George's Cathedral. But along this once elegant boulevard and in other sections of the city, the buildings reflect poverty, neglect and an absence of civic pride and discipline. The streets are disfigured by the mounds of rubbish which are allowed to accumulate at every corner, and the drainage canals which run alongside the carriageways are to-day lined with dead animals, household waste and detritus of every description. To witness all this and to listen to the lamentations of those Guyanese who remember Georgetown as 'the Garden City of the Caribbean' is an unhappy experience. And not only in Georgetown. New Amsterdam was to celebrate this year its bi-centenary by, according to the leading national newspaper, 'painting the Town Hall and having the drains unblocked'.

The amount of road traffic has greatly increased during the past three decades, but the roads have deteriorated hugely. Many of the traffic lights are broken, road signs defaced or missing; and outside the Capital the highways now consist of large areas of potholes linked by patches of tarmac or cement. The verges are in the main invisible and driving by night on the East Coast road or south towards the former Atkinson Field airport is an alarming experience on unlit roads with no warning signs and with dark skinned pedestrians and cattle wandering about on the carriageway. The transport system probably best reflects the appalling state into which the country has been brought; more so even than the inefficient telephone network or the unreliable electricity supply. A major folly, now openly admitted, was the removal of the railway which ran from Georgetown along the coast to New Amsterdam and its replacement by a fleet of road transport vehicles, including two hundred buses purchased from Yugoslavia and India. Soon after this decision had been implemented there occurred the oil price hike of 1973 which imposed a sudden and continuing drain on the Republic's currency reserves. Of the bus fleet acquired at that time only ten vehicles, we were told, remain on the road. The others can be seen rusting in great vehicle parks. Indeed one of the most distressing aspects of the current Guyanese scene is the multitude of motor cars, lorries, earth-moving equipments and farm machinery which litter the road-sides, derelict through lack of spares, cannibalization or misuse.

This inadequate transport system has especially evil consequences for children and their teachers who face daunting daily problems in getting to and from school; and the effects on the commercial life of the nation are plain to see.

Since Independence in 1966 the decline of the Guyanese economy has been very severe. When the Battalion was out there in 1953-54 the exchange rate was £1 = 8 Guianese dollars. Six months ago it was £1 = 187 Guyanese dollars; currently it is £1 = 225 dollars. This erosion of the currency now places Guyana as the cheapest labour market in the Caribbean and perhaps in the world. These devaluations have had a horrendous impact on pensioners and all those on fixed incomes, who have to struggle on pittances or, if lucky, on donations from relatives in North America or Europe. Savings have all been eroded: people who had invested in insurance policies in order to purchase a house at maturity now find that sum cannot even buy a toilet. The state of Guyana to-day is an awful warning of the condition to which the life and prospects of a nation can be reduced by bad government based on Marxist dogma and administered by persons for whom the population expresses distrust and contempt. Forbes Burnham, acknowledged as the architect of Guyana's decline, died in 1985. His devotees had intended that his body should be displayed, Lenin-like, in a public mausoleum. The Russian embalmers however proved to be inexpert and in consequence the first President of the Republic of Guyana now rests below ground in the Botanical Gardens. The airport at Atkinson Field, renamed Timheri International, is a forbidding place where the unsmiling officials outnumber the departing and arriving passengers, and where the facilities consist of two large huts with rows of plastic chairs but devoid of information boards, shops or the normal conveniences found at such establishments. The Duty Free Shop is a large cupboard totally empty save for one shelf holding three varieties of rum. Intending travellers take note!

Burnham and his colleagues have in twenty-five years of independence brought their country down to pretty near the bottom of the Third World pile. This is a tragedy, for the Guyanese are still a most friendly, hospitable people who speak of the British presence and contribution with gratitude and nostalgia. There are signs that his successor, Desmond Hoyt, is endeavouring to repair the economy with fresh financial and technical assistance from outside. Guyana is large, rich in certain resources and in the interior uniquely beautiful. The outlook is not hopeless.

Any significant improvement to the prosperity and quality of life of the Guyanese nation appears however to depend on three essential conditions. Firstly, the extent to which educated and successful Guyanese are willing to return to their birthplace from their domiciles overseas to play a part in the government and commerce and administration of their country. Secondly, the establishment of a reliable educational system, untained by politics and devoted to turning out qualified and honest civil servants, leaders and managers. Thirdly, the degree to which Guyanese governments succeed in attracting from the Developed World the amounts of capital and technical skill needed to create the base on which future generations of Guyanese can build.

JDCG
June 1991.

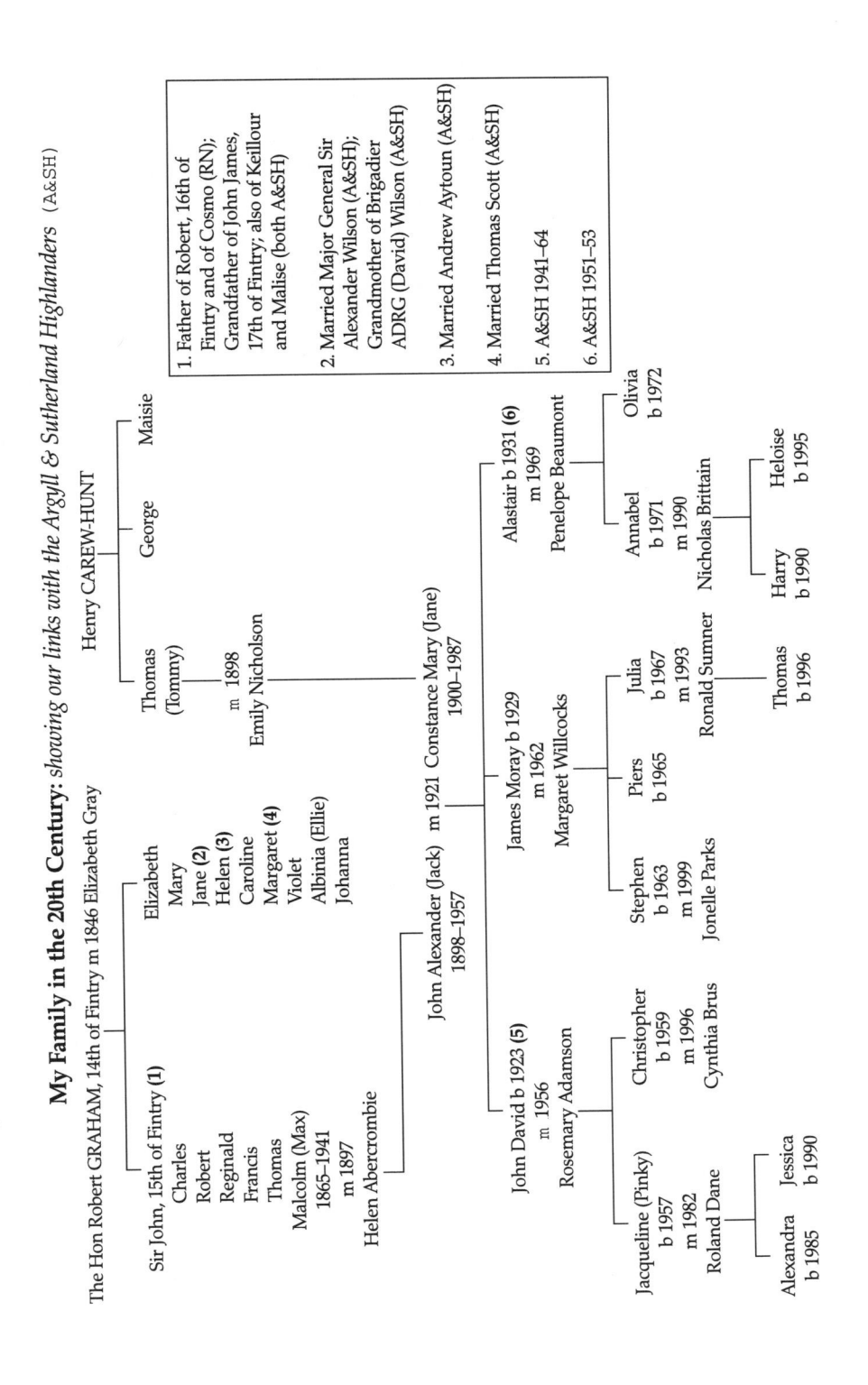

My Family in the 20th Century: *showing our links with the Argyll & Sutherland Highlanders* (A&SH)

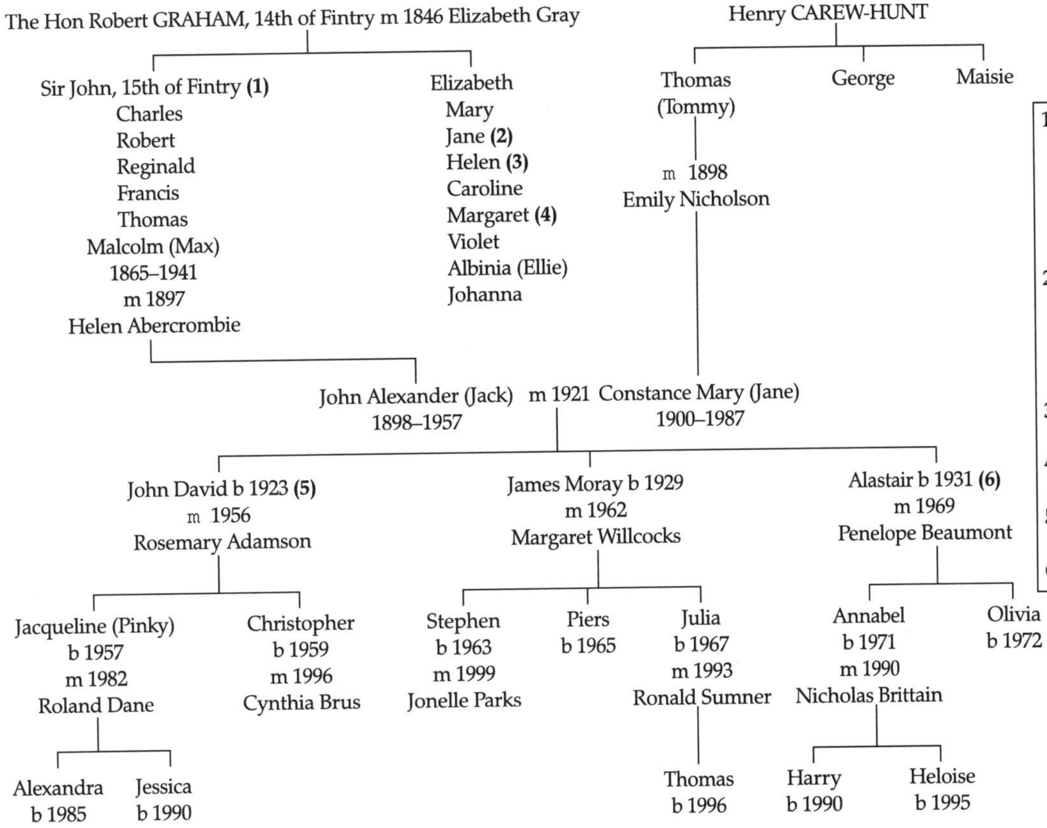
The Hon Robert GRAHAM, 14th of Fintry m 1846 Elizabeth Gray
Sir John, 15th of Fintry (1)
Charles
Robert
Reginald
Francis
Thomas
Malcolm (Max)
1865–1941
m 1897
Helen Abercrombie
Elizabeth
Mary
Jane (2)
Helen (3)
Caroline
Margaret (4)
Violet
Albinia (Ellie)
Johanna
Henry CAREW-HUNT
Thomas
(Tommy)
George
Maisie
m 1898
Emily Nicholson
John Alexander (Jack)
1898–1957
m 1921
Constance Mary (Jane)
1900–1987
John David b 1923 (5)
m 1956
Rosemary Adamson
James Moray b 1929
m 1962
Margaret Willcocks
Alastair b 1931 (6)
m 1969
Penelope Beaumont
Jacqueline (Pinky)
b 1957
m 1982
Roland Dane
Christopher
b 1959
m 1996
Cynthia Brus
Stephen
b 1963
m 1999
Jonelle Parks
Piers
b 1965
Julia
b 1967
m 1993
Ronald Sumner
Annabel
b 1971
m 1990
Nicholas Brittain
Olivia
b 1972
Alexandra
b 1985
Jessica
b 1990
Thomas
b 1996
Harry
b 1990
Heloise
b 1995

1. Father of Robert, 16th of Fintry and of Cosmo (RN); Grandfather of John James, 17th of Fintry; also of Keillour and Malise (both A&SH)

2. Married Major General Sir Alexander Wilson (A&SH); Grandmother of Brigadier ADRG (David) Wilson (A&SH)

3. Married Andrew Aytoun (A&SH)

4. Married Thomas Scott (A&SH)

5. A&SH 1941–64

6. A&SH 1951–53

INDEX OF PERSONALITIES
(Ranks shown are as they first appear in the text)

Adamson, Elaine Maud 155, 160, 404
Adamson, James Basil 155
Adamson, Rosemary Elaine 155 et seq Plates 25, 27, 37, 40, 41, 46, 63, 71, 78
Aitken, RSM Jim (5 PARA) 115
Akuffo, Colonel FWK (Fred) 383–4
Al Hosni, Sheikh Hilal bin Sultan 331–8, 478
Al Wahaibi, Lieut Said Salem (SAF) 334–9, 467–81 Plate 54
Amery, Mr Julian MP 193, 378 Plate 34
Anderson, Major RGH (Richard) ('The Drum') (SAF) 314, 470–2, 493
Archibald, Major DFM (David) (RHA) 269, 279–80, 282
Armitage, Major St John (SAF) 469, 493
Arthur, Sir Geoffrey (Political Resident Persian Gulf) 362
Ashley, Major Ted (PARA & SAF) 353 Plate 62
Aziz-Ur-Rahman, Captain (SAF) 353

Baker, Sqn Ldr Neville (SOAF) 359
Baldwin, Mr Stanley (Prime Minister) 11
Bandon, Air Chief Marshal The Earl of 191, 199–200 Plates 29, 33
Banks, Captain Geoffrey (PARA) 289
Baraik bin Hamood, Sheikh 322, 331–2, 334, 350, 360, 378, 478
Barber, Brigadier Colin 60, 74, 95
Barnes, Lt-Colonel (Brian) 476–7
Batra, Lt-Gen MN 383
Baxter, Captain David 343
Beale, Lt-Colonel Karl 325, 348, 364
Beauregard, Brigadier-General Costa de 189–212 Plates 28, 35, 38
Bedford-Roberts, Lt-Colonel John (2A&SH) 46, 49
Begin, Menachem 112
Beneš, Edouard (President of Czechoslovakia 1935–9) 125–6
Bernhard, Prince (of the Netherlands) 447
Best, Lt-Colonel AG (Tony) (SAF) 338, 353, 369
Bidwell, Sir Hugh (Lord Mayor of London) 446–8 Plate 73
Billière, Lt-Colonel Peter de la (SAS) 364–5, 375, 442
Bismarck, Count Otto von 1
Blair, WO2 HRA (Alex) (RASC) 128, 130, 133–4
Blake, Colonel Francis 128, 132, 138 Plate 20
Blériot, Louis (aviator) 6, 23
Blyth, Sgt Chay 308

Boyde, RSM Rex (Paddy) (1A&SH) 153–4
Boxhall, Major PG (Peter) (SAF) 353
Bradley, General Omar 72
Bridges, Sqn Ldr Alan (SOAF) 315, 342
Broadhurst, Air Chief Marshal Sir Harry 176, 180, 182
Brogan, Captain Sean (SAS) 359
Browning, General Sir Frederick ('Boy') 299
Browning, Lady (Daphne Du Maurier, authoress) 299
Bryers, Brigadier Dick 235, 255, 281
Brownrigg, Norman 12, 13, 18
Brus, Cynthia (Tia) 453 Plate 74
Budd, Colonel DJ (David) (RHA) 406–7
Bulganin, Marshal (of the USSR) Nikolai 132
Burrow, Mr Rene and Mrs Andrée (British Council) 137
Burt, CSgt Gordon (1 PARA) 274 Plate 45
Butler, Major-General Mervyn ('Tubby') 296–7, 302, 304
Butler, Mike and Robin (Dhofar Development Dept) 361

Caddow, Private 32
Callaghan, James (Prime Minister) 266, 411, 418, 421
Campbell, Captain Alan (RN) 148
Campbell, Captain Gordon (RA) 66, 102
Campbell, Lt-Colonel Lorne VC (A&SH) 148
Campbell, Captain MRA (Mike) (SAF) 352
Campbell-Baldwin, Major AN (Neil) (5 PARA) 115, 274
Came, Colonel KC (Ken) 306

Carew-Hunt, Ethel Emily (née Nicholson) 1–7, 20, 434
Carew-Hunt, George Ward 1
Carew-Hunt, Henry 1
Carew-Hunt, Mida (née Pantin) 26, 421 Plate 11
Carew-Hunt, Lt-Colonel TE (Tommy) 1–4, 14, 26, 216, 421, 434 Plates 1, 11
Carrington, Lord 424–7
Carver, General Sir Michael (CGS) 355, 363
Carver, Captain 'Splash' (RN) 226, 281
Cassels, Major General AJH (Jim) 115, 182, 189 Plates 29, 33
Cassidy, Captain George (5 PARA) 115
Castle, Mrs Barbara MP 162–3
Chabot, Captain Henri (R. Netherlands Army) 89
Challe, General Maurice (CINCENT) 178–98, 362 Plate 32
Chamberlain, Neville (Prime Minister) 11, 19, 23, 126, 193
Chapman, Lieut Ian (1 PARA) 289
Charles, Prince (of Wales) 418, 421, 424, 446, Plate 73
Chauncy, Leslie (Consul-General) 468
Chevening Personalities 422–31
  Trustees: Lord Hirshfield, Sir John Hewitt, Sir Roy Strong, Hugo Read, Lord Cornwallis, Robin Leigh-Pemberton, Lawrence Banks, Martin Pym, David Innes
  Staff: Frank & Joy Ennis, Ian Barker, Jim Goatham, John Eaton, Clive Barker, Bert Brain, Peter & Mary Gamble, Beryl Duncan, June Miles

Index

Village Residents: Geoffrey & Esmé Walford, Mollie Kohut, Simon & Rosie Claxton, Peter & Dorothy Jones, David & Ann Yeats-Brown, Bill & Margaret Foss, Michael & Rose Chavasse
Rector: Rev. Maurice Hewitt
Chiswell, Lt-Colonel PI (Peter) (3 PARA) 299, 408
Church, Lt-Colonel JC (Jim) (1A&SH) 143, 146, 152
Churchill, Major Jack (5 PARA) 115, 218–9
Churchill, Major General TBL (Tom) 218
Churchill, Winston S. (Prime Minister) 22–9, 51, 96–7, 122, 126, 177, 219, 264, 272–3, 366, 416, 441, 446
Cockcroft, Major Peter 297
Codner, Captain John (RA) 87, 94
Cole, RSM C (1 PARA) 275 Plate 43
Colley, Major HEP (Hugh) (SAF) 342 Plate 62
Colville, Major EC (Eddie) (2A&SH) 49, 52, 55, 69, 101
Cooper, Major JM (John) (SAF) 363, 474–5 Plate 52
Corbould, Captain WR (Bill) (5 PARA) 115, 254, 304–5
Cornwell, Major AJ (Tim) (SAF) 342
Cornwell, Major Vyvyan (RA) 65
Crawford, David (Consul-General) 338, 347, 349
Crawford, Sir Stewart (Political Resident Persian Gulf) 329
Crawshaw, Sqn Ldr Phil (RAF) 334
Creasey, Major General TM (Tim) 377
Crookenden, Lt-General Sir Napier 260

Cubbon, Major General John 257, 268
Cuneo, Terence (painter) 138, 447
Curtis, Major Leslie (4th/7th Dragoon Guards) 139–40

Daladier, Edouard (Prime Minister of France) 126, 193
Dane, RWS (Roland) 427, 434 Plate 69
Daniel, Major, AJ MacN (Jock) (2 PARA) 256, 259
Darling, General Sir Kenneth 274, 281 Plate 44
Darroch, Captain Duncan (1 A&SH) 295
Dawnay, Major Richard (1 PARA) 277–8, 282, 299
De Gaulle, General Charles 57, 175, 179, 204–13, 228, 272
De Klerk, FW (South African statesman) 191
Dempsey, General Sir Miles 49, 74
Dennison, Major Malcolm (SAF) 314, 331, 341, 345, 493 Plate 62
Dewar-Durie, Lieut Andrew 168
Dicharry, Captain 217–8 Plates 31, 36
Dimbleby, Richard 144
Dixon, Sir Pierson (Ambassador) 128 Plate 20
Doenitz, Admiral Karl 22
Dollmann, General Alfred 72
Douglas-Home, Sir Alec (Prime Minister) 265, 379
Dow, Sgt 33–4
Drummond, RSM Andrew (BW) 33–4
Duggan, Mr and Mrs 7
Duncan, Mrs Beryl 423–5
Dunning, Lieut Harry 47–8, 69 Plate 15

Eberhardie, Lt-Colonel CE (Ted) (2 PARA) 270
Edinburgh, Philip Duke of 140, 147, 414, 454,
Edward VIII, King 16
Edwards, Captain Lionel (RM) 148
Eichmann, Colonel Adolf 194
Eisenhower, General Dwight D. (Supreme Allied Commander) 51, 75, 77
Elizabeth, Queen (the Queen Mother) 16, 26, 27, 418
Elizabeth II, Queen 140–7, 156, 249, 414, 418, 445, Plates 21, 66, 67
Emson, Captain JB (James) (1 PARA) 268, 275
Ennis, Sgt Frank 423–5
Eon-Duval, Captain Loic (ADC) 205, 219 Plate 28
Erkel, Vice-Admiral van 176, 199–200 Plate 29

Farley, Lieut John C (US Army) 184
Farrar-Hockley, Lt-Colonel Anthony (TF-H) (3 PARA) 256–7, 276, 292, 293
Fee, Corporal (2A&SH) 84, 102
Felton, Captain Peter (SAF) 350
Ferber, General Ernst (CINCENT) 405–6 Plate 64
Ferguson, Captain & QM George (2 PARA) 256
Fergusson, Major Simon (2A&SH) 74–5, 102
Festing, Field Marshal Sir Francis (CIGS) 192
Fishwick, Matron 13
Fleming, Captain Jon (2 PARA) 251–2
Fletcher, Brigadier JS (Jack) (SAF) 376

Flood, Colonel GR (Bob) 254, 260, 298
Foch, Marshal (of France) Ferdinand 18
Forrester, Brigadier Michael 234, 245
French, Mr EJ and Mrs Sylvia 19
Freyberg, General Sir Bernard VC 103
Frost, Lt-Colonel JD (John) (2 PARA) 245, 269
Fyfe, Captain Alan (2A&SH) 56, 69, 72–3 Plate 15
Fyfe, Major Hugh (2A&SH) 62 Plate 15

Gagarin, Major Yuri (cosmonaut) 194
Gale, General Sir Richard 260, 302
Gamelin, General Maurice Gustave (French C-in-C) 195
Gandhi, Mrs Indira (Prime Minister of India) 400–2
Gandhi, Mohandas (The Mahatma) 381, 383
Gandhi, Rajiv 402
Gandhi, Sanjay 400
Gandhi, Mrs Sonia 402
Garroway, Private (1 PARA) 263, 274
Geddes, Sir Eric 10
George V, King 6, 10
George VI, King 16, 26–7, 42, 51, 133, 138, 140, 421, 448
Geraldine, Queen (of Albania) 125
Ghulam Hassan (Contractor to HM Forces) 236–7, 280 Plate 43
Gibbs, Brigadier RC (Roly) 251, 270–2, 293, 362 Plate 59
Gilbert, Major General GCA (Glyn) 449
Giles, Major JEN (Norrie) 278, 280, 297, 299, 302
Giri, Shri (President of India) 401

Index

Glazebrook, Lt-Colonel David (SAF) 343 Plate 57, 58
Goodfellow, Flt Lt W (Bill) (SOAF) 340 Plate 62
Gordon, Major ACS (Sandy) (SAF) 345
Gordon-Wilson, Lt-Colonel NF (Neale) (2 PARA) 230, 236, 249, 252, 260
Gore, Sir Ralph 29
Gort, General Lord VC 21
Gottwald, Klement (President of Czechoslovakia) 127, 132
Graham, Alastair 4, 14, 24, 28, 138, 144, 157, 209, 251, 333, 432, 489, 491 Plates 12, 19
Graham, Albinia Ellen (Ellie) 2, 157
Graham, Constance Mary (Jane) (née Carew-Hunt) 1–16, 23–37, 113, 157, 166, 192, 228, 251, 271, 281, 431, 434, 489–91 Plates 6, 7, 12, 44
Graham, Captain Cosmo Moray (RN) 17, 139, 234–43 Plate 8
Graham, Elspeth (née Sauer) 17, 139, 157, 274 Plate 10
Graham, Brigadier FCC (Freddie) 158, 227
Graham, Helen Magdalen (née Abercrombie) 2
Graham, Jacqueline Patricia Anne (Pinky) 160, 193–5, 214–7, 279, 293, 296, 300, 307, 388–9, 406, 416, 427 Plates 40, 63, 69
Graham, John Alexander (Jack) 2–7, 14, 31, 123, 157–60 Plate 5
Graham, John Christopher Malcolm (Christopher) 165–7, 279, 292, 296, 307, 388–9, 406, 416–7, 453 Plates 40, 63, 74
Graham, Major John James (17th Laird of Fintry) 272
Graham, 2nd Lieut Keillour (A&SH, Killed 1936) 17

Graham, The Hon. Mary (née Cathcart) 2 Plate 4
Graham, JMC (Moray) 4, 14, 24, 28, 157, 192, 209, 251, 432–3 Plates 12, 19
Graham, Colonel Malcolm David (Max) 2–4, 15, 23, 254 Plate 2
Graham, The Hon. Robert (14th Laird of Fintry) 2
Graham, Major General Thomas, of Balgowan (later Lord Lynedoch) 2, 31, 60, 159, 329 Plate 3
Grandmaison, Major Robert Allard de 177, 187, 199 Plate 31
Grandy, Air Marshal Sir John 198 Plates 29, 33
Grant, Lieut Angus (5 PARA) 115
Gray, Lt-General Sir Michael 444–5
Gray, Private Robert (1 PARA) 278–9
Greenbaum, Private (2A&SH) 40
Greenwood, Private (1A&SH) 111–2
Grivas, Colonel George 160

Hadow, Captain GAJ (Gerald) (5 PARA) 115, 205
Haig, General Alexander (SACEUR) 405 Plate 65
Haig, Field Marshal Sir Douglas 23
Hamed bin Hamood, Sheikh 338
Hamer, Major Peter 255, 282
Harington, General Sir Charles 302, 447
Harrison, CSM Jim (1A&SH) 173
Hartong, Frank, Lan and family 293, 375
Harvey, Lt-Colonel MG (Mike) (SAF) 319, 348, 351–76, 476 Plate 57
Harwood, Commodore (RN) 21
Hassan, 2nd Lieut Ehsan 368
Hausser, General Paul 64, 102

Hawley, Mr Donald (Ambassador) 349, 355, 370, 380 Plates 59, 62
Hawley, Major Jock (5 PARA) 115
Healey, Denis (Minister of Defence) 302, 304
Heath, Mr Edward (Prime Minister) 228, 328, 439
Henlein, Konrad 125
Henri, Prince (of Luxembourg) 447
Hepworth, Captain CF (Charles) (SAF) 325–6
Hewitt, Sir John 421, 439, 449
Heydrich, Obergruppenführer Reinhard 129
Hickman, Major Jeremy 448
Hildick-Smith, Lt-Colonel Donald (RE) 282
Hillary, Sir Edmund 143, 194
Hindenburg, Field Marshal Paul von (President of Germany) 55
Hirst, Wg Comd PJ (Curly) (SOAF) 342, 371
Hitler, Adolf (Chancellor and Führer of Germany) 14–27, 38, 50, 55, 72, 76, 96, 101–4, 126, 129, 172–7, 201–2, 331, 457
Hodges, Air Chief Marshal Sir Lewis 405 Plate 65
Holme, Brigadier MW (Michael) 255, 281–2
Holmes, Colonel Charlie (RAPC) 110
Holt, Major Toni (REME) 434–5
Hope-Thomson, Brigadier MRJ (Tim) 475
Horrocks, Lt-General Sir Brian 79, 92
Howard, Major John (Oxfordshire & Buckinghamshire LI) 260
Howe, Sir Geoffrey and Lady 427–31 Plate 70
Howlett, Sir Geoffrey 444, 448
Hughes, Francis 330 Plate 62
Hulme, Sqn Ldr PS (Peter) (SOAF) 371, 373

Hunt, Colonel HCJ (John) 143
Hurok, Mr Sol (impresario) 303–5
Hussein, King (of Jordan) 232, 377, 488
Hutchison, Miss Anne 425–6
Hynd, Major IM (Ian) 314, 375

Intelligence Section of 2A&SH: 47, 51 Plate 17
    Alf Horsley
    Maurice Lester-Mallinson
    Harry Oakley
    John Park
    Maurice Tucker

Isa bin Sulman Al Khalifa, Emir of Bahrain 232, 242–3, 277, 280–6 Plate 44

Isle of Wight Home Guard (Seaview Platoon) 29–31
Personalities:
    Neville Chichester Sgt
    Marcus Smith Cpl
    Mick Curran
    Jack Majorcas
    Reynolds, Allen, Henley
    Tom Love, Lieut

Jackman, Major Aubrey 415
Jacquot, Lieut Philippe 191, 198, 205, 211–13
Jacquot, General Pierre-Élie 189–225 Plates 28, 29, 34, 38
Jagan, Dr Cheddi 149
Jamieson, Padre (2A&SH) 61, 75
Jardim, Max and Joanne 449–50
Jeapes, Major AS (Tony) (SAS) 346–7
Jeschke, Korvetten-Kapitän Hubert 178, 223, 225 Plate 31,
Jones, Lt-General Sir Charles ('Splosh') 205
Jordan, Captain ME (Mike) (RASC) 193

INDEX

Jouhaud, General (French) 195, 197, 212

Kealy, Major Mike (SAS) 374–5
Kelly, Miss Grace (actress) 194
Kelway-Bamber, Major CG (Glen) (1A&SH) 173
Kennedy, John Fitzgerald, (President of USA) 183, 204, 229, 249–50
Kenneth, Major John (2A&SH) 52, 70–5 Plate 15
Kenny, Captain and QM John (2A&SH) 48, 63, 66, 82 Plate 15
Kerr, Lt-Colonel WW (Bill) (SAF) 364
Kettles, Lt-Colonel AR (Reggie) 329
Keynes, John Maynard (economist) 10
Khama, Sir Seretse 156
Khrushchev, Nikita (Soviet Statesman) 203, 229
King, Sgt 13
King, Sgt (2A&SH) 62–3
King, WL (schoolmaster) 16
Kirby, Daisy Alice (Nanny) 4, 11, 14
Kluge, Field Marshal Gunther Hans von 73, 102

Lambrecht, Colonel Wolf 184–6
Lammerding, Major General Heinz 222–3
Landon, Captain JTW (Tim) (SAF) 322–3, 331, 336–8, 345, 479
Lattre de Tassigny, General 201
Laval, Pierre (Head of French Vichy Govt) 57
Leopold, King (of the Belgians) 83, 166
Leslie, Cpl Jock 37, 115 Plate 18
Lewis, Colonel AD (Tony) (SAF) 475

Lewis, Major JC (John) (SAF) 375, 378
Lewis, Brigadier REC (Rudyard) (BDF) 452
Little, Christopher 19–20
Lloyd, Major JW (Jack) (2PARA) 236
Lloyd-George, David (Prime Minister) 9, 215
Lloyd-Owen, Brigadier DL 245
Lochore, Major John 63, 168
Lomas, Major THC (Tom) (SAF) 352
Lord, RSM John (PARA) 254
Luce, Sir William (Political Resident Persian Gulf) 234–5, 281, 284
Ludendorff, General Erich 55
Lutyens, Sir Edwin 5, 381

McDonagh, Colonel John (RAE) 383–4, 390, 399, 402–3
McDonald, Brigadier Gordon 409
MacDonald, Flt Lt AW (Mac) (SOAF) 352
McElwee, Major Bill (2A&SH) 61, 66, 91, 294 Plate 15
McFrederick, Major JJ (John) (SAF) 324
McGregor, Colonel JA (Hamish) 444, 446
Mackain-Bremner, Lt-Colonel AF (Fergus) (SAF) 348, 364, 491, 494 Plate 62
McKeown, Lt-Colonel John 312
Mackintosh-Walker, Brigadier Ronnie 48, 51, 69
McLeod, Private (2A&SH) 52 Plate 16

MacMillan, Major General GHA ('Babe') 49, 74, 158 Plate 21
MacMillan, Harold (Prime Minister) 204, 248–9, 439
Macpherson, Captain TA (Tim) and 'Mouse' 169–71 Plate 27
Malraux, André 206, 222
Mandela, Nelson (President of South Africa) 191
Marshall, General George C. (US Soldier and Statesman) 99
Martin, Lt-Colonel MJ (Mike) 435
Masaryk, Jan 127
Masaryk, Thomas (President of Czechoslovakia) 125
Mawle, Captain RG (SAF) 352
Maxwell, Colonel Colin (SAF) 314, 343, 363, 371, 415–6, 468, 477, 491–4
Mayfield, Major David 298
Meyer, Major General Kurt ('Panzermeyer') 258
Miller, Captain CR (Dusty) 165
Millington, Air Commodore Geoffrey 281
Milman, Major Claud 297
Mitchell, Captain Colin C. (1A&SH) 106, 159, 295, 299, 447, Plate 47
Mohammed Khalil (Ambassador) 372, 376, 488
Mohammed Shareef (Bearer) 330, 378
Molesworth, Major AJL (Tony) (SAF) 345, 364 Plate 62
Money, Brigadier Douglas 60
Montgomery, General Sir Bernard 49, 51, 70, 73–7, 102, 116, 118, 159, 181, 192–3, 200, 207, 266, 299, 458, Plate 47
Moore, Flt Lt DE (SOAF) 352, 354
Moore, Lt-Colonel John (SAF) 316, 339 Plate 62
Moreton, Major Law (2A&SH) 73, 81, 82, 102 Plate 15
Morgan, Major DR (Russell) (2A&SH) 49, 55, 65, 66, 70, 75, 88, 95, 100 Plates 14, 15
Morgan, Captain STG (George) (RHA) 290
Morrison, Major AGA (Alastair) (SAS) 358, 361, 425 Plate 62
Mountbatten, Admiral of the Fleet, Earl 193, 250 Plate 35
Muir, Major Kenny VC 100, 141
Muirhead, Captain Willie (2A&SH) 60, 61, 66 Plate 15
Mulley, Frederick MP 265–6, 418
Munro, Lt-Colonel Sandy (5 PARA) 115
Murray, Lieut Calum (1A&SH) 168
Mussalim bin Nufl 310, 346
Mussolini, Benito (Italian Dictator) (Il Duce) 14, 23, 27, 100, 177

Narindar Singh, Brigadier 399
Nasser, Colonel Gamel Abdel (President of Egypt) 178, 232, 276–7
Nehru, Jawaharlal (Prime Minister of India) 397, 401
Neill, Ivor (Chaplain-General) 273
Nelson, Major General EJB (John) 273
Nightingale, Major RC (Ray) 364, 376
Norfolk, Duke of (Earl Marshal) 144
Norstad, General Lauris (SACEUR) 174, 208 Plate 28

O'Connor, Lt-General Sir Richard 51, 68, 79
Oddie, Major WRA (Ric) (1 PARA) 276–9
Oglander-Aspinall, General Sir Charles 29
Ojukwu, Major Emeka 226–7

Index

O'Kane, Brigadier PJ (Pat) 291
Oldman, Colonel HRD (Hugh) 252-3, 306, 314-55, 366, 379, 475 Plate 49
O'Morchoe, Major DNC (David), The O'Morchoe 274, 286, 415

Paget, General Sir Bernard 50
Parker, Staff Sgt 192
Parnell, Major John (1A&SH) 149
Parsons, Anthony 235, 281, 285
Pearce, Sgt (RMP) 112
Pearson, Lt-Colonel AS (Alastair) 259, 269
Pearson, Major BA (Barclay) 74, 152
Pétain, Marshal Henri Philippe 57
Philipponnat, Captain Bernard (ADC) 191
Phipps, Captain JJJ (Jeremy) (SAS) 344 Plate 62
Pika, General (Czech) 129
Pirie, Major RM (Richard) (SAS) 358
Pitt, Thomas (Governor of Madras) 420
Pitt family links with Stanhopes 420
Pollock, Captain RM (Morton) (2 PARA) 256
Powell, Major NA (Spike) (SAF) 321 Plate 56
Prien, Leutnant Günther 22
Priestley, CT ('Jaw') 15
Purdon, Brigadier CWB (Corran) 305, 313-4, 317-9, 320-1, 323, 478

Qaboos bin Said (Sultan of Oman) 328-80, 415, 439-40, 477-80 Plates 51, 52, 53, 79

Rae, Captain SJ (SAF) 352
Rainier, Prince (of Monaco) 194
Rajab, Abdul Hafidh 376
Randall, Gp Capt WSO (Bill) 448
Ray, Lt-Col JB (Bryan) (SAF) 364, 376
Raybould, Lt-Comd JTG (Jeremy) (SAF) 316
Reagan, Ronald (President of the USA) 203, 454
Rees, Sgt Dai 118, 120
Richardson, General Sir Charles 283-4
Ridgway, Capt JM (John) 308
Ritchie, Lt-General Neil 68, 79
Ritchie-Williams, Mr 7
Roberts, Lt-Colonel JMH (John) (2PARA) 299
Robertson, General Sir Brian 119
Robertson, Brigadier JAR 472-5
Robinson, Sgt (RMP) 112
Robinson, Major AVO (Vyvyan) (SAF) 356 Plates 56, 58
Roman, Major Pierre (Belgian Army) 184
Rommel, Field Marshal Erwin 73, 102, 237
Rouse, Major Adrian (and Mrs Valerie) 228, 286, 292 Plate 41
Roosevelt, Franklin D (President of the USA) 10, 96, 126, 366
Rowallan, Lt-Col Lord 37
Roxburghe, Duke of 143, 145
Rundstedt, Field Marshal Gerd von 73, 90, 102

Said bin Taimur (Sultan of Muscat & Oman) 252, 277, 309-37, 350, 378-9, 493 Plate 48

Salan, General (French Army) 179, 195, 197, 212
Salote, Queen (of Tonga) 144
Sandilands, Lt-Colonel PS (Pat) (5 PARA) 115, 123
Savage, Sir Alfred 149 Plate 23
Saville, Private (2 PARA) 241
Scheurmier, Major Ian (1A&SH) 153
Schnell, General Dr Karl (CINCENT) 406 Plate 65
Schrader, Lisa 167, 171, 175, 193
Scorer, Gordon (surgeon) 139
Scott, Major RF (Dick) (and Mrs Jill) 270, 375, 404
Scott-Bowden, Major General Logan 385
Scott-Lyon, Lieut David (2A&SH) 47–8, 75, 84 Plate 15
Seely, Captain VR (Victor) (SAF) 353
Sengès, Colonel (French Army) 177, 188–9
Shelley, Major Andrew (SAF) 325
Shinwell, Emanuel MP 114, 266
Silva, Major Felix da 356–7
Slim, Field Marshal Viscount 97, 268
Slim, Major The Hon JD (John) (1A&SH) 163, 268
Smiley, Colonel D de C (David) 309, 321, 473
Slonkova, Mme Marketa 124
Speidel, General Dr Hans 176, 180–1, 199–200, 202, 208, Plates 29, 30, 33
Spencerley, Captain Tom (2A&SH) 52, 63 Plate 15
Spens, Lt-Colonel Hugh (1A&SH) 166–8, 173, 196, 208 Plate 26
Stainforth, Major General CH (Charles) 301–5
Stalin, Marshal Joseph (Ruler of the USSR) 22, 97, 100, 122–9
Stanhope, James Richard, 7th Earl 420–31
Starling, Major JG (Joe) 232, 291
Stewart, Lt-Colonel Ian (A&SH) 38
Stockwell, General Sir Hugh 180, 196, 227
Stoker, Sqn Ldr Bill (SOAF) 374
Storey, Captain & QM Charles (1 PARA) 264
Student, General Kurt 80, 102, 442

Tait, Corporal (PARA) 307–8
Tariq bin Taimur, Seyyid 326, 341–3, 354, 378, 471–2
Taylor, Major TEF (Ted) (SAF) 352
Templer, General Sir Gerald 394, 459
Tensing, Sherpa 143, 194
Thatcher, Mrs Margaret (Prime Minister) 229, 266, 415, 419, 424
Theobald, Tony (Philatelic designer) 448–9
Thomson, Lieut CG (Colin) (1 PARA) 269
Thornton, Captain Dudley 124
Todd, Richard (actor) 145
Todd, Sgt (master tailor) (2A&SH) 40
Thursby, Lt-Colonel PDF (Pat) (PARA) 232, 286, 296, 303
Tripp, Peter 235, 281
Troup, Major Alastair (1A&SH) 149, 152
Truman, Harry S (President of the USA) 100–101
Tucker, Sgt Maurice (2A&SH) 47, 51, 60 Plate 17

Tugwell, Major MAJ (Maurice) (1 PARA) 288
Turner, Joseph (painter) 48
Turnill, Lt-Colonel E (Teddy) (SAF) 321–53, 477 Plate 50
Tweedie, Lt-Colonel JW (John) (2A&SH) 49–50, 55–69, 73–4 Plate 13

Varnbuehler, Brigadier Freiherr von 218–9
Vaux, Lt-Colonel PAL (Peter) 168
Venn, Captain DJ (David) (SAF) 348
Vickers, Miss (assistant matron) 13
Vutirakis, Captain Eddie (SAF) 327

Wake, Hereward 15–17
Waldron, Brigadier JGC (John) 183–7
Walsh, Major JMH (Michael) (3 PARA) 256–7, 292, 299
Walton, Captain PS (Peter) (SAF) 340 Plate 62
Ward, Brigadier PJN (Philip) 362
Ward-Booth, Lt-Colonel AJ (Tony) 299
Warner, Major Bob (SAF) 314, 493
Waterfield, Brigadier Pat (SAF) 314, 470–3
Watkins, Major HBC (Bryan) 168
Watkinson, Harold (Minister of Defence) 193
Watts, Lt-Colonel JPBC (John) (SAS) 358, 360–4, 474
Wavell, General Sir Archibald 103
Webb, Lt-Colonel RL ('Squire') (1A&SH) 103–113
Welch, Colonel Courtney 363 Plate 61
Westwood, The Rt Rev. William, Bishop of Peterborough 446, 495–7
Wheeler, Captain GPMC (Guy) 128 Plate 20
Whitcombe, Mrs Angel 33
Whitfield, WO2 Harry (1 PARA) 280
Wildman, Major Bill (USAF) 177, 180, 207, 213–4 Plate 31
Wilhelm II, Kaiser (Emperor of Germany) 3, 172
Wilhelmina, Queen (of the Netherlands) 83
Willey, Mrs Maureen 251, 274, 425
Willey, Sqn Ldr RStJF (Richard) 251, 274
Williams, Drum-Major John (2 PARA) 245
Williams, Flt Lt JB (Barry) (SOAF) 354
Willows, Lieut Derek (5 PARA) 119, 121
Wilson, Major ADRG (David) (1A&SH) 109, 114
Wilson, Harold (Prime Minister) 265, 328
Worthy, Lt-Colonel Peter (SAF) 342, 345, 353, 364, Plate 62
Wright, Major PS (Paul) (SAF) Plate 61
Wynne, Flt Lt Jack (SOAF) 352

Young, Lt-Colonel (10 HLI) 69
Young, Robin (Dhofar Development Dept) 341, 361
Younger, Lieut JDB (David) (1A&SH) 168

Zand (Ambassador) 372, 377, 481
Zeller, General (French Army) 195–8
Zemanova, Mme 133
Zimmerman, Private (2 A&SH) 40
Zog, King (of Albania) 115